advantage

Dear Valued Customer,

We realize you're a busy professional with deadlines to hit. Whether your goal is to learn a new technology or solve a critical problem, we want to be there to lend you a hand. Our primary objective is to provide you with the insight and knowledge you need to stay atop the highly competitive and ever-changing technology industry.

Wiley Publishing, Inc., offers books on a wide variety of technical categories, including security, data warehousing, software development tools, and networking — everything you need to reach your peak. Regardless of your level of expertise, the Wiley family of books has you covered.

- For Dummies – The ***fun*** and ***easy*** way to learn
- The Weekend Crash Course –The ***fastest*** way to learn a new tool or technology
- Visual – For those who prefer to learn a new topic ***visually***
- The Bible – The ***100% comprehensive*** tutorial and reference
- The Wiley Professional list – ***Practical*** and ***reliable*** resources for IT professionals

The book you now hold, *Mastering Web Services Security,* shows you how to successfully develop and deploy secure Web services applications for both J2EE and .NET systems. The authors are involved in developing the — new security standards for Web services — which means you can be assured that this book is complete and authoritative. The book covers all of the key components of Web services security, including XML and SOAP security, as well as SAML (Security Assertion Markup Language), richly illustrating techniques with code examples and practical advice.

Our commitment to you does not end at the last page of this book. We'd want to open a dialog with you to see what other solutions we can provide. Please be sure to visit us at www.wiley.com/compbooks to review our complete title list and explore the other resources we offer. If you have a comment, suggestion, or any other inquiry, please locate the "contact us" link at www.wiley.com.

Finally, we encourage you to review the following page for a list of Wiley titles on related topics. Thank you for your support and we look forward to hearing from you and serving your needs again in the future.

Sincerely,

Richard K. Swadley

Richard K. Swadley
Vice President & Executive Group Publisher
Wiley Technology Publishing

Wiley Publishing, Inc.

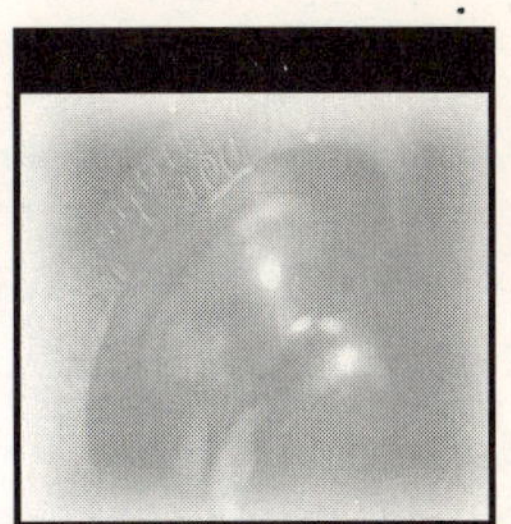

Mastering Web Services Security

Bret Hartman
Donald J. Flinn
Konstantin Beznosov
Shirley Kawamoto

WILEY

Wiley Publishing, Inc.

Publisher: Joe Wikert
Executive Editor: Robert Elliott
Editorial Manager: Kathryn A. Malm
Developmental Editor: Adaobi Obi Tulton
Managing Editor: Pamela Hanley
New Media Editor: Brian Snapp
Text Design & Composition: Wiley Composition Services

This book is printed on acid-free paper. ♾

Published by Wiley Publishing, Inc., Indianapolis, Indiana
Published simultaneously in Canada

For general information on our other products and services please contact our Customer Care Department within the United States at (800) 762-2974, outside the United States at (317) 572-3993 or fax (317) 572-4002.

Wiley also publishes its books in a variety of electronic formats. Some content that appears in print may not be available in electronic books.

Library of Congress Cataloging-in-Publication Data:

ISBN 0-471-26716-3

Printed in the United States of America

10 9 8 7 6 5 4 3 2 1

To Dana, Sarah, and Will.
—Bret

To Jane and Jason.
—Don

To Alla, Vladimir, Valerij, Olga, and Alissa.
—Konstantin

To Michael, Amanda, and Victoria.
—Shirley

Acknowledgments

The concepts discussed in this book represent the work of many people. In particular, an enormous amount of credit goes to the architects and engineers at the Quadrasis unit of Hitachi Computer Products (America), Inc., who were instrumental in developing new solutions for Web Services security and Enterprise Application Security Integration (EASI).

First, we would like to thank the Quadrasis engineering, sales, and marketing teams who conceived, implemented, and deployed the first-of-its-kind platform for application security integration called *EASI Security Unifier*: Barry Abel, Bob Atlas, Prasad Bhamidipati, Ted Burghart, Christopher Chaney, Jennifer Chong, Bob Clancy, Heather Cooper, David Cushing, Steve Cushing, Sean Dolan, Fred Dushin, Kurt Engel, Robert Frazier, Ian Foster, Ken Gartner, Harriet Goldman, Chris Green, Lakshmi Hanspal, Tim Heitz, John Horsfield, Bill Huber, Doug Hufsey, Peter Jalajas, Steve Jewkes, Jim Kelly, Chris Lavertu, Eric Maruta, Jon Mason, Geoff Matter, David Miller, Brian Moffat, Rick Murphy, Tim Murphy, David Murray, Hiroshi Nakamura, Patricia Prince, Ramanan Ramanathan, Hans Riemer, Kathleen Ruggles, Mark Schuldenfrei, Swati Shikhare, Narizumi Shindo, Sandeep Singh, Po Sun, Philip Teagle, Millind Thakre, Bill Thomas, Julie Trask, Stephanie Tyler, Rost Vavrick, Eric Wells, Mark Wencek, Robert Winant, and Jonathan Wu.

We would also like to thank Hitachi management who actively encouraged and supported the development of EASI Security Unifier: Bob Freund, Kiyoshi Kozuka, Kazuaki Masamoto, Soichi Oyama, Masato Saito, and Yousuke Tsuyuki.

Xtradyne is the development partner of Quadrasis for *SOAP Content Inspector*, a software Web Services firewall product. We appreciate the technical and business efforts from the entire Xtradyne staff, including: Jörg Bartholdt, Gerald Brose, Tim Eckardt, Uwe Eisert, Matthias Jung, Annette Kiefer, Philip Leatham, Marina Mueller, Nicolas Noffke, Frank Rehberger, Sebastian Staamann, Reimo Tiedemann, and Marcus Wittig.

We are grateful to Credit Suisse First Boston for helping us refine the concept of EASI and testing it in the real world, especially Kalvinder Dosanjh, Ted Gerbracht, and John Kirkwood.

The Security Assertion Markup Language (SAML) and WS-Security specifications, which are being defined by the Organization for the Advancement of Structured Information Standards (OASIS), are central to the content of this book. We thank the many members, representing over forty different companies, of the OASIS Security Services and Web Services Security Technical Committees for their ongoing efforts to define and evolve these important standards.

Thanks to Ian Bruce, Jeremy Epstein, Randy Heffner, Michael Howard, Emil Lupu, Marybeth Panock, and Zdenek Svoboda for reviewing various parts of this book and helping us keep at least most of our facts straight. Thanks also to the folks at Wiley who made this book possible: Robert Elliott, Pamela Hanley, Emilie Herman, and Adaobi Obi Tulton. We appreciate all of their support and feedback for these many months.

Finally, we especially want to thank our families: Dana, Sarah, and Will Hartman; Jane and Jason Flinn; Alissa Kniazeva and Olga Beznosova; and Michael, Amanda, and Victoria Hinchey. We know this writing has been a challenge for you, as you patiently put up with all of the late nights and lost weekends. We thank you for your understanding and support.

Foreword

A basic premise of this book is that applications requiring Web security services can utilize a unified security architecture. Authentication, authorization, accountability, administration and cryptography security services can be provided by a lightweight but robust architecture common to all defined applications.

This is an awesome concept. But does it work? In a word . . . YES.

At Credit Suisse First Boston, we have implemented the EASI unified security architecture. We carefully documented our requirements and mapped the specifications against requirements for 1½ years. In 2002, we implemented the EASI unified security architecture, carefully testing and validating each API, mapper, and component. In 2003, this architecture is set to be our standard for new application development, allowing us to reuse established security services, reduce time to develop and reduce cost of development efforts.

Our expectations are high for the EASI framework. Web Services are used extensively within Credit Suisse. If you can think of how it could be used, we probably use it that way within CSFB. Flexibility, ease of implementation, and robustness were critical to us when looking at any type of framework. Also, international regulatory and audit requirements strongly encouraged us to find ways to standardize and reduce complexity.

Like all truly awesome concepts, making a difficult and elusive "paradigm change" is required. There could be a separate book solely on management of the various types of cultural changes and challenges that accompany implementation. The approach that we used at CSFB was to create a strong interdepartmental team to coordinate efforts, monitor progress and deal with issues.

In the end, however, I believe implementation of such a unified architecture is inevitable. Resistance is truly futile. Redefining the security solution space for each developed application is no longer an option. Simply put, production environments have become too complicated for limited support resources. Security and trust are virtually impossible to maintain as applications must transverse legacy mainframe and client/server environments, complete with their known but daily updated vulnerabilities. The EASI architecture simplifies the environment to known, secured and trusted components.

Also, the useful life of legacy applications can be extended. Old security services can be retired and new security services integrated without rewriting applications.

Software companies understand the significance of these concepts. Microsoft via .Net Framework and Sun via Sun ONE have indicated their understanding and appreciation of the concepts by their commitment to providing common security architectural frameworks. At CSFB, we use the EASI architecture as our base and integrate .Net and Sun ONE into EASI.

I trust that you will come to appreciate the concepts presented in this book. I can personally vouch for the fact that many lost weekends were spent in its authorship. Bret and his team would occasionally show up at Credit Suisse bleary eyed from another weekend on "the book," trying to finish the writing, rewriting and edits.

When Bret asked me to write this foreword, I was personally pleased . . . but not for the reason you might initially think.

We have a fairly healthy back-and-forth, which started when we discovered we went to rival schools in Cambridge, by the river at the same time. So I can't resist this opportunity.

Bret, although you and your team are mostly MIT grads, I am reminded of the following quote from Anna Freud:

"Creative minds have always been known to survive any kind of bad training."

John Kirkwood
Director, Global Security Strategy and Architecture
Credit Suisse First Boston

Advance Praise for *Mastering Web Services Security*

"A much needed source for those building secure, next generation Web Services."

Michael Howard
Senior Program Manager, Security Engineering, Microsoft Corp.

"Without strong security, Web Services will, in the end, have but little impact on business. *Mastering Web Services Security* provides important practical guidance and theory for building secure services now and preparing for future secure Web Services standards."

Randy Heffner
VP & Research Leader, Giga Information Group

"The authors manage to cover an impressive collection of WS security topics in a no-nonsense, how-to style, while zeroing in on important techniques and critical points with specific source code examples and diagrams."

Max Levchin
co-founder, PayPal, Inc

"Bret Hartman and his fellow authors have set the standard for Web Services security books with *Mastering Web Services Security*. Their coverage is both broad and deep, discussing the range of security issues facing companies who are implementing Web Services, while delving into the difficult details of cryptography and application security infrastructures in a clear, understandable manner. Their balanced coverage of security on both the .NET and J2EE platforms is especially valuable, especially considering the solid chapters on interoperability, security administration, and building secure Web Services architectures. I recommend this book for all IT managers, architects, and enterprise security professionals who need a real understanding of how to build and manage secure Service-oriented architectures."

Jason Bloomberg
Senior Analyst, ZapThink LLC

"Web services are the next wave of business integration, with one major hurdle in their way: security. This comprehensive explanation of the state of the art in web services security will help remove that hurdle. Readers will learn both about the risks and the solutions. Not just a user's guide, this book explains the architectural issues in distributed systems, thus motivating the solutions. There's an alphabet soup of evolving standards, and this volume gives up to the minute coverage of all of them, including XML Signature, SAML, and WS-Security. Consistent examples that run through the book make it easy to apply the ideas to real systems. Important reading for anyone involved in web services."

Jeremy Epstein
Director of Product Security, webMethods Inc.

"In *Mastering Web Services Security* the authors provide us with an excellent technical and historical synopsis of the web services security environment and its historical relationship to other distributed computing environments. The book blends a presentation of the challenges of securing web services with descriptions of the security technologies developed to address these challenges. The major strength of the book is that it provides detailed examples of the use of these technologies to develop and deploy secure web services on the existing web services platforms. The book is also forward looking and presents for the reader a road map of the activities that will shape the future of web services security."

Ron Monzillo
Sun Microsystems.

Contents

Introduction

Web Services are a promising solution to an age-old need: fast and flexible information sharing among people and businesses. Web Services enable access to data that has previously been locked within corporate networks and accessible only by using specialized software. Along with the benefits of Web Services comes a serious risk: sensitive and private data can be exposed to people who are not supposed to see it. Web Services will never attain their tremendous potential unless we learn how to manage the associated risks.

Web Services represent the next phase of distributed computing, building on the shoulders of the previous distributed models. Widespread distributed computing started with the Transmission Control Protocol/Internet Protocol (TCP/IP). Using TCP/IP to build distributed products was hard work for application programmers, who just wanted to build business applications. To ease the burden of distributed programming the computer industry developed the Distributed Computing Environment (DCE) based on the client/server computing paradigm, followed by the Common Object Request Broker Architecture (CORBA). About the same time, Microsoft introduced the Component Object Model (COM), followed by Distributed COM (DCOM) using DCE technology as a base, and COM+. Sun, building on its Java language introduced the Java 2 Platform, Enterprise Edition (J2EE), with its popular Enterprise Java Beans (EJBs), using many concepts and research ideas from the previous technologies. Each step made distributed computing easier but each technology still lived, for the most part, in its own world, making interoperability between the different middleware technologies difficult.

Now Web Services have burst on the scene. There are two major Web Services goals—to make distributed computing easier for the business programmer and to enhance interoperability. These goals are aided by:

- Loose coupling between the requesting program and the service provider
- The use of Extensible Markup Language (XML), which is platform and language neutral

Hopefully, all the positive lessons that we learned from the previous distributed models will be incorporated into the Web Services model.

When all the past distributed models were being implemented, one technology, security, always seemed to be tackled last. The mantra was, "let's get the model working first, then we will worry about security." Inevitably, this resulted in poorly performing and difficult-to-use security. As we all know, distributed security is a tough problem.

What, if anything have we learned from our past experiences? For one thing, here we are at the early stages of Web Services, and we are able to bring you a book on the concepts of distributed security as it applies to Web Services. In it we detail the work of a number of specification groups and vendors that are working on security related to the basic technologies of Web Services: XML and SOAP. So, we have learned something from the past. However, you will see, as we describe Web Services security, that there are still limitations in the Web Services security model, and that parts of the model are not yet fully coordinated.

You can read new articles almost every day announcing that Web Services will not succeed without security. We hope that this book will help spread the word on what is needed for Web Services security and what is missing today. Hopefully, this book will also help you develop your own security solutions in the distributed world of Web Services.

It is not sufficient to limit Web Services security to your company's perimeter firewall. In today's world of electronic commerce, customers, suppliers, remote employees, and at times even competitors, are all invited into the inner sanctum of your computing system. Consequently, distributed security using the Web Services paradigm requires end-to-end security—a service request is made, which goes through the perimeter firewall, into your application servers and applications at the heart of your corporate network, to the persistent store of your sensitive data in the back-office. As we will show, the tentacles of Web Services reach deep into your system in many of the new architectural designs brought about by Web Services. Consequently, this book shows you how to secure your enterprise from end to end, using theory, examples, and practical advice.

Underlying end-to-end e-business is the broader technology of distributed computing and the various distributed security technologies. Everybody in the computing field and many typical computer users have heard of Hypertext Markup Language (HTML) and Secure Sockets Layer (SSL) but fewer have heard of EJB, COM+, or CORBA. But these technologies lie at the heart of modern distributed computing systems that are found behind the perimeter firewall. This area, which we call the mid-tier, is the most complex and most neglected area of end-to-end, enterprise security. Some recent government surveys have shown the mid-tier to be highly vulnerable to break-ins, resulting in significant financial loss. With the increasing e-business-driven movement toward letting outsiders into the mid-tier, the mid-tier is becoming even more sensitive to break-ins, with the potential for greater financial loss and privacy violations.

If you have any responsibility, direct or indirect, for any part of the security of your site, you owe it to yourself to read and study this book. Distributed security is not an easy subject, and Web Services security adds another level of complexity. It follows that parts of this book are not easy, but the returns for yourself and your company are significant if you master this complex subject.

We present material on how to use the architectures and technologies and how to understand the specifications that are available to build a secure Web Services system. Since this technology is rapidly changing, we present the theory behind the models and explain the thinking behind many of the security specifications that are at the forefront of the technology today. We are well positioned to do this since the authors are members of many of the committees and organizations writing these specifications, as well as doing hands-on work designing and building enterprise security products.

Our emphasis is on showing you how to build and understand the complexities of a secure end-to-end Web Services system. Consequently, we do not cover in depth some of the more arcane aspects of security such as cryptography, Public Key Infrastructure (PKI), or how to build the middleware systems themselves. We do, however, discuss these specialized security technologies in terms of how you use them in a Web Services system and give you an understanding of their features so that you can judge the best match for your needs.

This book gives you both a detailed technical understanding of the major components of an end-to-end enterprise security architecture and a broad description of how to deploy and use Web Services security technologies to protect your corporation and its interaction with the outside world.

Overview of the Book and Technology

Enterprise security is an ongoing battle. On the one side are those who want to break into your system, either for fun or for some advantage to themselves or their organization. On the other side are people like yourself who are putting up defenses to prevent these break-ins. This ongoing battle results in continuing changes to security solutions. Another dimension is that there is an evolving set of security requirements, such as giving a new group of outsiders controlled access to your system for e-business purposes. For these reasons we have concentrated on explaining the underlying thinking behind today's enterprise security solutions so that you can judge the worth of new solutions as they come on the scene and judge when old solutions are no longer good enough.

An important requirement for Web Services is to support secure interoperation between the underlying object models, such as .NET and J2EE, as well as to support interoperation between the perimeter security and the mid-tier, and between the mid-tier and legacy or back-office systems. To this end, we give significant detail describing the problems of maintaining secure interoperability and how you can overcome these problems. The distributed security community, as represented by the Organization for the Advancement of Structured Information Standards (OASIS), the World Wide Web Consortium (W3C), and the Internet Engineering Task Force (IETF), have offered the solutions to some of these problems in specifications that have been developed by the cooperative efforts of their member companies. Other organizations, such as the Web Services Interoperability Organization (WS-I) and the Java Community Process (JCP) have worked on additional solutions. We cover them all to bring to you the pertinent, distributed security work and thinking.

We look at solving the security problem from an end-to-end corporate viewpoint as well as from the major technical viewpoint for authentication, authorization, secure transport and security auditing. By presenting enterprise security from these two viewpoints, we give you both a top-down and bottom-up approach to understanding the problems and the solutions.

In some cases, there are no standard solutions. In such cases, we bring you the latest thinking and guidance towards solutions. The best solution is one where there is an open standard, because the solution will have gone through a rigorous examination and debate among the security experts in order to reach the status of a standard. However, standardization is a slow process, and we all are under pressure to solve the problem now. In situations where there is not yet a consensus, we put forth solutions that we or others have implemented, and describe the different possible solutions under debate in the distributed security community.

We have tried to balance the theory and understanding of Web Services security to give you the ability to determine when you can use today's solutions and when you should reject an inadequate solution and find something better. There is a saying to the effect that it is better to teach someone how to farm than to just give him today's meal. This is the philosophy that we have tried to follow. We hope that the knowledge you get from this book will prepare you to build secure systems that are ready for the new solutions, requirements, and threats that will always be coming down the road.

If you have read our previous book, *Enterprise Security with EJB and CORBA* (Hartman, Flinn, and Beznosov 2001), you will notice that some of the ideas and text have been derived and updated from this work. For example, the concept of Enterprise Application Security Integration (EASI) is a refinement of the Enterprise Security Integration (ESI) concept discussed in the previous book. Our work on Web Services security is a natural evolution from ideas in the previous book because we believe that Web Services security should be viewed in the context of an overall enterprise security architecture. Although there is a lot of new technology to discuss, the fundamental principles of building an enterprise security architecture remain the same.

You may also notice differences in writing styles and emphasis among the chapters. There are four authors of this book, and we all have different areas of security expertise and opinions about the most important issues to consider. We have worked to maintain consistency of terminology throughout the text, but variations are bound to appear in a book that covers such a variety of complex topics. We hope that our different perspectives will be useful to you by giving you several different ways to think about Web Services security solutions.

How This Book Is Organized

This book is divided into three major sections:

- Chapters 1–3 provide a basic introduction to Web Services and security issues to get you started. For securing very simple Web Services applications, this may be all the information you will need. Chapter 3 describes a Web Services application using .NET that provides limited Web Services security without the necessity to develop any security code.
- Chapters 4–7 describe the technology building blocks of Web Services security in detail. The chapters define the security technologies that support Web Services security, with particular emphasis on how security works with XML. These chapters will be of interest to people who want to get a good understanding of Web Services security and supporting infrastructure technologies but aren't necessarily interested in building secure applications.

- Chapters 8–12 compose the final section of the book, which goes into the details of how Web Services security is applied when building applications. Chapters 8 and 9 describe the features available when Web Services are implemented on the most popular application platforms, namely .NET and J2EE. The remaining chapters cover the advanced topics of interoperability, administration, and integration. Our final chapter on planning and implementing a complete security architecture pulls together all the concepts you have learned.

Chapter 1 introduces the subject of Web Services security and the new technologies that are used to solve the Web Services security problem. We lay the groundwork for understanding how the subsequent chapters fit into the whole solution. We introduce the concept of risk management in the balancing of system performance and complexity on one hand with the value of the resources being protected on the other hand. We introduce the concept of Enterprise Application Security Integration and how it supports end-to-end enterprise security. We wrap up with a description of our fictional enterprises, ePortal and eBusiness, which are used in a running example throughout the rest of the book.

Chapter 2 starts with a detailed description of Web Services and the benefits they can bring to distributed computing. It moves on to describe the language of Web Services, XML, followed by the XML messaging protocol, SOAP. After describing SOAP, this chapter introduces the Web accessible Universal Description, Discovery, and Integration (UDDI) service, which is used to discover a Web Service so that the requester is able to communicate with the service. The next component described is the Web Services Description Language (WSDL), which is an XML-based, machine-generated, and machine-readable document that details how to access a Web Service. As usual when one is interested in interoperability, there is a need for standards and standards bodies. This chapter covers the prominent standards bodies working in the area of Web Services.

Chapter 3 looks at the security technologies that are the basis of Web Services security. It introduces the fundamentals of cryptography, authentication, and authorization. There is a natural progression through these technologies. The most basic is the underlying cryptography, then authentication, which uses cryptography, then authorization, which depends on the principal having been authenticated. The chapter goes on to describe the uses of these security technologies to implement a simple Web Service using our ePortal and eBusiness example introduced in Chapter 1. This simple example uses only one of the Web Services technologies, namely .NET. While basic security measures may be used for protecting a simple system, Web Services systems may often be more complex. This chapter discusses the limitations of the basic approach and points the way to the complete set of security technologies described in the rest of the book, which are needed for enterprise deployments.

Chapter 4 discusses measures for securing XML and SOAP messages. Because many of these measures are based on cryptography, this chapter describes public key cryptography and explains how it is applied, in particular it discusses digital signatures as well as public key infrastructure (PKI). This chapter provides an overview of some of the more popular cryptographic technologies such as RSA, Diffie-Hellman, and DSA. Public key certificates, which are a necessary ingredient in establishing trust in a public key, are introduced. From there, it shows how encryption and digital signatures can be applied to XML documents. Finally, it discusses how such measures are being tailored to SOAP and Web Services and introduces the WS-Security specification, which may be used to secure SOAP documents.

Chapter 5 discusses the Security Assertion Markup Language (SAML) specification, which is directed at securing the basic credentials using XML. It describes how SAML is used in general and how it may be used in conjunction with Web Services. It takes a detailed look at the specifications for the various SAML assertions and the details of its request-reply model. The single sign-on (SSO) approach of the SAML browser/artifact profile is described. The chapter also looks at how SAML fits into a larger architecture. We describe the concept of distributed SAML authorities that perform the security functions of authentication, attribute retrieval, and authorization, and the protocols for accessing these authorities. The protocols for application-to-application transport of the SAML assertions are also covered. This chapter gives an example of a SAML-based solution to the issues of privacy, SSO, and federation by examining the Shibboleth project.

Chapter 6 brings together several of the previously defined security technologies and describes them within the context of the Web Services example introduced in Chapter 1. We divide the security solutions into connection-oriented and document-oriented solutions, look in more detail at possible security solutions, and determine how they fit into security for Web Services. After discussing the security of XML-based SOAP messages as they are communicated from one domain to another, we examine authentication, authorization, and data protection at the Web Services interfaces, and describe the relationship of the WS-Security and SAML specifications. Since Web Services are new and no best practices have yet been established, this chapter gives ways to analyze Web Services security needs and determine how to address those needs.

Chapter 7 gives an overview of the security in the various middleware technologies used to build Web Services applications. It discusses the middleware client-server and object paradigms, the basic building blocks of modern distributed architectures. The chapter then describes the distributed security fundamentals of authentication, message protection, access control, trust, administration, and fine-grained access control. It then explains the security mechanisms of the popular distributed middleware technologies that you will use for building Web Services applications: CORBA, COM+, .NET, and J2EE.

Chapter 8 describes how secure Web Services may be implemented using Microsoft technologies. It describes the different ways that you can create a Microsoft Web Service application using COM+, COM with the SOAP toolkit, .NET remoting, and ASP.NET. The chapter then explains the mechanisms available for securing Web Services based on ASP.NET—the most flexible and effective way to develop interoperable Web Services in the Microsoft world. We use our example, ePortal and eBusiness, in conjunction with ASP.NET to illustrate the security of ASP.NET-based Web Services.

Chapter 9 describes securing Web Services when the target Web Service is a J2EE application server or Java application. We look at what makes Web Services security different from traditional EJB security, and how one would secure an J2EE container in the Web Services environment. Throughout, we refer to the new JSRs that the JCP is developing and has developed to make Java compatible with Web Services. We then use our ePortal and eBusiness example to illustrate how to make a traditional application server Web Services aware. We introduce a product by Systinet that provides a Web Services development platform for application servers and discuss some of the security issues related to this approach. We also develop the same scenario using Sun's Java Web Services Developer Pack (JWSDP).

Chapter 10 discusses the difficult problem of achieving secure interoperability between Web Services implementations built on different application platforms and running in different policy domains. We look at the different security specifications for

Web Services and point out that these specifications still have limitations in some of the areas of secure interoperability, such as federation and delegation. We also enumerate and describe much of the security work that is underway in the area of Web Services. We show how SAML and WS-Security can be used together to secure Web Services messaging. We conclude that the security technologies available today are still lacking important features when one attempts to use Web Services over the Internet, except in very constrained cases. Our conclusion is that Web Services will be used first in the intranet, then move to the extranet, and finally, as the Web Services security community solves the problems in these domains, move on to applications used over the Internet.

Chapter 11 describes the security administration of Web Services in terms of the security of the underlying middleware, as well as the Web Services data protection methods. The chapter begins by discussing the basics of security administration, the grouping of principals by security attributes, and the use of the Role Based Access Control (RBAC) model, and how these may be used in Web Services. While RBAC is quite useful in access control, this chapter points out some of the difficulties and drawbacks in administering RBAC-based systems. We address the administration of delegation, while pointing out the risks of this approach and the necessity of careful assignment of delegation. Applying risk management to access control in complex systems, we recommend auditing as an integral part of the security system. The chapter then addresses the administration of data protection in SOAP messages.

Chapter 12 brings together the theory and approaches from the previous chapters using a practical example of securely deploying a Web Services business scenario. We walk you through the actual planning and deployment of our example, ePortal and eBusiness. We point out many of the pitfalls that could snare you in your deployment and describe how to avoid them. By providing a realistic scenario, we describe how firewalls, Web servers, browsers, EJB containers, .NET applications, the middleware infrastructure, and legacy systems all have to work together to secure an enterprise Web Services system.

Who Should Read This Book

This book should be read by anyone who has a responsibility for the security of a distributed enterprise computing system using Web Services. This includes managers, architects, programmers, and security administrators. We assume that you have some experience with distributed computing as applied to enterprise systems, but we do not expect you to have experience with security as applied to large distributed systems. In addition, some experience with XML, EJB, and .NET is helpful but not necessary.

Be forewarned that distributed security is not an easy subject, so don't expect to absorb some of the more technical chapters in a single reading. We also don't expect each of our audience members to read all the parts of the book with equal intensity.

Managers should read Chapters 1, 2, 3, 12, and the introduction and summary of the other chapters. Where managers have a special responsibility or interest, we invite them to delve into the pertinent chapters.

Architects and programmers should read all of the chapters, although programmers might only need to skim Chapters 1 and 3. Those who are familiar with ASP.NET security can skim Chapter 8, and those familiar with J2EE can skim Chapter 9. We recommend skimming those chapters even though you are familiar with the technology because some of the information is quite new and not readily available elsewhere.

Security administrators should pay particular attention to Chapters 4, 5, 10, 11, and 12. They should also read Chapters 3 and 7, and read at least the introduction and summary to the other chapters.

What's on the Web Site

Our Web site at www.wiley.com/compbooks/hartman contains the complete source code for securing the fictional corporations ePortal and eBusiness that we use as an example throughout this book. The Web site also contains any errata and updates to this book.

Since distributed security is an active, growing technology, we will, from time to time, update you on those security technologies that are expanding or those that are dying off, as well as the new technologies that come on the scene.

Summary

If you don't want your company to appear on the nightly news with the lead, "*<Your company>* has reported a break-in by hackers. The break-in resulted in large financial losses and the disclosure of privacy information of thousands of their customers, including stolen credit card numbers," you should learn how to protect your enterprise system. That is the purpose of this book, to teach you how to protect your enterprise when deploying Web Services. The technologies and concepts that we describe in this book begin with Web Services, and then move on to relating the Web Services interfaces to the security of the rest of your distributed system.

One weak link in the security of your enterprise can result in the failure of its security. Consequently, we describe the security of each part of your company, from the customers, suppliers, and partners beyond your perimeter firewall to securing the heart of your corporate system. By using both theory and examples, we educate you on how to build a secure Web Services system today and how to anticipate and be ready for the security systems of tomorrow.

We trust that you will be able to apply the theory, concepts, and approaches to distributed Web Services security that we discuss as you deploy and upgrade the security of your company's enterprise system. As you move deeper into this new computing paradigm of cooperative computing, you will need all the skills that you can muster to beat the bad guys. We hope our efforts in describing Web Services security will help you in this regard.

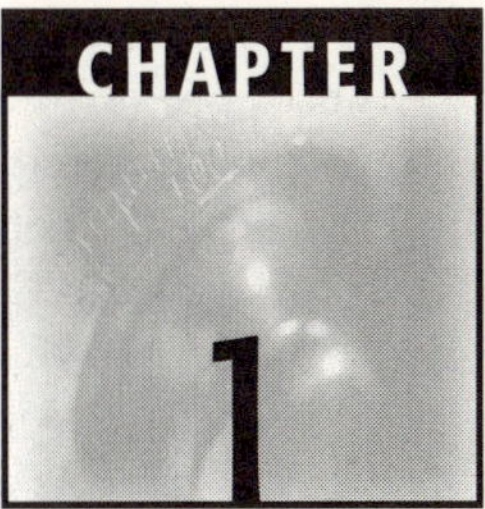

Overview of Web Services Security

In today's global marketplace, the Internet is no longer just about email and Web sites. The Net has become the critical conduit powering a growing list of revenue-generating e-business activities—from e-commerce and e-supply chain management to online marketplaces and collaboration. Web Services leverage the ubiquity of the Internet to link applications, systems, and resources within and among enterprises to enable exciting, new business processes and relationships with customers, partners, and suppliers around the world.

While early Internet applications helped *individuals* communicate with each other, Web Services are focused on helping *applications* communicate with each other. In the past, a purchasing agent might send a purchase order to a supplier via email. In the age of Web Services, a company's purchasing application communicates via the Internet directly with a supplier's warehousing application to check price and availability, submitting the purchase order to the supplier's shipping application—automatically, with little or no human intervention.

The benefits of Web Services are not limited to interactions between different companies. Business units within the same enterprise often use very different processing environments. Each policy domain (that is, scope of security policy enforcement) is likely to be managed differently and be under the control of different organizations. What makes Web Services so interesting is that they provide interoperability across security policy domains.

Web Services represent a fundamental shift, one that promises tremendous benefits in terms of productivity, efficiency, and accuracy. Indeed, corporate IT organizations are only just beginning to understand the full potential of Web Services. But, while they offer attractive advantages, Web Services also present daunting challenges relating to privacy and security. No longer is the "back office" hermetically sealed from the outside world. In exposing critical business functions to the Internet, Web Services can expose valuable corporate data, applications, and systems to a variety of external threats. These threats are not imaginary. They range from random acts of Net vandalism to sophisticated, targeted acts of information theft, fraud, or sabotage. Either way, the consequences can be catastrophic to the organization.

Given the potential risks, security must be a central focus of any Web Services implementation. Just as IT organizations are turning to proven Enterprise Application Integration (EAI) architectures to address systems integration issues, they can take advantage of new Enterprise Application Security Integration (EASI) architectures that enable end-to-end integration of scalable, best-of-breed security technologies for their Web Services. An overview of these architectures will be discussed later in this chapter.

What makes security for Web Services so challenging is the distributed, heterogeneous nature of these services. Web Services technology is based on the interoperation of many different software applications running on a variety of geographically dispersed systems in a complex, multidomain environment via the Internet. The Extensible Markup Language (XML); SOAP; Universal Description, Discovery, and Integration (UDDI); Web Services Description Language (WSDL); and other protocols and mechanisms are employed to enable platform-independent interaction across domains via the Internet.

Web Services Overview

Web Services are XML-based messages delivered via Internet standard protocols. XML is a text-based method for representing data, and will be discussed in greater detail in Chapter 2, "Web Services." Web Services messages can contain documents or procedure invocations. Specific definitions of Web Services vary widely, and range from "A web service is an application that exists in a distributed environment, such as the Internet" (Sun Microsystems FAQ) to "A Web Service is an interface that describes a collection of operations that are network accessible through standardized XML messaging." (Kreger 2001). Often, instead of defining a Web Service, an author describes the properties of a Web Service or defines it in terms of the protocols normally associated with it.

For the discussions in this book, we define a Web Service as an XML-based messaging interface to computing resources that is accessible via Internet standard protocols. We will even go a bit beyond this to say that the Web Services messaging protocol is SOAP, which we will describe in greater detail in Chapter 2. Please note that while Web Services may use "the Web," Web Services are not tied to a single transport protocol.

Although the most common way to exchange a Web Service request is via the Web transport Hypertext Transfer Protocol (HTTP), other transport protocols, such as File Transfer Protocol (FTP) or Simple Mail Transfer Protocol (SMTP), can also support Web Services.

Characteristics of Web Services

Web Services expand the Web from a user front end to an application service. With Web Services, the originator of a Web connection is no longer just the consumer or supplier of information. The originator can participate in a distributed application environment and issue remote procedure calls to request services. The use of Internet standard protocols and other standards by Web Services allows services to work across diverse environments, solving cross-platform interoperability issues.

Intranet and extranet applications are likely to be the major beneficiaries of Web Services. Consumer-oriented applications don't need the kind of access to distributed processing that Web Services promise. Distributed processing is more commonly needed for large-scale corporate applications. Additionally, for security reasons, companies aren't likely to allow access to the more powerful capabilities that Web Services can provide unless there is a larger measure of trust and partnership between the parties than exists for retail, consumer transactions.

Web Services facilitate the creation and resolution of requests involving parties from different organizations, whether the organizations are two separate companies or two business units within the same company. The actual requester of the service creates a request contained in an XML message. This message may be signed for authentication purposes by the requester, as we discuss later in this chapter.

Web Services Architecture

Web Services are an Internet protocol-based interface to processing. As one would expect, Web Services are generally stateless and follow a request/response model of interaction. Web Services standards provide a way to locate interfaces and exchange data in an understandable way. For Intranet applications, SOAP messages may be received directly by application servers. For extranet applications, because of security concerns, SOAP messages are likely to be received by Web Servers or integration servers that pass the messages on to the appropriate applications.

Other than the interface to the service, there are no requirements as to how the services are provided. For instance, a Web Services front end can be added to an existing information-processing infrastructure. This is particularly useful for organizations that have an existing infrastructure in place. Figure 1.1 shows an example of how Web Services can be provided in this way. Alternately, applications can be engineered to use a consistent Web Services model in all tiers.

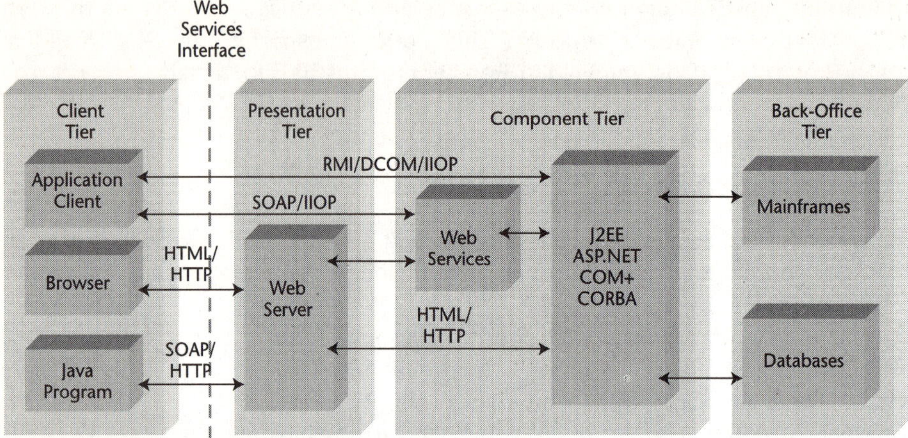

Figure 1.1 Typical Web Services environment.

Security as an Enabler for Web Services Applications

Corporations are discovering the power of Web Services-enabled e-business applications to increase customer loyalty, support sales efforts, and manage internal information. The common thread in these diverse efforts is the need to present end users with a unified view of information stored in multiple systems, particularly as organizations move from static Web sites to the transactional capabilities of electronic commerce. To satisfy this need, legacy systems are being integrated with powerful new Web Services-based applications that provide broad connectivity across a multitude of back-end systems. These unified applications bring direct bottom-line benefits. For example:

On the Internet. A bank cements relationships with commercial customers by offering increased efficiency with online currency trading. This service requires real-time updates and links to back-office transactional and profitability analysis systems.

On extranets. A bank and an airline both increase their customer bases with a joint venture—a credit card that offers frequent flyer credits sponsored by the bank. This service requires joint data sharing, such as purchase payment and charge-back information, as well as decision support applications to retrieve, manipulate, and store information across enterprise boundaries. Additionally, employees from both companies need to access information.

On an intranet. A global manufacturer accelerates the organizational learning curve by creating a global knowledge sharing system for manufacturing research and development. Plant engineers on one continent can instantly share process breakthroughs with colleagues thousands of miles away.

On the other hand, these new e-business applications can have a dark side. They can open a direct pipeline to the enterprise's most valuable information assets, presenting a tempting target for fraud, malicious hackers, and industrial espionage.

Appropriate protections are a prerequisite for doing business, both for maintaining an organization's credibility with its stakeholders and for protecting its financial viability. For example:

- The bank offering currency trading needs to protect the integrity of its core systems from unauthorized transfers or tampering.
- The bank and airline in a joint venture may compete in other areas or through other partnerships. A secure barrier, permitting authorized transactions only, must be erected between the two enterprise computing environments.
- The manufacturer posting proprietary discoveries needs to ensure that competitors or their contractors cannot eavesdrop on the system. Attacks from both the outside and the inside must be blocked.

Enterprises rely on information security mechanisms to safeguard their Web Services applications.

Information Security Goals: Enable Use, Bar Intrusion

Information security focuses on protecting valuable and sensitive enterprise data. To secure information assets, organizations must provide availability to legitimate users, while barring unauthorized access. In general, secure systems must provide the following protections:

Confidentiality. Safeguard user privacy and prevent the theft of enterprise information both stored and in transit.

Integrity. Ensure that electronic transactions and data resources are not tampered with at any point, either accidentally or maliciously.

Accountability. Detect attacks in progress or trace any damage from successful attacks (security auditing and intrusion detection). Prevent system users from later denying completed transactions (nonrepudiation).

Availability. Ensure uninterrupted service to authorized users. Service interruptions can be either accidental or maliciously caused by denial-of-service attacks.

To provide these four key protections, information security must be an integral part of Web Services system design and implementation.

Web Services Solutions Create New Security Responsibilities

The breadth of information security in Web Services applications is broader than you might expect. Many system architects and developers are accustomed to thinking about security as a low-level topic, dealing only with networks, firewalls, operating systems, and cryptography. However, Web Services change the risk levels associated with deploying software because of the increased ability to access data, and as a consequence, security is becoming an important design issue for any e-business software component.

The scope of Web Services security is so broad because these applications typically cut across lines of business. There are many examples of new business models that drive security needs:

E-commerce sites on the Internet. These rely on credit card authorization services from an outside company. A federated relationship between an e-commerce company and a credit card service depends on trustworthy authenticated communication.

Cross-selling and customer relationship management. This relies on customer information being shared across many lines of business within an enterprise. Cross-selling allows an enterprise to offer a customer new products or services based on existing sales. Customer relationship management allows the enterprise to provide consistent customer support across many different services. These e-business services are very valuable, but if they are not properly constrained by security policies, the services may violate a customer's desire for privacy.

Supply chain management. This requires continuing communication among all of the suppliers in a manufacturing chain to ensure that the supply of various parts is adequate to meet demand. The transactions describing the supply chain that are exchanged among the enterprises contain highly proprietary data that must be protected from outside snooping.

Bandwidth on demand. This allows customers to make dynamic requests for increases in the quality of a telecommunications service and get instant results. Bandwidth on demand is an example of *self-administration*, in which users handle many of their own administrative functions rather than relying on an administrator within the enterprise to do it for them. Self-administration provides better service for customers at a lower cost, but comes with significant security risks. Because corporate servers, which were previously only available to system administrators, are now accessible by end users, security mechanisms must be in place to ensure that sensitive administrative functions are off-limits.

In each of the preceding cases, one enterprise or line of business can expose another organization to increased security risk. For example, a partner can unintentionally expose your business to a security attack by providing its customers access to your business resources. As a result, security risk is no longer under the complete control of a single organization. Risks must be assessed and managed across a collection of organizations, which is a new and very challenging security responsibility.

Risk Management Holds the Key

A large middle ground exists between the options of avoiding e-business applications based on Web Services altogether, fatalistically launching unprotected systems, or burdening every application with prohibitively costly and user-unfriendly security measures.

This middle ground is the area of risk management. The risk-management approach aims not to eliminate risk but to control it. Risk management is a rigorous balancing process of determining how much and what kind of security to incorporate in light of business needs and acceptable levels of risk. It unlocks the profit potential of expanded network connectivity by enabling legitimate use while blocking unauthorized access. The goal is to provide adequate protection to meet business needs without undue risk, making the right trade-offs between security and cost, performance, and functionality.

Consider four different Web Services users: an Internet service provider (ISP), a hospital administrator, a banker, and a military officer. Each has a different security concern:

- The ISP is primarily concerned about availability, that is, making services available to its customers.
- The hospital administrator wants to ensure data integrity, meaning that patient records are only updated by authorized staff.
- The banker is most concerned about accountability, meaning that the person who authorizes a financial transaction is identified and tracked.
- The military officer wants confidentiality, that is, keeping military secrets out of the hands of potential enemies.

The challenge is to implement security in a way that meets business needs cost-effectively in the short term and as enterprise needs expand. Meeting the challenge requires a collaborative effort between corporate strategists and information technology managers. Understanding the business drivers for information security helps clarify where to focus security measures. Understanding the underlying application architecture—how components work together—clarifies the most practical approach for building system security.

Industrial experience in managing e-business information security is generally low. Security technology is changing rapidly, and corporate management is not well equipped to cope with risk management changes caused by technology changes. New versions of interconnected Web Services systems and software product versions continue to appear, and with each release, a whole new set of security vulnerabilities surfaces.

Managing security risk in distributed Web Services applications is daunting, but following some basic rules for building security into component-based applications lays the groundwork for a solid risk management approach. Although this book does not provide detailed advice on security risk management, we do describe principles for building secure Web Services applications that are independent of any specific technology and will continue to be a guide for you as technologies evolve. Other chapters in this book, particularly Chapter 12, "Planning and Building a Secure Web Services Architecture," supply many insights on Enterprise Application Security Integration (EASI) that will place your risk-management approach on a firm foundation.

Information Security: A Proven Concern

Information security is a serious concern for most businesses. Even though the reporting of computer-based crime is sporadic because companies fear negative publicity and continued attacks, the trend is quite clear: Information security attacks continue to be a real threat to businesses. According to a recent Computer Security Institute Survey, 90 percent of interviewed businesses reported that they had detected computer security breaches in the last year. In addition, 74 percent of the businesses reported that the attacks caused financial losses, such as losses from financial fraud or theft of valuable intellectual property.

Threats to businesses result from both internal and external attacks. In the same survey, 71 percent of businesses said that they detected insider attacks (by trusted corporate users). This last statistic is very important from the perspective of this book—to meet corporate needs, a complete end-to-end security solution must address insider attacks.

Web Services solutions blur the line between the inside world containing trusted users and the outside world containing potentially hostile attackers. As we've discussed, a primary purpose of Web Services architectures is to open up the corporate network to the external world, thus allowing valuable corporate resources to be accessible to outsiders. Outsiders (such as business partners, suppliers, or remote employees) may have data access rights to corporate information very similar to those of many insiders. As a result, protection mechanisms must be in place not only at the external system boundaries, but also throughout the enterprise architecture.

According to a META Group survey, 70 percent of businesses view information security as critical to their corporate mission. Because of the continuing threat, many businesses are increasing their spending on security; large corporations are increasing their spending the most.

We're concerned about the way businesses spend their money on security. We've seen many of them address security using a fragmented, inefficient approach, in which various corporate divisions each build their own ad hoc security solutions. Piecemeal security solutions can be worse than no security at all because they can result in:

- The mistaken belief that the system *is* secure
- Redundant spending across the organization
- Point solutions that don't scale or interoperate
- Increased maintenance, training, and administration costs

Applying security products without thinking about how they all fit together clearly does not work. We believe that businesses should build and leverage a common security infrastructure that is shared across the enterprise. A unified approach to Web Services security is the only way to address complex multitier Web Services applications, which we'll explain later in this chapter.

Securing Web Services

The pervasive reach and platform-agnostic nature of Web Services demands a security framework that enables enterprises to secure and control access to applications and data, without impeding the exchange of data that is essential for successful Web Services.

Web Services Security Requirements

Let's begin by defining some core security services that are fundamental to end-to-end application security across multitier applications. They are:

Authentication. Verifies that principals (human users, registered system entities, and components) are who they claim to be. The result of authentication is a set of *credentials*, which describes the attributes (for example, identity, role, group, and clearance) that may be associated with the authenticated principal.

Authorization. Grants permission for principals to access resources, providing the basis for access control, which enforces restrictions of access to prevent unauthorized use. Access controls ensure that only authorized principals may modify resources and that resource contents are disclosed only to authorized principals.

Cryptography. Provides cryptographic algorithms and protocols for protecting data and messages from disclosure or modification. Encryption provides confidentiality by encoding data into an unintelligible form with a reversible algorithm, which allows the holder of the decryption key(s) to decode the encrypted data. A digital signature provides integrity by applying cryptography to ensure that data is authentic and has not been modified during storage or transmission.

Accountability. Ensures that principals are accountable for their actions. Security auditing provides a record of security-relevant events and permits the monitoring of a principal's actions in a system. Nonrepudiation provides irrefutable proof of data origin or receipt.

Security administration. Defines the security policy maintenance life cycle embodied in user profiles, authentication, authorization, and accountability mechanisms as well as other data relevant to the security framework.

All security services must be *trustworthy* and provided with adequate assurance. That is, there must be confidence that security services have been implemented correctly, reliably, and without relying on the secrecy of proprietary mechanisms. We will discuss the concept of building trustworthy security architectures in Chapter 12.

Moreover, all of the critical security services must be provided on an end-to-end basis. Each Web Services transaction must be traceable from its origin through to its fulfillment, maintaining consistent security across processing tiers and domains. This is no simple feat when one considers the potential diversity of applications, systems, and business processes involved in a typical Web Services transaction—and when you consider that these distributed systems may be managed in very different ways.

Access to enterprise Web Services search and discovery mechanisms, such as UDDI, also needs to be managed. While much of the Web Service information listed in a Web Services directory is appropriate for all the applications or developers in the enterprise, it is also important to provide a robust security mechanism for user authentication and authorization. This facility is used to limit the set of users who may either access or update Web Services directory entries, and can be managed at a central point.

Web Services security must be flexible enough to identify all participants in a transaction based on a variety of authentication mechanisms. Web Services security must also be able to establish a *user security context* at each processing tier. (A user security context is the combination of a user's identity and security-relevant attributes.) Sophisticated authorization policies using the security context will be needed. The Web Services security facility must perform auditing so that an accurate record of the steps that occurred to fulfill a request and the identities of the responsible parties is maintained.

Finally, in order to achieve end-to-end security, the Web Services security must pass the security context between domains or tiers, thereby establishing a consistent security context for the entire transaction. Without this consistent security context, there is no way to attribute actions to the right individual later. Passing the user security context also eliminates the need for a user to reauthenticate each time his or her request crosses from one tier to another. Thus, an additional benefit of the seamless integration of security with Web Services is to provide single sign-on (SSO), even across organizations using different security technologies.

Web Services require the ability to use different authentication mechanisms, establish a security context, implement sophisticated authorization policies, and attribute actions to the proper individuals. Consistent security must be maintained across processing tiers and domains in the Web Services world. Flexible ways to create, pass, and establish security contexts are needed for end-to-end security in a Web Services environment.

Providing Security for Web Services

Given the diverse nature of these distributed environments, it is not surprising that Web Services security efforts to date have taken a "patchwork" approach. This patchwork may include a range of existing, standalone Web security mechanisms, together with operating system security (domain logins), communications security (SSL), applications environment security (J2EE, COM+, .NET, or CORBA), and SSO (Netegrity SiteMinder, IBM/Tivoli Policy Director, or others) solutions. Even electronic mail systems can support Web Services. The problem is that each of these solutions has evolved to solve a specific problem within a single tier or domain. While there have been attempts to extend these solutions beyond their original scope, the results have not been very rewarding.

Historically, ad hoc solutions have evolved informally to handle multitiered security. This is especially true in going from one processing tier to another. For instance, user identities can be passed from a Web Server to a business application as HTTP header variables. This is generally done without encryption "in the clear," based on a trust relationship between the Web server and the business application. Once at the application, programmatic security is used for authorization. It is up to the application developer to decide on the authorization policy that must be enforced and to implement it correctly. Infrastructure-provided security services are not generally used. Informal solutions such as these tend to weaken overall system security by making it discretionary and leaving the strength of the implementation up to the skill of the application programmer, who typically isn't experienced implementing security.

How have Web Services affected this security picture? First, interactions are more complex and take place between more diverse environments. When interactions were limited to browsers alone, they required only a transfer of data, and there were still many security problems. Widespread use of Web Services means that direct invocation of services can be performed over HTTP. Web Services are used to invoke distributed procedure calls. Moreover, these requests can come from different domains, from users and servers we know relatively little about.

Although this book concentrates mainly on the delivery of Web Services via HTTP, they could be delivered by other protocols as well, because Web Services are based on XML-based documents. For example, email or message systems can transport Web Services requests and responses. These options make Web Services an even more flexible way of delivering processing capabilities.

Finally, in traditional Web interactions, the actual user is at the other end of a virtual connection. While HTTP itself is stateless, Web SSO systems go to great lengths to create and maintain the notion of a session that maintains a secure connection between the user and Web server. In such sessions, users are available to authenticate themselves using passwords, certificates, or other mechanisms. However, with Web Services, the originator of the request may not be available for authentication on an interactive basis. For instance, the originator may choose to authenticate the request by signing it. The system must be flexible enough to use identity derived in different ways to make access control decisions.

The following diagram (Figure 1.2) illustrates new and existing security mechanisms for securing Web Services at different security tiers. For instance, where access to the Web Service is through a Web Server, Secure Sockets Layer (SSL) and Web SSO can be used. At the application level, Security Assertion Markup Language (SAML) can be used to support authentication and authorization across domains. Finally, access to a mainframe is needed to complete the request, and a mainframe authentication system is in place.

Existing security solutions have tended to concentrate only on one tier because they evolved to solve a single-tier security problem. As the processing model has changed to incorporate Web Services, so has the nature of the security problem. While new solutions have been devised to address the Web Services model, existing security solutions have not been replaced as system implementers have tried to leverage existing investments. The challenge lies in weaving together this patchwork of standalone solutions into an integrated, end-to-end security solution.

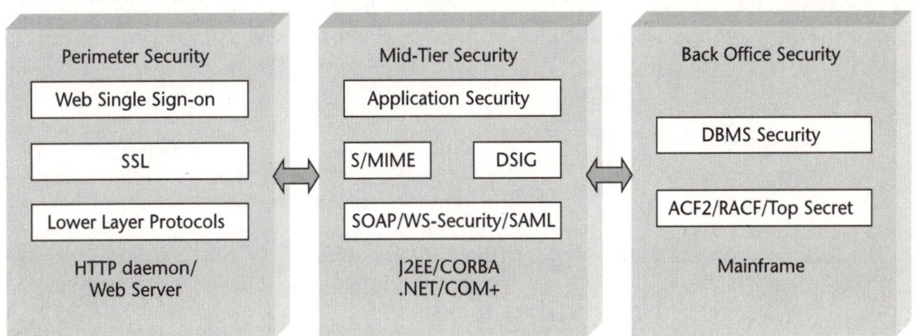

Figure 1.2 Example of Web Service security implementation.

Unifying Web Services Security

As e-business environments have evolved to Web Services models, security technologies have been trying to keep up. As you'll see throughout this book, we believe that most of the pieces of the security puzzle exist, but that it still takes considerable effort to put all these pieces together to build an integrated solution. Figure 1.3 provides an overview of the different security technologies that need to be integrated.

Twenty years ago life was reasonably simple for the security professional. Sensitive data resided on monolithic back-office data stores. There were only a few physical access paths to the data, which were protected by well-understood operating system access control mechanisms. Policies, procedures, and tools had been in place for many years to protect legacy data stores.

Then, several years ago, Web-based applications burst onto the scene. With the advent of e-commerce in this environment, secure access to Web servers was extremely important. Today, there are many mature perimeter security technologies, such as SSL, firewalls, and Web authentication/authorization servers, that enforce security between browser clients and corporate Web servers.

Companies are now building complex e-business logic using Web Services in application platforms in the mid-tier. These application platforms are commonly called *application servers* or *integration servers*. (To simplify terminology, this book uses the term *application server* to indicate any type of mid-tier application platform.) As we've discussed, the business motivation for this development is compelling: Web Services business logic allows accessibility to back-office legacy data in ways never imagined; the opportunities for increased interaction among all kinds of buyers and suppliers seem endless.

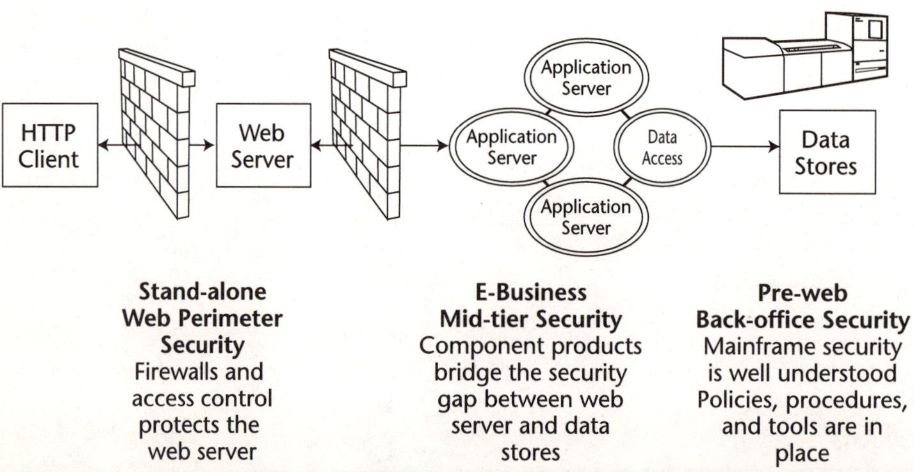

Figure 1.3 Web Services require EASI across multiple security technologies.

Security gets much more interesting when we introduce Web Service-enabled components. Although there are many technologies that hook up Web servers to back-office legacy systems via a middle tier, the security of these approaches is often nonexistent. In fact, several recent publicized attacks have been caused by weaknesses in mid-tier security that have exposed sensitive back-office data (for example, customer credit card numbers and purchase data) to the outside world. Companies are usually at a loss for solutions to middle tier security problems.

To solve the thorny issue of securely connecting Web servers to back-office data stores, we introduce the concept of end-to-end Enterprise Application Security Integration (EASI). EASI is a special case of EAI (Ruh, Maginnis, Brown 2000).

EAI is a technique for unifying many different applications by using a common middleware infrastructure. EAI provides an application "bus" that allows every application to communicate with others via a common generic interface. Without EAI, an application would need a separate interface for every other application, thus causing an explosion of pairs of "stovepipe" connections between applications. EAI allows application development to scale to a large number of interchangeable components.

We recognize that the integration of end-to-end security requires EAI techniques. Many different security technologies are used in the perimeter, middle, and back-office tiers. Typically, these security technologies do not interoperate easily. As a result, we face exactly the same problem that application integrators face: A separate ad hoc interface to connect one security technology to another causes an explosion of stovepipe connection pairs between security technologies.

EASI (Heffner 2001) provides a common security framework to integrate many different security solutions. We use Web Services security to bridge the security gap between perimeter and back-office security. By using EASI, new security technologies in each tier may be added without affecting the business applications. We'll further explore the concept of EASI in the next sections.

EASI Requirements

A key issue in enterprise security architectures is the ability to support end-to-end security across many application components. End-to-end security is the ability to ensure that data access is properly protected over the entire path of requests and replies as they travel through the system. The scope of end-to-end security begins with the person accessing a Web browser or other client program, continues through the business components of the middle tier, and ends at the data store on the back-office legacy system. The path may travel through both public and private networks with varying degrees of protection.

In the enterprise architecture shown in Figure 1.4, a user accesses an application in the presentation layer (for example, a Web browser client sends requests to a Web server), which communicates to mid-tier business components (such as Web Service-enabled application servers). Frequently, the client request is transmitted through a complex multitier chain of business components running on a variety of platforms. The request finally makes it to one or more back-office legacy systems, which access persistent data stores on behalf of the user, process the request, and return the appropriate results.

To provide end-to-end security, each link in the chain of requests and replies must be properly protected: from the initiating client, through mid-tier business components, to the back-office systems, and then back again to the client. There are three security tiers that make up any end-to-end enterprise security solution:

Perimeter security technologies. Used between the client and the Web server. Perimeter security enforces protection for customer, partner, and employee access to corporate resources. Perimeter security primarily protects against external attackers, such as hackers.

Mid-tier security technologies. Used between the mid-tier business components. Mid-tier security focuses primarily on protecting against insider attacks, but also provides another layer of protection against external attackers.

Back-office security technologies. Address the protection of databases and operating-system-specific back-end systems, such as mainframe, Unix, and Windows 2000 server platforms.

EASI Solutions

EASI solutions integrate security technologies across the perimeter, middle, and back-office security tiers. An EASI solution first and foremost consists of a security framework, which describes a collection of security service interfaces that may be implemented by an evolving set of security products. We'll spend most of this section describing our approach for defining an enterprise security framework. As you read the rest of this book, keep in mind that we use this security framework to integrate interfaces into all of the Web Service security technologies discussed.

In addition to the framework, an EASI solution also contains the software and hardware technologies for securing e-business components. Chapters 3, 4, 5, 6, and 7 describe digital signatures and encryption for XML documents, WS-Security, SAML, J2EE, CORBA, .NET, COM+, and many other security technologies that may be used to secure Web Services components.

Finally, an EASI solution contains integration techniques, such as bridges, wrappers, and interceptors, that developers can use to plug security technologies into a middleware environment. To hook together different security technologies, EASI must solve a key problem: defining a secure association between clients and targets that establishes a common security context. The security context, which contains a user's identity and other security attributes, must be transferred across the system to a target application. A user's identity and security attributes form the basis for authorization decisions and audit events, and must be protected as they are transmitted between perimeter, middle, and back-office tiers, as shown in Figure 1.4. Because each technology in these tiers represents and protects a user's security information differently, integration of the security context can be a rather difficult problem.

So how can one get a patchwork of different security technologies to interact with and augment one another? The Organization for the Advancement of Structured Information Standards (OASIS) is defining standards called WS-Security and SAML to address this issue. WS-Security defines a standard way to attach security information

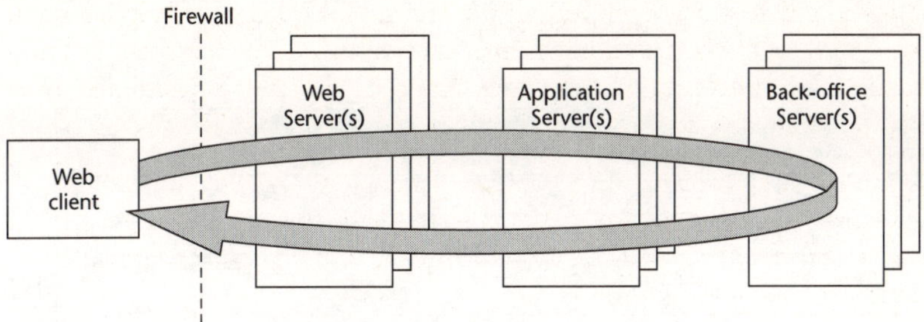

Figure 1.4 Key e-business challenge: end-to-end EASI.

to SOAP messages, while SAML defines a format for exchanging authentication, authorization, and attribute assertions. The combination of these two specifications provides a description of the security context that can be passed across the tiers of an architecture. WS-Security and SAML together are a standards-based approach for expressing the security context that is not tied to any particular vendor's application environment or security product. Designed specifically for distributed security environments, WS-Security and SAML are important building blocks for any Web Services security framework. In Chapter 4, "XML Security and WS-Security," and Chapter 5, "Security Assertion Markup Language," we'll explore WS-Security and SAML in depth; in Chapter 10, "Interoperability of Web Services Security Technologies," we'll look at how WS-Security and SAML facilitate the exchange of an interoperable security context across multiple Web Services security technologies.

EASI Framework

The EASI framework specifies the interactions among the security services and the Web Services components that use those security services. By using common interfaces, it's possible to add new security technology solutions without making big changes to the existing framework. In this way, the EASI framework supports "plug-ins" for new security technologies. Key aspects of the framework are shown in Figure 1.5.

Applications

The security framework provides enterprise security services for presentation components, business logic components, and back-office data stores. The framework supports security mechanisms that enforce security on behalf of *security-aware* and *security-unaware* applications.

Security-aware application. An application that uses security Application Programming Interfaces (APIs) to access and validate the security policies that apply to it. Security-aware applications may directly access security functions that enable the applications to perform additional security checks and fully exploit the capabilities of the security infrastructure.

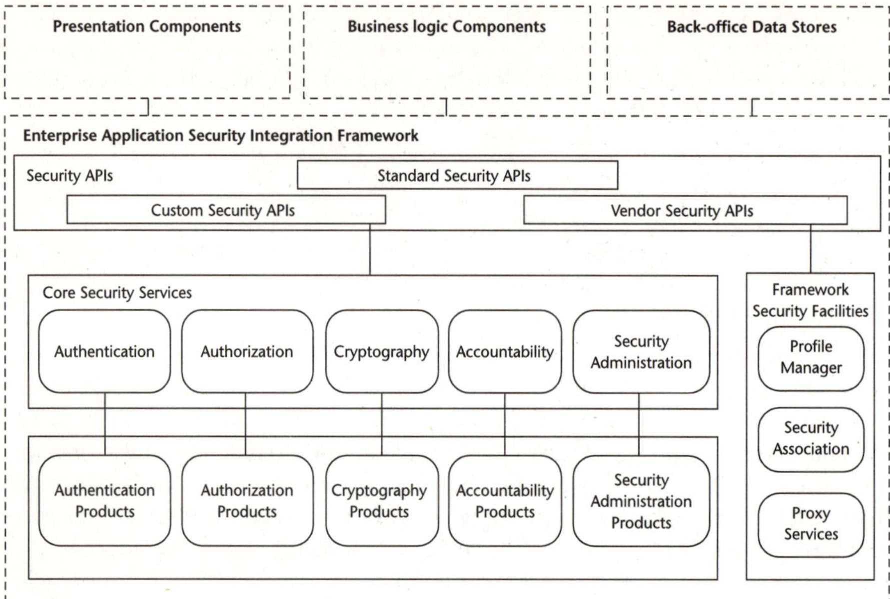

Figure 1.5 EASI framework.

Security-unaware application. An application that does not explicitly call security services, but is still secured by the supporting environment (for example, J2EE or COM+ container). Security is typically enforced for security-unaware applications by using interceptors, which transparently call the underlying security APIs on behalf of the application. This approach reduces the burden on application developers to implement security logic within applications and lessens the chance of security flaws being introduced.

Other applications, called *security self-reliant applications,* do not use any of the security services provided by the framework. A security self-reliant application may not use the security services for two reasons: because it has no security-relevant functionality and thus does not need to be secured or because it uses separate independent security functions that are not part of the defined EASI security framework.

APIs

The framework security APIs are called explicitly by security-aware applications and implicitly by security-unaware applications via interceptors. Security APIs provide interfaces for access to the framework security services. The framework supports standard, custom, and vendor security APIs.

Standard security APIs. We encourage support for APIs based on open standards or industry de facto standards. Examples of such standards are the J2EE and COM+ security APIs described in this book in Chapter 7, "Security of Infrastructures for Web Services." These standards should be used whenever possible because they are likely to provide the most stability and the most portability across many different vendors' products.

Custom security APIs. Custom APIs may be implemented when an enterprise's needs cannot be met by existing standard APIs. Custom APIs are required especially when an enterprise uses a security service that is tailored to its business, for example, a custom-rule-based entitlements engine developed internally by an investment bank.

Vendor security APIs. As a last resort, vendor-specific proprietary APIs may be used where open standards have not yet been defined. We recommend avoiding the use of proprietary security APIs in applications if at all possible. Proprietary APIs make it very difficult for the developer or administrator to switch security products. Although vendors may think this is a great idea, we believe that security technology is changing much too rapidly for an enterprise to be confined to any one product. As an alternative, we recommend wrapping a vendor's proprietary API with a standard or custom API.

Core Security Services

The next layer of the security framework provides core security services enabling end-to-end application security across multitier applications. Each of the security services defines a wrapper that sits between the security APIs and the security products. The security services wrappers serve to isolate applications from the underlying security products. This allows one to switch security products, if the need arises, by simply creating a new wrapper, without affecting application code. The key security services are authentication, authorization, cryptography, accountability, and security administration, which we defined previously.

Framework Security Facilities

The framework provides general security facilities that support the core security services. The framework security facilities include the profile manager, security association, and proxy services.

Profile manager. Provides a general facility for persistent storage of user and application profile and security policy data that can be accessed by other framework services.

Security association. Handles the principal's security credentials and controls how they propagate. During a communication between any two client and target application components, the security association establishes the trust in each party's credentials and creates the security context that will be used when protecting requests and responses in transit between the client and the target. The security association controls the use of delegation, which allows an intermediate server to use the credentials of an initiating principal so that the server may act on behalf of the principal. (Delegation is discussed in considerably more detail in Chapter 11, "Administrative Considerations for Web Services Security.")

Security proxy services. Provide interoperability between different security technology domains by acting as a server in the client's technology domain and a client in the target's domain.

Security Products

Implementation of the framework generally requires several security technology products that collectively constitute the enterprise security services. Examples of such required security products include firewalls, Web authentication/authorization products, Web Service and component authentication/authorization products, cryptographic products, and directory services. Several of these product categories are discussed in this book. We describe CORBA, COM+, .NET, and J2EE security in Chapter 7, and we survey other relevant security technologies in Chapter 12.

EASI Benefits

At this point, the benefits of using a framework to address enterprise application security integration should be clear. Our approach focuses on standards, which are the best way to maintain Web Service application portability and interoperability in the long run. Products and technologies will come and go, but generally accepted security standards for fundamental security services will be much more stable. A standards-based set of security APIs allows you to evolve security products over time without needing to rewrite your applications. Designing your applications for evolving security products is important because we believe that your business requirements and new security technologies will continue to be a moving target. You might choose a great product that satisfies your needs for the present, but you'll probably want to change the product in the future, and most people don't want to be stuck with any one vendor's product for too long.

Having a security framework also means that you don't need to implement everything at once. The framework allows you to start small by selecting the security services you need and building more sophisticated security functionality when and if it's required. The framework provides you with a roadmap for your security architecture, helping to guide you on how to choose products and technologies that match your needs over time.

Finally, the framework puts the security focus where it should be—on building a common infrastructure that can be shared across the enterprise. Custom-built security that is hand-coded within applications is expensive to implement and maintain and is likely to have more security vulnerabilities. A single security infrastructure with APIs that can be used by all of your applications avoids multiple, duplicate definitions of users, security attributes, and other policies. You can focus your limited time and money on building a few critical interoperable security technologies rather than coping with a mass of unrelated security products that will never work together.

After we have fully explored the many aspects of Web Services security, we will return to the theme of EASI at the end of this book. In Chapter 12, when we explain how to plan and build integrated Web Services systems, we use EASI concepts to bring the various security technologies together into a coherent security architecture.

Example of a Secure Web Services Architecture

Throughout this book, we use a simple e-commerce example to illustrate Web Services security topics. Several of the chapters start with the basic scenario described here and then extend the example in a variety of ways to emphasize specific security issues. In this section, we introduce the basic example and provide an overview of its business security requirements.

Business Scenario

Our application is a simple online storefront provided by *ePortal*, shown in Figure 1.6. The store sells its products to *customers*, who can electronically place and settle orders for products through customer *accounts* represented by *shopping carts*. *Members* are a category of customers who get special treatment. Members have access to product deals that are not available to regular customers. We also have two other classes of users that access the storefront: *visitors* are casual browsers of the site, and *staff* administer the storefront applications.

Users have two potential ways to access the services provided by ePortal. In the typical consumer scenario, users access ePortal directly via a browser client. Browser clients may reside anywhere on the Internet, and access the ePortal services via HTML over HTTP (or HTTPS when SSL is used). Alternately, in a business-to-business (B2B) scenario, ePortal users who are employees of a separate company, namely *eBuyer*, access ePortal via Web Services applications. In this case eBuyer employees do not access ePortal directly using a client browser; instead special-purpose applications in eBuyer access ePortal services on behalf of the employees (who may use either a Web browser to access the eBuyer application or perhaps use a customized user interface). The applications access ePortal services via SOAP over HTTP (or HTTPS).

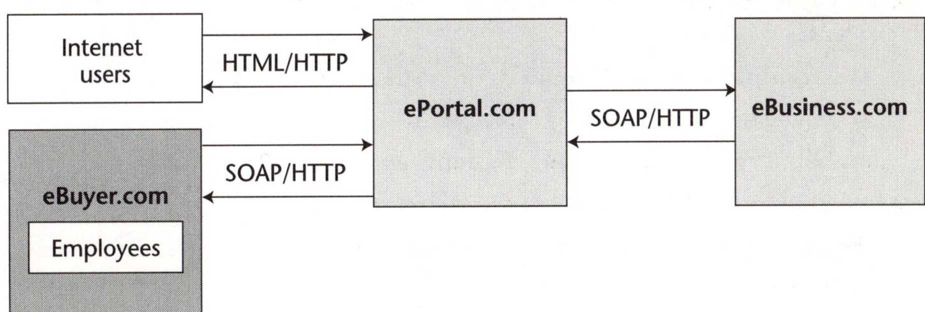

Figure 1.6 eBuyer, ePortal, and eBusiness.

The services provided by ePortal are actually implemented by a third company, *eBusiness*. ePortal accesses the eBusiness services via SOAP over HTTP (or HTTPS). eBusiness stores information about products and prices, and also processes the orders received by ePortal.

Why wouldn't customers access the eBusiness services directly rather than going through ePortal? There are several possible reasons. eBusiness may not be interested in providing a direct Web presence for a large number of consumers, since such a service requires maintaining authentication information for all users, protecting against denial-of-service attacks, and other complexities of a large-scale Web deployment. Furthermore, ePortal may consolidate service offerings from many other companies besides eBusiness. In this case, ePortal may provide the recognized consumer brand (such as those provided by Amazon or eBay), and the consumer may not even be aware that eBusiness exists.

Web Services Interfaces

Figure 1.7 provides an overview of the Web Services implemented by eBusiness. As we just described, eBusiness provides Web Services to ePortal, which in turn provides these services to users.

The list below describes the eBusiness Web Service interfaces along with the methods (operations) that each interface supports. For simplicity, we have omitted the operation signatures that describe arguments and return values because these have little relevance to the security policies that we will define.

- **ProductManager** is the object manager that returns **Product** instances.
  - **getProducts** returns a list of **ProductIDs** that represents the inventory of products that eBusiness is selling. (To keep the example simple, we don't provide an interface to add new products to the list.)
  - **lookup** returns a Product instance based on a supplied **ProductID**.
- **Product** represents a product that eBusiness is selling.
  - **getPrice** returns the price of **Product**.
  - **setPrice** sets the price of **Product**.
- **AccountManager** is the object manager that returns **Account** instances. This manager stores accounts (shopping carts) so a customer may retrieve them for later use.
  - **create** makes a new **Account** based on the **CustomerID**.
  - **delete** removes an existing **Account**.
  - **lookup** retrieves an existing **Account** based on the **CustomerID**.
- **Account** represents a customer's shopping cart, which is a list of product orders.
  - **placeOrder** puts an order into **Account**.
  - **deleteOrder** deletes an order from **Account**.
  - **listOrders** lists the orders in **Account**.
  - **settleOrder** allows the customer to pay for the orders in **Account** with a credit card.

For this scenario, we assume that the preceding interfaces have been implemented on an application server containing J2EE, CORBA, COM+, or .NET components. A typical interaction would go something like this: A customer is first authenticated to ePortal.com, and ePortal then gets a list of products and prices from eBusiness, using **getProducts** and **getPrice**. The customer then places an order for products into his or her account, which ePortal requests from eBusiness.com, using **placeOrder**. Sometime later the customer settles the orders with a credit card number, which ePortal requests from eBusiness.com by calling **settleOrder**.

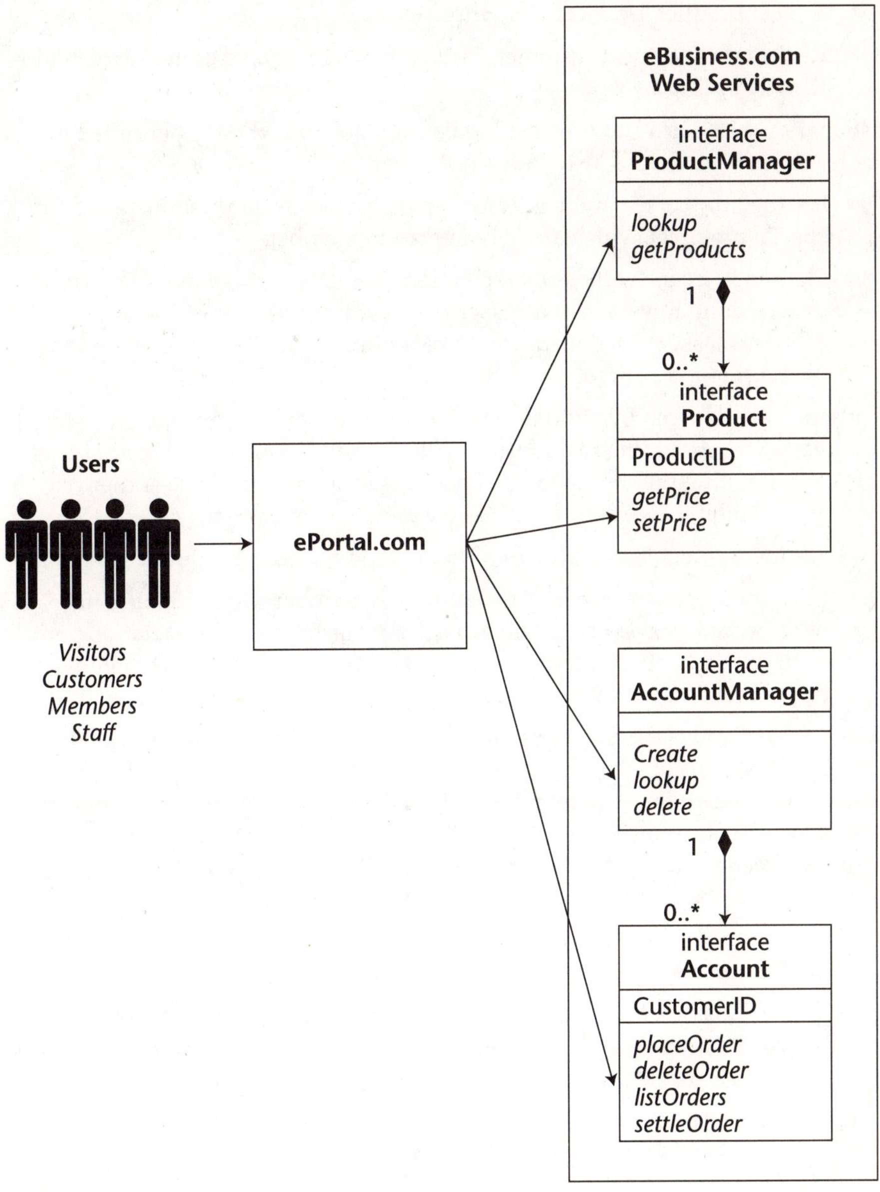

Figure 1.7 eBusiness Web Service interfaces.

Scenario Security Requirements

The Web Service security policies that we define in later chapters are based on the business requirements for this example. Generally, it's the combination of ePortal and eBusiness security mechanisms that enforces the overall business requirements for our example. We describe the business requirements for each class of user below.

Visitors. To entice new customers, ePortal permits visitors who are unauthenticated users to browse the site. Visitors are permitted very limited access. Visitors may:

- See the product list, but not their prices.
- Register to become a customer. Visitors may create an **Account**, which turns the visitor into a **Customer.**

Customers. Most users accessing ePortal are customers who are permitted to order regular products. Customers may:

- See the product list and prices for regular products, but not the prices for special products, which are only offered to members.
- Place, delete, and settle (pay for) orders. A customer may not delete his or her **Account**, however, and must ask someone on the ePortal staff to perform this task. ePortal wants to make it difficult for customers to remove their affiliation with the company.

Members. If approved by ePortal, some customers may become members. Members have a longstanding relationship with ePortal and are offered price breaks on special products. Other than having access to special products and prices, members exhibit the same behavior as customers. Members may:

- See the product list and prices for regular and special products.
- Place, delete, and settle (pay for) orders. A member may not delete his or her **Account**, however, and must ask someone on the ePortal staff to perform this task. ePortal wants to make it difficult for members to remove their affiliation with the company.

Staff. ePortal and eBusiness company staff members are responsible for administering all aspects of the site. However, ePortal and eBusiness are concerned about someone on the staff committing fraud by creating fictitious customers and using stolen credit card numbers to order merchandise. To prevent this exposure, people on the staff are not permitted to settle orders on behalf of customers or members. Staff may:

- See the product list and prices for regular and special products and set product prices.
- Assist a customer or member by placing, deleting, or listing orders on their behalf. Staff may not settle orders, however—customers and members must settle their own orders.
- Administer customer and member accounts, including the creation, deletion, and looking up of the accounts.

Summary

In this chapter, we covered a large expanse of material to introduce you to the wide world of Web Services security. We started with a quick overview of Web Services and described how they are focused on helping applications communicate with each other, enabling interactions between applications residing in different companies using different processing environments.

We then described how security is an enabler for many Web Services applications: without a good security solution in place, many new e-business opportunities would not be feasible. We also discussed the concept of risk management, which balances the level of security that is required according to the business factors of cost, performance, and functionality. We showed that information security is a serious concern for many businesses, in terms of both external and internal (insider) attacks.

Next, we described the need for controlling access to Web Services data without impeding the exchange of data. We described Web Services security requirements in terms of authentication, authorization, cryptography, accountability, and security administration. We then enumerated the patchwork of security mechanisms that can be used to support Web Services security: operating system security, digital signatures, J2EE, CORBA, COM+, .NET, SSO, WS-Security, and SAML, among others.

We introduced Enterprise Application Security Integration (EASI), which we use to unify the many different security technologies needed to secure Web Services. We defined perimeter, middle, and back-office tiers of security and described how they all work together to provide end-to-end security. We defined an EASI solution in terms of a security framework, technologies, and integration techniques that hook those technologies together. Recall that the EASI framework consists of a number of layers, including the applications, APIs, core security services, framework security services, and underlying security products. The EASI framework enables architects to design security systems that are flexible and able to meet future needs as business requirements and technologies evolve.

Finally, we introduced the eBuyer, ePortal, and eBusiness business scenario, Web Services interfaces, and security requirements. This example will be used as the basis of our security discussions in several of the later chapters.

In the rest of this book we'll expand on many of the concepts that we've just introduced. Hopefully, this chapter has laid the groundwork for your basic understanding of the security issues of Web Services.

In several of the chapters, you'll see code and XML fragments that refer to security integration technology. Rather than focus on any specific set of products, this book addresses issues that are relevant to many different application servers and security products. At Quadrasis, we have worked on a variety of Web Services security solutions, so we explain what we have learned about integrating security into J2EE, CORBA, COM+, and .NET environments. Our work is based on security integration in many application platform environments, including Microsoft .NET and COM+, BEA WebLogic, IBM WebSphere, Sun FORTE and JWSDP, Sysinet WASP, Hitachi TPBroker, Iona Orbix, and Inprise Visibroker. We've integrated application servers with many different security products, including Quadrasis Security Unifier, Netegrity SiteMinder, Entrust getAccess, and IBM/Tivoli PolicyDirector to name a few.

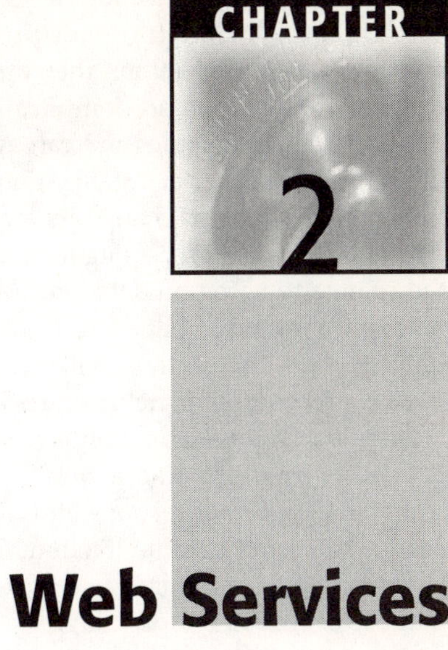

Web Services

Web Services provide a way to access business or application logic using Internet-compatible protocols such as HTTP, SMTP, or FTP. Because of the widespread adoption of these protocols and formats such as XML, we expect Web Services to address many of the requirements for interoperability across independent processing environments and domains. Web Services can overcome differences in platforms, development languages, and architectures, allowing organizations to perform processing tasks cooperatively. Using XML and SOAP, systems from different domains with independent environments, different architectures, and different platforms can engage in a distributed endeavor to address business needs.

Distributed Computing

Pressures to share information and cooperatively share processing lead to the notion of distributed processing. Traditional distributed processing models assume that there is a common environment or architecture between cooperating entities. When both parties try to accomplish a processing task using J2EE or COM+, a common architecture exists for the invocation of operations or sharing of data. This makes it relatively easy to connect applications. While a common architecture does not guarantee interoperability, it makes it easier to achieve.

It isn't always possible for all the participants in distributed processing activities to use the same architecture and processing environment. When processing must be spread across organizations, their architectures, platforms, and development languages are likely to be different. Complications arising from mismatches in environments can exist between companies and can even exist between departments or divisions within the same company. An organization with a large investment in an existing infrastructure cannot afford to change its architecture and processing capabilities, even if successful distributed processing depends on it. And, if one organization is willing to make the change to accommodate another organization, there are probably other groups it needs to work with that can't make such an all-encompassing change. As a result, it's unlikely that organizations will be able to use a common environment.

Current processing architectures are single domain, but multitiered. That is, the processing load within a domain is spread among several systems, each handling a well-defined portion of a transaction. The systems can work sequentially or in parallel. A common division of responsibility is to have a front-end processor that handles data presentation and user interaction, a middle tier that is responsible for implementing business logic, and a back-end system that may be a data repository or a mainframe that performs batch processing.

A logical extension of multitiered processing is multidomain processing. A processing domain is a computing facility under the control of a single organization. A domain may include many computers and utilize different processing architectures. A department or a division within a company may control a domain, or a domain may be under the control of a company. Within a large company, there may be an accounting domain and a purchasing domain. We want the accounting system to know of purchases occurring in the purchasing system so that the bills can be paid automatically. Between companies, it may be desirable for a purchasing system to request bids from and send purchase orders to vendors' systems.

Multidomain processing is generally very difficult to implement because of the disparate platforms, environments, and languages in different domains.

One notable attempt at achieving multidomain processing is Electronic Data Interchange (EDI). EDI is a standard format for exchanging financial or commercial information. Two versions of EDI are in use. They are Accredited Standards Committee (ASC) X12 and the International Standards Organization's Electronic Data Interchange for Administration, Commerce, and Transport (EDIFACT). The latter standard is often referred to as UN/EDIFACT, since it was originally developed by a United Nations working party.

With EDI, a company can transmit a purchase order to its vendor. Banks use EDI to send funds transfer information to financial clearinghouses. Value-added networks are used to transfer the EDI messages. EDI has existed since about 1980, and it has been used successfully by many companies.

By dealing with the structure and format of data exchanged, EDI frees each party to the transaction from the requirement for a uniform computing environment. So long as the sender can construct the correct message, it does not matter what platform, operating system, or application created the message. Likewise, on the receiving side, so long as the receiver can parse the message, identify the elements of interest, and process them appropriately, the processing environment at the receiver's end is of no consequence. The transaction has been processed by two loosely coupled systems located in two separate domains.

There are several reasons why EDI is not used more widely. EDI messages are rigid. The data is not self-defining, and it is presented in a prescribed order with a fixed representation. This rigid structure often needs modification when users discover needs that cannot be accommodated by the existing fields. However, EDI's rigidity makes changes, such as adding new fields, difficult to implement. This leads to a multitude of vendor- and customer-specific implementations.

Another reason for EDI's limited acceptance is that specialized software is required, which can be very expensive. EDI documents are often transferred via specialized, value added networks, increasing cost and support requirements. Implementing EDI can be very costly, and a company needs a very compelling reason before choosing to adopt it.

Distributed Processing across the Web

Extensible Markup Language (XML), which is a platform-independent way to specify information, is the foundation of Web Services. SOAP, which originally stood for Simple Object Access Protocol (newer versions of the specification do not use it as an acronym), builds on XML and supports the exchange of information in a decentralized and distributed environment. SOAP consists of a set of rules for encoding information and a way to represent remote procedure calls and responses, allowing true distributed processing across the Web. XML and SOAP enable platform- and data-independent interfaces to applications. Because Web Services are usually built on HTTP, they can be delivered with little change to existing infrastructures, including firewalls.

UDDI and WSDL also support Web Services. Universal Description, Discovery, and Integration (UDDI) is a mechanism for discovering where specific Web Services are provided and who provides them. Web Services Description Language (WSDL) specifies the interfaces to these Web Services, what data must be provided, and what is returned. SOAP, UDDI, and WSDL are the underlying technologies upon which Web Services are based. Using these protocols (shown in Figure 2.1), systems from different domains, independent environments, or with different architectures can engage in a cooperative manner to implement business functions. SOAP, UDDI, and WSDL are built using XML and various Internet protocols such as HTTP.

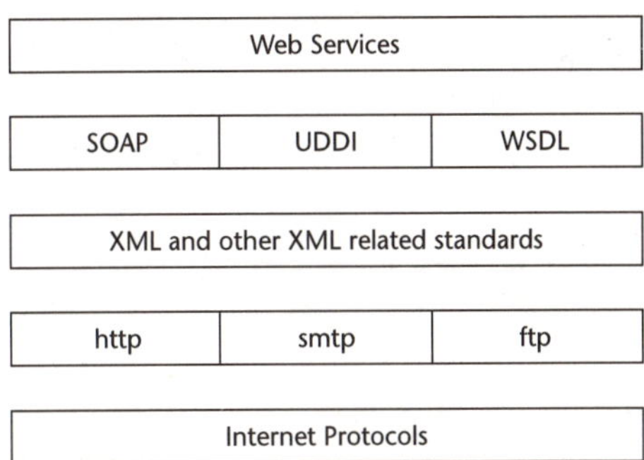

Figure 2.1 Web Services building blocks.

SOAP, UDDI and WSDL are used in different phases, called publishing, finding, and binding, in the Web Services development cycle. The Publish, Find, and Bind Model is shown in Figure 2.2.

The model begins with the publish phase, when an organization decides to offer a Web Service (1). The Web Service can be an existing application with a new Web Service front end, or it can be a totally new application. Once an enterprise has developed the application and made it available as a Web Service, the enterprise describes the interface to the application so that potential users interested in subscribing to it can understand how to access it. This description can be oral, in some human language such as English, or it can be in a form, such as WSDL, that can be understood by Web Services development tools. To facilitate automated lookups, the service provider advertises the existence of the service by publishing it in a registry (2). Paper publications or traditional Web Services can provide this service, or UDDI directories can advertise the existence of the Web Service.

The next step of the model is the find phase. Once the service is advertised in a UDDI registry, potential subscribers can search for possible providers (3 and 4) and implement applications that utilize the service (5). Potential subscribers use the entries in the registry to learn about the company offering the service, the service being offered, and the interface to the service.

The final phase of the model is the bind phase. When a subscriber decides to use a published service, it must implement the service interface, also called binding to the service, and negotiate with the service provider for the use of the service. The negotiation can cover mutual responsibilities, fees, and service levels.

When the application has been implemented and the business relationships resolved, the Web Service is utilized operationally. The only participants at this point are the service subscriber, who requests the service (6), and the service provider, who delivers the service (7). WSDL and UDDI registries are generally only used during the initial discovery of the service and the design of the application.

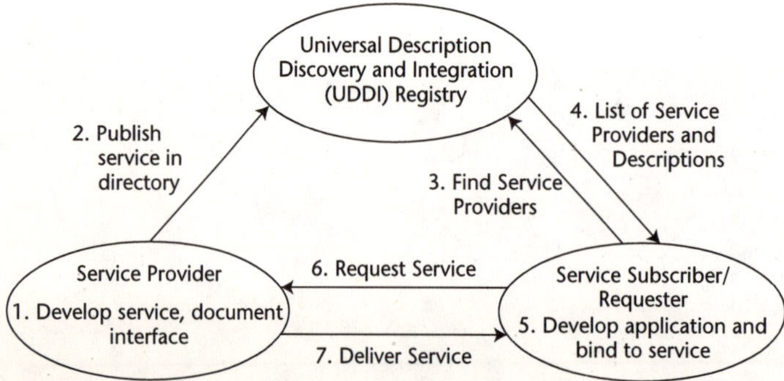

Figure 2.2 Web Services development phases.

Web Services Pros and Cons

Web Services have many advantages that were not enjoyed by earlier attempts at cross-domain interoperability. Since Web Services are in the early phase of adoption, we cannot readily point to many actual implementations that prove Web Services live up to expectations. Nevertheless, Web Services have many characteristics that set them apart from solutions that came before them and make Web Services more likely to succeed. The advantages of Web Services are:

- Web Services processing is loosely coupled. Earlier attempts to address cross-domain interoperability often assumed a common application environment at both ends of a transaction. Web Services allow the subscriber and provider to adopt the technology that is most suited to their needs to do the actual processing.
- Web Services use XML-based messages. Web Services using XML have a flexible model for data interchange that is independent of the computing environment.
- Participating in Web Services does not require abandoning existing investments in software. Existing applications can be used for Web Services by adding a Web Services front end. This makes possible the gradual adoption of Web Services.
- Software vendors are coming out with tools to support the use of Web Services. Organizations can use currently available tools from vendors such as IBM, Microsoft, Sun, and others. There is no delay between interest in the technology and the availability of tools to implement and use Web Services.
- There is a lot of emphasis on the interoperability of Web Services. Web Services tool developers are working to demonstrate interoperability between implementations. It's likely that this will pay off and allow developers to choose tools from one vendor and be confident that they will be able to interoperate with other implementations.
- The modular way Web Services are being defined allows implementers to pick and choose what techniques they will adopt. Other than having a basis in XML, SOAP, UDDI, and WSDL, the building blocks of Web Services have related, but independent capabilities. They are not tightly coupled and don't depend on each other to function.
- Use of Internet standard protocols means that most organizations already have much of the communications software and infrastructure needed to support Web Services. Few new protocols need to be supported, and existing development environments and languages can be used.
- Web Services can be built and interoperate independently of the underlying programming language and operating system. In organizations where there isn't a single standard, Web Services make interoperability possible, even when one part of the organization uses .NET, while another portion uses Java, to build their Web services, and other organizations use other technologies.

Reservations about Web Services fall into two categories. First, Web Services are not proven technology; there is some suspicion that Web Services are the fashionable solution of the day. That is, some think that Web Services are the current fad, and like many other solutions to the distributed processing problem from the past, they will not deliver. While we cannot disprove this, the advantages that Web Services have over past solutions are significant.

The second reservation about Web Services centers on its reliance on XML. While there are many advantages to XML, size is not one of them. Use of XML expands the size of data several times over. The size of a SOAP message translates into more storage and transmission time. The flexibility of SOAP means that more processing is needed to format and parse messages. Do the advantages of XML outweigh the additional storage requirements, transmission time, and processing needed? The answer is a qualified yes. The flexibility offered by XML is required when trying to connect two dissimilar processing environments in a useful way. Spanning processing domains requires a flexible representation. However, once a message is within a single environment, on either side of the connection, implementers must decide the extent to which XML is required. XML will not always be the choice to represent data within a single processing domain.

Extensible Markup Language

In order to understand Web Services, the reader must understand XML. Much of what we'll be discussing in this chapter, and other chapters in this book, is based on XML. You'll see it in many of our examples.

XML is a derivative of the Standard General Markup Language (SGML) (ISO 1986). SGML is an international standard for defining electronic documents and has existed as an ISO standard since 1986. SGML is a meta document definition language used for describing many document types. It specifies ways to describe portions of a document with identifying tags. Specific document types are defined by a document type definition (DTD). A DTD may have an associated parser, which is software that processes that document type.

HTML, an SGML application, has been well accepted on the Web but regarded as limited because of its fixed set of tags and attributes. What was needed was a way to define other kinds of Internet documents with their own markups, which led to the creation of XML. Work on XML began in 1996, under the auspices of the World Wide Web Consortium (W3C). The XML Special Interest Group, chaired by Jon Bosak of Sun Microsystems, took on the work. It was adopted as a W3C Recommendation in 1998 (W3C 2000).

XML is a specialized version of SGML used to describe electronic documents available over the Internet. Like SGML, XML is a document definition metalanguage. Since XML is a subset of SGML, XML documents are legal SGML documents. However, not all SGML documents are legal XML documents.

XML describes the structure of electronic documents by specifying the tags that identify and delimit portions of documents. Each of these portions is called an element. Elements can be nested. The top-level element is called the root. Elements enclosed by the root are its child elements. Each one of these elements can, in turn, have its own child elements. In addition, XML provides a way to associate name-value pairs, called attributes, with elements. XML also specifies what constitutes a well-formed document and processing requirements. XML, like SGML, allows for DTDs. But, DTDs are not used with SOAP, which will be discussed later in this chapter. Instead, SOAP uses XML Schemas, so our examples will be based on XML Schemas rather than DTDs.

XML elements begin with a start tag and end with an end tag. Each document type has a set of legal tags. Start tags consist of a label enclosed by a left angle bracket (<) and a right angle bracket (>). The corresponding end tag is the same label as in the start tag prefaced by a slash (/), both enclosed by the left and right angle brackets. For instance, a price element looks like *<price>123.45</price>*. Unlike HTML, every start tag must be matched by a corresponding end tag.

Start tags may also contain name-value pairs called attributes. Attributes are used to characterize the element between the start and end tags. In our previous example, a currency attribute could be included in the start tag to designate the currency of the price, *<price currency="USdollars"> 123.45</price>*. There are several kinds of attributes. Those most commonly encountered are strings. A specific predefined attribute that will be important later in this chapter is *ID*. The *ID* attribute associates a name with an element of an XML document.

XML defines a small number of syntax restrictions such as requiring an end tag to follow a start tag. These restrictions enable the use of XML parsers, which must be flexible enough to work with any XML-specified document. Any document that follows these restrictions is said to be well formed.

The term XML is used in the literature in several ways. The common uses are:

- The metalanguage specified in (W3C 2000). In our examples, this will involve the use of XML Schemas as well.
- An XML specification for an application-specific document type.
- A specific document created using the application-specific markup language.

To clarify these uses, let's consider the case of a developer wishing to implement a purchasing application. This developer wants to describe a purchase order and decides to use XML, the metalanguage, for this purpose. So, the developer uses XML, the metalanguage, to define the tags that identify the elements of a purchase order. The developer defines an *order* as a sequence of *element*. Then, she defines tags for the elements. These elements are *orderNum*, *itemDescription*, *quantity*, *unitPrice*, and *aggregatePrice*. The developer also defines an attribute called *currency*, which can be applied to *order*. If the attribute is used, the purchase order application will associate the currency of order with the price elements. The resulting XML specification is shown below:

```
<?xml version="1.0" encoding="UTF-8"?>
<xs:schema targetNamespace="www.widgets.com"
    xmlns:xs="http://www.w3.org/2001/XMLSchema"
    xmlns="www.widgets.com"
    elementFormDefault="qualified"
    attributeFormDefault="unqualified">
    <xs:element name="order">
        <xs:complexType>
            <xs:sequence>
                <xs:element name="orderNum"/>
```

```
                <xs:element name="itemDescription"/>
                <xs:element name="quantity"/>
                <xs:element name="unitPrice"/>
                <xs:element name="aggregatePrice"/>
            </xs:sequence>
            <xs:attribute name="currency"/>
        </xs:complexType>
    </xs:element>
</xs:schema>
```

An instance of a purchase order is an order for five widgets, part number 9876, for $34.23 each. This XML purchase order document is shown below. Note that each name is now a tag. Values associated with each tag are sandwiched between the start tag and its corresponding end tag. We also use the attribute to designate prices in dollars.

```
<?xml version="1.0" encoding="UTF-8"?>
<order currency="USDollars"
    xmlns="www.widgets.com"
    xmlns:xsi="http://www.w3.org/2001/XMLSchema-instance"
    xsi:schemaLocation="www.widgets.com>
    <orderNum>9876</orderNum>
    <itemDescription>widgets</itemDescription>
    <quantity>5</quantity>
    <unitPrice>34.23</unitPrice>
    <aggregatePrice>171.15</aggregatePrice>
</order>
```

Supporting Concepts

XML relies on several other concepts to be effective. Two important concepts used within the XML specification are Uniform Resource Identifiers (URIs) and the XML namespace. XML Schemas, a separate W3C Recommendation, is used with XML to provide greater control over data types. In fact, we've already been using all three in our examples.

Uniform Resource Identifiers

URIs identify abstract or physical resources. The resource can be a collection of names that has been defined by some organization or it can be a computer file that contains that list. A URI follows the form: *<scheme>:<scheme-specific-part>*.

The most familiar form of a URI is the Uniform Resource Locator (URL). It usually specifies how to retrieve a resource. It denotes the protocol used to access the resource and the location of the resource. The location can be relative or absolute, but it must be unambiguous. For URLs, the scheme is usually a protocol to access the resource, and the scheme-specific part is the user's name when accessing the resource, the password that allows access, the host of the resource, the port, and the URL path. Not all of the constituents of the scheme-specific part are required. Typically, a URL looks like this: *http://www.widgets.com.*

In addition to complete resources, URLs can be used to refer to an element of an XML document. In order to do this, an ID attribute must be used with the element to associate a unique name with the element. Then, the URL string ends with the *ID* string. We modified our purchase order to include an *ID* attribute.

```
<?xml version="1.0" encoding="UTF-8"?>
<order currency="USDollars"
     ID="ThisPO"
     xmlns="www.widgets.com"
     xmlns:xsi="http://www.w3.org/2001/XMLSchema-instance"
     xsi:schemaLocation="www.widgets.com>
     <orderNum>9876</orderNum>
     <itemDescription>widgets</itemDescription>
     <quantity>5</quantity>
     <unitPrice>34.23</unitPrice>
     <aggregatePrice>171.15</aggregatePrice>
</order>
```

External references to the element must be qualified by the complete URL to the document followed by # and the *ID* string. An example of this is: *http://www.mysys.com/ThisOrder.xml#ThisPO*. If the element is being referenced from within the XML document, the URL can be shortened to *#ThisPO*.

The other form of URI is the Uniform Resource Name (URN). Unlike a URL, the URN is not location dependent. There are no requirements that a URN be locatable. It can be purely logical and abstract. It does have to be globally unique and persistent. Global uniqueness is ensured by registering the URN. For a URN, the scheme is *"urn:"*, which is fixed. The scheme-specific part consists of an identifier followed by a ":" and then a namespace-specific string, which is interpreted according to the rules of the namespace (this is described in the next chapter). An example of a URN is: *urn:ISBN:0471267163*. In this case, *ISBN* identifies the namespace as an International Standard Book Number and the number identifies a particular book.

Namespaces

As XML-based applications are implemented, a developer may wish to use elements defined by the service developer. But, XML documents are likely to consist of a combination of elements and attributes from several different sources, each source working independently of the others. It should be possible to associate elements and attributes with specific applications, while eliminating confusion due to duplication of element or attribute names.

To make it easier to use elements or attributes associated with specific applications while resolving possible ambiguity over the use of an element or attribute name, namespaces are used (W3C 2002c). A namespace is a collection of names. An element or an attribute can be associated with a namespace, thereby identifying it as having the semantics of the elements or attributes from that namespace. Qualifying a local name with a namespace eliminates the possibility of misunderstanding what a name denotes or how its value should be formatted. Qualifying a name is accomplished by declaring a namespace, then associating the namespace with a local name.

Namespaces are identified by a URI, usually a URL. An example of a namespace declaration is: *<order xmlns:acct="http://www.widgets.com/schema">*. This declaration allows elements and attributes within the scope *order* to identify their membership within the namespace by prepending *acct:* to the element or attribute name. The URL in the declaration does not always resolve to a location that can be reached over the Internet. It may simply serve to make any names qualified in the namespace unique.

The following example takes our purchase order and illustrates how to qualify names. Two namespaces are declared. The first is used for elements defined by the purchasing department, which includes the purchase order number and the item description. The second declares a namespace defined by the accounting department, which includes the number of units and the prices. To make this example more meaningful, we've changed the element name *orderNum* to *num*, and *quantity* to *num*. Now, without some assistance, we wouldn't be able to differentiate the two elements named *num*. This is where namespaces are useful.

```
<?xml version="1.0" encoding="UTF-8"?>
<order currency="USDollars"
      xmlns="www.widgets.com"
      xmlns:orderform="http://www.widgets.com/purchasing"
      xmlns:acct="http://www.widgets.com/accounting"
      xmlns:xsi="http://www.w3.org/2001/XMLSchema-instance"
      xsi:schemaLocation="www.widgets.com>
      <orderform:num>9876</orderform:num>
      <orderform:itemDescription>widgets</orderform:itemDescription>
      <acct:num>5</acct:num>
      <acct:unitPrice>34.23</acct:unitPrice>
      <acct:aggregatePrice>171.15</acct:aggregatePrice>
</order>
```

In this example, two additional namespaces are declared for use within a purchase order. The first is designated *orderform*, and the second is *acct*. Neither of the URLs that specify the namespace have to be reachable via the Internet nor do they even have to exist as files. Their purpose is to uniquely qualify names and attributes as belonging to the purchasing namespace or the accounting namespace. Later, two child elements *orderform:num* and *acct:num* are specified. Because they are qualified, we know that the 9876 is a purchase order number and that 5 is a number of units.

XML Schema

XML Schema (W3C 2001d, W3C 2001e) is a language used with XML specifications to describe data's structure, the constraints on content, and data types. It was designed to provide more control over data than was provided by DTDs that use the XML syntax. While XML Schema and DTDs are not mutually exclusive, XML Schema is regarded as an alternative to DTDs for specifying data types. SOAP, which we will discuss later, explicitly prohibits the use of DTDs.

In many ways, XML Schema makes XML interesting. XML provided two ways to aggregate elements: sequence and choice. A sequence of elements requires that each element of the sequence appear once in the order specified. Choice requires that a single element be present from a list of potential elements. With XML Schema, the language designer can specify whether an element in a sequence must appear at all, *minOccurs*, or whether there is a maximum number of appearances, *maxOccurs*.

XML Schema datatypes are primitive or derived. A primitive datatype does not depend on the definition of any other datatype. Many built-in primitive datatypes have been predefined by XML Schema. They include integer, boolean, date, and others. Derived datatypes are other datatypes that have been constrained, explicitly listed, or combined (the actual term used in the specification is "union"). Constrained datatypes take an existing datatype and restrict the possible values of the datatype. The derived datatype *belowSix* consists of integers restricted to values between 0 and 5. The restriction on the datatype is called a facet. A datatype may consist of a list of acceptable values. A datatype of U.S. coins contains penny, nickel, dime, and quarter. The union of U.S. coins with U.S. paper denominations results in all United States currency denominations.

XML Schema is useful for several reasons. First, the built-in datatypes of XML Schema support the precise definition of data. With facets, schemas can constrain the values of XML data. Finally, a definition that is more precise can be achieved with derived datatypes. Once a schema has been defined, schema processors are able to validate a document to ensure that the document corresponds to the schema's structure and permissible values. This checking can eliminate a source of many of the vulnerabilities that plague Web-based systems.

We have modified the purchase order example to show some of the features we've just discussed. Up until now, we have conveniently avoided discussing lines 2–4 of the example. What they do is identify this XML document as an XML Schema document that defines the namespace *http://www.widgets.com*. Line 4 also declares the default scope of the names in the schema to be *www.widgets.com*. We've been using XML Schema all along. In this example, each of the elements is now associated with an appropriate data type. In addition, we have specified that the *itemDescription* element is optional and does not have to be in the sequence.

```
<?xml version="1.0" encoding="UTF-8"?>
<xs:schema targetNamespace="www.widgets.com"
     xmlns:xs="http://www.w3.org/2001/XMLSchema"
     xmlns="www.widgets.com"
     elementFormDefault="qualified"
     attributeFormDefault="unqualified">
     <xs:element name="order">
          <xs:complexType>
               <xs:sequence>
                    <xs:element name="orderNum" type="xs:string"/>
                    <xs:element name="itemDescription" type="xs:string"
minOccurs="0"/>
                    <xs:element name="quantity" type="xs:integer"/>
                    <xs:element name="unitPrice" type="xs:decimal"/>
                    <xs:element name="aggregatePrice"
type="xs:decimal"/>
               </xs:sequence>
               <xs:attribute name="currency" type="xs:string"/>
          </xs:complexType>
     </xs:element>
</xs:schema>
```

There are many other aspects to XML Schema. A good overview is contained in *XML Schema Part 0: Primer* (W3C 2001c). XML Schema are placed in a separate schema document so that type definitions can be reused in other XML documents. This can lead to confusion when the term *XML schema* is used. This confusion is comparable to what occurs when *XML* is used. When a separate XML schema document is used, references to the XML schema instance must be namespace qualified so that the XML schema processor can determine that a separate schema instance is being referenced. This is usually done by declaring an XML namespace using an attribute with *xmlns:* for a suffix. The location of the schema instance can be declared eliminating any possibility of ambiguity. We've been declaring the namespace in our order examples using the *xmlns:* attribute.

The advantage of using this schema is that there are schema processors that check the values of elements to ensure that the values comply with the facets in the schema. This reduces the possibility of using improperly formed input as a means of compromising the security of an XML-based system.

SOAP

We are now ready to discuss SOAP. SOAP is a unidirectional, XML-based protocol for passing information. (As of draft version 1.2, SOAP is no longer an acronym.) Despite being unidirectional, SOAP messages can be combined to implement request/response processes, or even more sophisticated interactions. In addition to the sending and the receiving nodes of a SOAP message, SOAP message routing includes intermediary nodes. SOAP intermediaries should not be confused with intermediaries in any underlying protocol. For instance, HTTP messages may be routed through intermediaries. However, these intermediaries are not involved in the processing of SOAP messages. SOAP intermediaries play a role in the handling or processing of a message at the application level.

SOAP describes an XML-based markup language "for exchanging structured and typed information." The information passed in a SOAP message can either represent documents or remote procedure calls (RPCs) that invoke specific procedures at the service provider. A SOAP document could be a purchase order or an airline reservation form. On the other hand, an RPC can invoke software to charge a purchase. There are no clear guidelines to determine when a document or an RPC should be used. The system designer will make this decision.

Web Services using SOAP have gained popularity very quickly. The concept of an XML RPC was created in 1998 by David Winer of Userland Software. The XML-RPC specification was released in 1999 and was the work of Winer, Don Box of DevelopMentor, and Mohsen Al-Ghosein and Bob Atkinson of Microsoft. While the specification was published as XML-RPC, the working group adopted the working name SOAP. Soon after, SOAP .9 and 1.0 were released. In March 2000, IBM joined the group and worked on the SOAP 1.1 specification. The 1.1 version was adopted by the W3C as a recommendation. SOAP version 1.2 currently exists as a series of working drafts (W3C 2002e, W3C 2002f). In addition to the working drafts, there is a SOAP 1.2 Primer (W3C 2002d) that takes the information in the working drafts and describes SOAP features using actual SOAP messages.

The discussion in this section is based on the SOAP 1.2 working drafts. The discussion is not meant to be all encompassing and is a brief overview of the protocol. The reader should consult the W3C drafts or other books on SOAP to get further details.

As with any other protocol, there are two portions to the SOAP Protocol: a description of the messages that are to be exchanged, including the format and data encoding rules, and the sequence of messages exchanged. As the reader will see, there isn't a lot of specificity to SOAP. This is by design. Rather than overspecifying and trying to anticipate every possible outcome, the SOAP designers took a minimalist approach. SOAP specifies the skeleton of a message format—very little else is required. This approach allows messages to be tailored to application-specific uses. In addition to the protocol, there are protocol bindings that describe how SOAP can be transported using different underlying transport protocols. Currently, HTTP is the only underlying protocol with a binding referenced in the SOAP specification, but others are possible and not excluded by the specification.

SOAP Message Processing

The two main nodes in processing a SOAP message are the initial message sender and the ultimate message receiver. In addition, SOAP intermediaries, who are message receivers that later forward the message toward the ultimate receiver, also have a role in the processing of a SOAP message. For instance, in Figure 2.3, the buyer's system may send a purchase order to the seller via the buyer's accounts payable system. The accounts payable system records the details of the purchase so that, when an invoice from the seller is received, the information needed to authorize a payment is already entered. The accounts payable system is an intermediary. When the accounts payable system completes its tasks, it is responsible for transmitting the purchase order to the seller.

The buyer's system can target portions of the SOAP message at different receivers. The body of the message is, by definition, intended for the ultimate receiver of the message. Other receivers may examine the body and process information in it but must not modify it. The ultimate receiver must be able to understand and process the body. If it can't process the message, a SOAP fault is generated and returned to the sender. Unlike the message's body, elements in the message's header can be:

- Explicitly targeted at specific receivers via a URI
- Targeted at a receiver based on its relative position in the processing chain
- Targeted using some application-defined role

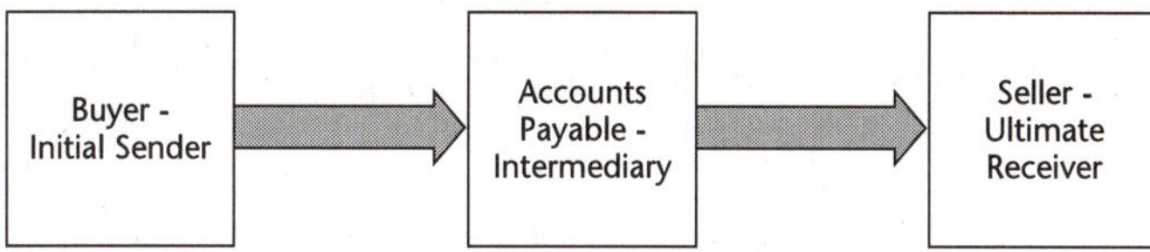

Figure 2.3 SOAP message-processing nodes.

Except for the ultimate receiver, all other receivers of the SOAP message are SOAP intermediaries. When a URI is used, the URI can specify a unique and concrete receiver, say by using a URL receiver.

When the relative position is used to specify a target, two predefined roles, *next* and *ultimateReceiver*, are available. *Next* is a role assumed by the next receiver of a message. *UltimateReceiver* is the ultimate receiver of the message. If no role is associated with the element, the ultimate receiver is assumed to be the target.

A third predefined role, *none*, indicates that no receiver should process the element. An element targeted at *none* may not be processed by any receiver but may contain data that is examined in the course of processing other elements.

The third option for targeting a header element is application specific. But, it will probably be used to target header elements to nodes performing an application-specific function, such as manager or accounting.

It is possible for a receiver to fill more than one role. For instance, an element could be targeted at a receiver based on a URL and based on its role as the next receiver.

The creator of the header element can specify that the targeted receiver must process the header or whether it is acceptable for the targeted receiver to ignore the header element. If the targeted receiver must process the header, it is said that the receiver must understand the header. If there is a requirement to understand the element but the receiver does not understand it, the receiver must stop all processing of the message and return a SOAP fault code. By marking a header as must understand, the creator can force a receiver to process the header. This is useful for making sure that security-related information is properly processed.

Processing order

SOAP prescribes an order for processing the SOAP-specific parts of a message. This description follows the *SOAP version 1.2 Part 1: Messaging Framework* (W3C 2002e). Processing of the SOAP message must be performed as though it were done in the following order. First, the receiver must decide what roles it will play. Is it only the next receiver or is it also the ultimate receiver? The node can use information contained in headers or the body to make the decision.

Next, the node must identify header elements targeted at it and that it must understand and decide whether it can process these blocks. If it cannot, all processing must end and a SOAP fault generated. For the ultimate receiver, processing of the body should not be considered at this step in deciding whether to generate a fault.

If all mandatory headers can be processed, the node should process the headers and, in the case of the ultimate receiver, process the message body. The node can choose to ignore header elements that are not mandatory for it to process. Other faults may be generated during this phase.

Finally, if the recipient is an intermediary, it must remove header elements targeted at it, insert any new header elements needed, and pass the message on to the next receiver with the body unmodified.

Open items

After this description of SOAP message processing, you may be curious to know:

- How does a receiver know what role it is playing? The recipient of a message is always the next receiver, but is it also the ultimate receiver?
- How does a receiver decide what order it is going to use to process the headers?
- How does a node know who the next receiver is so that the message can be routed to it?

These are all very good questions, but the SOAP specification does not answer them. These decisions can be determined using some algorithm programmed into the application, or determined by some other method that is outside the scope of SOAP.

Once these decisions have been made, instructions that reflect the answers can be contained in the headers of the message itself. For instance, the originator of the message can include routing information and more detailed processing instructions in the header. Or each node can insert instructions for the next.

Message Format

The basic minimal form of a SOAP message is shown in the XML document below. A data encoding using only built-in types and no additional definitions or declarations is recommended in the specification. This minimal schema allows SOAP message validation without XML Schema documents. However, application-specific XML schemas are allowed, which may require additional validation. DTDs are explicitly disallowed. Each SOAP message is identified as an XML 1.0 document that has one element with the local name *envelope*. It is qualified with the namespace *http://www.w3.org/2002/06/soap-envelope*. Besides qualifying the namespace as a SOAP namespace, the URL identifies the version of SOAP used. In this discussion, we use the June 2002 version of SOAP 1.2. Attributes are also qualified by the *soap-envelope* namespace. The *envelope* has child elements of an optional header and a required body that we will describe later.

```
<? Xml version='1.0' ?>
<env:Envelope xmlns:env="http://www.w3.org/2002/06/soap-envelope">
     <env:Header>
          ...
     </env:Header>
     <env:Body>
          ...
      </env:Body>
</env:Envelope>
```

Beyond what we have just discussed, there are no required elements within the SOAP envelope that convey the meaning or intent of the message. There is no requirement to include the identity of the sender or the receiver, the time or date the message was created, or a message title. It is expected that each application will define these elements, if they are required.

While the SOAP specification describes how an RPC can be represented in a SOAP message, there is no requirement to use the representation described. And, even if the encoding is used, there is no indicator in the message itself that the message body represents an RPC. With the exception of guidance on how to encode arguments to an RPC, the receiver is left to determine how to interpret the contents of the message. It is expected that the receiver does this, in part, through the use and understanding of namespaces that associate elements and attributes with the application implemented by the receiver.

SOAP Message Header

A SOAP Message Header, shown in a modified version of the message from above, is an optional part of a SOAP message. Its local name is *header*, and it is qualified using the same namespace as the envelope, *http://www.w3c.org/2002/06/soap-envelope*. The header can contain zero or more namespace-qualified child elements. Two attributes, *role* and *mustUnderstand*, can be associated with child elements of the header. In the example, *hdr1*, is qualified in the *www.widgets.com/logging* namespace.

```
<? Xml version='1.0' ?>
<env:Envelope xmlns:env="http://www.w3.org/2002/06/soap-envelope">
     <env:Header>
               <sec:hdr1 xmlns:sec="http://www.widgets.com/logging"
                       sec:role="http://www.w3.org/2002/06/soap-
envelope/role/next"
                       sec:mustUnderstand="true">
                       ...
              </sec:hdr1>
     </env:Header>
     <env:Body>
               ...
     </env:Body>
</env:Envelope>
```

Unlike the message's body, which may not be modified, the message's header is a dynamic part of the message. Intermediaries are required to delete header elements targeted at them and can add header elements as needed. Adding the same header back in that was deleted is acceptable.

Role

SOAP header elements are targeted at SOAP nodes. A node performs some function in processing or routing the message. The value of the SOAP *role* attribute can be designated explicitly via a URI or relatively via three predefined values, *next*, *ultimateReceiver*, or *none*. These relative values correspond to the roles described previously in the section on SOAP message processing. That is, if the header is targeted at *next*, then the next receiver processes the header. If the header is targeted at the *ultimateReceiver*, then the ultimate receiver processes the element. Finally, if *none* is the role targeted, no receiver processes the element. If no role attribute is specified, the default is *UltimateReceiver*, the ultimate receiver. In the example above, the header is targeted at the next recipient. The namespace of the header hints that the header is targeted at a logging intermediary that will log the order before it goes to the seller.

Each header element will be processed by at most one role. However, nodes playing other roles may examine headers not targeted at them. If the node is an intermediary, it must delete from the message any header elements targeted at it and may add other header elements for subsequent receivers before passing it on. It is not considered a fault if the ultimate receiver receives the message and there are header elements that are not targeted at it. A receiver must decide for itself whether it is the next receiver or the ultimate receiver.

MustUnderstand

Besides identifying a header element as intended for a particular receiver, the creator of a header element may designate that the targeted receiver *mustUnderstand* it. In other words, the receiver must know what to do with the header. The receiving software must understand the semantics of the names in the header element and be able to process the element accordingly. The header in the previous example, *hdr1*, must be understood by the recipient. If the header namespace is not known to it, the receiver must stop processing the message. Ideally, the processing node should return a SOAP fault to the requester. But, depending on the protocols used and the routing, there are conditions where this is not possible.

SOAP Message Body

A message body must have the local name of *body*. It must be associated with the *http://www.w3c.org/2002/06/soap-envelope* namespace. Child elements are optional, and multiple child elements are allowed. No body-specific attributes are defined. The message body is targeted at the ultimate receiver, who must understand the body.

Remember that SOAP is a unidirectional protocol. It is often difficult to keep that in mind. It is natural to think of SOAP as a request/response protocol. But, there is no requirement to return a response for a message received. Still, message body child elements have been defined that are the logical consequence of certain inputs. Because of this, our discussion of the message body will be divided into request message body elements and response message body elements. However, the reader should keep in mind that the SOAP protocol regards communication in each direction as separate and unrelated events. A discussion of the options for returning a response to a SOAP request is discussed in the section on protocol bindings.

Request message body elements

A SOAP request message body may contain zero or more child elements. If multiple child elements are present they can represent a single unit of work, multiple units of work, or some combination of work and data. Request body elements can be divided into two categories, document type and RPC type. The distinction is subtle. There is nothing that distinguishes an RPC message body from a document body.

Document body elements are analogous to paper documents. Most likely, they will be forms that have an understood structure such as purchase orders, invoices, itineraries, or prescriptions. In order for the document to be processed correctly, it is important that the ultimate receiver be cognizant of the namespace that defines the elements of the document.

RPC message bodies are XML-based remote procedure calls. *SOAP Version 1.2 Part 2: Adjuncts* (W3C 2002f) describes how to encode data structures used by programming languages to convey parameters in procedure calls. SOAP does not mandate the use of these encoding rules and acknowledges the possibility of using other encoding rules. However, use of other encodings will adversely impact the interoperability of the RPC.

Two options exist for encoding the arguments of an RPC. First, the SOAP RPC invocation can be a struct where the name of the struct corresponds to the procedure or method name. Each input or in/out argument to the procedure is a child element structure with a name and type corresponding to the name and type of the parameter in the procedure signature. The second RPC encoding method is to encode each argument as an element of an array. The name of the array corresponds to the name of the procedure and the position in the array corresponds to the position in the argument list. If problems occur, several RPC specific faults have been defined which will be described later.

The following example invokes an RPC called buy. This RPC is in the form of a structure and takes two arguments, the *order* and the *shipInfo*. Note that there is no explicit indication that this is an RPC invocation.

```
<? Xml version='1.0' ?>
<env:Envelope xmlns:env="http://www.w3.org/2002/06/soap-envelope">
     <env:Header>
               <sec:hdr1 xmlns:sec="http://www.myCompany.com/logging"
               sec:role="http://www.w3.org/2002/06/soap
envelope/role/next"
               sec:mustUnderstand="true">
                        ...
               </sec:hdr1>
     </env:Header>
     <env:Body>
           <buy xmlns="http://www.widgets.com/purchasing"
                 env:encodingStyle="http://www.w3.org/2002/06/soap-
encoding">
                 <order xmlns="http://www.widgets.com"
                         currency="USdollars">
```

```
                <orderNum>4567</orderNum>
                <quantity>6</quantity>
                <unitPrice>3.25</unitPrice>
                <aggregatePrice>19.50</aggregatePrice>
            </order>
            <shipInfo>
                <name>My Company</name>
                <streetAddress>234 Main St.</streetAddress>
                <city>Boston</city>
                <state>MA</state>
            </shipInfo>
        </buy>
    </env:Body>
</env:Envelope>
```

Response message body elements

The content of response message bodies can be documents, RPC responses, or a SOAP fault. Just as a document can be received, a document can result from the receipt of a document. For instance, a reservation request can result in the creation of an itinerary. Using SOAP to transmit a document has already been described, so the discussion will not be repeated here.

The response to an RPC can be a structure or an array. The name of the structure is identical to the name of the procedure or method that is returning the information. If the procedure or method returns a value, it must be named *result*, and it must be namespace qualified with *http://www.w3.org/2002/06/soap.rpc*. Every other output or input/output parameter must be represented by an element with a name corresponding to the parameter name. If an array is used, the result must be the first element in the array. The *result* element, if there is one, is followed by array elements for each out or in/out parameter, in the order they are specified in the procedure signature. The following example illustrates the response to the RPC invocation from the previous section. For this response, there is no special header targeted at the recipient. A result is returned indicating the status of the RPC invocation.

```
<? Xml version='1.0' ?>
<env:Envelope xmlns:env="http://www.w3.org/2002/06/soap-envelope">
    <env:Body>
        <ns:buy xmlns:ns="http://www.widgets.com/purchasing"
            env:encodingStyle="http://www.w3.org/2002/06/soap-
encoding">
            <result xmlns="http://www.w3.org/2002/06/soap-
rpc">okay</result>
        </ns:buy>
    </env:Body>
</env:Envelope>
```

A SOAP output message may also contain a SOAP fault. SOAP faults are generated in response to errors or to carry other status information. This is the only body child element that is defined by SOAP. The element must have a local name of *fault* and a namespace of *http://www.w3.org/2002.06/soap-envelope*. Only one *fault* element may appear in the message body. Child elements of *code* and *reason* are required within the *fault* element. Other child elements, *node* and *role*, and details are optional. *Code* is a structure that consists of a value that designates the high-level fault and an optional *subcode* that provides additional details on the fault. *Reason* is a human-readable representation of the fault. *Node* identifies the SOAP node that encountered the fault. *Role* identifies what role the node was operating in when the fault occurred. Finally, *detail* carries application-specific fault information. SOAP defined faults are:

- Version mismatch.
- Inability to understand or process a mandatory header.
- A DTD was contained in the message.
- A data encoding was referenced that is not recognized by the processor.
- The message was incorrectly formatted or did not contain needed information.
- The message could not be processed for some reason other than that the message was malformed or incomplete.

For SOAP RPC, additional fault codes have been defined. Fault codes can be extended to handle application specific needs.

SOAP Features

Key to SOAP's future success is the ability to add capabilities to it and extend it. SOAP features are abstract capabilities related to the exchange of messages between SOAP nodes. These capabilities can include reliability, guaranteed delivery, and security.

If a feature is implemented within a SOAP node, the feature is implemented by modifying the SOAP processing model. If the feature affects the interaction between two successive nodes, the feature is implemented as part of the SOAP protocol binding. One limitation of a protocol binding is that it relates two nodes connected by a single transmission. End-to-end transmission may be implemented using different protocols, requiring multiple transmissions. In these cases, the feature should be expressed in SOAP header blocks and implemented by the processing model.

Features are expressed as modules or Message Exchange Patterns. Modules are expressed as SOAP header blocks. The content and semantics of the header blocks must be clearly and completely stated. In addition, if the operation of the module affects the operation of other SOAP features, these effects must be identified.

A Message Exchange Pattern (MEP) is a template, defined in the SOAP specification (W3C 2002f) used to describe the exchange of messages between SOAP nodes. A major part of specifying a binding is to describe how a protocol is used to implement any MEPs it claims to support. Two MEPs, Request-Response and Response, have been defined so far. The request-response MEP is exactly what we'd expect and is used for RPCs. The response MEP is the sending of a SOAP response after receiving a non-SOAP request. The MEP describes actions from the point of view of both the requesting and the responding nodes.

The MEP is a distributed state-based specification of a node's operation. At any particular point in a message exchange, a node is in a specific state. Upon receipt of an input, sending an output, or the arrival of some other event, the node enters a new state and undertakes some processing.

HTTP Binding

Many underlying protocols can be used to transmit SOAP messages. The selected underlying protocol may also provide additional features such as assured delivery, correlation of a response to a request, or error correction and detection that enhance SOAP. In addition, the underlying protocol may support patterns of message exchange that are more complex than the simple one-way exchange specified by SOAP.

A SOAP protocol binding describes how an underlying transmission protocol is used to transmit the SOAP message. A binding framework is used as a formal method to describe the relationship between SOAP and its underlying transmission protocol. It describes the operation of one node as it exchanges and processes a single message. Other functionality supported by the binding is also described in the framework.

SOAP defines a default HTTP binding (W3C 2002f). Unless otherwise agreed to, SOAP over HTTP is transmitted using this binding. The binding supports the request-response and Response MEP and specifies how HTTP is used to implement the pattern. For the request-response MEP, the HTTP protocol binding describes how requests are transmitted using HTTP by the requesting node and how the responses are sent in the responding state at the responding node. SOAP request messages are sent using HTTP POST requests. The HTTP URL identifies the target node as well as the application that receives the message. The SOAP message is carried as the body of an HTTP POST. The HTTP content-type header must be *application/soap*. The corresponding response is returned using the HTTP response. This provides a natural way to correlate the SOAP request with its response.

In the HTTP binding, the SOAP response message is sent in the response to an HTTP request. For the request-response MEP, the SOAP request message is sent in an HTTP POST request. For the SOAP response MEP, the request is transmitted as an HTTP GET request. The HTTP binding only supports this MEP to request information. When used in this way, the interaction will be indistinguishable from conventional HTTP information retrieval. The MEP can only be used when there are no intermediaries between the initial sender and the ultimate receiver. The information retrieved must be identified by the URL alone because there is no SOAP message envelope to transmit additional identification to the service provider.

SOAP Usage Scenarios

SOAP is a very simple protocol, but this simplicity supports many kinds of interactions, some of them very complex. To illustrate the variety of ways that SOAP can be used, the W3C, XML Protocol Working Group has sponsored the creation of *SOAP Version 1.2 Usage Scenarios* (W3C 2002g).

SOAP Usage Scenarios span the basic, one-way SOAP message transmission to request/response to intermediaries. The scenarios also cover the provision of features such as caching, routing, and quality of service. Familiarity with these scenarios gives more appreciation of the ways that SOAP can be used.

Universal Description Discovery and Integration

One perceived obstacle to widespread, easy access to Web Services is limited ability to locate suitable Web Services. If an enterprise needs a service that it doesn't already use, how does it discover providers that offer the service? Today, enterprises make use of various directories to identify a vendor or products or services of interest. The directories offered by the phone company are an example of one such type of directory, but industry-specific directories are also possible. To provide information on Web Services available over the Internet, a comparable type of Internet facility has been conceived.

A consortium of companies, including Ariba, IBM, and Microsoft, began developing the concept of an Internet business directory. The result is the UDDI Project. UDDI continues to be a collaborative effort of concerned businesses. Unlike the topics that have been discussed so far, UDDI is more than a specification or standard. It encompasses an infrastructure that implements the standard and allows Internet-wide, all-inclusive search and discovery of Web Services.

UDDI includes a structured way to describe a business, the services that are offered by the business, and the programmatic interface to the services. Data is organized so that a business may offer multiple services, and a service (which may have been developed by a separate organization) may be offered by more than one business.

UDDI is a Web accessible directory and is built on SOAP over HTTP. A UDDI registry is basically a Web Service. Two sets of SOAP interfaces have been defined. One set of interfaces for potential subscribers supports searching for services or direct retrieval of details about known services of interest. While UDDI is built on SOAP, it should be pointed out that the services described in the directory are not required to be SOAP services. The directory's discovery services can also be used to mitigate problems that occur during runtime access of the registered Web Service. If a service is not accessible at a previously published location, the registry can be updated to refer to a location where the service can be accessed. Service subscribers can then update their location caches. The second set of interfaces is for use by service providers and supports saving descriptions, deleting descriptions, and security for access to these services.

The infrastructure conceived by the UDDI Project is a single, distributed network of directory operators called the UDDI Business Registry. Business and service descriptions published by the Business Registry are intended to be publicly available to anyone without restriction. Publishing and deleting information are subject to authorization checks. Publishing a description at one node results in the description being propagated to and available at all nodes. IBM, Microsoft, SAP, and HP operate nodes.

An alternative to public business registries are private registries that make Web Services known to a community of potential subscribers. The community can be based on a common line of business, such as building construction or manufacturing lawn furniture, or the community could be a single company. Private registries cater to subscribers who have common interests and needs. Unlike the business registry, access to a private registry may not be open to everyone, and controlling access to the information becomes important.

A business registry contains a variety of company-specific data so that a potential subscriber can decide whether it wants to do business with the service provider and, if it does, what must be done to use the service. Besides the name of the company, the registry can include other identifying information, such as tax number, a text description, and contact information. Industry segment or business categorization descriptors support use of the registry for searches based on industry. Potential subscribers can locate companies that offer the type of services they need. Finally, the registry can contain technical and programmatic descriptions of the Web Services offered by the company so that programmers have the information they need to interface with the Web Services offered.

Five structures have been defined for UDDI entries. They are *businessEntity*, *businessService*, *bindingTemplate*, *tModel*, and *publisherAssertion*. The diagram in Figure 2.4, taken from UDDI Version 2.0 Data Structure Reference, UDDI Open Draft specification 8, June 2001, illustrates their relationship.

The *businessEntity* structure represents a business. The structure is made up of a Universally Unique ID (UUID) that is assigned to each business entity, and can also include a business name, description, and the contacts that are in the white pages. These identifiers and categories are descriptors that can be used to classify businesses and the services they provide. Finally, the structure optionally includes one or more *businessService* structures.

The *businessService* structure includes data about a service being offered by the business. This structure contains a UUID that is assigned to each business service, an optional text-based description of the service and category descriptors, and zero or more binding templates.

The *bindingTemplate* structure identifies how and where a service can be accessed. Each binding template is assigned a UUID and contains an address that can be used to call a Web Service. This address can be a URL or an e-mail address. The *tModelInstanceDetails* element of the binding template identifies a specific *tModel* that contains the details of the interface used to access the Web Service. The *bindingTemplate* includes zero or more *tModels*.

The *tModel* structure contains the technical specification of the Web Service interface. It contains a UUID for the *tModel*, a name, and a description. *tModels* can contain identifier and category descriptors.

The *publisherAssertion* provides a way for two businesses to assert a joint relationship. For this to work, both businesses must agree to the assertion before it is published.

While UDDI depends on SOAP for its API structure, the services listed in a UDDI Registry need not be limited to SOAP-based services. Likewise, SOAP subscribers are not limited to using UDDI registries to locate Web Services. Subscribers can learn of the existence of a Web Service through word of mouth, from an advertisement, or by looking up the desired service in a paper-based phone directory. Once the service has been located, details of the service can be provided to the subscriber by email, on a floppy disk, or in a manual. There is no tight coupling between SOAP and UDDI. UDDI is not needed in order for SOAP to succeed. For all these reasons, adoption of UDDI is not happening as quickly as its backers expected. As we will see in the next section, the same holds true for the relationship between UDDI and WSDL.

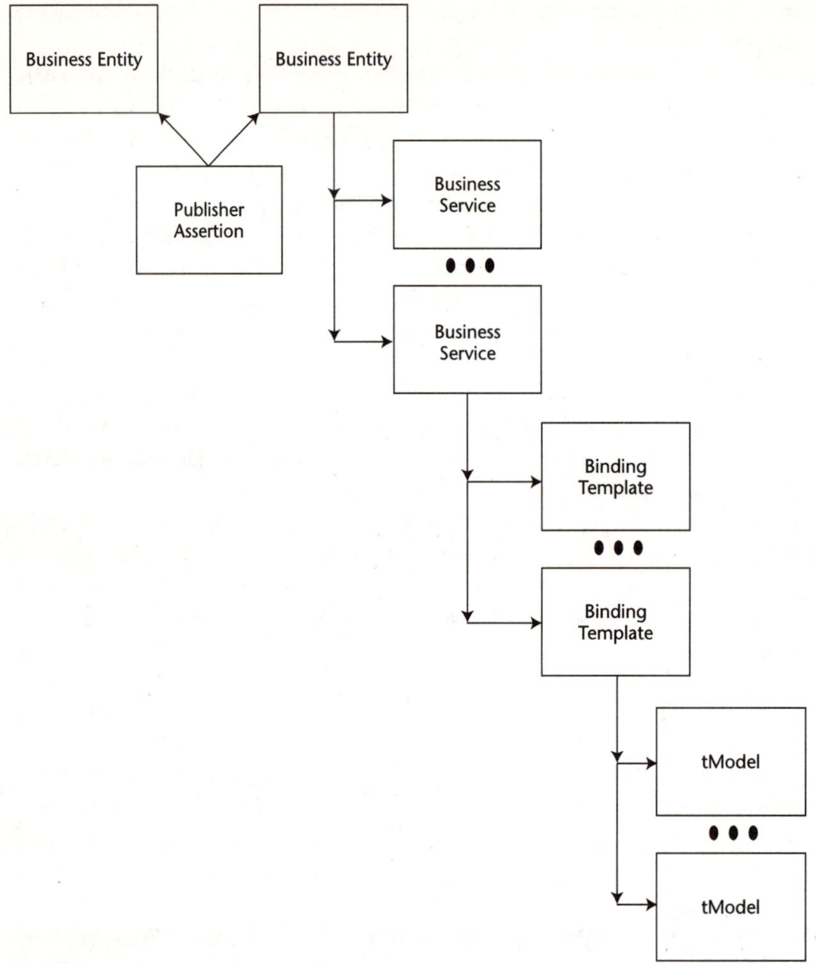

Figure 2.4 UDDI data structure relationship.

WSDL

To ease the burden of developing SOAP code, a vendor standard for an XML-based language to describe the SOAP interface has been developed. The initial *Web Services Description Language (WSDL)* (Microsoft 2001) specification was a joint development of Ariba, IBM, and Microsoft. The WSDL 1.1 specification was turned over to the W3C, which published it as a note (W3C 2001b) in March 2001. The W3C Web Services Description Working Group is now working on further development of the language.

Earlier, we discussed concerns about the verbosity of XML. WSDL expands XML several times over. Luckily, WSDL is usually only used during design and development of Web Services applications. We should also note that even though WSDL is text-based, human beings were not meant to comprehend WSDL. It is a machine-generated and machine-processed markup language used with software development tools. Finally, WSDL is its own markup language. It is not SOAP. So if someone looks at it and it does not look familiar, this is understandable.

Since we don't expect that human beings will have to dissect a WSDL specification, we won't go into the details of WSDL. Instead, we'll discuss its structure and describe how it specifies the interfaces to Web Services.

WSDL documents describe logical and concrete details of the Web Service. The logical part of the WSDL document describes characteristics of Web Services that are determined by the service developer and are valid regardless of the actual implementation. The concrete part of the document describes aspects of the service that are decided by the service provider. This supports the independent development of Web Services that may be offered by different service providers. Figure 2.5 shows the parts of a WSDL document.

To define an interface with WSDL, we begin by defining the types of data exchanged across the interface. The type portion of a WSDL document declares the namespaces and datatypes used in the Web Services messages that constitute the service. It defines application-specific data types. Data is then organized into messages. In the case of SOAP, message descriptions only apply to the body of the SOAP message. Headers are defined elsewhere within the WSDL document. portType defines the operations supported by a logical endpoint and the messages sent or received. For instance, a SOAP service provider receives a message and generates a response to the received message. The messages received and sent in response are defined in the message portion of the WSDL message.

Up to this point, no implementation-specific information should be specified. For instance, the protocol used to transmit the messages, the encoding used for the data, and the location of the actual ports that are the connection points should not have been given. These features are regarded as differentiators for different Web Services providers. The service provider rather than the service developer makes these choices. The bindings, ports, and service portions of a WSDL document specify this information. First, bindings are used to specify the underlying protocol used to transport the messages in a portType (portTypes were previously defined in the logical portion of the WSDL document). The binding also specifies the encoding for the messages that are part of the operations in the portType. A port specifies the address at which the service is available. Finally, a service specifies the ports at which the service is available.

WSDL is not tightly coupled to SOAP, and the interface WSDL describes can be accessed via other protocols. Several bindings extend WSDL to account for differences in underlying transport protocol. There is a SOAP binding, an HTTP GET or POST binding without SOAP, and an SMTP binding. The SOAP binding describes how to specify whether a message body is a document type or an RPC type. If the message is an RPC, it describes how to identify arguments. The SOAP binding also includes the definition of header elements and header fault elements.

Because Web Service descriptions allow independently specified components, there is a lot of redundancy in a WSDL document. Operations reference messages. Bindings reference operations, and messages further define how the operations and messages are transmitted. This redundancy, combined with the use of XML, is responsible for the large size of a WSDL document compared to the actual SOAP messages it defines. This is the price of modularity.

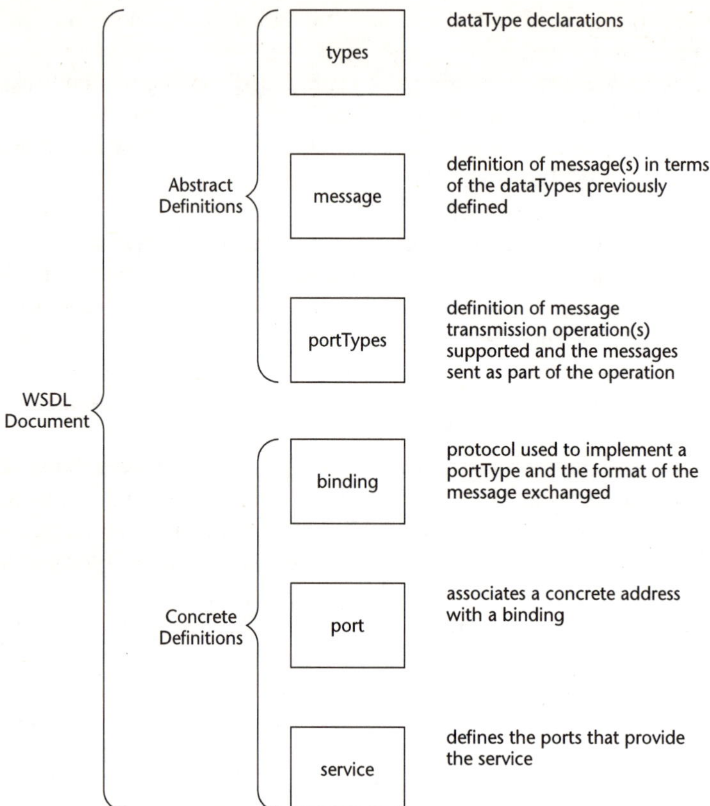

Figure 2.5 WSDL document components.

WSDL is loosely coupled with SOAP and UDDI. There is a SOAP binding for WSDL, but there are also HTTP GET and POST bindings and an SMTP binding. SOAP interfaces can be specified by other means. There is guidance for using WSDL to provide the tModel and binding template of a UDDI entry, but UDDI could be used with other description languages, and there are other ways to distribute WSDL interface specifications.

A SOAP service provider is not required to use WSDL. WSDL's verbosity makes it difficult for human beings to understand and is an impediment to its acceptance. Developers who use WSDL are those using development tools that automatically generate and consume WSDL interface descriptions.

Other Activities

SOAP, with its minimalist style, encourages the formation of other, complementary activities. In this section, we will identify organizations and standards that extend and complement SOAP-based Web Services.

Active Organizations

We've already discussed several standards and the groups that developed them. The most influential group in Web Services is the W3C. It defined XML, XML-schema, and SOAP. It is now working on WSDL and Web Services architectures. We've also mentioned UDDI.org. UDDI and WSDL are the results of vendor collaboration.

The Organization for Structured Information Standard, OASIS, is a consortium that "drives the development, convergence and adoption of e-business standards" (from http://www.oasis-open.org/who/). It has also been very active in Web Services. It currently sponsors several working groups concentrating on XML-based capabilities that can also be used with SOAP. Included in these activities are SAML, XACML, and WS-Security, which are XML security specifications. We'll have more on these specifications later in this book. It also includes SOAP-based applications, one of which we will discuss later in this section.

One of the concerns about adopting any standard is ensuring the interoperability of two standard-compliant products. Most standards have optional features that can interfere with interoperability. Even if a product complies with a standard, there is no guarantee that it is interoperable with another product that is compliant with the same standard.

A recent development in this area is the Web Services Interoperability Organization (WS-I). This is an industry consortium for fostering the development and use of interoperable Web Services. WS-I is not a standards development group. Instead, it endorses the use of existing standards, and collects complementary standards into profiles. To date, one profile for WS-I Basic Web Services has been defined. This profile includes XML-Schema 1.0, SOAP 1.1, WSDL 1.1, and UDDI 1.0. Other profiles are likely. However, anyone who has tried to use a standard in the hope that conformance with a standard is sufficient to guarantee interoperability understands that compliance to a standard is not enough. The WS-I group goes further by recommending choices for optional parameters that make interoperability more likely. These recommendations are covered in implementation guidelines. Finally, the WS-I will develop two tools to monitor Web Services communications traffic (The Sniffer) and then verify that the service implementation is free of errors (The Analyzer).

One very interesting activity is the SOAPBuilders interoperability testing. SOAPBuilders is an ad hoc group that started with the SOAPBuilders mailing list (soapbuilders@yahoogroups.com). It has developed a suite of compliance tests. Testing participants range from large companies, such as Microsoft, to small companies to individuals. Several rounds of interoperability testing have taken place. The results are posted on several Web sites. Some of these sites are PocketSoap, http://www.pocketsoap.com/weblog/soapInterop/; WhiteMesa, http://www.whitemesa.com/interop.htm; and XMethods, www.xmethods.net/ilab/.

Other Standards

The work of most of the organizations previously discussed is to produce a standard. These standards address workflow, reliable delivery, and a host of other needs. The W3C, at http://www.w3.org/2000/03/29-XML-protocol-matrix, keeps a list of other XML-based protocols being developed. This list was compiled in 2000 and is somewhat dated. However, it's a start. There are many other protocols currently being developed, but we will not go into them here.

One area we have not touched on is application-specific activities. One notable effort is the ebXML project.

ebXML is a joint activity of OASIS and the United Nations Center For Trade Facilitation and Electronic Business (UN/CEFACT). It is an ambitious effort aimed at defining standards for the formatting and transmission of electronic commerce data, the description of business processes, and the negotiation of business terms and responsibilities. Because it relies on Internet standard protocols and uses XML, the specifiers expect that the cost of implementing ebXML will be less than the cost of EDI.

Besides XML, ebXML specifies SOAP as its message format. It goes beyond SOAP by defining elements for routing, trading partner information, and quality of service requirements. ebXML includes a registry and repository that is similar to, but not the same as, a UDDI registry. Two documents, the Collaboration Protocol Profile (CPP) and the Collaboration Protocol Agreement (CPA) are critical to establishing the business-to-business interoperability. The CPP specifies the interface available at a service provider, and the CPA defines the actual interface agreed to by two trading partners. Beyond this, ebXML also makes use of the Unified Modeling Language (UML) to describe the steps for designing an ebXML business process specification.

The reach of ebXML into the business process can be large. However, businesses are not required to adopt it in its entirety and can choose the parts they are comfortable adopting.

ebXML uses XML Digital Signature and XML Encryption for message security and specifies how to tailor the two standards for use with ebXML. Other security standards, such as S/MIME and PGP MIME, are options for message security. In addition, the Security Assertion Markup Language (SAML) assertion is being considered as a vehicle for conveying user information for the purpose of making authorization decisions. We will discuss these standards in subsequent chapters of this book.

Summary

Web Services are SOAP-based interfaces to computing resources using Internet standard protocols. SOAP is built on XML and XML Schema with very few required elements. It is a very simple protocol that can be carried on HTTP or other Internet transport protocols. SOAP takes advantage of underlying transport protocols to provide additional transport services. There are a number of complementary standards to fill in the gaps left by SOAP. UDDI registries spread the word about specific Web Services. WSDL is a formal way to describe a Web Service interface.

While Web Services make it possible for applications to interoperate, they complicate the security landscape. A new dimension is added to the security problem. Where end-to-end security previously meant spanning processing tiers, security must now span processing domains. The minimalist approach taken by SOAP means that the security requirements for SOAP messages are harder to understand and implement. We will discuss approaches to securing Web Services in the chapters that follow.

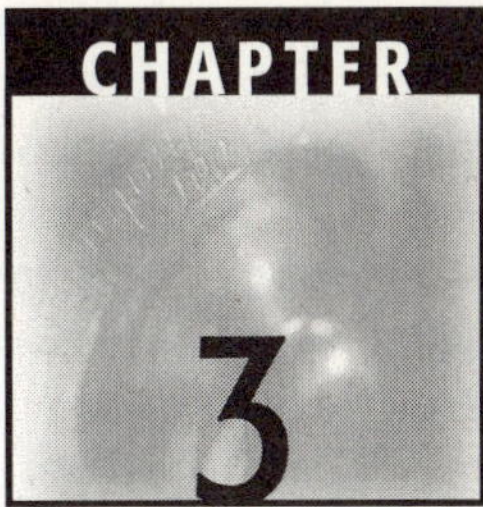

Getting Started with Web Services Security

Many architects and developers will look at the diverse and complex topics described in this book and think, "I'm just building a simple Web Service application for my company, and we don't care that much about protecting sensitive data. I don't need anything very fancy. Do I really need to deal with all of the security issues that you describe throughout this book?"

Perhaps not—your Web Services application may need only the bare minimum of security. If so, you may not need to implement anything more than what is described in this chapter. We give you an introduction to what you need to know to provide the most basic Web Services security solution with a minimum of effort.

Although you can work within the solution defined here, we do think that it's important to understand what you're *not* getting when you implement something so simple. We provide several cautions and describe inherent vulnerabilities in the approach. In this manner, you can decide if a simple version of Web Services security is enough for you. If not, you will know why and have plenty of motivation for reading the more advanced topics in later chapters.

Although many people begin by experimenting with a simple Web Services deployment, we expect that these applications are likely to evolve into more advanced architectures. After all, the primary purpose of Web Services is to enable many different applications to share data across a heterogeneous environment. Web Services are expressly targeted at distributed applications that cross corporate boundaries and, consequently, are likely to have challenging security requirements. So, although you may be starting with a "harmless" Web Services application within a corporate network that doesn't need much security, keep in mind that your architecture may need to evolve over time to work in a more hostile environment with sensitive data.

We begin this chapter by describing security fundamentals that are the basis of all security architectures. Whether you are building a Web Service application for a small mom-and-pop storefront or a huge multinational conglomerate, you need to understand these fundamental security requirements. We then walk you through a Web Services security example that takes advantage of the basic security functionality provided by .NET.

Security Fundamentals

There are a number of security technologies that repeatedly arise in diverse corporations when they identify their security requirements. We provide an overview of these common security requirements, explain how the collection of security technologies solves a host of diverse problems, and offer some general recommendations on their use.

Figure 3.1 expands on the description of the enterprise security technologies that were introduced in Chapter 1, "Overview of Web Services Security." As you may recall, perimeter security serves as the first line of defense and primarily protects against hostile attackers outside of an organization. Mid-tier security serves as the second line of defense, providing another layer of protection against external attackers, and also protecting against attackers who are located within an organization. Back-office security provides the third layer of defense by protecting the back-office legacy servers that contain an organization's most valuable resources. The combination of these three tiers of security makes it extremely difficult to mount an attack; even if one tier fails, the other tiers will still serve to defend against the vast majority of attacks.

There are a number of security services that are used within these tiers. These security services include:

- *Cryptography,* which protects communications from disclosure or modification by using encryption or digital signatures
- *Authentication* of principals by means of passwords, tokens, public key certificates, or secret keys
- *Authorization* of access to resources, including sending/receiving packet transmissions, access to a specified Uniform Resource Locator (URL), invocations on a target component interface/operation, or access to a back-office resource (that is, a file or database record)
- *Security association* to establish trust between client and target components
- *Delegation,* which allows a delegated principal to use the identity or privileges of an initiating principal so that the delegate may act on behalf of the initiating principal
- *Accountability,* which provides a record of security-related events to permit the monitoring of a client invoking on a target or accessing back-office resources
- *Security administration,* which maintains the security policy embodied in user profiles, access control lists (ACLs), passwords, and other data relevant to the security technology

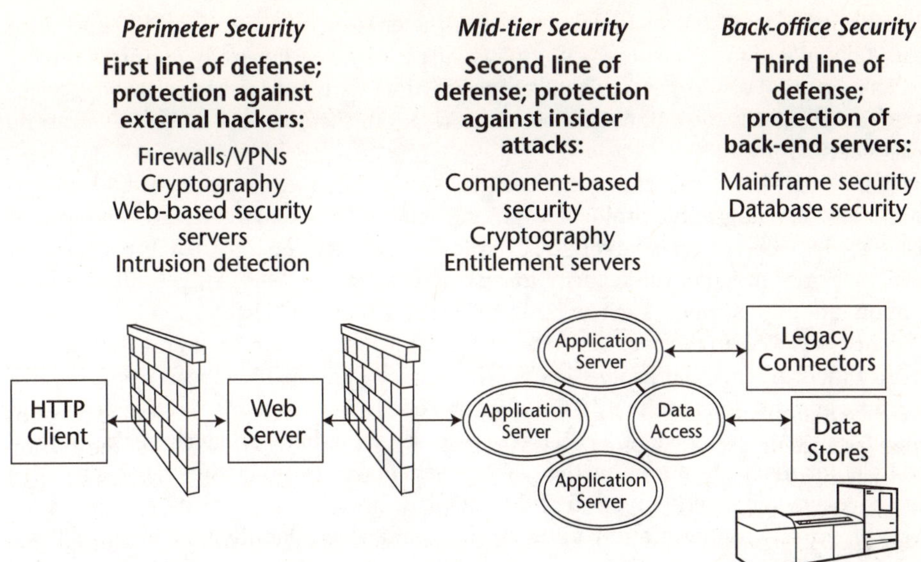

Figure 3.1 Enterprise security technologies.

Security services in the perimeter tier face outward toward an external network, which is typically the Internet. Because the perimeter may need to accommodate requests from virtually any client on the Internet, perimeter security mechanisms are designed for high performance and are usually coarse-grained. By coarse-grained, we mean that the decision of whether a client is authorized to perform a request is based on a simple criterion, such as whether the client may use a protocol on a specified port. Perimeter security services focus on cryptography, authentication, and authorization.

Technologies that support the security services at the perimeter include operating systems, Web servers, single sign-on (SSO), cryptographic protocols, firewalls/VPNs, and intrusion detection. Since this chapter concentrates on the basics of Web Services security, we focus our discussion on several of these perimeter technologies that are needed in virtually any Web Services deployment. We discuss firewalls/VPNs and intrusion detection in Chapter 12, "Planning and Building a Secure Web Services Architecture."

Next, we briefly describe mid-tier and back-office security so you have some perspective on how Web Services security relates to other security mechanisms used throughout the enterprise. For more advanced applications, you'll need to understand in more detail how Web Services security fits together with other security technologies as part of a complete end-to-end solution. Chapter 12 discusses this topic in depth in the context of building integrated Web Services systems.

Security services in the mid-tier provide a general set of protection mechanisms for the business logic. Mid-tier security technologies are, in effect, extensions to the underlying operating system because they provide security at the application layer similar to the security that operating systems provide to protect underlying platform resources (for example, files and devices). Mid-tier security does not focus on providing protection against outside attackers, as is the case in perimeter security. Instead, mid-tier security treats all business components as potentially suspicious, and generally requires security checks as part of any component-to-component interaction. Mid-tier security services focus on cryptography, authentication, authorization, security association, delegation, and accountability.

Technologies that support mid-tier security services include component-based security servers, cryptographic protocols, and entitlement servers. We discuss component-based security servers extensively in Chapter 7, "Security of Infrastructures for Web Services," since much of the security infrastructure for Web Services is built on top of component-based systems such as J2EE, COM+, .NET, and CORBA.

Security services in the back-office tier protect the resources in back-end servers. The security mechanisms that protect back-office legacy systems have been in place for a long time and are quite mature. In the past, these security mechanisms have been used to guard against direct client/server access to sensitive back-office server resources. Today, enterprises are adapting the same mechanisms to guard against back-office server access via the perimeter and middle tiers. Back-office tier security services focus on cryptography, authentication, authorization, and accountability.

Technologies supporting back-office security services include mainframe security and database security, which we discuss in Chapter 12.

In the sections that follow, we provide the basics on a set of security technologies for the perimeter tier that will be enough to get you started with Web Services security. We concentrate on technologies supporting cryptography and authorization, but we also give you an overview of authorization.

Cryptography

The first important security technology that you'll need to secure a Web Service is a way to protect the sensitive data as it travels over open networks. Cryptography may be used to encrypt messages to protect them from disclosure; that is, to prevent someone from reading the message data as it passes by on the wire. Cryptography also can ensure the integrity of messages; that is, prevent someone from modifying, deleting, or inserting bits into the message data without this being detected by the legitimate recipient of the message.

Most people think of cryptography as a way of making information unreadable, or encrypted, and, later, of reversing the operation so that the information is again understandable, or decrypted. It is used as a way to protect information, usually when it is being communicated from one spot to another. Cryptographic keys, which are nothing more than very large random numbers, control the process. There are many books you can read for further information on this topic, for example (Smith 1997).

Secret Key Cryptography

In traditional cryptography, the same cryptographic key is used to encrypt and decrypt information. This is known as *secret key* or *symmetric key* cryptography because the two parties who want to communicate securely use the same key to encrypt and decrypt messages. They both get their keys through secure means and must protect their keys to make sure that only authorized individuals can use the information. Keeping track of all these keys is difficult. Also, since the parties both use the same key, one side of the communication can't be distinguished from the other, so it's not possible to prove who originated a message. Common secret key algorithms are the Data Encryption Standard (DES) (NIST 1988) Triple DES (3DES), and Advanced Encryption Standard (AES) (NIST 2001), standardized by the US National Institute of Standards and Technology (NIST).

Public Key Cryptography

Another approach to cryptography is called *public key* or *asymmetric cryptography*. This form of cryptography uses two different but mathematically related keys. One key can't be used to discover the other. With public key cryptography, the public key can be made public to anyone wishing to conduct transactions with the holder of the private key. Distribution of the public key is easy. The private key must be kept private and held only by its owner. A popular public key algorithm is RSA, invented by Ron Rivest, Adi Shamir, and Leonard Adleman.

When public key cryptography is used for encryption, the public key is used to encrypt data and the private key is used to decrypt data. Any of the holders of the public key can encrypt data meant to go to the private key's owner, but only the private key's owner can decrypt the information.

Public key cryptography may also be used to create unforgeable digital signatures based on a user's private key. We discuss digital signatures and present public key algorithms in more detail in Chapter 4, "XML Security and WS-Security," when we investigate how public key cryptography is applied to XML security.

While public key cryptography is a great breakthrough, it comes with a price. Even with today's computers, public key cryptography is relatively slow because it requires complex computations. With a common key size of 1,024 bits, we are dealing with numbers that are 15 times larger than can be handled by double-precision multiplication routines. Public key algorithms perform several multiplications per key operation as well as exponentiation. In practice, public key cryptography routines encrypt small amounts of information, such as a DES or triple DES key. This second key is then used with a secret key algorithm that does the bulk of the encrypting at higher performance.

For public key cryptography to work, private keys must be properly protected. There are various schemes to provide this protection; smart cards are one effective means for securely carrying the client's private key. Technology for PC smart card readers is readily available and reasonably priced; in the future these readers are likely to be built into many Internet appliances.

Finally, it's important to make sure that the correct public key is being used for encryption or for verifying a signature. Proper identification of the public keys is the motivation for *public key certificates*. Certificates provide a strong binding between a public key and the owner of that key, so users can be confident that they are using the public key that is associated with the owner. A Certificate Authority (CA) is a trusted issuer of certificates and vouches for the identities contained in the certificates. Public key infrastructure (PKI) builds on the services of a CA by providing an environment for trusted key and certificate management. We discuss these topics in more detail in Chapter 4.

Authentication

Cryptography is a tool necessary for the protection of data as it traverses over networks, but for most Web Services cryptography by itself is inadequate. To maintain a secure Web Service, you also need to know the identities of the parties who are establishing a Web Service connection. *Authentication* provides such a service, and can give you confidence that the requester of a Web Service is who he or she says and not an imposter.

In this section, we explore the categories of authentication. We then examine authentication protocols that are built on cryptography, specifically SSL (Secure Sockets Layer) and Kerberos. We also discuss a variety of authentication systems that use these mechanisms.

Categories of Authentication

Authentication mechanisms fall into two basic categories: password and challenge-response. Although password-based authentication is popular, it has some inherent limitations, as we will explain. Challenge-response based authentication can be more complex to set up, but it provides a significantly higher level of security.

Password Authentication

The simplest kind of connection-oriented authentication uses a shared secret in the form of a password, a personal identification number (PIN), or passphrase. The most significant characteristic of password-based systems is that the authentication does not depend on information sent by the side performing the authentication check.

We are all familiar with password-based systems. Operating system logons are password based. HTTP basic authentication is another example of such a system. If the user requests a protected resource and does not provide authentication information, the Web server rejects the request. This rejection causes the user's browser to request the user's ID and password. The browser reissues the request with the user ID and password. Then, if the user ID and password are acceptable, the Web server delivers the requested content.

One disadvantage of this system is that the password is sent over the network and is potentially exposed while in transit. Cryptography should be used to protect the password when it traverses any open network. The most common client authentication for Web-based applications establishes an encrypted session using SSL, and then uses a conventional password protected by SSL encryption to authenticate the user. We describe SSL in more detail later in this chapter.

Another problem with passwords is that so many of them are needed, which makes it very difficult for users to keep track of them. Often, each application requires its own user ID and password, leading to the "yellow sticky note syndrome," in which passwords are written down and stuck to the user's workstation. Poorly chosen passwords (an English word, for example) are easily guessable by a hostile attacker. To reduce the risk of vulnerabilities when using passwords, it's good practice to change your passwords periodically.

Since the password is available at the authenticating system, the server application can then use the password to impersonate the original authenticated entity when interacting with another party. This approach can provide a lot of flexibility, but it can also be abused if applications impersonate users for unauthorized operations (say, emptying the user's bank account). We discuss the concepts of impersonation and delegation further in Chapter 11, "Administrative Considerations for Web Services Security."

Passwords provide a simple-to-implement identity check. However, passwords can be forged, cracked, or spoofed if the password is poorly selected or if the password is not protected while in transit and in storage. This mechanism is appropriate for low-risk applications. Although continued support for Web-based password authentication is important, it's a good idea to begin planning for an evolution to PKI-based client authentication. The weaknesses of passwords are well known, and they are even more vulnerable to attack in distributed systems.

Challenge-Response Authentication

In challenge-response systems, the side performing the authentication check first sends out a challenge. The client system trying to prove the user's identity performs some function on the challenge based on information only available to the user/client and returns the result. If the result is as expected, the user is authenticated. The notable characteristic of these systems is that the response depends on the challenge. HTTP digest authentication is an example of a challenge-response system. In this approach, the client sends a response to the server that is derived from a random value provided by the server as well as the password.

Challenge-response systems are more secure than password systems because they do not expose the authenticating information over the network. The authenticating information originally provided by the user never leaves the client workstation. Another advantage is that since the challenge, which is chosen by the authenticating side, varies with each authentication, the response will vary as well, thereby eliminating replay attacks. Challenge-response systems generally cannot support impersonation of the authenticated party by the server application, which makes challenge-response more secure but less flexible than passwords alone.

Challenge-response systems perform authentication without sending a password over a network. However, this approach does not eliminate passwords. Unlocking authentication information stored on the client usually requires a password. In contrast to password authentication, however, neither the password nor the authentication information ever leaves the user workstation in a challenge-response system.

Cryptographic Protocols

Most of the popular challenge-response authentication systems are implemented using *cryptographic protocols*. These protocols build upon the cryptographic mechanisms that we have previously discussed, namely secret key and public key cryptography. The protocols define how clients and servers should exchange key information to establish a secure authenticated session. A client and server then use the established session to exchange data that is protected from disclosure and/or modification.

The most common cryptographic authentication protocols are SSL and Kerberos, which we discuss next.

SSL/TLS Protocol

In public key algorithms, the principal keeps his or her private key secret. For that reason, a principal's signature on a message using the principal's private key constitutes a proof of identity. When public key technology is used to authenticate the principal to a Web server, the principal sends the server its public key certificate after server authentication is complete and the session key has been established. The principal also sends its signature on a combination of server- and client-provided information. The server verifies the signature on the principal's public key certificate and verifies the client's signature on the combined data. If the signature is verified, the client is authenticated, and the encrypted session can begin using a shared secret session key.

The widest application of a public key authentication protocol scheme for Web access is the Secure Sockets Layer (SSL) protocol. SSL is now officially called Transport Layer Security (TLS) (IETF 1999). (In this book, we'll continue to call the protocol SSL since this is the most commonly used name.) Several books are available that describe the details of SSL and TLS, for example (Rescorla 2000).

SSL is a transport security protocol positioned above TCP but below the application layer of a communication protocol stack. It was originally developed by Netscape to provide security for Web-based HTTP transactions. In addition to HTTP, SSL can also be used to provide secure transport for Telnet, FTP, and other application protocols. SSL is generally used to enforce confidentiality and integrity for end-user access to the Web, and should be based on 128-bit triple Data Encryption Standard (3DES) or RC4 session keys. For adequate protection, Web server public keys should be at least 1,024 bits.

The operation of SSL is normally transparent to the application that sits above it. However, once a user has been authenticated, the application can obtain information about the client's certificate through application programming interfaces (APIs) provided by the Web server. We will talk more about certificates in Chapter 4.

One thing of note about SSL is that the protocol supports mutual authentication. That is, SSL authenticates the server to the client and can also optionally authenticate the client to the server. While many authentication systems only authenticate the client to the server, with Web Services it is often more important to authenticate the server to the client. Users trying to connect to a Web server need to be confident that they are communicating with a trustworthy server before sending sensitive information such as credit card numbers.

Kerberos/DCE Protocol

In secret key algorithms, a principal's identity is verified by testing whether the principal can correctly encrypt a message using a key that is shared only between the verifier and principal. Thus, the verifier must also possess the key in order to perform verification. Unlike public key protocols, secret key protocols can be difficult to scale to large applications because each principal must have a different secret key for every other principal it would ever want to authenticate.

To deal with the problem of pair-wise keys for all applications, practical versions of secret key authentication protocols have a trusted third party that maintains keys for a collection of principals. All principals in that collection have to trust only that third party to protect their secret keys.

The most popular representative of secret key authentication protocols is Kerberos (IETF 1993, Neuman 1994), which was developed at MIT. After a client and server have used Kerberos to prove their identity, they can also encrypt all of their communications to ensure data confidentiality and integrity.

Kerberos has been incorporated into Distributed Computing Environment (DCE) (Gittler 1995, OSF 1996) and adopted with extensions by Microsoft for Windows 2000 environments. You can find a good overview of Kerberos and its followers in (Oppliger 1996).

Kerberos is commonly used in the middle tier within corporate networks. Kerberos allows a principal to prove its identity to a server without sending authentication data (such as a password) that might allow an attacker to subsequently impersonate the principal. The client application provides a secret key that is derived from a password as the basis of authentication. The secret key may potentially be stored on a hardware token (DES card) for stronger authentication and may also be derived from a public key certificate.

To use a Kerberos security service, the client first sends the principal's identity to the authentication server, which sends back a credential called a ticket-granting ticket (TGT). The TGT has been encrypted so that only the legitimate principal who possesses the correct password is able to decrypt it and use it at a future time.

When the client wishes to access a server application using Kerberos, the client sends the TGT to the Key Distribution Center (KDC). The KDC returns a session ticket, which contains a secret session key and client identifier. The client uses the session ticket to establish a secure authenticated TCP/IP session with the server application. The session ticket is protected by encryption and is not exposed over the network.

Kerberos optionally provides encryption and integrity services for messages exchanged between clients and server applications. Kerberos uses DES for encryption and RSA MD4/MD5 for integrity. Kerberos is capable of supporting 128-bit keys, which is the current recommended key length for most applications.

DCE extends Kerberos functionality, and has been used extensively in corporate networks in which its rich feature set and high-performance secret key authentication technology are critical requirements. DCE 1.1 security is a mature product that provides powerful and flexible support for all aspects of security: login, authentication, message protection, authorization, delegation, audit, and key management. DCE begins with Kerberos V5, which provides basic secret key (DES) authentication and message protection. DCE then adds Registration Servers and Privilege Servers to provide additional services.

Secret key authentication using Kerberos and DCE security are known and proven technologies with good performance in corporate networks. However, it is generally accepted that secret key distribution and management is not tractable for very large numbers of users. Even with the Kerberos-based design of Microsoft Passport, the protocol still receives criticism for its inability to handle the scale and loosely federated nature of the Internet-based Web Services.

Authentication Systems

There are several different authentication systems for Web Services that use the security authentication mechanisms we've described. These systems are listed below. Although some of these systems are focused on authenticating human beings rather than Web Services applications, they are relevant to this topic because Web Services applications need to be able to handle user information that originates from any of these systems.

Operating system-based authentication. Web Services are usually requested and delivered via HTTP. Therefore, Web Services systems often have Web servers as front ends. Some Web servers perform authentication by using the facilities of the underlying operating system. This is the way that Microsoft's Internet Information Server (IIS) performs authentication. IIS offers a variety of methods for authentication. This includes username and password with HTTP basic authentication; NT LAN Manager (NTLM) and HTTP digest authentication, both of which are challenge response-based; SSL authentication; and Kerberos authentication. As a result of successfully completing IIS authentication, the user is known to the operating system and the facilities of the operating system can be used for authorization. This is a very powerful capability, but not all system implementers want to establish Windows operating system accounts for Web users.

Web server-based authentication. Web servers generally come with a built-in authentication capability to handle the authentication requirements for HTTP, namely HTTP basic authentication (which is password based) and HTTP digest authentication. Depending on the Web server, the authentication information used can be the same as that used by the operating system, stored in a separate file contained on the same platform as the Web server, or stored in a separate user repository (Lightweight Directory Access Protocol [LDAP]-based). The key point about this type of authentication versus the operating system-based authentication described previously is that a successfully authenticated user will not be known to the operating system. Operating system mechanisms cannot be used to enforce access control. In these cases, the Web server itself enforces access control.

Token-based authentication. With token-based systems, the user must possess a physical token that plays some part in the authentication process, which makes this approach a lot stronger than passwords by themselves. Tokens are frequently used for remote access to privileged services because they provide two-factor authentication (physical possession of the token card and knowledge of a PIN). Tokens, however, are more costly and complex to implement than IDs and passwords. Sometimes the token displays a value that must be verified by an authentication server. The token may have a keypad so that a challenge can be input to the token. The token may also have a physical connection to the workstation so that the challenge is automatically entered into the token and the response is automatically sent from the token to the workstation during the authentication protocol. Examples of tokens include CRYPTOCard and RSA SecurID.

Web single sign-on. Authentication is needed just as much for HTTP transactions as for other electronic transactions. The difficulty with HTTP is its statelessness and inability to keep track of a user session. Each request to a Web server is treated as a new request and the user must, theoretically, be authenticated again. A solution to this problem is to have the Web browser cache authentication information and present it with each request to the Web server. This relieves the user from having to reenter it multiple times. However, this compounds the problem of a clear text password traversing the Internet and makes it the problem of a clear text password traversing the Internet with every access to the Web server. Other problems, such as using the same authentication information with different Web servers in the same Web server cluster, still require that the user be authenticated again. In answer to this need, Web SSO systems like Netegrity SiteMinder, Microsoft Passport, Entrust getAccess, and RSA ClearTrust were developed. Web SSO systems maintain a session between HTTP requests to the same server or server cluster. The user logs in once and can access any other Web server in the cluster without logging in again for the duration of the session. If the authentication check passes, the security server creates an encrypted cookie, which contains the username, IP address, browser, time, and expiration time. The Web server returns the cookie to the client browser, which then uses the cookie for subsequent authenticated HTTP requests. The length of a session is governed by the site's policy. Web SSO systems allow customized and branded login screens. Most Web SSO systems support a variety of authentication mechanisms such as password, RSA SecurID, Windows NT domain login, and public key certificate. They also provide authorization services. Since Web servers implement intercepts at key points during the serving of an HTTP request, including authentication, Web SSO systems can easily be integrated with Web servers.

Client/server single sign-on. Just as Web interactions need SSO capability, client/server systems need SSO. In fact, since client-server systems were developed before Web browsers and servers, the need for a client/server SSO was identified earlier. Kerberos is the most common approach for client/server systems, and is used, for example, in Microsoft COM+, described in Chapter 7.

Biometrics. When enterprises need very strong evidence of a user's identity, they often turn to biometrics. Biometrics includes mechanisms such as retina scanners, voice recognition systems, and palm or fingerprint readers. These provide strong authentication, but can be costly and need to be evaluated with respect to false negatives as well as social acceptance. Biometrics are most commonly used at controlled facilities or for highly critical applications with limited users. When used with Web authentication servers, biometrics generally require custom integration.

Authorization

As we've discussed, cryptography and authentication are required for virtually any secure Web Services application, no matter how simple the security requirements might be. The last security technology that is generally needed is authorization. *Authorization* grants permission for principals to access Web Services resources, providing the basis for access control. Authentication is performed mainly to support authorization. The primary reason for a server to authenticate an identity is so the server can make a decision, based on that identity, to grant access to the requested Web Service resource.

The challenge of understanding authorization is the vast diversity of policy granularity. Coarse-grained authorization policies can be very simple; fine-grained policies, which distinguish among many different resources, become increasingly complex. The simplest "all-or-nothing" coarse-grained authorization policy is based solely on whether an authentication is successful. That is, if a principal has been successfully authenticated to the server, the principal is permitted to access the resource. (Some people say there is no authorization policy in this case, but that's not accurate—the authorization policy is simply equivalent to the authentication decision.) This coarse-grained policy is not too useful, since it would give Jack the Ripper and the Queen of England the same access to resources, as long as they both were authenticated. However, if the population of authenticated users is very small and all of them are equally trustworthy, an authentication check may be all that is needed.

Typical authorization policies permit access to different resources based on distinct collections of authenticated users, such as roles, groups, or privileges. Authorization policies restrict access to many different collections of resources: hosts, files, Web pages, application interfaces, methods, instances, and database records, to name a few. Authorization policies may also restrict access based on a global context (such as time of day), transactional context (such as no more than three withdrawals per day), or data values (such as trading no more than one million shares of stock). These types of fine-grained authorization policies can be very complex to define and manage, and they are certainly well beyond the basic security needs of a typical application. We discuss advanced models for authorization in Chapters 7 and 11.

Web authorization servers focus on controlling users' access to Web pages (URLs), although authorization servers can support more general classes of access policies. The authorization policy supports user groups for scalability and is also extensible to allow customized access policies.

Web authorization servers generally support access control at the directory and page level. This means that the entire page or a URL can be protected, but not a portion of it. To effectively provide personalized Web content or provide different levels of security for specific functions or information, a finer level of access control may be required. Fine-grained access control is supplied by mid-tier authorization products, which are described in Chapters 7 and 11. Some issues of granularity can be addressed by carefully designing security for Web pages to ensure that information with different protection requirements is isolated, thus reducing the number of authorization decisions.

Walk-Through of a Simple Example

Now that you're versed on the security basics of cryptography, authentication, and authorization, you have everything you need to understand a simple application of Web Services security. For this scenario, we've chosen to use ASP.NET, since Microsoft has created an environment that allows developers to deploy their basic Web Services applications securely with as little trouble as possible.

Our example illustrates the basic requirements for Web Services security as well as the limitations and risks of such a simple approach. You may start out thinking that you're building an application similar to our example with simple security needs, but this chapter may change your mind. Prepare yourself; when we are finished going through the example, the variety of issues that we uncover will make you think long and hard about the complexity of your application security needs.

Example Description

As you may recall from Chapter 1, our e-commerce example describes an online storefront provided by *ePortal*. The store sells its products to *customers*, who can electronically place and settle orders for products through customer accounts represented by *shopping carts*. *Members* are a category of customers who get special treatment: members have access to product deals that are not available to regular customers. *Visitors* are casual browsers of the site, and *staff* administer the storefront applications. In this chapter, we focus on users accessing ePortal services directly via a browser client using HTML, as shown in Figure 3.2.

The services provided by ePortal are implemented by eBusiness. ePortal accesses the eBusiness services over the Internet via SOAP. eBusiness stores information about products and prices, and also performs the processing of the orders received by ePortal.

To implement this example we're using ASP.NET. Chapter 8, "Securing .NET Web Services," covers the topic of .NET in detail and expands considerably on this example, so we will give only a very quick overview here. ASP.NET provides a full environment for building Web Services and is the preferred way to build these services using Microsoft technologies. We use ASP.NET to implement our example as shown in Figure 3.3. For more information on ASP.NET and more advanced security scenarios, please refer to Chapter 8.

The client browser accesses ePortal services that are running on an IIS Web server. When ePortal needs to request services of eBusiness concerning products, prices, or order processing, the IIS Web server sends a SOAP/HTTP request to a SOAP server called StoreFrontService that is running on eBusiness. This server provides a bridge between the Web Service and the COM+ implementation of the eBusiness business logic.

Figure 3.2 ePortal and eBusiness.

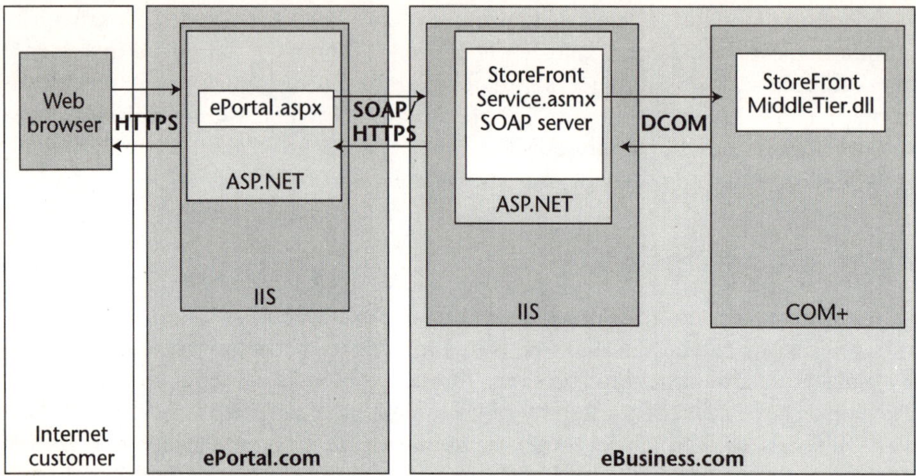

Figure 3.3 Providing Web Services access to eBusiness using ASP.NET.

The basic security requirements that we will address here, which are a subset of those we described in Chapter 1, are:

Cryptography. All network traffic between the client Web browser and ePortal, and between ePortal and eBusiness, should be encrypted to maintain message confidentiality and integrity. Data confidentiality must be enforced to maintain consumer privacy and to prevent disclosure of credit cards. Data integrity must be enforced to prevent tampering with any transactions by a hostile attacker.

Authentication. Customers, members, and staff should be authenticated, and their roles should be distinguished.

Authorization. Customers, members, and staff should only be permitted to access specific authorized services for each role (as described in Chapter 1).

Security Features

As shown in Figure 3.3, we have two potential boundaries where we can enforce our security requirements: the HTTP connection between the browser and ePortal, and the SOAP/HTTP connection between ePortal and eBusiness. For this discussion, we rely mainly on eBusiness for security enforcement. The ePortal server serves as a pass-through to forward the browser's credential information to eBusiness. This approach keeps security functionality very simple, but, as you'll see later, it does have its limitations.

On the positive side, this example requires the Web Services developer to write very little security-specific code. By deploying ASP.NET properly on ePortal and eBusiness, existing Microsoft security mechanisms handle all of the security issues. It can't get much easier to deploy a secure Web Service. Let's examine the security features that are provided:

Cryptography

All network traffic between browser and ePortal, and between ePortal and eBusiness, is protected by SSL. Consequently, clients are required to access the Web servers via HTTPS (defaulting to port 443), which encrypts all message traffic. To enforce this requirement, the IIS Web servers on both ePortal and eBusiness need to be configured to require a secure channel when accessing any resource. This requirement is part of the *Secure Communications* dialog box used during IIS set up. The SSL connections will enforce our message confidentiality and integrity requirements.

Authentication

We use HTTP basic authentication in our scenario, since this type of authentication is built into the Microsoft environment and is easy to configure. Customers, members, and staff all have individual usernames and passwords, and are required to login before accessing protected resources. These users are all recognized as Windows users and are mapped to Windows operating system (OS) user accounts. Visitors to the site are permitted to access unprotected resources using anonymous access; these users are not required to login. The *Authentication Methods* dialog box of IIS is used to define these requirements and is discussed further in Chapter 8.

Using HTTP basic authentication by itself would expose passwords on the Internet. By using basic authentication in conjunction with SSL, we ensure that the passwords are protected from snooping as they travel over the network.

In this example, IIS on ePortal does not actually perform a password authentication check, but simply impersonates the user and forwards the username and password on to eBusiness. The ASP.NET configuration file on eBusiness is set up to use an authentication mode of Windows, which means that ASP.NET Web Services will use the authentication performed by the IIS Web server on eBusiness.

Authorization

To protect our StoreFrontService on eBusiness, we use Windows discretionary access control lists (DACLs). (Windows DACLs are described further in Chapter 8.) The DACLs provide file-level protection for the file that defines the StoreFrontService SOAP server implementation. We use the *Access Control Settings* dialog box to set up permissions so that customers, members, staff, and anonymous visitors can read the appropriate Web Services files. When a client requests access to a particular Web Service method (such as getting the price for a product), Windows will use the authenticated identity as provided by IIS and check whether the user is permitted to access the requested service according to his or her role.

Limitations

This example manages to provide a reasonable degree of security for ePortal and eBusiness. However, our security scenario does have several limitations, which we explore below.

We have set up this example with Microsoft technology exclusively. Using technology from any one vendor is always the easiest, because vendors want to ensure that the solutions they provide are self-contained. However, a single-technology solution is not acceptable for many Web Services deployments. In fact, one of the main advantages of Web Services is their ability to support cross-vendor applications, such as .NET systems connecting to J2EE environments. Users of Web Services want to connect applications across enterprise lines of business, or across enterprise boundaries. If the security technologies used by Web Services clients and servers are required to be identical, this limitation eliminates one of the primary advantages of Web Services. Much of this book discusses how to apply Web Services security when Web Services clients and servers use different and potentially incompatible security technologies. We discuss techniques to support secure interoperability in Chapter 10, "Interoperability of Web Services Security Technologies."

Our example relies heavily on IIS security mechanisms, both to authenticate users and protect traffic. Web servers from all vendors, and from Microsoft in particular, have come under heavy attack as sources of vulnerability. We see a constant stream of Web server patches to address new vulnerabilities, which continue to be discovered at an alarming rate. This is not a surprise, considering the extensive and complex features offered by Web Services products—there are plenty of ways to inadvertently create security holes in any complex software. Because a primary purpose of Web Services is to enable flexible remote procedure call (RPC) access to applications, the stakes for Web server vulnerabilities become much higher. A weakness that is exploited in the Web server could expose your entire corporate network.

If IIS security were compromised in this sample system, eBusiness applications would be wide open, and attackers could potentially commit fraudulent purchases. A better approach would be to provide additional layers of protection so that if an IIS security weakness were exploited other protective mechanisms would limit the damage that could occur. Many of the later chapters in this book discuss techniques to enforce security at multiple tiers in the architecture and avoid a single point of failure.

Our example provides no accountability service to record accesses in a security audit log. Such a service would be valuable for tracing the source of an attack after it has occurred. Because Web Services are so new there is little available in terms of security auditing. However, as described in Chapter 7, many of the underlying infrastructures for Web Services provide a basic security auditing capability.

Cryptography

Our example uses SSL, which does a fine job of protecting the contents of a message as it travels across the network. However, security mechanisms like SSL have their limitations.

First, because SSL works at the transport layer, it's all-or-nothing security—either the entire message body is encrypted or none of it is. For small messages, encrypting the entire message is acceptable, but for very large messages the overhead of encrypting the entire message may make the process too slow. In cases where a lot of data is transmitted but only a small fraction of it needs to be protected, transport layer security is not a good solution.

In addition, SSL transport layer protects traffic in a point-to-point fashion, but it exposes the data contents at intermediate locations. In our example, the HTTP traffic is encrypted when traveling from browser to ePortal, decrypted and exposed within the ePortal site, reencrypted when traveling from ePortal, and then decrypted at eBusiness. When ePortal is a completely trustworthy site, permitting it to view all traffic content is an acceptable risk, but in some cases this model may not be appropriate. For example, eBusiness may not be willing to permit ePortal to view credit card information, even though ePortal provides this information on behalf of its clients. In our example, there is no reason for ePortal to have access to credit card information since eBusiness is handling the order processing.

In both of these cases, a better approach is to encrypt only the small portion of the message that needs to be protected rather than relying on SSL transport. Allowing clients to selectively encrypt data lets them send data through ePortal to eBusiness without ePortal being able to view or manipulate the data. This approach requires message-level security, which we describe in Chapter 4.

Authentication

The password authentication mechanism we use for the example is easy to set up, but it has a number of problems that you should be aware of.

As we have mentioned previously, password-based authentication provides weak security, and it is risky to use for high-value transactions. The human-engineering issues relating to passwords are difficult to address. On one hand simple passwords are easy to guess; on the other hand complex passwords are easy to steal (no one can remember them, so people write them down). At least our example ensures that the passwords are not exposed on the Internet, which would make them highly vulnerable.

A more subtle limitation is the impersonation model used by the example. The client sends its username and password to ePortal, and ePortal impersonates the user when making the SOAP request to eBusiness by forwarding the same username and password. As far as eBusiness is concerned, it thinks it is receiving the request directly from the user. If the eBusiness StoreFrontService needs to access other applications (such as the COM+ server), StoreFrontService will again impersonate the user by forwarding the same username and password.

It doesn't take much thought to realize that this approach can cause passwords to proliferate to many different servers. In fact, there is no way to tell where a user's password may end up. This model assumes that all servers are equally trustworthy, and that is a bad assumption to make in most distributed systems. If an attacker compromises any one of those systems, all of the passwords will be discovered, and the rest of the systems will fall like dominoes. Further, there is nothing to prevent an insider attack on a server like ePortal, to abuse its ability to impersonate users and perform actions that were not intended by the user, such as buying extra merchandise that disappears off the loading dock.

As we discussed earlier, sharing the same password authentication technology between ePortal and eBusiness made this example easy to implement and allowed us to use Microsoft products that can transparently handle the password credentials.

However, it would be more likely for Web Services applications to use different authentication mechanisms and databases. If ePortal and eBusiness were different companies, there would not be much of a chance that they would share their database of users and passwords as they do in this example. Furthermore, authentication schemes like this one that are tightly coupled to OS accounts do not scale well to very large distributed applications with many thousands of users. Web Services applications with large numbers of users would probably not use OS-based authentication, and would use a Web SSO authentication system instead.

A more typical cross-enterprise scenario would be for ePortal to authenticate the user with its own database, and then pass evidence of that authentication (rather than the password itself) to eBusiness. In addition, ePortal might keep track of the customer, member, and staff role memberships, and pass both the user's identity and role to eBusiness. In this case, eBusiness would not need to reauthenticate the user but instead would verify that the user and role information came from a trustworthy source (namely ePortal) that vouches for the authentication information. We describe cross-enterprise security issues in Chapters 6 and 10.

Authorization

Finally, we come to our choice of authorization, which is barely adequate even for this simple example. We chose to use DACLs to enforce security based on Windows file system OS protections. Windows will perform this check transparently for us, but the difficulty in the granularity of the access check is that file system access is too coarse for our Web Services model. We want to enforce access to different Web Services methods based on the user roles, but file system protections will not provide this for us. All methods for an ASP.NET Web Service are defined within the same file, so the OS cannot tell the difference between one method and another.

Consequently, we will have a very difficult time enforcing the authorization policy we want in our example. We could split up our single StoreFrontService into separate ones for visitors, customers, members, and staff, but this approach would be awkward and would require redundant implementations for the methods that are used by more than one role. We discuss better and more sophisticated approaches to enforce fine-grained authorization in Chapters 7, 8, and 9.

Summary

In this chapter, we provided an overview to a variety of security technologies that are the basis for all security architectures. We gave an overview of perimeter, middle, and back-office tier security services. Perimeter security serves as the first line of defense and primarily protects against hostile attackers who are outside of an organization. Mid-tier security serves as the second line of defense, providing another layer of protection against external attackers, and also protecting against attackers who are within an organization. Back-office security provides the third layer of defense by protecting the back-end servers, ensuring that an organization's most valuable resources are safe from unauthorized access.

We then concentrated on the set of perimeter security technologies that are the starting point for Web Services security: cryptography, authentication, and authorization. We introduced the concepts of secret and public key cryptography, and public key certificates. Authentication starts with passwords and then expands to stronger forms of security that have cryptographic foundations, such as the SSL and Kerberos protocols. The various authentication mechanisms may be used to provide authentication systems such as OS-based, Web server-based, token-based, Web SSO, Client-server SSO, and biometrics. Authentication, in turn, serves as the foundation on which to make authorization decisions. The security services described in this chapter define only the bare essentials; several subsequent chapters expand on these topics and explore more advanced security mechanisms.

We then walked you through a Web Services security example that takes advantage of the basic security functionality provided by .NET. This example gives a fairly complete initial view of Web Services security issues and demonstrates that security doesn't have to be very complex to implement. However, we describe several significant limitations of the example that should help you think through your own Web Services security requirements. We hope that these limitations give you motivation to read on through the rest of the book, which provides guidance and solutions for the issues we raised in this chapter.

The next chapters explore a number of different aspects of Web Services in the real world that are well beyond the simple example we presented here. Chapters 4, 5, 6, and 7 discuss the underlying technologies for securing Web Services including XML document security, Security Assertion Markup Language (SAML), Web Services security principles, and application platform security infrastructure. When you get through these chapters, you will have a good understanding of what makes a Web Service secure, and you will be ready for the advanced topics described in the remaining chapters.

CHAPTER 4

XML Security and WS-Security

This chapter discusses measures that can be used with XML and SOAP messages to secure them. As you will see, these measures are based on cryptography. In Chapter 3, "Getting Started with Web Services Security," we introduced the basic concept of public key cryptography. In this chapter, we expand on this topic and show how cryptography can be applied to XML. Finally, we discuss how such measures are being tailored to SOAP and Web Services using WS-Security.

Public Key Algorithms

As you recall from Chapter 3, *public key* or *asymmetric cryptography* uses two different, but mathematically related, keys. There are several public key algorithms. Although there are differences in their operation, they can be divided into two general approaches for encryption and two for digital signature.

ENCRYPTION

- RSA
- Diffie-Hellman (DH) or Elliptic Curve Diffie-Hellman (ECDH)

DIGITAL SIGNATURE

- RSA
- Digital Signature Algorithm (DSA) or Elliptic Curve DSA (ECDSA)

When a public key algorithm is incorporated into a system, it is combined with a faster algorithm that makes the system useable with large amounts of data. We will first discuss encryption and then digital signatures.

Encryption

Encryption provides confidentiality. It does this by preventing data from being understood except by the intended recipient. This is true even if the encrypted data falls into the hands of unintended recipients. Encryption provides a form of access control by virtue of the management of keys. Only the intended recipient or recipients have the keys needed to decrypt the data and thus access it.

There are two generally used public key techniques that support the encryption of data: RSA and Diffie-Hellman. We say support because public key algorithms are too computationally expensive to use for data encryption. That is, using public key cryptography for encryption is time consuming and eats into performance. So, instead of encrypting data directly, public key algorithms are used with a symmetric key algorithm to protect data.

RSA

RSA, named for Ronald Rivest, Adi Shamir, and Leonard Adleman, the developers of the algorithm, is the best known of all the public key algorithms. When people are asked to describe public key cryptography, they describe the operation of RSA. The key feature of RSA is that it is a reversible algorithm. (Technically, RSA, or any public key algorithm, is not reversible. Public key algorithms are one-way functions. We say RSA is reversible because the data that was transformed with one key can be recovered with a different key.) With RSA, we can use a private key to recover the data that was previously encrypted using the public key. This concept is illustrated in Figure 4.1. With RSA, the public key is used to encrypt data. The private key is used to decrypt the data. Since the public key is available to anyone, but only the owner of the key pair has the private key, anyone can encrypt data meant for the key's owner, and only the key's owner can decrypt the data.

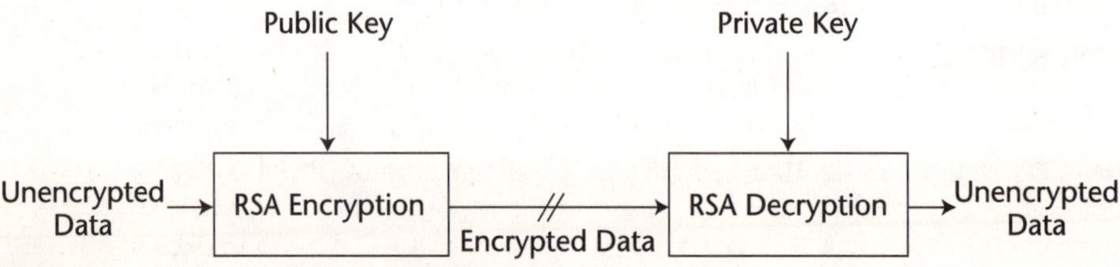

Figure 4.1 RSA encryption and decryption.

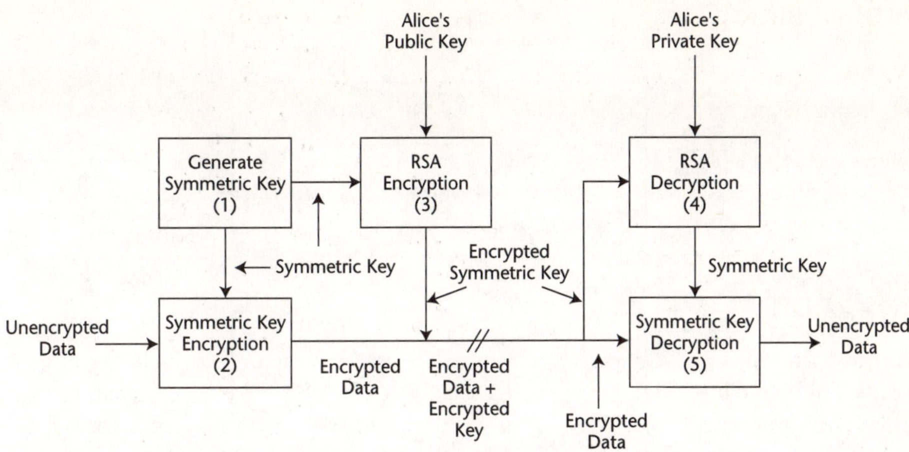

Figure 4.2 RSA-based encryption and decryption system.

When implemented as part of an encryption system, RSA is used to encrypt a symmetric key that actually encrypts the data. This is illustrated in Figure 4.2. In this example, Bob wants to send Alice information in such a way that only Alice is able to understand it.

1. Bob begins by generating a symmetric key.
2. He uses this key to encrypt the data with a symmetric algorithm such as DES.
3. Using Alice's public key, he encrypts the symmetric key, which is then appended to the encrypted message. This encryption ensures that only Alice can decrypt and make use of the symmetric key.
4. Once the message is received, Alice extracts the encrypted symmetric key from the message and decrypts it using her private key.
5. Using the recovered symmetric key, Alice decrypts the entire message.

Diffie-Hellman, Elliptic Curve Diffie-Hellman

Diffie-Hellman (DH) and Elliptic Curve Diffie-Hellman (ECDH) are key agreement algorithms. The algorithm is named for Whitfield Diffie and Martin Hellman, the developers of the algorithm. In key agreement, two parties exchange information that allows them to derive a shared secret. Unauthorized parties can intercept the information exchanged but they are not able to determine the shared secret. This shared secret can then be used as a key for a symmetric algorithm. The DH key agreement process is shown in Figure 4.3. In the figure, two parties, Bob and Alice, wish to exchange sensitive information so they use encryption.

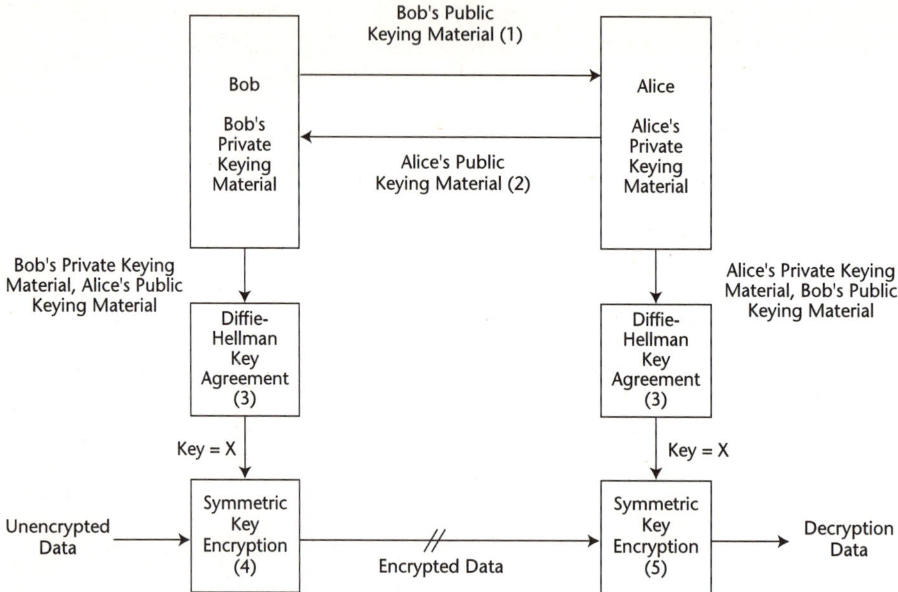

Figure 4.3 Diffie-Hellman key agreement.

1. Bob sends Alice his public keying material. (This isn't a key. Instead, it is information that allows a key to be derived.)
2. Alice sends Bob her public keying material.
3. Each uses this information and the DH algorithm to derive a common secret.
4. Bob uses the secret as a key to encrypt data sent to Alice using a symmetric key algorithm.
5. Alice uses the secret to decrypt the data Bob sends.

Figure 4.4 shows how DH can be used as part of an encryption system. The exchange of the keying material does not have to be as interactive as the previous discussion implies. It does not have to be synchronous. Public keying material can be published in a well-known location, well in advance so that one party can readily pick up the data when he or she needs it, rather than counting on the other party to send it. The following scenario demonstrates an asynchronous exchange:

1. Alice places her keying material in a directory for Bob to pick up when he wants.
2. Bob gets Alice's DH public keying information from the directory.
3. He generates unique keying material for this particular exchange. This is distinct from the keying material that he may already have published for himself in a directory. It prevents the reuse of the same symmetric key for all communication between the two of them.

4. Bob uses his private keying material with Alice's published, public keying material to derive the symmetric key for this message exchange.
5. Using the symmetric key, he encrypts the message to Alice.
6. He appends his public keying material for this message exchange onto the encrypted message and sends the combination to Alice.
7. She extracts Bob's keying information, combines it with her private keying material and derives the symmetric key.
8. She uses this key to decrypt the message.

One drawback to the Diffie-Hellman system is that the symmetric key used for the encryption depends on information sent from the sender and the receiver. If a message is destined to go to multiple recipients, it must be encrypted multiple times. With RSA, the message is encrypted once, and only the symmetric key is encrypted multiple times, once using the public key of each recipient.

The preceding discussion used Diffie-Hellman as the key agreement algorithm. If we had used ECDH, the process would have been very similar. However, in elliptic curve cryptography, we use points defined by an elliptic curve in a finite field rather than using the integers modulo, some prime number, as in Diffie-Hellman.

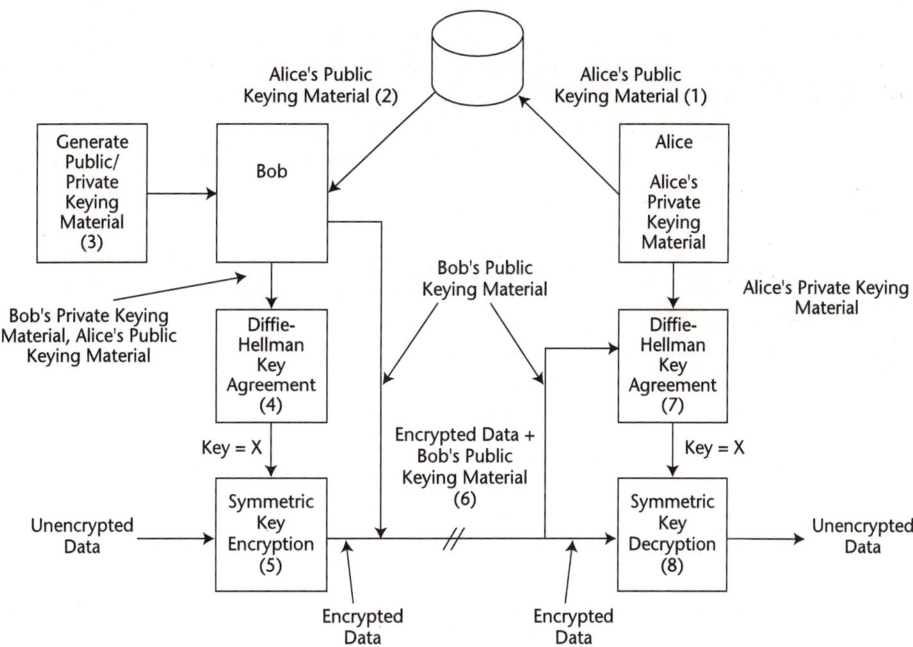

Figure 4.4 Diffie-Hellman-based encryption system.

Digital Signatures

Because only a key's owner holds a private key, a function that uses the private key is considered the work of the key's owner and no one else. This fact has opened up the world of cryptography to the concept of digital signatures. A *digital signature* is created by using the owner's private key to "sign" electronic data in a way that can't be forged. One party, the private key's owner, can create a properly implemented digital signature. Digital signatures are stronger than handwritten signatures because the signature is mathematically tied to the data signed. A digital signature can't be cut from one document and pasted into another. Also, any modification of the signed data invalidates the signature. A digital signature is created from the data being signed and the signer's private key. The signature is appended to the message. Anyone receiving the message performs another related function, using the public key and either the signature or the data as input, depending on the algorithm. If performing this function yields the expected result, the signature is considered valid.

Digital signatures provide several security services. They authenticate the message as having originated with the signer since only the owner of the key—that is, the holder of the private key—can sign the message. A digital signature also protects the message from unauthorized modification by serving as an integrity check. If a digital signature cannot be verified as having originated with the claimed signer, then the contents of the message are assumed to have been modified. While a digital signature by itself is not sufficient for establishing nonrepudiation, a properly constructed digital signature can play a key part in establishing nonrepudiation.

Message Digests

Before we discuss digital signature algorithms, we will discuss message digest algorithms, also known as hashing algorithms. In our discussion of encryption, we described how symmetric algorithms, such as DES, are used to do the bulk of the data encryption, while public key algorithms are used to protect or derive the symmetric key. This keeps the speed of encryption acceptable. A similar accommodation must be made for digital signatures. This accommodation consists of creating a digest of the data being signed.

A message digest algorithm takes input of any size and transforms it into a fixed string size. Since a million bytes or more of data is reduced to 128 or 160 bits, information is lost and the transformation is not reversible. A major property of a digest is that given a known input string, it is computationally infeasible to discover a different input string with the same digest.

Since public key algorithms are so computationally expensive, the digest of a message is signed rather than the entire message. With a suitable digesting algorithm, the security properties of the message are not affected. The signature on the message still authenticates the message, and a valid signature still verifies that a message hasn't been altered.

Two message digest algorithms are commonly used: MD5 and SHA-1. MD5 produces a 128-bit digest. Some theoretical concerns have been raised about MD5, but nothing concrete has been demonstrated. SHA-1, the Federal Information Processing Standard (FIPS), produces a 160-bit digest.

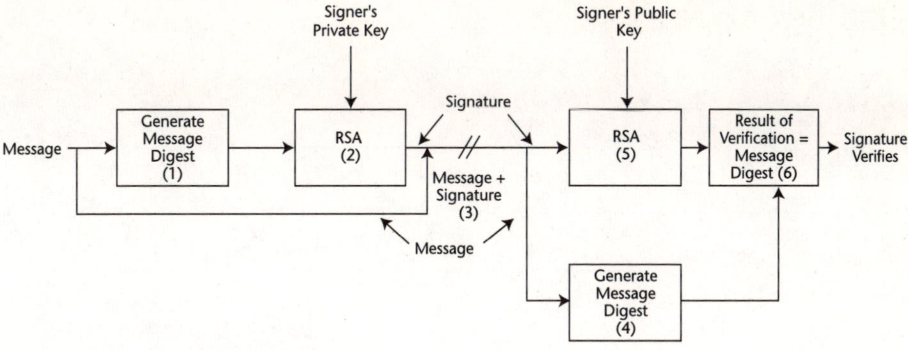

Figure 4.5 RSA digital signature.

RSA

The exact same RSA algorithm used for encryption can be used for digital signatures. Using RSA for a signature is shown in Figure 4.5.

1. First, a message digest is calculated.
2. The private key is used to sign the digest of the message.
3. The signature is appended to the message and transmitted to the recipient.
4. The recipient calculates the digest of the received message.
5. Then, verifying the signature requires extracting the signature from the message and using RSA on the signature with the public key.
6. If the result of the transformation and the newly calculated digest are equal, the signature is valid.

DSA

The National Institute of Standards and Technology developed the Digital Signature Algorithm (DSA). It was developed to provide an alternative to RSA that could be used for signatures but not for encryption. The U.S. government has been concerned about the proliferation and uncontrolled use of encryption. The government's position was that strong encryption was only for use by the government or other institutions. Use of encryption by others interferes with the government's ability to eavesdrop on the activities of lawbreakers. An alternative to RSA that could be used for digital signatures but not encryption was needed.

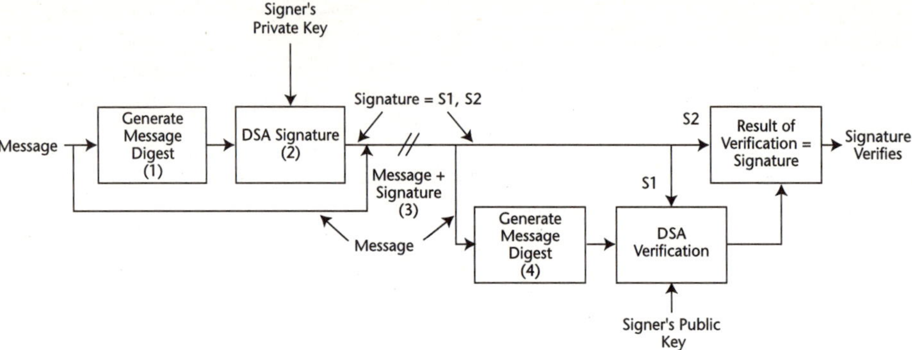

Figure 4.6 DSA signature and verification.

The DSA algorithm meets this requirement. Figure 4.6 describes its operation. With DSA:

1. The message is first used to create a message digest.
2. The message digest is signed. The signature itself is composed of two parts.
3. Then the signature and other supporting information are appended to the message and transmitted to the recipient.
4. The recipient calculates the digest of the message and performs a function based on the signer's public key, the digest, and the signature. If the result of this operation is equal to part of the signature, the signature is valid.

Public Key Certificates

While public keys can be distributed freely and held by anyone, they must still be secured to avoid misrepresentation. For the system to work, users of public keys need to be sure who the owner of the key is and that the key is correct and hasn't been modified. If it were possible for one person's public key to be substituted for another's, then the user of the key could be fooled into conducting a transaction with someone other than the person he or she is expecting.

In human society, we use introductions as a way to handle similar situations. Someone we know and trust will introduce us to someone we don't know. When this can't be done in person, letters of introduction are used. In this way, a network of trust is built.

In the electronic world, public key certificates play the role of letters of introduction. Certificates are a way for a trusted organization, known as a certificate authority (CA), to introduce us to an individual, by vouching for his or her public key. The certificates make it possible for the recipient of a public key to know with confidence who the owner of the key is and to be sure that the key has not been modified. It is a way for the CA to link an individual with his or her public key in a way that makes tampering without detection impossible.

The CA maintains a (logically) centralized database of all published public keys. It distributes public key certificates. Each certificate is essentially a statement by the authority describing the principal's public key. The CA vouches for an individual's public key by using its private key to sign a public key certificate, which is an electronic document that contains, among other information, the user's name and public key. The CA's signature on the certificate indicates that the public key belongs to the named user. Depending on its policy, the signature may also convey other information, such as the CA's vouching for the creditworthiness of the user. Each CA should have a Certificate Practices Statement (CPS). The CPS describes the operation of the CA, how it authenticates an individual or organization before issuing a certificate, and what kind of liability the CA assumes.

The signed certificate also prevents the undetected modification of the user's public key. If the holder of a public key certificate trusts the CA, and the CA's signature on the certificate is valid, the holder can then be confident that the public key belongs to the person named in the certificate and that the public key is correct. The holder may then use the certificate to authenticate a message that was sent by the person named in the certificate and signed with his or her corresponding private key.

It's unlikely that one CA organization in a very large community will know everyone who wants to communicate securely. Consequently, there may be many CAs. The CAs within a particular community are organized into a hierarchy. For instance, there could be a hierarchy of banks or of insurance companies. Anyone in a hierarchy can use a certificate issued by a CA within the hierarchy to meaningfully exchange cryptographically protected data with other individuals in the hierarchy.

An individual may choose to belong to several hierarchies. One hierarchy may apply stricter standards of identification than other hierarchies to an individual before issuing the individual a certificate. Its certificate would be regarded as more trustworthy than another hierarchy's that is less strict. A hierarchy may support the users of a particular application. A certificate from one organization, for instance an ISP, may be acceptable for everyday correspondence. But, an introduction from another, say a bank, may be needed to buy something. When we use a Web browser and a message pops up on the screen asking if we wish to accept a CA certificate, we are effectively joining a certificate hierarchy, even if the hierarchy only has one CA.

An individual in one hierarchy may need to communicate with an individual in another hierarchy. This individual may choose to belong to both hierarchies, if he or she can. Another option is for nodes of the two hierarchies (possibly the root nodes) to cross-certify each other. Through cross-certification, the nodes provide a way for certificate recipients in one hierarchy to verify a certificate from another hierarchy. Cross-certification needs to be done carefully to ensure that the policies applied by the CAs are compatible.

Setting up a certificate hierarchy and CAs needs to be done carefully. There are the usual cost, performance, and functionality issues associated with these systems. But there are also liability issues that need to be understood. CAs may need to back their certificates with monetary guarantees. Security is critical to the correct implementation of the system and can't be stressed enough. Standard practice calls for a CA to issue a certificate practices statement, which describes the practices of the CA and its liability.

Verisign and Entrust are examples of popular CA products. Identrus, a global network of financial institutions, is an example of a consortium-sponsored CA. Identrus provides standards for banks that act as trusted third parties for e-commerce transactions. From a CA perspective, Verisign, Entrust, and Identrus provide the root CA, which is at the top of an inverted CA hierarchy tree. The root CA has a self-signed certificate. Beneath the root are other CAs that have certificates signed by the root. Additional levels can exist to provide finer-grained associations or to distribute the workload. CAs at each level have certificates signed by the next highest level. Eventually, we reach a level with CAs that sign user certificates. Some hierarchies consist of the root and users certificates. Others may have several levels in addition to the root and user nodes.

Another solution to the problem of distributing public keys, although one that is not very popular in business enterprises, is to use a form of decentralized networks of trust, as in Pretty Good Privacy (PGP)-based environments. With PGP, users distribute their own keys directly via secure means to those with whom they will communicate. Secure means could be putting the certificate on a floppy and personally handing the floppy to a user's communicant. Also, with PGP, a trusted party, someone we already know and trust, can sign a certificate for another individual who wishes to be known to us. By carefully accepting keys and certificates, an individual can extend his or her trusted circle of communicants.

Certificate Format

There are several alternate formats for public key certificates. Data encoding, trust models, and specific content can differ among the alternatives. We will concentrate on the X.509 certificate format in this section. X.509 certificates are arguably the most common form of public key certificate.

Besides the owner's public key, a public key certificate consists of the CA's signature on the public key and the CA's own public key. Other information in the certificate includes the certificate's version, the key owner's name, the key owner's organizational affiliation, the CA's name, the certificate's validity period, the algorithm used to sign the certificate, and key parameters.

X.509 public key certificates are encoded in Abstract Syntax Notation 1 (ASN.1). It was developed for use with the ISO X.400 email standard. It is a platform-independent method for specifying and representing data. The hopes for ASN.1 when it was developed were very similar to those for XML now. However, it does not have the flexibility of XML. One problem with ASN.1 is that elements are not tagged. Consequently, an application must know exactly what elements are in the data structure and what order they are in to correctly parse the data. Despite the difficulty of working with ASN.1, many applications of the time were built with the assumption that it was the encoding format. Today, many of these applications have been left behind, and attention has switched to XML as the solution for platform-independent data representation. But, public key certificates continue to be encoded in ASN.1.

ASN.1 elements consist of a type, a length, and a value. Several basic types are specified. They include bit strings, octets, character strings, and Booleans. Complex types can be built up using the basic types. In addition to specifying data abstractly, two methods of encoding ASN.1 data, Basic Encoding Rules (BER) and Distinguished

Encoding Rules (DER), are used. With BER, the same piece of data can be represented in several different ways. This is analogous to 1, 1.0, and 1.00 all representing the same value. DER only allows one representation. Using the same analogy, in DER encoding, only one representation, say 1, is allowed. DER encoding is used when a precise, consistent representation is required, such as for digital signatures.

Public Key Infrastructure

Public key certificates require a management infrastructure to support certificate generation, distribution, and revocation. This infrastructure is called a public key infrastructure (PKI). Because certificate management is often tied to keys, PKIs often include the management of keys as well.

There are several components to a PKI. There is the CA, which we've discussed previously. There can also be a registration authority (RA) and a directory. In addition to the software components, there is usually a certificate practices statement (CPS) that describes the operation of the PKI, its security measures, and the extent of the CA's liability.

There are many ways that a PKI can operate. One PKI operational concept is shown in Figure 4.7.

1. Alice starts the process by generating a public key-private key pair.
2. Software on her system inserts her public key into a certificate request. She will usually sign the certificate request with her private key, the mate of the public key in the request.
3. The self-signed certificate is sent to an RA, since a self-signed request may not be sufficient proof of identity for a CA to issue a certificate.
4. Before the CA issues a certificate, Alice must convince the RA, a trusted operative of the CA, that she is who she claims to be. The RA usually consists of a person and software used to create certificate requests. The RA's most important function is to verify the identity of the presenter. For instance, if Alice is able to convince the RA that she is Sue and the RA requests a certificate for Sue with Alice's public key, then Alice will be able to impersonate Sue.
5. Once Alice's identity is verified, the RA takes Alice's self-signed public key certificate request and signs it. Alternatively, Alice can act as her own RA and sign the certificate request herself if the receiver of the signature is willing to accept the risk. Alice's signature on the original request proves that she possesses the private key matching the public key in the request. Sometimes, to ensure that keys are properly generated, the key holder must create his or her key pair in the presence of the RA.
6. The RA sends the certificate request to the CA.
7. Upon receipt of the certificate request, the CA verifies the RA's signature on the certificate request and verifies that the RA is entitled to make the request. Assuming that the RA is authorized, the CA takes the public key in the certificate request, creates a public key certificate with it, and signs the certificate.

8. The certificate is returned to Alice, and she inserts it in a signed e-mail, with SSL, or wherever she needs her signature verified and the protocol in place permits it. Assuming that he trusts the CA, Bob, the recipient, can use the public key certificate to verify Alice's signature.
9. The CA may also take the certificate and place it in a directory so that anyone wishing to communicate with Alice securely or wishing to verify her signature can retrieve her public key certificate independent of any direct communication with her.

If, for some reason, Alice's keys are compromised because they've fallen into the wrong hands or her certificates are compromised because they have been inappropriately modified, the CA must be notified, and Alice's certificate must be revoked. Once the CA is notified that the certificate is no longer valid, it places this certificate on its certificate revocation list (CRL) together with a date and time indicating when the certificate ceased being valid. Transactions completed before this time are assumed to be good. Transactions after this time may be compromised. The CA generates this list periodically and posts it in a Lightweight Directory Access Protocol (LDAP) directory that holds certificate and CRLs in a tree-structured, hierarchical organization. Individuals or organizations wishing to communicate securely with a user in the hierarchy can retrieve the user's certificate from the directory and verify the certificate's validity by checking the CA's CRL. In theory, anyone wishing to use Alice's key should consult her CA's CRL before using the key. In practice, since locating and then accessing the CA's directory can be difficult (most applications that use public key cryptography do not support this feature), most certificate users do not do this, leaving open a potential security problem.

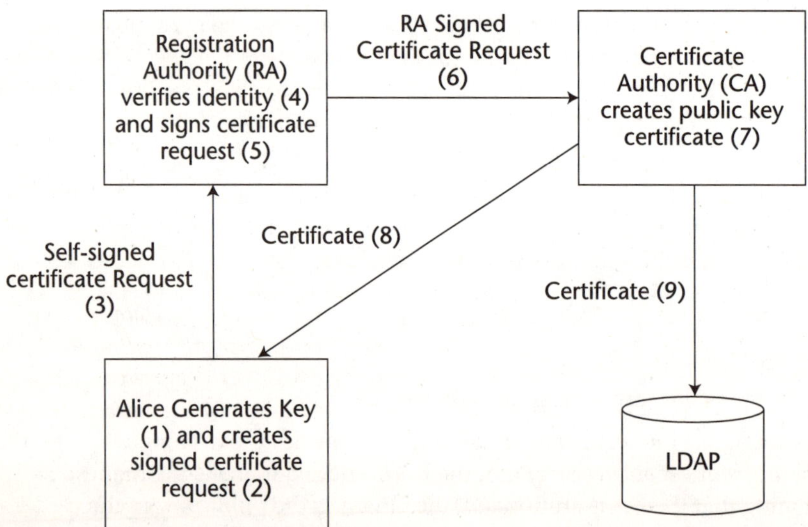

Figure 4.7 Public key infrastructure.

The original hope for PKIs was that there would a single, global, hierarchy of CAs. That way, the credibility of a CA could be validated, even if the recipient of a public key certificate did not formally know the specific CA. The reality is that most PKIs are independent of other PKIs. Cross-certification (one CA vouching for another CA) is sometimes used when individuals in different PKIs must exchange information securely.

XML Security

Since XML represents messages, XML security focuses on message security. Message encryption and digital signatures are the principal techniques used. While email- or file-encryption techniques can be used with XML messages, XML-specific techniques are more suitable for the way XML messages and SOAP messages are processed.

The W3C leads most of the XML security standardization efforts. A digital signature standard exists in the form of a W3C recommendation. There is also a candidate recommendation for XML encryption.

XML Encryption

The *XML Encryption Syntax and Processing* candidate recommendation (W3C 2002i) defines a process for encrypting digital data and the way the resulting encrypted data should be represented in XML. While the data being encrypted is intended to be more general than XML, XML data is the natural fit for XML Encryption. XML Encryption supports the encryption of an entire XML document or only selected portions of an XML document. The smallest unit of information that can be encrypted is an element. It supports the superencryption of data. That is, already encrypted data can be encrypted. XML Encryption provides for the identification or transfer of decryption key information.

The W3C recommendation focuses on defining the process for creating and representing XML-encoded encrypted data. Naturally enough, it also looks at the decryption process. It does not try to define new algorithms. It specifies existing algorithms for encryption/decryption, key agreement, message digests, message authentication, and other cryptographic applications (except for digital signatures, which are covered in a separate document). It addresses both symmetric and asymmetric cryptography.

Format/Structure

An encrypted element is contained in the structure *CipherData*. *CipherData* minimally consists of the encrypted data. *EncryptionMethod*, *KeyInfo*, and *EncryptionProperties* are all optional. XML Encryption allows the sender and the receiver of encrypted data to preselect cryptographic parameters, including keying data so that the parameters do not have to be exchanged when encryption is actually used.

The *CipherData* can be represented in either of two ways. It can be contained in the XML document, the most usual case. The encrypted data that is no longer comprehensible as text is base64 encoded. The second way is for the *CipherData* to reference the encrypted object.

The *EncryptionMethod* element contains the encryption algorithm and the key size. *KeyInfo* provides the information needed by the receiving application to decrypt the cipher data. If it is omitted, the receiving application is expected to know how to perform the decryption, including what key to use. XML Encryption supports all options specified by XML Signature for specifying keys. This includes a key identifier, the decryption key itself, a reference to the location where the decryption key is available, or the receiver's public key certificate that was used to encrypt the data. Several certificate formats are supported, including X.509. However, some key representations are not useful for encryption. For instance, sending an unencrypted decryption key with the same data that it unlocks is counterproductive. As an alternative, XML Encryption extends the options of XML Signature and adds an option for an *EncryptedKey*. If *KeyInfo* is not included, the application must know what key to use to decrypt the message. Finally, *EncryptionProperties* holds additional information related to the encryption.

Procedure

To encrypt XML elements:

1. Select the encryption algorithm and parameters.
2. Obtain the key. If the key is going to be identified, construct a *KeyInfo* element. Encrypt the key, if it will be sent with the encrypted data, and construct an EncryptedKey element. Place it in *KeyInfo* or in some other portion of the document.
3. Encrypt the data. For XML data, this can involve a transformation to UTF-8 encoding and serialization. The result is an octet string.
4. Build the *EncryptedType* structure. Where the encrypted data is actually stored in the structure, instead of being referenced, the encrypted data must be base64 encoded.
5. Replace the unencrypted element in the XML document with the *EncryptedType* structure.

To decrypt XML elements:

1. Process the element. Unspecified parameters must be supplied by the application.
2. Obtain the decryption key. This may require using a private key to decrypt a symmetric key or to retrieve the key from a local store.
3. Decrypt the data in *CipherData*.
4. Process the decrypted data. This requires that the application restore the decrypted data, which is in UTF-8, to its original form. It must be able to replace the *CipherData* structure in the XML document with the results of the decryption. In some cases, additional processing is required.

Example

The following code fragment is an example of encrypted content. Encrypted content replaces the original clear text content of the XML document. In this case, the fragment represents payment information. The name on the credit card and the credit limit are being transmitted in the clear. However, the credit card number is encrypted. The encryption algorithm is triple DES in cipher block chaining mode. The key that can be used to decrypt the credit card account number is *MyCompany*'s key. In this case, the key for MyCompany was preplaced with the receiver of the message. The encrypted data appears as *CipherValue*.

```
<PaymentInfo xmlns='http://example.org/paymentv2'>
  <Name>John Smith</Name>
  <CreditCard Limit='5,000' Currency='USdollars'>
      <EncryptedData xmlns='http://www.w3.org/2001/04/xmlenc#'
           Type='http://www.w3.org/2001/04/xmlenc#Content'>
           <EncryptionMethod
              Algorithm='http://www.w3.org/2001/04/xmlenc#3des-cbc'/>
           <ds:KeyInfo xmlns:ds='http://www.w3.org/2000/09/xmldsig#'>
               <ds:KeyName>MyCompany</ds:KeyName>
           </ds:KeyInfo>
           <CipherData>
                <CipherValue>A23B45C56</CipherValue>
           </CipherData>
     </EncryptedData>
  </CreditCard>
</PaymentInfo>
```

Issues

The primary issues with using XML Encryption for Web Services are:

Out-of-band agreements between the sender and the receiver. XML Encryption is very flexible and allows many parameters to be omitted from the *CipherData* structure. For instance, *KeyInfo* is optional. For the most part, we consider this flexibility a positive feature. If the data is decrypted immediately and does not have to persist, this is not a problem. However, if the encrypted data must be stored to protect confidentiality or if signatures have been applied to encrypted data and it is important to preserve a record of the signatures, leaving information out of the structure can lead to decryption problems at a later time. In general, including the encryption parameters in the structure is preferable.

Choice of algorithms and key lengths. XML Encryption does not mandate the use of particular algorithms or key lengths. It is the user's responsibility to ensure that the right choices are made. The system implementer should carefully consider how long the encrypted data must be retained, how much use the keys will have, and the preferred algorithm, then decide on the appropriate key length.

Application in SOAP. XML Encryption specifies encryption for XML documents. It does not describe how XML Encryption data and structures are implemented within the SOAP message structure.

XML Signature

The XML Signature recommendation (W3C 2002j) defines how digital data is signed and how the resulting signature should be represented in XML. While the data to be signed is intended to be more general than XML, XML data is the principal application for XML Signature. With XML Signature, all or selected portions of an XML document can be signed.

The recommendation defines the process for creating and representing an XML signature and then verifying the signature. It relies on existing algorithms for the signature, message digests, and message authentication codes. It offers several established alternatives for certificates, including X.509. It can also be used without certificates. This represents a departure from established thinking about public key cryptosystems, but it can be justified under certain circumstances. The recommendation references other standards for transformation such as *canonicalization*, rendering the data in a standard way that eliminates inconsequential differences in representation, and encoding/decoding.

Digital signatures are much more complex to implement than encryption. Because signatures are tied to the representation of the data being signed, caution must be exercised to ensure that the representation of the signed data and the verified data are consistent. Signature processing is much more subtle than encryption and is very sensitive to changes in data representation and processing order. Even if the signature was valid at the time it was created, it may not be verifiable because of changes that occurred as the message was routed.

Format/Structure

An XML signature consists of two required elements, *SignedInfo* and *SignatureValue*. There are also two optional elements, *KeyInfo* and *Object*.

SignedInfo. This includes the *CanonicalizationMethod*, which is discussed in the next section, for the *SignedInfo* element itself, the algorithms (usually a digest algorithm and a signature algorithm) used to produce the signature, and one or more references to the data being signed. Each *Reference* element includes a URI identifying the data being signed, the transforms that process the data (we will describe some transforms in the next section), an identifier of the digest algorithm used with the referenced data, and the value of the message digest.

SignatureValue. This is the value of the digital signature. It is base64 encoded.

KeyInfo. This provides the information needed by the receiving application to validate the signature. If it is omitted, the receiving application is expected to know how to validate the signature. For instance, two business partners may have previously exchanged public keys through some other means, thereby eliminating the need to include the public key as a child element of KeyInfo. If this hasn't been done, KeyInfo can contain a key identifier, the signer's public key, a reference to where the public key is available, or the signer's public key certificate. Several public key certificate formats are supported.

Object. This is a structure that carries any other information needed to support the signature.

Transformations

Before data is signed, it usually goes through a transformation process or processes. These transformations render the data suitable for signature. For instance, one well-known transformation is base64 decoding. This is used so that the raw version of base64-encoded data can be signed. In addition, there are several other transformations important for XML and XML signatures. We will discuss XPath, Canonical XML, and Decryption Transform for XML Signature in this section.

Canonical XML can be applied to *SignedInfo*. In addition, each *reference* element in *SignedInfo* can contain transformations that are applied to the referenced elements. One or more transformations can be specified for each referenced element. The input to the first transform is the data identified by the *SignedInfo* URI. Its output becomes the input to the second transform, and so on, until the output of the last transform becomes the input to the message digest algorithm.

While XML Signature does not mandate the use of these specific transformations, the functionality that they provide is needed to ensure that digital signatures function correctly. Even if the application designer does not want to use these specific algorithms, a functional equivalent must be found. We do not encourage the use of alternatives because this limits the interoperability of XML signature.

XPath/XPointer

It must be possible to selectively sign portions of XML documents. Unlike email or files where the entire message or file is meant for a specific recipient, many recipients can handle XML documents and especially SOAP documents. Each may choose to sign or verify the part of the document that is of concern to him or her. This is different from the selective encryption capability of XML Encryption. With XML Encryption, the encrypted data replaces the plaintext data in the XML document, and it is appropriately identified. It will be obvious which data has been encrypted. With digital signatures, the signed data is not transformed and replaced. Instead, an additional structure is created that probably resides elsewhere in the document. A method is needed to identify which elements of the document the signature applies. XPath is used for this purpose. While XPath can be used for other functions, digital signatures make use of XPath's location path to identify the signed nodes.

XML Path Language (Xpath) Version 1.0 (W3C 1999) is a query language that searches for, locates, and identifies parts of an XML document. It was originally developed for use with Extensible Stylesheet Language Transformations (XSLT). The algorithm identifier for XPath is http://www.w3.org/TR/1999/REC-xpath-1999116. Work is also proceeding on *XML-Signature XPath Filter 2.0* (W3C 2002k). This is a specialized version of XPath, currently in working draft state, tailored for use with digital signatures. The following discussion is based on XPath Version 1.0.

For XPath to work, the XML document must be organized into a tree structure. A SOAP message modeled as such a tree is shown in Figure 4.8. The contents of this tree are close to, but not identical to, the original XML document. We won't go into all the details here, but the tree contains the elements, attributes, comments, namespaces, and processing instructions of the XML document. It also has a root node that is logically above what we normally consider the root of the document. This allows the inclusion of comments that appear before the start of the XML document. However, it does not contain the XML declaration statement `<?xml version="1.0"?>`.

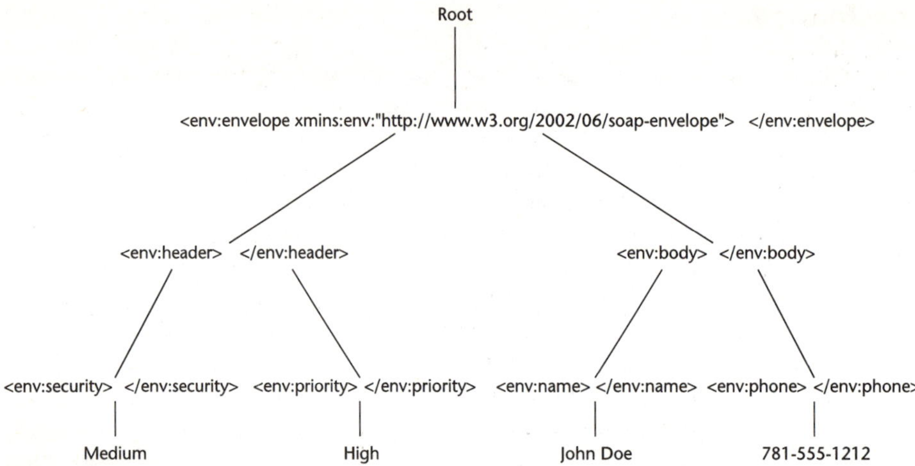

Figure 4.8 SOAP message tree.

The location path identifies a node in the tree by specifying directions for getting to the node of interest from a starting node. The location path can be absolute or relative. If it is absolute, the path starts from the root node of the document. If the path is relative, the path starts at another node, called the context node, in the tree.

From this point, XPath steps along the tree to identify nodes of interest. Each location step consists of a direction, called an axis, to search relative to the context. Searches may go up the tree from the starting node, or they may go down the tree, and particular relationships can be required. For instance, the step can specify namespace nodes two generations away. For digital signatures, descendants of the context node are the only nodes of interest. The location step also includes a node test. The node test selects a candidate comment, processing instruction, or text nodes. Finally, operations called predicates filter the selected nodes and further narrow them down. Predicates are relational operators (equal, not equal, greater than, and so on). They test for specific node content. So, in a purchasing application using XPath, we can identify the total value of the PO and the account number for signature but exclude all other portions of a SOAP purchase order document body. The results of one location step can be the input to another step, thus becoming the context for the next step.

XPointer (W3C 2001c) is a W3C candidate recommendation. It extends XPath so that XPointer can be used as a URI. We are most interested in the bare-name form of XPointer. A bare name references an element that has an ID attribute identical to the bare name. In the following code, the element *demo* has an attribute *refNode*. A URI referencing *demo* only needs to use *refNode*.

```
<signedInfoRef URI="#refNode">
...
</signedInfoRef>
<demo ID="refNode">
...
</demo>
```

This form of the bare name XPointer is used when *refnode* is in the same document as *demo*. When a node in an external document is referenced, the bare name is appended to the document-identifying URI. The bare-name XPointer is used to indicate signed elements within the document.

XML Canonicalization

Digital signatures are dependent on the representation of the data being signed. What a person regards as an inconsequential change in the document, say the addition or deletion of white space, would be read by a system as a significant alteration and could cause a signature not to be verified. To avoid this possibility, XML documents are transformed into a standard representation before being signed or verified.

Canonical XML Version 1.0 (W3C 2001a) provides a standard way to determine if two documents are identical. It defines rules for transforming an XML document into a standard representation. Another document with the same canonical representation is considered identical to the first. There are two variations on Canonical XML. One version does not include comments, and its algorithm identifier is http://www.w3.org/TR/2001/REC-xml-c14-20010315. The other version includes comments, and its algorithm identifier is http://www.w3.org/TR/2001/REC-xml-c14-20010315#WithComments.

A second document, *Exclusive XML Canonicalization Version 1.0* (W3C 2002b), a candidate recommendation, addresses the need to sign parts of a document in such a way that the signed portion can be extracted and placed in another document. For instance, if the signed portion of the document uses a default namespace, Exclusive XML Canonicalization copies the namespace into the subdocument being signed.

The canonical representation of a document is a handy representation to sign, because the canonical rules applied to the received XML document eliminate inconsequential changes that occur as the document is passed among nodes and result in a standard form of the document. Canonical XML transforms data by utilizing a standard character encoding (UTF-8). It normalizes line feeds and attributes, replaces references, removes unnecessary namespace references, adds default attributes, and performs other functions that eliminate unnecessary constructs and resolve potential ambiguity.

When used with digital signatures, canonicalization must transform data prior to signing. Then, it is used to transform data prior to signature verification, thus eliminating the possibility of verification failing for spurious reasons. Also, since canonicalization can use up computational resources, only those portions of the document that will be signed are canonicalized.

XML Decryption Transform for Signature

When a digital signature is combined with encryption, it is necessary to know whether a signature was applied to encrypted data or to unencrypted data that was subsequently encrypted. In the first case, the encrypted data must be left encrypted for the signature to be verified. In the second case, the encrypted data must be decrypted before the signature is verified. *Decryption Transform for XML Signature* (W3C 2002a) is a W3C candidate recommendation that specifies how the signer of a document can inform the signature verifier which signed portions of a document must be left encrypted so that a signature will be verified. All other portions of the document should be decrypted before the signature verification is attempted. This procedure is not a separate transform. Instead, it is an instruction to the signature verifier that is used during the decrypt transform. (Since it applies to signature verification, we've chosen to discuss it here rather than in the encryption section.) Therefore, an element containing the excluded, encrypted node must be inserted as a child element to the transform element. An example taken from the candidate recommendation is:

```
<Transform Algorithm="http://www.w3.org/2001/04/decrypt#">
      <Except xmlns=http://www.w3.org/2001/04/decrypt# URI="#enc1"/>
</Transform>
```

In this example, node *enc1* was encrypted before the signature was applied. Other portions of the document were encrypted after signature. To verify the signature, the other portions of the document must be decrypted first, but node *enc1* must be left intact until the signature is verified. If necessary, it can be decrypted after the verification is complete.

Signature Creation/Verification Process

To create a digital signature:

1. Apply the transform or transforms to the data object to be signed. Transforms are applied in the order they are specified.
2. Calculate the message digest of the output of the transforms.
3. Create a reference element that includes the URI of the data object (optional), the transforms used, the digest algorithm, and the digest value. As many reference elements as needed may be created. This occurs if one signature covers several nodes of the document.
4. Create the *SignedInfo* element. Include the *SignatureMethod*, the *Canonicalization-Method*, and the references previously generated.
5. Apply the *CanonicalizationMethod* to *SignedInfo*.
6. Use the algorithms specified by *SignatureMethod* to create the signature. This usually means applying a message digest algorithm to the canonicalized SignedInfo and then signing the resulting digest.
7. Create the *Signature* element that contains the *SignedInfo*, the *SignatureValue*, *KeyInfo* (if needed), and *Object* (if needed).
8. Note that a different canonicalization algorithm or message digest algorithm can be applied to each referenced element.

To verify a signature:

1. Canonicalize the *SignedInfo* element according to the *CanonicalizationMethod* specified in SignedInfo.
2. For each reference element, obtain the data object referenced.
3. Process each data object according to the specified transforms.

4. Digest the result according to the digest algorithm specified for the referenced element. Compare the result with the value stored in the corresponding reference element. If the two are not equal, the verification fails.
5. Obtain the necessary keying information. It may be available in *KeyInfo*, or it may have been preplaced.
6. Apply the signature method using the previously obtained key to confirm the *SignatureValue* over the canonicalized *SignedInfo* element.

Example

The following code fragment is an example of an XML signature. This is called a detached signature because it is not part of the document being signed. *SignatureMethod* specifies the signature algorithm and the message-digesting algorithm, DSA and SHA-1, respectively. That XML Canonicalization used to transform the input is also specified. The actual data being signed is identified by the URI attribute of *Reference*. In this case, there is only one *Reference* element, and it identifies a separate document called *order*. The message digest applied to the document, SHA-1, and the transformation, XML Canonicalization, applied to the document are child elements of reference. *DigestValue* contains the SHA-1 message digest of the order. *SignatureValue* is calculated based on *SignedInfo*. Finally, the DSA public key, that can be used to verify the signature, is appended. Note that if there were several data items being signed, each of them could have its own canonicalization and message digest algorithms. The signature itself could also be calculated using a different message digest algorithm. Our simple example uses only the public key for verification rather than a public key certificate. This provides minimal security for the signature format, since the receiver of the SOAP message has no way to verify that the holder of the key is the expected individual. If the overhead of a PKI is not acceptable, a better way to handle this is to preplace the public key with the receiver and reference the key in the message.

```
<Signature xmlns="http://www.w3.org/2000/09/xmldsig#">
<SignedInfo>
    <CanonicalizationMethod Algorithm="http://www.w3.org/TR/2001/REC-
xml-c14n-20010315"/>
    <SignatureMethod Algorithm="http://www.w3.org/2000/09/xmldsig#dsa-
sha1"/>
    <Reference URI="http://www.mycompany.com/order/">
        <Transforms>
            <Transform Algorithm="http://www.w3.org/TR/2001/REC-xml-
c14n-20010315"/>
        </Transforms>
        <DigestMethod
Algorithm="http://www.w3.org/2000/09/xmldsig#sha1"/>
        <DigestValue>j6lwx3rvEPO0vKtMup4NbeVu8nk=</DigestValue>
    </Reference>
</SignedInfo>
<SignatureValue>MC0CFFrVLtRlk=...</SignatureValue>
```

```
<KeyInfo>
     <KeyValue>
          <DSAKeyValue>
               <P>...</P><Q>...</Q><G>...</G><Y>...</Y>
            </DSAKeyValue>
     </KeyValue>
</KeyInfo>
</Signature>
```

Issues

There are several topics for consideration when implementing a digital signature system for Web Services.

Signature syntax vs. semantics. The XML Signature Recommendation deals with the syntax and technical process for creating an XML digital signature. Signatures have a meaning from a legal and business point of view. It is important to consider what need the signature meets and then ensure that the signature is being applied to the appropriate parts of the document to satisfy the need. For instance, we may want a secure signature to authorize charging $50 for two shirts. In this case, the signature must cover the charge account number, the amount, and the two shirts. This prevents the account number and the amount from being reused in a different context. In addition, the signature should also include a unique identifier, which will not be used again, to protect against possible replay attacks.

Out-of-band agreements between the signer and the verifier. The XML Signature Recommendation is very flexible and allows many parameters to be omitted from the signature. For instance, *KeyInfo* is optional. For the most part, we consider this flexibility a positive feature. However, leaving information out of the signature means that there can be problems with signature verification at a later time or if the verifier changes. In general, including signature parameters in the signature element is preferable.

Choice of algorithms and key lengths. XML Signature does not mandate the use of particular algorithms or key lengths. It is the user's responsibility to ensure that the right choices are made. The system implementer should carefully consider how long the signature must be retained and the preferred algorithm, and then decide on the appropriate key length.

Application in SOAP. XML Signature specifies encryption for XML documents. It does not describe how XML Signature data and structures are implemented within the SOAP message structure.

WS-Security

IBM and Microsoft have begun a joint initiative to define an architecture and roadmap to address gaps between existing security standards and Web Services and SOAP. The first results of the initiative have been published in *Security in a Web Services World: A Proposed Architecture and Roadmap* (IBM and Microsoft 2002a) and *Web Services Security (WS-Security), Version 1.0* (IBM, Microsoft, and Verisign 2002b).

WS-Security has been submitted to OASIS for standardization, and OASIS has formed a technical committee to refine the standard. Bringing WS-Security into OASIS is a significant development for Web Services security because it allows WS-Security and SAML, which we will discuss in the next chapter, to fit together in a standardized way. We will talk further about the relationship of WS-Security and SAML in Chapter 5, "Security Assertion Markup Language," and Chapter 10, "Interoperability of Web Services Security Technologies."

The WS-Security initiative defines a single security model that abstracts security services, thereby separating the functional security characteristics of the system from the specifics of the implementation. The model serves as a means to unify formerly dissimilar security technologies such as PKI and Kerberos. The model as shown in the Architecture and Roadmap paper is illustrated in Figure 4.9.

In this model, the requester requests resources from the Web Service. But, the Web Service requires proof of some claims before satisfying the request. These claims could be an identity or a permission. If the requester has the needed proof, it will be sent to the Web Service in a security token. If the requester does not have the proof, the service provider will try to get the proof from a security token service, which is also a Web Service.

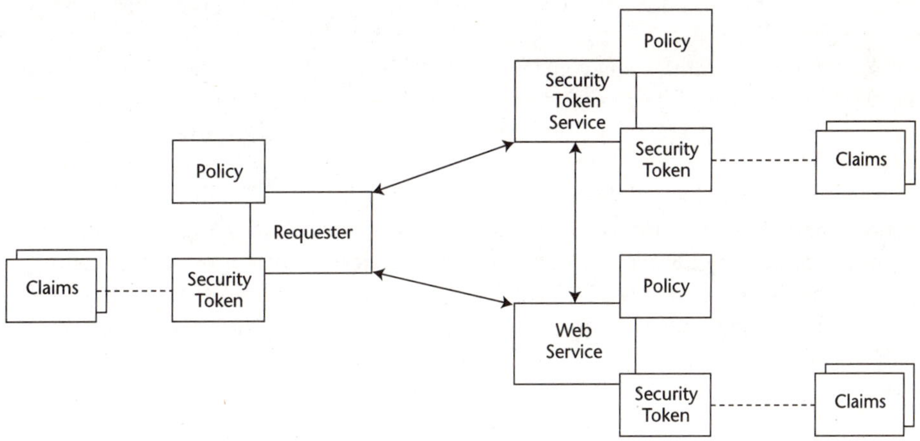

Figure 4.9 The general WS-Security messaging model.

The joint effort will result in several specifications. The initial specifications are:

WS-Security. How to attach signature and encryption information as well as security tokens to SOAP messages

WS-Policy. How to specify the security requirements and capabilities of Web Services nodes

WS-Trust. How to establish trust in a Web Services environment, either directly or indirectly using a security token service

WS-Privacy. How to specify the privacy policies in place and privacy preferences

Additional specifications are:

WS-SecureConversation. How to authenticate the subscriber, the provider, or both

WS-Federation. How to support federation (that is, how to make dissimilar security systems interoperate)

WS-Authorization. How to specify and manage access control policies

The goals of this effort are admirable and ambitious. At this time, IBM and Microsoft have only published one specification. It is too early to determine whether the goals will be met. But, given its backing, the project deserves your attention.

Functionality

The WS-Security specification is already available. It addresses single-message, end-to-end security. There are specific security services for ensuring Web Services message integrity and confidentiality and for associating security-related claims with Web Services messages.

The specification team extensively leveraged XML Signature and XML Encryption for Web Services message integrity and confidentiality. WS-Security requires compliance with both these specifications, including support for the same algorithms and certificate types. The specification goes beyond these two standards by tailoring them for SOAP messages. In other words, WS-Security fills in some of the gaps left when XML Signature and XML Encryption are used with SOAP. It also provides additional guidance.

Claims are used by the Web Service to make security-relevant decisions. A claim is a statement made about a subject by the subject or another party. It can assert an identity, a role, or the ownership of a key. A special type of claim is the proof-of-possession claim. This claim shows that the sender has some knowledge that should only be in the possession of the sender. A security token is a collection of claims.

A Web Service can require that the subject offer proof of a set of claims before honoring requests from the subject. A claim endorsed by a trusted authority is acceptable proof. The trusted authority normally endorses the claim by digitally signing the claim. An unendorsed claim is acceptable if the sender and the receiver have established a trust relationship. The subject can provide the proof, or a security token service can provide the proof. Sometimes, proof-of-possession in combination with other claims will be accepted as adequate proof.

Security Element

WS-Security defines a security element of the SOAP message. The security element is contained in the SOAP message header and is targeted at a specific *role*. This means that there can be multiple security elements in the header. However, each *role* can have at most one security element.

The *Security* element contains all claims or other message security information that is relevant to the *role*. Claims can include the sender's identity. Other message security information includes *Signature* elements and *EncryptedKey* elements for encryption. When *EncryptedKey* is in the *Security* element, it must contain a *ReferenceList* so that the receiver will know how to associate keys with the encrypted data.

If a SOAP node needs to communicate security-relevant information to a node acting in a *role*, it looks to see if a *Security* element targeted at the role already exists. If it does, the information is prepended to the information already in the element. If a *Security* element does not exist, it creates a new *Security* element for the role and adds it to the header. There is no requirement to process the components of the *Security* element in a particular order. However, prepending information ensures that the elements may be processed in the order in which they are encountered.

Structure

The *Security* element can contain several types of subelements. They are *UsernameToken, BinarySecurityToken, SecurityTokenReference, KeyInfo, Signature, ReferenceList*, and *EncryptedData*.

The *UserNameToken* is a way to include the user's name and an optional password in the *Security* element. *BinarySecurityToken* is a non-XML security token such as an X.509 certificate or Kerberos ticket. *SecurityTokenReference* is a set of claims or a reference to claims. We've already discussed *KeyInfo* and *Signature*. In our previous discussion, *ReferenceList* is used within *EncryptedKey*. The purpose of *ReferenceList* is to identify encrypted elements within the message that are encrypted using the same key. In WS-Security, this structure does not hold. *EncryptedData* must replace the unencrypted data, or it may be referenced. *EncryptedData* may be in the *Security* element.

Example

The following code fragment shows a SOAP message with a WS-Security *Security* header, signature, and encrypted content. The security header is targeted at the next recipient and must be understood by the recipient. *Security* includes a signature and encryption key information. The entire body of the SOAP message is encrypted.

```
<? Xml version='1.0' ?>
<env:Envelope xmlns:env="http://www.w3.org/2002/06/soap-envelope"
     xmlns:wsse="http://schmas.xmlsoap.org/ws/2002/04/secext"
     xmlns:sig="http://www.w3.org/2002/02/xmldsig#"
     xmlns:enc="http://www.w3.org/2002/03/xmlenc#">
     <env:Header>
```

```
          <wsse:Security
               env:role="http://www.w3.org/2002/06/soap-
envelope/role/next"
               env:mustUnderstand="true">
               <wsse:BinarySecurityToken
                    ...
               </wsse:BinarySecurityToken
               <sig:Signature>
                    ...
               </sig:Signature>
               <enc:EncryptedKey>
                    ...
               </enc:EncryptedKey>
          </wsse:Security>
     </env:Header>
     <env:Body>
          <enc:EncryptedData>
               ...
          </enc:EncryptedData>
     </env:Body>
</env:Envelope>
```

Summary

In this chapter, we've described cryptographic techniques used to protect XML and SOAP messages. We described how to encrypt and decrypt XML documents and how to sign and verify signatures on XML data. We also went over supporting techniques such as XPath, XPointer, and Canonicalization, and security-related issues that must be addressed when using these techniques. Finally, we discussed WS-Security and how it tailors these XML techniques to SOAP.

In the next chapter, we will discuss Security Assertion Markup Language (SAML), an XML standard for representing security data so that it may be exchanged across different enterprises or lines of business. Several of the later chapters describe various ways that the XML security and WS-Security standards may be used to secure Web Services implementations.

CHAPTER

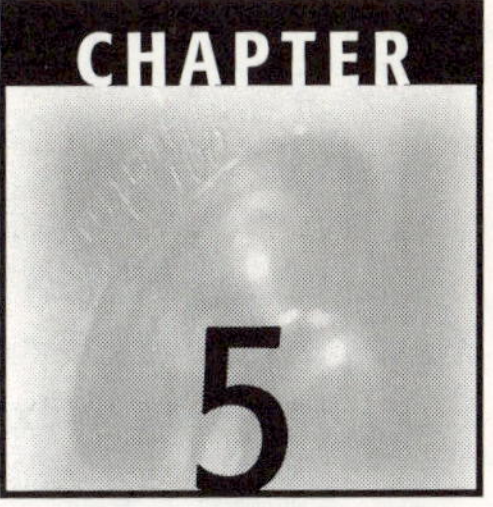

5

Security Assertion Markup Language

One of the main problems that needs to be solved in distributed Web Services security is how to unambiguously interpret security context information when that data has been transferred from a source to a target application. If the two locations are in the same division of the same company using the same application security technology, for example, J2EE security, then the problem is not difficult. This is so because a given application security technology is usually designed to work between different processes running the same middleware system. However, if one tried to get a J2EE application to interact securely with a COM+ application, the COM+ application would not recognize the security data sent from the J2EE application. The problem gets worse when two companies try to interoperate since their security policies will probably be different.

A second problem is that people want single sign-on (SSO) capability. That is, people want to be able to log on to a system once and then access different Web Services applications without requiring additional logons.

A solution to these problems is to have a standard representation of security data that different application security services will recognize no matter what security policy or technology they are using. This is what the Organization for the Advancement of Structured Information Standards (OASIS) has attempted to do with the release of its Security Assertion Markup Language (SAML) specification. The success of SAML will depend on its acceptance by the vendor community that deals with security in distributed computing. Most major software middleware vendors, including Microsoft, are members or backers of the group defining the SAML model. Achieving interoperability with Microsoft's .NET, which we will discuss in Chapter 8, "Securing .NET Web Services," will be easier with Microsoft's planned support for WS-Security and SAML. However, there are still interoperability issues, as we discuss in Chapter 10, "Interoperability of Web Services Security Technologies."

This chapter describes SAML assertions, which are XML representations defined by the SAML specifications. We describe how the assertions may be used and transmitted, and put this in context with a number of common scenarios that require an interoperable secure conversation. This description of SAML is not directed at the vendors who are implementing SAML products but at you, the end user of the middleware application products that use SAML. SAML is an important technology in Web Services security, so it is important that you understand SAML so that you can select and use the new breed of SAML-based products that are hitting the market.

In addition, this chapter will briefly discuss another OASIS specification, the Extensible Access Control Markup Language (XACML). XACML is a specification for expressing access control policies over the Internet.

OASIS

Before we get into the details of SAML, we will take a brief look at the parent organization of the SAML Technical Committee (TC). The SAML TC, as well as the Web Services Security TC and the XACML TC, are organized under the OASIS international consortium. The stated purpose of OASIS is to create interoperable standards based on XML. SAML, Web Services Security, and XACML are not the only TCs that work under the OASIS umbrella. There are a handful of other TCs on security and about 25 other TCs concentrating on areas other than security, with new ones emerging all the time.

The modus operandi of OASIS is to encourage open debate to develop standards that represent the interests of the community of vendors and users of the resultant products. At present OASIS has some 170 members that span the globe and range from small companies to some of the largest ones in the world. A stated goal of OASIS is to complement the work of other standards bodies and thus they desire—in their words—to be cordial, cooperative and complementary to other standard bodies. Consequently, SAML, which is driven by the goals of OASIS, strives to be inclusive of other specifications and organizations. OASIS's policy, reinforced by customer demand, will help ensure vendor-neutral specifications.

What Is SAML?

SAML is a specification (OASIS 2002) that defines a standard way to represent authentication, attribute, and authorization information that may be used in a distributed environment by disparate applications. All the security services that comply with the SAML specification will be able to interpret the security data sent from one security service to another security service.

Version 1.0 of the SAML specification, which is the latest version as of this writing, does not address all the problems associated with the interoperable transfer of security data, but it represents significant progress. SAML does not yet address the interoperable transfer of authentication evidence itself, although the TC is working on that problem. Another difficulty with the initial SAML specification is that it emphasizes perimeter security with little attention given to middle and back-office tier security. However, these limitations are temporary and are overshadowed by the ability of SAML to bridge the gap between different security models.

The heart of the SAML specification is the XML Schema that defines the representation of security data, which can be used as part of a general solution to pass the security context between applications. This representation of security data is an assertion by a trusted third-party security service that the activity of authentication, attribute retrieval, or authorization is correct as represented. For example, the authentication assertion is a representation by a third party that the subject of the assertion, the security principal, has been authenticated. As long as the target trusts this third party, it can accept the assertion as true and can accept the principal named by the authentication assertion as authenticated.

The designers of the SAML specification did not intend it to work alone. They wished to incorporate as much of the complementary work that was being carried out in other specification groups as was appropriate. Therefore, SAML is designed to work with other specifications, such as the digital signature specification (XML Signature Syntax and Processing, W3C, 2002) or the HTTP and SOAP specifications created by the World Wide Web Consortium (W3C).

How SAML Is Used

When SAML is used, it is envisioned that third-party services will act as trusted sources to assert the correctness of a particular authentication, authorization, or attribute activity and return to the requesting parties SAML assertions related to these activities. For example, a client may have authenticated itself with one of these trusted third parties. When the client attempts to access some target, it will pass along the SAML assertion from the third party. The target can then verify that the assertion is from a third party that it trusts, and if this is so, it can use this information as assurance that the user has been authenticated.

The target, having accepted the SAML authentication assertion, could then go to another third-party service and request an attribute assertion for the authenticated user, passing in the authentication assertion. The returned attribute assertion will contain the attributes for that user, which will be guaranteed to be correct by the trusted third-party attribute service.

Finally, the target may go to an authorization service, and upon passing the attribute or authentication assertion, ask if the principal is permitted to perform an activity on a certain target resource. The authorization service is likely to be a local service of the target company, although the enterprise could use an external SAML authorization service. In general, authorization can be more complex than authentication or attribute retrieval. SAML has recognized this and constructed a more complex system for the authorization model. In fact, the umbrella organization for SAML and other XML-related activities has another closely related TC, XACML, which has defined an access control policy model and language.

XML Basis

XML is rapidly becoming the lingua franca of the new, distributed computer paradigms. The marriage of XML and distributed systems is a step in the right direction, but it does not, by itself, simplify the complexity of security data transfer between processes. When it comes to security, the existing models (that is, the pre-Web Services models) are rigid and require inflexible interface contracts between two parties. This is caused by the fact that those security models are designed only for their own paradigm, and are, in many cases, platform- and/or programming language-specific.

SAML is written in XML and thus incorporates XML's advantages of platform and language independence. Please refer back to the description of XML given in Chapter 2, "Web Services," for details on the usage and advantages of XML.

Scope of SAML

As stated above, SAML's goal is to define security documents that will be used in a distributed environment. The specification itself does not describe all the aspects and supporting services of the environment, but it does indicate what such an environment might be like. Figure 5.1 depicts what a distributed system that supports SAML services could look like. The shaded rectangles are the XML documents that SAML has defined in its specification. (Note that the unshaded Credentials Assertion indicates that the current version of SAML has not yet defined the authentication credential. This credential is the document that contains the evidence for authenticating the principal.) The handling of the authentication and attributes follow the outline we described above. Authorization requires a few more entities, a policy decision point (PDP), and a policy enforcement point (PEP), which we'll discuss later in this chapter.

Note that the SAML specification does not define all of the architecture shown in Figure 5.1, but it does, in a non-normative way, describe how one would use such services. (Specification writers use the term non-normative to indicate those portions of a specification that are not required for conformance but that help to make the specification clearer.) The specification does define how to talk to the SAML services. It uses the term *bindings* to describe a standard way to request authentication, attributes, or authorization decisions from the appropriate SAML-compliant service or authority and for the authority to respond to the requester. The two bindings defined so far are a SOAP binding and an HTTP binding. Another term that we will run across is *profiles*, which are the descriptions of how protocols transfer SAML assertions from one application to another.

Let's use Figure 5.1 to gain a better understanding of how SAML may be used. We start out with a client wishing to make a secure request on some target. The client will first authenticate itself. Once the client has been authenticated, it can ask the authentication authority to return a SAML assertion as proof of its authentication (line 1). The means by which the authentication authority determines that the client making the request has been authenticated is out of scope for the SAML specification. The manner by which any of the other authorities carry out their tasks is also not defined by the specification.

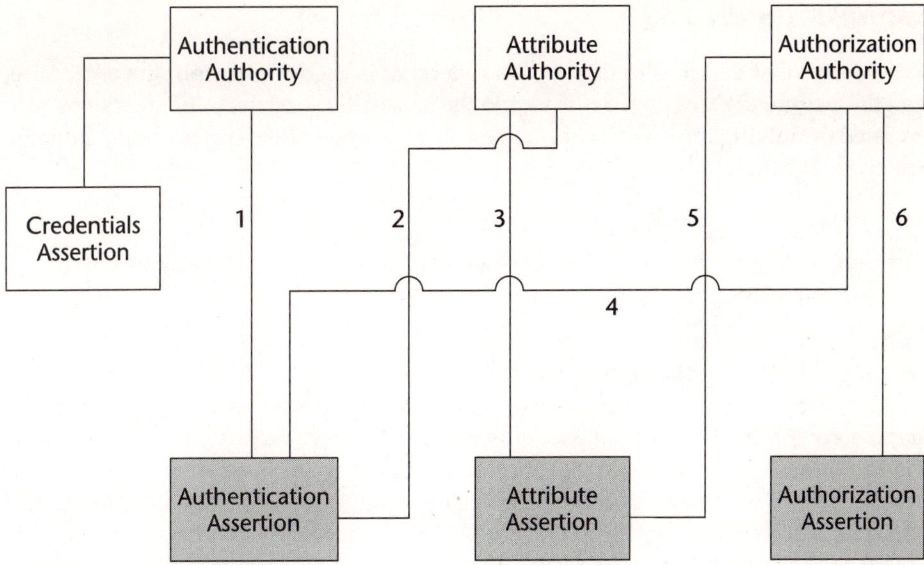

Figure 5.1 SAML scope.

When an organization uses a SAML-based authentication authority, the organization does not have to know how to carry out intricate security calculations or decisions. It can use external SAML-enabled authorities to implement its security procedures, thus avoiding the complex development of its own security services.

Going back to our example, the customer request arrives at the target organization carrying a SAML authentication assertion that the client retrieved from the authentication authority when that client was authenticated. (We do not depict the transfers between the client and target in Figure 5.1, to keep the diagram simple.) The target organization, which receives the request, first examines the authentication assertion and satisfies itself that the assertion is genuine and from an authority that it trusts. The target organization may then go to a SAML attribute authority, passing the authentication assertion to the attribute authority (line 2) and request a SAML attribute assertion. The attribute authority returns the customer's attributes in the attribute assertion to the requesting organization (line 3). Alternately, the client may retrieve the attribute assertion from the attribute authority and push it to the target.

In either case, the target organization sends a SAML authorization request to the authorization authority, along with the named resource that the client wishes to access, as in line 6 in Figure 5.1. The authorization request may contain an assertion, which may have authentication and attribute statements or possibly just an attribute statement. The authorization authority reaches an access decision and returns a grant or deny decision.

This description is simplified, skipping many of the subtleties and variations of the full use of SAML. The remaining portion of this chapter will expand on the different aspects of this example, fully fleshing out the details of SAML.

Emphasis on Web SSO

While the goal of SAML is to develop a model that is used throughout the enterprise, from the perimeter through the mid-tier to the back-office tier, the initial work has concentrated on solving the Web SSO problem at the perimeter tier. This is understandable for two reasons:

- Today users are highly focused on Web SSO perimeter security.
- The perimeter tier is, to a large extent, underspecified, with many proprietary solutions dominating it.

SAML has defined profiles that define the protocols for transferring the SAML assertions from one Web application to another. The first of these profiles, which are defined in the initial SAML specification, describes a protocol for a browser to target secure Web interaction. The profile does not explicitly attempt to cover security requirements specific to the other two tiers, such as application-to-application security, delegation, or secure access to mainframes or databases. Although the profiles for the first release of the specification concentrate on solving the perimeter-tier Web problem, we believe that SAML will ultimately be used to secure Web Services across all tiers. Later in this chapter, we will discuss ways that you can use SAML in the middle and back-office tiers and what extensions you need to make SAML work seamlessly through all three tiers.

Perimeter security is a tough problem, especially when it is combined with the desire to have SSO. Some of its difficulties lie with the limited nature of browsers and the request/reply paradigm of HTTP. Another problem is the uncontrolled expanse of the perimeter, when, for example, a company deals with hundreds of thousands of customers who access the company using a wide variety of client programs that are not under the control of the target company. We will delve into these problems later in the chapter.

Given these problems, one of the important, positive steps towards an end-to-end security solution is to have a standardized format for a security token that carries security context data that is universally recognized throughout all three tiers. Once this token is well defined and accepted by the different security models in the other tiers, we will have reduced the interoperability problem to a much more manageable size.

The Rationale for Understanding the SAML Specification

Standard specifications are esoteric things that rarely enter the thoughts of application developers and designers, so why should you need to think about them? There are several reasons for understanding the security standards that underlie the distributed architecture of your business systems:

- If you want your applications to interoperate with anyone but yourself, you should be sure that your implementation meets the pertinent standard specifications.
- To squeeze the last drop of performance out of your distributed system, knowing the ins and outs of the specifications will let you maximize performance without sacrificing interoperability with customers, partners and suppliers.

- When it comes to purchasing third-party products, you will want to know to what degree they conform to the standards so that you can satisfy the requirements presented in the first two bullets.
- Since the specifications that we are talking about relate to security, your selection of standards-compliant third-party products ultimately determines the level of security of your company's systems.
- Security is a constantly changing technology. Understanding the thinking behind the specifications lets you predict and prepare for the changes and improvements that are coming down the road.

While you don't need to know the details of the underlying specifications, it is important that you know enough to make rational judgments with respect to the issues outlined above. Our goal is to provide you with enough of the SAML specification details so that you will feel comfortable with satisfying these responsibilities.

Why Open Standards Like SAML Are Needed

Security is a tough subject, and distributed security raises the bar by a few orders of magnitude. The job of the information technology (IT) staff of your company is to solve the business problems of the corporation. They do not have the time to become security experts to the degree that their adversaries have. Therefore, the solution is for security experts to pool their knowledge and produce standard specifications like SAML that can be used by companies that have the security expertise to produce security products that implement the specifications. You can then incorporate these third-party products into your infrastructure and get the benefits of distributed security without having to develop it yourself.

It has been shown over and over that to have a solid security model, the model must be publicly available and must be analyzed thoroughly. As many people as possible should be involved in trying to find security holes in the model. This can only be done with an open process where the full model is available for all to examine.

Security Problems Solved by SAML

We stated above that the initial version of the SAML specification concentrates on perimeter Web SSO. However, the broader problems that it is designed to solve pertain to end-to-end security, company-to-company security, SSO, and privacy. SAML addresses a specific, important aspect of these problems.

To explain where SAML fits into the security process, let's look at a message as it moves from one process to another, where the two processes may be in the same company or in different companies. For the message and the actions related to the message to be secure, it is necessary that several crucial types of security information be transferred between the processes. These segments of information fall into the well-known security categories of authentication of the principal, attribute information about the initiator of the request, and authorization information about the particular resource that is to be accessed.

Let's take a look at the first of these categories, authentication. Here, a principal, which may be a human being or a computer process, is authenticated when it presents some evidence (such as a password) to prove who it is. In the SAML model, in many cases a trusted third party evaluates this evidence. On the basis of the evaluation, the trusted third party authenticates or declines authentication of the principal. In the case of approval, verification of the approval is passed along with the request as it goes from process to process. Each process in the chain examines this verification of approval. If the process trusts the third party that did the authentication and accepts the confirmation of the authentication, the process will accept that the principal is who it claims to be.

The problem in distributed computing is that the confirmation or proof of authentication differs between the different security systems that may be in use for different parts of the distributed system. For example, in the CORBA model, the proof of authentication takes the form of a credential with specific syntax and semantics that cannot be understood by, for example, a COM+ application, and vice-versa. The same holds true for interoperability between most other security models. (An exception is Enterprise Java Beans and CORBA, which recently completed an interoperability specification called Common Secure Interoperability version 2 (CSIv2). Unfortunately, this example is the exception rather than the rule.)

In many cases today, a token or container holds the authentication evidence that is passed from application to application. This requires the principal to be reauthenticated at each target application. In this case, the authentication evidence (for example, a password) is available to each application and can be stolen by a malicious process. If a malicious process has the authentication evidence, the malicious process can be authenticated as the initiating principal and thus impersonate that principal.

Authorization and attribute values can also be passed in the distributed scenario. One of the primary problems that SAML solves is defining a standard format for passing authentication, attribute, and/or authorization proof from process to process. As long as the different models understand SAML, we can have interoperability between security models. SAML's open platform and language-neutral constructs make it acceptable to most security models.

Single Sign-On

SSO is the holy grail of distributed computing for many people. One of their complaints is the need to remember a multitude of different passwords for the various applications that they need to access simply to do their job. "Why," the cry goes up, "can't I have just one password for all the applications that I have to access?"

The reason is that noninteroperable security credentials, which contain proof of authentication and attributes, are used in many of the security models available today. If one model cannot understand the credentials passed from another model, then the second model will have to force the user to log in again, that is, it will have to ask the user to again input a password. One can build bridges between the models to try to solve this problem, but these will be proprietary, nonextensible, and different for each combination of security models.

An even worse problem exists when the credentials themselves are proprietary, as they are in many of the existing security products. In many of these cases, one cannot even build bridges, since the format is unknown and potentially encrypted.

The SAML SSO model uses an openly specified assertion that is being adopted by many security implementations and models. Given widespread acceptance of SAML assertions, the proof of authentication, specifically a SAML authentication assertion, can be passed from application to application and thus abolish the need to log in more than once.

A First Detailed Look at SAML

Now that we have an idea of what SAML is and how it may be used, let's begin to describe the technical details. SAML has defined an XML document that can be used as proof of authentication, attribute assignment, or authorization. XML, as we discussed in Chapter 2, is platform- and language-independent, so different security models can use it and do not have to depend on their specific model format. XML is very popular, partly due to its simplicity and the abundance of parsers.

Using XML, more accurately the XML schema, SAML has specified a set of documents called assertions by which a third party *asserts* that a particular fact related to security is true. In the case of authentication, the trusted third party asserts that the principal, called the Subject, has been authenticated. In addition to the assertion of authentication, other information is contained in the assertion, such as the identity of the third party who makes the assertion, digital signatures, validity times, and so on. There is sufficient information in the assertion for the proof of authentication, attribute, or authorization to be self-contained.

SAML defines one XML structure for each of the assertion types. This structure contains an authentication, attribute, or authorization statement. For simplicity, we will call an assertion that contains an authentication statement an authentication assertion. Likewise, we will use the term attribute assertion for an assertion that contains one or more attribute statements, and authorization assertion for assertions that contain authorization statements.

We've talked about authentication assertions, so now let's outline the importance and usage of attribute assertions. In distributed security, an attribute is a property of a principal that can address two different requirements:

- The need for a collection property whereby many individual principals can be categorized under one heading and for security purposes treated as one
- The need for a permission to perform an action

The first usage of an attribute supports scaling. For example, you can group all your customers as belonging to the category *customer*. Where appropriate—for example, for looking at certain Web pages, you do not have to authorize at the individual level but can authorize users based on the category *customer*. This category may incorporate hundreds of thousands of individuals. Alternately, the attribute can imply a permission, such as the attribute *chiefTeller*, which would group all of the chief tellers at one particular bank into a category and grant all of them the permission to look at a bank customer's balance.

The distinction between these two definitions is not very obvious, since they are both ultimately used for authorization. You can think of the first usage of attributes as groups and the second as roles. If you look in the literature, you will find a lot of ambiguity in this area. So, this distinction is more one of intent than of strict definition. You can think of customers as having certain permissions, while you can think of the grouping of all your head tellers under the role *chiefTeller*. The important point here is that an attribute has a dual role, and in certain cases the grouping function is more important, while in other cases the intent of granting a permission is more important. However, it is important that you understand that an attribute can have these two different purposes so that you use an attribute appropriately.

While these various uses of attributes are important in deciding which attributes to assign to which principals, the SAML model does not differentiate among any of them.

This ambiguity is not the only difficulty with attributes. A fundamental problem is encountered when we begin to look at federation or the security between two or more disjoint companies. Each company will have its own syntax and semantics for similar attributes. For example, company A may have an attribute *admin* that allows principals to have permission to manipulate all aspects of security, whereas company B may have an attribute *admin* that allows only limited security functions. What does company B do with a principal that comes into its domain with an attribute of *admin*, and vice versa? We will look toward XACML in the future for the details of the solutions for these problems. SAML's job is to define the assertions themselves.

The third area that SAML supports is authorization. In this case, SAML defines an XML schema for a third-party assertion on whether an authenticated principal who has certain attributes can perform a given action on a particular resource. The concept of authorization is straightforward, but the "devil is in the details." While SAML defines the assertion that carries the accept or deny decision, there is still a lot of work in defining the interaction of multiple security policies with the requested actions to be carried out on some resource. The details of a policy model and the definition of a policy language that can be used to express the policy will be addressed by XACML.

In addition to defining assertions, SAML describes how assertions may be transmitted by applications through bindings and profiles.

Bindings describe the way to request and deliver assertions from third-party security services. Bindings define how to pass the assertion in a messaging protocol. The two bindings defined in the initial specification are SOAP and the HTTP POST protocol.

Profiles define the way to use SAML assertions to support the security of the transactions between applications. Specifically, a SAML profile describes how to embed assertions in and retrieve them from the protocol that is used to communicate between the applications. There are two defined profiles for SAML:

- The browser, artifact profile
- The browser, POST profile

An artifact is a token that is passed from a Web browser to a Web server that allows the Web server to get the appropriate assertions from a trusted third party. We will describe the artifact profile later in this chapter. The browser POST profile describes how to securely pass the assertions in an HTTP, POST request.

An important section of the SAML specification is called "Security Considerations." Since there is no such thing as perfect security in the distributed world, this section of the specification details the areas in which security risks exist and describes ways to mitigate those risks.

Having completed this overview of SAML and the portion of the distributed security problem that it is attempting to solve, we will now investigate SAML in more detail.

SAML Assertions

We have established reasons why we need a standard container to carry security context information between applications in different tiers and different companies. We have also stated that SAML defines containers that would be suitable for the job and would be acceptable to various parties and domains involved in these transactions. So, let's look at what that SAML containers are.

SAML defines these containers as assertions about authentication, attributes, and authorization. In addition, SAML uses XML as its language. While SAML is not designed solely for Web Services, its use of XML makes it a nice fit for the security needs of Web Services. In fact, there is close cooperation between the technical committees working on Web Services and SAML.

The SAML assertion itself may be divided into two general areas. The first portion is common to all SAML assertions and contains items like the version number, the security principal involved in the transaction, some required conditions, and an optional advice field. The second portion contains one or more of the actual statements about authentication, attributes, or authorization.

Let's now move to the description of the details of each of these parts of a SAML assertion.

Common Portion of an Assertion

Each assertion has a set of data that is common to all assertions. There is the typical bookkeeping data such as the version number of the specification that this particular assertion supports, what namespaces define the originating organization, and what other specifications this assertion uses.

The common portion contains the identity of the security principal of this assertion, called *subject* by SAML. The subject can have a domain and a name. There is another aspect of subject called *subject confirmation*. This can be used as an alternate way of identifying the subject and/or as a means by which the target can confirm the authentication of the subject of the assertion. For example, a subject could be identified as the holder of the private key associated with the X.509 certificate contained in the subject confirmation. The subject confirmation authentication evidence theoretically could be used by a third party to authenticate the subject. This last point is interesting in that SAML has not yet defined an XML schema for authentication. However, using the subject confirmation for authentication is not the intention nor would it be in conformance with the specification.

Let's take a look at a fragment of the XML schema that defines the subject and the subject confirmation. Below is the schema fragment from the SAML specification that defines the *SubjectType*. (The full specification schema may be found at the OASIS Web site at http://www.oasis-open.org/committees/security/docs/cs-sstc-schema-assertion-01.xsd.)

```
<element name="Subject" type="saml:SubjectType"/>
<complexType name="SubjectType">
  <choice>
    <sequence>
```

```
        <element ref="saml:NameIdentifier"/>
        <element ref="saml:SubjectConfirmation" minOccurs="0"/>
      </sequence>
      <element ref="saml:SubjectConfirmation"/>
    </choice>
  </complexType>
```


The first line in the schema fragment defines an element, which is a basic type in XML, whose name is *Subject*. The *Subject* is of type *saml:SubjectType*. The *saml:* means that the *SubjectType* is defined by SAML. The first part of the schema, which hasn't been shown here, defines a number of Uniform Resource Identifiers (URIs). One of the defined URIs is *saml*. The URI in this definition points to the SAML namespace.

On the second line, we see the beginning of the definition of *SubjectType*. It is a *complexType*, which means that it is composed of a number of other definitions. This is in contrast to a simple type that can consist of only one element such as a string or an integer. The third line says that the things that compose the *SubjectType* are a choice of, in this case, two elements. The first choice is a sequence of a *NameIdentifier* followed by a *SubjectConfirmation*.

The *ref=* that proceeds the *NameIdentifier* and the *SubjectConfirmation* means that these elements are defined elsewhere in the schema. You will notice that the *SubjectConfirmation* is followed by a *minOccurs="0"*. This means that the *SubjectConfirmation* is optional. There is also a term *maxOccurs* that tell how many times the element can occur. The default value of both *minOccurs* and *maxOccurs* is 1.

The second choice for *SubjectType* is to identify the *Subject* only by the *Subject Confirmation*.

The definition of the *NameIdentifier* is:

```
<element name="NameIdentifier" type="saml:NameIdentifierType"/>
<complexType name="NameIdentifierType">
  <simpleContent>
    <extension base="string">
      <attribute name="NameQualifier" type="string" "use=optional"/>
      <attribute name="Format" type="anyURI" use="optional"/>
    </extension>
  </simpleContent>
</complexType>
```


We can see that the Subject name in SAML is made up of the name itself, which is a simple string, and two optional attributes *NameQualifier* and *Format*, which are both strings. The syntax of an attribute is a little different from that of an element. It must be a simple type. Also, note an attribute is optional by using use="optional", rather than maxOccurs=0 as with elements. By default an attribute is required. The Name itself is a little tricky when looking at the schema in that it doesn't appear to be there. However, it is the value of the element *NameIdentifier* and is a string.

That should give you a good idea of how to read a schema. There are other constructs that we will explain as we come across them. In addition, there some obtuse schema constructs that schema lawyers can argue about, but the casual reader can ignore.

The schema for the *SubjectConfirmation* has a few more terms, but you should be able to get the meaning. It is:

```
<element name="SubjectConfirmation"
                    type="saml:SubjectConfirmationType"/>
<complexType name="SubjectConfirmationType">
  <sequence>
    <element ref="saml:ConfirmationMethod" maxOccurs="unbounded"/>
    <element ref="saml:SubjectConfirmationData" minOccurs="0"/>
      <element ref="ds:KeyInfo" minOccurs="0"/>
  </sequence>
</complexType>
<element name="SubjectConfirmationData" type="anyType"/>
<element name="ConfirmationMethod" type="anyURI"/>
```


There are a few new terms here. The element *KeyInfo* is proceeded by *ds:* where *ds* refers to the digital signature specification developed by W3C. *KeyInfo* contains elements to enable one to retrieve the keys used in conjunction with the specific SAML assertion. For example, the key, if present, would be the one held by the subject of the SAML document. The format of the information may range from an X.509 certificate to the value of the key itself to a means to retrieve the key from some other place.

The *SubjectConfirmationData* may be a base64-encoded password, or other simple security evidence such as a digest.

The common portion of an assertion also requires the issuer of the assertion and the date/time that the assertion was issued be included. An assertion may also be digitally signed, in which case the digital signature is specified by the digital signature specification. There is also an optional element, called *Condition*, that, if included in the assertion, must be understood by the target. If the elements of the condition are not valid, the assertion must be rejected. If any subelements of the condition cannot be evaluated, the assertion is said to be indeterminate. At present, the *Conditions* element contains the time for which the assertion is valid, the audience to which the assertion is directed, and the target restrictions. More conditions may be added in the future since the *Conditions* element can be expanded.

The final element in the common portion of an assertion is an element called *Advice*. The *Advice* element may contain assertions or IDs for assertions, or any type of information that the creator of the assertion wants to include. It allows nonstandard information to be inserted into the assertion. There is no requirement that a receiving party understand information in the *Advice* element. Therefore, information in the *Advice* element may be ignored.

We will now move on through the assertion description and explain the statement portion of an XML assertion.

Statements

The top-level statement portion of an assertion is an abstract element. An XML document that contains only abstract elements is not valid and must contain concrete, derived elements. Therefore, a valid assertion must contain one of the three statements defined by SAML, authentication, attribute, or authorization. These will make up the concrete representation of the abstract element *StatementAbstractType*. Another important point about the abstract statement element is that it can be used as an extension point, that is, additional concrete statements beyond those defined may be constructed as extensions to an abstract element, the statement element in this case.

Authentication Statement

The authentication statement is derived from the abstract *SubjectStatementAbstractType* that, in turn, is derived from an abstract *StatementAbstractType*.

In the common portion of the assertion we have already assigned to the assertion a particular *Subject*, stated who the issuer is, and signed the assertion. (We really can't sign the assertion until we have a complete assertion, so this is just a statement that has a slot for an optional signature in the common portion.) What else do we need to create an authentication assertion? The *AuthenticationStatement* is shown in the schema fragment below:

```
<element name="AuthenticationStatement"
                           type="saml:AuthenticationStatementType"/>
<complexType name="AuthenticationStatementType">
  <complexContent>
    <extension base="saml:SubjectStatementAbstractType">
      <sequence>
        <element ref="saml:SubjectLocality" minOccurs="0"/>
        <element ref="saml:AuthorityBinding" minOccurs="0"
                                            maxOccurs="unbounded"/>
      </sequence>
      <attribute name="AuthenticationMethod" type="anyURI"
                                              use="required"/>
      <attribute name="AuthenticationInstant" type="dateTime"
                                               use="required"/>
    </extension>
  </complexContent>
</complexType>
```


Note that there is a new term in the above schema fragment, *extension base*. This is the XML schema's way of expressing inheritance. So, this fragment of SAML inherits the elements of the *SubjectStatementAbstractType*.

The optional information in the *AuthenticationStatement* includes the *SubjectLocality*, which is defined as an IP and DNS address of the entity that has been authenticated. Since this address may be relatively easily spoofed by a sophisticated attacker, this is not looked upon as much of a security deterrent, but the TC recognized that people want to use these addresses, so they provided that option. Another element is what is called an *AuthorityBinding*. This is information that may be used to contact the SAML Authority that made the assertion in case the target wanted to get additional information on the authentication.

The *AuthenticationMethod* identifies the type of authentication that was carried out, while the *AuthenticationInstant* contains the time that the authentication took place. All times in the schema are in Coordinated Universal Time (UTC).

Attribute Statement

The attribute statement returns the attributes that the issuer of the assertion asserts are associated with the *Subject* identified in the common portion of the assertion. The schema definition of an attribute is:

```
<element name="AttributeStatement" type="saml:AttributeStatementType"/>
<complexType name="AttributeStatementType">
  <complexContent>
    <extension base="saml:SubjectStatementAbstractType">
      <sequence>
        <element ref="saml:Attribute" maxOccurs="unbounded"/>
      </sequence>
    </extension>
  </complexContent>
</complexType>
```

Where the attribute element contains the AttributeValues as shown below:

```
<element name="Attribute" type="saml:AttributeType"/>
<complexType name="AttributeType">
  <complexContent>
    <extension base="saml:AttributeDesignatorType">
      <sequence>
        <element ref="saml:AttributeValue" maxOccurs="unbounded"/>
      </sequence>
    </extension>
  </complexContent>
</complexType>
```

Similarly to the *AuthenticationStatement*, the *AttributeType* inherits from the *AttributeStatementType*. The *AttributeDesignatorType* is included below.

```
<element name="AttributeDesignator"
              type="saml:AttributeDesignatorType"/>
<complexType name="AttributeDesignatorType">
  <attribute name="AttributeName" type="string" use="required"/>
  <attribute name="AttributeNamespace" type="anyURI" use="required"/>
</complexType>
```

You may have noticed that it is easy to run into some terminology confusion in this fragment. The XML schema defines a term called an attribute, which we first encountered in the fragment describing the *SubjectConfirmation*. Security also defines the term attribute, which is associated with a security principal. These two usages of the term attribute have totally disjoint meanings, so try not to be confused by them.

As can be seen from the two schema fragments, the required elements of a security Attribute are a sequence of attribute values for that type. Attribute values may be of any type, which means that the type of an attribute value may be of any valid XML type, including structured types.

Since the attribute is derived from an *AttributeDesignator*, an attribute inherits an *AttributeName* and an *AttributeNamespace* in which the *AttributeName* is defined.

The representation of the attributes of a subject in the SAML schema is relatively straightforward. The problem lies in the interpretation of the attributes when the domain of the sender and receiver are not the same. We will discuss this problem in Chapter 10.

Authorization Statement

SAML authorization deals with conveying the decision on whether some action or actions may be performed on some resource. The algorithms necessary to reach an authorization decision may be very complex, but SAML itself is only concerned with delivering the outcome of that decision.

Since the infrastructure for authorization may be complex, SAML does define a few additional constructs that can be involved in an authorization decision. These are a PEP, which is responsible for enforcing the results of an authorization decision. There also exists a PDP, where the authorization decision is carried out. In order to satisfy an authorization request the PEP makes a request on the PDP, passing authentication and/or attribute assertions as evidence that the PDP can use to make an authorization decision. SAML doesn't say much about the decision-making process—this is left up to the XACML specification or some other access decision specification.

The authorization statement portion of the SAML schema defines additional elements that are used in making an authorization decision. The first of these is an action element that is used to describe what is to be done to the second element, the resource. The action has *maxOccurs="unbounded"*, so you can have multiple actions on a resource. A simple example is authorization to read, write, and execute a file, where the file is the resource to be acted upon. Actions are not limited to the traditional operating system paradigms. An action may be the attempt to countersign a contract, where the action is countersign and the resource is the contract. Actions, like subjects, may be qualified by a namespace. As you can imagine, the authorization model is potentially very rich.

In addition to the actions and resource, the specification lets you pass evidence to aid the PDP in making or confirming the authorization decision. The evidence takes the form of an assertion. As a result, you can pass an attribute assertion and/or an authentication assertion as evidence.

Of course, since this is an authorization, we need an element to indicate whether the authorization was granted or not. Therefore, the schema also provides a decision element.

A fragment of the authorization statement is presented below:

```
<element name="AuthorizationDecisionStatement"
         type="saml:AuthorizationDecisionStatementType"/>
<complexType name="AuthorizationDecisionStatementType">
  <complexContent>
    <extension base="saml:SubjectStatementAbstractType">
      <sequence>
        <element ref="saml:Action" "maxOccurs ="unbounded"/>
        <element ref="saml:Evidence" minOccurs="0/>
      </sequence>
      <attribute name="Resource" type="anyURI" use="required"/>
      <attribute name="Decision"
            type="saml:DecisionType "use="required"/>
    </extension>
  </complexContent>
</complexType>
```


There is nothing very new in this fragment, so you should be able to figure out what this schema means. We've described the meaning of all the elements except the *Decision*, which returns the results of a decision. A *Decision* element may take one of the values:

- Permit
- Deny
- Indeterminate

Assertion Example

Now that we have gone through a detailed explanation of the SAML assertion schema, let's take a look at what a simple assertion itself would look like. The following XML document is an attribute assertion that says that *dflinn* has the attribute *Payroll Administrator.*

```
<saml:Assertion xmlns:saml="urn:oasis:names:tc:SAML:1.0:assertion"
        MajorVersion="1" MinorVersion="0"
        AssertionID="4bef456bba6"
        Issuer="http://www.quadrasis.com/easi"
        IssueInstant="2002-08-20T10:30:32Z" >
  <saml:Conditions
        NotBefore="2002-08-20T10:28:32Z"
        NotOnOrAfter="2002-08-20T11:28:32Z" >
    <saml:AudienceRestrictionCondition>
      <saml:Audience>
        http://www.bigbiz.com/accounting
      </saml:Audience>
    </saml:AudienceRestrictionCondition>
```

```
    </saml:Conditions>
    <saml:AttributeStatement>
      <saml:Subject>
        <saml:NameIdentifier
          NameQualifier="www.quadrasis.com"
          Format="urn:oasis:names:tc:SAML:1.0:assertion
                                  #WindowsDomainQualifiedName" >
          ne\dflinn
        </saml:NameIdentifier>
      </saml:Subject>
      <saml:Attribute
          AttributeName="role"
          AttributeNamespace="http://www.quadrasis.com/easi" >
        <saml:AttributeValue>
          PayrollAdministrator
        </saml:AttributeValue>
      </saml:Attribute>
    </saml:AttributeStatement>
  </saml:Assertion>
```

The code starts out defining this as a SAML assertion, version 1 0. It then gives a unique ID for the assertion followed by identifying the issuer and issue time. This satisfies the common portion of the assertion. We next add some condition elements that identify the time period for which this assertion is valid and who the intended audience is.

The next section of the assertion is an attribute statement that identifies the subject of the assertion, *ne\dflinn*, and states his attribute as the role *PayrollAdministrator*. Notice that the format of the name uses one of the standard formats defined by the specification, a *WindowsDomainQualifiedName*. The definition of a *WindowsDomainQualifiedName* is an optional Windows domain, *ne* in our case, followed by the Windows user name, *dflinn*.

SAML Protocols

The SAML usage model, as opposed to the SAML specification, discusses services or authorities that issue the authentication, attribute, and authorization assertions and attest to the truth of their assertions. As a consequence, a necessary part of the specification is to define a protocol for requesting assertions from such third parties and returning the completed assertion in a response message.

How the service authorities carry out their mission is not in the province of SAML, just the standardization of the request and reply messages and the means of transporting these messages. SAML calls the means or protocols for transporting the messages to and from the authorities the SAML bindings.

In addition to getting the SAML assertions, there needs to be a means of transporting the assertions from the initiator of a request to the target of the request. That is, what protocols does SAML use to transport the assertion and where does one place the

SAML assertions in the message protocol used between the initiator and the target? These protocols are called SAML profiles.

We cover the format of the request and responses as well as the bindings and profile protocols in this section.

SAML Request/Response

As you might imagine, there are three variants of SAML request and response, one each for authentication, attributes, and authorization. Similar to the assertions themselves, the requests and responses are XML documents and have a header portion that is common, a portion that is specific to a request, and a portion that is specific to a response.

The header portion of a request/response contains a definition of the namespaces used and the import of other specification schemas used by the SAML request/response. In the present specification, these imported schemas are the digital signature specification, the SAML assertion schema, and the XML schema itself. Following the header portion, the request schema is defined, followed by the definition of the response schema.

Both the request portion and the response portion of the SAML request/response schema begin with an abstract element. As we described above, in an XML schema, as in a programming language, one cannot have only abstract elements. There has to be a concrete portion that derives from the abstract portion to have a valid schema. In addition, abstract elements can be used as an extension point. SAML defines the *RequestType* as inherited from the abstract *complexType*, *RequestAbstractType*. Since *RequestAbstractType* is abstract, other elements or complex types could be derived from it in the future. Similarly, all responses are inherited from the abstract element *ResponseAbstractType*.

In the next two sections, we take a look at the SAML request and response in more detail.

SAML Request

A SAML request is a format used by SAML to ask specific questions of an authentication, attribute, or authorization authority. For an authentication authority, the question is: Has this subject been authenticated? The requester is expecting a response in the form of a SAML authentication assertion. For an attribute authority, the question is: What are the attributes for this authenticated subject? The requester is expecting an answer in the form of a SAML attribute assertion. For an authorization authority the question is: Can this subject perform the specified action on the specified resource optionally using the supplied evidence? The requester is expecting an answer in the form of a SAML authorization assertion.

The request portion of the SAML protocol starts out with an abstract type called the *RequestAbstractType*. This is followed by the version of the specification and the time of issuance of the request.

Optionally, the request may be digitally signed. The digital signature must follow the W3C Digital Signature specification.

The *RespondWith* element in the request is a statement by the requestor that it can handle the responses set in this element. The responder must conform to this request. The types of responses that are defined for the *RespondWith* element are *AuthenticationStatement, AttributeStatement,* and/or *AuthorizationStatement.* Multiple statements are indicated by multiple *RespondWith* elements. *RespondWith* is an optional statement. If it is not sent then the responder may send any assertions with any statements.

The request element fragment of the schema is shown below.

```
<element name="Request" type="samlp:RequestType"/>
<complexType name="RequestType">
  <complexContent>
    <extension base="samlp:RequestAbstractType">
      <choice>
        <element ref="samlp:Query"/>
        <element ref="samlp:SubjectQuery"/>
        <element ref="samlp:AuthenticationQuery"/>
        <element ref="samlp:AttributeQuery"/>
        <element ref="samlp:AuthorizationDecisionQuery"/>
        <element ref="saml:AssertionIDReference"
                                  maxOccurs="unbounded"/>
        <element ref="samlp:AssertionArtifact" maxOccurs="unbounded"/>
      </choice>
    </extension>
  </complexContent>
</complexType>
```


You can see from the schema that the request type is derived from the *RequestAbstractType.* You might have noticed that several of the choices are prefixed by *samlp* rather than *saml.* This is the namespace for the SAML Protocol schema.

A request type can take any of seven forms. It can be a:

- Query
- SubjectQuery
- AuthenticationQuery
- AttributeQuery
- Authorization Query
- AssertionIDReference
- AssertionArtifact

The *Query* and the *SubjectQuery* are both abstract types, with the *SubjectQuery* derived from the *Query.* Therefore, they cannot be the only choice, and both of these elements may be used to define new elements in the request. In the specification, the remaining choices are derived from the abstract element *SubjectQuery.* The Query element is simply an extension point, whereas the SubjectQuery contains the SAML Subject that we discussed earlier, as well as being an extension point.

The SAML *SubjectConfirmation* in the request raises some interesting points. As we mentioned earlier, SAML does not explicitly define a means to request that an authentication be carried out. However, the SAML assertion defines the *SubjectConfirmation* that contains the *ConfirmationMethod*, the *SubjectConfirmationData*, and the *KeyInfo* elements. According to the specification, these elements are not to be used to authenticate the subject, only to verify the authentication. Since authentication is not defined by the initial SAML specification, a principal is expected to authenticate itself to the authority in such a manner that the authority is able to unambiguously assert that the authentication has taken place. One way that this can be done is to have the authentication take place in the same session as the request for authentication. For example, a client could perform mutual SSL authentication at the same time it requests the SAML assertion, or it could use one of the HTTP authentication methods. At the very least, the authentication authority must associate the SAML authentication with absolute knowledge that the authentication has successfully taken place.

The next three additional elements in the choice are what you would expect: authentication, authorization, and attributes. The next to last element in the choice, *AssertionIDReference*, lets you use an assertion ID to point at an assertion, that is, the assertion may be external to this request.

The last element in the request, the *AssertionArtifact*, is something that we have not run across before. This is a somewhat complex construct that is used to help solve the "dumb browser" problem. By "dumb," we mean that when it comes to security, today's browsers do not have sufficient capabilities to operate at the level of security that we would like in a Web Services environment. The artifact construct, which we will discuss a little later in this chapter, attempts to mitigate this problem.

AuthenticationQuery

The *AuthenticationQuery* element of the SAML request asks the question, to quote from the specification, "What authentication assertions are available for this subject?" The schema for the *AuthenticationQuery* only adds the element *AuthenticationMethod* that has been defined in the SAML assertion. This is a URI that identifies the type of authentication that has been performed.

The specification identifies a number of authentication methods that may be used in the *AuthenticationMethod*, which include:

- Password
- Kerberos
- Secure Remote Password
- Hardware Token
- SSL/TLS certificate-based client authentication
- X.509 Public Key
- SPKI Public Key
- XKMS Public Key
- XML Digital Signature
- Unspecified

Each of the *AuthenticationMethods* is assigned a URI by the specification.

AttributeQuery

An *AttributeQuery* extends (that is, derives from) the *SubjectQueryAbstractType.* It is used to request that an attribute authority return certain attributes in an attribute assertion. The schema for the *AttributeQuery* is quite straightforward. There are only two elements added to a request for the *AttributeQuery.* They are an optional *AttributeDesignator* that was defined by the SAML assertion schema and an optional resource. The schema is shown below.

```
<element name="AttributeQuery" type="samlp:AttributeQueryType"/>
<complexType name="AttributeQueryType">
  <complexContent>
    <extension base="samlp:SubjectQueryAbstractType">
      <sequence>
      <element ref="saml:AttributeDesignator" minOccurs="0"
                                   maxOccurs="unbounded"/>
      </sequence>
    <attribute name="Resource" type="anyURI reference"use="optional"/>
    </extension>
  </complexContent>
</complexType>
```


The *AttributeDesignator* is used to tell the attribute authority what attributes the requestor wants returned. In order to make this request, the *AttributeDesignator* contains an attribute name and a namespace in which the attributes are defined. For example, one could ask for all the attributes of type "role" in the namespace "J2EE". As you can see from the schema, one can ask for the attributes related to an unlimited number of types.

The resource element is an optional field that the requester can use to tell the attribute authority that this request is made in response to an authorization request for access to a particular resource.

It should be noted that the XACML TC is working on fully defining the access control and a language for access control. This will have the effect of more fully defining attributes and authorization.

AuthorizationQuery

An *AuthorizationQuery* is used to request that the authorization authority answer the question of whether the particular subject is permitted to perform the stated actions on the given resource, optionally based on the evidence sent in the request.

The elements in the *AuthorizationQuery* are the name of the resource, the actions to be performed, and optional evidence. The resource is defined by a URI. Both the *Actions* and the *Evidence* are defined in the SAML assertions. The schema for the *authorization decision query* is:

```
<element name="AuthorizationDecisionQuery"
              type="samlp:AuthorizationDecisionQueryType"/>
```

```
<complexType name="AuthorizationDecisionQueryType">
  <complexContent>
    <extension base="samlp:SubjectQueryAbstractType">
      <sequence>
        <element ref="saml:Action" maxOccurs="unbounded"/>
        <element ref="saml:Evidence" minOccurs="0"
                                     maxOccurs="1"/>
      </sequence>
    <attribute name="Resource" type="anyURI" use="required"/>
    </extension>
  </complexContent>
</complexType>
```


Here we see that *Actions* are composed of a sequence of potentially many *Action* elements and optional *Evidence*, both of which are defined by the SAML core.

The authorization authority may use the assertions in the *Evidence* attribute in making its authorization decision.

SAML Response

The response, similarly to the request, starts out with a common portion that contains many of the same elements, such as version number, *Subject*, and so on. The new attributes in the response common section are the *ResponseID* and the *InResponseTo* attributes.

The purpose of the *InResponseTo* attribute is to tie the response to its corresponding request, if any. This is accomplished by setting the *InResponseTo* attribute of the response equal to the *RequestID* of the request to which it is responding.

The *Response* element itself follows a structure similar to the request in that it is derived from the *ResponseAbstractType*. The main element returned in a SAML response is the appropriate assertion or assertions.

The other major element returned in a *Response* element is a sequence of statuses, which can be one of *Success*, *VersionMismatch*, *Requestor*, or *Responder*. The meaning of the first two is pretty obvious. The *Responder* status needs some explanation. This means the request couldn't be performed because of an error at the receiving end. The *Requester* status indicates that the request couldn't be performed because of an error in formulating the request.

In addition to the status errors, SAML defines a number of optional sub statuses. The element *SubStatusCode* has defined the following values, the meaning of which should be obvious:

- RequestVersionTooLow
- RequestVersionTooHigh
- RequestVersionDepreciated
- TooManyResponses
- RequestDenied
- ResourceNotRecognized

There is also an optional *StatusMessage*, which is a string that allows an explanatory message to be returned.

Bindings

The protocols that carry the request or response message to or from the SAML authentication, attribute, or authorization authorities are what SAML calls bindings. In addition to the binding protocols defined in the specification, other binding protocols can be defined. The specification details the steps required to propose a new binding.

There is only one binding protocol defined in the first version of SAML, the SOAP binding. We will discuss this binding next.

SOAP Binding

We have discussed the details of the SOAP protocol in Chapter 2, so we will not go into the details of SOAP here. Our purpose in this section is to talk about how SOAP is used to transport the SAML request and responses.

The SOAP specification states that security information for a SOAP message is to be carried in the SOAP header. However, the purpose of a SAML SOAP binding is not to secure the SOAP message but to request and receive SAML security information, specifically SAML assertions. Therefore, the SAML information, in this case, is the message and is to be carried in the SOAP body, as is the case for any other SOAP message.

There must not be any data other than the SAML request or reply in the SOAP message body when it is used to send a request or response for SAML assertions to or from a SAML authority. To keep the protocol simple, there cannot be more than one request or response in the SOAP message. The response is a SOAP message containing either a SAML response in the SOAP body or a SOAP fault code. The SOAP fault code is returned when the responder cannot process a SAML request. If there is an error in the processing of the SAML request or response, then a SOAP fault code is not sent, but a SAML error is returned.

Establishing the security of the SOAP message used in a SAML binding is optional and is outside the SAML specification. From a system security point of view, this is an important consideration. You should treat the SOAP binding message as you would any other sensitive message, and perform authentication between the SAML authority and the requestor. Similarly, you should look at the confidentiality and integrity of the SOAP binding message and assess its security needs.

Profiles

A SAML profile is the description of how a SAML assertion is to be transported from one application to another. The SAML TC has submitted a SOAP profile to the Web Services Security TC, which is working on supporting transport of SAML assertions in a WS-Security token element. The effort of the Web Services Security TC is just beginning as of this writing. We will discuss the topic of WS-Security and SAML at the end of this chapter.

There are two profiles defined for the initial SAML specification, the Browser Artifact profile and the HTTP POST profile. Both of these profiles are browser-based and are intended to support SSO. The browser is assumed to be a common commercial browser.

The architecture for the browser-based profiles is depicted in Figure 5.2. The browser accesses what the specification calls a source site. This is some authority that can generate SAML assertions to be used by the browser for consumption by some target. The browser accesses the source site by some means not defined by the specification. It may reach the source site by being redirected there by the target when the target discovers that the browser request does not have the required SAML assertion(s). Alternately, the browser may access the source site on its own to obtain the necessary security evidence to access a target. The browser must authenticate itself to the source site by some means, which is also outside the specification. It may accomplish this by using SSL/TLS, basic authentication, or any authentication method common to the source site and the browser. The source site itself is assumed to have a means of keeping track of an authenticated browser such as retaining session information or some other means outside this specification. Given this, the browser will only be required to log in to the source site once for the length of a session.

Once an authenticated browser accesses the source site, Step 1 in Figure 5.2, the source site generates some evidence for the browser and returns it to the browser. The browser then contacts its intended target, Step 2 in Figure 5.2, presenting the evidence received from the source site. The target evaluates the evidence, optionally contacting the source site, Step 3, to gather additional evidence to ascertain whether to accept the evidence presented. If it accepts the evidence, then the browser is deemed to be authenticated.

The browser may use the evidence from the source site to access other targets and to make additional calls on these targets. Thus, the browser will have accomplished SSO for the length of the session held by the source site.

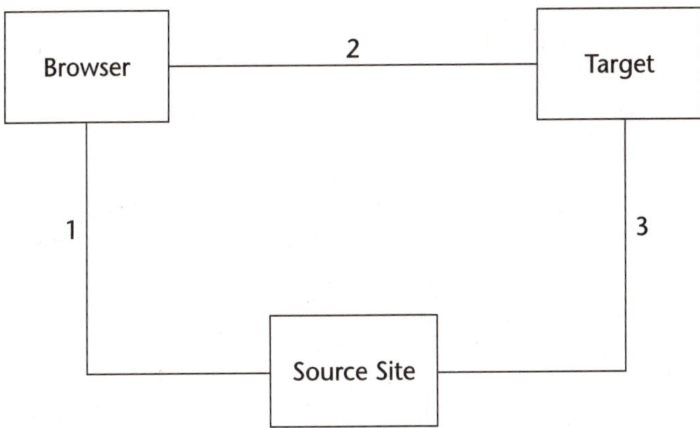

Figure 5.2 Browser artifact profile.

SAML Artifact

The first of the two profiles defined by version 1.0 of SAML uses a level of indirection in presenting its security evidence. The browser first obtains from the source site a small identifier called an *artifact* by SAML.

Artifacts are used so that SAML assertions may fit into an HTTP URL from a Web browser. Typically a browser would pass security information in a cookie. However, cookies cannot be used in cross-domain applications, so the URL may be used instead to pass security data. Browsers put a limit on the size of the URL length that they will support, and SAML assertions containing a large number of attributes may not fit into a URL. Note that the browser manufacturers, not the HTTP specification, impose a limit on the URL size. For example, Microsoft Internet Explorer imposes a limit of 2 KB on the HTTP URL size. We discuss the topic of session tracking on the Web in more detail in Chapter 6, "Principles of Securing Web Services."

We will first describe the format for an artifact and then describe how it is used.

SAML Artifact Structure

The artifact structure consists of a mandatory 2-byte field followed by optional additional data and is defined as follows:

```
SAML_artifact := B64(TypeCode RemainingArtifact)
TypeCode := Byte1Byte2
```

The B64 notation means that the artifact is base64 encoded. Base64 encoding transforms any binary representation to text by substituting ASCII text character groups for any non-ASCII characters, thus allowing you to treat binary encodings as text.

The TypeCode is defined as:

```
TypeCode := x0001
```

The *RemainingArtifact* field is composed of a *SourceID* followed by an *AssertionHandle* where:

```
SourceID := 20 byte sequence
AssertionHandle := 20 byte sequence.
```


Thus, for this release of the SAML specification, the artifact is 42 bytes long.

The *SourceID* is to be used by the target to determine the identity of the source site. This encoding is not defined, but it is assumed that the target will store a table of source site identifiers keyed by *SourceID*. The source site identifier must be rich enough for the target to identify and contact the source site.

The source site uses the *AssertionHandle* to locate an assertion for a particular browser user. It is assumed that the source site will keep a table of assertions or sufficient information to construct a particular assertion keyed by *AssertionHandles*. The requirement is that, when a source site is presented with an artifact, it will be able to return the correct assertion to the requestor.

Using the SAML Artifact

Given that we now understand what an artifact is and how it may be used, we can trace how a browser can use the artifact protocol. The browser wishes to initiate a conversation with some target. There are two ways that a secure, SSO connection can be initiated using the Browser Artifact Protocol.

1. The browser can try to access the target without an artifact, and the target will cause the Browser request to be redirected to a third-party authority, called the source site in the protocol.
2. The browser can access the source site on its own and request an artifact.

In either case, the browser must authenticate itself with the source site. This may be done before the request is sent to the target or, in the first method, the target may force the authentication.

In the first case, the browser reaches the source site by redirection and requests an artifact by presenting information on the target to be accessed. If the browser is not authenticated to the source site, the browser is required to log in. This will be the only login request for this session with the source site and thus the rationale for the claim of SSO. The source site constructs an artifact and returns the artifact to the browser, Step 1 in Figure 5.2, and redirects the browser to the target.

In the second case, the browser accesses the source site, either having logged on previously or at the time of access, and requests an artifact for a target.

The browser presents the artifact(s) to the target. Note that the browser may send more than one artifact. The target dereferences the artifact, determines the location of the source site, and makes a SAML request to the source site, sending the artifact(s) that it received from the browser. The target must use the SAML binding protocol in accessing the source site. The request is a SAML request asking for one or more assertions that are associated with the artifact or artifacts sent.

The source site inspects the artifact(s) and creates or retrieves the proper assertion(s) and returns them to the target in a SAML response. The source site must return one assertion for each artifact in the request. The target may make additional requests on the source site, depending on what it is trying to accomplish. For example, the target may request a SAML authentication assertion, and then, after assuring itself of the authenticated user's identity, it may make an attribute and/or authorization request. These requests may be made to the same source site if it handles both types of requests, or the requests may be sent to other SAML authorities. Once the target has the proper assertions, it may perform other security functions such as authorization. These will be carried out using the appropriate SAML methods.

There are a number of potential security threats to the browser artifact protocol that the specification describes and makes recommendations on how to mitigate. The threats described are:

Stolen artifact. If an attacker can obtain an artifact, then that attacker has a very good chance of impersonating the user. To counter this threat, the specification states that the exchange must have confidentiality and integrity protection. This can be accomplished by using SSL/TLS. If the bad guy defeats this, say, by compromising the DNS and redirecting the browser to a malicious site, then a short validity time can be used to limit the time available to the attacker. For example, the source site can check the time between the request from the target and the creation time of the corresponding artifact. The specification recommends that this time should be set to a few minutes. This, of course, means that the time clocks of the source site and the target must be synchronized. Given this constraint, the time that an artifact is valid must be greater than this chosen delta time. The target may also set a valid time limit on the time span during which it will accept a valid assertion. Another, albeit weak, approach is to check the IP address of the browser if it is included in the assertion.

Attacks on the exchange. The stealing of the artifact being sent from the target to the source site by man-in-the-middle and replay attacks may compromise the exchange between the target and the source site. These attacks may be defeated by good distributed security practices such as encrypting messages using, say, SSL/TLS, mutual authentication, and signing the message.

Malicious target. Someone with bad intent may set up a malicious target. If so, that site could turn around and imitate the user. If this target is not one that has a relationship with the source site, mutual authentication will defeat this attack. Note that the target must establish trust with the authenticated source site. If the target has a relationship with the source site, the source site should check whether the request has come from the site to which it sent the artifact. Remember, the target is named in the artifact.

Forged artifact. Some sites may try to create a bogus artifact. The algorithm that the source site uses to create the artifact should contain enough randomness to make constructing an artifact very difficult.

Exposure of the browser state. The artifact may be stolen from the browser and reused. The use of an artifact should be checked by the source site, and it should only allow the artifact to be used once. The specification recommends a short lifetime for an artifact. Thus, the exposure time of the artifact is limited to this short lifetime.

SAML POST

A second profile defined by the SAML specification uses the HTTP POST protocol to transmit assertions from the browser to the target. The POST method does not impose any size limits, so you are not forced to invent a method to keep the size of the security information small, as is done in the artifact profile described previously.

In the POST profile, the browser makes a request to the source site, passing the requested target the browser wishes to access. The source site constructs one or more SAML assertions and puts them in an HTTP form. The source site returns the form that contains the assertion(s) to the browser with a redirect to the target. The assertions must be digitally signed, and it is further recommended that the transfer between the browser and the source site and the browser and the target be protected by SSL/TLS or some other mechanism to ensure confidentiality. Further, the target must ensure that the assertion can be used only once. This may require the target to hold a lot of state for an indeterminate time.

This profile faces security threats similar to those faced by the artifact, with the difference that an assertion is sent rather than an artifact.

In the next section, we will take a brief look at an endeavor named Shibboleth that is working on SAML-based solutions for some of the harder problems in distributed security.

Shibboleth

Internet2/MACE and IBM are working on a research and development project called Shibboleth (Erdos 2001) to provide security for interaction between a number of universities. Internet2 is a consortium of some 200 universities that are working with industry and the government to develop and deploy advanced networking technologies. Specifically, the Shibboleth project is investigating practical technologies to support institutional sharing and access control to Web-based services. It is a goal of Shibboleth to use open standards in its solutions. Shibboleth explicitly states as one of their key concepts that they will use the message and assertion formats and protocol binding developed by SAML. What makes this project especially interesting is the scope and difficulty of the security problems that Shibboleth is attempting to solve. This section will give an overview of Shibboleth as an advanced example of some solutions to some of these hard security problems.

Let's first walk through the Shibboleth model, and then we will discuss three important problems for which Shibboleth is attempting to derive solutions. The Shibboleth model is shown in Figure 5.3.

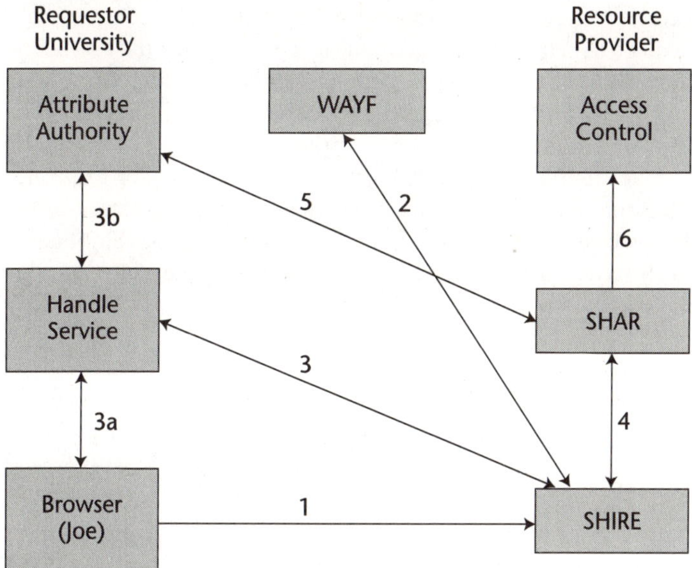

Figure 5.3 Shibboleth Model.

Starting at the lower left of Figure 5.3, we see a user, Joe, at his browser in the requestor university, say, MIT, attempting to access some resource at the resource university, say, Harvard. When Joe makes his request he connects with the Shibboleth Indexical Reference Establisher (SHIRE), line 1. Since one of the aims of Shibboleth is privacy, Joe does not identify himself to the SHIRE at Harvard. Instead, the SHIRE, noticing the lack of any SAML authentication assertion, redirects Joe's request (2) to Where Are You From (WAYF), which looks up the handle service (HS) that is associated with MIT. Joe will have previously registered his handle service with the WAYF service. The WAYF service returns the URL for Joe's HS to the SHIRE. The SHIRE redirects Joe's request to the MIT HS through Joe's Browser (3).

If Joe has not authenticated himself previously with the MIT HS, he is required to do so at this point (3a). The handle service looks up the correct attribute authority, AA, that handles Joe's attributes (3b) and creates an object that identifies Joe. This object, called an attribute query handle (AQH), contains a reference to Joe that is opaque to the SHIRE but can be interpreted by the AA to identify Joe's attributes. The AQH also contains the URL to the attribute service that handles Joe's attributes. The HS returns the AQH to the SHIRE. Note that the SHIRE does not know Joe's identity. It only has the opaque reference to Joe, which it cannot interpret.

The SAML request/reply protocols are used for these messages, while the browser uses the POST profile of SAML to access the SHIRE. The package that makes up the AQH contains the URL to the AA and a SAML authentication assertion. When the SHIRE receives the AQH, it carries out a number of security checks on the SAML assertion to assure its validity, such as valid time and signature checks. The HS is required to digitally sign the SAML assertion.

The SHIRE passes the AQH to the Shibboleth attribute requestor (SHAR), which contacts the MIT attribute service returning the AQH and its own URL. The SHAR uses a SAML attribute query request in the return call to the AA to request Joe's attributes. The attribute service decodes the AQH, identifies Joe's attributes, and returns Joe's attributes to the SHAR, using a SAML response containing a SAML attribute assertion. The SHAR then passes the attributes to the access control at Harvard, which uses them to grant or deny access. As noted, Shibboleth uses SAML assertions and protocols as a standardized way to pass much of the data between entities.

The various services must establish out-of-band trust relationships—for example, between the SHIRE and HS and between the SHIRE and the Attribute Service.

Having completed this overview, we will now look at the approach that Shibboleth uses to satisfy the goals of privacy and federation, and some special services that the attribute service can offer.

Privacy

There are two aspects of privacy:

- Keep my identity secret.
- Don't share any of my private information with anyone else unless I authorize it.

The Shibboleth model as described above puts forth one solution to these requirements. Sending only a set of attributes to Harvard satisfies the first goal. The system does not reveal Joe's identity, since Harvard cannot derive Joe's identity from the information that is sent to the SHIRE. Shibboleth uses the subject element in all SAML assertions in such a way as to represent the blinded name of Joe. However, Joe also might not want to reveal to Harvard that he is a full professor in the Astronomy department, for example, which is one of his attributes. This is the second privacy problem.

This second type of privacy, honoring the amount of information sent to another party, is accomplished in a different way by Shibboleth. Joe can arrange with the AA at his MIT attribute service which attributes to reveal to which requesting party. When the SHAR at Harvard sends a request to the AA at MIT, the protocol requires that it send its URL with the request and that it has authenticated itself to the AA at MIT. This is done prior to any requests for attributes. Therefore, the AA at MIT only sends the attributes that Joe has permitted it to send to Harvard.

There is another aspect of the second type of privacy—can Joe trust the AA to only reveal what Joe has authorized the AA to release? This is out of the scope of Shibboleth, or for that matter any automated system. This trust must be established between the authority keeping a user's information and the user. The question then becomes, "Do you trust that organization?" The fact that the AA is within Joe's organization makes this a solvable problem.

Federation

The definition of federation that we will discuss in the context of Shibboleth is the ability of a party from one organization to securely communicate with another organization, while maintaining independent repositories of users. Since Harvard has a relationship with some 200 other universities, does the administrator at Harvard have to keep the authentication information on every visitor to be able to perform authentication on each individual? This would be a huge task for the administrator because of the large number of potential users from the other universities and the need to keep the data up to date.

As we see from the Shibboleth model, this is solved by the simple expedient of each university keeping its own faculty and student data. This, of course, means that Harvard must trust the HS at every university with which it establishes a relationship. In establishing this trust relationship, Harvard will perform mutual authentication with the visiting HS, meaning that Harvard must be able to authenticate the various HSs. This is a much smaller problem, maintaining some 200 authentications, rather than trying to authenticate some 100,000s of student and faculty at the other universities.

Single Sign-on

The Shibboleth model only requires a user to sign on once to its home site. When Joe attempts to access Harvard for the first time, the HS at MIT must have an authenticated session with Joe or else it will force Joe to log on. Once Joe has established an authenticated session with the HS at MIT, he may request a resource from Princeton or any other university in the consortium without logging on again. All the universities with which Joe wishes to establish a secure session will be directed to the HS at MIT to complete the transaction.

The Trust Relationship

In order for this model to work, all of the universities in the consortium must establish trust with all the other HSs at other universities. They can establish that they are talking to the correct HS by means of mutual authentication. However, this does not mean that they trust the other HSs and AAs to have authenticated their respective users and to send the correct security data. Therefore, there are out-of-band trust relationships that must be set up.

This trust model becomes even more difficult when we expand this to federation between companies that set up ephemeral relationships with other companies for one-time transactions. In that case, the HS and AA might have to be a trusted third party. In the general business case, this will mean full employment for the companies' respective lawyers.

Related Standards

In this section, we will briefly introduce XACML and describe how it works with the SAML model. We will also describe the relationship of SAML to WS-Security.

XACML

The XACML TC is working under the OASIS consortium, and has the charter to develop an access control specification based on XML. The TC has taken the SAML authorization model as a jumping-off point and is developing a rich policy language and model to be used for access control. The intent is to work with the SAML specification and have seamless integration of the two specifications. As XACML develops its language and model, it may have to ask the SAML TC for some extensions to SAML. This is a contingency that both TCs expect and are prepared to address.

XACML is a general purpose access control language based on XML but not limited to work only with SAML. To this end, the XACML TC has specified its language so that it is insulated from the application environment by a canonical representation of the inputs and outputs. The XACML specification calls this insulating layer the XACML Context. The specification states that the actual methodology to convert from a specific application's environment to XACML is out of scope, but suggests that one automated way is to use Extensible Stylesheet Language Transformations (XSLT).

In SAML, we have seen the definition of an authorization request, a reply, and an authorization assertion. These permit you to construct a simple request to ask the question: Can this subject perform this action on this resource? XACML's intent is to refine and expand the SAML authorization request to work with the access control model and a language it is developing.

WS-Security

SAML is used in a SOAP profile that is being developed by another OASIS technical committee, the Web Services Security TC. That profile uses a specification called WS-Security, which we discussed in Chapter 4, "XML Security and WS-Security." The

SAML TC has submitted a specification to the Web Services Security TC to include a SAML token. The Web Services Security TC has accepted this proposal and is working it into the WS-Security specification.

SAML and WS-Security are naturally complementary. SAML assertions need a protocol to be transmitted from one application to another in some secure, standard way. WS-Security can address this need, since it is designed to transmit security data from one application to another application in a SOAP header.

WS-Security defines an XML document that, among other things, identifies tokens that carry security information. WS-Security has defined some tokens, such as the *UserName* token element, which carries the username and optionally the password, and a *BinarySecurityToken*, which could contain an X.509 certificate or a Kerberos ticket. The specification permits other tokens to be defined, such as a SAML assertion. Consequently, there are few technical obstacles for aligning SAML and WS-Security.

In Chapter 10, we will provide further detail on how SAML and WS-Security support interoperability, and give examples of the combined approach.

Summary

This chapter has described an XML-based specification, SAML, that defines the syntax and semantics of statements supporting the security of message exchanges in a distributed system. The statements are assertions by trusted third parties relating to the authentication, attributes, and/or authorization of principals in a distributed system.

The set of distributed security problems that SAML helps solve includes:

Interoperability. The ability to communicate between security systems within the different tiers that support enterprise applications

Privacy. The ability to protect a user's identity and personal data, such as credit card numbers and medical records, from unwanted disclosure when making a request

Federation. The ability of different companies to securely exchange requests and data with each other

SSO. The ability to log in once and use that login to access disparate applications

We described two aspects of the SAML specification:

- The SAML assertions and how they may be used
- The means by which the SAML assertions can be transported from application to application, called SAML profiles, and the means by which a SAML assertion can be requested and returned from a trusted third party, called SAML bindings

We delved enough into the SAML specification so that you, as a user of SAML assertions and request/replies, could understand their capabilities and make judgments on how they are being supported by a security service that you might contemplate using or purchasing.

We described a project called Shibboleth that addresses some solutions to some of the hard problems faced when one is trying to achieve secure, distributed computing using SAML. The problems that we talked about were privacy, federation, and single sign-on.

SAML provides an important contribution to solving the overall problem of secure Web Services interoperability. SAML's contribution to interoperability is its ability to define a standardized format for security information, and a standardized way of transmitting security data among different applications. A prime requisite for any hope of interoperability, beyond proprietary bridges, is to have a standard credential that different tiers and security models know how to interpret.

The next chapter will discuss principles for securing Web Services that will tie together the security concepts we introduced in the last few chapters: XML security, WS-Security, and SAML.

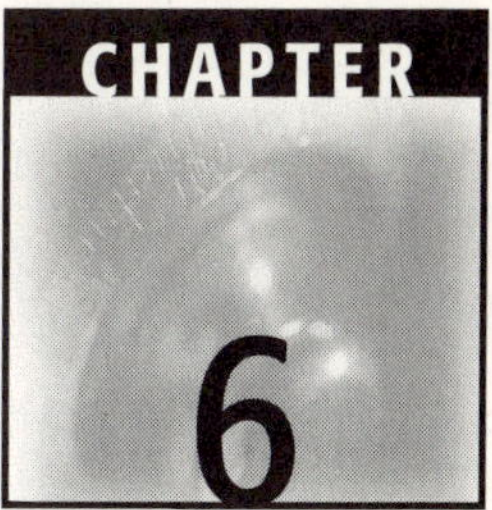

Principles of Securing Web Services

In earlier chapters, we defined security services and explained how they could be provided. In this chapter, we would like to focus on several of these security services and describe them within the context of Web Services. We will also look in more detail at possible security solutions and determine how they fit into security for Web Services. We will do this by considering a Web Services usage scenario and seeing how the security solutions can be applied.

For this discussion, we will limit our scope to the Web Services interface. That is, we will look at the security of XML-based SOAP messages, as they are communicated from one processing domain to another. This does not mean that we aren't concerned about events that occur before or after communication across the interface. At the Web Services interface, we are concerned about authentication, authorization, confidentiality, and integrity.

Web Services Example

In our discussion of some of the details of securing Web Services, we'll start with the Web Services online storefront example introduced in Chapter 1. We will extend the original purchasing scenario to provide an opportunity to discuss a variety of Web Services security issues. In this version, we add the concept of the eBuyer user who accesses ePortal via a Web Services client purchasing system in addition to using a browser. Figure 6.1 illustrates the purchasing example.

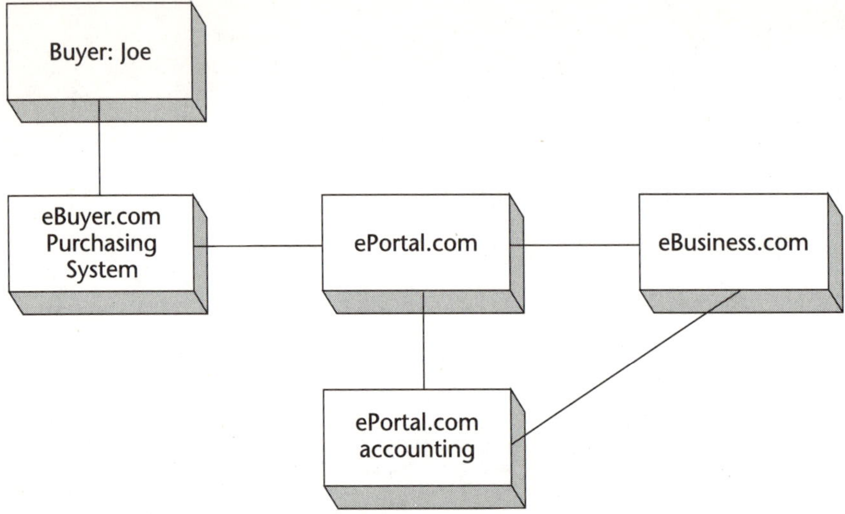

Figure 6.1 Web Services purchasing example.

Web Services operations can be complicated and can involve many different entities. There is the initiator of the Web Services transaction, who may use a generic browser rather than a Web Services client to start the transaction going. Then, there is the Web Services subscriber, who will be a business or a business unit. There are two Web Services subscribers in the example. First, the eBuyer purchasing system is a service subscriber to ePortal. eBuyer users may also be initiators of transactions at ePortal. Second, ePortal is a subscriber to services provided by eBusiness. eBusiness responds to product and pricing requests and buy requests from ePortal.

Functionally, ePortal takes in a buyer's purchasing requirements, solicits proposals from multiple vendors, and presents the offer that comes closest to the buyer's purchasing criteria. eBusiness produces merchandise. It receives inquiries from ePortal about merchandise, price, and availability. It also receives orders from ePortal.

There may be intermediaries who handle Web Services messages and may even affect the content of the message. A SOAP intermediary receives a SOAP message and may process SOAP headers addressed to it, but leaves the SOAP body intact. ePortal has an accounting system that is such an intermediary. It will receive buy requests on the way to eBusiness and record the transactions so that funds can be collected from eBuyer and paid to eBusiness, but it leaves the message body intact.

Another kind of interaction occurs when a SOAP node receives a message as the ultimate receiver. It may extract part of the body and send it on as part of another SOAP message. ePortal.com is such a node, and it creates new messages with information extracted from messages received from eBusiness or eBuyer.

As we analyze this example, many possible security solutions will present themselves. Each solution is valid given a set of assumptions. A goal of this chapter is to guide the reader through the analysis process to understand how to choose among the possibilities. We will choose a set of solutions for our example, but keep in mind that other possibilities will be more appropriate, depending on a system's specific requirements and environment.

Authentication

In discussing authentication, our analysis will focus on the interaction between ePortal and eBusiness and what these entities need to operate securely. The authenticated identity of several entities involved in producing and satisfying the Web Services request will be required. Ways to determine those identities are not obvious and require the cooperation of the participants in the process.

Authentication Requirements

The authenticated identities of several entities are needed to process and fulfill a request. ePortal must verify the identity of the buyer, Joe, before initiating the request. That is, a customer of ePortal wants to see how much 5,000 ball bearings will cost. Before ePortal starts to process the request, it makes sure that it knows who made the request so that it can decide if the request is legitimate. In this particular example, Joe uses a browser.

While we have chosen to use a person at a browser, the reader should keep in mind that another computer could represent the customer. Rather than using a browser, the customer could use a special-purpose client, or the customer may even have emailed a purchase order to ePortal. This is the case with eBuyer. However the request was received, ePortal must verify the identity of the sender, even if the sender is another computer.

When ePortal determines that it must request a Web Service from eBusiness, eBusiness now needs two authenticated identities. First, it needs to verify who sent the request. This is important because eBusiness's business relationship is with ePortal, and only companies with which it has a business relationship are entitled to make requests. eBusiness also wants to make sure that it will be paid for providing the Web Service, and ePortal is responsible for payment.

Second, eBusiness needs to know who initiated the request. This is particularly important when eBusiness must take action on behalf of the initiator. For instance, eBusiness may not mind responding with pricing information and sharing it with Joe. But, it doesn't want to ship merchandise unless it knows that Joe is a legitimate buyer.

Web Services complicate business-to-business authentication because the path from ePortal to eBusiness may not be direct, and intermediaries (SOAP and otherwise) may be in the path, handle the SOAP message, and even modify the message. However many entities have touched and relayed the message, we need to make sure that the requests in the message came from a business partner of ePortal's.

In our scenario, it is not possible for eBusiness to directly authenticate Joe. As a workaround, eBusiness agrees to accept ePortal's customer authentication. The two companies have established a trust relationship. Since ePortal has already authenticated and authorized the initiating user, eBusiness can carry out the request based on ePortal's word that Joe is who he says he is, and ePortal's authority to request the Service.

Passing a user's identity is more complicated in a multidomain application than in a single-domain, multitiered application. In the case of a single-domain, multitiered application, which is shown in Figure 6.2, a Web server can authenticate a user, and rather than the application server's authenticating the user again, the application server trusts the identity passed to it by the Web server. Often, this identity is passed in the clear between the two systems. That is, the identity is not encrypted as it passes across the internal network from one system to the other. Also, there is no authentication that the source of the identification information was the Web server.

The reason that this approach is so popular is that the user does not want to go through authentication multiple times, and it is also burdensome for the application server to have to maintain a list of users and their passwords, essentially duplicating functionality already performed at the Web server. While there is some risk in accepting the user's identity without authenticating its source, many organizations feel that the risk is acceptable, since the data is being moved over internal networks, not the Internet.

For Web Services, which operate in the multidomain, multitiered environment shown in Figure 6.3, messages flow across the more hostile Internet. Passing the customer's identity in the clear and without any further protection is more difficult to accept. eBusiness has to trust ePortal to authenticate the initiator. However, since the two companies are not connected over internal networks but, instead, are connected over the Internet, passing this information can no longer be done in the clear, without any authentication of the source of the information.

Finally, eBusiness would like to make sure that it is exchanging information with ePortal and ePortal alone. It wants to know that it is sending potentially sensitive information to the correct receiver.

We have identified at least four requirements for authenticated identity during the interaction between eBusiness and ePortal, and others may be needed. The four required authenticated identities are:

- ePortal must know who the initiator is.
- eBusiness must be sure that it received a SOAP request from ePortal.
- eBusiness must reliably know who the initiator is.
- ePortal must be sure that eBusiness sent the SOAP response.

Of these requirements, the first, ePortal knowing that the initiator is Joe is not, strictly speaking, a Web Services issue since it does not occur at the Web Services interface. Nevertheless, it is significant and we will discuss why later.

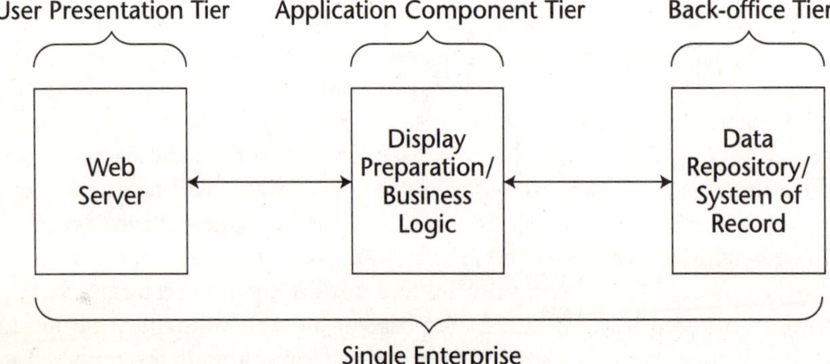

Figure 6.2 Single domain, multitiered environment.

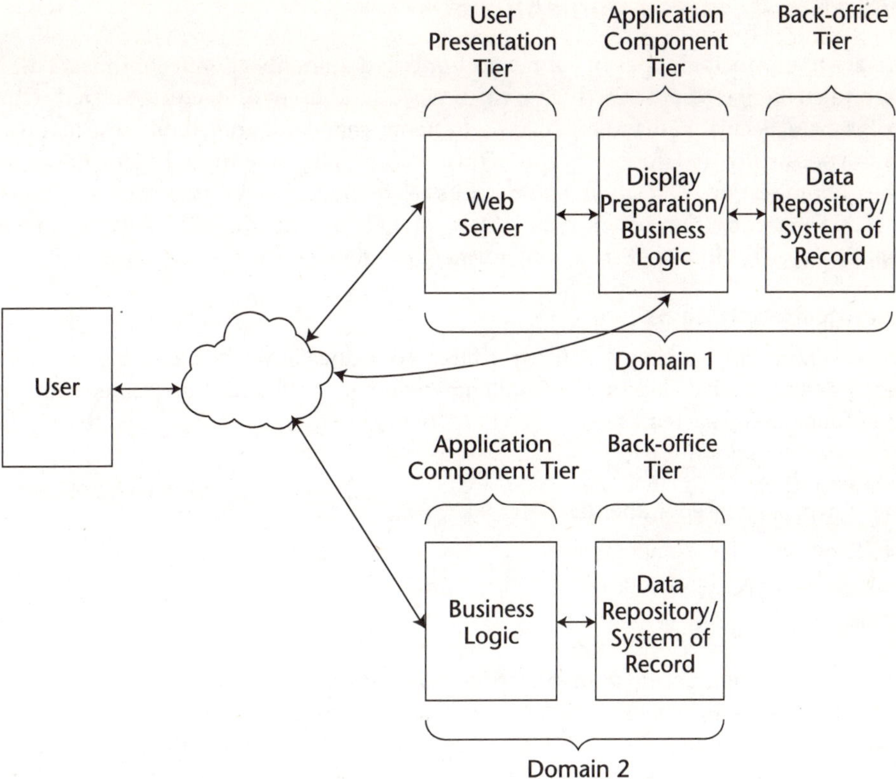

Figure 6.3 Multidomain, multitiered environment.

Options for Authentication in Web Services

Options for authentication are divided into two categories: connection oriented and document oriented. Connection-oriented systems identify who or what is at the other end of a connection. Even where the communication protocol does not support a sustained connection, some connection-oriented systems maintain the concept of a session by using cookies or URL extensions so that users do not have to authenticate themselves each time they make a request on a server.

Document-oriented authentication systems attach or embed an authentication token or tokens with a message. Messages and their authentication tokens may be transported using any number of protocols. HTTP, SMTP, and FTP are all candidate transport protocols. Messaging systems such as MQ may also be used. The significance of the authentication information contained in the token varies and must be negotiated by the sender and the receiver of the message. For instance, authentication information may pertain to the sender or it may pertain to the initiator, the system user, who caused the message to be sent. A single message may contain authentication information on both.

Connection-Oriented Authentication

There are two principal types of connection-oriented authentication techniques, password and challenge-response, which we described in Chapter 3, "Getting Started with Web Services Security." Password-based systems send authentication information, such as a password, that does not depend on any data being sent from the side that will do the authentication. With challenge-response authentication systems, the side that is doing the authentication sends data, called a challenge, to the side wishing to be authenticated. This information is transformed and returned as the response.

Authentication Systems

With one exception, which we will cover later, all connection-oriented authentication systems are built on password or challenge-response authentication. Categories of such authentication systems are:

- Operating system-based authentication
- Web server-based authentication
- Token-based authentication
- Web single sign-on (SSO)
- Client/server SSO

Operating system-based authentication relies on underlying mechanisms supported in the operating system, such as Microsoft Windows. Web server-based authentication uses capabilities that are built into HTTP, such as passwords. Token-based authentication requires the user to possess a physical token, such as a smartcard, that plays some part in the authentication process. Sometimes the token displays a value that must be verified by an authentication server. Sometimes, the token has a keypad so that a challenge can be input to the token. The token may have an electrical interface. Web SSO authentication supports many different authentication methods and, in addition, maintains an authenticated session that can be used to access a collection of Web servers within a domain. Finally, client/server SSO defines an authenticated session based on cryptographic authentication protocols such as Kerberos. For further detail on any of these authentication mechanisms, please refer to Chapter 3.

Two noteworthy Web SSO proposals are the Liberty Project and Microsoft's Passport. While they differ in the specifics, they both address the problem of SSO across domains.

The Liberty Alliance Project (www.projectliberty.org), founded by Sun Microsystems and several other companies, is a consortium that has developed a specification for defining federated network identities. Liberty appears to have broad industry support. Liberty calls for an open, decentralized system and accommodates a variety of authentication mechanisms. *Federation* is the approach taken by the Liberty Alliance, which means that authentication information can be shared among a group of trusted peers, thus enabling SSO. Liberty is built on and extends the OASIS Security Assertion Markup Language (SAML) specification. Two methods to share authentication information across a domain are described. These methods are based on the SAML profiles described in Chapter 5, "Security Assertion Markup Language." The first is an artifact, a small piece of data that is appended to URLs and that is subsequently used to request authentication data about an individual. The second uses a form, containing authentication data, sent to the Web site that needs it using an HTTP POST.

SESSION TRACKING ON THE WEB

HTTP access is stateless. That is, each access is meant to be a complete transaction. The next time the same Web site is accessed, the request is treated as a new transaction with no information being retained from the previous access. This makes HTTP simple, but there is an undesirable consequence to this mode of operation. It is inefficient. Authenticating the user with each request takes time and resources.

Several mechanisms have been devised to keep track of a previously performed authentication. They are all based on sending the browser information that is returned at a later time. They are cookies, URL extensions, and hidden fields. Each has its strengths and weaknesses.

Cookies. Cookies are defined for use with the HTTP protocol (IETF 1999a, Netscape). They are a mechanism used by the Web server to send information to the browser for storage. The cookie carries information about where the cookie can be returned. When the browser accesses the domain and path specified in the cookie, the cookie will be returned to the Web server.

- Either the cookie is stored in the browser for the duration of the browser session, in which case the cookie is never written into persistent storage, or it is retained for a defined period set by the Web server, in which case the cookie is written to persistent storage. Many users are reluctant to accept cookies because they are concerned about the misuse of cookies.
- Cookies can carry a maximum of 4,096 bytes. A Web site may send multiple cookies. A maximum of 20 cookies will be accepted per domain. Browsers are obliged to store a maximum of 300 cookies. If this maximum is exceeded, the least recently used will be eliminated.
- The biggest limitation of cookies is that they are restricted to being read by the same site at which they were generated. So, while they are useful for maintaining state within the same domain, they aren't useful for maintaining state across domains. Authentication information from one domain is not useable at another domain.

URL extensions. With URL extensions, the Web server can append a name-value pair to the end of URLs that are sent to the browser. When the browser subsequently accesses the URL, the name-value pairs are sent to the Web server. Name-value pairs can consist of information that allows the Web server to track the user's session.

- The size of the URL can be limited to as little as 2,048 bytes. Unfortunately, URL extensions are a popular way to attach session data, so URL space cannot always be counted on.

Hidden fields. Hidden fields in forms can be used to keep session information. If a form is sent to the browser for the user to fill in, it can contain data that is not displayed. When the form is sent back to the Web server, using an HTTP POST, the hidden fields, together with the other information in the form, will be sent. This technique does require that an HTTP POST be used to communicate with the Web server, something that is not always efficient to do.

Whichever method is used, keep in mind that the session tracking data still needs to be protected from eavesdropping. The session data in all three approaches is relatively easy to discover and can be modified easily.

Microsoft's Passport is a single sign-on service and takes a centralized approach to cross-domain SSO. If a user wishes to access a Passport-enabled Web site, the user is redirected to a .NET Passport login server. Once the user is successfully authenticated, encrypted authentication data is appended to the URL as query string parameters, and the user is redirected to the original Web site. At the receiving Web site, a COM component, called the .NET Passport Manager, deciphers the authentication information, authenticates the user at the site, and uses it to authorize access to protected resource. Passport can manage other security relevant data. The closed nature of Passport, together with privacy concerns, is an obstacle to wider acceptance.

Document-Oriented Authentication

Document-oriented authentication systems embed information about an entity in the body of the document. This information allows the receiver to authenticate the creator of the document or a trusted third party vouching for the identity of an entity who is related to the document. The exact relationship of the entity to the document can vary and must be agreed to previously. We will discuss two document-oriented approaches. They are digital signatures and tokens.

Digital Signatures

With digital signatures, one or more parties sign the entire message or parts of the message using a digital signature algorithm such as RSA (ANSI 1998a). or DSA (NIST 2000). We discussed standards for signing messages in Chapter 4, "XML Security and WS-Security." These standards specify what portions of the message are signed, how the data is encoded, what algorithms are used, and other cryptographic parameters. For Web Services, XML Signature and WS-Security are the logical formats to use. They are tailored to SOAP and XML-based documents and have the flexibility that is needed for SOAP messages.

The other option for signing an XML-based Web Services document is the Cryptographic Message Syntax (CMS) (IETF 1999b). CMS is used with Secure Multipart Internet Message Extension (S/MIME) (IETF 1999c). CMS and S/MIME were developed by the IETF as ways to secure email. They assume that the input is text but not XML. They do include standards for signing and encrypting text-based messages and also include a specification for encoding a signature and certificates so that they can be handled by e-mail systems.

Standards such as WS-Security, XML Signature, and CMS concentrate on format and identification of algorithms. However, the logical relationship of the signer to the SOAP message is still not defined. More generally, standards do not cover the significance of the signature. A signature may designate many things. It may identify the creator of a message, or it may be attached to ensure that the message is not subsequently modified. The signer may or may not be endorsing the contents of the message, and the signer may not be authorizing the receiver to take action based on the message. Resolving the intent of the signer is complex and varies from document type to document type. These relationships are not within the scope of a standard. For Web Services, the signer and receiver of a signed message must make sure that they agree on the meaning of a signature.

While certain aspects of securing the signature are covered by the specification, others are not. These aspects are more system-oriented. For instance, a signed message should include a timestamp and/or nonce to keep the message from being replayed. The application system needs to keep track of the time or the nonce used to ensure protection against replay attacks.

Tokens

The last option for embedding authenticated identity information in a document is to insert a token bound to a subject. One token type is the SAML assertion, which we described in detail in Chapter 5. Unlike signatures, which are devoid of application context, SAML assertions are specifically defined to carry security-relevant information. An authentication assertion describes when and under what conditions the subject is authenticated. The attribute assertion identifies characteristics of the subject, and the authorization assertion identifies the subject's privileges with respect to a resource and an action. SAML assertions can be embedded in the header of a SOAP message. A specific insertion point for SOAP messages has not yet been standardized, but is in progress, as we discuss later.

Although a token is more narrowly defined than a digital signature, some of the same considerations still apply. The assertion subject's role is most likely that of the request initiator. However, this need not always be the case. In cases of complex workflow, several tokens may be present in the security header of a message. The relationship of each identity to the message may not be obvious. It is up to the application to resolve ambiguities.

A second option is WS-Security which is tailored to SOAP and recognizes several token types such as Passport, Kerberos, and X.509. We expect that WS-Security will incorporate the SAML assertion as a WS-Security token in the near future, thus identifying the insertion point and rules for the SAML assertion. As with the SAML assertion alone, the context of the WS-Security token must be resolved separately.

System Characteristics

Given what we know about the possible security solutions, we need to understand some key characteristics of our system.

> **What authentication is already performed and can the results be used for Web Services?**

Most applications require some kind of authentication. Since Web Services require cooperation between multiple components across multiple domains, life would be much simpler if the authentication system that came with the application were flexible enough to accept authentication information from the previous application and to pass it on to the next application. This is seldom done now, although this is changing.

A key aspect of using authentication or other assertions from another source is whether we trust the other source to have done its work correctly and whether we trust the information to be delivered securely. Making these decisions requires detailed knowledge of the operation of the other site and legal agreements defining liabilities. For our Web Services scenario, we will assume that ePortal uses a Web SSO system to authenticate Joe. This system uses Liberty and creates a SAML assertion that can be embedded in the SOAP message to indicate the initiator of the transaction.

Is the entity being authenticated directly connected to the authenticator?

As described earlier, many authentication systems require that the participants be directly connected to each other and able to interact on a real-time basis. For instance, the client may need to respond to a challenge in order to be authenticated. On the other hand, some authentication systems require a token or a password to be passed on as proof of identity. This information could be passed through intermediate relay points so long as the information is protected or the relay is trusted.

There are times when ePortal is directly connected to eBusiness, and there are times when it isn't. When requesting product or pricing information, ePortal connects to eBusiness directly. However, when an order is sent to eBusiness, ePortal's accounting system becomes a SOAP intermediary so that billing and payment information can be recorded.

Is software to support the authentication process acceptable at the client?

This is a big factor in deciding what authentication method to use. Since the client workstations are not generally administered by the same organization as the server, it is common for application developers to be told that no additional software can be installed on the initiator's workstation. With Internet applications, the initiator's ties to the server's organization are loose at best. Requiring the initiator to load more software on her workstation, when there is nothing to enforce compliance, is problematic. Additional software requirements at the client may turn customers away.

Additional software at Joe's browser, in any form, is not acceptable. This is usually the case with users connected to servers with browsers over the Internet. Additional software at ePortal and eBusiness is acceptable. Both entities had software developed for this application. Security should be part of the requirements.

Must authentication be performed transparently to the application? Or, can the application be modified to add authentication?

Some applications provide interception points. These are predefined points during program execution, including one for authentication, which can be used to insert code to customize the application. Other applications that don't have these intercept points require access to source code in order to support additional security measures. Adding authentication systems to such applications cannot be done transparently to the application. Adding security to such applications requires access to source code. In such cases, the application can be responsible for authentication.

Can the application be front-ended or wrapped with code that can support the needed authentication?

When the answer to previous questions is no, this is the solution of last resort.

For our example, only the Web server has interception points that are available. This allows a Web SSO system to authenticate Joe. SSL authentication is a candidate for use to meet some of our other authentication requirements. Many applications come SSL enabled, so SSL authentication would not require significant work to implement.

Finally, message-based techniques will generally require additional application code to implement.

Must the authentication system support subsequent impersonation?

In some multitiered applications, it is desirable for the user's authenticated identity at one tier to be useable for requesting processing at the next tier. The current tier impersonates the user to the next tier to get work done securely under the identity of the user. This topic will be covered in greater detail in Chapters 7, "Security of Infrastructures for Web Services," 8, "Securing .NET Web Services," and 10, "Interoperability of Web Services Security Technologies," with a discussion of the several possibilities for supporting impersonation.

The authentication system can provide a token for use in establishing the authenticated identity at the next tier. The token securely represents a previously completed successful authentication. A forwarded Kerberos ticket is such a token. Another approach is to pass on the actual authenticating information so that the current tier can authenticate itself to the next, thereby establishing its identity. While this approach works, it leads to potential security and administrative problems and isn't generally recommended. Authentication techniques that rely on passing around authenticating information, such as passwords, are able to support impersonation. Authentication systems that keep the information at the client, such as challenge-response systems, do not. In our example, there is no requirement for impersonation.

Authentication for ePortal and eBusiness

We return to the four requirements we listed earlier.

ePortal must know who the initiator is. ePortal's authentication of the initiator does not occur across the Web Services boundary. But, the authenticated identity of this individual may be important to eBusiness. The Web server, possibly using operating system authentication, or a Web SSO system will authenticate Joe. He interacted with ePortal using a conventional browser and established a connection to ePortal. Joe did not need any additional software, helper apps, plug-ins, or applets, at his workstation. This is an important reason for the popularity of Web SSO systems. Once Joe is authenticated, a SAML assertion is created. The user's identity is passed on to the ePortal application system using the assertion. The application server establishes the user's security context. This is done assuming that the application server has established a trust relationship with the Web server and its SSO system. Different authentication methods may be used. This includes passwords, one-time passwords, and SSL client-side authentication.

eBusiness must be sure that it received a SOAP request from ePortal. eBusiness must know that it is getting its SOAP request from ePortal. Since we are using HTTP to transmit the message, a connection-oriented authentication system is a possibility. However, there are times when messages are routed through an intermediary, the accounting system. At these times, connection-oriented techniques can't be used to authenticate ePortal, and another technique must be used.

XML Signature, a document-authentication technique, can be used to authenticate the message even if the message is routed through an intermediary. Signing authenticates the source of the message rather than the other end of the connection. In this case, the distinction is not significant. But, because the message is authenticated, it doesn't matter what transport is used. It also doesn't matter that other servers between the originator and the destination may relay the message. Since the digital signature is part of the message, the signature has persistence that allows it to be used to authenticate the message at a later time. Software to sign the message can be included on the eBusiness server.

eBusiness must know who the initiator is. In general, eBusiness will need the authenticated identity of the request initiator. However, since the initiator is not directly connected to the eBusiness, connection-oriented authentication techniques cannot be used. Since the initiator used a generic browser without any special-purpose software, there was no way to create a digital signature and attach it to his HTML document. Of course, doing so only makes sense if the document has an obvious relationship to the SOAP message that was actually sent to eBusiness. This may not be true. What Joe, the initiator, saw on his screen and submitted was formatted to be meaningful to him and probably looked nothing like the message that was sent. So, even if there was a way for him to sign his HTML document, it might not mean much to eBusiness.

In setting up Web Services between ePortal and eBusiness, mutual trust has been established between them. Since ePortal authenticated the initiator, eBusiness will take ePortal's word for the identity of the initiator. In fact, eBusiness will also accept ePortal's attributes for Joe. We must make sure that this information is passed to eBusiness in a secure and meaningful way. That's where SAML comes in. When ePortal authenticated the initiator, it requested a SAML authentication assertion. Later, when ePortal knows it is going to make a Web Services request to eBusiness, it requests an attribute assertion with the attributes that eBusiness needs to decide whether Joe is authorized to order the merchandise. If the message has been signed, the assertion will be bound to the message, and no one will be able to separate the assertion from the message without detection and use it with another message. (Of course, we also want to make sure that the entire message can't be reused either.)

ePortal must be sure that it is sending its SOAP request to eBusiness. Finally, we must make sure that eBusiness's authenticated identity is known to ePortal. The most common method in use is SSL with server-side authentication. During the establishment of the SSL session, the server normally provides authentication to the client by using public key cryptography. But, if ePortal is not directly connected to eBusiness, the possibility of using SSL server authentication is not feasible. ePortal's ability to ensure itself of eBusiness's identity before it sends a message to eBusiness is limited. Even if it could authenticate eBusiness, it still has other concerns. Since there are intermediaries that can handle the SOAP message, it must ensure that the message gets to eBusiness intact. Without authenticating eBusiness, ePortal could encrypt the SOAP message so that eBusiness and only eBusiness can decrypt the message. If the message gets into the wrong hands, it doesn't matter because they couldn't decrypt the message in a practical length of time.

Data Protection

Since the SOAP message between eBusiness and ePortal is used to transact business, we consider the data to be sensitive and not for general release. We must protect it from eavesdroppers and those who would modify the data for unauthorized reasons. We must also protect our Web Services system from inappropriate messages.

In this discussion, we will consider the interactions between eBuyer, ePortal, and eBusiness. As before, eBuyer is an automated purchasing system for an ePortal corporate customer, and SOAP is used for communication between the parties.

Data Protection Requirements

In our eBusiness scenario, sensitive data is exchanged between eBuyer and ePortal. Sensitive data is also exchanged between ePortal and eBusiness. Each sender wants to make sure that only the intended recipient can understand the data being sent. We must ensure that messages will not be modified in transit. Finally, we want to protect eBusiness from improperly formatted messages.

While the basic requirement for message protection is straightforward, protecting Web Services messages is more complicated. The flow of a Web Services transaction may mean that the message may be passed to several parties and that each may affect the message content. Portions of the message may be meant for one recipient but not for another. SOAP intermediaries may delete SOAP headers and add new SOAP headers.

In response to a request for information from eBuyer, ePortal solicits a bid from eBusiness. Along with product information and pricing, eBusiness sends a payment instruction to ePortal. After receiving the offer, ePortal may send the offer, including the payment instruction to eBuyer. But, under normal circumstances, neither ePortal nor eBuyer may be allowed to understand the payment instruction.

In the opposite direction, eBuyer may send its accounts payable information in its acceptance of eBusiness's offer. ePortal receives the acceptance and sends it to eBusiness. This message is routed through ePortal's accounting system. Although they both possess the information, neither ePortal nor eBusiness should be allowed to understand the payment information unless there is some dispute. However, the ePortal accounting system must be able to understand the data. It is responsible for ensuring that money is collected from eBuyer and the money is paid to eBusiness. A SOAP header instructs the accounting system to record the contents of the message and make entries into the accounts payable and the accounts receivable systems. Then, since the header is no longer needed, the audit system passes the SOAP message on without the audit header.

SOAP messages may be created from other, previously received SOAP messages. The dynamic nature of SOAP messages means that portions of the document have to be protected from some parties and not others and that this needs to be done carefully or the intended recipient will not be able to use the data.

Many of the vulnerabilities of Web systems are the result of improperly formatted messages. Everyone has heard of buffer overflow problems. Arguments that are too long or out of range can cause unforeseen and disastrous consequences.

For this application, we must ensure that:

- Data sent by eBusiness should only be understandable by the intended recipient, which varies according to the purpose of the data.
- Data sent by eBusiness should be protected from modification in transit. The intended recipient should be able to verify that the data was not modified.
- Data sent by eBuyer should only be understandable by the intended recipient. Again, the recipient will vary.
- Data sent by eBuyer should be protected from modification in transit. The intended recipient should be able to verify that the data was not modified.
- Input data is inspected to ensure compliance with expected types, including size, range, and values.

Options for Data Protection in Web Services

To protect the data, we must provide two security services: confidentiality and integrity. We must ensure that the contents of the message are not revealed to unauthorized personnel and we must ensure that the contents of the message are not altered. These services usually require cryptography. Encryption is used to provide confidentiality, and digital signatures are used to ensure message integrity. Keyed Message Authentication Codes (NIST 2002), another cryptographic technique, can be used for message integrity but does not scale well and is not suited for use across domains, for example, between eBuyer and ePortal.

Again, the approaches can be connection-oriented or message-oriented. Connection-oriented approaches protect the messages while they are being transmitted between systems. While in storage, application or operating system mechanisms are used to protect the data. Message-oriented approaches protect messages in transit or in storage. Connection-oriented solutions include SSL and IPSec. Message-oriented solutions include XML Encryption and S/MIME.

A security mechanism may provide more than one service. Many of the same solutions previously discussed are also candidates to provide confidentiality and integrity services as well. For instance, a digital signature can authenticate the source of a message, but it also protects the integrity of the message. A security system is often designed to provide several related security services.

Both SSL and IPSec are used to securely transmit data from endpoint to endpoint. A connection is established between two communicating parties. The data is encrypted as it moves from one party to the other. At the destination site, it will be decrypted so that the receiver can process the request and pass it on, if necessary. With Web Services, the message may need to pass through other hands before arriving at its intended destination. We may not know who has access to each of these systems or how well managed they are. If the contents of the Web Services message must be protected from eavesdroppers, connection-oriented solutions, such as SSL and IPSec, are useful but may not be sufficient to the job.

Another issue with connection-oriented approaches is that the entire message is protected in transit. So, while the message is being transported, it is protected from eavesdropping and modification. But, at the endpoint, the whole message is exposed. There is no ability to hide parts of the message from the endpoint or to protect parts of the message from modification. Depending on the situation, this level of protection may be adequate. In other cases, connection-oriented protection may need to be augmented by other protective mechanisms.

XML Encryption and XML Signature work together to provide message-oriented data protection. Since we have covered XML Signature, we will not repeat the explanation here, except to point out that since the signature is tied to the message representation (the hash of the message), a change to the message invalidates the signature, thereby serving as a way to detect that the message was altered.

An advantage of XML Encryption is that portions of the SOAP message can be encrypted. The encrypted portions of the message may or may not overlap with the signed portions of the document. This means that a message containing an offer to sell some equipment can include encrypted payment instructions that should be hidden from the potential buyer. But, the entire message can be signed so that the buyer can verify the seller's signature on the offer.

The other accepted method of protecting messages is CMS. Its origins are in message protection. While it protects text-based information, it was not designed for XML. CMS operates on the entire message. There is a SOAP binding for MIME. So, if email is used to transmit the SOAP message and the granularity is acceptable, CMS is an option for message protection.

XML Schema processors are able to check XML documents for compliance with the associated schema. This is a powerful capability as a flexible method for specifying datatypes. There are two drawbacks to the approach. First, application developers may not always generate a schema for each message type. Second, inspection of the elements and attributes in each message will be time-consuming. Protection against malformed messages may be appealing but many will forgo it because of the reduced performance that will result. Otherwise, applications will have to handle input checking, much as they do now.

System Characteristics

Before we describe the solutions for eBusiness, we need to answer some questions about the situation.

Between eBusiness and eBuyer, will other parties handle the message?

The offer from eBusiness is first sent to ePortal. At ePortal, the offer is extracted and sent to eBuyer in a message that may include offers from other possible vendors. The payment portion of the offer needs to be kept private, even from eBuyer. Once eBuyer selects eBusiness as its vendor, it sends its acceptance along with its account information to ePortal, which sends the acceptance to eBusiness. Again, neither ePortal nor eBusiness should be able to understand this part of the message. A reasonable question to ask at this point is why the information is sent if the payment instruction must be hidden from the other receivers. In this case, each side signs its message as a single unit. Removing the payment instruction from either message makes it impossible to verify the signature.

As discussed previously, SOAP messages may be routed through SOAP intermediaries that have responsibilities for support of the SOAP message processing. SOAP headers are used to convey information to intermediaries but the entire message is accessible to an intermediary. In our example, the intermediary is the ePortal accounting system. Payment instructions are encrypted so that they can be decrypted by the accounting system. The accounting system uses this information to collect payment from eBuyer and pay eBusiness.

What protocol(s) will be used to transfer the SOAP message?

SOAP messages may be sent using any protocol that handles text messages. HTTP is the most likely protocol, but candidates also include FTP and SMTP. If there are intermediaries, different protocols may be used between each segment. HTTP is used between all of the participants in this transaction. EBuyer, ePortal, and eBusiness use HTTP to transmit the SOAP message.

Are the recipients/handlers of the message allowed to understand some parts of the message but not others? If yes, what parts of the message are each allowed to understand?

In the purchasing example described above, some information must be kept confidential from nodes that are handling the information. This is shown in Figure 6.4. First, eBusiness's payment instruction must be kept from ePortal and eBuyer. When the offer is presented, the vendor does not want to make its banking information known except to those who need the information. The payment information is only needed by ePortal's accounting system if Joe, the buyer, accepts eBusiness's offer, so that the funds can be transferred to the correct account. eBuyer's payment instruction must be kept from ePortal and eBusiness. eBuyer's account information is also needed by ePortal's accounting system to collect payment, but eBuyer wants to limit knowledge of its bank account number to those entities that have a need for the information. The ePortal accounting system needs the information to collect the amount owed by eBuyer.

Besides financial data, medical data or other sensitive personal data is a good example of information that might be transferred in SOAP messages where intermediaries handle messages but should not be allowed to understand parts of them.

What parts of the message are related so that they must be sealed as a group using a digital signature?

In the example, the description of the offer and the payment instruction need to be signed together. This protects the vendor from having the financial terms cut from the specification of the materials promised and attached to other merchandise. When the buyer accepts the offer, the payment instruction being sent to ePortal's accounting system, including the seller's payment information, should be signed.

In what order are the encryption and digital signatures to be applied?

If the signed portion of a message includes encrypted data, a decision has to be made whether the encryption happens before or after the signature. A digital signature applied after encryption must be clearly called out. With WS-Security, the order in which cryptographic functions were performed is implied by the order in which the key information is appended to the security header. Keys are prepended to the header element as they are used. Therefore, the key for the most recently performed cryptographic operation is closest to the security header element start tag.

When eBuyer accepts eBusiness's offer, eBuyer signs the offer as well as its acceptance, linking them so that they cannot be used separately. Since eBusiness's offer included eBusiness's payment instruction, eBuyer signs encrypted data. The description of the signature must exclude eBusiness's payment instruction from decryption before eBuyer's signature is verified.

Does an XML Schema specification exist for the SOAP messages exchanged?

Existence of the schema for the messages makes it possible to use XML Schema processor to check the validity of a message. Otherwise, the application programmer must take responsibility for this.

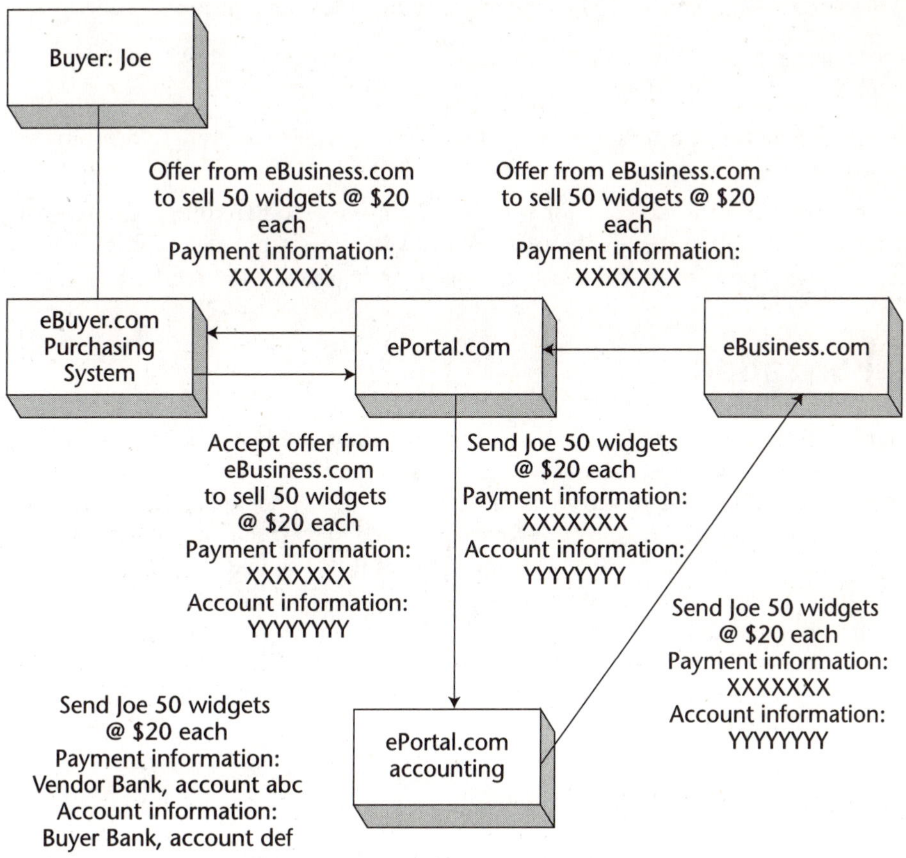

Figure 6.4 Encrypted data flow between nodes.

eBusiness Data Protection

We are now going to look at the data protection requirements for our eBusiness example:

- Data sent by eBusiness should only be understandable by the intended recipient, ePortal. When eBusiness sends ePortal data, only ePortal's accounting system should be able to understand and use the payment instruction, even if the message is sent to eBuyer as well.
- Data sent by eBusiness should be protected from modification in transit. The intended recipient should be able to verify that the data was not modified.

eBuyer and ePortal must agree that eBuyer's signature on the acceptance message authorizes ePortal to have eBusiness ship the merchandise and signifies eBuyer's agreement to pay for the merchandise. When eBuyer sends the acceptance message, eBuyer signs the message, including the offer from eBusiness.

- Data sent by eBuyer should only be understandable by the intended recipient.
- Data sent by eBuyer should be protected from modification in transit. The intended recipient should be able to verify that the data was not modified.

These two requirements are handled in the same way as the first two requirements. We will not duplicate the description.

- Input data is inspected to ensure compliance with expected types, including size, range, and values.

We do not have the schema for our SOAP messages. Therefore, we cannot do schema checking. Even if the schema were available, we might not wish to pay the price of reduced performance that schema checking requires.

Authorization

In our example, we concentrate on eBusiness's authorization needs. There are two aspects to authorization. eBusiness wants to ensure that it is only allowing ePortal to utilize the services it intends to make available. In fact, since eBusiness provides a range of services and ePortal may not have contracted to use them all, eBusiness needs to make sure that it restricts ePortal to the services it has signed up for. ePortal may have signed up to broker some products but not others.

Second, in the course of supplying the service, eBusiness wants to make sure that the initiator is entitled to request the service on its behalf. If the initiator is Joe Smith, the account used for the transaction should be the one Joe is entitled to use. It should not be Jane Brown's.

Authorization Requirements

The basic authorization requirements that exist for eBusiness are:

- eBusiness wants to ensure that ePortal is entitled to use the services it has requested.

- eBusiness wants to ensure that the initiator, Joe, has the authority to purchase the merchandise.

Rules for authorization can be quite complex and require that we know the authenticated identity of the initiator or the service provider, the target of the request, and the action requested. Depending on the application, other entities may have a part to play in the authorization process as well. In concrete terms, the target could be merchandise, and the action could be a sale. So, we want to know if the requesting party is authorized to buy 5,000 items. This is the minimum information required. In practice, we may need even more information to make the authorization decision. We may need to know more about the requestor, the target, the action, or the environment in which this is all taking place.

We might care whether the time is outside of regular business hours or whether the purchase is larger than the amount allowed for retail customers such as Joe. In many cases, the service provider knows for itself most of the information it cares about. It knows about the environment, the target, and the action. It needs the attributes of the service subscriber, ePortal, or the initiator, Joe. Once they are made available to eBusiness by ePortal, eBusiness can interpret them as appropriate.

The authentication we performed earlier gave eBusiness the identity of the service subscriber or initiator. Using an identity to make authorization decisions doesn't usually scale well, and rather than basing an authorization decision on the identity of the requestor, most security systems collect users into groups or roles with identical privileges and then make the decision based on the user's group or role. For instance, managers can sign timesheets or a project leader can authorize a purchase.

With Web Services, the privileges of a person called manager in ePortal may not be the same as the privileges of a person called manager at eBusiness. It is difficult for a large company to standardize names for groups or roles, let alone decide on a standard set of privileges for each. Standardization of groups or roles across two companies is practically impossible. Then, when another Web Services subscriber or even more subscribers must be accommodated, practically impossible becomes impossible.

For now, rather than using standard designations for groups or roles, these differences are likely to be resolved by pair-wise negotiation between the Web Services provider and the Web Services subscriber that identifies how to map attributes from eBuyer to attributes in ePortal. This isn't very satisfying and does not scale well. But, other more practical options have not presented themselves. The Web Services provider will have to understand how each subscriber wishes to map its attributes to attributes that are meaningful to the provider.

Earlier in this chapter, we discussed how to determine the needed authenticated identities for each company. If the SOAP message was signed, we assumed that the signer was an application or a person signing it on behalf of ePortal and that the subject whose SAML assertion was in the header was the initiator. But, this is not assured. At this time, there is no standard guidance on if or how authentication information should be associated with the contents of the SOAP message. SOAP messages can involve more than one initiator, multiple companies, and one or more intermediaries. Additionally, multiple RPCs in the SOAP request can make sorting out the relationship of all the signers and assertions even harder. The relationship of various entities involved in the request must be negotiated, together with an understanding of how the information is to be conveyed.

The first thing to do is identify the entity that has the business relationship with eBusiness and determine if that entity is authorized to request the service. In this case, ePortal and eBusiness have the business relationship. ePortal has discovered that eBusiness, possibly through eBusiness's business registry entry, offers some service or product that ePortal wants to offer its customers. ePortal and eBusiness have negotiated terms for use of the Web Services and probably signed some contract to formalize the relationship. The negotiation may entitle ePortal to receive a percentage of the sale for bringing the buyer to eBusiness.

Assuming that eBusiness is satisfied that ePortal originated the message, eBusiness can then verify that ePortal is authorized to send the document or make the request. If ePortal was able to authenticate itself directly to the operating system, then the operating system can be used to enforce authorization requests. If ePortal was authenticated by the Web server, which did not use the operating system for authentication, or it was authenticated by a Web SSO System, enforcement of authorization begins with those two systems. These systems are usually set up to protect URLs, so the target needs to be a URL. The granularity represented by the URL varies from system to system.

Additional authorization checks may need to be implemented by the Web Service. How the user identity and whatever attributes are provided depends on the environment in which the code executes. In some cases, there are automatic, transparent ways to pass the identity and use it to create a user context at the Web Services implementation. In other cases, there are no transparent ways to pass the identity and set up a user context. Instead, passing the identity and establishing the user's context become the responsibility of the application.

Now that it's known that ePortal can make these requests, eBusiness sets about fulfilling them. However, it now needs to authorize the initiator. Since the initiator was never directly connected to ePortal, we assume that information about the initiator is contained in the message. The initiator's identity could actually be an argument to the RPC for an RPC type message, or it could be contained in the document for a document style of message. Another option is to insert the initiator's identity and some attributes for the initiator in a SAML assertion in the SOAP message header. There could be more than one SAML assertion in the SOAP header. In such cases, it is up to the parties, ePortal and eBusiness, to agree on a way to distinguish the initiator's assertion from the other assertions that are in the header. In addition, there must be some understanding as to what roles the other assertions represent.

For our example, we will use the SAML assertion. It is a flexible way to include information about the initiator and allows ePortal to include attributes about the user as well. ePortal's signature on the message must cover the assertion as well as the document or the RPC calls. This binds the assertion to the requested actions. When eBusiness verifies ePortal's signature, it can also be confident that ePortal intended that the subject of the SAML assertion be the initiator of the transaction. eBusiness should also be confident that ePortal authenticated the initiator. These understandings should be carefully negotiated before the two companies agree to conduct business.

Besides the initiator's identity, the assertion contains some of the initiator's attributes in ePortal. For instance, Joe could be a Gold customer in eBuyer. Unfortunately, this isn't very useful in ePortal. But, because the two companies have worked out a mapping of the attributes in eBuyer to ePortal, ePortal can map the Gold attribute to a $50,000 purchase limit attribute for the user in eBusiness. eBusiness is now able to decide whether to go ahead and process the transaction.

It is unlikely that the initiator's authority to request the transaction will be enforced by the operating system or the Web server. Depending on the implementation, the authorization could be performed by the application system or even the application itself with the aid of an entitlement engine. Again, the exact mechanism depends on the components that make up the system.

Options for Authorization in Web Services

There are several methods that can be used to enforce authorization. They are:

Operating system- or platform-specific mechanisms. If the user being authorized to take action is known to the operating system, the operating system can be used to authorize the action and then enforce the authorization. This usually happens when the operating system authenticated the user on the platform where the authorization is taking place. The service subscriber must be directly connected. The advantages of using the operating system to enforce authorization are that it can all be done transparently, and the application environment may be able to accept the operating system context and use it for authorization within the application server. Again, this can be transparent to the application. This option is only available where the system components are compatible, when, for instance all components are from a single vendor.

Web server mechanisms. Web server mechanisms, including Web SSO systems, are designed to protect Web pages. If protected resources can be mapped to URLs, then using Web server mechanisms can be effective. In order to take advantage of Web server mechanisms, the service subscriber must be directly connected to the Web server, because Web server authentication is based on connection-oriented authentication. A disadvantage of this approach is that the user's authenticated identity is only known to the Web server authentication and authorization system. Authorization at any component beyond the Web server, because, say, finer-grained authorization is required, requires explicitly passing the user's context to the component. Facilities for passing and accepting the context vary from system to system.

Application server mechanisms. Application servers are able to perform authorization based on the authentication they perform or the identity that is passed to them by front-end components. This assumes that the identity can be used to establish the user's context in the application server's environment. In most cases, this authorization is limited to allowing access to object methods, based on user roles. This is usually acceptable; but may be too coarse grained in some circumstances. The passing of context from one application server to another may be handled automatically or may need to be handled explicitly, depending on the specific implementation.

Application mechanisms. Applications alone or with the aid of a separate authorization system can enforce authorization. Since the application has intimate knowledge of the resource being protected, application-based authorization offers the finest-grained authorization when used together with policies that can be customized to the application. Authorization criteria can take advantage of user, resource, and environmental attributes. The biggest disadvantage of this approach is that the application programmer, who is probably not well acquainted with the requirements of security programming, must implement security mechanisms. Another disadvantage is that the security for each application is usually implemented from scratch and does not take advantage of previous efforts.

The implementation of many of the techniques we have discussed in this chapter is the responsibility of the application. Document-oriented techniques must be exercised by applications. XML Signature and XML Encrypt are examples of security services explicitly invoked by applications. Since most options for passing initiator information require inserting information about the initiator in the SOAP message, the application or its agent is the most likely decision point for authorization of the initiator of request.

System Characteristics

Let's spend some time determining some of the authorization characteristics of this system.

What enforces the decision as to whether ePortal is permitted to make the SOAP request(s)?

Web Services architectures vary considerably. The Web server, the SOAP gateway that determines which application is actually invoked, the application system, and the application itself are potential candidates to make authorization decisions. But the granularity of the decision built into each component is different. While the Web server received the HTTP POST that delivered the SOAP request, the URL referenced may only allow coarse-grained authorization decisions.

The SOAP gateway or the application system is able to differentiate between specific applications referenced in the SOAP message. Therefore, it can authorize use of specific applications.

Finally, the application itself is able to exercise the finest granularity of control. However, while the other components can potentially perform authorization transparently, application-enforced security will usually require the inserting of code into the application. Initiator-based authorization, specifically making decisions based on the identity of the buyer being Joe, is application enforced. In addition, if encryption is used, the data must be available in decrypted form before any decision to authorize based on the encrypted data can be made.

While front-end components, such as the Web server, can be used to make some authorization decisions, since we have decided to use signatures and assertions, the application will need to be part of the authorization process.

What relevant attributes are established for the initiator by ePortal?

What attributes of the initiator will be useful to ePortal in making authorization decisions? Is the user a preferred customer? What is the user's customer ID number in eBuyer? eBuyer must be prepared to send this information to ePortal in some mutually agreed-to format.

In this example, the initiator, Joe, is a gold customer who is able to purchase up to $50,000 worth of merchandise.

What is the mapping of attributes in ePortal to eBusiness?

If the user is a preferred customer in eBuyer, what does that translate to in privileges at eBusiness? Does that mean that he/she is allowed to buy $100 worth of merchandise or $10,000 worth of merchandise? This translation will, in all likelihood, vary for each of the service provider's subscribers. This limit may also be different if eBuyer is the initiator rather than Joe. Again, this is a negotiated value and rules must be in place in ePortal to translate the preferred customer status to that of an initiator who is allowed to buy $50,000 of merchandise.

What granularity of authorization is needed and what attributes are needed to make this decision?

Is it sufficient to authorize the service subscriber to send a SOAP message or request the RPC, or is the authorization to perform some action on an instance of an object? As a rule of thumb, the finer the granularity, the closer to the application the authorization must be done. Ultimately, this means that some authorization decisions must be performed by the application, with or without the assistance of a separate authorization engine.

In our Web Services example, we must ensure that Joe is entitled to buy through ePortal. This is coarse-grained authorization and could be done by a Web server, assuming that the Web server receives the POST. We also need to ensure that Joe is entitled to purchase the quantity of merchandise specified. Is Joe a customer who is authorized to commit this amount of money? This is a fine-grained decision that is specific to this particular transaction. The attribute needed to make this decision is Joe's buying limit.

eBusiness Authorization

We'll now see how authorization for eBusiness can be conducted.

- ePortal wants to ensure that eBuyer is entitled to use the services it has requested.

eBuyer's signature on the message will authenticate it as the creator of the SOAP message. Message signatures must be handled explicitly by an application level function. The application must include code to parse the SOAP message, identify the signature, verify the signature, and verify that the signer is an entity authorized to send SOAP messages to ePortal. In addition to the signing code, this requires that eBusiness be part of some PKI so that it can be certain that the certificate is valid and hasn't been revoked. It must also verify that the signer of ePortal's certificate is trusted to vouch for ePortal's public key. Lastly, the application must either maintain a list for itself of ePortal's privileges or use some authorization engine to render the final decision as to whether eBuyer is entitled to issue this message.

eBusiness wants to ensure that the initiator is entitled to request the services on the information. eBusiness must extract the SAML assertion from the SOAP header. The assertion includes information about the initiator's authentication at ePortal or its attributes at ePortal. The specific contents are determined by negotiations between ePortal and eBusiness. The assertion itself may be signed. In which case, the signature on the assertion and the certificate of the signer need to be verified. If the assertion is an authentication assertion, we will assume that the authorization decision is based on the initiator's identity. If there are attributes, then the authorization will be based on the initiator's attributes. As with verifying ePortal's authorization, Joe's authorization will be performed by application layer software. This software will determine whether Joe's attributes in ePortal need to be converted to attributes meaningful to eBusiness. We know that as a gold customer in ePortal, Joe will need a purchasing limit of $50,000. Finally, with the help of some authorization engine, the application will decide if Joe is authorized to make the purchase.

Summary

Web Services are new, and there are very few solid guidelines concerning security. Best practice has not been determined. The other complicating factor is that there are so many different ways Web Services can be implemented that it is difficult to identify common patterns to use to formulate guidelines for security. What we've tried to do is explain how to analyze specific Web Services security needs and determine how to address those needs.

In this chapter, we've identified three critical aspects of securing Web Services: authentication, message protection, and authorization. We discussed specific requirements for each, solutions that can address the requirements, factors affecting the choice of a solution, and the proposed security solution for ePortal and eBusiness.

In many cases, we decided to utilize document-oriented solutions. This was because they are tailored to XML documents and offer the most flexibility. However, a connection-oriented technique such as SSL is widely implemented and can be utilized easily. It should be given very serious consideration before another approach is adopted.

While we analyzed technical solutions, the reader should be aware that understanding business practice is critical to securing Web Services. The service provider and the service subscriber must agree on the relationship of various entities to the Web Services transaction, how each entity can be authenticated, how needed security information is passed between the two, the meanings of any digital signatures, if any, and other relationships.

The next two chapters on .NET and J2EE describe how to use some specific technologies to implement the measures discussed in this chapter.

CHAPTER

7

Security of Infrastructures for Web Services

Middleware technologies are the software foundation of modern enterprise computing systems, which process the requests coming through Web Services gateways. Understanding the middleware security mechanisms that are available to you is the first step toward achieving end-to-end security for applications exposed as Web Services. This chapter covers the security mechanisms in the mainstream middleware technologies: Common Object Request Broker Architecture (CORBA), Component Object Model (COM+), .NET, and Java 2 Platform, Enterprise Edition (J2EE). If you are already familiar with middleware security, just skim through and move on to the next chapter.

We recommend that you read the entire chapter to understand the security mechanisms of other technologies. However, if you only use one technology, such as J2EE, or combine only a few distinct yet similar technologies, such as COM+ and .NET, feel free to skip the other technologies in this chapter—but focus on understanding the security of what you have. You should have a general understanding of the fundamentals of computer security before you tackle this chapter. For a good introduction to this subject, we suggest: Amoroso (1994), Golmann (1999), and Russel (1991).

We will start with the main concepts of distributed system security and introduce you to necessary and common terms. This should give you a good basis with which to approach the security of any middleware technology, as well as what you need to identify the similarities and differences between the security mechanisms of CORBA, COM+, .NET, and J2EE. Describing all the features of each of these modern and complex technologies would take multiple volumes. To avoid overwhelming you with huge amounts of information, we focus on the material essential for understanding the rest of the book. If you would like to master any of these technologies further, or need answers to some specific questions, we have also provided an extensive list of references.

We have derived some of the material in this chapter—particularly information on the security of EJB and CORBA, as well as CSIv2, delegation, and security policy domains—from our previous book, *Enterprise Security with EJB and CORBA* (Hartman et al 2001). Please refer to that text for more details on these topics.

Distributed Security Fundamentals

If you survey a selection of middleware technologies, you will find that there are many similarities, such as groups, roles, and other user attributes, as well as unique functions or features, such as CORBA's required rights. Other functions or features, such as EJB method-permissions and .NET principal permission attributes, may appear different but are really different terms with similar meanings. Yet, there are also terms that look misleadingly similar, such as the principal in JAAS and DCOM+, but that have very different semantics. This section begins by defining the elements and principles of middleware security in technology-neutral terms. Later sections will describe how these basic concepts are instantiated in concrete technologies. But first, let's cover the basic terms.

Security and the Client/Server Paradigm

The dominant feature of most commercial distributed systems today is the client/server paradigm, which is the foundation for the remote procedure call (RPC) model that allows a client program to send a procedure call request to a target server. In each interaction, a client initiates the request, and a server receives and processes the request. Take a look at Figure 7.1, which illustrates the client/server and RPC models. Client A sends a request to server B, which sends a response back to A. A acts as a client and B only as a server.

Does this scheme seem to be too simple? Let's look at the same figure from the security perspective, using the computer security terminology with which you are already familiar. Server B might want to control whether or not it processes requests from client A—the concept of *access control*. To do so, B needs to know whom a request comes from, which requires *request authentication*. Client A, in its turn, might decide whether or not to send requests to and receive responses from B—the concept of *trust*, which in its turn requires the ability to know who a response comes from—*response authentication*. A or B might want to make sure that, while in transit, their requests and responses are not modified by anybody unauthorized to do so—*integrity protection*—or eavesdropped upon—*confidentiality protection*. B might want to hold A accountable for making requests because, for instance, B wants A to pay for the service it provides to A—a security functionality known as *accountability*. The latter can be implemented in a weak form of *security audit*, which is usually used also for monitoring system security health and for detecting intrusions. Accountability can also be implemented in the form of *nonrepudiation* evidence that can be taken to court to prove that a request (and response) did take place.[1] As you have probably realized, even in this simple client/server interaction, security adds quite a bit of complexity.

[1] The digital forms of nonrepudiation available today are still very difficult to use as legal evidence (at least in the U.S.). In addition, a full implementation of a nonrepudiation service is generally too expensive to be justifiable for the overwhelming majority of commercial companies.

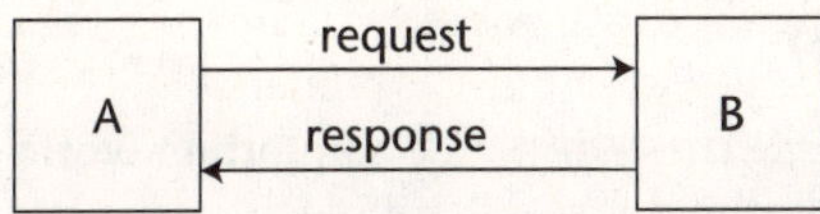

Figure 7.1 Basic client/server paradigm and RPC model.

Keep in mind that the relationship between a client and server is always associated with a particular invocation. For example, in Figure 7.2, B acts as a server when it is invoked by A, and as a client when it invokes C. If B invokes C while processing the request from A, it demonstrates a *request propagation*—a request travels from A to B and then, possibly changed, to C. This is also referred to as an *invocation chain*, in which B acts as an *intermediate*, as opposed to C, a *target*.

Invocation chains introduce new aspects to the security of distributed systems and make the security picture much more complex. If B invokes C while processing a request from A, several questions arise. First, should B use its own identity, and the accompanying attributes, when it calls C? Or should it use A's, so that C believes it received a request from A? *Credentials delegation* takes different forms, from a very simple *impersonation*, in which C does not even know that the request is actually from B, to very complex *composite delegation*, in which C knows the credentials of all the intermediates through which the invocation was propagated. In the case of composite delegation, C's access control and other security policies become significantly more complex to accommodate *compound principals*. Second, should A trust B to use A's credentials to call others? Some middleware security models give A this level of control over whom B can call on behalf of A, which is known as *constrained delegation*.

Some RPC models support "fire-and-forget" invocations—for example, in Figure 7.2, if B sends a request to C, and no response is sent back. One example is CORBA's one-way functions, whereby the client does not expect any response from the server and is not even guaranteed that its request will be processed at all. This is also the case for the world of SOAP-based Web Services, where, if a method does not return anything, no response message is sent to the client.

NOTE If you want to learn more about client/server computing, we recommend *Client/Server Survival Guide, Third Edition,* by Robert Orfali, Dan Harkey, and Jeri Edwards (Orfali 1999)—a fun-to-read and very comprehensive introductory book.

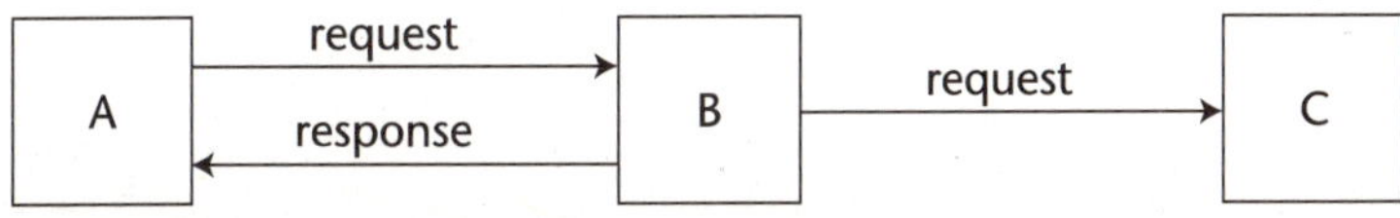

Figure 7.2 Propagated and "fire-and-forget" invocations.

Security and the Object Paradigm

CORBA, COM+, .NET, and J2EE are all *object-based*. These days, the computing world takes for granted that any modern computational technology—distributed or not—has inherent support for objects. For the purposes of this section, we assume that you have a good grasp of objects, and are familiar with terms such as "class," "method," "encapsulation," "polymorphism," and "inheritance." For a good book on the basics of objects, we recommend Taylor (1997).

When you add objects to a client/server computing model, there are significant effects on the overall security infrastructure of your enterprise. Objects tend to be of fine granularity, that is, they encapsulate small amounts of data and provide diverse methods to manipulate that data. Object-based systems usually have many more objects of many different varieties, increasing the number of resources in your systems that you need to protect, compared to conventional, procedural systems. The number of resource-operation pairs also skyrockets even higher.

An object-based security architecture must support large numbers of protected resources. Traditionally, this has been done via resource groupings. Objects are grouped, and policies are defined on those groups. Objects with similar names, or those that reside in the same location, should not be required to belong to the same group, since policies do not necessarily follow your application's topology or naming organization. The same is true for objects to be assigned to the same group; name similarity and co-location should not be required for being governed by similar policies.

There are also transient and short-lived objects, such as those implementing shopping carts in the ePortal example used throughout this book. Such objects are likely to be nameless and created without administrator's control. Manually assigning transient objects to security policies would be unrealistic.

In addition, object-based systems tend to have less rigid naming hierarchies, and the naming mechanism may allow an object to have more than one name. Also a concern is the object identity in some systems, in which two opaque object references may be reused by middleware, making it difficult to determine if the objects they point to are different or the same. Whatever middleware security architecture is in place, it must allow security administrators to define security policies without assuming that they know the name of every object in the system. Even if an object has more than one name, the same policy should be applied to it no matter what name is used.

Of additional security concern is that the methods on objects are no longer limited to just two or three universal "read," "write," and "delete" operations. The methods could be very complex and potentially involve many diverse activities. Consequently, security administrators should not have to understand the semantics of the methods on objects to secure them.

Due to encapsulation and other advanced techniques—such as dynamic binding and on-demand reincarnation of object implementations—that make large distributed systems scalable and simpler to design, it is difficult to understand which actual resources are manipulated behind an object interface. While the job of client developers is simplified by using objects, the encapsulation makes it difficult to determine which security policies should govern access to which application objects. The security architecture of object-based systems must also have some mechanisms in place that help with this problem.

Bob Blakley (1999) has a good introductory chapter on object security, which provides some additional information on this topic.

What All Middleware Security Is About

The next sections will describe the four middleware security technologies individually, how they implement the security functionalities for client/server systems, and how they address the requirements specific to object-based systems. To unify this discussion, we treat every technology described as an instance of the same scheme. No matter if it is .NET or Java, COM+ or CORBA, each middleware technology reduces to this one scheme, shown in Figure 7.3, which we put together to help you understand the general concepts.

NOTE Because applications written for COM and COM+ have a lot in common, we will refer to COM and/or COM+ v1.0 as COM(+) when we do not need to distinguish between the two.

In the list below, we explain the levels of the middleware stack as depicted in Figure 7.3:

Client application. Makes RPC-like calls to the server. Because of the abstraction provided by the proxy of the server object, the client application does not have to be aware of any layers below the proxy.[2]

Server application. Receives RPC calls, serves them, and returns replies.

Application server. The runtime environment that provides important services to the critical high-performance and high-scale business applications. Its presence in the stack distinguishes CORBA component model (CCM) from plain CORBA, COM+ from COM, and J2EE from Java 2 Platform, Standard Edition (J2SE). If you have ever tried to implement a business application using plain COM, Java, or CORBA, you are familiar with how much you need to do to manage the object life cycle, engage in distributed transactions, and implement load balancing and fault tolerance. The application server layer handles those functions in CCM, COM+, and J2EE. Due to its complexity, the layer is often tightly integrated with the ORB and object adapters (defined below) and therefore comes bundled with them.

Proxy. A local implementation of the remote server object on the client. It isolates the application from all the details and complexities of the RPC implementation by realizing syntactically the same interface as the object on the target. A proxy marshals requests to and unmarshals responses from the server, and could perform some other housekeeping work. A client must have a proxy for each interface it uses on the server. Proxies are usually compiled out of the interface descriptions. These are interface definition language (IDL) files in COM(+) and

[2] Technically, the application code has to perform some steps to initialize the middleware layer: via CoInitialize call and its friends in COM(+), and ORB.init() in CORBA. We omit such details to keep the discussion at the higher abstraction layer for now.

CORBA, WSDL files in Web Services, files with Java interfaces extending EJBObject in J2EE, and "remoted" class files in .NET.

Skeleton. The server's counterpart of the proxy. Also created from the interface definition, a skeleton performs marshaling/unmarshaling of the call parameters and return values, and hides specifics of the particular ORB implementation.

Object adapter. Sits on top of the object request broker (ORB) and accepts requests on behalf of the server's objects. It provides the runtime environment for instantiating server objects, passing requests to them, and assigning the object IDs, called *object references*. The object adapter also registers object implementations with the ORB and, sometimes, with the implementation repository, so that the server objects can be discovered at run time. Not all middleware technologies (for example, COM(+)) distinguish object adapters from their ORBs, although the adapters are still there.

Object request broker (ORB). Constitutes the core of the middleware layer and implements most of the plumbing, including composition of the messages given to the network layer for sending, determining where to send messages based on the object reference, establishing virtual (session) channels with other ORBs, and dispatching requests to the server objects. An ORB could be implemented just as a library (like most CORBA ORBs), or could be a set of system services (as in COM+). It cooperates with various services, such as naming, fault tolerance, transactions, and load balancing, to make the life of clients and servers easier. In this discussion, we concentrate on the security service.

Security service. Often tightly integrated with the ORB, the service intercepts the client's and server's interactions to enforce various security policies. Some of them, such as access control, have request granularity and therefore are enforced by *request security interceptors*. Other policies, such as integrity and confidentiality protection, are commonly enforced by *message security interceptors*.

Security mechanism implementation. An implementation of generic network security technology such as Kerberos, NTLM, SSL, or IPSEC. By and large realized as a set of libraries, a security mechanism implementation generates session keys and performs authentication, encryption/decryption, data signing, and validation.

OS and network layers. Perform their usual roles of transmitting the actual messages between client and server.

Figure 7.3 is an adequate abstraction of the middleware security, although it is not always completely accurate. For example, it shows all the elements in one elegant stack, whereas this is not the case in real situations; the ORB, security service, and security mechanism layers have a more complex interaction topology, and most elements in the figure interact with the OS. Some applications, due to their security requirements, could also call the ORB security service and even the security mechanism directly. Nonetheless, keep this figure in mind when you read about the implementation of client and server security services and the secure channels connecting them.

The client and server security services and mechanisms, in cooperation with their ORBs, are the basis for three abstractions very useful for reasoning about distributed systems' security: client security service, secure channel, and target security service. We will explain them next.

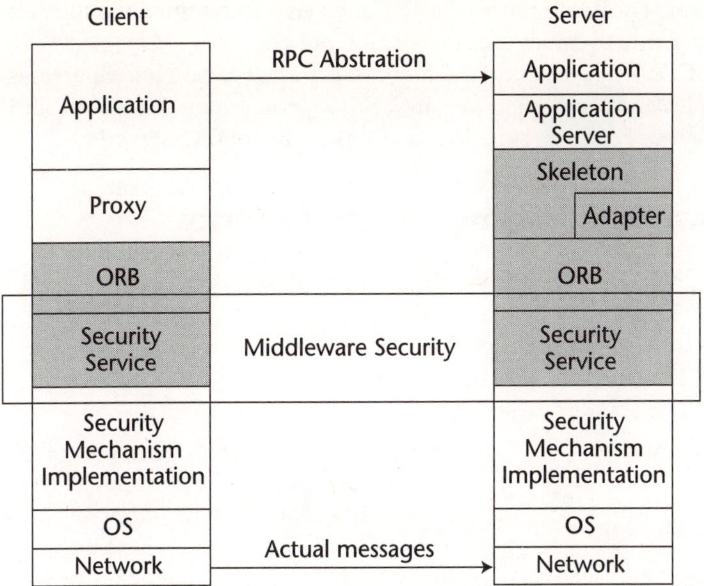

Figure 7.3 Security stack of middleware-based distributed applications.

Roles and Responsibilities of CSS, TSS, and Secure Channel

The security structure of most distributed systems that are based on the client/server paradigm is composed of a *client security service* (CSS) and a *target security service* (TSS), which are connected by one or more secure channels. Their roles are based on the security requirements for client/server systems (discussed in the previous section, *Security and the Client/Server Paradigm*). As we discuss what's expected from these three elements, keep the generic scheme for middleware security from Figure 7.3 in mind.

To enforce client security policies, a CSS should be able to establish and maintain secure channels with TSSs and enforce client-side trust, message confidentiality, and integrity, as well as delegation control and audit policies. To perform these tasks, a CSS relies on client application authentication to obtain the credentials used to represent the principal on behalf of whom requests on the server are made. To enforce trust and delegation control policies, a CSS also needs to authenticate the target. Once a CSS and TSS have authenticated each other, both can negotiate the level of channel protection.

A *secure channel* is a useful abstraction that encompasses the functionality necessary for message confidentiality, integrity, and authenticity protection. To retain a channel's state, CSS and TSS must establish and maintain a security association. The security association establishes the trust in each party's credentials and creates the security context that will be used when protecting requests and responses in transit between the client and the target.

TSS responsibilities are similar to those of a CSS and have an additional obligation to enforce access control and, possibly, nonrepudiation policies.

Although CORBA, COM+, .NET, and J2EE all have different security architectures, they implement the roles and responsibilities of CSS, TSS, and secure channel in similar ways. We describe these common security functions in the following section.

How Middleware Systems Implement Security

The main distributed security functionalities are:

- Authentication
- Message protection
- Access control
- Audit
- Delegation
- Trust
- Administration of all the above

Even though some of these functions are more critical than others, it is important to employ all of them to implement a complete security solution for your system.

Distributed Authentication

Authentication is mainly used by middleware security services to verify the origins of incoming requests and responses. Acting on behalf of the principals, CSS and TSS first authenticate each other using the credentials of the principals (on behalf of which they participate in the exchange of application messages), generate a channel-specific session key, and use it to encrypt the traffic through the channel. Therefore, the messages comprising requests and responses received from the channel are authenticated by the virtue of being encrypted with the session key. Although, strictly speaking, there are multiple principals involved on each side (the channel, the host, the OS, the ORB, the application, and the user—if any—using the application) and there are even theories of principal calculus (Abadi 1991; Lampson 1991), in practice, those who use the corresponding entities assume that everything but the applications and their users can be trusted. This assumption, though not always justifiable, allows significant simplifications of the administration of access control and other policies that rely on authentication, and of the authentication protocols themselves.

Authentication Protocols

Authentication in a distributed system environment is performed using an authentication protocol, which consists of cryptographic computations and a message exchange protocol. All authentication protocols can be classified according to the cryptosystem they use. Since most popular cryptosystems today are either symmetric (secret key only) or asymmetric (private and public keys), the authentication protocols also fall in one of the two groups. We described symmetric and asymmetric authentication protocols in detail in Chapter 3, "Getting Started with Web Services Security."

NOTE Surprisingly, the authentication of most of today's commercially distributed systems still relies on sending a plain username and password to the server, possibly using secure channels or hashing the password with a digest algorithm.

To perform authentication, a CSS and TSS first need to determine the authentication protocol to be used. The next section briefly describes available methods.

Choosing an Authentication Protocol

There are commonly two ways to determine which protocol and its parameters should be used for authenticating a CSS and TSS to each other. One way is for the TSS to advertise the protocols it wants to use. The other is to employ a special negotiation phase when establishing a secure channel. A customary place for the information about supported authentication protocols is the target's object reference. Despite being inherently insecure, an object reference is considered an adequate solution for most systems.

NOTE Those security service implementations that employ the Simple Authentication and Security Layer (SASL) protocol (IETF 1997b) specify the type of authentication mechanism they support. This means that the client and server can be configured to negotiate and use one of the standard or customized mechanisms for authentication, depending on the level of protection desired by the client and the server.

SASL supports the Generic Security Service (GSS) API, which is a popular programming interface that supports many different authentication protocols. Another method of negotiating a GSS-API-based authentication protocol is to use Simple and Protected GSS-API Negotiation Mechanism (SPNEGO) (IETF 1998). This standard negotiation protocol enables GSS-API peers to determine in-band whether their credentials share common GSS-API security mechanism(s), and, if so, to invoke normal security context establishment for the selected mechanism. The protocol allows negotiating different security mechanisms, different options within a given security mechanism, or different options from several security mechanisms. Once identified, the security mechanism may also negotiate mechanism-specific options during its context establishment.

Message Protection

Once CSS and TSS authenticate each other, they can establish a shared secret session key to be used for verifying message origin authenticity and protecting the integrity and confidentiality of the messages. Using the same principle as in the symmetric key authentication protocols, the sender encrypts the message and the receiver decrypts it with the session key generated as a result of their mutual authentication and known only to them. This ensures that the message was sent by the other peer, a property known as *message origin authenticity.*

Encrypting messages using the session key also provides *message confidentiality* protection (secrecy). *Message integrity* is commonly protected by tagging a key-dependent message authentication code (MAC) onto a message before it is sent. Upon receipt, the MAC is recomputed and compared with the one attached to determine if the message has been altered in transit.

All three protections do not have to be enforced on all messages flowing between a CSS and TSS. Some objects on a TSS might not require protection for the messages comprising requests and responses for those objects. Some might require only message authenticity. Message protection enforced on each side is governed by the corresponding policies. Who defines those policies depends on the capabilities of a particular middleware security technology. Generally speaking, there are several stakeholders who define message protection policies: object owners, system owners, and principals (users). Object owners decide what protection they need for the information supplied to and sent back from the methods on their objects. System owners mandate the protection policy for the messages flowing back and forth from their systems. Principals interacting with remote objects decide what is an acceptable protection level for the information they send to and receive from the servers. Therefore a CSS and TSS need to determine message protection policies for each stakeholder and determine the level that satisfies all parties.

In this and the previous sections, we discussed CSS and TSS authentication and protection of the messages flowing between them. The next important element of secure middleware-based computing is controlling access to the server objects.

Distributed Access Control

Access control in middleware consists of two functions: (1) the TSS making an access decision and (2) enforcing it. See Figure 7.4. The enforcement part is fairly easy since the ORB gives the TSS an opportunity to intercept an invocation and enforce the policies. The hard part here is the access control decision (authorization). Authorizations are challenging because they have to be quick to reduce security-related overhead, but depending on the authorization policies and the number of objects in the application system, the decision process can be quite complex.

First, we need to figure out what policies should govern authorization decisions for the request in question. Since the policies are needed for message protection, auditing, and other security functionalities, this task is not as trivial as it might sound. The reason is that objects are often organized into groups, each protected by a distinct policy, to achieve scalability in middleware object-based systems. The groups are then organized in complex relations so that large numbers of objects with similar security requirements can be governed by a few base policies. Policies for objects with peculiar requirements could be obtained through some composition of the policies according to the group relations. An example of such relations is the use of hierarchies, where each node is associated with a policy and leaves in the hierarchy are objects "hanging off" the nodes. This object hierarchy approach allows you to impose base policies near the hierarchy root and to fine-tune the protection of some objects located down the tree. A simple example illustrating object hierarchies is shown in Figure 7.5.

Besides the difficulty of determining policies due to the scale, as you remember from the section on the object paradigm, some objects may have many names and some may be anonymous, making it difficult to identify what group(s) they belong to. Additionally, object encapsulation and method semantic complexity make objects and their methods opaque to the outside world (at least to the poor security administrators), which then means that an extra level of indirection is required to compute those attributes of objects and methods that can be used for calculating applicable policies. Every middleware security technology described in this chapter categorizes methods into related groups in some way. We will discuss the techniques for determining object group membership and method categorization for each technology.

Then, various policies governing access to the object's method might have to be composed into one "ultimate" policy that is evaluated to come up with a final access decision. The composition may not be trivial since the policies could contradict each other, with one policy granting and the other denying access. Consequently a "metapolicy", which is a policy about composing policies, is required to resolve the conflicts. How a resulting policy is computed depends on the semantics of the relation and varies from technology to technology. For some, more specific policies take higher priority. For others, all policies are compiled into a list and those at the top of the list take precedence over later ones. There are other strategies as well.

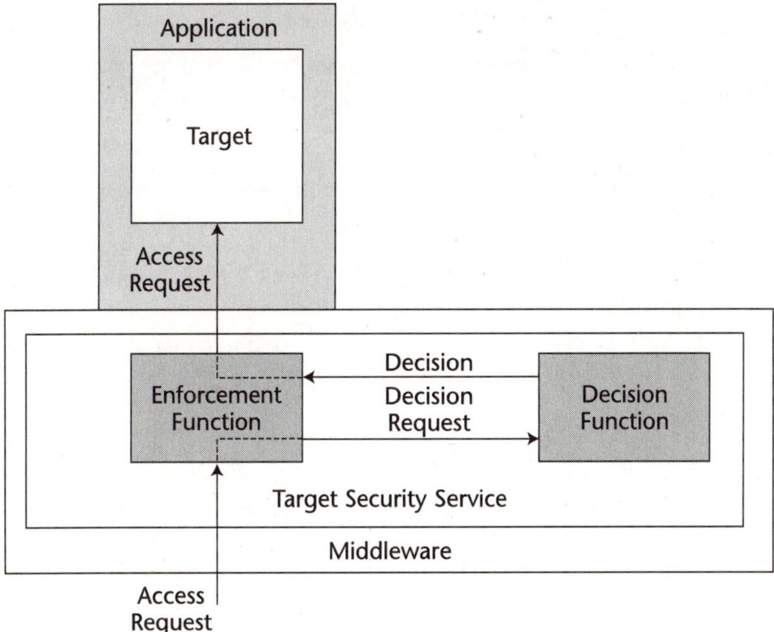

Figure 7.4 Access control is a combination of decision and enforcement functions.

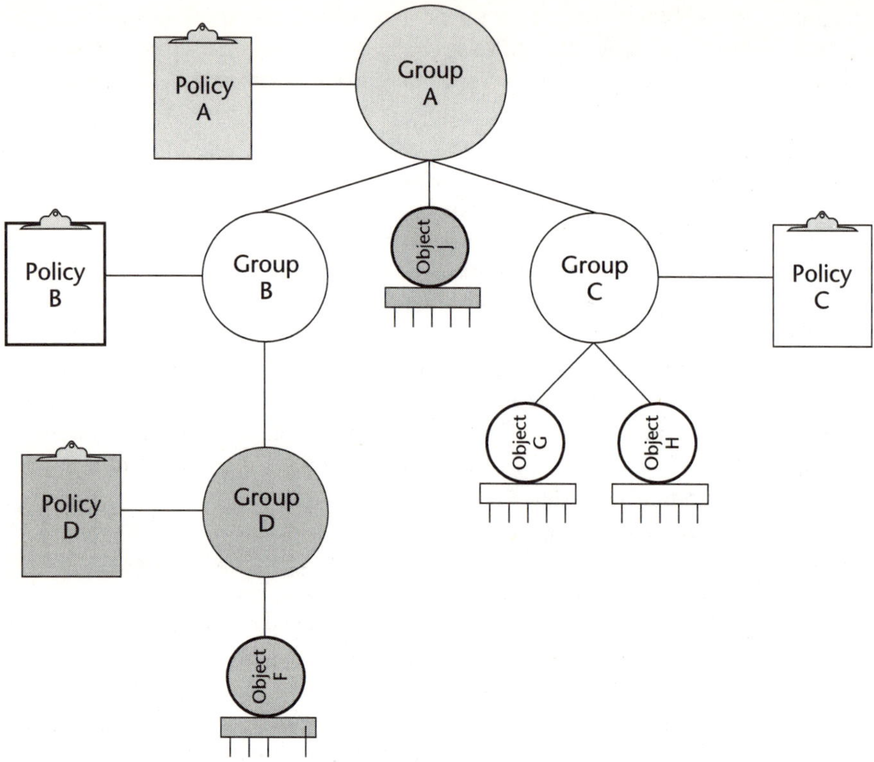

Figure 7.5 Sample hierarchy of object groups.

Most practical security policies consist of statements that either grant or deny access. The statements usually contain references to one or more of the following:

- *Subject attributes* such as groups, identity, roles, and clearance, age, location
- *Resource attributes* such as name, the owner identity, security label, location
- *Operation* on the resource
- *Environmental information* such as time of day, day of week, global state (for example, emergency, under terrorist attack)
- *History information,* such as how many times the principal has accessed the resource before
- *Request information,* such as the level of the channel protection through which the request came and through which the response will be sent back
- *Obligations* that specify additional conditions to be satisfied before access is granted, such as an agreement to be signed by the end user, auditing the transaction, or availability of funds.

These references need to be resolved before their values can be used in policy evaluation. The CSS and TSS gather the values in two ways:

Push model. In this mechanism, information is "pushed" to the TSS although it was not requested. For instance, the CSS may send an access request including the subject attributes as well as the operation name to the TSS.

Pull model. Not all information can be obtained by the CSS beforehand, due to, for example, the cost associated with retrieving it, the inability to do so, or even the low trust that the TSS has in client-provided information. In this situation, a pull model becomes indispensable. The TSS will need to request this security information to have it "pulled" from a security policy server.

Some information, such as environmental data, is better to "pull." At the same time, one can find a combination of push and pull models for a principal or resource attributes. A good example of mixing the push and pull models is the Dynamic Attribute Service (DAS) object in the Resource Access Decision (RAD) architecture (Hartman et al 2001). With RAD, before an access request is dispatched to the policy engines, all principal attributes pushed with the access request are sent to a DAS along with the resource name. The DAS could "pull" additional attributes, which are specific to the access request in question, and add them to the "pushed" ones. It could even replace "pushed" attributes with "pulled" or even drop some, depending on the governing logic.

Since access control plays a key role in both middleware and Web Services security, we devote a significant amount of material to the subject in this chapter and several others.

Distributed Auditing

For any distributed computer system, the purpose of security auditing is to provide support for:

Accountability. That is, holding users of a distributed system accountable for their actions

Detection of security policy violations. That is, the detection of attempts by unauthorized individuals to access the system and by authorized users to misuse their access to the system

Security auditing is usually implemented by means of an audit service called by the security, OS, and application layers. The audit records are created and collected by the service in a repository called an audit log. The audit log may be used to re-create a global picture of the security-related activities in the system and reveal which users performed which activities. Analysis of this picture, either in real time or after the fact, permits security administrators and auditors to detect violations of security policies or to make system users accountable for their actions.

Many components of distributed systems now include some form of security-auditing or event-logging capability, used by applications and middleware to record security-relevant events. These services are provided via component-specific interfaces and use component-specific audit record formats.

The distributed nature of middleware systems makes security auditing a more challenging task because of the following related factors:

- Within distributed systems, security-relevant activity is not isolated within individual components but spans many components. For example, intrusion attempts may be made via multiple entry points rather than a single point of entry. It is therefore necessary to monitor activity across and between distributed components. As a result, audit records from the components need to be stored in a central place to re-create the state of the whole system and see what happened to it.
- It is difficult to maintain global time across distributed components. The order of the audit records in the central log, and even their timestamps, do not necessarily reflect the order of the events captured in those records.
- Since audit records are sent over the network to a central place, it might take a while before the recording is completed. Synchronous audit calls are usually prohibitively expensive from a performance point of view. To remedy this, modern distributed audit techniques employ store-and-forward solutions and allow asynchronous calls to an audit service.
- The lack of guarantees that an event has been logged in the audit repository potentially exposes a system to intrusion attacks. The system could be attacked, but the corresponding audit records may not be logged because the attacker shut down the audit service during the first phase of the intrusion.

Another challenge for security auditing in today's object-based middleware systems is due to the fine-grained nature of the resources and operations on them. Because there are many more methods invoked during each transaction, the amount of collected audit records is increased significantly. This makes the audit log far more difficult for security administrators to understand. For that reason, selective use of audited events becomes critical and deserves a security *audit policy*, which specifies which events in what circumstances should be recorded in the audit log. Audit policies are commonly encapsulated into *audit decision objects* that decide if a given event should be audited.

When we describe the security of the four middleware technologies later in the chapter, we will explain how they implement audit channels, what audit policies they support, and how the policies can be queried via audit decision objects.

Distributed Delegation

As we described earlier in our section, *Security and the Client/Server Paradigm*, there are situations in which it is necessary for an intermediate object to use the attributes of the initiating client in a chain of invocations on objects. These situations call for delegation, which allows an intermediate object to act on a principal's behalf.

Strictly speaking, there are two commonly used meanings for "delegation" in the context of distributed applications. One is the delegation of *privileges* (responsibility) from one person to another. The second is the delegation of *credentials* in a security context from one application to another.

Delegation of privileges from one person to another is a common security requirement, but it is not itself a security service. Delegation of credentials in a security context, which is the focus of this section, is a security service that is supported by the CSS and TSS.

To implement delegation of privileges from one person to another, a developer could use delegation of credentials, but this is unusual. Typically, delegation between people is accomplished by granting one person a privilege (for example, "I grant John Smith the privilege of security officer for the next week"). This approach only requires that the user's security profile be updated via the security administration service; it does *not* require the use of delegation of credentials between applications.

Delegation of credentials defines how a principal's security attributes are transmitted to other objects to allow them to act on the principal's behalf. It is of particular relevance in distributed object systems. Since an object invocation frequently results in a whole chain of calls on other objects, it is common for a target object in the call chain to use the client's privileges, which allows the target object to pass the access control checks and perform an operation on behalf of the client. See Figure 7.6.

As illustrated in Figure 7.6, when an intermediate object receives a client request, it also receives credentials for the client, which are known as *received credentials*. The TSS uses the received credentials for making access control decisions to determine if the client is allowed to call the intermediate. The intermediate object also has its *own credentials*, which contain the intermediate's own security attributes for use when the intermediate acts as a client. When the intermediate then calls the next target, it makes use of *invocation credentials*, which consist of its own and received credentials. The composition of the invocation credentials depends on the type of the credential delegation implemented by the middleware technology and the delegation policy that governs the invocation chains in your system.

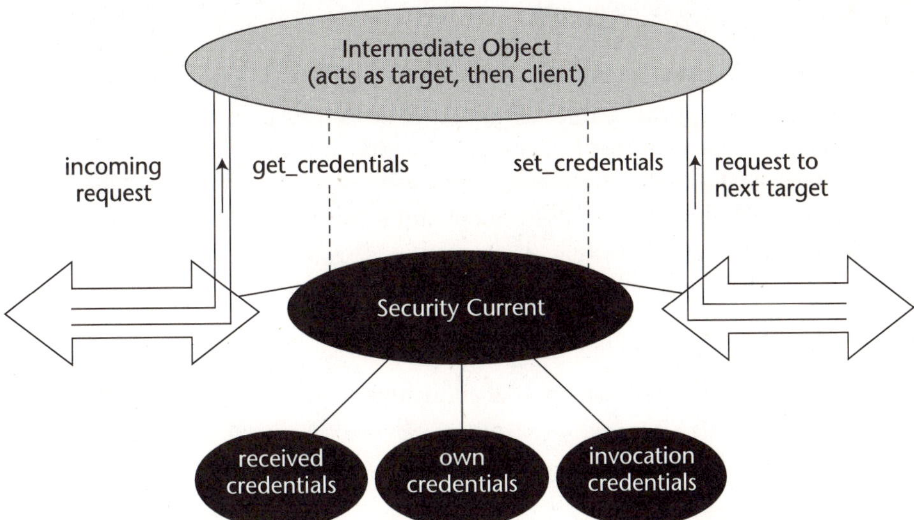

Figure 7.6 Use of credentials by intermediate objects during delegation.

Motivations for Using Delegation

One reason to use delegation of credentials is to preserve accountability. Allowing the initiator's credentials to propagate through the middle-tier components enables the final target application (typically a back-end system) to learn the true identity of the original requester. Without delegation, the target application only learns the identity of an intermediate component application. Thus, delegation allows authorization or auditing to be performed based on the original requester rather than an intermediate application.

A second reason to use delegation is to allow an intermediate application's credentials to be set at run time. It allows an initiator's credentials to be dynamically assigned to the intermediate application so that the intermediate may access a resource on behalf of the client. Delegation of security context provides the intermediate application with great flexibility because the intermediate can access resources on behalf of clients unknown in advance.

Levels of Delegation

Most middleware security technologies support one or more of the following options (illustrated in Figure 7.7) for delegating credentials to other objects:

No delegation. The client does not permit its credentials to be delegated to another object. Thus, the intermediate's invocation credentials are always the same as its own credentials.

Simple delegation. The client permits an intermediate object to assume the client's credentials and pass them on or delegate them in subsequent invocations, allowing the intermediate to access objects using the client's credentials. In this case, the intermediate's invocation credentials are the same as the ones it received from the client. There are two variations of simple delegation:

> **Controlled (constrained or restricted) delegation.** The client restricts the intermediate object's use of the credentials (that is, it controls which privileges are delegated or which objects may use the privileges).
>
> **Impersonation (unconstrained or unrestricted delegation).** The client passes the credential to an intermediate object with no controls. In this case, a subsequent target cannot distinguish between an invocation from the original client and a delegated invocation from the intermediate.

Composite delegation. The client permits the intermediate object to use the client's credentials as in simple delegation, but both the client's (that is, received) and the intermediate's (that is, own) credentials are passed in subsequent invocations, allowing for access checks based on both sets of credentials.

Traced delegation. The credentials of all the intermediates as well as the initiator's are passed.

The initiator can use different credentials when it is accessing a target directly and when its credentials are delegated to an intermediate. Thus, the initiator may limit the use of credentials when they are delegated, reducing the privileges an intermediate can use when acting on the initiator's behalf.

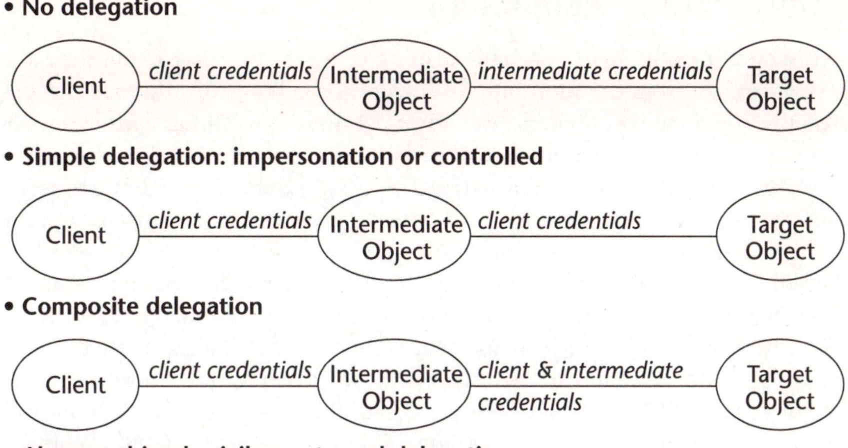

Figure 7.7 Delegation options.

Delegation can be harmful to your system's security. On the other hand, in almost all complex systems, delegation is either needed or very difficult to replace with an alternate solution. In later sections, we will describe the supported delegation options for each of the middleware security technologies.

> **DIFFERENCES IN TERMINOLOGY**
>
> **Please keep in mind that different technologies use inconsistent delegation terms, and there is no universally accepted definition of delegation. Since this book needs to define these terms in a uniform way across a variety of technologies, we use the definitions from the CORBA Security specification, which is one of the few standard definitions that we are aware of. We use the terms consistently across all chapters in this book for both Microsoft and Java technologies.**
>
> **There are major differences between our definitions for delegation and impersonation and the definitions used by Microsoft. In particular, in the Microsoft world impersonation refers to what we describe in this book as simple delegation constrained to a local resource. That is, in Microsoft literature, if a server "impersonates" the client, the server can access local resources on the client's behalf. The ability for a server to access resources on remote machines on behalf of the client is referred to in Microsoft literature as delegation. Note that in this book, we describe this as simple unconstrained delegation, which we also refer to as impersonation. The inconsistent and confusing use of these terms by different technologies reflect the inherent complexity of the problem.**

Distributed Security Administration

No matter how good the security mechanisms of a middleware system are, they are useless if you cannot properly configure and administer them to implement your organizational security policies. Inadequate administrative capabilities cause the cost of ownership of any distributed application to skyrocket, and also result in a proliferation of security breaches due to human errors. This is why for each middleware security technology described in this chapter, we explain provisions for configuring and administering available security mechanisms.

Independent of technology type, security mechanisms are configured and administered through changes to *security policies*. The policies could be presented to the administrators and application deployers as textual configuration files that drive corresponding security mechanisms, as GUI windows that provide more restricted interface to the files, as APIs, or as any combination of the three. Next, we will discuss the administrative capabilities of the middleware security—that is, what organizational security policies you can express and how difficult it is to do so.

Security policies are commonly categorized according to the types of security mechanisms:

- *Authentication policies* define which authentication protocols should be employed with which particular parameters to authenticate principals.
- *User attribute assignment policies* govern the security attributes that are assigned to authenticated users.
- *Message protection policies* govern authenticity, confidentiality, and integrity protection of the messages traveling between system components.
- *Authorization policies* are responsible for defining which principals have access to a particular resource in the distributed application. Authorization policies are usually structured according to one or more access control models, such as military clearance/label based, discretionary owner based, role based, identity and group based, and so on.
- *Audit policies* determine which events must be recorded in the audit log under what circumstances.
- *Credentials delegation policies* specify how intermediates use received credentials for making downstream calls and accessing other resources on behalf of the client's principal.

Although one language and data model could possibly be used for all types of security policies, it is common practice to have specific ones for each type of security function. For that reason, we will explain each type of security functionality, along with the corresponding policy capabilities, when describing security technologies.

It is hard to imagine having one global policy that would effectively govern access to all resources in a large enterprise. Most of the time, security requirements are so diverse within an enterprise that different policies are needed. It is next to impossible to keep a variety of security policies consistent if the only way to configure them is on an object-by-object or some other small-scale basis. Therefore, the means of administering the security of your distributed applications should scale with the number of resources, the number of users, and the number of resource locations.

A common way to achieve security administration scalability is to introduce an additional level of indirection via *policy domains*, or just *domains* for short. With domains, enterprise resources and users can be partitioned into groups containing elements of similar security requirements. Policies can then be assigned to the domains instead of directly to the resources and users. Policy domains (1) facilitate administration and protection of resources with similar security requirements, (2) help to achieve scale in distributed applications, and (3) enable delegated administration, where local security administrators, as opposed to central ones, administer local resources and users.

Depending on the particular model for policy domains supported by a given technology, domains could be completely disjointed, have hierarchical relationships, or have more complex relationships. Domain boundaries for policies of different types could coincide or be independent. For example, there could be only one authentication policy domain for an organization, a couple of disjointed authorization domains, and three hierarchically organized audit policy domains.

Normally you find security mechanisms provided by middleware to be well suited to your needs in securing your application. However, there are particular classes of applications that require fine-grained control of access to enterprise resources. In such cases, just using middleware security would not provide adequate security. The next section explains how to handle such situations.

Enforcing Fine-Grained Security

Let us use the eBusiness example to illustrate situations when you might need to enforce fine-grained security specific to a particular application. As you recall from the eBusiness example described in Chapter 1, "Overview of Web Services Security," users may access information about accounts and products. If you go back and look at the security requirements more carefully, you may notice that they do not prevent any user from accessing another user's shopping carts (accounts). This permissive policy is definitely not desirable, since it does not protect user privacy. There are several alternate solutions for separating users' accounts, and some require you to build security-aware applications or custom security logic. We discuss the options below.

One way to protect shopping carts from access by others is to have one separate policy domain per user. This solution keeps your application from being security-aware. However, requiring as many policy domains as users may result in very slow authorization checks that would kill your performance. More significantly, administrative overhead would soar, and in a matter of months your security administrators would quit out of frustration.

Another alternative is to implement your own authorization logic that would be smart enough to find out which customer a cart belongs to and use this information for access decisions. This approach still keeps your application from being security-aware, although it requires the middleware security to be capable of using your custom authorization logic. Besides developing your own authorization logic, you will also need two things: a means for your custom logic to find out the cart owner, and a way to configure your middleware security to use custom authorization logic. Although these seem to be fairly straightforward capabilities, most middleware security technologies lack them, and there is a strong chance that your middleware product will not allow you to implement this approach.

One common practice is to create a security-aware application and change the shopping cart implementation logic so it checks whether the accessing user is the owner of the corresponding account. Because this allows us to get back to only one policy for all shopping cart objects, we avoid performance scalability problems, and most importantly, make the life of the security administrators in eBusiness much easier. However, the burden is now shifted onto application developers, who need to code the authorization logic within the shopping cart implementation. We recommend that, whenever possible, your security-aware applications perform security checks by calling an authorization server, which separates application logic from authorization logic.

The final alternative for fine-grained access control is to use delegation to allow a separate back-office server to enforce the check based on the caller's credentials. In many cases, the enterprise may already have fine-grained policies defined in a back-end database or other enterprise repository. We will discuss this alternative further in Chapter 12, "Planning and Building a Secure Web Services Architecture."

As you can see, there are many ways of supporting security policies that protect fine-grained application-specific resources. Depending on the capabilities of your middleware security, you may be in a position to employ some of them. In addition to describing CORBA, COM+, .NET, and EJB in the next few sections, we will explain how these technologies support fine-grained security.

CORBA

This section explains CORBA security, which defines the security service for the CORBA component model (CCM) as well as all other CORBA objects. (Because CORBA security protects all CORBA objects, we'll use *objects* interchangeably with *components* for the remainder of the section.) Hopefully our brief description of CORBA security will provide the most essential information you might find in the 400-plus-page specification and related OMG documents.

The CORBA security specification (CORBASec) defines a framework for providing security services to applications via the CORBA object request broker (ORB). The security service is one of several Common Object Services defined as part of the CORBA standard.

CORBASec defines two conformance levels for ORB security. Any product compliant with CORBASec must support Level 1 or both Level 1 and Level 2:

Level 1

- Support *security-unaware* applications
- Have ORB-enforced authentication, secure invocation, authorization, and auditing
- Perform simple delegation

Level 2

- Support *security-aware* applications
- Have the ability to select quality of protection, change credentials, select delegation options, and use audit services
- Support administration interfaces using security policy domains

There are also the following optional functions:

Nonrepudiation. Application interface for generating and checking evidence of claimed events

Replaceability of security services. Allows replacement of security services that are enforced by the ORB

Security services. Standard set of object security interfaces

ORB services. Low-level interceptor interface within the ORB to extend beyond security

Security ready. The ORB has security interfaces, but no implementation; designed for future extensions

The rest of this section provides a high-level description of CORBASec so you can see how its security functionality can fit into a Web Services security architecture.

How CORBA Works

CORBA technology, including the CORBA security service, defines a general-purpose language and OS-independent infrastructure for developing and deploying distributed object-based systems in a broad range of specialized application domains. Application systems and the CORBA infrastructure, including the security service, are defined using standard CORBA declarative facilities.

Declarative Part

All entities in the CORBA computing model are identified with interfaces defined in the OMG Interface Definition Language (IDL). CORBA IDL resembles C++ in its syntax and constructs. A CORBA interface is a collection of three elements: operations, attributes, and exceptions. Interface definitions can inherit other interfaces to allow interface evolution and composition. The following IDL fragment from our eBusiness example shows the interface Product:

```
typedef string ProductID;

exception InvalidPrice
{
   string description;
};

interface Product
{
   attribute ProductID ID;
   float getPrice();
   void  setPrice(in float NewPrice)
      raises InvalidPrice;
};
```

The interface defines the following:

- Attribute ID of type ProductID, which is an alias for a native type string.
- Operation getPrice(), which returns the price of the product associated with a particular instance of the interface.
- Operation setPrice(), which allows the product price to be set. If the price value is out of the supported range—for example, negative—the operation throws a user-defined exception InvalidPrice.

The CORBA standard defines how IDL constructs are translated into various programming languages. It allows multiple language bindings, which means that CORBA objects can be coded in different programming languages and yet interoperate with clients and each other. Because of this, objects from different environments residing on different machines with different computing architectures can be integrated and shared among clients, which makes IDL-based objects inherently distributable.

Runtime Part

When CORBA objects are deployed, they reside in OS processes and utilize CORBA middleware in the form of ORBs to make their functionality available to the clients as well as to receive and process invocations and return the results. Objects can act as clients as well, that is, make invocations on other objects, creating chains of invocations. Clients and targets may reside in the same or different processes or in different hosts.

A CORBA ORB is responsible for core middleware functions, such as:

- Registering, keeping track of, and finding interface implementations
- Introducing clients to needed server objects
- Providing communication transport from a client to a target

Wire Protocol

CORBA ORBs communicate with each other, including sending object requests, by means of a special protocol for inter-ORB communications called Generic Inter-ORB Protocol (GIOP). Because GIOP is a connection-oriented protocol and requires reliable service and presentation of communicated data as a byte stream, GIOP messages are delivered over the TCP in TCP/IP networks. Defined by the OMG, Internet Inter-ORB Protocol (IIOP) is a specialization of GIOP using TCP. GIOP messages sent between the sender and receiver ORBs are translations of request/response interactions between the corresponding CORBA client and server object.

From a security point of view, it's important to note the following about GIOP Request messages:

- To identify an object, the server uses an object key that is opaque to anybody except the hosting server. The client obtains the object key from the object reference.
- A list of *service contexts* accompanies all request and reply messages; it's a place for passing request-related data that different services, such as transaction and security, need to exchange.

Security service passes all its data related to a particular request or reply in the form of a service context list element in GIOP Request and Reply messages. We'll discuss this in more detail later in the chapter when we discuss CORBA secure channels.

Object Reference

In order for a CORBA object to be accessible to its clients, it needs to have some equivalent of an address. Object addresses are presented in the form of interoperable object references (IORs). The ORB that hosts the object, working together with the object adapter, can create such references using the host IP address, the TCP port number, and other information essential for locating the object inside the ORB. Obviously, this information is specific to the TCP communication protocol because the IP address and the port number are part of the address. The information is also specific to the ORB that created the reference, because the object key is ORB-specific. To make such references understandable across ORBs from different vendors, the OMG defined a format for IORs.

From a security perspective, the most interesting part of the IOR is the list of components, which allows additional information to be attached to the IOR so that it's available when the client establishes a connection with the server to make object invocations. Several standard components are specifically defined for supporting security, and we'll discuss them in the following sections.

If you want to look further into CORBA, books include Orfali (1997), Ruh (1999), Siegel (2000), and Pope (1998).

Roles and Responsibilities of CSS, TSS, and Secure Channel

One of the objectives of CORBA CSS, TSS, and secure channel architectures is to provide totally unobtrusive protection to applications. Most CORBA objects should be able to run securely on a secure ORB without any active involvement within the application code. In the meantime, it is possible for an object to exercise stricter (application-specific) security policies than the ones enforced by CORBA security run time. In this section, we provide an overview of the CORBA CSS, TSS, and secure channel.

The CORBA CSS provides the following security functions:

- Obtaining the principal's credentials by authenticating the user or retrieving credentials from the session environment if the principal has already been authenticated, and managing the principal's credentials created as a result of the authentication.
- If necessary, translating the principal's credentials into those accepted by the TSS, before they are "pushed" to the server.
- Creating a secure channel with the TSS. While doing this, the CSS could authenticate the TSS if the client's policy requires it to do so.
- Protecting request messages and verifying response messages, depending on the message protection policy.
- Performing audit of the invocations.
- Implementing client's nonrepudiation policy.

The CORBA TSS provides security functions that are very similar to those of CSS as well as enforcing access control:

- Authenticating clients and verifying their credentials if they are "pushed," or obtaining them if they are "pulled."
- Obtaining credentials used to authenticate the target to clients, usually by retrieving credentials from the session environment or from trusted and secure storage for principals not associated with people.
- Creating a secure channel with the CSS. While doing this, it could authenticate the CSS if the target's policy requires it to do so.
- Verifying request messages' protection and securing response messages, depending on the target's message protection policy.
- Performing an access control check on the requested object and method, based on the received credentials.
- Performing an audit of the invocations.
- Implementing a target's nonrepudiation policy.

The state of CORBA secure channel is maintained by CSS and TSS and managed via service context in GIOP messages. As described in the earlier section on the runtime part of CORBA, any GIOP Request/Reply message contains a list of service context data, which is used by different services for inserting service-specific information into the stream of communications between client and server. CORBASec defines a *SecurityAttributeService* (SAS) data type as an element of GIOP message service context, which may be used to associate security-specific identity, authorization, and client authentication contexts with GIOP Request and Reply messages.

Common Secure Interoperability Version 2

The objective of the CSIv2 specification is to define the interoperable wire protocol for CORBA and J2EE secure channels. CSIv2 defines the format and rules to send the security information from a client to a server, running on either CORBA or J2EE, to support the secure interoperability between the client and server.

CSIv2 defines the following three logical layers that are used to transfer the security data from a CSS to a TSS:

1. The authorization layer (or attribute layer)
2. The authentication layer
3. The transport layer

The first two layers are the subject of a new protocol defined by CSIv2, the Security Attribute Service. The transport layer supports the security mechanism that you choose, for example TLS/SSL or DCE/RPC. All three layers work together to support passing the security data so that the target can satisfy all of its security requirements.

The first part of the protocol, passing the authorization security information, uses the service context in the request or reply header as defined by the GIOP protocol. The SAS protocol defines how authorization data will be passed from the client to the target. At the attribute layer, the principal privilege (roles and groups) and identity (access and audit identity) attributes are passed from CSS to TSS, using a cryptographically signed Privilege Attribute Certificate (PAC) in a format defined by the IETF Attribute Certificate specification (IETF 2002b). The attribute layer is also responsible for supporting delegation.

CSIv2 supports both forms of simple delegation. In constrained delegation, the CSS names the intermediates that it trusts in an extension field of the PAC called *proxy attributes*. The TSS checks this field and makes sure that an intermediate has a right to delegate the client's credentials. Unconstrained delegation is indicated through a special value of this PAC field, "Any."

The second layer of CSIv2 supports authentication. In some cases, the security mechanism in the transport layer handles authentication. For example, SSL will support client authentication if the target requires that the client provide authentication based on a public key certificate. This may not be desirable in all cases, because an enterprise may not want the expense of purchasing SSL certificates for all its clients, customers, and suppliers. In cases where the underlying security transport does not support authentication, CSIv2 will do the job, since its authentication layer supports any GSS-API request/reply mechanism, such as Kerberos, as well as simple username and password.

The third layer defined by CSIv2 is the transport layer. In this layer, CSIv2 authors chose Transport Layer Security, TLS/SSL, as the security mechanism, which all conformant security services should support. A CSIv2 security service can work with other secure transports such as DCE/RPC or CORBA's Secure Inter-ORB Protocol (SECIOP), but it must support TLS/SSL so that the client and target have at least one security mechanism in common.

In summary, CSIv2 has three layers that support secure channel in CORBA and EJB systems, and the layers match the basic trio of security—authorization, authentication, and message protection. Once the security context is safely established between the CSS and the TSS using CSIv2, it is used on the server to protect target objects.

In the next sections, we will explain how CSS and TSS responsibilities are fulfilled via security mechanisms implemented by the CORBA security service.

Implementation of Security Functions

Similar to other middleware security technologies, security policies in CORBA are enforced completely outside of an application system. Everything, including obtaining information necessary for making policy decisions, is done before the method invocation is dispatched to the target object. As Figure 7.8 shows, the security enforcement code is executed inside of a CORBA security service when a message from a client application to a target object is passed through the ORB.

Authentication

A principal may be authenticated in a number of ways—the most common of which for human users is a password. For system entities, on the other hand, authentication data, such as a long-term key, must be associated with the corresponding object. In CORBA, a principal has at least one and possibly several different identities. When a principal is being authenticated, it normally supplies:

- Its security name
- The authentication data needed by the particular authentication method used
- Requested privilege attributes (although the principal may change them later)

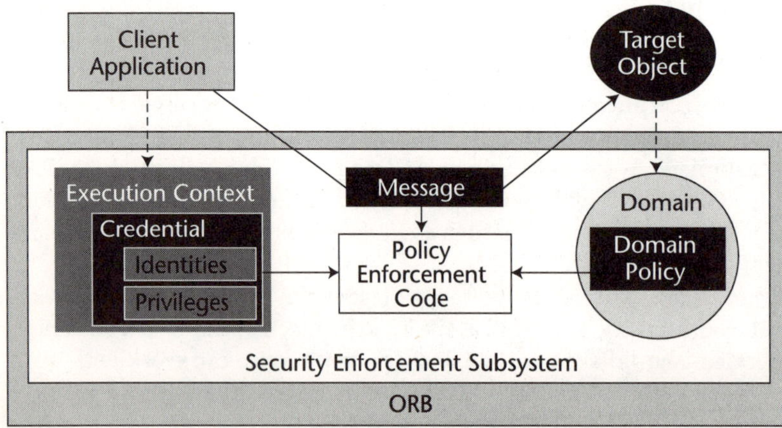

Figure 7.8 Enforcement of policies in CORBA security.

The principal may have privilege attributes that the TSS can use to decide what the principal can access. A variety of privilege attributes may be available, depending on access policies. The privilege attributes that a principal is permitted to take are known to the system. At any given time, the principal may be using only a subset of these permitted attributes, chosen either by the principal (or an application running on its behalf) or by using a default set specified for the principal. There may be limits on the duration for which these privilege attributes are valid and controls on where and when they can be used. Because CORBASec defines an extensible privilege attribute model, it enables access control policies based on roles, groups, clearance, and any other security-related attributes of the principal. These attributes, once established through principal authentication, are carried from CSS to TSS in the CSIv2 attribute layer.

Message Integrity and Confidentiality Protection

Although the CORBASec architecture does not have any explicit provisions for message origin authenticity protection, it is performed implicitly if the other entity is authenticated and messages are encrypted with the session key, or if the message came through one of CSIv2's secure transport layers from an authenticated party. As for message confidentiality and integrity protection, they are both supported by CORBA security and referred to as quality of protection (QoP). Similar to other technologies described in this chapter, CORBA's QoP is set by policy, and has four possible values: no protection, integrity protection only, confidentiality protection only, and both integrity and confidentiality protection.

Access Control

CORBA security has an extensible model for subject security attributes to enable security run-time and administration scaling with possibly large numbers of subjects. Another application of grouping in CORBA security is policy domains that allow scaling on the number of objects. Domains are used for most security policies in CORBA. A third grouping mechanism, which is also specific to access control, introduces required and effective rights and allows scaling on the number of operations. The role of all three grouping mechanisms in CORBA is illustrated in Figure 7.9.

Being the finest level of access control granularity in CORBA, operations could proliferate in your system and cause scaling problems. You might not realize that the number of methods accessible on distributed objects in your enterprise is quite large. In the complete version of our eBusiness example, we have over 20 different operations, so you can easily imagine that in real enterprises there are hundreds of distinguished operations on distributed objects. Any security administrator can tell you that it's common to grant the same access to more than one resource in the enterprise. As a result, an administrator's job can be significantly eased if the operations that are alike in security requirements can somehow be grouped and administered at a group level instead of using individual operations. In addition, the use of such groups prevents security administrators from having to understand the semantics of methods. This is exactly what CORBA's required rights do.

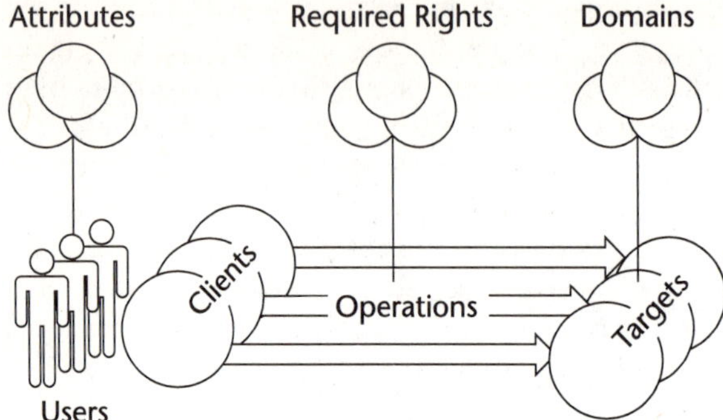

Figure 7.9 Users, operations, and target objects are grouped via attributes, rights, and domains.

In CORBA, every operation has a global set of associated *RequiredRights*. This set, together with a combinator *(all* or *any* rights), defines what rights a subject has to have to invoke the operation. CORBA security defines standard rights, *get* (g), *set* (s), *manage* (m), and *use* (u), that are likely to be understood by administrators without expecting administrators to understand detailed semantics of the corresponding operations. However, these standard rights are not the only ones permitted. They may be extended using the *ExtensibleFamily* attribute. Examples of required rights can be found in Table 7.1, which shows some of the settings for our eBusiness example.

Depending on the *domain access policy* (DAP) enforced in a particular access policy domain, a subject is granted different rights *(GrantedRights)* according to what privilege attributes it has. We show the granted rights for our eBusiness example in Table 7.2. For instance, Johnson is only granted right "g" (get) in the Products domain, so he can't invoke Product::setPrice because the operation requires "s" (set) and "m" (manage). However, if Johnson invokes Account::deleteOrder on an object belonging to the Accounts domain where he is granted both "s" and "u" (use) rights, then the invocation will succeed, since that operation requires only "s."

Table 7.1 Examples of Required Rights for eBusiness

INTERFACE NAME	OPERATION NAME	REQUIRED RIGHTS
Product	getPrice	g (all)
Product	setPrice	s m (all)
Account	settleOrder	u (all)
Account	placeOrder	s (all)
Account	listOrder	s (all)
Account	deleteOrder	s (all)

Table 7.2 Examples of Granted Rights for Different Domains in eBusiness

PRIVILEGE ATTRIBUTE		DOMAINS AND GRANTED RIGHTS	
TYPE	VALUE	ACCOUNTS	PRODUCTS
AccessID	Johnson	s, u	g
GroupID	Marketing	s, m	s

CORBA access policy domains are encapsulated in DAP objects, one per domain, which define what rights are granted for each security attribute. Security administrators are responsible for defining granted rights on a per domain basis.

Auditing

The audit service of CORBA security is represented through an *AuditChannel*, used to write audit records, and an *AuditDecision* object, which is queried for audit decisions.

The *AuditChannel* implementation may filter records, route them to appropriate audit trails, and cause event alarms. Different *AuditChannel* objects may be used to send audit records to different audit trails. Applications and system components both invoke the *audit_write* operation on an *AuditChannel* object to send audit records to the audit trail. A CORBA application can either obtain a reference to the default *AuditChannel* from the *AuditDecision* object—which, in turn, is discovered through the application's security context—or it can create its own audit channel with the help of the audit service APIs.

AuditDecision objects make audit decisions according to CORBA audit policies defined via audit administrative interfaces. Specifically, administrators define, by specifying *audit selectors*, which security related events result in audit records generated by the audit service. However, the specification does not define the behavior, or the policies governing the behavior, of a CORBA ORB if an audit record cannot be recorded or otherwise processed by the audit subsystem, or if another type of audit service failure occurs. CORBASec leaves this up to the implementation of the security service. Audit policies specify which events should be audited under what circumstances. The specification divides all events into two major classes: system and application security events. Furthermore, it defines types of system-related audit events that reflect major points in the system life cycle, such as authentication, success or failure of object invocation, object creation and destruction, changes in the system security settings, and so on.

Delegation

Although CORBASec specifies all of the options of delegation we have outlined earlier, not all implementations have the same support for these options. First, different compliance levels of CORBASec require support for different types of delegation, and second, different technologies used to implement CORBASec also have different support for delegation. CORBASec level 1 includes simple delegation, which allows an object to assume the identity of its invoker, whereas CORBASec level 2 requires the ability to select delegation options.

The CSIv2 defines support for the CORBASec delegation options in the following ways:

CSIv2 authorization token-based delegation. Uses the PAC passed in the CSIv2 attribute layer to implement *simple restricted (constrained) delegation*. The PAC allows the client to delegate selected attributes to an intermediate. The PAC's proxy attributes allow the client to delegate only to selected intermediates, thus constraining delegation. If the PAC's proxy attribute is set to "Any," delegation is not constrained and thus the security service implements *impersonation*.

CSIv2 identity assertion-based delegation. Uses the identity token passed in the CSIv2 attribute layer to implement *impersonation*. The identity token allows the client to delegate its identity (and potentially its attributes) to an intermediate, but the client cannot constrain where its privileges are delegated. A subsequent target may check whether an intermediate that uses an impersonated identity is trustworthy.

Administration

CORBASec administration architecture rests on three constituents—*administrative interfaces*, defined on *policy objects*, each associated with a *policy domain*. At run time, CORBA security subsystem intercepts an invocation, determines what domain(s) a target or a client belongs to, and enforces the policies associated with the domain(s).

Policy Objects and Administrative Interfaces

CORBASec specifies administrative interfaces for managing most security runtime mechanisms described above, except authentication. (For authentication, an administrator can still specify if a target can be authenticated and/or requires its clients to authenticate.) As with anything else in CORBA, these interfaces are defined in CORBA IDL. Since the mechanisms for user management are beyond CORBASec's scope, the interfaces for administering user attribute assignment policies are as well.

Policy Domains

The semantic models of most policies share the same common concept—policy domains. Policy domains are the way CORBA security runtime and administration mechanisms achieve scalability on the number of objects in a system. Policies of more than one type (for example, authorization, audit, QoP) can be associated with the same domain, and each object can belong to more than one policy domain. Domains can be organized in federations or hierarchies. Policy decisions and enforcement can be object specific if each object is located in a separate domain, or a large group of objects can be associated with one policy domain. This means that the model scales (in terms of performance as well as administration) very well without losing fine granularity. Unlike most other middleware security technologies, CORBA objects residing on different computers can belong to the same domains, because CORBA security policy domains span multiple computers, and therefore can be governed by the same security policies.

Enforcing Fine-Grained Security

There are several interfaces available to security-aware applications for enforcing application-specific security policies. Accessible at run time, they allow an application code to perform the following tasks:

- Authenticate the application to the CORBA security run time and obtain a *Credentials* object as a result of a successful authentication.
- Manipulate the application's own credentials by:
  - Inspecting, refreshing, and copying credentials
  - Inspecting and specifying secure invocation options for those object invocations in which these credentials are used
  - Inquiring and modifying privileges and other principal attributes in the credentials
- Inspect credentials of the immediate client who invoked the application target, as well as the properties of the security association that has been used for the invocation. This includes obtaining a list of the security attributes associated with the received credentials.
- Perform the same inspection of credentials but with respect to those of the target with whom an application has established a secure association.
- Specify what security policy options a client wants to apply when communicating with a target object by performing operations on the target object's reference and the binding object associated with it.
- Check with the audit service, represented via the *AuditDecision* object, if a particular event is supposed to be audited, and write to an audit channel using the *AuditChannel* object.
- Generate and verify nonrepudiation evidence, if the CORBASec environment implements the optional nonrepudiation service.

To perform these tasks, an application obtains references to the needed objects by querying its runtime process or thread-specific security context. Since CORBASec administrative facilities are defined in the form of run-time interfaces, an application can use them at run time as well.

As you can see, CORBASec defines a comprehensive set of security mechanisms for an ORB security subsystem to protect distributed applications and for allowing security-aware applications to enforce their own policies. It is a far-reaching specification of a middleware security, but, unfortunately, it is short on implementations. There are only a few products supporting less then half a dozen CORBA ORBs that could claim some compliance with the CORBA security standard. The next section describes a solution of a different type—defining a technology through its implementation. Supplied with every installation of Microsoft Windows 2000, COM+ is a de facto standard application server platform for the homogenous world of Microsoft systems.

COM+

The architectures of CORBA and EJB are independent of the OS type, so their implementations are available for many different platforms. At the same time, the integration of CORBA and EJB applications with a particular OS infrastructure is highly challenging to standardize. COM+, on the other hand, is tightly integrated with the MS Windows platform, which allows leveraging the OS infrastructure but also creates dependence on it and prevents portability to other platforms. If your applications live in a pure Microsoft technology world, then COM+ naturally becomes the component platform of choice. However, it is problematic, to say the least, to make COM+ applications interoperate with other worlds. This is when Web Services could come to the rescue by serving as a gateway to the COM+ applications.

How COM+ Works

COM+ is the next generation in the evolution of the Microsoft distributed computing architecture. The previous one, Component Object Model (COM)—a binary standard for interoperation—in its turn builds upon Microsoft's Remote Procedure Call (MS RPC) client/server architecture. Since COM is inherently distributed, an application could be developed using just COM, where client and server communicate over DCOM (Rubin 1999, Grimes 1997) networking mechanisms, which are part of the current COM architecture.

Introduced in Windows 2000, COM+ v1.0 integrates Microsoft Transaction Server (MTS) into COM and provides a messaging alternative, based on Microsoft Message Queue (MSMQ) technology, for COM calls.

NOTE In this section, we refer collectively to COM, MTS, and COM+ v1.0 as just COM+, to simplify the terminology. Also, we describe only COM+ version 1.0, given that COM+ v1.5 became available on Windows .NET Server and Windows XP Pro just at the time when this book was being written.

The end result is that now applications developed for COM+ can use the following enterprise computing services:

- Transactions
- Thread synchronization
- Security
- Queued components
- Loosely coupled events
- Component load balancing

COM+ makes these services available for an application, without the application explicitly calling the services, through interception that enables COM+ to intervene when it needs to. That is, an application could be developed by following the COM+ rules of the game and registered with the COM+ infrastructure. After that, the application's transactional, security, and other characteristics could be administered via COM+ administrative mechanisms and not coded inside of the application. This is a significant step forward compared to COM and MS RPC.

In short, COM+ is an application server platform for MS Windows applications, just as EJB is an application server platform for Java applications, and CORBA Component Model (CCM) is the same in the CORBA world. The difference is that EJB and CCM are defined by a specification, while COM+ is defined by the Microsoft implementation.

Declarative Part

As with CORBA, a COM(+) component consists of one or more objects, each implementing one or more interfaces. The objects and the interfaces exposed by a COM(+) component can be described in Microsoft Interface Definition Language (MS IDL).[3] A COM(+) interface is a collection of methods decorated with metadata attributes. The following MS IDL fragment from our eBusiness example shows the interface Product.

```
[
        object,
        uuid(832BC8B3-1B5E-4F50-AC05-0B5A24DD7B5A),
]
interface IProduct : IUnknown
{
        HRESULT GetPrice([out, retval] double* price);

        HRESULT SetPrice([in] double SetPrice);
};
```

The interface defines the following:

- Interface attributes (in square brackets) that set metadata for configuring the COM(+) runtime environment correctly. You will see in the next section that the concept of metadata configured by the means of decorative attributes is carried much further by the .NET architecture.
- Method GetPrice(), which returns the price of the product associated with a particular instance of the interface.
- Method SetPrice(), which allows the setting of the product price.

Heavily influenced by C, the COM computational model does not have exceptions, so all errors are delivered to the caller as return values of type HRESULT. As a consequence of this error indication mechanism, all data returned from a call is defined as *out* parameters, which are indicated as parameter attributes in square brackets. For example, if the price value is out of the supported range—let's say, negative—method SetPrice() could be programmed to return either a custom error code or predefined

[3] Unlike the CORBA architecture, which uses interface definitions expressed in IDL as a primary binding contract between servers and clients, COM is based on client/server contracts in binary form and uses IDL as a complementary human-readable description of the binary contract.

E_INVALIDARG. Notification that access to an object has been denied is also returned through this HRESULT mechanism.

A COM+ application is a collection of one or more dynamic link libraries (DLL), each of which contains business logic for one or more classes—called components in COM terminology—and additional logic for creating objects and marshaling invocations on their methods. Every class implements one or more interfaces.

A COM+ programmer declares the environment in which a component must run by specifying the configuration attributes for the component. An application is registered with COM+ Catalog, where these attributes, as well as any other configuration information, are stored. The content of the Catalog is manipulated through administrative tools or the corresponding API.

The advantages of COM+ over COM start to become more apparent when it comes to configuring the characteristics of distributed applications important for enterprise-scale computing. COM+ can support security administration of anything between an individual class method and the whole application just using administrative tools with no restart of the application required. Once various constraints are set, COM+ services with the use of the interception mechanism take care of running the application.

Runtime Part

The novelty of the COM+ runtime architecture, in comparison to COM, lies in the notion of runtime *context*. A context can be thought of as a set of runtime constraints imposed on all those incoming calls and their outgoing results that cross the context boundaries. Each COM+ object exists in a context. Consequently, if the caller and the target are located in the same context, no constraint checks are performed, freeing invocations from any overhead. If they are running in different contexts, the incoming call goes through an interceptor, which can do whatever is necessary to satisfy the runtime constraints. The outgoing message also goes through the interceptor for any needed postprocessing. The result is that the application server mediates the calls only when needed. The downside is that a call chain can propagate freely from object to object in the same context once it gets through security checks at its entry point. This makes the task of designing secure applications with COM+ tricky.

When an object is created based on a client's request, COM+ checks the Catalog to see if the corresponding class is registered and if there is configuration information for it—that is, if it is a "configured component." If there is, the object is placed within a context that matches the configuration settings for its component. If the client of a COM+ component is in a different context, COM+ uses interception to enable the incompatible components to work together. If the component and the client have identical runtime requirements, the component is placed in the same context as the client, and no interception is performed. If a class to be instantiated is not registered with the Catalog, it is placed in a context for unconfigured components. After object activation and placement have been done, the client starts making invocations. If the client and the target are not on the same machine, the invocation is performed over DCOM.

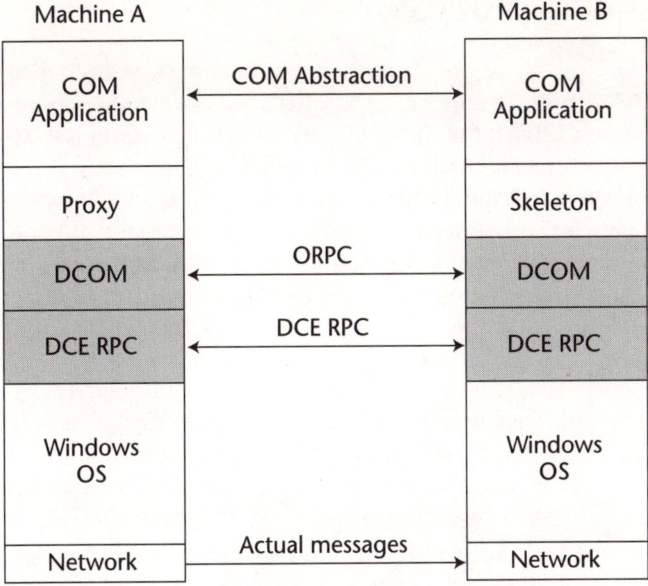

Figure 7.10 DCOM wire protocol adds support for objects to DCE RPC.

Wire Protocol

Viewed by some as the "Microsoft ORB," DCOM extends COM to distributed computing by adding support for location transparency, remote activation, connection management, concurrency management, and security. The DCOM wire protocol, referred to as Object RPC (ORPC), extends MS RPC (Microsoft's implementation of DCE RPC) by adding support for objects. The relationships among COM, DCOM, and DCE RPC are illustrated in Figure 7.10. Because COM was designed to be distributed, it is often confusing to distinguish DCOM from COM. This is why many use the name DCOM to refer to just the DCOM wire protocol.

For the sake of brevity, we will not describe the DCOM wire protocol, which you can find in Kindel (1998). If you want to look further into COM(+) architecture and its services, you can find numerous books about it. We recommend Thai (1999), Tapadyia (2001), and Grimes (1997). You are welcome to stop at this point and read more on COM(+), using these and other sources, if you find it necessary, before continuing with COM(+) security architecture.

Roles and Responsibilities of CSS, TSS, and Secure Channel

COM+ is an extension of COM, which came out of MS RPC, just as COM+ security architecture can be traced back to MS RPC security. Neutral to network protocols, MS RPC will load whatever protocol the client and the server have agreed upon. It will also load corresponding libraries that contain the selected Security Service Provider (SSP) and call them to complete an authentication handshake, as long as an authentication protocol can be negotiated by both sides through some means. Depending on the capabilities of the selected SSP and on how the client application has configured MS RPC run time through security APIs, the run time could:

- Perform mutual authentication
- Use different client credentials from call to call
- Restrict delegation of the client identity to the server
- Ensure message protection

The server application receives all authenticated and unauthenticated calls and decides which ones should be processed and which should be denied. The server can look up the client's authenticated identity, if any, the type of authentication, and the message QoP. The flexibility of MS RPC comes at a significant programming cost, as all security functionalities need to be explicitly configured or even programmatically enforced by the client and server applications.

In addition to the functionality of MS RPC, COM adds APIs that allow the server application to set some basic checks to be performed automatically on each incoming call. The COM interception layer does the checks when a call is about to be dispatched to the application. The client-side COM layer also adds value by letting the application know what authentication and message QoP levels are acceptable by the server. To make such information accessible to the client, the server COM layer encapsulates appropriate data into the interface pointer of its objects before handing them to the client. The client application can also set process-wide settings for all of its calls once it initializes CSS. If the client does not initialize CSS, then reasonable default settings will be used. TSS can also be given a security descriptor containing a DACL and perform process-wide coarse-grained access checks against the DACL and security tokens of the clients on all incoming calls. Clearly, even though COM architecture makes CSS and TSS do more work than in basic MS RPC (and in its later versions, COM even supports external security configuration), the client and server applications still have major responsibilities. For example, all object or method level access control has to be done programmatically. COM+ security architecture moves further towards declarative configuration while providing fine-grained access control.

Not making any noticeable improvements to CSS, COM+ uses interception mechanisms to enable TSS to support complete administration of the server security. Besides supporting access checks up to the level of object methods, COM+ TSS enforces access policies whenever a call crosses dynamic link library (DLL) boundaries, even in the same process. Unfortunately, any control stops at those boundaries and cannot be enforced on calls between components co-located in one DLL. These require very careful analysis of intralibrary invocation chains to avoid inadvertently opening entry points to protected components.

Implementation of Security Functions

As with CORBA, COM+ security functions are enforced outside of the application through security interceptors. There is one difference, though. Since the COM+ interception architecture is both proprietary and nonextensible, custom security subsystem implementations are not supported. Depending on your business needs and the security risks involved, this could be good or bad. For example, since COM+ does not support auditing for security-unaware applications, developers have to resort to complex tricks (see Brown 1999, for one) to implement consistent auditing in large applications. However, the built-in security implemented in COM+ provides a variety of functionality that you can be sure will be available in any deployment. The following subsections contain more details on COM+ security functions.

Authentication

Despite its COM heritage, COM+ does not provide a means for changing the SSP. It uses either Kerberos, if the server host is in a Windows 2000 domain, or Windows NT LAN Manager (NTLM) SSPs for authentication. If the component is configured to be launched in a separate process (that is, an "out-of-process" component), client authentication could be performed:

- Never, and the client will have anonymous identity
- At the time of establishing a secure channel
- On every call
- With every network packet, even when several packets constitute only one call

The same authentication level is used for all components in the same process. Also, a machine-wide authentication level that will be used by all COM+ servers can be set using administrative tools, unless the server's configuration is explicitly set to a different value. For in-process components, COM+ can be configured not to authenticate the caller at all, or to use the process-wide authentication level.

If a COM+ component is activated in the process of the caller, then the component inherits the identity of the hosting process. For a component configured to run in a process separate from the client, it is possible to choose between running it under a predefined OS account or with the identity of whoever is conducting the interactive session on the server machine. If a component calls another COM(+) object, credentials associated with its current identity will be used to authenticate the target.

Message Integrity and Confidentiality Protection

The COM+ TSS can be configured to the following levels of message protection:

- Authentication and integrity protection of every packet
- Authentication, integrity, and confidentiality protection of every packet

Just as with CORBA, means to control the strength of the protection are not documented. As already described, interface pointers contain information necessary for the client CSS to find the minimum protection level the server will accept.

Access Control

If a COM+ application is configured with access control enforced (radio button in the Authorization area in Figure 7.11), TSS could check every call coming not only into the process but also into each DLL. A TSS erects three barriers that every client must overcome before its call will be successfully dispatched to the server object:

1. The COM+ server needs to be launched before any method can be invoked. If the server application is already running due to a previous invocation, then this barrier is not applicable. Otherwise, the client needs to have sufficient permissions (we'll discuss them later) for the target-side machinery to activate the server process.
2. Checks are made when the call enters a running server process. If the application security is configured to perform access checks only at the process level (see Figure 7.11), then this will be the last roadblock.

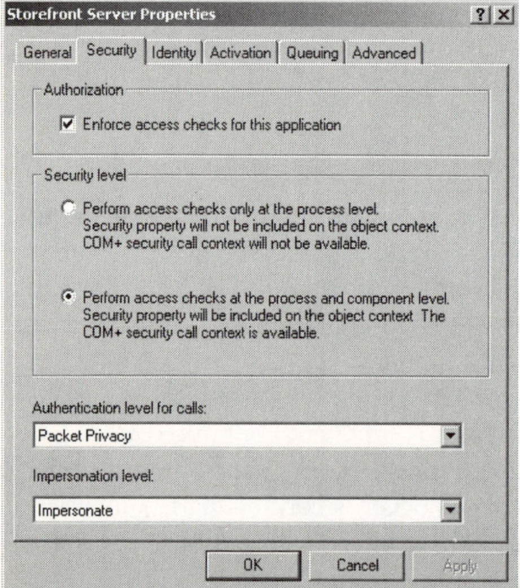

Figure 7.11 Security configuration for a COM+ application.

3. Access checks are performed when a call enters a DLL hosting the target object. Once inside the DLL, the TSS performs no further access checks.

Authorization can be specified at the granularity of the component (all class instances), interface, or method. In the case of component- or interface-level authorization, if a client is permitted to access a component, then that client can invoke any of its methods. Rights on interfaces are scoped by the components implementing them, which means that different clients could have different access rights to the same interface implemented by different components.

Auditing

Having no COM+ support and left to perform an audit on their own, applications can use Windows event log mechanisms to write their own audit records. As with all security-aware applications built on top of any middleware security technology, this requires at least high maintenance costs and good programming discipline, which still would not ensure against human errors.

Delegation

The intermediate can perform simple unconstrained delegation, or "impersonation" as it is also known in Microsoft terms, if the underlying SSP supports it and the immediate client allows it. In COM+ v1.0, only Kerberos SSP completely implements impersonation, whereas NTLM, with its challenge-response authentication handshake, does not let impersonation go beyond the first hop.

A client can always specify one of four delegation options for all or selected pointers to remote objects, something also done administratively on COM+ applications. It will limit what the server is able to do with the client's credentials. The options that can be specified are:

1. The server does not get the client's identity at all, which makes most of the access control policies problematic to implement.
2. The server can obtain the client identity but not use it (default).
3. The server can impersonate the client on the server's machine, but not when accessing other computers.
4. The server can impersonate the client everywhere, including other machines. (This is supported only by Kerberos SSP.)

Administration

COM+ is not as flexible as MS RPC and COM, but it surpasses them by significantly simplifying the life of developers and security administrators. It provides administrative GUI to the component Catalog. Enabling even access control administration, the GUI hides most of the security infrastructure's complexity.

Administrators use the GUI to specify:

- Minimum level of authentication and message protection a COM+ application would accept
- What identity the application should be launched with (no support for launching under the client's identity, however)
- How servers can use the application's identity when it calls other COM(+) components
- If access checks are performed, and at what level—process or DLL
- Access control checks (see below)

The COM+ access control model achieves scalability in a number of ways. First, it has several levels of permission granularity. One can specify access rights for a whole component (that is, all class instances), its interface, or interface method.

Second, COM+ allows permission grouping. Like EJB, it does so by introducing the notion of permission groups, dubbed "roles." However, since such roles are specific to the application under which they are defined and do not reflect the application users' organizational roles, they should be treated as just aggregated permissions. In any case, the COM+ administrative GUI allows creating these permission groups and specifying which Windows users or user groups are granted which permission groups. If a user is granted any of these "roles" for a COM+ application, the user automatically gets the right to launch that application.

COM+ has made great progress with the administrative GUI. However, it is still difficult to perform cross-machine administration. If you deploy the same COM+ application on several computers and you need to change security settings, you will have to do the changes for every application installation. Another drawback is the lack of the capability to group different applications into one CORBA-like policy domain, and administer that instead of the individual applications. It is possible to set machine-wide default authentication and delegation control levels, but this is not enough for enterprise-scale security.

Enforcing Fine-Grained Security

Thanks to MS RPC and COM heritage, COM+ clients and servers can do programmatically almost everything that can be configured via administrative GUI and more. In addition, a server application can obtain a pointer to the security context of the call. The context interface has methods to do the following:

- *IsSecurityEnabled()* — Check if the access controls are enabled or disabled on the application
- *IsCallerInRole()* — Check if the caller is granted a particular permission grouping
- Inspect the security data of the invocation chain (if the channels are configured to track it), specifically:
  - The number of hops in the chain

- The security information about each of the calls in the chain that crossed an application boundary, such as the caller's security identifier and name, the authentication service, authentication level, message QoP, and the delegation option used by the caller
- The lowest authentication level used in the chain
- Information about the first and last caller in the chain

In addition to COM+ infrastructure, an application can always use Windows security APIs if it wants to take advantage of the OS protection mechanisms.

There are many more aspects of COM+ security that we have omitted. If you plan on dealing with COM+ security, make sure to look at Brown (2000) for more details.

.NET Framework

Very new to the world of business enterprises, the .NET Framework is positioned to become the computing environment of choice for at least all those developers who create applications using COM(+) today. This means that, sooner or later, .NET-based systems will pop up in the Web, middleware, and back-office tiers. The .NET Framework is part of a bigger picture, the .NET Platform, as shown in Figure 7.12.

Built on top of the framework with the use of generic building blocks, .NET enterprise services are envisioned to become part of the organizational computing infrastructure. Although the .NET Framework SDK is freely available from Microsoft, developers will typically use some IDE product, such as Visual Studio.NET.

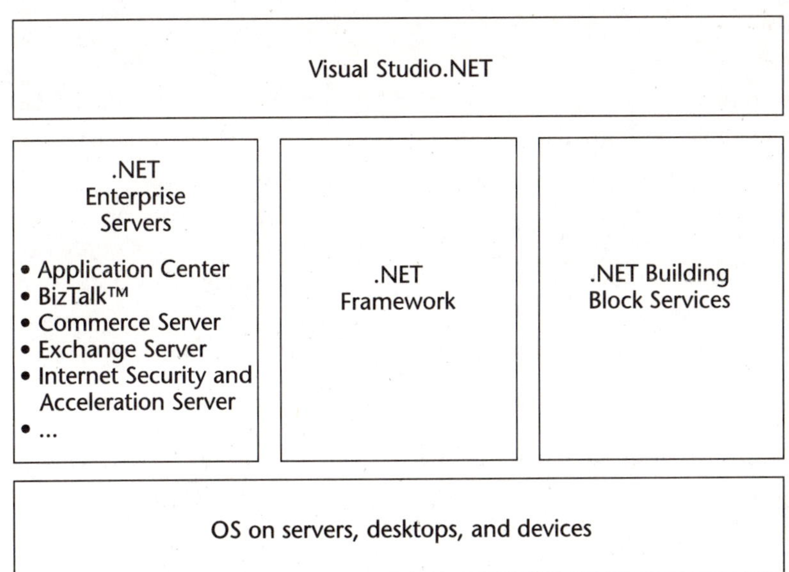

Figure 7.12 .NET platform is composed of the .NET Framework and other parts.

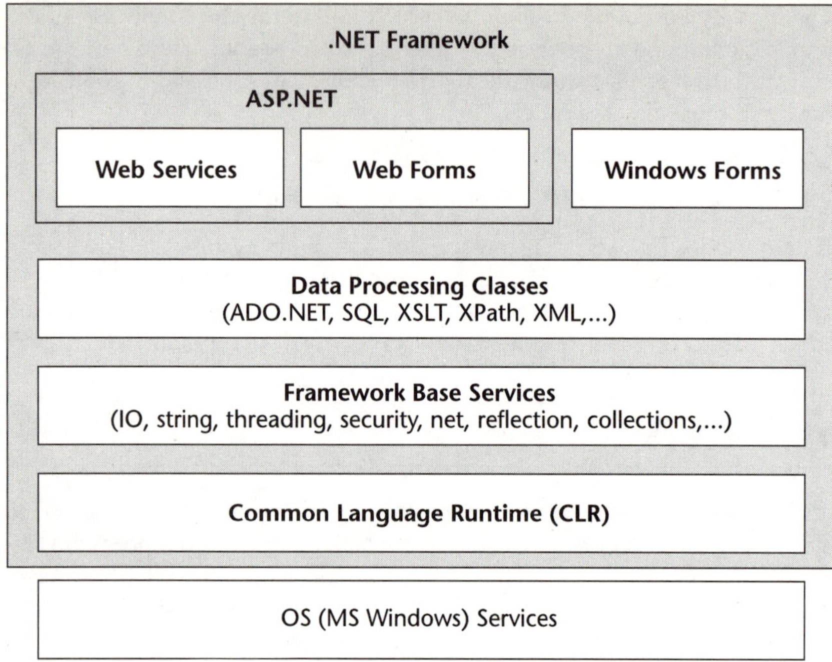

Figure 7.13 .NET Framework main elements.

Since .NET technology is relatively new, we will take a brief tour around the framework as shown in Figure 7.13 and describe its main elements:

- *Common Language Runtime (CLR)*, the framework foundation, manages code at execution time, providing core services such as memory management, thread management, and distributing computing support, while also enforcing strict type safety and other forms of code accuracy that ensure security and robustness.
- The next layer is a set of *base classes* providing supporting functionality for data processing.
- On top of the base classes, there are more sophisticated *data processing classes* for working with back-end data stores and other persistent storage, querying databases, and manipulating XML documents. The Java-world analogy to the base and data-processing classes is the J2SE APIs.

Finally, the classes for building SOAP, Web, and Windows GUI applications extend the framework base and data-processing classes. The former two constitute what is known as ASP.NET, the next iteration of Microsoft's Active Server Pages technology.

Microsoft advertises a number of .NET's key technical features:

- Simpler (distributed) component development process due to less plumbing code, compared to COM(+), to be written by programmers. A developer simply defines classes without worrying about DLL initialization, object life-time management, interface advertisement, resolution, or many other necessities in COM(+) programming.
- The COM binary contract model gives language independence. .NET aims at language integration with common data type representation across multiple languages, and mechanisms for defining, managing, and using new types across applications possibly written in different languages, as well as cross-language inheritance. According to Microsoft (Angeline 2001), they are working with various companies on integrating 15-20 languages. Since not every language can be integrated with CLR to the same extent, there are various levels of integration.
- CLR-supported memory and thread management, type safety, dynamic binding, array boundary checks, and other features of modern computing environments (similar to JVM, the Java Virtual Machine), simplify programming for .NET significantly. The code managed by CLR is referred to as "managed" in Microsoft documentation, and so we'll use this term, too.
- Extensive support for distributed application development not only with classes supporting XML, SOAP, HTTP, and other popular protocols but also with the ORB layer built into CLR, which is called "remoting" in .NET terms.
- COM-based DLL architecture causes developers and users a lot of headaches, which were even nicknamed collectively "DLL hell." Hopefully, the .NET new side-by-side versioning architecture and extensive use of metadata in assemblies will make deployment simpler.
- A new .NET security model, which we will discuss later, supplied with permissions, code groups, declarative and programmatic checks, and other features.

Shown in Figure 7.14, the development and execution process of .NET intermediate language (IL) code is very similar to the bytecode execution by the JVM. The main difference is that the "managed native" code to be executed by CLR, while having "hooks" for memory, thread, and other management functions, is specific to the processor architecture.

If you want to dig into the .NET and CLR architecture, you can start with a good introductory book by Thai and Lam (Thai 2001) and go from there. The rest of this section will concentrate on the distribution and security mechanisms available in .NET for building distributed applications.

How .NET Works

To develop a distributed service application with .NET technology, and eventually expose it through Web Services, one could go either of the following routes:

- Make .NET assemblies COM+-enabled and install them as COM+ components
- Use CLR object remoting mechanisms to make some of the objects accessible over the network

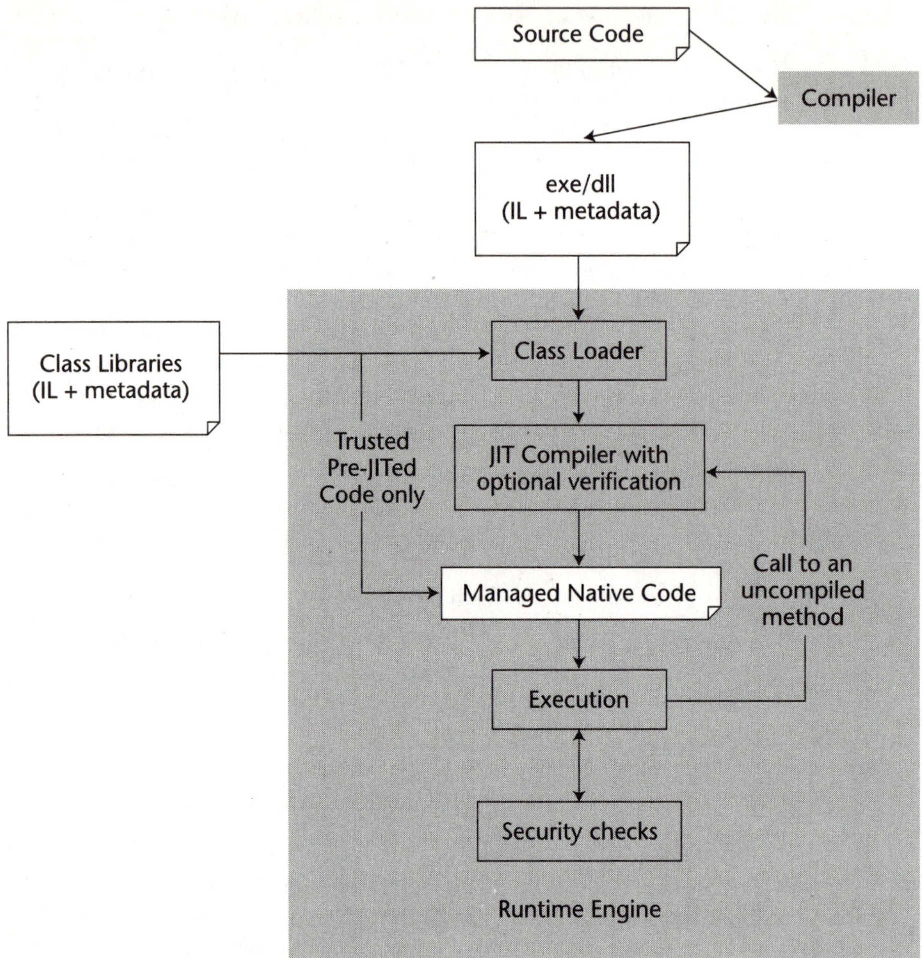

Figure 7.14 Development and execution of .NET managed code.

Exposing .NET Objects as COM+ Components

Installing .NET assemblies as COM+ components is the method to employ if .NET components need to be used from COM clients, or if you want to take advantage of COM+ transaction, security, load-balancing, object life-cycle management, and other services of this application server platform. With the metadata configurable through attribute-based declarative programming, it becomes very straightforward—although with some limitations and restrictions—to make a .NET assembly COM+-enabled. You just derive your COM+-component classes from the *System.EnterpriseServices.ServicedComponent* class, and the compiler will generate all necessary metadata and plumbing code. All other configuration information, including security settings, needed for COM+ infrastructure to host such a component uses default values and can be configured through native COM+ administrative tools. You can control the metadata through a number of attributes added at the assembly, class, interface, or method level. The following C# code fragment illustrates this by showing method *GetPrice* on class *Product*, which implements interface IProduct.

```
using System.EnterpriseServices;

namespace Ebusiness.StoreFrontMiddleTier {

  [GuidAttribute("0761670B-9F43-4458-9BED-A4F0B2337B5C")]
  [ComponentAccessControlAttribute(true)]
  [SecurityRoleAttribute("Staff", false)]
  public class Product : ServicedComponent, IProduct
  {
     [SecurityRoleAttribute("Customer", false)]
      public double GetPrice() {
             //Implementation goes in here
```

This fragment also provides an example of how optional attributes are used for:

- Specifying specific GUID under which COM+ clients will "know" instances of *Product*
- Requiring authorization checks for invocation requests on *Product* objects
- Giving role *staff* access to all *Product* objects
- Allowing role *customer* to invoke method *GetPrice*

These attributes serve as a complementary mechanism to the one provided in a GUI form through the Component Services Administrative Tool snap-in, used for configuring COM+ servers, in Microsoft Management Console (MMC). We described the snap-in in the COM+ section of this chapter. The attributes do not introduce anything new to the already discussed COM+ architecture and its security mechanisms, so after the assembly is installed as a COM+ server with the tools from .NET Framework SDK, COM+ and .NET clients can use it right away. This is a great help for those developers, like most of us, who need to reinstall and reconfigure an application numerous times during coding and testing phases, and is helpful for streamlining application deployment. If you know COM+ and its security, you already know how to develop secure .NET-based distributed servers and expose them as COM+ components.

Since COM+ is quite a rich application server platform and significantly more mature than object remoting, which is discussed in the next section, it is the primary candidate for hosting middleware applications, as long as you can confine yourself to the Microsoft-only world. Even though this way of developing distributed servers with .NET seems to be very pleasant and painless, it is constrained by the COM/DCOM computational and distribution models. For example, only the object default constructor (that is, no parameters are provided by the caller) can be used, and an application server is accessible only via DCOM (unless it is deployed on Windows XP Pro or Windows.NET, where SOAP/HTTP is also supported by COM+ v1.5). The alternate approach, albeit new and not widely used, is the remoting architecture of .NET CLR.

Object Remoting

Just as the RMI architecture in the Java world gives you a means to "connect" two applications running in different JVMs, object remoting (or just "remoting" for short) enables remote invocations between .NET objects in application domains located in the same or different processes, or on different machines. Although other means, for example, COM and bare TCP sockets, are always an option, remoting is tightly integrated with the .NET data and computational architectures, which makes it almost transparent to programming. The client's code uses regular methods, such as via function *new()*, to create a remote object and uses it as if it were a local one, since everything is hidden in the local proxy representing the remote object.

A .NET developer usually follows the following steps to develop a distributed application with the use of remoting:

1. Writes remotely accessible business logic classes and compiles them into a .NET DLL
2. Configures a managed executable (.EXE) to host those classes
3. Writes and configures the client(s) that call the remoted classes

Let's briefly look at each of these steps. Writing a remoted class is no different from coding any other .NET class, except that the former needs to be derived from *MarshallByRefObject*. While objects derived from *MarshallByRefObject* can be referenced by remote clients, it is also possible to pass objects by value. To do this, an object either has to implement interface *ISerializable* or to have the metadata attribute [Serializable] declared on the object's class. In the latter case, the remoting mechanisms will do a member-wide recursive copy of an object's public and private member variables.

Once the remoted classes for an application server are implemented, an application that will host them needs to be configured. Any .NET managed executable can be used as a host as long as it can do two things:

- Configure a remoting transport channel through which clients will access the server objects
- Register each remoted class

It is easy to do both tasks either programmatically or via a configuration file passed to a .NET base class that implements remoting service. Here, you have several options.

First, you need to choose the type of channel and data formatter (that is, the format that will be used for marshaled data). Version 1 of .NET Framework comes with HTTP and bare TCP channels (which are much faster than HTTP). As for types of data formatting, either proprietary binary or limited SOAP formats can be used .[4]

Second, the hosting application needs to know how the objects are activated. An object can be activated either as a *singleton*, when the same instance serves all calls, as a *singlecall*, when each client call is serviced by a new object instance, or as *client activated*, when a client creates, uses, and releases a particular instance of the remote object.

[4] It is not clear from Microsoft documentation if a SOAP formatter can be used with the TCP channel.

You can either write your own hosting application or use Microsoft's Web server IIS to host your remoted objects. Since IIS is itself not a managed application, it forwards all requests for remoted objects to ASP.NET. With the mandatory choice of the HTTP channel, either of the two formats can be used. SOAP formatting allows remoted objects to be exposed as Web Services, but with limitations: the inability of SOAP clients to use client activated objects, the use of RPC SOAP encoding, and the lack of support for object constructors with parameters.

To use a remoted object type, a client registers an object's proxy with the run time and specifies the URL where the remoted object can be found. Again, both programmatic and configuration file options are available. Once this is done, a client handles a remoted object as a local one.

Now you are probably thinking, "This is all well and good, but what about security?"

Securing Remoted Objects

Remoting, unlike COM(+), does not have any security mechanisms beyond those available to all other .NET applications. To secure a distributed application built using .NET remoting, you need to rely on the protection provided by the .NET security mechanisms and the application hosting the remoted objects.

For example, if IIS hosts your remoted objects or you need to protect ASP.NET Web Services, then IIS and ASP.NET security mechanisms are put to use. These mechanisms are described in detail in Chapter 8, "Securing .NET Web Services." At this point, we will explain what support you get from .NET security for protecting remoted objects.

.NET Security

As in the case of other modern distributed computing technologies hosted by an OS, such as Java and CORBA, .NET security rests on OS protection mechanisms, which it trusts unconditionally. However, the CLR does not trust the managed code it executes. Before it executes the code, the run time verifies and validates it, then checks whether the code and the user identity associated with the code runtime context have sufficient permissions.

The implementation of all these checks is founded on the five cornerstones of the .NET security model:

- Code access security
- Permissions
- Policies
- .NET principal and identity
- "Role-based" access control

CLR verifies the IL code before compiling it into native binary form and executing it, and validates the assembly metadata. In addition to type-safety checks, the IL verification algorithm in the run time also checks for the occurrence of a stack underflow/overflow, correct use of the exception-handling facilities, and object initialization.

Even if the code is successfully verified and its metadata is validated, both the code group and the principal associated with the execution context must have sufficient privileges to access a resource or perform a privileged operation. This is when code access security comes into the picture. The CLR classifies all code into code groups according to one or more of the following membership conditions:

- Zone
- Site
- Assembly "strong name"
- Publisher
- URL
- Hash value of the assembly
- Skip verification
- Directory within the application
- User-specified conditions

Code groups are organized into a hierarchy with the least privileged group at the root, and then the other more powerful groups in descending order.

Any .NET resource or privileged operation can be associated with one or more permissions. Permissions represent authorizations to access protected resources or to perform protected operations. A security-aware application can require that a particular permission be present in the granted permission set. If the permission is not present, a security exception is thrown at run time by the CLR. An application can also deny or assert permissions, which causes them to be added or removed from the granted permission set. .NET declarative mechanisms allow a programmer to specify a minimum set of permissions through attributes, without which the application will not run at all. In keeping with good principles of extensibility, custom permission classes can also be defined.

Administrators and users grant permissions to code groups by modifying policy files. Each installation of .NET Framework has one policy file per policy level: enterprise, machine, and the individual user. The enterprise, machine, and user policy levels are configured by security policy administrators and users. The application domain policy level can be programmatically configured by hosts. When a .NET application is executed, the policy files of the user—whose OS identity is assigned to the application's process—the machine, and the enterprise are used to compute permissions granted to the code groups. First, the permission set for enterprise, machine, and user levels is computed, and then their intersection is used as the result.

NOTE It is possible to specify in an enterprise or machine policy file that any policy below that level should not be evaluated. In that case, no "lower" policy level would produce a permission set.

An obvious question is how enterprise security policy is administered. .NET security architects provide the following solution, which maintains consistent policy from machine to machine across the whole enterprise: an enterprise security administrator uses the .NET Framework configuration GUI to create a security policy deployment package, and then installs it across multiple machines.

Synchronization of machine-level policies and changes to the enterprise policies are done the same way. Since the whole technology is so new, it's hard to predict how this relatively low-tech way, with questionable administration scalability, will be accepted by enterprises.

Code access security is devised to protect against Trojan horses and other malicious code, but it is not as effective in protecting middleware servers as the other mechanism of the .NET security model—access checks against the identity of the executing context. Its core abstractions are principals and identities.

Identity represents the user on whose behalf the code is executing. This could be a logical user as defined by the .NET application or developer, and not necessarily the user associated with the operating system process in which the application is running. A principal is an aggregation of a user and the user security attributes, called "roles" in .NET. There is only one principal per thread, and one identity per principal. Note that the same principal can be associated with several threads, and the same identity can be related to several principals, as shown in Figure 7.15.

Since a thread's principal and the associated identity are not bound to the Windows identity of the process, a piece of code, provided it has enough privileges, can replace both the principal and the identity on its thread with any other implementation of the interfaces. This makes the whole model of .NET principal and identity very flexible and provides opportunities for custom authentication schemes to be integrated with built-in access control—a key enabler of electronic commerce applications. At the same time, the flexibility demands very careful permission administration to avoid opening security holes in .NET.

The UML class diagram in the figure also shows public methods and properties that can be used to inspect the corresponding interface implementations. A security-aware application can check if a principal has a particular attribute by invoking method *IsInRole(string attribute)*, and obtain a reference to the corresponding identity via property Identity. Identity interface implementation can be queried if it has been created as a result of an authentication, the type of authentication used, and the name.

Thanks to the .NET declarative attributes that can decorate assemblies, classes, interfaces, and methods, it is possible to instruct the CLR security to ensure that a class, interface, or method is accessed by code only if the principal associated with the running thread has required attributes. As shown in the code below, the developer only needs to put the attribute *PrincipalPermissionAttribute* in front of the protected element.

```
public class Product : IProduct
 {
     [PrincipalPermissionAttribute(SecurityAction.Demand,
                                            Role="customer")]
     public double GetPrice()
     {
```

It is also possible to use the Microsoft Windows security model, if developers wish. In this situation, users and roles are tied to those on the hosting machine; therefore, accounts may need to be created on the hosting system.

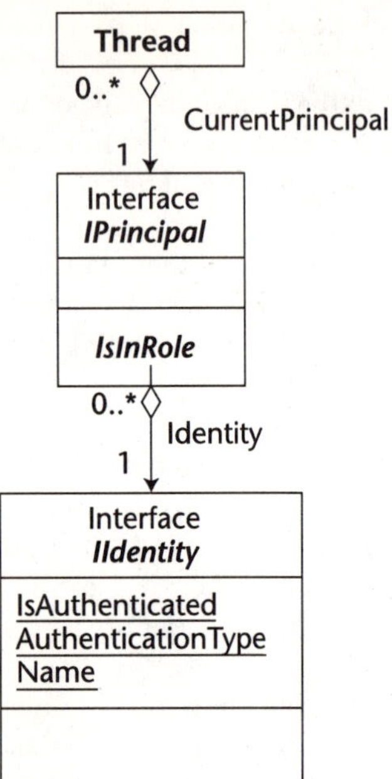

Figure 7.15 Relationships among .NET thread, principal, and identity.

Regarding accountability, developers can program an application to send log records to the Windows event log service on a local or remote machine, using the *EventLog* class that comes with .NET SDK libraries. It even allows an application to receive an event when an entry is written to a log. Unfortunately, there are no declarative means to make .NET Framework perform an audit for security-unaware applications.

The .NET security model follows the modern trend towards practicality, simplification, flexibility, and extensibility of security mechanisms. Its architecture is tailored for practical problems, not for academic challenges. Because it is not as extensive as COM(+) and CORBA security, it is closer to Java in its relative minimalism and extensibility. More an execution framework than a middleware platform, .NET with its remoting mechanisms does not implement authentication, message protection, and other functionalities essential for distributed applications. Instead, it relies on the hosting application server platform, such as IIS and COM+, to complete the protection task. Similarly, J2EE serves as an application server platform for distributed Java applications. You can find a detailed description of .NET Framework's security architecture in LaMacchia (2002).

J2EE

Java 2 Platform, Enterprise Edition (J2EE) is gaining popularity as a platform for server-side Java deployments. Like CORBA, J2EE is a specification that defines a contract between application developers and vendors of the runtime infrastructure and services. In addition to the specification, Sun Microsystems—which defines J2EE, with the help of Java Community Process member companies—provides a test suite, a reference implementation, and "BluePrints" documents. The latter describe how to use the J2EE technologies together. The current version of J2EE, v1.3, contains the following groups of APIs that can be used by server application developers:

Enterprise Java Beans (EJB). These define a standard contract between server-side components and the application servers.

Java Remote Method Invocation (RMI) and **RMI-IIOP.** The latter is the API for standard RMI over IIOP wire protocol used between J2EE components.

Java Naming and Directory Interface (JNDI). For accessing naming and directory services.

Java Database Connectivity (JDBC). For accessing relational databases.

Java Transaction API (JTA) and Java Transaction Service (JTS). Used for utilizing transactional services by applications.

Java Messaging Service (JMS). For communicating via message-oriented middleware (MOM) such as IBM MQSeries or Microsoft Messaging Queue.

Java Servlets and Java Server Pages (JSPs). For programming presentation logic in Web servers.

Java IDL. For programming with Sun's CORBA ORB.

JavaMail. For sending email messages from inside of applications.

J2EE Connector Architecture (JCA). For accessing existing enterprise information systems.

Java API for XML Parsing (JAXP). For working with XML documents.

Java Authentication and Authorization Service (JAAS). For accessing authentication and authorization services.

To improve your understanding of this multitude of services and the relationships among them, we show the key elements in Figure 7.16.

For our discussion, the most interesting items in the list are EJB and JAAS. Even though Java Servlets are the first entry point for SOAP requests, Enterprise JavaBeans are the focal middle-tier point in J2EE applications because they contain the main business logic. Therefore, in the next sections, we will describe the EJB security architecture. We will cover JAAS when we discuss J2EE support for authentication.

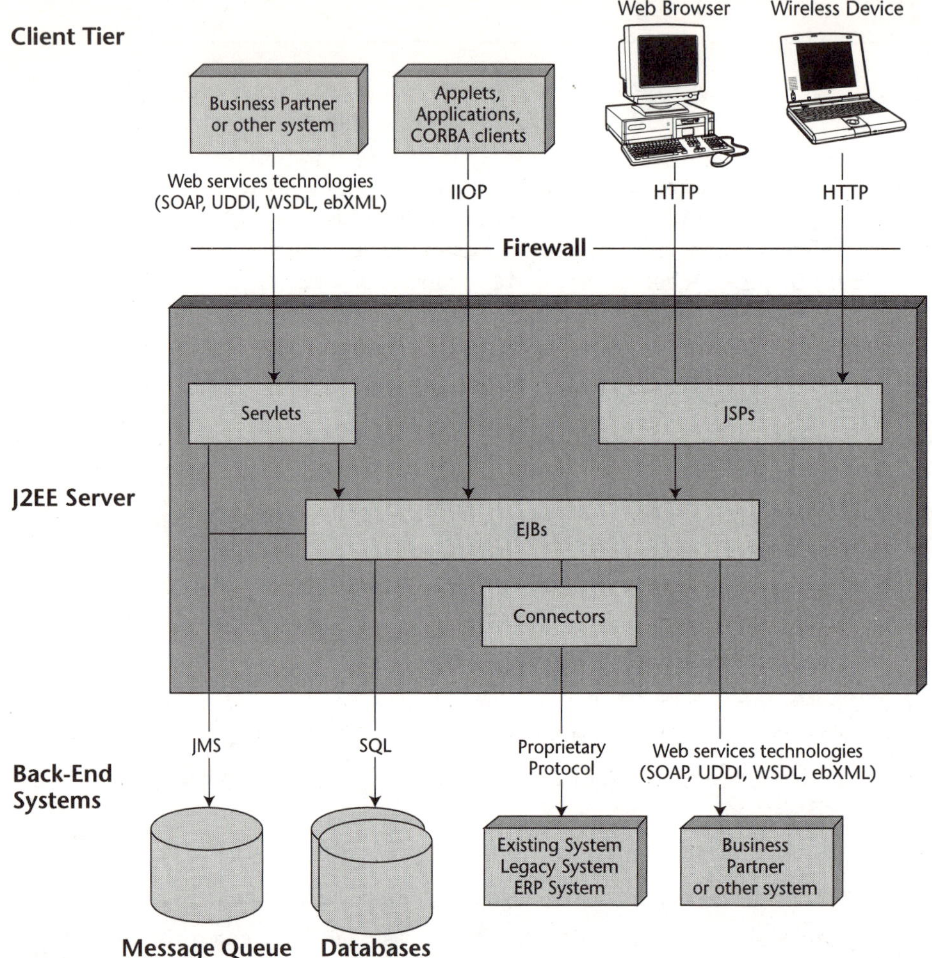

Figure 7.16 A J2EE deployment (adopted from Roman, Ed. Mastering Enterprise JavaBeans, 2e. Wiley 2002).

How EJB Works

The EJB standard is an architecture for deployable server-side components in Java. Serving as an agreement between components and application servers, this standard consists of the specification and the APIs. Products based on the EJB specification have compelling advantages:

- They shield application developers from many of the low-level object service details (such as transactions, state management, persistence management, load balancing, security, and others).

- They enable enterprise beans to be ported to another environment with minimal effort.
- They are interoperable with other EJB products.

Fully compliant EJB products support the IIOP protocol, leveraging IIOP and CSIv2 capabilities and allowing CORBA clients (that can be written in languages other than Java) to access enterprise bean objects.

EJB architecture has the following basic parts, as illustrated in Figure 7.17:

Enterprise bean. A special Java component that implements business logic executed in the runtime environment provided by the component's container.

EJB container. Where the EJB component "lives." An EJB container provides services such as transaction and resource management, versioning, scalability, mobility, persistence, and security to the enterprise beans it contains. Multiple enterprise beans typically exist inside a single container.

EJB server. Provides runtime environment to one or more containers. Since EJB does not explicitly define the separation of roles between containers and servers, containers and servers usually come inseparable in one system.

Remote interface. The remote interface of an enterprise bean represents the bean's business logic to remote clients. That is, the clients access the bean business logic via its remote interface.

EJB object. Provided by the container and serving as an interception point where most of the work for serving the bean is done. Implements the remote interface on the way to the bean.

Home interface. Provides factory methods that allow remote clients to request that an instance of an enterprise bean be created and initialized.

Home object. Implements the methods specified in the home interface.

Local interface and EJB local object. Provide local access to the bean from other enterprise beans running in the same container.

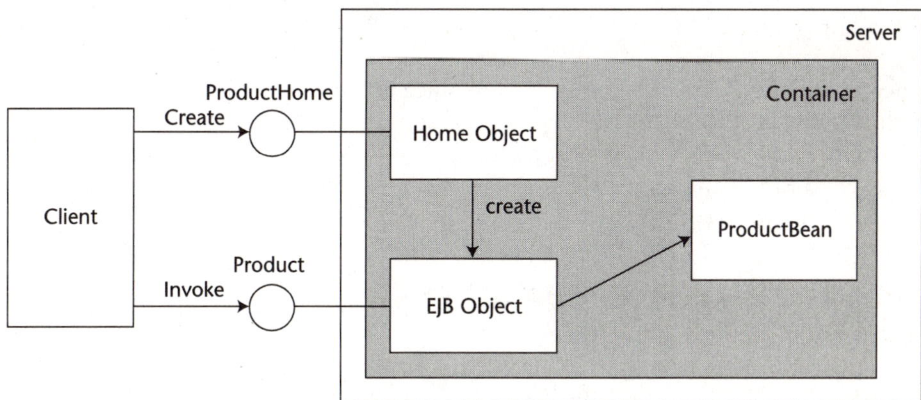

Figure 7.17 Main parts of EJB architecture.

Declarative Part

Defining remote, home, and local interfaces as well as implementing the business logic in EJB is as easy as in standard Java. Here, for example, is the definition of the remote interface for the Product enterprise bean.

```
package com.ebusiness;

public interface Product extends javax.ejb.EJBObject
{
      public float getPrice();
      public void setPrice(float newPrice)
throws InvalidPriceException;
};
```

The product interface, to be an eligible remote interface, inherits from the *EJBObject* interface, which defines additional methods needed by an EJB container. Other than that, it is regular standalone Java code that can use all the capabilities including standard or application-specific exceptions, inheritance, method overloading, and so on.

A bean developer specifies transactional, security, and other requirements for the application in the deployment descriptor—an XML file with predefined syntax that holds all the explicit metadata for the assembly. The descriptor can be later augmented and altered in other ways by an application assembler and deployer, who also play specific roles in the life cycle of enterprise beans predefined by EJB specification.

If you want to extend your knowledge of EJB, we recommend reading a definitive guide, *Mastering Enterprise JavaBeans* by Ed Roman (Roman 2002).

Runtime Part

While the remote object model for EJB components is based on the Remote Method Invocation (RMI) API, all invocations between J2EE components are performed using IIOP. The use of the RMI remote invocation model over the IIOP wire protocol is usually referred to as RMI-IIOP. When EJB components use RMI-IIOP (mandatory for EJB 2.0), the standard mapping of the EJB architecture to CORBA enables interoperability with multi-vendor ORBs, other EJB servers, and CORBA clients written in a language other than Java.

Because of the IIOP, the same object reference used for CORBA is used in the EJB world. Moreover, it would not be surprising if your EJB server uses a CORBA-like ORB as an underlying layer that handles networking for the server. The similarities between CORBA and EJB lie in their use of a secure channel, as well as their client and server security layer architectures.

Roles and Responsibilities of CSS, TSS, and Secure Channel

The basic security model for EJB, as depicted in Figure 7.18, is conceptually simple: When the client program invokes a method on a target EJB object, the identity of the subject associated with the calling client is transmitted to the EJB object's container—

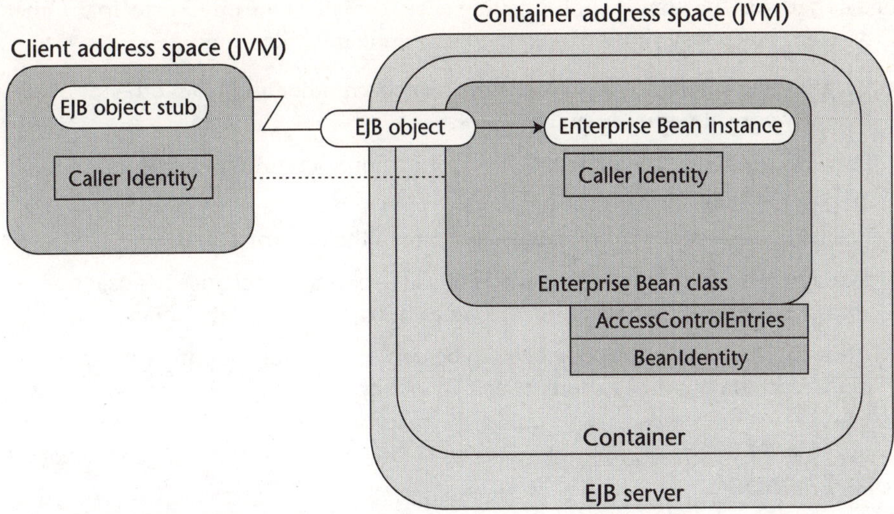

Figure 7.18 The EJB security model.

the major part of an EJB application server. The container checks to see whether the calling subject has a right to invoke the requested method. If so, the container permits the invocation on the method.

Client Security Service

Because of the use of IIOP and CSIv2, the responsibilities of an EJB CSS are similar to those of a CORBA CSS: (1) creating a secure channel with the TSS and (2) obtaining the user's authenticated credentials or passing username and password over the CSIv2 context to TSS, as well as (3) protecting request messages and verifying response messages.

The main distinction is that EJB does not mandate that the client or server security subsystem be compliant to CORBASec. Therefore, as long as CSS and TSS can "talk" to each other using CSIv2 level 0, they can be implemented in any form. This also means that neither CSS nor TSS has to implement auditing or nonrepudiation functions, or any of the CORBASec APIs, for the client or server to enforce application-specific security policies. However, as will be described later, the server container provides a number of methods useful to security-aware applications.

Target Security Service

Treated by the EJB security model as an integral part of the server container, a TSS establishes and maintains a secure channel with the clients, verifies authenticated credentials or performs client authentication itself, implements message protection policies, and performs access checks before an invocation is dispatched to an enterprise bean. Depending on the application configuration, which is done through the deployment descriptor, the container associates the runtime security context of the dispatched method either with the identity of the calling client or with some other principal. Other security-related responsibilities of a container include the following:

- Isolating the enterprise bean instances from each other and from other application components running on the server
- Preventing enterprise bean instances from gaining unauthorized access to the system information of the server and its resources
- Ensuring the security of the persistent state of the enterprise beans
- Managing the mapping of principals on calls to other enterprise beans, or on access to resource managers, according to the defined security policy
- Allowing the same enterprise bean to be deployed independently multiple times, each time with a different security policy

Secure Channel

The secure interoperability requirements for EJB v2.0 and other J2EE v1.3 containers is based on the CSIv2 specification that we discussed in the CORBA section of this chapter. J2EE requires CSIv2 Level 0 conformance, which defines the base level of secure interoperability that all CSIv2 implementations are required to support. This includes SSLv3.0/TLSv1.0 protected connections with all mandatory TLS (and their SSL equivalent) cryptographic mechanisms. Level 0 implementations are also required to support the Security Attribute Service (SAS) layer with stateless CSS and TSS, and with support for username/password client authentication and identity assertion by using the service context protocol.

Implementation of Security functions

The EJB 2.0 specification focuses largely on authentication and access control. It relies on CSIv2 level 0 for message protection, and it leaves support for security auditing to the discretion of container vendors.

Authentication

Although EJB v2.0 does not mandate any particular mechanism or protocol for client authentication, it suggests using the Java Authentication and Authorization Service (JAAS) (Sun 2001) API. JAAS provides a standard and uniform interface behind which authentication modules, each responsible for a particular authentication mechanism, can acquire client credentials. Adhering to the JAAS interface, such modules can be provided by different parties and used in concert in the same runtime environment on the client side.

Unfortunately, the JAAS specification does not define how client credentials, authenticated via JAAS, are passed from CSS to TSS. JAAS is a generic architecture used not only by J2EE but also by J2SE applications. It leaves the transport of client credentials to the EJB server implementation, which could jeopardize secure interoperability between heterogeneous implementations. This is where CSIv2 comes in. As you remember from its description at the beginning of the chapter, CSIv2 enables client credentials or authentication data to be transported to the TSS in an interoperable form. If a TSS receives authentication data (only username and password for CSIv2 level 0) or credentials from a client over CSIv2, it can again use JAAS APIs to authenticate the client or verify the received credentials. Once the container knows the authenticated identity of the client, it enforces access control policies as defined by EJB specification.

Access Control

The EJB access control model is undergoing an update from the predefined model configured in the deployment descriptor to a new one, which will allow third-party authorization engines supporting different access models to be used by EJB containers. The committee of Java Specification Request (JSR) involving 115 experts had just submitted a proposal on this topic for public comments at the time this book was written, so it is too early to know exactly what the upcoming changes will be. For that reason, we recommend that you track the work of this JSR at the Java Community Process Web site (http://www.jcp.org), where you will find the latest version of the "J2EE Authorization Contract for Containers" specification. The rest of this section describes the current version of the access control model for EJB, which is quite straightforward.

Configured by an application deployment descriptor, the container controls access to enterprise beans down to the level of an individual method on a bean class, although not a bean instance. If different instances of the same bean have different access control requirements, they should be placed in different application assemblies. This means that the scope of the EJB's policy domain is the application assembly. In addition, it is possible to grant different permissions for methods with the same names but different parameter types.

The EJB access control model allows us to group methods with "method permissions" and grant access on all methods in a method permission group to one or more "security roles." Both method permissions and security roles enable administration scalability, which we will describe in detail in the section on security administration for EJB.

Delegation

EJB v2.0 requires containers to support simple unconstrained delegation, when a bean method is executed in a context with the caller's identity. It is possible to configure each bean to either impersonate the caller or to run as a particular security role. This delegation is supported in remote calls through the CSIv2 protocol.

Administration

Some security administration tasks of EJB servers are performed through changes in deployment descriptors. This includes definition of security roles, method permissions, and specification of security identity, either delegated or predetermined, for dispatching calls to bean methods. Other tasks, such as mapping users to roles, specifying message protection, administering an audit, and authentication mechanisms, are beyond the scope of the EJB specification and are therefore left up to the vendors of container products and deployment tools.

Defined independently in each deployment descriptor, access control and delegation policies have natural limits on their effects—all the beans are located in the same EJB JAR file. However, this does not preclude development of administrative tools that can ensure consistency of the policies across deployment descriptors in multiple JAR files.

Access Control Policy

A deployment descriptor, besides other things, specifies the access policy for the corresponding application composed of one or more enterprise beans. An application access policy is constructed using sections called "security roles" and "method permissions." Although called a "security role," it is in fact "a semantic grouping of permissions that a given type of users of the application must have to successfully use the application" as the EJB v2.0 defines it. These permission groupings could have different meanings in each assembly and should be treated as unrelated in most cases.

The following deployment descriptor fragment depicts the security portion that would be created for our eBusiness company. In this example, there are four security roles nested in the *<assembly-descriptor>* element, and a role name and an optional description are nested in each *<security-role>* element. Also, note that the names of the tags, such as *<role-name>*, have been defined by the specification and should be used as specified.

```
<assembly-descriptor>
     <security-role>
          <description>
               This role includes the members of the online
               business who are allowed to access the
               special products application. Only users
               who have the role member can access the special
               products.
          </description>
          <role-name>member</role-name>
     </security-role>

     <security-role>
          <description>
               This role includes the customers of the online
               business. This role is only allowed to
               access the regular products.
          </description>
          <role-name>customer</role-name>
     </security-role>
     <security-role>
          <description>
               This role should be assigned to the personnel
               of the online store who are authorized
               to perform administrative functions.
```

```
        </description>
        <role-name>staff</role-name>
    </security-role>
        ...
</assembly-descriptor>
```

This portion of the deployment descriptor defines the security roles called *member*, *customer*, and *staff* and provides a description of each. The EJB specification deliberately leaves the mapping between user identities and these roles up to the EJB container implementation or the employed security technology. Once roles are defined, they can be used in "method permissions" to specify who can invoke what methods. A "method permission" element of a deployment descriptor defines a permission to invoke a specified group of methods of the enterprise beans' home and remote interfaces. Here is an example showing how one could define access rights for the roles *customer*, *member*, and *staff* on *Product* beans.

```
<method-permission>
    <role-name>staff</role-name>
    <method>
        <ejb-name>Product</ejb-name>
        <method-name>*</method-name>
    </method>
</method-permission>

<method-permission>
    <role-name>customer</role-name>
    <role-name>member</role-name>
    <method>
        <ejb-name>Product</ejb-name>
        <method-name>getPrice</method-name>
    </method>
</method-permission>
```

Here, we grant full access on both bean classes to staff, and allow customers and members to obtain product prices. Access control is one of the few security policies that can be administered through standard deployment descriptors.

Delegation Policy

Delegation is another policy configurable via the deployment descriptor. The *<security-identity>* element, which can be defined for each bean, serves two purposes. If it contains the *<use-caller-identity>* element, then the bean impersonates the caller while serving requests, providing simple unconstrained delegation. If, on the other hand, *<security-identity>* contains the *<runAs-specified-identity>* element with a nested role name, then no delegation takes place, and the specified role is associated with the runtime context of the bean for processing all invocations. Here is a usage example that specifies that the security role *customer* should be used by *ShoppingCart* beans. Keep in mind that access to a bean is controlled independently of the bean's identity.

```
<enterprise-beans>
    ...
    <session>
        <ejb-name>ShoppingCart</ejb-name>
        ...
        <security-identity>
            <runAs-specified-identity>
                <role-name>customer</role-name>
            </runAs-specified-identity>
        </security-identity>
        ...
    </session>
    ...
</enterprise-beans>
```

There is one more security setting available in EJB deployment descriptors. Since it is useful only to security-aware applications, we describe it in the following section.

Enforcing Fine-Grained Security

EJB supports fine-grained application-specific access control by defining the following methods, similar to those in COM+ and .NET, on the runtime context available to the business logic:

- *getCallerPrincipal()* returning implementation of the *Principal* interface, which can be used for obtaining its name and hash code, associated with the execution context
- *isCallerInRole(String roleName)* testing if the current caller is in the specified role

NOTE These methods perform their checks on the principal associated with the caller, not the principal that corresponds to the <security-identity> element of the executing bean.

EJB makes the life of application deployers easier by having provisions for bean developers to specify in the deployment descriptor what roles an application checks in the calls to *isCallerInRole()*. It also defines syntax for linking these roles with the ones defined for the application.

As you can see, the overall support for fine-grained application-specific security policies in EJB is limited to the basic tasks. However, container vendors could have proprietary extensions supporting more demanding applications.

Summary

We hope that this long and dense chapter helped you to get familiar with the security of today's commercial middleware technologies—CORBA, .NET and Java—and application server platforms—CCM, COM+ and EJB. Understanding the security of your middle tier is a prerequisite to the advanced task of safely exposing the mid-tier functionality through SOAP gateways.

The first section explained the security aspects of client/server and object paradigms and traced a recognizable pattern in all of them: client and server security services, along with a secure channel, constitute a security layer that implements the security functionalities used by the ORB layer. The majority of the discussed technologies implement (to different extents) the main groups of mechanisms, particularly authentication, message protection, access control, credentials delegation, auditing, and administration.

All other sections reviewed CORBA, COM+, .NET, and EJB in the light of the framework we described in the first section. Through these sections, you could see a multitude of ways security functions are designed. CORBA and COM+ security is mostly defined through APIs. .NET and EJB mix APIs with declarative policy files. COM+ and .NET are defined through implementations, whereas CORBA and EJB are specified by standards.

COM(+) and CORBA belong to approximately the same generation of middleware technologies and provide a similarly rich—though complex and harder to use—functionality. Part of a newer wave, EJB and .NET focus more on flexibility and extensibility, including security design, which enables us to hide the complexity behind configurable interfaces and bundling basic implementations for the majority of users, while letting more sophisticated users plug in complex logic. Users building client/server and simple point-to-point systems can be satisfied with the protection models of .NET and EJB, while those with advanced requirements will need to extend the technologies or use CORBA and COM+, which is more suitable for their end-to-end scalable security needs. This is yet another example of having to make trade-offs: programming models of EJB and .NET are more modern and hide quite a bit of complexity of distributed application development, and yet CORBA and COM+ have more advanced distributed security mechanisms exposed to security developers and administrators.

Next, we shift our emphasis away from an overview of available security technologies that support Web Services. In the following chapters, we will discuss how those security technologies can be applied when building a Web Service generally, and our ePortal and eBusiness Web Service example in particular. We will begin by examining how to secure a Web Services implementation using .NET.

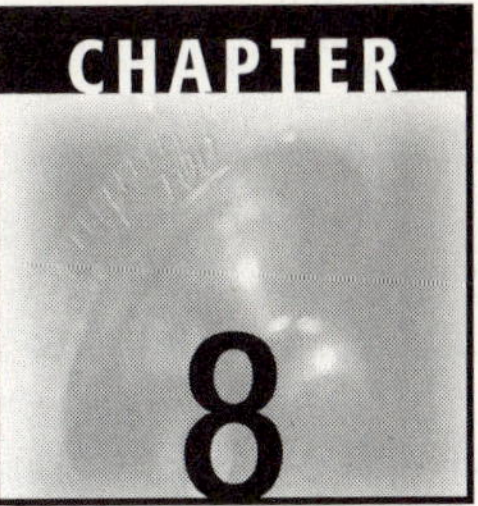

Securing .NET Web Services

The previous chapters discussed the security needs of Web Services and ways of addressing them in general. Your specific Web Services security solution depends on the security mechanisms available on your selected application platform. This chapter describes the security features you can use when your Web Services are implemented using the Microsoft .NET framework. You'll see that not only are there multiple options for building a Web Service with .NET, there are also multiple alternatives for protecting Web Services applications. To help you with the multitude of decisions you will face, we describe at the end of the chapter a prospective approach for protecting our sample eBusiness Web Service when using .NET. This chapter requires basic knowledge of the .NET framework and its security mechanisms, which were explained in Chapter 7, "Security of Infrastructures for Web Services."

IIS Security Mechanisms

We begin by providing you with a brief background on the security features of Microsoft's Internet Information Server (IIS). An important building block of Microsoft's Web Services solutions, IIS plays a critical role in protecting the hosted .NET Web Services that we will describe in this chapter. The security mechanisms IIS provides can be classified in the following basic groups: authentication, message protection, access control, logging, and fault isolation, which we describe below.

Authentication

IIS authentication mechanisms are not that much different from what most other Web servers provide. For each directory, one or more authentication options, shown in Figure 8.1, may be selected.

All of the features, except the last method in the figure, are likely to be found on any other vendor's Web server. Tailored specifically to Windows environments not separated by firewalls, integrated Windows authentication can use either NTLM or Kerberos V5 and only works with Internet Explorer 2.0 and later. When a user with an IE browser attempts to access a protected resource, IIS negotiates with the browser, and one of the two mechanisms gets used.

All these methods authenticate incoming HTTP requests. If, however, the server is configured with SSL/TLS support, then client connections could be authenticated with client X.509 certificates mapped into OS accounts (Microsoft 2000). Even without client certificates, use of SSL/TLS is always a good idea in the case of basic and digest authentication, because it protects the exchange of authentication data, otherwise vulnerable to eavesdropping and/or replay attacks.

We provided background on these authentication mechanisms in Chapter 3, "Getting Started with Web Services Security." If you are looking for additional information, Microsoft 2001a provides a brief summary and also lists pros and cons for each. Distinctive to IIS is the way it implements anonymous authentication. It is important to understand that any, even anonymous, HTTP request is handled by some HTTP handler running with a particular identity recognized by the OS. If simple delegation, also known as impersonation, is not turned on, then all handlers use the same identity as the IIS itself. Once the administrator enables impersonation, the handlers start working with the identity of the authenticated user. But anonymous requests don't have any identity, you might guess. Wrong! (See Figure 8.2.)

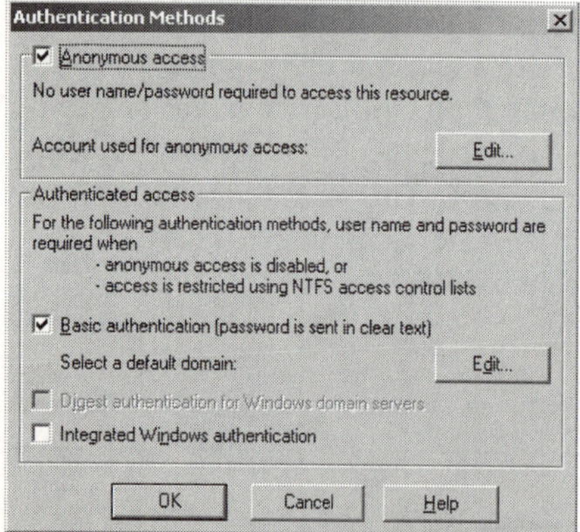

Figure 8.1 Per-directory authentication methods available for IIS-hosted applications. (Courtesy: Microsoft Corporation).

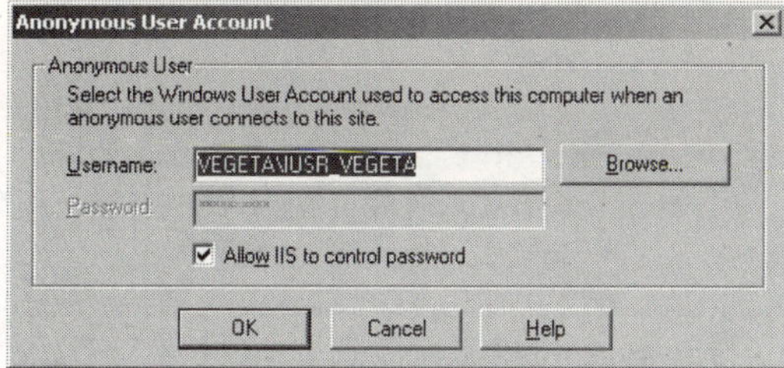

Figure 8.2 IIS uses a configurable user account for anonymous requests. (Courtesy: Microsoft Corporation).

As Figure 8.2 illustrates, IIS provides stored credentials to Windows using a special user account, IUSR_<machinename>, which can be changed to any other account. Even for anonymous requests, HTTP handlers impersonate a legitimate user account, which is assigned particular privileges and granted some permissions. Whether or not IIS controls the password, the check box at the bottom of Figure 8.2, affects the permissions the anonymous user has. When IIS controls the password, Windows authenticates the user and creates a network logon that prevents the user from accessing resources on other machines. When IIS does not control the password, it uses slightly different means and, as a result, a local logon is created instead. A local logon makes it possible for the corresponding HTTP handler to impersonate an anonymous user while accessing network resources, including calls to remote COM and COM+ components. With natively supporting multi-hop delegation Kerberos, introduced in Windows 2000, things became even trickier. At the end of the day, all this requires you to be even more careful while designing distributed applications with Microsoft technologies.

Protecting Data in Transit

Authenticity, confidentiality, and integrity protection of messages in transit between HTTP clients and IIS can be implemented using either SSL/TLS, by configuring the Web server, or IPSEC (IETF 2002, Microsoft 1999), if this technology is part of your company's (and your partners') infrastructure. Since SSL is a mature technology that every Webmaster is familiar with these days, we will skip the description of particular steps necessary to configure an IIS server for SSL. If you need detailed instructions, there are numerous sources of information. Just for starters, read "Configuring SSL/TLS" in Chapter 5 of Howard (2000), and you can get up-to-date information by searching for "IIS SSL" at the Microsoft MSDN Web site (http://msdn.microsoft.com). Keep in mind that both approaches give, at most, point-to-point protection, which may or may not be sufficient, depending on your use of Web Services, as we discussed in Chapter 6, "Principles of Securing Web Services."

Access Control

All these efforts by IIS—to use a system account for anonymous requests, map clients authenticated with X.509 certificates into user accounts, and support impersonation by HTTP handlers—are mainly for the sake of leveraging native OS access control mechanisms for protecting IIS resources. When an HTTP handler accesses an HTML or any other file in order to process the corresponding HTTP request, Windows file system permissions in the form of a discretionary access control list (DACL) are used by the OS to enforce access control policies. Keep in mind that this mechanism is only available on NTFS file systems. If a file to be accessed resides on a FAT partition, no access checks are done.

Two other access control mechanisms—Web permissions and IP-based restrictions—could be used in addition to DACL controls, if any. Web permissions allow you to set coarse-grained authorization policies per Web site, virtual directory, directory, or file. Since user identity is not taken into account in Web permissions, the same policy applies to all requests, which could be useful when you need to set a common low watermark for a branch of your IIS resources. Web permissions allow tweaking the following options that are important for Web Services, shown also in Figure 8.3:

- Read - Data can be read or downloaded.
- Write - Data can be written to or files can be uploaded using HTTP PUT verb.
- Directory Browsing - Clients are able to receive directory listing.
- Execute Permissions:
  - None—ASP (.ASP) files and executable (batch, .EXE, and .DLL) files will not run.
  - Scripts Only—ASP, but not executable, files will run.
  - Scripts and Executables—Both ASP and executable files will run.

Even more coarse grained is the IP address and domain name restriction mechanism provided by IIS on Windows Server installations. Using it, you can grant access to all hosts other than specified, or reversibly, deny access to all but particular hosts. As with Web permissions, this mechanism can be configured to control access to an entire Web site or down to specific files.

Logging

Security auditing is not an option for IIS, although its logging facilities can serve as a partial substitution. If configured to do so, IIS logs information in text format about HTTP requests into %winnt%\system32\LogFiles\W3SVC<n>, where <n> is the number of the Web site instance. You can select, per Web site instance, what information is recorded about processed requests. There are around 20 request-specific details and a number of process accounting properties that could be recorded on each request. Figure 8.4 shows the logging properties selection window.

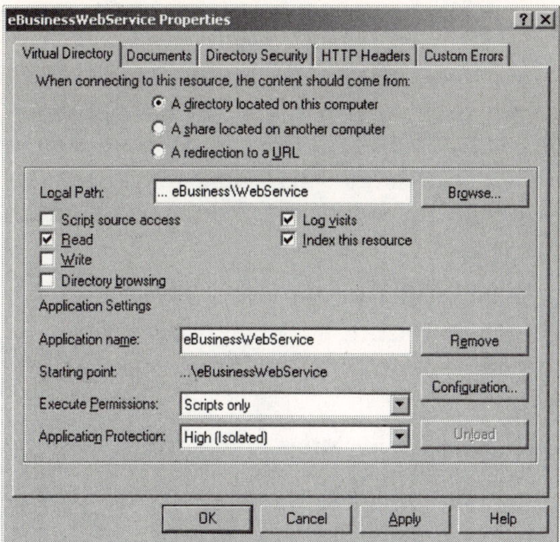

Figure 8.3 Web permission options for a virtual directory.
(Courtesy: Microsoft Corporation).

Whether to log a request to a particular IIS resource is determined by the option "Log visits," shown in Figure 8.3. You can turn this inheritable switch on or off per Web site, virtual directory, subdirectory, or file.

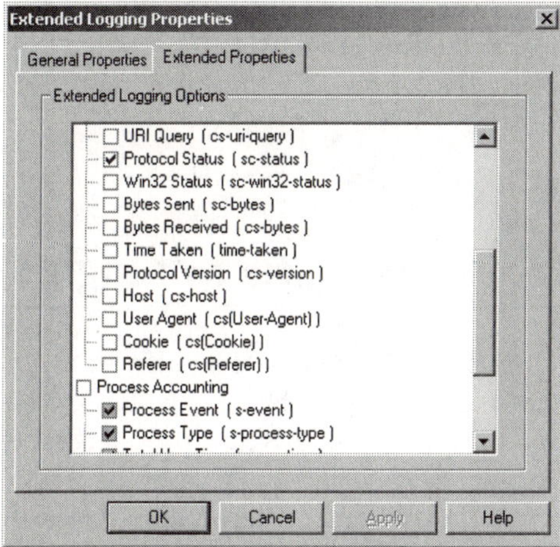

Figure 8.4 Selecting information to be logged on each HTTP request.
(Courtesy: Microsoft Corporation).

Fault Isolation

Fault isolation can be considered as a part of the group of security mechanisms known as *service continuity*. Although IIS does not offer full-blown service continuity solutions, at least it provides a way to isolate HTTP handlers from the main process in which IIS is executing, InetInfo.exe, and from each other. This is done through configuring applications in virtual directories to run with one of the following options (supported by IIS v5):

IIS process. All requests to the files in the virtual directory are handled in the space of InetInfo.exe. Having the best performance, this option does not offer any fault isolation. That is, if the handler crashes because of an error in the application code, IIS will crash as well.

Pooled. Requests to the resources of all virtual directories configured with this option run in the same process external to InetInfo.exe. The process runs under the identity of an account controlled by IIS, IWAM_<machinename>. This offers the best performance versus robustness trade-off, because if a Web application crashes, it takes down only other applications, but not InetInfo.exe, which will be able to relaunch the pool process on the next request that needs one of the pooled handlers. This is the default option.

Isolated. Executes each Web application in its own process that runs under the IWAM_<machinename> account. This option has the highest level of fault isolation—no faulty application could bring down any other application—but it is not as fast as the previous one.

As you can see, IIS security mechanisms provide a regular set of functions consisting of authentication, message protection, authorization, logging, and fault isolation. All these functions are integrated with user accounts and file system access controls. If you want to find out more about IIS security, look at Howard (2000). The last chapter of Brown (2000), contains a lot of useful details on this subject as well.

In the next section, we will describe the role of IIS in hosting and protecting a variety of Web Services implementations on COM+ and .NET.

Creating Web Services with Microsoft Technologies

You will need to understand how to build a Web Service if you have a business application running on a Windows machine and need to expose it to SOAP clients. Or, you may be designing a Web Service from scratch and want to use this new product called .NET but are not sure how to go about it.

You have four options to create Web Services with Microsoft technologies, which will be explained in this section at a level of detail that will allow you to understand how to secure the resulting application. We have already prepared you in Chapter 7 with a description of the supporting infrastructure for building secure Web Services. In this chapter we will show you the connections back to what was discussed previously, and spend the rest of the chapter discussing additional security mechanisms that support ASP.NET-based Web Services.

Creating Web Services out of COM+ Components

The easiest way to create a Web Service using a Microsoft technology is to use COM+ v1.5 (Lowy 2001), available on Windows.NET Server and Windows XP Pro platforms. Turning on SOAP support with this newest version of Microsoft's application server technology is just a matter of selecting a check box in the application properties window and filling in the name of the IIS virtual directory where the application objects will have their endpoints published, as shown in Figure 8.5. Selection of the check box induces the COM+ infrastructure to provide the necessary adapters, install the Web Services bridge with IIS, and generate the proper Web Service configuration and information files. You should note that IIS must be installed on your machine to enable SOAP activation mode for your application. After that, all the application's components become available via DCOM as well as SOAP/HTTP. In addition to exposing objects via SOAP, your newly created Web Service will get all of the support for the object life cycle, just-in-time activation, object pooling, and, most important, the security of COM+, as we described in Chapter 7.

This does not mean, however, that SOAP clients will access COM+-based services via a secure channel. Unfortunately, message integrity, confidentiality, and authenticity protection, provided with DCOM-based secure channels, are not available to SOAP/HTTP channels unless the use of SSL is turned on.

Besides the ease of turning SOAP support on, you are also getting an HTTP-based alternative to DCOM wire protocol for client/server communications. This becomes handy in those situations when COM+ clients and servers are separated by a firewall and you want to reduce the DCOM-related burden of firewall administration. DCOM support could be hard on firewall administrators because each COM+ server host requires one statically configured TCP and/or UDP port for Service Control Manager (SCM), which activates objects and makes them ready to invoke, and a range of ports—one per active COM+ object. This port range needs to be large enough to accommodate bursts in the client's activity and object population. Access to COM+ objects via SOAP/HTTP, on the other hand, requires administration of only one port (traditionally, TCP port 80). However, this port has to be better protected because, as with any tunneling solution, once a client is allowed to send its requests to the server, a simple TCP firewall cannot control what objects on the other side of the tunnel the client is accessing.

Even with all the ease and benefits available for COM+-based Web Services, there are some limitations and drawbacks. The foremost limitation is due to the difference between COM and SOAP distribution and computational models. Unlike service-based SOAP, COM is object-based, and passing object references as method *in* and/or *out* parameters is a common and widely used practice for COM applications. This is not the case with SOAP, which has no direct counterpart of an object reference. Additionally, the COM computational model allows multiple return values via *out* parameters. This all means that you cannot take an arbitrary COM+ application server and publish all its components as Web Services and still expect strict interoperability with SOAP-compliant clients.

Also, if a COM+ component has to be placed in a transaction context, it will not work with SOAP clients, because transactions are not supported in SOAP. Therefore the use of COM+ components as SOAP endpoints requires compliance with Web Services design guidelines that limit design of COM+ applications.

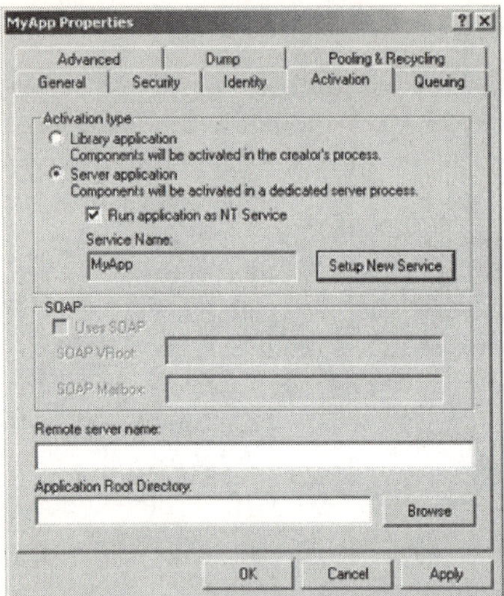

Figure 8.5 Turning on SOAP support for COM+v1.5 applications via the properties window.
(Courtesy: Microsoft Corporation).

As we have already pointed out, the two key advantages of Web Services based on COM+ v1.5 components are the ease of creating Web Services and the strong COM+ security. Additionally, you don't have to do anything special to protect such Web Services—just use the same methods described in Chapter 7 on COM+ security.

This approach may be straightforward, but what if you don't use Windows.NET Server or Windows XP Pro in your production environment, so COM+ v1.5 is out of the question? In that case, "wrapping" your application's COM DLLs using tools from the Microsoft SOAP toolkit could be an option, as we describe next.

Creating Web Services out of COM Components Using SOAP Toolkit

If the previous option of creating Web Services with Microsoft technologies is the easiest, the one that we describe in this section is the most affordable. You don't need to have COM+ components, or Windows.NET Server, or Windows XP Pro machines, or even the .NET framework, for that matter, to create Web Services this way. All you need is your application developed as a set of COM components, and SOAP Toolkit version 2 or higher from Microsoft's Web site. This is a good way to reuse existing COM components that may not have been developed with Web Services in mind.

Once you have IIS and Microsoft SOAP Toolkit installed, simply launch the WSDL generator GUI tool from the toolkit, and select the name of the COM library where your application components reside. Note that another Web server besides IIS could be used to host a COM-based server, as long as the generic Internet Server Application

Programmer's Interface (ISAPI) and Active Server Pages (ASP) listener from the SOAP toolkit can be registered with such a Web server, as discussed below.

The WSDL generator asks to check the methods and objects that will become available through the wrapper. On completion, the tool generates a Web Service Meta Language (WSML) file, with extension WSML, used by the runtime environment to find out which COM objects serve which SOAP requests. Another file it generates is in standard WSDL format and describes the newly configured Web Service. The last step left is creating a virtual directory and putting the generated WSDL and WSML files in that directory.

The runtime part is as straightforward as the setup. With the installation of the SOAP toolkit, a SOAP handler in the form of an ISAPI or ASP (depending on the options selected while running the WSDL generator) listener is registered with IIS. When an HTTP message that contains a SOAP request and points to the endpoint corresponding to the virtual directory you have created comes in, IIS dispatches the body of the HTTP message to this listener, as shown in Figure 8.6. The WSDL and WSML files, which were created by the WSDL generator at configuration time, drive this generic listener. Specifically, the WSML file contains information necessary for the listener to perform the work of loading the DLL, creating an object responsible for serving the request, converting request parameters into a format suitable for calling the object's method, invoking the method, and shipping the returned data back to the SOAP client.

As with the previous way of creating Web Services, while SOAP Toolkit 2.0 may allow you to expose existing COM objects through SOAP, this is not true in all cases (Microsoft 2001c). The main roadblocks are support for *Dispatchable* interfaces only, and no support for user custom types, such as MS IDL *struct*. Again, many DCOM features such as lifetime-management, passing objects by reference, and some COM data types are not supported since they don't have counterparts in the current SOAP specification.

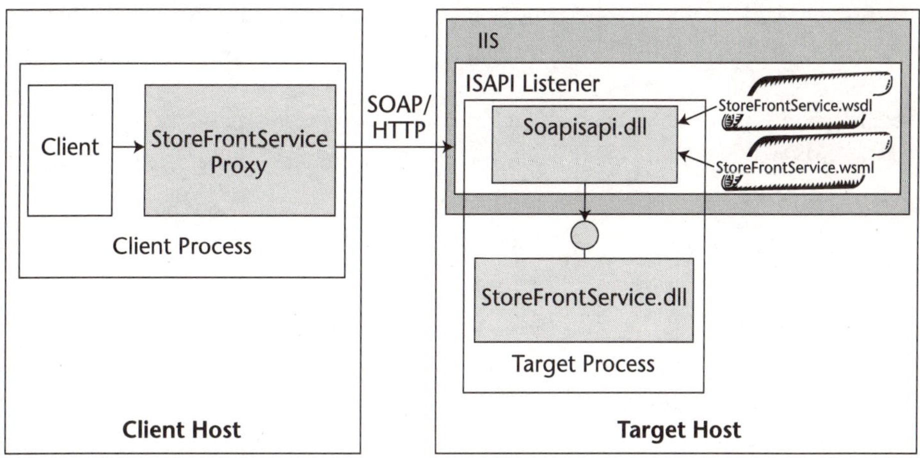

Figure 8.6 Processing SOAP requests by a SOAP listener and dispatching them to the COM objects.

Now, when you have a COM-based Web Service, the question is, what options do you have for protecting it? One is that you can make your application security-aware and invoke security APIs defined in COM, which we described in Chapter 7. In addition to the extensive description of those APIs, Keith Brown, in his book *Programming Windows Security* (Brown 2000), explains how to use the DCOM configuration tool to set some security properties, such as authentication and message protection, of remotely accessible COM objects. However, any reasonably fine-grained access control, and all audit calls, would have to be programmed inside of your COM objects, because COM security mechanisms are not very sophisticated. Custom security development within COM objects is usually not what you want.

To avoid programming security into your COM objects, you may also use the security mechanisms of IIS that we described previously. Since any SOAP/HTTP request to your objects comes through IIS, the Web server is a good candidate to intercept requests for the purpose of enforcing security policies.

Creating Web Services with .NET Remoting

.NET remoting mechanisms provide yet another way to create Web Services using Microsoft technologies. In Chapter 7, we described remoting and what you need to do to use it in your .NET distributed applications. You can also make your remotable objects accessible over SOAP, and thus make them effectively Web Services. We also noted some limitations of this approach—the inability of SOAP clients to use client-activated objects, the use of RPC SOAP encoding, and the lack of support for object constructors with parameters.

The most straightforward way to host remotable objects in IIS is by taking the following steps:

- Create a virtual directory where the remotable objects will be accessible.
- Put the DLL containing the remotable objects into the \bin directory of the virtual directory created in the previous step, or put it in the global assembly cache (GAC).
- Register your remotable objects in one of the two following ways:
  - Put the remoting configuration section into the web.config file in the virtual directory. Here is the configuration section:

```
<configuration>
  <system.runtime.remoting>
    <application name="eBusiness">
      <service>
        <wellknown mode="SingleCall"
          type="Ebusiness.SOAPServer, ProductInfoManager"
          objectUri="StoreFrontService.soap" />
      </service>
    </application>
  </system.runtime.remoting>
</configuration>
```

This configuration file specifies the eBusiness application with one *singlecall* object implemented in class *ProductInfoManager* under namespace *Ebusiness.SOAPServer*. The endpoint for the class is created by concatenating the virtual directory URL and "StoreFrontService.soap."

- Alternately, place registration code into the Application_Start() function of the global.asax file. The registration code there is the same as in regular .NET-based hosting applications for remotable objects.

Be careful to adhere to IIS hosting restrictions:

- You should not specify a channel in the configuration section because IIS already listens on port 80.
- Specifying a port for a channel causes exceptions to be thrown when new HTTP handler processes are started.
- Web Services URIs must end with .rem or .soap extensions in order for IIS to dispatch requests to the right ISAPI/ASP listeners.

In order to program a client to use a Web Service, one needs a WSDL file defining the service. For Web Services based on .NET remoting, their WSDL files could be obtained by making a query on the service endpoint URL appended with "?wsdl". For example, if the Web Service described in the above configuration file were located in virtual directory StoreFrontService on machine www.eBusiness.com, then the URL for the WSDL file would be:

http://www.eBusiness.com/StoreFrontService/StoreFrontService.soap?wsdl.

As Chapter 7 explained, .NET remoting does not provide any additional security mechanisms other than those available for .NET code and provided by the hosting application. This makes it clear that if you need to protect Web Services based on .NET remoting, you have four groups of security mechanisms available: Windows OS, .NET, IIS, and ASP.NET. The last may be used as a broker between IIS and remotable objects. .NET security is described in Chapter 7, and IIS protection was discussed in the previous section. After introducing ASP.NET in the next section, we will explain in depth how to employ ASP.NET security for creating secure Web Services.

Creating Web Services Using ASP.NET

All three techniques for creating Web Services discussed so far have their own advantages, but despite this, they share one problem—their computational and distribution models don't match that of SOAP Web Services. For example, COM and COM+ natively support passing object references in and out of remote calls, while parameterized object construction by clients is supported in .NET remoting. Neither of these features is supported by standard-compliant Web Services. And these are just a few examples of their incompatibility. The bottom line is that you cannot take an arbitrary COM or COM+ component, or .NET remotable object, and expose it as an interoperable Web Service. If you use the ASP.NET-based approach discussed in this section, however, you will not have any of these problems, because SOAP Web Services are the natural RPC model for ASP.NET applications. Combined with IIS as a hosting platform and .NET CLR as a runtime environment, ASP.NET offers a compelling option of developing Web Services with Microsoft technologies.

As with .NET remoting, you need to have the .NET framework SDK and IIS installed on the machines where a Web Service will be developed and where it will be deployed. Upon the SDK installation, an ASP.NET_ISAPI.DLL listener is registered with IIS, which allows it to receive HTTP requests for URLs ending with specific extensions, the one for ASP.NET Web Services being ".asmx".

As shown in Figure 8.7, while running in unmanaged code, IIS forwards a request to the ASP.NET_ISAPI.DLL first. An inter-process communication (IPC) bridge is formed between IIS and managed code, and the DLL passes the request on to ASP.NET, where the request passes through registered HTTP modules acting as invocation interceptors, and reaches the Web Service Handler Factory. The factory uses the information in the URL to determine which Web Service implementation should handle the request. If the handler has not been compiled from the source into intermediate language representation, ASP.NET does so at this point, then loads the handler in CLR and dispatches the request. Although not used only for performing security functions, the HTTP modules will be discussed later when we talk about ways to protect ASP.NET Web Services.

In addition to taking advantage of IIS and .NET security, Web Services created with ASP.NET are the solution most compliant with the SOAP standard, out of all Microsoft technologies. They are also very simple to develop. Let us briefly walk through the development process, as shown in Figure 8.8.

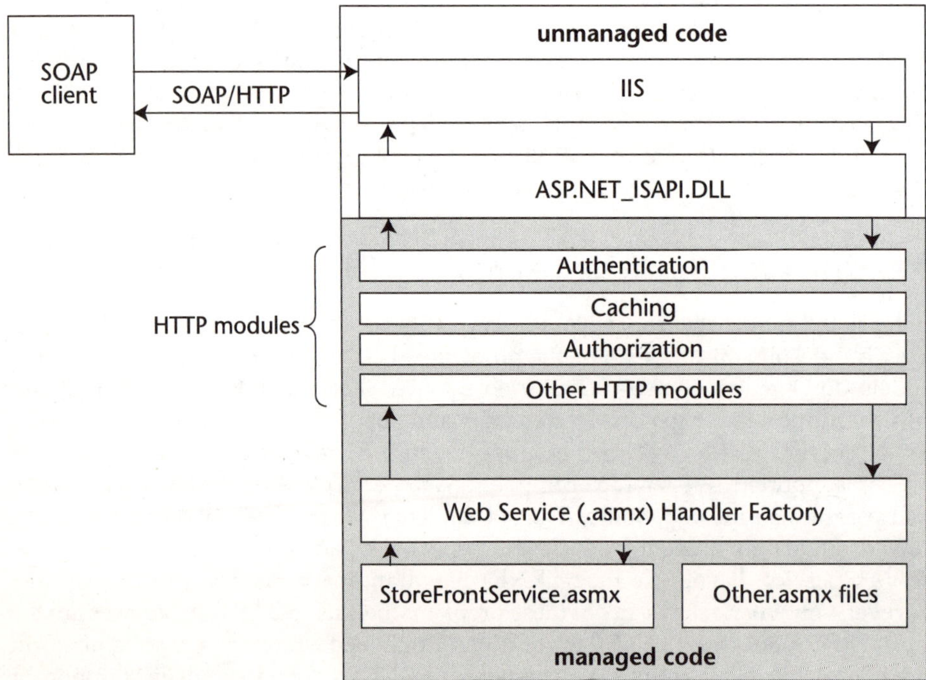

Figure 8.7 Request handling by ASP.NET Web Services.

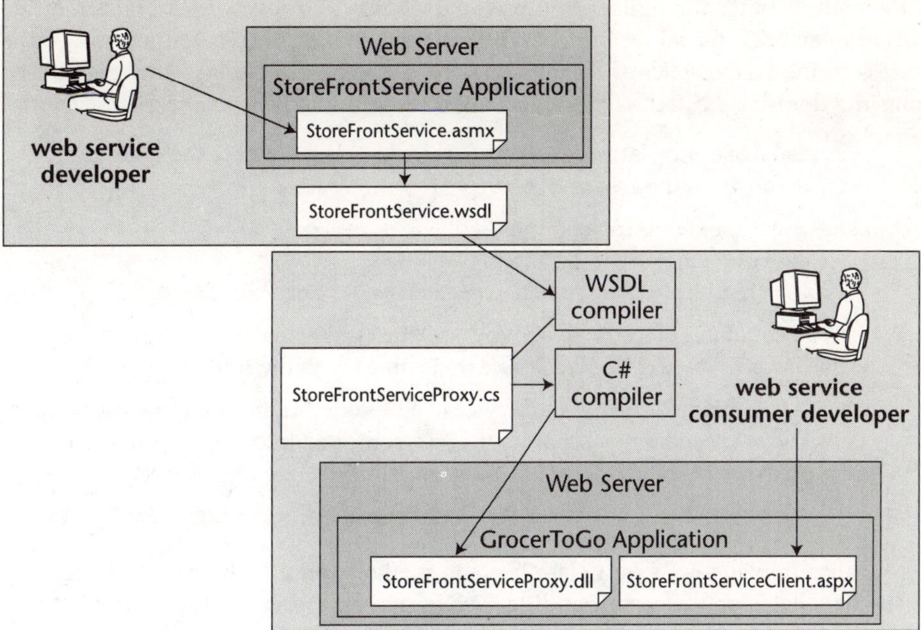

Figure 8.8 ASP.NET Web Services development process.

1. Unlike IDL-based technology such as COM or CORBA, an ASP.NET Web Service is developed first, and the WSDL file (StoreFrontService.wsdl in the figure) that defines the contract for that service is generated automatically later. Once a compilable source code file for the Web Service (StoreFrontService.asmx) is placed in the corresponding virtual directory, IIS will return the WSDL file on any HTTP GET request with the Web Service URL and "?wsdl" suffix, for example: http://localhost/eBusinessWebService/StoreFrontService.asmx?wsdl. This trick is done with the help of ASP.NET, which compiles the service source and creates the WSDL file "on the fly."
2. The WSDL file is fed into the WSDL compiler by the developer of the Web Service client. The compiler produces source code (StoreFrontServiceProxy.cs) for the proxy. The source code language can be selected via command line options.
3. The proxy source code is compiled into a library (StoreFrontServiceProxy.dll), which is used for building the client application (StoreFrontServiceClient.aspx). In our example, the client is yet another ASP.NET application. However, this could be any type of application.

As you can see from Figure 8.8, service and client development processes are connected via the WSDL file. This is the only point of dependency. Since WSDL files, produced out of ASP.NET Web Service applications, are compliant with the standard, the client and service could be developed using different Web Service products.

Depending on what language you use for Web Services development on top of the .NET framework, you might perform different steps. Just to give you a sense of the process in the case of Microsoft languages, here are the three things that need to be done in order for a .NET class to become a Web Service if it is developed using C#:

1. A special declarative attribute "WebService" is placed before the class definition, as shown in the C# code below:

```
namespace Ebusiness.SOAPServer {
     [WebService]
          public class ProductInfoManager : WebService  {
```

2. As you could guess from the above code, the class also needs to be derived from the .NET base class *WebService* that comes with the framework SDK.

3. The class implementing a Web Service can be coded right in the corresponding asmx file or placed into a separate file and compiled into a library. In the latter case, an asmx file referring to the class contains just one line of code:

```
<%@ WebService Class="Ebusiness.SOAPServer.ProductInfoManager" %>
```

Not all public methods of a class become methods on a Web Service. To make a method available on the corresponding Web Service, a special attribute *WebMethod* is declared before the method definition.

We will summarize the description of ASP.NET Web Services by listing the main building blocks used. As depicted in Figure 8.9, ASP.NET Web Services rely upon ASP.NET, .NET Framework, IIS, and, underneath it all, the Windows platform. This figure oversimplifies the architecture and does not show all the complex interdependencies that exist among all the elements, but it will be helpful to keep the figure in mind when we discuss the choices for ASP.NET protection mechanisms. We will discuss the protection mechanism options right after describing an implementation of the ePortal-eBusiness scenario using ASP.NET Web Services, which comes next.

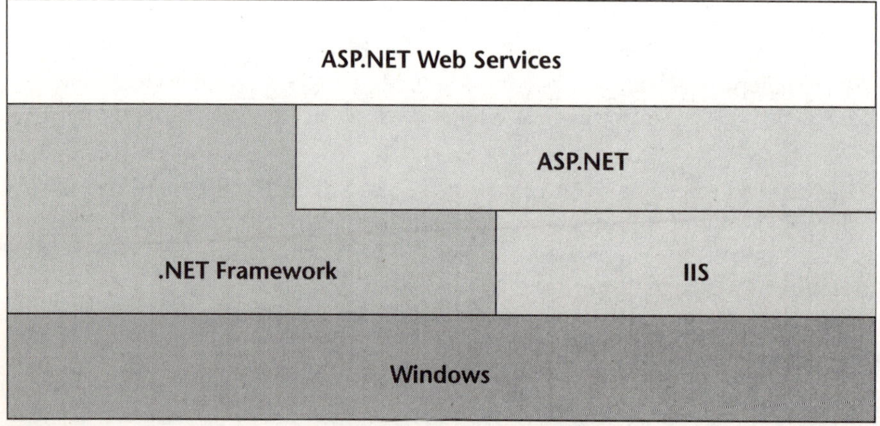

Figure 8.9 Main building blocks for ASP.NET Web Services.

Implementing Access to eBusiness with ASP.NET Web Services

To illustrate the use of ASP.NET in building Web Services, we implemented a subset of the e-commerce scenario used throughout the book. The purpose of the Web Service for this implementation is to provide access to eBusiness's online store over SOAP/HTTP by serving as a SOAP gateway to the middle-tier application. This enables the use of eBusiness services by other businesses such as ePortal, which acts as a broker between human users and sites like eBusiness.

The implemented scheme is shown in Figure 8.10. All of the business logic of eBusiness is concentrated in the middle tier, which is implemented as a COM+ application, and is therefore accessible over DCOM wire protocol and protected by COM+ security mechanisms, described in Chapter 7.

StoreFrontService not only links divergent wire protocols but also bridges the distribution and computational models of COM+ and Web Services. For example, each product's information at *StoreFrontMiddleTier* is encapsulated into a separate *Product* object created on the fly by the *ProductManager* component. The Web Service hides this from SOAP clients by providing a single method, *ProductInfo GetProductInfoById(int id)*, where *id* is the product identifier unique in eBusiness. You can download this example from this book's Web site and see the details of mapping methods of *StoreFrontMiddleTier* into those of *StoreFrontService*.

We also used ASP.NET for implementing the browser interface on ePortal. The interface gives visitors a common shopping experience where they can browse products sold by eBusiness and brokered by ePortal. Visitors are able to see particular categories, find product descriptions and prices, and see pictures of products. A selected product can be added to the customer's shopping cart. Quantities of items in a shopping cart can be changed and the total recalculated before checkout. A screen shot illustrating the customer experience is shown in Figure 8.11.

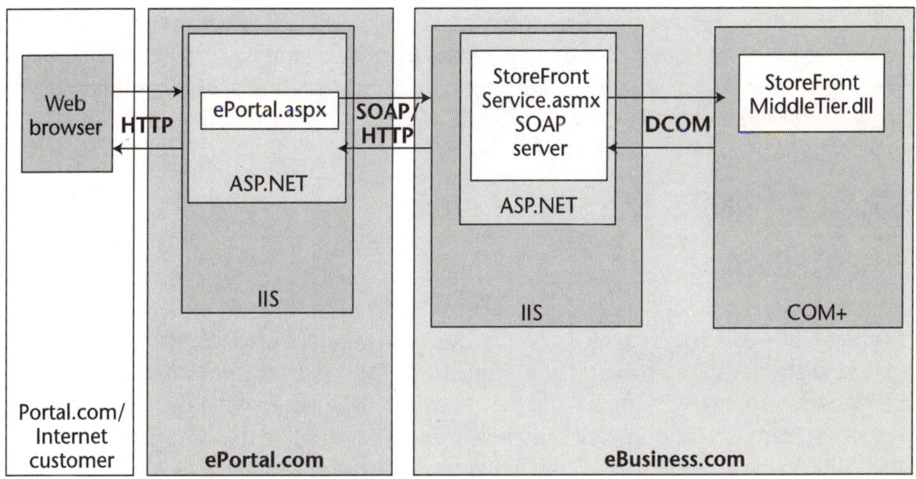

Figure 8.10 Providing SOAP/HTTP access to eBusiness services by means of ASP.NET Web Services.

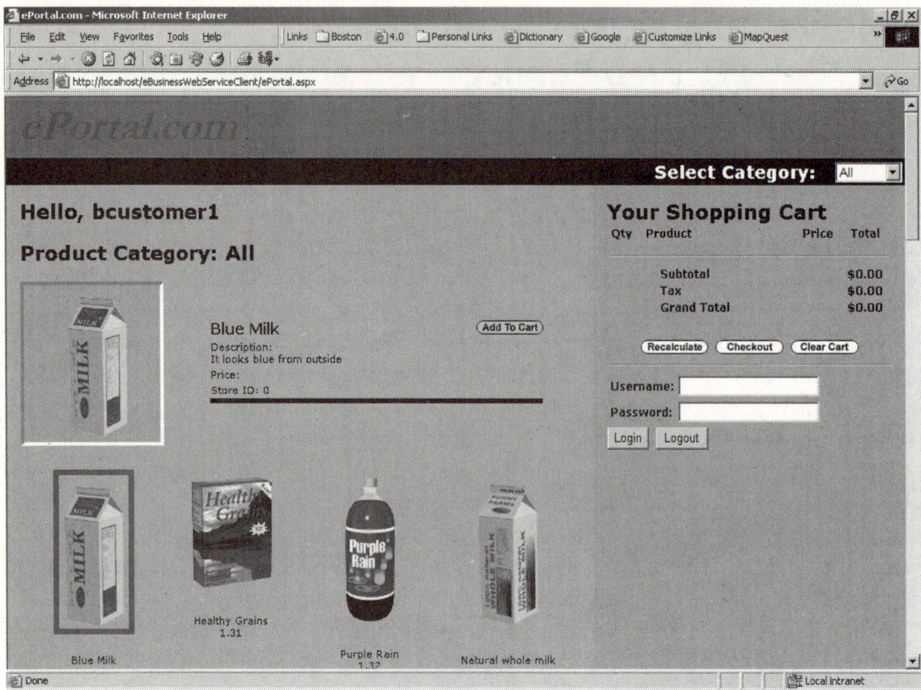

Figure 8.11 Sample screen shot showing the ePortal shopping experience.
(Courtesy: Microsoft Corporation).

The presentation logic at ePortal obtains all information about products and the customer's shopping cart from eBusiness's *StoreFrontService* by making corresponding invocations via SOAP/HTTP. The latter, in turn, calls the *StoreFrontMiddleTier* application via DCOM. This sample application system is an example of how middle-tier services with their security infrastructure can be exposed securely over HTTP transport to the business partners by means of SOAP gateways. The latter are implemented using Web Services technologies. How security mechanisms are used to protect this sample system will be described after we first explain the security of Web Services built with ASP.NET.

ASP.NET Web Services Security

The security mechanisms of ASP.NET Web Services consist of the security available for the building blocks of these services and SOAP security, as shown in Figure 8.12.

We have already covered most of the mechanisms in Figure 8.12. We described SOAP security in Chapter 6, and the security of .NET's common language runtime (CLR) was described in Chapter 7. Finally, you became familiar with IIS security mechanisms earlier in this chapter. The only new topic we will introduce here is the security of ASP.NET. We will also explain how it all works in concert. We will describe ASP.NET security while explaining how all these mechanisms could be selected and mixed together to secure your Web Services.

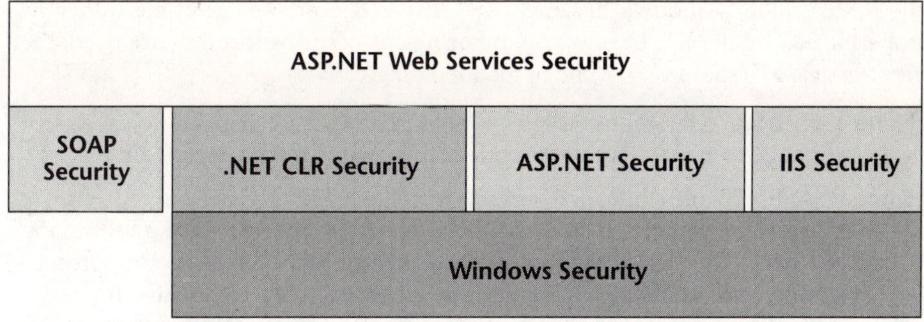

Figure 8.12 Building blocks for ASP.NET-based Web Services security.

In the following sections, we explain each security service addressed by ASP.NET Web Services mechanisms: authentication, data protection, access control, and auditing.

Authentication

There are three ways to do authentication with ASP.NET Web Services: IIS, ASP.NET (sometimes on top of IIS), and SOAP headers. IIS can perform authentication of HTTP requests by means of basic, digest, certificate, or integrated Windows authentication. Discussed previously in this chapter, IIS-based authentication is a widely implemented and understood approach. As long as the Web Service clients support one of the defined mechanisms, IIS is the simplest way to support authentication. The main disadvantage with IIS authentication is the necessity of having corresponding user accounts on the Windows system hosting a Web Service. Depending on the nature of the service—for example, self-registering consumers—this could be a real roadblock. The use of ASP.NET authentication services and HTTP modules doesn't have this limitation.

ASP.NET Authentication Services

ASP.NET authentication facilities can either ride on top of IIS authentication or get by without it. First of all, if IIS authentication is used, then ASP.NET can be configured to accept the authenticated identity so that Web Services will have access to it. This is done through the following element in the ASP.NET configuration file, web.config:

```
<configuration>
     <system.web>
          <authentication mode="Windows"/>
     </system.web>
</configuration>
```

Use of the value "Windows" instructs ASP.NET to take advantage of the authentication performed by the IIS. If, however, other means of authentication are used, then *authentication mode* should have one of the following values:

None. Used when authentication is implemented by a mechanism other than based on IIS, forms, or Passport—for example, a third-party Web SSO.

Forms. ASP.NET authentication services manage HTTP cookies and redirect unauthenticated users to a logon page. IIS is usually configured to allow anonymous access. The main advantage of the technique is the ability to support self-registering consumers because no system accounts have to be created for new users. It requires the use of HTTP cookies as well as human intervention on the client side, such as acquiring the correct cookie at the beginning of a session by providing authentication data at a logon page. Since most Web Service clients are expected to run unattended, forms-based authentication enjoys only limited applicability. Cookies by themselves raise concerns in the privacy community because they are sometimes abused by Web portals (Berghel 2001). In addition, many in the security community believe that cookie-based authentication schemes are vulnerable to forgery by malicious clients and replay attacks (Sit 2001).

Passport. (See Microsoft 2001b.) This is another way to avoid managing system accounts and creating additional code to handle forms-based authentication. Passport authentication is a centralized authentication service provided by Microsoft. When you use Passport, you do not need to implement your own authentication code, logon page, or user table in some cases. Passport works by means of a cookie mechanism. Currently, Microsoft completely controls this authentication technology, and this becomes an issue for heterogeneous solutions. Although ASP.NET is purely Microsoft technology, it does not follow that the clients of such Web Services are all based on Microsoft products, too. In addition to the above drawbacks, Passport is not yet widely used, and the technology has its own vulnerabilities, some already discovered (Slemko 2001) and others possible in the future. All these issues may make Passport risky to use in a commercial deployment.

HTTP Modules

If you are not satisfied with any of the above methods of authentication, you still have one more option available in ASP.NET. The interceptor-like architecture of its HTTP modules makes it possible to implement custom authentication schemes. If you go back to Figure 8.7, you will notice that HTTP modules intercept HTTP requests dispatched to ASP.NET handler factories. This architecture enables stackable "filters," each dedicated to a specific task. Tasks could vary from support for transactions to caching. From the "protecting Web Services" point of view, HTTP modules are a convenient place to enforce various security policies (for example, access control, data protection, and audit) and perform authentication. As a matter of fact, forms and Passport authentication providers are implemented in ASP.NET through prebuilt authentication modules—*FormsAuthenticationModule* and *PassportAuthenticationModule* in *System.Web.Security* namespace—that come with every installation of ASP.NET and can be turned on and off via the *authentication mode* element of the configuration file.

Each ASP.NET authentication provider handles an *OnAuthenticate* event that occurs during the authentication process. The primary purpose of this event is to attach a custom object that implements the .NET *IPrincipal* interface to the request's context.

Here's what a custom authentication module for Web Services would do at run time, provided that ASP.NET is configured to use it:

- The module parses HTTP messages to check whether they are SOAP messages.
- If the module detects a SOAP message, it checks for authentication data in the request. Depending on the authentication scheme, authentication data can be in different parts of the request, including, but not limited to, HTTP header, SOAP header, and even SOAP body, for example in the form of a digital signature of the SOAP message.
- If the HTTP request with the SOAP message contains authentication data, the module performs authentication, and dispatches a new event containing the authenticated identity.
- The identity is used by the event implementation to create and initialize a custom or default instance of a principal object.
- The principal is later set on the runtime context used to serve the request.

To be more specific and give you an idea of the technique, here are the steps one would go through in order to implement authentication using HTTP modules. First, you write a module that implements interface *IHttpModule*. The module is implemented in the form of a class, like the one shown in the C# code fragment below, that defines two key public methods—*OnAuthenticate()* and *OnEnter()*:

```
namespace eBusiness.Authentication {
  public class FooAuthModule : IHttpModule {
  private FooAuthenticationEventHandler myEventHandler = null;

    public event FooAuthenticationEventHandler Authenticate {
      add {
        myEventHandler += value;
      }

      remove {
        myEventHandler -= value;
      }
    }

    public void Init( HttpApplication app ){
      //Add my event handler to AuthenticationRequest event.
    app.AuthenticateRequest += new EventHandler(this.OnEnter);

      // Do other initialization steps.
      ...
    }
```

```
        private void OnAuthenticate( FooAuthenticationEvent e ) {
          // Uses authentication information off the event
          // to set principal information on the execution context
          if (myEventHandler == null){
            e.Authenticate();
          } else {
            myEventHandler(this, e);
          }

          if (e.Context.User != null)
          {
            e.Context.User = e.Principal;
          }
        }

        void OnEnter( Object source, EventArgs eventArgs ) {
          // Authenticate using authentication data found
          // in the request.
          ...

          // Raise the custom global.asax event.
          OnAuthenticate(new FooAuthenticationEvent
            (context, authIdentity));
          return;
        }
      }
    }
```

You also need to implement a custom authentication event, which method *OnEnter()* supplies when it eventually calls *OnAuthenticate()*:

```
    namespace eBusiness.Authentication {
      // The custom event
      public class FooAuthenticationEvent : EventArgs {
        private IPrincipal  principal;
        private FooIdentity identity;
        private string[] roles;
        ...
        public FooAuthenticationEvent(HttpContext context,
         FooAuthenticatedIdentity authIdentity){
          identity = authIdentity();
        }

        public IPrincipal Principal{
          get{
            return iprincipal;
          }

        set{
          iprincipal = value;
          }
      }
```

```
        ...
        public void Authenticate(){
          // Create principal and set it on the current thread.
          principal = new GenericPrincipal(identity, roles);
          context.User = principal;
        }
      }
    }
```

Then, you register the module with ASP.NET by adding the following to the configuration file:

```
<configuration>
  <system.web>
    <httpModules>
      <add name="FooAuthenticationModule"
        type="eBusiness.Authentication.FooAuthModule,
        eBusiness.Authentication" />
    </httpModules>
    <authentication mode="None" />
    <authorization>
      <deny users="?" />
    </authorization>
  </system.web>
</configuration>
```

The element *httpModules* contains information necessary for ASP.NET run time to locate the module and place it at the interception point for all incoming HTTP requests. The use of value "None" in the *authentication mode* section instructs the run time to turn off preinstalled ASP.NET authentication modules. The element *authorization* will be explained in the section on access control.

Once you have a place for intercepting HTTP requests, some of which are carrying SOAP messages, you have few constraints on what your code can do and what authentication schemes it can implement. This does not take the responsibility of implementing a sound authentication scheme off your (or your authentication solution provider's) shoulders. For an example of a custom authentication scheme implemented with the use of ASP.NET HTTP modules, look at Wagner (2002). One side effect of any nonstandard authentication protocol surfaces in the coupling between the entities using the protocol. If a server resorts to custom authentication, its clients must support the same protocol.

This approach has a number of important advantages. First, it enables support for authentication against user accounts stored in third-party repositories and therefore frees developers from using Windows accounts. Second, since the modules can parse the content of HTTP requests, they can perform authentication on the data that comes with SOAP messages, thus enabling independence of the authentication schemes from HTTP transport. Transport independence of an authentication mechanism becomes important in scenarios where authentication-related data needs to travel along with its SOAP message over different transports. The third, and most important from our perspective, advantage of HTTP modules lies in the fact that the first two advantages can be achieved while the decoupling of authentication and business logic can still be maintained by putting the authentication logic in (possibly independently developed) modules and placing the business logic in the Web Service classes. Thanks to the flexible and extensible design of CLR Principal and Identity (which is also used for access control in .NET), HTTP modules have another important advantage—once authentication performed by such a module succeeds, the value of the authenticated identity and its security attributes can be set on the execution context. The context will be automatically used by the .NET access control mechanism. We will discuss further details later, in the section on access control.

Although this approach appears to be straightforward to implement, HTTP modules still require significant effort, especially when your authentication scheme requires processing of SOAP headers. This is due to the general SOAP-neutral architecture of HTTP modules. If, after performing a risk analysis of your system, you decide that a simple scheme with clients passing their authentication tokens in SOAP headers is sufficient (we presume that you at least use SSL for data protection in such cases), then a less demanding implementation could be done with the help of the SOAP-header-processing capabilities provided by ASP.NET classes.

Custom Authentication with SOAP Headers

The IIS authentication mechanisms authenticate HTTP requests or, in the case of client certificates, the underlying SSL/TLS channel. Therefore, they are specific to the HTTP transport, whereas SOAP is transport independent. As we discussed in Chapter 6, it might sometimes be necessary to forward a SOAP request from one processing entity to another while keeping data authenticating the originator of the SOAP request together with the SOAP message. Or, in other situations, the same SOAP message could travel by the means of different transports, thereby making it necessary to employ transport-independent authentication. One way to implement transport-independent authentication is through the use of SOAP headers. Since SOAP headers allow the inclusion of almost any out-of-band data, which does not have to be related to the semantics of the information in the body of the message, the header information can be processed by any intermediary, including the ASP.NET runtime infrastructure as well as the Web Service method itself.

The simplest way to employ SOAP headers for authenticating originators of ASP.NET Web Services is by requiring the clients to include authentication data in the header of each request, as shown below:

```
using System.Web.Services;
using System.Web.Services.Protocols;

public class AuthenticationHeader : SoapHeader {
  public AuthenticationData AuthData;
}

public class FooService : WebService {
  public AuthenticationHeader AuthHeader;
```

```
    [SoapHeader("AuthHeader", Required=true)]
    public string foo() {
      if (AuthHeader == null) {
        return "ERROR: Please supply authentication data";
      } else {
        AuthenticateRequestor(AuthHeader.AuthData);
      }
      //Perform business
    }
  }
```

As you can see from this C# code fragment, the Web Service developer will need to define a data structure corresponding to the header element first. Then, the header is declared in the *SoapHeader* attribute, followed by the method definition. Because this header element is declared as *required,* the run time will return a SOAP Fault message back to the client if it is not present in the header. Method *Foo()* implementation can refer to the elements of *AuthHeader*.

Since the corresponding WSDL file contains *AuthHeader* definition, clients, when written using .NET, populate the header and call the service using code along the following C# lines:

```
FooService h = new FooService();
AuthHeader myHeader = new AuthHeader();
myHeader.data = myAuthData;
h.AuthHeader = myHeader;
String result = h.foo();
```

Depending on the technology used for implementing a Web Service proxy, there could be different means for setting custom SOAP header content. As you can see, ASP.NET provides convenient ways for clients and servers to deal with elements of SOAP headers, including their use for authentication. The Web Service implementation, however, has to be programmed explicitly in each method to perform requestor authentication. Not only does this mix the business and authentication logic, but it also increases the chances of programmer's error. As we have repeatedly advocated in this and our previous book (Hartman 2001), it is important to keep your business applications as little aware of security as possible.

To maintain separation between authentication and business logic and yet implement transport-independent authentication of SOAP requests, the HTTP modules technique fits very well for passing authentication data in SOAP headers. You already know from the previous section how to implement a custom authentication scheme using an HTTP module. Here we only show the method from the authentication HTTP module that contains code specific to the authentication scheme based on the SOAP header:

```
namespace eBusiness.Authentication {
  public class FooAuthModule : IHttpModule {
    ...
```

```
void OnEnter(Object source, EventArgs eventArgs) {
HttpApplication app = (HttpApplication)source;
HttpContext context = app.Context;
Stream HttpStream = context.Request.InputStream;

            AuthenticationData data;
            FooAuthenticatedIdentity identity;

// Save the current position of stream.
long streamPosition = HttpStream.Position;

// Expecting special server variable in the request
// if there is a SOAP message
if (context.Request.ServerVariables["HTTP_SOAPACTION"]
   == null)
return;

// Load the body of the HTTP message into an
// XML document.
XmlDocument dom = new XmlDocument();

try
{
  dom.Load(HttpStream);

  // Reset the stream position.
  HttpStream.Position = streamPosition;

  // Get the authentication data.
  data =
  dom.GetElementsByTagName("AuthData").Item(0).InnerText;

  // Authenticate the SOAP request and create
  // the corresponding identity.
  identity = Authenticate(data);
}
catch (Exception e)
{
                   // Handle any unpredicted errors.
           }

           // Raise the custom global.asax event.
           OnAuthenticate(new WebServiceAuthenticationEvent
                        (context, identity));
           return;
      }
  ...
}
```

While reading through this section, you might have wondered how the problem of binding authentication data with SOAP messages is addressed. Indeed, if, for example, one inserts just the username and password into a SOAP message header, even when they are encrypted, then the authentication data can be replayed by an attacker. Thus there is a need to make sure that the authentication data and the SOAP message are bound together. Another obvious problem stems from the fact that an unprotected SOAP message can be modified by an unauthorized party and, therefore, will not represent the original intent of the requestor whose authentication data is in the header. These and other problems related to the secrecy, integrity, and authenticity of SOAP message content are addressed via data protection mechanisms available to developers of ASP.NET Web Services, which we will describe in the following section.

Data Protection

We discussed the requirements and general forms of the solutions to data protection in Chapter 6. This section describes the means of data protection available specifically for systems built with ASP.NET.

Let us start with the simplest approach. If you want the data in transit between clients and your Web Services to be protected with a minimum effort, then simply configure IIS to use SSL for all requests addressed to the virtual directory where the asmx files of your service reside. We briefly discussed the use of SSL and another technology—IPSEC—earlier, in the section on IIS security. A widely available and mature technology, SSL only provides connection-oriented point-to-point protection of SOAP messages. The same limitation holds for IPSEC. Depending on the specific requirements and risks for your Web Service, this type of data protection may be adequate. In other cases, connection-oriented protection may need to be augmented by message-oriented data protection.

Options for securing message-oriented data become complicated. You can use HTTP modules and other interception mechanisms—such as IIS and Internet Security and Acceleration server (ISA) filters—that, due to their versatility, can perform virtually any inspections and transformations of incoming and outgoing HTTP requests, including SOAP message authenticity, confidentiality, and integrity protection. If you are ready to roll up your sleeves and implement a complex intercepting inspector, then you could potentially implement the WS-Security specification (Atkinson 2002) described in Chapter 4, "XML Security and WS-Security," and Chapter 10, "Interoperability of Web Services Security Technologies."

Keep in mind, however, that the implementation will not be easy. First, the cryptographic protection of XML documents in general and SOAP messages in particular is still very new and naturally lacks product support. Second, as we discussed back in Chapter 6, SOAP cryptography is more complex and tricky than cryptography for opaque blobs of data because only some elements of a SOAP message might have to be cryptographically protected.

If your business and security requirements don't call for all of the advanced features of WS-Security, you could consider using Microsoft's recent release of a preview version of the Web Services development kit (WSDK). WSDK (Microsoft 2002) implements limited support for WS-Security. Its HTTP module *Microsoft.WSDK.HttpModule*, once installed in the ASP.NET run time, processes WS-Security and related elements (such as those related to XML encryption and XML Signature) in ASP.NET messages. For incoming SOAP messages, the results of the processing become available to the receiver through .NET CLR data types and interfaces. This allows an ASP.NET application to inspect the data related to WS-Security. For outgoing messages, corresponding data types and interfaces enable creation and manipulation of the security data that will become part of the SOAP message once it leaves the sender.

WSDK also supports the creation, validation, and extraction of security tokens that hold passwords (in clear text or digest forms) and X.509 certificates. It can bind them to the message, and thus provide proof of the key possession as well as message integrity protection, by signing the message with the corresponding key. We expect that other token types, such as SAML, will ultimately be supported.

Since, as of this writing, we have had a chance to see only a preview version of the development kit, we hope that the current limitations of WSDK will be addressed soon in the first full releases. However, if you are concerned with just signing/verifying and encrypting/decrypting everything present in a SOAP body, then you will find WSDK very helpful.

Another potential caveat is not addressed yet, due to the recent release of the WSDK: a third-party HTTP module may not be able to take advantage of the WSDK interfaces and data. If not, then ASP.NET applications have to be programmed to explicitly use the functionality provided by the kit. However, if an HTTP module can use the WSDK, then business applications may be able to avoid security-aware code, because all security-related code can be eliminated from applications and put into HTTP modules.

Access Control

There are a number of options for ASP.NET Web Services access control mechanisms. The options can be classified into two groups, according to whether they need to impersonate the client. (The topic of impersonation was introduced in Chapters 6 and 7.) Let's first look at those that don't require client impersonation.

First of all, there are Web permissions and IP-based restriction mechanisms provided by IIS, which we described previously. Restrictions based on the client's host address can also be enforced at the level of the Windows OS. If the granularity of the control is sufficient for your security policies, then these would be the most cost-effective and high-performance solutions. One point to keep in mind, however, is the possibility of attackers spoofing permitted IP addresses, unless the proper IPSEC infrastructure is in place, allowing strong authentication of incoming IP traffic. Unfortunately, IPSEC is not an option yet for Internet scenarios with large and diverse client populations.

Another way of controlling access without performing client impersonation is through inspecting SOAP/HTTP requests by means of an HTTP module. Although complicated to implement, this approach enforces fine-grained and expressive access control policies without being within the application business logic. We expect that vendors will offer software products that provide this functionality, so that end users will not have to implement it themselves. In general terms, the implementation is similar to authentication via HTTP modules, except that the authorization handler uses the *AuthorizeRequest* event.

The group of mechanisms that don't use client impersonation has either high performance and coarse-grained control, or complex implementation and fine-grained control. The impersonation-based approaches that we describe next are in between these two extremes. Before we explain impersonation-based access control, we will first discuss what impersonation means in ASP.NET and how it can be configured.

Impersonation

Impersonation (or more precisely, simple unconstrained delegation, as discussed in Chapter 7) allows an intermediate to access objects using the client's privileges with no limitations on their use. In this case, the invocation credentials used by the intermediate server are the same as the ones it received from the original caller. Depending on the underlying network authentication protocol (NTLM or Kerberos, in the case of Windows 2000) and its configuration, the server may or may not use the client's identity to access resources and services located on other computers. You can find detailed discussions of the limitations of impersonation implementations in Windows systems in Howard (2000) and Brown (2000).

In contrast to the previous version of ASP, HTTP handlers do not impersonate clients in ASP.NET unless an application is configured to do so. In order to turn on impersonation mode, you need to set the *identity* element of the application's web.config file to "true," as shown in the following fragment:

```
<configuration>
  <system.web>
<identity impersonate="true" />
  </system.web>
</configuration>
```

With impersonation mode turned off, your Web Service serves requests with the identity of the account under which IIS runs (predefined special account <MACHINE_NAME>\ASPNET). This is what the top screen shot in Figure 8.13 shows. Once impersonation mode is turned on, all requests are processed with the identity of the client. The bottom screen shot shows output from code in an ASP.NET page executing under the identity of the special account used for anonymous visitors (<MACHINE_NAME>\IUSR_VEGETA).

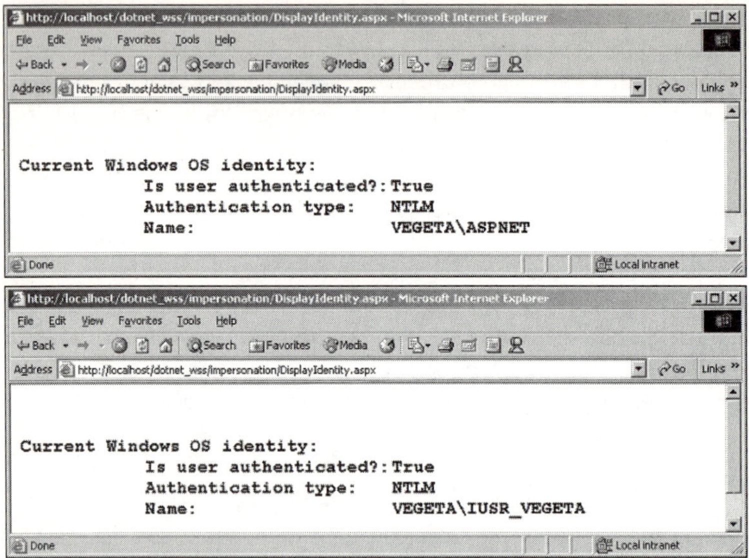

Figure 8.13 Identity of the processing thread in an HTTP request handler with impersonation mode turned off (top) and on (bottom).
(Courtesy: Microsoft Corporation)

Even though impersonation blindly hands most of the client's privileges (without its consent!) to the Web Service (which is always very risky for the client if the server is not totally trusted), it enables access control enforcement with better granularity and with less effort than HTTP modules require.

Impersonation-Based Access Control Methods

Once you have impersonation mode turned on, you have three more ways to control access to your Web Service functionality. They differ in their granularity and reliance on OS accounts. Let's begin with the most familiar mechanism.

Windows Access Control Lists

Controlling access to a Web Service with Windows discretionary ACL (DACL) is the simplest way to achieve file-level granularity, provided that the clients are mapped into OS accounts. All you need is to grant read and execute permissions on the corresponding asmx file to those OS accounts that should have access to the service. We illustrate this in Figure 8.14, which shows the window with permissions granted to customers, members, visitors, and staff on file StoreFrontService.asmx.

Even when impersonation is turned on, a special low-privileged account, automatically installed with .NET SDK and called {machine name}\ASPNET, has to have *read* permission to the service's asmx file. In addition to that special account, this example grants all members of groups *bcustomers*, *bmembers*, *bstaff*, and *bvisitors read* permission. However, we have explicitly denied account *bmember1* the permission, so the corresponding client would not be able to access the service, even though *bmember1* is a member of group *bmembers*. This example illustrates the ease of administering the DACL mechanism and the degree of its expressiveness. It has, however, a number of drawbacks. First, the DACL granularity is a file. Since a service in the ASP.NET Web Services architecture is composed of one asmx file, even when it has more than one method, DACL-based access control cannot be used to grant different permissions for different methods in the same service.

Another downside is in the low scalability of the DACL administration. If you only create a few Web Services, you will not notice the problem. But once you try to administer, say, an application service provider (ASP) with hundreds of Web Services, you will realize before long that it's a daunting task to set a DACL for each asmx file and make sure the settings across all these files truly implement the required authorization policies. As you remember from Chapter 7, the administration of security mechanisms for any distributed system with numerous protected entities needs some means to group those entities according to their security requirements, and not necessarily their location. The most the Windows DACL model gives in terms of grouping is inheritance of access permissions in the file system tree, which is still grouping by location, not by security requirements.

Another disadvantage is due to the requirement to have a mapping from Web Service clients to OS accounts, for DACL protection to work. In other words, you have to create accounts for all of the clients distinguishable from the point of view of authorization, authentication, and audit policies. Again, the problem occurs with large-scale systems, depending on the size of the client population. If you have hundreds of different clients accessing your Web Services, the use of OS accounts is a recipe for disaster, especially if you want your users to be able to do self-registration or manage their accounts, such as by changing passwords. In this case, you might want to consider the technique described in the next section.

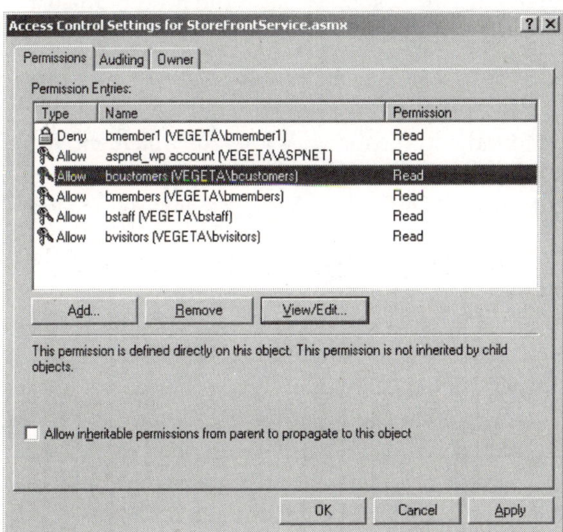

Figure 8.14 Protecting access to a Web Service with Windows DACLs.
(Courtesy: Microsoft Corporation).

ASP.NET URL Authorization

Similar to DACLs, this technique does not require that clients' identities be mapped into OS accounts. ASP.NET URL authorization also expresses protected resources in terms of URIs (and URLs in particular) instead of files. For any Web Service endpoint, you can specify what identities and groups can access the service, as illustrated in the following fragment from a web.config file:

```
<configuration>
  <location path="StoreFrontService.asmx">
    <system.web>
      <authorization>
        <allow roles="bcustomers, bmembers, bstaff, bvisitors"/>
       <deny users="bmember1" />
       <deny users="*" />
      </authorization>
    </system.web>
  </location>
</configuration>
```

The above settings achieve a result similar to those shown in the example with DACLs. There are two special identifiers for users. A question mark (?) means anonymous users, and an asterisk (*) means all users. The latter identifier had to be denied access in this example because of the following order of evaluating the grant/deny rules:

- Rules at lower levels of the URL hierarchy take precedence over rules at higher levels. The system determines which rule takes precedence by constructing a merged list of all rules for a URL, with the most recent (nearest in the hierarchy) rules at the head of the list.
- Given a set of merged rules for a URL, the system starts at the head of the list and checks rules until the first match is found.
- The default configuration for ASP.NET contains an <allow users="*"> element, which authorizes all users. If no rules match, the request is allowed unless otherwise denied. If a match is found and the match is a <deny> element, it returns 401. Applications or sites can easily configure a <deny users="*"> element at the top level of their site or application to change the default behavior.

If the location tag is omitted, then the authorization section applies to all the URL resources in the current directory and its subdirectories.

Since this technique is implemented using an HTTP module—specifically URLAuthorizationModule, provided in .NET SDK—OS accounts are generally not used to evaluate the name and roles of the impersonated client. However, OS accounts can be used if a Web Service application is configured to use IIS authentication by specifying "Windows" in the *authentication* element of the web.config file (described in the earlier section on ASP.NET authentication). If you use some non-IIS authentication, then URLAuthorizationModule picks up an instance of IPrincipal and makes access checks against the principal's name and roles. Therefore, the technique is open for integration with third-party authentication systems.

The URL Authorization mechanism remedies one drawback of DACLs—coupling with OS accounts—but leaves the other major limitation unaddressed: neither of them allows enforcement of different authorization requirements for methods implemented by the same Web Service. The problem of too coarse granularity is solved by the role-based access control enforced by .NET CLR.

CLR's Declarative Role-Based Access Control

Discussed briefly in Chapter 7's section on .NET security, role-based access control can be enforced outside of an ASP.NET Web Service business logic if its implementation has appropriate metadata. The metadata is specified in the source code via *PrincipalPermission* attributes that can be declared for classes, interfaces, or methods. Depending on particular parameters set on the attribute, CLR checks against roles of the principal associated with the executing thread or the identity name of the principal. The following C# code shows an example of specifying what role can invoke what methods. Here, being in role *visitor* is a prerequisite for invoking any method on Web Service *ProductRetrievingService*.

```
[WebService(
   Namespace="http://xml.eBusiness.com/StoreFront/",
   Name="ProductRetrievingService")
]
[PrincipalPermissionAttribute
(SecurityAction.Demand, Role="visitor")]
public class ProductInfoManager : WebService  {

   [WebMethod]
   public double GetProductPrice(int id) {
      ...
   }

   [WebMethod]
   [PrincipalPermissionAttribute
   (SecurityAction.Demand, Role="staff")]
public bool SetProductPrice(int id, double newPrice) {
      ...
```

The code illustrates the additive nature of attributes as well as the use of the *PrincipalPermission* attribute. Method *GetProductPrice* does not demand any additional role, so anybody who is in role *visitor* can invoke it. (You will note that this policy does not conform to our original scenario requirement, where customers and members were permitted to get prices, but visitors were not. We will correct this problem in a moment.) On the other hand, to invoke method *SetProductPrice*, the client has to be in roles *visitor* and *staff*.

As you can see, the granularity of access checks with this technique is up to the method—a significant improvement over DACLs and URL Authorization mechanisms. Because, as in URL authorization, the CLR principal is used, this approach does not require authenticated clients to be mapped into OS accounts. By these criteria, CLR role-based access control is ahead of other impersonation-based methods.

One dangerous caveat with this technique, which you need to keep in mind, is the lack of a way to change the parameters for the *PrincipalPermission* attribute outside of the source code. The .NET documentation does not indicate any alternate way to set *PrincipalPermission*. If, for instance, you decided later that in order to invoke the *GetProductPrice* method, the caller has to be in roles *visitor* and *customer*, then you would have to add an additional *PrincipalPermission* attribute to the method by modifying the source code, recompiling the application, and redeploying it.

There is a workaround that could overcome this constraint. If you treat .NET roles not as user roles but as fixed logical groupings of permissions that can be granted to users when they are being authenticated (the same way the EJB security model treats method permissions in deployment descriptors), then your code can determine at the time of constructing an *IPrincipal* object what permissions the authenticated client has, and can initialize the principal with the .NET roles representing those permissions. However, such a solution could lead to confusing role definitions in your system, if not used carefully.

Another limitation of the .NET *PrincipalPermission* attribute is illustrated by the following simple policy applied to the above code: Our scenario requires the client to be either in *member* or in *customer* role (but not *visitor*) in order to be permitted to invoke method *GetProductPrice* on *ProductRetrievingService*. Although quite simple and natural to define, this policy cannot be expressed by declaring *PrincipalPermission* attributes. The only way to implement this policy with CLR's roles is to give up on their declarative use and to add program checks in your application, as we discuss next.

CLR's Imperative Role-Based Access Control

If you do want to use CLR's roles but find the expressiveness of their declarative checks too limited, programming checks inside of your Web Service is the last resort. In the C# fragment below, we show how one would implement a policy that allows anybody in either *member* or *customer* role to invoke the *GetProductPrice* method.

```
[WebService(
        Namespace="http://xml.eBusiness.com/StoreFront/",
        Name="ProductRetrievingService")
]
public class ProductInfoManager : WebService  {
  [WebMethod]
  public double GetProductPrice(int id)
  {
    if (Thread.CurrentPrincipal.IsInRole("customer") == false ||
        Thread.CurrentPrincipal.IsInRole("member") == false)
   then
     throw new SecurityException("User is not customer or member");
   ...
```

Another way to achieve the same effect is to use the *PrincipalPermission* object and *Union* method to indicate that any role would suffice:

```
[WebMethod]
public double GetProductPrice(int id) {
  PrincipalPermission memberPerm =
  new PrincipalPermission(null, "member");
  PrincipalPermission customerPerm =
  new PrincipalPermission(null, "customer");

  memberPerm .Union(customerPerm ).Demand();
  ...
}
```

The imperative role-based control adds not only more flexibility but also granularity of access checks that is even finer than method-level. However, developers pay for these benefits by making their application code security-aware, which is a high price unless you develop very limited applications with a small number of methods and security policies that never change. If you don't want the trouble of coding access checks into your Web Service methods, consider instead implementing authorization enforcement by a specialized HTTP module, as described earlier.

This concludes the discussion of the building blocks of access control in your ASP.NET Web Services. Depending on your application security requirements and design, you might find some built-in features sufficient for your needs—such as IP-based restriction mechanisms (preferably combined with IPSEC), Windows DACLs, and ASP.NET URL authorization. On the other hand, you might have to resort to .NET roles (using them either declaratively or programmatically) or HTTP authorization modules, or even a combination of several mechanisms. Each mechanism has its own advantages and disadvantages, which hopefully have been explained to you well enough to allow you to make the right decisions when designing secure ASP.NET Web Services.

No matter how well the access control solution has been designed and implemented, it is never perfect. This is why it is imperative to implement a secure audit mechanism that makes users of Web Services accountable for their actions and detects security breaches.

Audit

As with other security mechanisms available in ASP.NET Web Service implementations, the potential choices you have for implementing auditing are Windows OS, ASP.NET itself, CLR, SOAP Security, and IIS. ASP.NET and SOAP Security don't define any functionality specific to auditing, leaving you with the other three. Out of the three, as in the cases of access control, data protection, and authentication, you have the dilemma of choosing between simplicity and capability. We describe the options in the following subsections, starting with the simple ones.

Audit on Windows Files and IIS URLs

Audit mechanisms for the Windows file system allow configuring the generation of audit records on file access. For the purpose of ASP.NET Web Services auditing, you can turn on auditing for read access on asmx files, as shown in Figure 8.15.

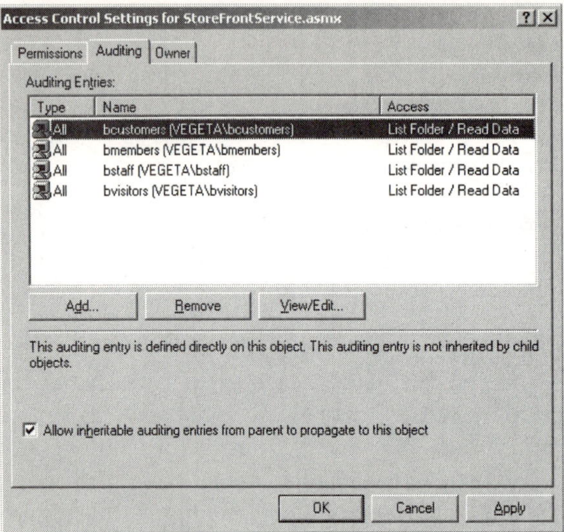

Figure 8.15 Setting audit on a Web Service file. (Courtesy: Microsoft Corporation).

A sample security audit event, which would be generated for each invocation executed by the specified clients on a Web Service, is shown in Figure 8.16.

This solution for security auditing of ASP.NET Web Services is similar in its capabilities, advantages, and weaknesses to the audit provided by IIS, which we described earlier. The major difference between the two is the security-oriented nature of file access auditing, and the performance and access statistics orientation of IIS logs.

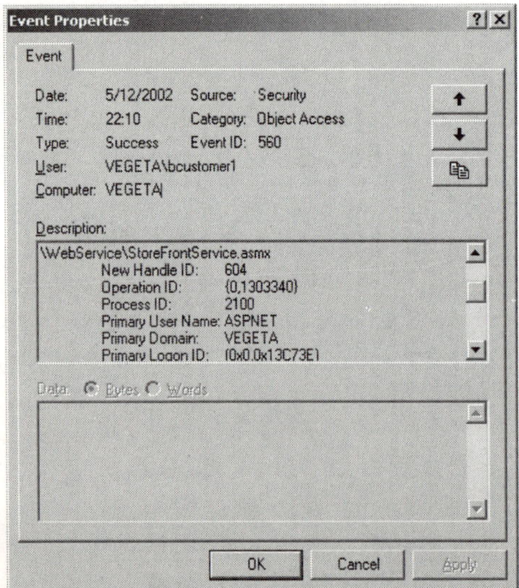

Figure 8.16 A sample event generated as a result of an invocation on StoreFrontService. (Courtesy: Microsoft Corporation).

Both are an easy way to turn on basic auditing for your Web Services without spending much effort. As with many other approaches this book describes, since the approaches are simple, they are not very powerful. What does this mean in the case of auditing? The main limitation is granularity. Since each file or URL is an ASP.NET Web Service with one or more methods, there is no way to set up these audit mechanisms so that only access to particular methods triggers generation of audit/log records. Another important issue is the level of information provided by the audit. An audit or log record does not contain information about what method was invoked and with what parameters. If non-OS accounts are used for clients, then client identity will not be recorded either. So, these two techniques, although simple, don't provide very effective security auditing of ASP.NET Web Services. Alternately, you can "manually" create audit events using .NET basic service classes.

.NET Log Classes

Event-logging classes that come with the .NET Framework SDK provide a programmatic way for your ASP.NET Web Services to record important events, not necessarily related to security. Windows platforms come with a standard user interface for viewing the logs, the Event Viewer, shown in Figure 8.17. Using the CLR's *EventLog* class, you can connect to existing event logs on both local and remote computers, and write entries to these logs. You can also read entries from existing logs and create your own custom event logs with this class.

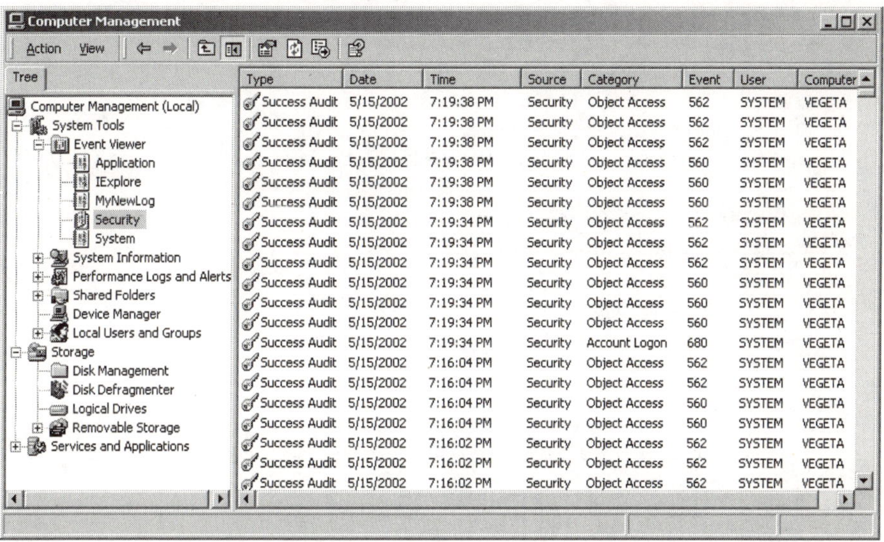

Figure 8.17 Windows Event Viewer, integrated into Microsoft Management Console, provides event-viewing capabilities.

(Courtesy: Microsoft Corporation).

If you write to an event log, you must specify or create an event *Source*. The *Source* registers your application with the event log as a valid source of entries. You can only use the *Source* to write to one log at a time. The *Source* can be any random string, but the name must be distinct from other sources on the computer. However, a single event log can be associated with multiple sources. Windows 2000 has three default logs: Application, System, and Security. Other installed applications and services can have additional event logs. You can use *EventLog* to create custom event logs. For example, the code below creates a custom event log "StoreFrontApp" first, as a side effect of creating a new event source.

When writing to an event log, in addition to sending the message, you can specify the type of the log entry, to indicate whether the message is an error, a warning, or information. You can also specify an application-defined event ID and category to display in the Type and Category columns of the event viewer. Finally, you can also attach binary data to your event entry if you need to associate additional information with a given event. The code below illustrates steps an application would take to prepare and write to a log.

```
using System;
using System.Diagnostics;
class LoggingSample {

  public static void Main(){
    string sourceName;
    string logName;
    string eventText;
    short category = 11;

    sourceName = "StoreFrontWebService";
    logName = "StoreFrontApp";
    eventName =
      "SetProductPrice for product with id=3510934 was called";

    // Create the source, if it does not already exist.
    if (!EventLog.SourceExists(sourceName))
      EventLog.CreateEventSource(sourceName,logName);

    // Write an informational entry to the event log.
    EventLog.WriteEntry(sourceName,eventText);

    // Create an EventLog instance and assign its source.
    EventLog myLog = new EventLog();
    myLog.Source = sourceName;

    // Another way to write detailed entries
    byte[] myByte=new byte[10];
    for(int i=0;i<10;i++)
    {
      myByte[i]= (byte)(i % 2);
    }
```

```
        myLog.WriteEntry(eventText, EventLogEntryType.Information,
            0, category, myByte);

        // Delete source -- optional
        EventLog.DeleteEventSource(sourceName);
    }
}
```

The code sample above generates two events, the latter of which is shown in Figure 8.18.

When you develop your application service with the use of Event Log, keep in mind that an application has to have additional privileges to be able to write to *Security* log. Also, most of the unprivileged accounts, such as ASPNET, would not be able to create their own source. An account with more privileges (for example, Administrator) would have to do it for them. Another feature of Windows logging facilities is that records from any log, other than *Security*, can be erased, making the logs an unreliable place for storing security audit records.

One of the items in our wish list for ASP.NET security is the provision of audit records generation outside of a Web Service. We think this is important to have in order to achieve a Web Service with good audit characteristics. Why? To have an effective audit service in your applications it is important to control audit generation without getting inside of the applications. The only way to do this with ASP.NET Web Services today is to write your own HTTP module responsible for auditing incoming SOAP requests.

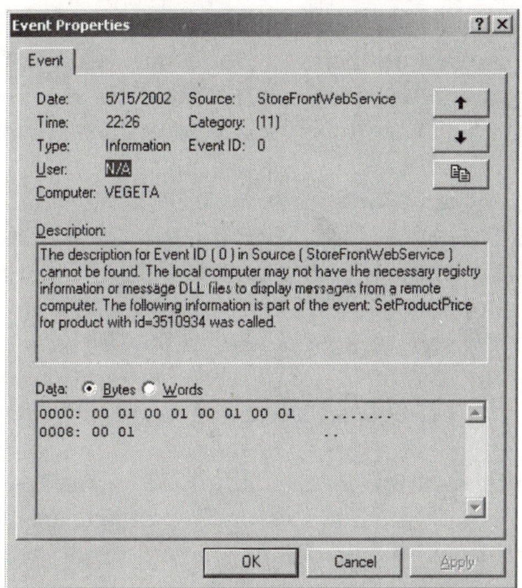

Figure 8.18 A sample event generated by the accompanying code fragment and viewed using Event Viewer.

(Courtesy: Microsoft Corporation).

This concludes our discussion of the building blocks of ASP.NET Web Services security. We hope you now have a fairly good idea of what you can do and how you can use various means to protect your Web Services. We deliberately avoided prescribing any specific approach because you have choices for every type of security functionality—authentication, data protection, access control, and auditing—and the way you combine the choices depends largely on the specific risks in your application domain and on your business requirements. To give an example, we show in the next section how these choices were made for our sample application, eBusiness/ePortal. This is also an example of putting everything together and implementing protection for a concrete system based on ASP.NET and other Microsoft technologies.

Securing Access to eBusiness

Since *StoreFrontService* acts as a SOAP gateway to the actual business logic and data access layer implemented as a COM+ server, *StoreFrontMiddleTier*, the middle tier, enforces access control policies. The Web Service only authenticates the incoming SOAP requests, as shown in Figure 8.19.

If a user of ePortal wants to see the prices of the items and potentially purchase them, the user has to log in by providing a username and password. The presentation tier at ePortal does not authenticate the user. Instead, it uses the authentication data to perform HTTP basic authentication when making SOAP/HTTP invocations to the eBusiness Web Service hosted by the IIS. Impersonation in this case comes in very handy, for it enables the Web Service to use the client's identity when calling the COM+ server and accessing other resources. The main drawback of this schema is the necessity of mapping ePortal customers and members into OS accounts at the machines running the Web Service and COM+ server at eBusiness. Moreover, both these machines have to share the account database by, for example, being in the same Windows domain. We did not show in this example how to use Microsoft technologies to perform document-oriented authentication using HTTP modules architecture, since this is far from trivial.

SSL is used for protecting data in transit between ePortal and eBusiness, whereas all invocations between the Web Service and COM+ server are protected by DCOM wire protocol cryptographic protection. Given the business scenario for the example, there was no need for message-oriented protection of data.

We did not define any comprehensive audit service. Implementing SOAP-specific auditing at the Web Service and at ePortal would require a significant amount of work. Therefore, we just enabled IIS-based logging of requests accessing corresponding URLs.

Service continuity has been increased by configuring corresponding IIS and COM+ applications in ePortal and eBusiness to run in individual processes. This allowed us to isolate faults and make sure that, for example, IIS would not crash even if the Web server process failed.

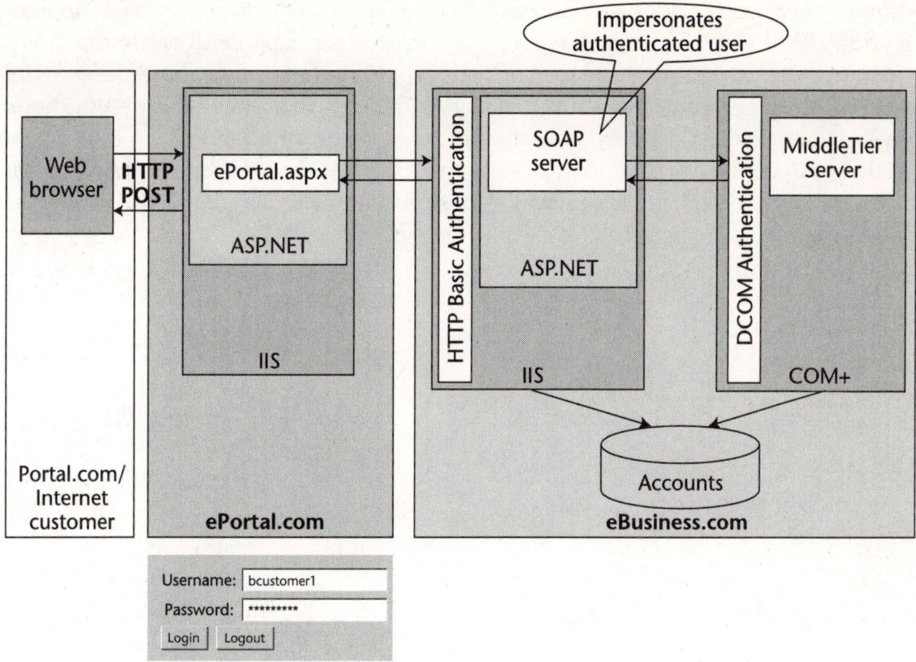

Figure 8.19 eBusiness enforcement of authentication and access control.

Summary

The purpose of this chapter was to give an example of concrete mechanisms available in the Windows world that realize various security functions for protecting Web Services. We described four ways of creating Web Services using Microsoft technologies. You can make COM+v1.5 components available to SOAP clients, wrap COM DLLs with configurable bridges provided in the SOAP toolkit, use .NET remoting, or take advantage of ASP.NET. After illustrating the use of ASP.NET for building Web Services on a sample ePortal/eBusiness application, we described the options you have for securing such services. The options match the building blocks of ASP.NET Web Services: Windows OS, IIS, .NET, and ASP.NET. Once more, we illustrated these concepts by describing the protection of our sample system.

Overall, Microsoft products provide a convenient family of technologies to support the security of modest-sized applications with little effort. As soon as your requirements for authentication, access control, accountability, and availability grow to the enterprise scale, you will need either significant amounts of in-house development or additional third-party products and services to fill the gap. Fortunately, .NET in general and ASP.NET in particular have a good architecture capable of accommodating various security extensions quite well. If you want to find out more about the security of ASP.NET in general and the security of its Web Services in particular, the online book from Microsoft (2002b) is a good collection of relevant information.

In the next chapter, we will describe how to secure Java-based Web Services. As you will see, the style of security solutions for those environments is significantly different than it is for .NET Web Services.

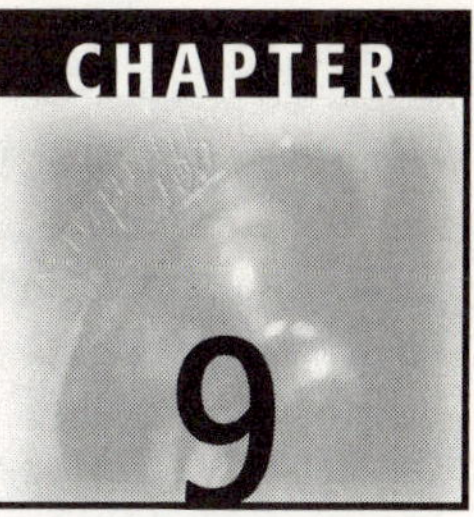

Securing Java Web Services

In this chapter we will describe how Java platforms may be used to secure Web Services. One of the promises of Web Services is the ability to make your existing server applications available to your employees, customers, and partners whether they are local or remote, establish a casual connection, or have a long-term relationship with your company. It would seem that Java 2 Platform, Enterprise Edition (J2EE), including Enterprise Java Beans (EJB), would fit well within this new distributed paradigm. This chapter will show you how the Java community is working to define security to bring the Web Services vision to a reality. While the principles in this chapter apply to a variety of Java implementations, we will often use application servers since they are typical services platforms in Java Web Services scenarios.

In the larger context, EJB, defined originally by Sun Microsystems, has gained wide acceptance as the open standard for server component architectures. Products based on the EJB specification have compelling advantages: They shield application developers from many of the low-level object service details (such as transactions and security), they enable enterprise beans to be moved to another environment with minimal effort, and they are interoperable with other EJB products. All of these capabilities are desirable in a Web Services environment.

The software system that supplies the EJB-related services to the application developer is the *application server*. Application servers, which provide a convenient environment for building distributed business applications, are widely available from a number of vendors, including IBM, BEA, Oracle, Sun, and Iona. Most of these vendors have upgraded their application servers to be Web Services aware. Because application servers are targeted at enterprise deployment, it's no surprise that security is generally addressed in these architectures. Without a good security solution protecting the corporate data on an application server, most businesses would not be willing to make their data accessible to Internet Web clients.

This chapter assumes that you have worked with Java applications and EJB, have written programs for some application server, and are familiar with the existing Java security mechanisms as described in Chapter 7, "Security of Infrastructures for Web Services." We are going to look at how security can be handled in a Java-enabled Web Services environment. Although EJB is, for the most part, a server-side architecture, an enterprise bean can act as a client and call upon other beans, thus fully participating in a Web Services scenario.

This chapter will examine how Java applications, as well as EJB servers, can be used in conjunction with Web Services. We will also use the ePortal-eBusiness example that we have been developing in previous chapters to give concrete examples of using Java with Web Services. We will limit detailed examination of our example to the path from the ePortal Web server to a Java server supplying prices for products at eBusiness.

The previous chapter used our example to describe how to secure a Web Services system based on Microsoft's technologies. In this chapter we will replace the COM+ portion of the example with a Java platform. We will also use a Web server other than the Microsoft IIS Web server, and we'll replace the .ASP layer with the J2EE equivalent.

You will notice that the discussion of Web Services security for Java is substantially different from our previous chapter on .NET. The chapters differ because the two technologies approach Web Services in very different ways. .NET provides a specific concrete Web Services solution that is defined and implemented by a single vendor: Microsoft. On the other hand, Java Web Services represent a whole family of different solutions from a variety of vendors. To ensure that this chapter is relevant across different products, we focus on the Java standards that define common system features as well as the security mechanisms of a typical Java application server. Although this chapter spends less time than the previous one on specific Web Services security product solutions, we do describe the approaches of a few different representative vendors: Sun and IBM as examples of Web Services-enabled Java vendors, and Systinet as a Web Services development platform vendor for non-Web Services applications.

Using Java with Web Services

Even though Java is a platform-neutral system, it has a few areas that do not yet fully address Web Services requirements. For example, until recently there was no specification on how to handle SOAP messages, which is one of the basic message protocols of Web Services as they are commonly defined. Ongoing work by the Java Community Process (JCP) is defining a number of these missing pieces. These extensions to Java take the form of Java Specification Requests (JSRs). Some JSRs that are pertinent to Web Services are:

- JSR 31 defines a facility for compiling XML schema into Java Classes that parse, generate, and validate documents.
- JSR 67 defines APIs to transport Web Service messages.
- JSR 101 defines APIs that support XML-based RPC.

- JSR 110 defines APIs to handle WSDL.
- JSR 155 defines APIs to exchange SAML assertions.
- JSR 183 defines facilities for enabling Java applications to handle secure SOAP messages.

As you can see from this sampling of JSRs, Java is being positioned for smooth integration with the Web Services paradigm.

The Java model fits well in most cases when it is used as a Web Service. One of the new issues for Java-based Web Services concern the nature of access to a Java container, e.g. a servlet, or an EJB container. Traditionally, a request to a Java container used the HTTP protocol with the request in the HTTP header, cookie, and/or the HTTP POST message. In the Web Services case, the message format is SOAP.

The Java container must be prepared to handle SOAP security. However, be aware that traditional Java servers cannot even handle plain SOAP messages, let alone SOAP security, without some upgrading. For example, EJB containers based solely on EJB 2.0 are not able to handle SOAP and SOAP security and thus are not able to participate as a secure Web Service without external help. However, Java containers that have implemented the above JSRs are able to handle SOAP security. If you are going to use an EJB application server for deploying a Web Service, be sure that you check whether the version that you will use has been upgraded to be compliant with the pertinent JSRs. If your container has not been upgraded, which will be the common case for some time, don't lose hope. A number of products on the market will bridge between a Web Service request and a traditional EJB application server. We will describe such an approach in our example in a later part of this chapter.

Compared to .NET, Java is a mature technology that has been in use for several years. On the other hand, Java has not been used in Web Services until recently. In addition, as you can see from the new JSRs that we just discussed, more work is necessary to allow Java to become a full-fledged member of the Web Services world.

The transition of the Java security model to Web Services is evolutionary, and builds on existing security mechanisms. The evolutionary approach holds not only for the Java model but also for .NET. Both Java and .NET have concentrated first on perimeter security, as supported by Web servers such as IIS in the case of .NET, and Apache Tomcat in the case of Java. We will describe the more complete Web Services security model for both Java and .NET in Chapter 10, "Interoperability of Web Services Technologies," where we address interoperability based on SAML and WS-Security.

Let's now look at a few of the traditional EJB security features and see where they differ when the EJB container is accessed as a Web Service. By "traditional features," we mean those security features that were defined in the EJB 2.0 Specification.

Traditional Java Security Contrasted with Web Services Security

The traditional security model for J2EE, as described in Chapter 7, contains a simple and elegant access control policy. EJB security emphasizes a declarative authorization security model called method permissions. Method permissions are specified in the J2EE deployment descriptor.

When the client program invokes a method on a target object, the identity of the user (that is, the principal) associated with the calling client is transmitted to the object's container. The container checks to see whether the caller's role is in the access control entry associated with the server's method, as described in the deployment descriptor. If the caller's role is in the access control entry, the container permits the invocation on the method.

Authentication in J2EE is less specified. The specification says that the credentials of an authenticated client may be passed in from a client in the client security context, or authentication may be supplied by a third-party security service. It's up to the vendor of the J2EE platform to define how to handle authenticated credentials.

In the following sections we will discuss how Java-based security relates to Web Services security requirements for authentication, data protection, and access control.

Authenticating Clients in Java

Before you check whether an entity is allowed access to a resource, you must determine whether that entity is who it says it is—that is, authenticate the requesting entity, the client. Therefore, we need to obtain the client's identity and authenticate it.

The security mechanism used between the client and server determines how the user's identity is passed from client to server. For example, if Secure Sockets Layer (SSL) is used for client authentication, SSL passes the client's identity in the form of a public key certificate, if requested by the server.

In the Web Services' case, the user's identity is passed as part of SOAP security within the message. We described the various security concepts related to SOAP messages in Chapter 6, "Principles of Securing Web Services." As you remember, one aspect of SOAP security addresses the security information related to the accessing client, that is, its authentication information and security attributes. The authentication information may be passed as the authentication evidence itself (for example, a password) or as some evidence that the authentication has taken place (for example, a SAML assertion, as described in Chapter 5, "Security Assertion Markup Language").

If you are the requesting party, passing the authentication evidence itself is usually not good security practice, but it is frequently used because it is the easiest method. If this method is used, be sure to guard against the possibility of the evidence being stolen or compromised. Remember, you are handing the security evidence to the Web Service, which may send your security evidence through many intermediates before it reaches its intended target. Therefore, this method should be weighed against the value of the items or information requested and your desire for privacy.

Passing a SAML assertion is a more secure method than passing a password, but you still have to guard against stolen or compromised assertions. Therefore, the assertion should be signed by the issuer and tied to the SOAP message body by means of a digital signature, allowing a more secure check on the validity of the assertion.

Data Protection

Another aspect of SOAP security, also described in Chapter 6, is the security of the message itself. All or parts of the message may be signed and/or encrypted. Message confidentiality (encryption) and message integrity (digital signature) are not explicitly provided by the Java security model, and are assumed to be provided by the underlying security mechanism.

Controlling Access

Once we have authenticated the caller from the incoming SOAP message and protected the data in transit, we may then rely on the Java infrastructure to handle authorization in its normal manner.

For instance, one of the capabilities of a traditional EJB server is the ability of the container to provide the caller's identity as part of the request's context. If an enterprise bean instance needs to determine the caller identity (say, to perform additional checking), the bean can call *getCallerPrincipal* and *isCallerInRole* on the javax.ejb.EJBContext interface. The process for defining which callers are in which roles is not specified by the EJB security model, and is left up to each container implementation. However, EJB does specify that the container provider supply a tool that the deployer can use to map the roles to specific users.

In the EJB security model, the enterprise bean provider sets up the security policy for the bean as part of the deployment descriptor in an EJB jar file. When the bean is deployed, container tools read and interpret the security policy in the deployment descriptor to enable the container to enforce the specified security policy for all bean instances. The container may allow the deployer and system administrator to modify the bean security policy so that it may be customized beyond what was originally set up by the bean provider. More and more container providers, for example, furnish an EJB deployment wizard that includes the security policy setup for the deployment descriptor. The EJB deployment wizard may be used later to modify the security policy.

Access control entries are an aspect of security policy defined in the bean's deployment descriptor. The deployment descriptor may include a *method permission* for each individual bean method. The descriptor may also include a method permission for the entire bean that applies to all methods. A method permission associates a bean's method with a list of logical privileges or roles. The identities of the requestor are mapped to the roles that are allowed to invoke the method.

Credentials, which contain system-certified user information such as identities and roles, are not explicitly represented in EJB, but are supported by the underlying security mechanism (for example, SSL or Kerberos) that provides the secure authentication between client and server. Because EJB access policy is normally defined in terms of roles derived from the user identity, the credentials usually contain only that identity. However, this is not mandated by EJB.

In a Web Services case where SAML is used, both the user's identity and attributes (such as roles) may be passed in a SAML attribute assertion.

How SAML Is Used with Java

As you remember from Chapter 5, SAML is XML-based and is a natural mechanism to be used as a security extension for Web Services. But, what about its compatibility with Java? The JCP has released JSR 155, which deals specifically with the use of SAML in Java, in addition to other JSRs that deal with the other Java / Web Services interactions.

JSR 155 defines an API for manipulating each of the SAML assertions. In addition, this JSR uses the work of other JSRs to complete the Java use of SAML. For example, JSR 155 uses JSR 105 which, in turn, defines APIs to carry out XML signatures as referenced in the SAML specification. XML signatures are ultimately defined in the digital signature specification that has been released by the World Wide Web Consortium (W3C).

JSRs that are used by JSR 155:

- JSR 109 implements Web Services.
- JSR 105 defines APIs for XML signature.
- JSR 106 defines APIs for XML encryption.
- JSR 104 defines the XML trust services.
- JAXRPC defines APIs to use XML-based RPC mechanisms in the Java paradigm.
- JAXM defines APIs for XML messaging.
- JSR 110 defines the APIs for the WSDL.

There is a lot of reuse of the work of other standards organizations as well as the various JSR technical committees that are working on Web Services and XML security.

These JSRs, taken together, comprise a complete set of APIs for Java programmers building secure systems for use in the Web Services world. We will not go any deeper into the various JSRs since we are interested in using the Java infrastructure that is built by the providers, not in building the Java systems themselves. The important point is that the Java system you purchase or plan to purchase should follow or plan to follow the specifications previously listed, so that your Java system can have secure interoperability with other Web-Service-enabled processes that are in your enterprise and with clients that wish to use your services.

While your particular Java provider may not have the full range of specifications implemented, they should have a well-defined road map as to when these JSRs will be implemented in their product, if you intend to use that particular brand of Java application as a foundation for your Web Services.

Even if your Java provider does have the ability to handle SOAP messages, this does not mean that it can seamlessly handle secure SOAP messages. You should investigate two areas:

1. How does it accept the user identity? Does it accept a standardized format for the user identity—for example, defined by the WS-Security specification—or does it have some proprietary way of getting the user identity?
2. How does it handle user attributes? Can it accept user roles sent in the request, or does it rely on the pre-Web Services method of requiring you to associate users with roles?

Even though your Java provider may advertise itself as Web Services enabled, it may not be Web Services *security* enabled, or it may require that you bridge different methods of authentication and authorization. Most of these potential problems arise because the client and service are disjoined from each other. They may be in different companies or in different divisions of the same company that do not use the same Web

Services security protocol as your application, if it is not fully compliant with the pertinent protocols. We will delve into the interoperability problem in the next chapter.

In addition to receiving and interpreting SAML assertions, a Java application may have a need to make requests for authentication, attribute, and authorization assertions from SAML authorities. SAML defines binding protocols for handling these requests and responses, which we discussed in Chapter 5. At present, the SAML bindings only support SOAP and HTTP Post as a means for contacting the services. While these methods could be used, they are not standard messaging protocols for Java. For example, the EJB specification dictates the use of CSI v2 for secure container-to-container transport. Thus, if the SAML authority is an EJB application server, the binding between the source container and the authority container is caught between two differing specifications.

We recommend that you discuss this area with your Java platform provider to determine their solution to this problem. Most application servers do not address this problem. Therefore, you will need to use some third-party product or build an in-house system for accessing the SAML authorities. The most common authority that an application server will want to use is an authorization service. Thus, you will want to construct a SAML authorization query and pass that query to the authorization service. Both of these steps will probably entail some work on your part. Does your application server have the capability to construct an authorization query? If it does, what protocol does it support to interact with the authorization authority? Does this protocol match the expected protocol of the authorization authority that you intend to use?

Next, we will enumerate a few of the steps you should take to determine how difficult or easy it would be to use a particular application server for Web Services.

Assessing an Application Server for Web Service Compatibility

If your Java platform does not support the JSRs outlined in the previous section, then you will have to create a bridge between the incoming Web Service message and your application. There are some products, such as Systinet WASP, that help you do this. The example that we give later in this chapter uses just such a product. We believe that the example will help you to find a way to bridge between the new world of Web Services and the "old" world of traditional Java applications.

In this section, we will look at how to assess application servers that claim to support Web Service security and what that might mean when you attempt to use them. We recommend a three-step approach to assessing the security capability of the application server or any Java application that you intend to use as a Web Service provider. We'll discuss these in the next three subsections.

JSR Compliance

The list of JSRs that we provided earlier in this chapter provides a convenient way for you to assess whether your application server is Web Service ready. In checking the compliance of your candidate application servers against these JSRs, you might have to contact the sales representative or customer support for the application servers. If you follow this route, have them describe and possibly demonstrate the product's compliance with any JSRs that their literature does not explicitly declare they support.

It is highly likely that your application server provider does not fully implement all the JSRs. If this is the case, you should then assess your requirements against the missing functionality. For example, JSR 110 specifies the APIs for WSDL. You may have decided that you do not intend to advertise your services by means of WSDL, since you are setting up your Web Service system to work only in an intranet. You should also assess whether you will expand your Web Services capability to your suppliers or customers. If future expansion of your Web Services capability is probable, you should get a firm road map from your application server supplier as to their future plans on supporting such capabilities as WSDL. You could also decide to use a WSDL compiler and tools from a vendor other than your application server supplier.

Another compliance example is whether encryption of the XML messages themselves is important in your work. If you believe that it will be, then compliance with JSR 105 is important to you. There are some additional complications associated with the encryption capability. As in our previous example, are you intending to deploy intranet or Internet Web Services? In both cases some sort of Public Key Infrastructure (PKI) is necessary. However, the reduced complexity of an intranet deployment can require a simpler PKI than an Internet deployment. You will need to ask your potential provider about their PKI features so you can determine how well the supplied PKI will support your XML encryption needs.

In summary, as you go through each of the JSR compliance points with your application server provider, you should determine:

- Which JSR capabilities you require now and in your future Web Services plans
- Whether the provider supplies the capabilities to meet your present and future Web Services requirements
- Whether they have plans to provide the missing capabilities, if they do not currently meet your requirements

You should go to a third-party provider or develop the missing capability yourself if your requirements are not on your application provider's road map.

Authentication

A critical security requirement for Web Services is the ability to authenticate the client. Because Web Services support application-to-application communication, a live user at the client end of the request may not be available to type in the password. One of the requirements of Web Services is that unattended processes can make requests on your Web Service and receive a reply. The reply may be a fulfillment of some expensive order or the transfer of funds. Therefore, the sender of the SOAP request must be authenticated to a level that matches the risk.

Both SAML and WS-Security are attacking this problem. The groups defining the specification are working on ways to combine and coordinate their respective realms of security coverage. Their integration into Web Services security will be discussed in more detail in the next chapter. You should ask your application server vendor whether their product supports both of these specifications. If the answer is no, then you should ask how they support Web Service security. The importance of this question again revolves around whether you intend to use Web Service beyond a closed system within your company. You can work around this constraint by using a third-party Web Service authentication mechanism, but you usually will have to do more work to make the third-party authentication product work with your application server. Our example later in this chapter will give you a good feel for the concepts required for a secure connection to your application server in a Web Services environment.

Authorization

Once you have an authenticated user, the Web Service must authorize the user to use a resource. You can use the authorization method described in the EJB 2.0 specification—that is, method permissions—or you could use a third-party authorization service. Authorization itself is not specifically a Web Services problem and is covered in other books (for example, Hartman 2001). The tough problem lies in getting the proper attributes for the authenticated user that match the authorization method that you will use.

Any large-scale implementation will determine the access permissions based on security attributes of the requestor, to solve the potentially large scaling problem associated with using access policies based on individual users. EJB uses the *role* attribute to address scaling.

Bean portability adds additional complexity to role-based security. The provider of a bean from one company may sell that bean to a number of other companies. The bean provider does not know the specifics of how a particular role will fit into the policy of a purchasing company. Therefore, a role defined by the producer company is a logical construct that can be used by the different purchasers of the bean. The purchaser of the bean can then give a concrete representation to the logical role that is meaningful to the purchasing company.

Roles in EJB take the form of permissions that are granted to a group of entities—that is, if a user is given the role of administrator, then the user will have administrator permissions when the time comes to check whether the user is authorized to perform a particular function.

The challenge with attributes in Web Services is that the attributes may be defined in the scope of the client, which may be different from the scope of the service. Since the client of a Web Service can be from another company and use a different security model, the syntax and semantics of the user's attribute may not match those at the service provider company. Authorization can fail if the target system does not understand the initiator's security attributes, or it may give an incorrect authorization decision if it misinterprets the role data. We will address this problem in the next chapter when we look at secure interoperability.

Java Tools Available for Web Services

Since the Web Service's goal is to make the use of services easily available to their users, there need to be software tools to make this job easy for developers. The tool vendors listened to customers and have supplied products that simplify the job of building Web Services applications with Java. We'll look at some typical tool environments to give you an idea of what is available now, or will be in the near future.

There are development environments from two of the largest companies that support Java and Web Services: the Java development tool from Sun called FORTE, Sun's Java Web Services Developer Pack (JWSDP), and a tool set from IBM contained in their WebSphere Development Environment. We will also discuss a development environment specifically focused on Web Services, called the Web Application and Services Platform (WASP), offered by Systinet.

There are many other developer tool kits that may be a better fit for your needs. However, you can use the products from Sun, IBM, and Systinet as a comparison point for these other tool sets.

Sun FORTE and JWSDP

Sun provides two ways that you can write Web Service clients and services in Java: their enterprise development system FORTE and their developers' kit called the Java Web Services Developer Pack (JWSDP). Of course, when using Web Services, the client and service do not have to use the same platform; that is, you could develop one side using Java and the other side using Microsoft's .NET.

FORTE

FORTE is a software development environment from Sun Microsystems that aids you in developing Java programs, including EJB applications. The FORTE development environment has added capabilities and extensions by third parties to generate the ancillary programs necessary for deployment of Web Service systems. You can find the FORTE environment at http://wwws.sun.com/software/Developer-products/ffj/ .

In addition to their production-level development environment, Sun provides a lot of documentation, sample code, and individual tools in their Java Developer Connection. This can be accessed at http://developer.java.sun.com/.

Java Web Services Developer Pack

Sun has released a software developers' kit (SDK) called JWSDP. The JWSDP is a free download that contains the reference implementation of the Java Web Services JSRs that we discussed earlier. There are four basic parts of the developer pack, which correspond to the four major Web Services JSR categories. These are:

- Java Messaging (JAXM), which supports the construction and delivery of SOAP messages. It provides a number of Java APIs for creating SOAP messages. The infrastructure takes care of transmitting the messages to the service, using HTTP. Similarly, on the service side there are APIs to retrieve the information from the SOAP message. We will give an example of JAXM use later in this chapter.
- Java Remote Procedure Call (JAX-RPC), which supports construction and delivery of SOAP messages. In contrast to JAXM, when using the JAX-RPC you write normal Java RMI calls that the JAX-RPC converts to SOAP and transmits using HTTP. When the call is received at the SOAP service, the HTTP message is converted back into an RMI call on your Java object. While this will be more

familiar to Java developers, it does not give you the control over the security details of the message that JAXM gives.

- Java API for Registries (JAXR) is an implementation of the UDDI. The JWSDP includes an implementation of a UDDI and a set of APIs to register your service and retrieve that information. There is also a capability to do SQL searches on the registry. JAXR uses messaging based on JAXM to access UDDI.
- Java APIs for XML Processing (JAXP) provides the supporting infrastructure for the developer pack. Its APIs are also available to you for any detailed XML work that you may want to implement. The JAXP supports both the Simple API for XML Parsing (SAX) and the Document Object Model (DOM), specifications for parsing XML documents. The parsers are below a pluggable layer that allows you to substitute your favorite parser if you wish. JAXP also supports the XML Stylesheet Transformations Language (XSTL) specification that allows you to format the presentation of XML data or to translate the XML into another language or protocol.

This package gives you the ability to write your Web Services using native Java APIs, reducing the complexity by letting you work in a familiar language and structure. There is also a tool, called the xrpcc, which converts WSDL files to Java and the inverse. This is mostly used at the lower layers to create the stubs to prepare the data for interprocess calls. If you input a WSDL file to the xrpcc, it will produce RMI interfaces, and if you input RMI interfaces it will produce a WSDL document.

The JWSDP also supports a declarative security model that, in conjunction with a deployment descriptor, will support the security model as defined in both the Java 2 Platform, Standard Edition (J2SE) and J2EE specifications.

In this chapter we will provide a basic example of how JWSDP may be used to implement a secure Web Service. We will also describe a more advanced example using JWSDP in Chapter 10 when we discuss cross-platform interoperability.

IBM WebSphere and Web Services Toolkit

IBM has extended its flagship Java development environment, WebSphere, to aid you in developing your Web Services applications. IBM also has a Web Services toolkit (WSTK) that is part of their alphaWorks initiative. You can download WSTK to get familiar with a number of Web Services technologies such as SOAP, UDDI, and WSDL. The toolkit comes with a number of examples to let you see how these components work together. You can find WSTK at http://www.alphaworks.ibm.com/tech/webservicestoolkit and the WebSphere environment at http://www-3.ibm.com/software/ad/studioappdev/. IBM does not intend the WSTK to be used for production-level code. They recommend that you use their WebSphere product when deploying an enterprise Web Services application.

IBM has released its WSTK Version 3.2.2, which contains WS-Security technology. Included in the toolkit is a demo that uses WS-Security. In this demo, a browser authenticates the user by means of HTTP basic authentication. The username and password are extracted from the HTTP request at the sender side, which then constructs a SOAP document that includes a WS-Security element with a username password token. The Web Services receiver extracts and uses the WS-Security element to enforce authorization.

Using WSTK you can produce a SOAP XML document that contains header code including the WS-Security element. A snippet of the header would look something like the following XML code. This snippet defines a SOAP header with a WS-Security element included.

```
              ...

1.  <SOAP-ENV:Header>
2.     <wsse:Security xmlns:wsse=
                  "http://schemas.xmlsoap.org/ws/2002/04/secext">
3.      <wsse:UsernameToken>
4.         <wsse:Username>bhartman</wsse:Username>
5.         <wsse:Password>mypassword</wsse:Password>
6.      </wsse:UsernameToken>
7.     </wsse:Security>
8.  </SOAP-ENV:Header>
              ...
```

In this example, other code typical of a SOAP message would come before the start of our snippet. Line 1 of the snippet is the start of the SOAP header element, followed on line 2 by the *wsse:Security* element that is the beginning tag of the WS-Security. wsse:Security is the identifier that the specification has defined for WS-Security. Line 3 starts the username token. Following this on the next two lines are the username and password elements. The next three lines close the token, WS-Security, and the header. The body of the SOAP message would follow.

In addition to the Web Services security capabilities, which are our main interest, the toolkit has full support for Web Services, including the SOAP specification, UDDI, and WSDL.

IBM has demonstrated two versions of Web Services support, a Java server page and a WebSphere version. The Java server page version uses a username/password token. The WebSphere version covers a lot more of the Web Services security technology, using X.509 certificates, digital signature, and XML encryption. The WebSphere version also has an additional interesting feature that allows you to supply WebSphere with an XML configuration file that directs WebSphere as to which security functionality to include.

These examples show IBM's initial capabilities and commitment to supporting WS-Security. Although IBM has not yet provided support for SAML-based Web Services, IBM is actively involved in the WS-Security TC and the SAML TC at OASIS, and has a strong commitment to WS-Security. Since the WS-Security TC has accepted SAML as one of the tokens in WS-Security, it is highly likely that IBM will support the combination of WS-Security and SAML in the future.

Systinet WASP

The third product that we will discuss is called the Web Application and Services Platform (WASP) system from Systinet. You can download the WASP system for free from http://www.systinet.com/download.html, as long as you don't use it for commercial purposes.

WASP is a Web Services development platform that allows users to build interoperable Web Services applications that run on existing enterprise servers. WASP supports both Java and C++ environments and several J2EE application servers. WASP also supports a UDDI registry. Systinet products are targeted on integrating existing enterprise applications across a variety of platforms using Web Services technologies.

WASP provides three layers of security: low-level, XML, and Web Services security. The low-level security consists of many of the security models that we described in Chapter 7, as well as Kerberos, SSL, and servlet-based security such as HTTP basic auth and digest. The Java version of WASP server can also integrate with JAAS and Java Cryptography Extension (JCE). The second layer of security, XML security, is based on XML signature and encryption, XML Key Management Specification (XKMS), WS-Security, and SAML. The third layer of security in WASP supports single sign-on (SSO).

Systinet has an administrative GUI that lets you manage users, public and private keys, X.509 certificates, and other security policies to support a range of authentication methods. The administration console also lets you manage user roles for authorization. In addition, you can use the Java *SecurityManager* and *AccessController* interfaces as well as Microsoft's Active Directory for access control.

The Java Web Services Examples

Now that we have presented how Java security and Web Services work together, we will present two examples of Java in a Web Services setting, using the ePortal-eBusiness scenario that we have discussed throughout this book. The first example will use WASP and a Java application server that does not support SOAP. Since there are many implementations of applications servers that are not based on Web Services and are not SOAP-enabled, we will use WASP both to provide a Web Services interface and to secure the connection. Our second example discusses a SOAP-enabled application server; in this case, we will use Sun's JWSDP.

The examples in this chapter will show how to use the traditional J2EE security methods that we described in Chapter 7, since many of the application platforms available today do not yet support the newer Web Services security models. In Chapter 10, we will describe the emerging Web Services security interoperability models based on WS-Security and SAML.

Example Using WASP

Our example will use WASP to provide a secure SOAP interface to an existing application server that does not support SOAP. We will not go too deeply into WASP, as we are interested in the security for Web Services, not in building Web Services applications themselves, but we do need some understanding of the Web Services model to demonstrate the security.

Please refer to Figure 9.1 for a representation of the setup of the example used in this chapter. The shaded portions of the diagram, namely the ePortal.com Web server, the StoreFrontService application server, and the WASP server, represent our areas of interest.

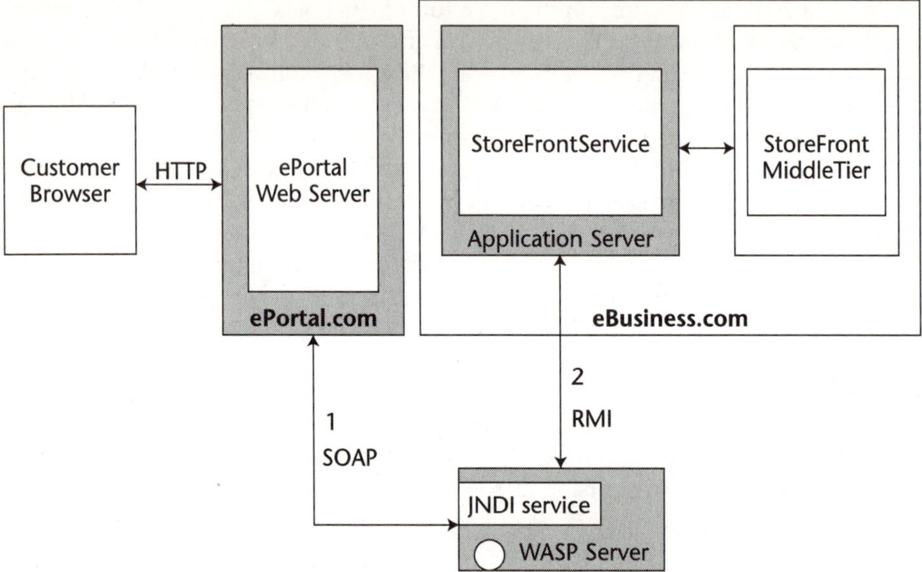

Figure 9.1 ePortal-eBusiness example on Java platforms.

In Figure 9.1, you can observe a customer using a browser to access ePortal to retrieve some pricing from eBusiness related to the product items. Rather than access an IIS Web server in eBusiness, as discussed in Chapter 8, in this case ePortal will access a Java application server in eBusiness. The application server may have an EJB that will carry out the implementation of the price retrieval. This bean may call out to a legacy system or to another application server. These secondary calls are outside the context of Web Services. If you wish to study the security solutions of EJB in the non-Web-Services case, please refer to Hartman (2001).

In Figure 9.1, the paths that we are interested in for this example are labeled 1 and 2. Path 1 goes from ePortal to the WASP Server. The message then follows path 2 from the WASP server to the application server in eBusiness. It's now time to describe the WASP Server.

For the most part, all but the newest releases of Java application servers do not yet speak SOAP. Although there is a SOAP specification for EJB APIs, it takes time for any enterprise to upgrade its application servers. We also realize that upgrading your application servers to support SOAP in a production environment is often not feasible, so incremental support for Web Services using a product like WASP may be a more viable near-term alternative. Given that fact, we need a way for application servers to communicate in the SOAP-based Web Services world. We will use WASP to bridge from a SOAP request to an RMI request to an application server. See Figure 9.2.

Figure 9.2 shows the conceptual architecture that will be used in this example. This figure expands on the shaded areas of the architecture in Figure 9.1, which are the areas of concentration for this Java example.

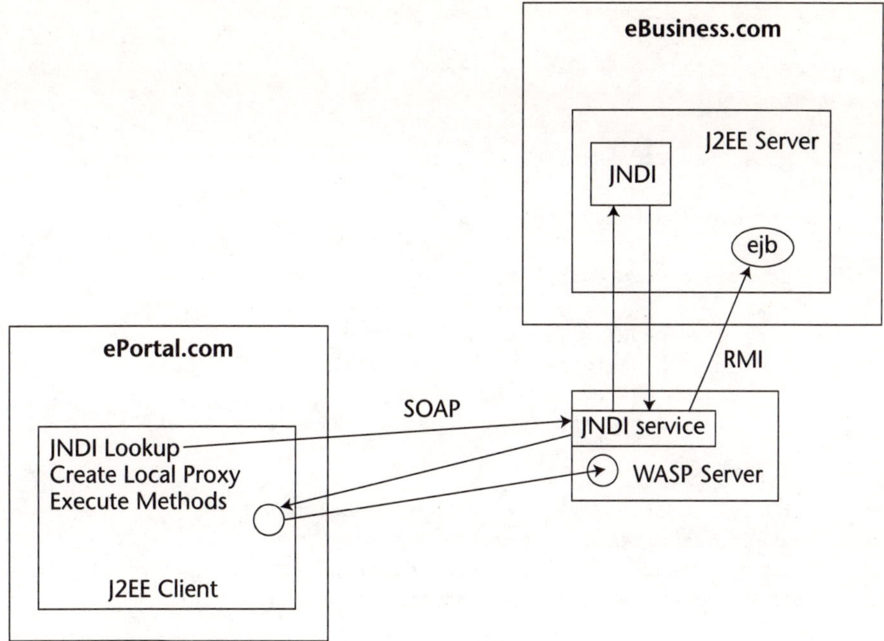

Figure 9.2 Java Web Service conceptual architecture.

We'll first trace the message at a high level. On the left side of Figure 9.2 we have a Java client. This may be either a separate Java process that was called by the ePortal Web server or, more likely, a plug-in to the Web server. Before the Java client was called, the browser had previously called in to the Web server and authenticated itself (refer to Figure 9.1). The browser authentication could be any of the standard browser-to-Web-server authentication methods—for example, basic authentication, forms-based authentication, or even the SAML Browser Profile described in Chapter 5. Since this step is outside of our interest for this example, we skip its details.

After successful authentication of the browser to ePortal, an HTTP message from the client goes to the Java code in ePortal. This is the point where our example of Java Web Service security starts. The Java client calls the WASP server, asking for information from eBusiness. The WASP server connects to the application server in eBusiness and makes a call on the pertinent EJB to get the information that it needs—for example, methods *GetProductPrice*, *GetAllProducts*, and the like.

StoreFront Client

In this first Web Services example, we have a simple Java client at ePortal calling on an application server in eBusiness, asking for a price for a product that has a *product id* of "2." The following is the Java client code:

```
1.    import org.idoox.webservice.client.WebServiceLookup;

2.    public final class StoreFrontClient
3.    {
4.     /**
5.      Lookups StoreFrontService, use it and print out the response
6.      from it.
7.      @param args  not used.
8.     */
9.     public static void main(String[] args) throws Exception
10.    {
11.      String serviceURI = System.getProperty(
                        "idoox.storefront.service.uri");
12.      if(serviceURI == null)
13.         serviceURI = "http://localhost:6060/ProductManager/";

14.      // lookup service
15.      WebServiceLookup lookup = (WebServiceLookup)
         Context.getInstance(Context.WEBSERVICE_LOOKUP);
16.      ProductManager storeFront = (ProductManager)
         lookup.lookup(serviceURI, ProductManager.class);

17.      // Call service and print out a response message from
18.      //  ProductManager Service.
19.      System.out.println(storeFront.GetProductPrice (2));
20.    }
21.   }
```

The first thing that we see is that on line 1 of the client example we need to import the client lookup class from WASP. Line 2 defines our StoreFrontClient class that will call on eBusiness. Line 11 retrieves a Java property that identifies the URI of the WSDL document, which identifies our storefront implementation for ProductManager at eBusiness. If we haven't set that property, we will set a default URI to contact the WASP server on our local host at port 6060 at lines 12 and 13. The WASP server by default listens on port 6060.

Next we have to set up the means to find the class that we are interested in calling at eBusiness. We do this by contacting the WASP server that will access the eBusiness class of interest. The client first looks up a reference to the class of interest that has been registered, or, to use the terminology of WASP, deployed in the WASP server. The class that we are interested in for this example is the ProductManager class. Our first step in performing the lookup is to find the lookup service in the WASP context. We do this at line 15. At line 16, we use the reference to the lookup service to get a reference to *the* ProductManager in the WASP server, line 16.

Now that we have a reference to the ProductManager service, we can use it to call its methods. Therefore, in line 19, we make our call to the *GetProductPrice* method, asking for the price of item with *id* 2. This call goes through the proxy to the WASP server that delivers the request to the actual server in eBusiness. The eBusiness implementation determines the price and returns it back along the original path.

For all this to happen, a lot goes on behind the scenes. First, we need a proxy (also called a stub) to handle the local call from the client and send the request to the WASP server. This proxy is created from information supplied by the eBusiness server. In Web-Services-speak this information is contained in a WSDL file, which was described in Chapter 2, "Web Services." As you recall, that WSDL file is an XML document that is created and made available by the supplier of the Web Services, in this case eBusiness. The WSDL describes the methods that can be called on eBusiness through the Web Services, what their format is, and where they can be reached. We'll cover how the WSDL file is created in the next section.

Now let's take a closer look at the messages exchanged between the Java client and the WASP server. Referring to Figure 9.2, we see that the client sends a SOAP message to the JNDI service supplied by the WASP server. The JNDI Web Service contacts the JNDI in the application server in eBusiness and retrieves the home reference to ProductManager. It then gets the remote interface to ProductManager from the home interface and returns this to our client. The client uses this reference to call on the ProductManager remote interface through the WASP server. At each of these steps, the WASP server can be set by policy to call in to the security service to authenticate each of the calls to eBusiness. The next step is to create the WSDL file for the StoreFront service.

StoreFront Service

We now have to move over to eBusiness to set up the code to be a service. The developers at eBusiness have written a number of implementations of the services that eBusiness supports. Let's look at one of the service implementations. As with the client, we'll use a standalone Java application to simplify this example. The implementation code for our ProductManager class follows:

```
package StoreFront.Service;

public class ProductManager
{
    public double GetProductPrice(int id) {
                return 2.20;
    }
    public boolean SetProductPrice(int id, double newPrice) {
                m_id = id;
                m_newPrice = newPrice;
            return true;
    }
private
    int m_id;
    double m_newPrice;
}
```

Our ProductManager server class only has two methods, rather than the full functionality of eBusiness, so that we can concentrate on the Web Services functionality. The first method returns a price of $2.20 for any product requested. This method is

GetProductPrice on line 4. *ProductManager* also has a method that lets one set a price for any product ID, *SetProductPrice,* line 6. Using this class we will create a WSDL file. Then using the WSDL file, we will create a proxy that clients can use to access eBusiness's service implementations.

WASP supplies a script, Java2WSDL, that we will use to create the WSDL file. The Java2WSDL script is supplied for both Windows and Unix. We will use the Windows version.

The command line for the Java2WSDL script is:

```
Java2WSDL.bat -d ../wsdl StoreFront.Service.ProductManager
```

The first parameter to Java2WSDL, *-d ..\wsdl,* tells the script where to write out the WSDL file. The second parameter is the full package name of the class. The resultant WSDL file is:

```
<?xml version='1.0'?>
<wsdl:definitions name='StoreFront.Service.ProductManager'
 targetNamespace='http://idoox.com/wasp/tools/
                  java2wsdl/output/StoreFront/Service/'
xmlns:xsi='http://www.w3.org/2001/XMLSchema-instance'
xmlns:soap='http://schemas.xmlsoap.org/wsdl/soap/'
xmlns:tns='http://idoox.com/wasp/tools/java2wsdl/
                  output/StoreFront/Service/'xmlns:xsd='
                  http://www.w3.org/2001/XMLSchema'
xmlns:SOAP-ENC=
        'http://schemas.xmlsoap.org/soap/encoding/'
xmlns:http='http://schemas.xmlsoap.org/wsdl/http/'
xmlns:mime='http://schemas.xmlsoap.org/wsdl/mime/'
xmlns:wsdl='http://schemas.xmlsoap.org/wsdl/'>
<wsdl:message name=
    'ProductManager_SetProductPrice_Request'>
      <wsdl:part name='p0' type='xsd:int'/>
      <wsdl:part name='p1' type='xsd:double'/>
</wsdl:message>
<wsdl:message name=
      'ProductManager_SetProductPrice_Response'>
   <wsdl:part name='response' type='xsd:boolean'/>
</wsdl:message>
<wsdl:message name=
      'ProductManager_GetProductPrice_Response'>
    <wsdl:part name='response' type='xsd:double'/>
</wsdl:message>
<wsdl:message name=
    'ProductManager_GetProductPrice_Request'>
    <wsdl:part name='p0' type='xsd:int'/>
</wsdl:message>
<wsdl:portType name='ProductManager'>
    <wsdl:operation name='SetProductPrice'
                        parameterOrder='p0 p1'>
```

```
    <wsdl:input name='SetProductPrice' message=
    'tns:ProductManager_SetProductPrice_Request'/>
    <wsdl:output name='SetProductPrice'
 message='tns:ProductManager_SetProductPrice_Response'/>
</wsdl:operation>
<wsdl:operation name='GetProductPrice'
                                  parameterOrder='p0'>
<wsdl:input name='GetProductPrice'
 message='tns:ProductManager_GetProductPrice_Request'/>
<wsdl:output name='GetProductPrice'
 message='tns:ProductManager_GetProductPrice_Response'/>
</wsdl:operation>
</wsdl:portType>
<wsdl:binding name='ProductManager'
  type='tns:ProductManager'>
<soap:binding
transport='http://schemas.xmlsoap.org/soap/http'
style='rpc'/>
<wsdl:operation name='SetProductPrice'>
    <soap:operation soapAction='' style='rpc'/>
    <wsdl:input name='SetProductPrice'>
        <soap:body use='encoded'
encodingStyle='http://schemas.xmlsoap.org/soap/encoding/'
namespace='http://idoox.com/wasp/tools/java2wsdl/output/
StoreFront/Service/ProductManager'/>
    </wsdl:input>
    <wsdl:output name='SetProductPrice'>
        <soap:body use='encoded'
encodingStyle='http://schemas.xmlsoap.org/soap/encoding/'
namespace='http://idoox.com/wasp/tools/java2wsdl/output/
StoreFront/Service/ProductManager'/>
    </wsdl:output>
    </wsdl:operation>
    <wsdl:operation name='GetProductPrice'>
        <soap:operation soapAction='' style='rpc'/>
        <wsdl:input name='GetProductPrice'>
            <soap:body use='encoded'
encodingStyle='http://schemas.xmlsoap.org/soap/encoding/'
namespace='http://idoox.com/wasp/tools/java2wsdl/output/
StoreFront/Service/ProductManager'/>
        </wsdl:input>
        <wsdl:output name='GetProductPrice'>
            <soap:body use='encoded'
encodingStyle='http://schemas.xmlsoap.org/soap/encoding/'
namespace='http://idoox.com/wasp/tools/java2wsdl/output/
StoreFront/Service/ProductManager'/>
        </wsdl:output>
        </wsdl:operation>
</wsdl:binding>
<wsdl:service name='JavaService'>
```

```
85. <wsdl:port name='ProductManager'
86. binding='tns:ProductManager'>
87.     <soap:address location='urn:unknown-location-uri'/>
88.     </wsdl:port>
89. </wsdl:service>
90. </wsdl:definitions>
```

Let's look at the elements in our generated WSDL file (please refer to Chapter 2 for further details on WSDL). The WSDL file starts out with definition of a number of namespaces that are used in the WSDL XML document on lines 1 through 14. Line 15 contains the first interesting part of the WSDL file, the message portion. There are two message formats declared in lines 15 through 31. These lines declare the messages that will be sent in the SOAP document. Lines 16 through 18 declare the *SetProductPrice* request. You can see the declaration of the two parameters to *SetProductPrice* on lines 17 and 18. The name of the parameter is *wsdl:part*. The types of the parameters are int and double, which was initially declared in the Java server code. Lines 21 and 22 declare the response for SetProductPrice and declare a Boolean return value.

Lines 24 through 31 declare the response and request for the other method in our server, *GetProductPrice*.

Line 32 starts the declaration of the portType, which represents the interface semantics for ProductManager. This runs through line 47. In this section of the WSDL, you can see the Interface and methods of our server code. On line 33 we see the *SetProductPrice* method of the *ProductManager*. This method is sent using the message request on lines 16 through 18.

Line 50 begins the binding declaration, which is set to SOAP over HTTP in line 51, and declares the style as rpc in line 52. The WSDL declares the type of operation on our methods as rpc on lines 54 and 69. The rpc style handles the marshaling and demarshaling of the parameters of our methods.

Creating the WASP Proxy

Now that we have our WSDL file, we can use it to create a proxy that will receive the local calls from our client application. We do this by running another WASP script:

```
WSDLCompiler.bat -i -d ../../src -p StoreFront.Client
                            Definitions_StoreFront_Service.wsdl
```

This script produces the following Java Interface file from the WSDL file that we previously produced: The interface file will be used as the WASP proxy.

```
package StoreFront.Client;

/**
 * No documentation found for interface
 */
public interface ProductManager {
```

```
    /**
     * No documentation found for method
     */
    boolean SetProductPrice(int p0, double p1);

    /**
     * No documentation found for method
     */
    double GetProductPrice(int p0);


}

/*
 * Generated by WSDLCompiler, (c) 2001, Systinet, Inc.
 *                            http://www.systinet.com
 */
```

We will compile our client code using this interface and then run the Java client. As we described in our high-level description of the scenario, the call from the client will access the WASP server that will access the eBusiness Java server.

Securing the WASP Example

Now let's turn to securing our example. There are two general ways that you can secure Java-based Web Services:

- Traditional J2EE security, as described in Chapter 7
- Emerging Web Services messaging security based on WS-Security and SAML

We will use our examples to illustrate how J2EE security can be used to secure Web Services that do not yet support the emerging WS-Security and SAML standards. We will cover Web Services messaging security in Chapter 10, since messaging security helps solve a number of the security interoperability problems in Web Services.

In general, the advantages of the traditional security technologies used in J2EE are that they are mature, their strengths and weaknesses are well known, and they are supported by many implementations. However, these technologies generally lack the ability to support end-to-end security, especially for highly distributed Web Services systems that span multiple companies. For example, SSL encrypts a message from point A to point B. If the message is to travel to point C, the message must be decrypted at point B, reencrypted, and sent to point C. If any of the intermediaries along the way are compromised, security breaches could range from eavesdropping to attackers modifying the message for their benefit.

However, in a trusted environment—for example moving a request from department to department in a bank—a multi-hop scenario protected by SSL would be adequate. As we have repeatedly said, security is, at its core, risk management. If the exposure to attack is not high, then the security risk at an intermediate may be acceptable.

Going back to figure 9.1, we will now describe a security scenario for WASP relying on J2EE security. The customer at the browser makes a call to the ePortal.com Web server. The Web server at ePortal requires the client to log in over SSL, using HTTP basic authentication, whereby the client's username and password are passed using SSL encryption. Depending on the value of the activity that the client wants to access, less stringent types of authentication may be used. If a visitor is just asking to look at the services that ePortal offers, ePortal may permit anonymous access.

Once ePortal has authenticated the client for, say, purchasing a product from eBusiness, it performs a coarse-grained authorization check on the user to see if he or she is permitted to make a purchase. ePortal then constructs a SOAP message, which it sends to the WASP server. ePortal also needs to send the identity of the original client to the WASP server. Since we don't have WS-Security and SAML in our scenario, ePortal needs to use some alternate means, for example using HTTP basic authentication to transmit the client identity. (The password field can have a dummy value, since it is not actually being used for authentication, and we may not want the WASP server to have access to the ePortal password repository for validation.) This approach is an ad hoc delegation solution that allows ePortal to impersonate the client to the WASP server.

The message from ePortal to the WASP server is protected by SSL with mutual authentication, which allows the WASP server to be certain that the message came only from ePortal. The WASP server, after receiving the SOAP message from ePortal, sends an RMI message to eBusiness's Application Server. The WASP server extracts the client identity from the HTTP header and creates a JAAS context containing the identity that is included in the RMI message. The application server at eBusiness uses the JAAS context to extract the username, gets the roles associated with the user, and, using the method permissions in its deployment descriptor, determines whether the user can access the requested resource. If the WASP server is under eBusiness's control, this is an acceptable risk. Alternately, if the WASP server is under ePortal's control and the business agreement establishing ePortal's responsibilities and penalties is in place, this approach will also be an acceptable risk.

If the user is allowed access, the EJB makes a call to the StoreFront middle tier to carry out the required purchasing activity. When both the application server and the processes in the mid-tier are within eBusiness, and the value of the purchase is not excessive, eBusiness may decide that no security is required in this hop. Of course there is the risk of an insider attack, but because of the low value, eBusiness has determined that any potential loss is an acceptable risk.

As you can see from this description using traditional J2EE security, there are a number of trust points that must be set up. As the number of trust points increases, the security becomes more cumbersome and the potential for a security failure increases. In the following chapter we will use Web Services messaging security, which will reduce the requirement for many of the discrete trust points, making the security model simpler and more secure.

Example Using JWSDP

Now that we have developed our example using WASP, we will show you how you would do the same thing using Sun's JWSDP. In this case, however, we assume that the Java platform on eBusiness does support SOAP, and the ePortal client may access the eBusiness server directly rather than via an intermediate SOAP server.

StoreFront Client

First we will develop our StoreFrontClient code for ePortal using JAXM. You will find a lot of similarity with the previous client example. The main difference is that you have more control over the SOAP document itself. For the most part, the code is pretty straightforward and follows the model in the Sun tutorial.

```
package com.StoreFront;
import javax.xml.soap.*;
import java.util.*;
import java.net.*;
public class StoreFrontClient {
 public static void main(String [] args) {
 try {
 SOAPConnectionFactory scf =
   SOAPConnectionFactory.newInstance();
SOAPConnection con = scf.createConnection();
MessageFactory mf = MessageFactory.newInstance();
SOAPMessage msg = mf.createMessage();
          // Access the SOAP Body object.
SOAPPart part = msg.getSOAPPart();
SOAPEnvelope envelope = part.getEnvelope();
SOAPHeader header = envelope.getHeader();
          // Either create the header security element or
          // set the header to null.
         //Create SOAP Body Element request.
SOAPBody body = envelope.getBody();
Name bodyName = envelope.createName("request-prices",
          "RequestPrices", "http://ebusiness.com");
SOAPBodyElement requestPrices =
          body.addBodyElement(bodyName);
Name requestName = envelope.createName("getPrice");
SOAPElement request =
          requestPrices.addChildElement(requestName);
request.addTextNode("Send updated price list.");
msg.saveChanges();
          //Create the endpoint and send the message.
URL endpoint = new URL(
          "http://localhost:8080/grocery supplier/
                 getProductPriceList");
SOAPMessage response = con.call(msg, endpoint);
con.close();
           // Get contents of response.
Vector list = new Vector();
SOAPBody responseBody = response.getSOAPPart().
getEnvelope().getBody();
Iterator it1 = responseBody.getChildElements();
          // Get price-list element.
while (it1.hasNext()) {
 SOAPBodyElement bodyEl = (SOAPBodyElement)it1.next();
 Iterator it2 = bodyEl.getChildElements();
         // Get coffee elements.
```

```
41. while (it2.hasNext()) {
42.   SOAPElement child2 = (SOAPElement)it2.next();
43.   Iterator it3 = child2.getChildElements();
44.          // Get the price list.
45. while (it3.hasNext()) {
46.   SOAPElement child3 = (SOAPElement)it3.next();
47.   String value = child3.getValue();
48.   list.addElement(value);
49. }
50. }
51. }
52. //  Now that we have the contents of the response, we can
53. //  do something with price list we received.
54. }
55. catch (Exception ex) {
56.   ex.printStackTrace();
57. }
58. }
59. }
```

Since we have described the process in the former example, we need less explanation. Line 2 imports the SOAP library to set up the message. The other imports are not new, and you should be familiar with them. Lines 8 through 10 set up a SOAP connection for us.

One difference between this example and the WASP example is that the JWSDP JAXM makes the SOAP header available to the application developer. Therefore you may construct the security element and put it in the header. We will cover this approach in Chapter 10.

The second line of attack to securing a JWSDP application in a traditional Java environment is to use security mechanisms such as SSL, Kerberos, HTTP basic authentication, and so on. We will describe how to secure a JWSDP application using this approach later in this chapter. But first let's look at the code for a Web Service using JAXM.

StoreFront Service

On the service side we will use an Apache Tomcat servlet container where we retrieve the SOAP message from the HTTP input stream. The code example is a snippet from a full server showing just the retrieval of the SOAP message.

```
public SOAPMessage onMessage(SOAPMessage message) {
  try {
    System.out.println("Here's the message: ");
       message.writeTo(System.out);
           // Retrieve the SOAP envelope.
       SOAPEnvelope env = message.getSOAPPart().getEnvelope();
      SOAPBody body = env.getBody ();
          // Do your normal processing of the SOAP message.
    } else {
```

```
            // construct a SOAP Fault
8.      }
9.      return msg;
10.         } catch(Exception e) {
11.             logger.error(
            "Error in processing or replying to a message", e);
12              return null;
        }
    }
```

The SOAP message is passed to the onMessage JWSDP callback as per the servlet examples in the JAXM tutorial that comes with the JWSDP developer kit from Sun. You could extract the header once you have retrieved the envelope in line 5, just as you did with the client code. Having the header, you could extract the WS-Security element, provided the client had inserted it, and use the data for access control. We will discuss this advanced interoperability approach in Chapter 10. Alternately, you could use traditional J2EE security, which we will cover next.

Securing the JWSDP Example

As we discussed earlier, there are certain Web Services situations where the use of traditional security for securing Web Services is a reasonable approach. Figure 9.3 depicts a scenario for JWSDP similar to the one used for WASP, with the exception that the WASP server is not required and a Web server is used as the receiving process in eBusiness.

Much of the security discussion that we had in the WASP example also applies here. We use HTTP basic authentication between the browser and the ePortal Web server as before, line 1 in Figure 9.3. If the user is authenticated, the Web server will call either a JWSDP plug-in or a JWSDP application to make a SOAP call to eBusiness. Similar to the WASP example, the JWSDP application at ePortal could make the call to the Web server at eBusiness impersonating the client. In this case, before ePortal and eBusiness start their computer interactions, they would have set up a trust relationship whereby eBusiness trusts that ePortal will have authenticated the client, as we pointed out in the WASP example.

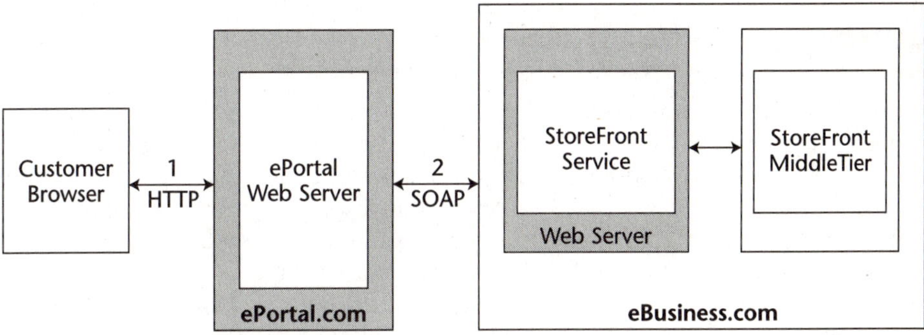

Figure 9.3 JWSDP example.

After having authenticated the user at the Browser, ePortal securely connects to the Web server in eBusiness, using an SSL connection with mutual authentication, line 2 in Figure 8.3. At this point the application in ePortal will be authenticated to the Web server in eBusiness and vice-versa. As a result of the previously established trust relationship and the mutual authentication between ePortal and eBusiness, the application at eBusiness will be able to transitively trust the authentication of the user at the remote browser, if the application at ePortal declares that the user has been authenticated.

Next we have to establish a way for the application at ePortal to declare the authenticated user identity to eBusiness. One way to do this is for ePortal to pass the user identity to eBusiness using HTTP basic authentication, potentially using a dummy password so that the password is not transmitted to eBusiness. This approach brings with it all the caveats that we have previously described for impersonation, and depends on the SSL mutual authentication to ensure eBusiness that it is actually receiving the requests from ePortal.

Once eBusiness has assured itself of the user's authentication, it then must determine whether the user is permitted to perform the action that the user requests (for example, getting a product price). The documentation for the JWSDP initial release discusses performing access control based on deployment descriptors, as we described in Chapter 7. To use the method permission access control approach, the server has to be in a Java container, that is, a J2EE application server or a Web server that supports the servlet specification. The JWSDP includes Tomcat, which is an open source servlet container that has been developed by the Jakarta Project. (The URL for Tomcat is http://jakarta.apache.org/tomcat/.) When using Tomcat from the JWSDP, you add the onMessage callback class to your servlet code to capture the SOAP message, as shown in the JWSDP Web server example.

Recently, a number of application servers have begun to support SOAP and continue to use method permissions access control, for example, the latest releases of WebLogic and WebSphere. In this case, ePortal could send its HTTP SOAP call directly to the eBusiness application server rather than via an eBusiness Web server, which would then call the application server. From a security point of view, we would prefer that eBusiness use a Web server in its DMZ to receive any inbound calls.

As in the WASP example, eBusiness could permit unsecured access to the mid-tier or, depending on the exposure of the application, use traditional security between the perimeter Web server and the mid-tier application server.

Summary

This chapter described how Java application platforms can be used in conjunction with the Web Services security principles that we have presented in the earlier chapters of this book. We first described the theory and practice of integrating security into Web Services when the applications are implemented in Java.

We then discussed the different security specifications, called JSRs, related to Web Services that have been defined by the Java Community Process. We discussed how they work together and how you can use these JSRs to judge whether a particular Java server will meet your needs for a secure Web Service. We discussed how SAML assertions might be used to carry security data through the complex path that a Web Service message may follow.

We described how Java application servers that do not support Web Services can be SOAP-enabled and secured using the WASP product from Systinet. Since tools are available to construct Web Services in Java, we also presented an example of a Java application server that supports security and Web Services using Sun's JWSDP. In both of these examples, we described how to use traditional J2EE security to secure the transactions. We attempted to point out some of the issues behind the examples so that you may use this as a template for understanding the security principles involved. Both of these examples represent technology offerings that require code development to provide security. As products that implement WS-Security and SAML services become more readily available, Web Services security will become easier to use and more transparent to developers.

The next chapter will look at the problem of interoperability between the different Web Services technologies and the interoperability between different companies that wish to communicate securely using Web Services. In particular, we will discuss how WS-Security and SAML may be used within an EASI framework to provide cross-technology secure interoperability.

CHAPTER

10

Interoperability of Web Services Security Technologies

One of the dreams for Web Services is to allow seamless interoperability between entities making a request for some service and the providers of that service. This paradigm, like many advances of computer technology, is built on distributed systems. In the case of Web Services, the lineage has progressed through a series of technologies: the distributed protocol TCP/IP and the concept of RPC were used by the Distributed Computing Environment (DCE), which led to the Common Object Request Broker Architecture (CORBA) and Enterprise Java Beans (EJB). There were some parallel steps along the way. Microsoft's MSRPC, COM, DCOM, and COM+ evolved from DCE and ultimately led to .NET. Each of these predecessors worked to make distributed computing transparent to the business programmer. Each step, while getting closer to the dream of transparency and interoperability, fell short. The latest attempt, Web Services, is another step towards this goal, building on the experience and technologies of its predecessors.

The computing community made a number of strategic errors building these technologies. For example, one of the authors was involved in the early days of a DCE implementation. Everyone involved was struggling to get the technology to work. Then, when we finally got a working system, we said, "What about product installation?" So, we quickly assigned a junior engineer to slap together an installation script for this complex system. As you know, installation is the first impression of a product, and a poor experience with the installation, especially of a complex product, gives that product a bad reputation. Needless to say, the user community was not thrilled by the "afterthought" installation of DCE, and we believe that DCE suffered from that, as well as other "nontechnical" decisions. However, as we progressed through each of these technologies, and the business application programmers struggled to use them and gave us feedback on our attempts, we learned more of what was needed for success.

A great deal of progress has been made in getting distributed systems to interoperate. However, there is one glaring sticking point—getting the security aspects of the different models to work together. At each step forward, the security portion was addressed last. That is, the basic technology was developed and made to work, and then security was tacked on as an afterthought. This led to certain discontinuities between the base technology and security. Without a solid security model, the dream of interoperable Web Services will never be practical. No one will want to carry out substantial transactions with another company without having solid security in place.

Since Web Services aim to be platform and language independent, so too must the security that Web Services uses. This means that the security model must interoperate between the different Web Services models, platforms, and languages. This chapter will look at the various security interoperability problems and ways that you can implement security in the Web Services world so that it is interoperable.

The Security Interoperability Problem

Until recently, security mostly operated in its own homogeneous world. The security that companies used was designed and constructed to solve a single security problem in a subset of a distributed business process. We can divide these islands of security isolation into three general areas. It is at the boundaries of these areas that we run into interoperability problems. Islands of security can be delineated by the boundaries between different:

1. Security tiers (perimeter, middle, and back office)
2. Security technologies
3. Processing domains, that is, corporate enterprises or business units

We have touched on each of these boundaries in Chapter 1, "Overview of Web Services Security." In this chapter, we will dig deeper into these problems and present solutions. Where there are standard security specifications, we will recommend their use. Specifications are important for security because, in this area more than any other, we need to use techniques that have been designed and tested by independent security professionals and that have withstood the assaults of these professionals for some time. Security is complex and requires the skill and experience of specialists to design a model in which the subtle and not-so-subtle vulnerabilities are avoided. Finding flaws becomes even more complex when we try to get security to interoperate across the different boundaries.

In the next two sections, we will cover the first two interoperability problems, between-tier and between security technologies. We will leave the last problem, that of interoperability between processing domains, for later in this chapter, since that is the most difficult and will not be completely solved in the near term. We believe that secure Web Services will first be used between business units of a single enterprise. Next, major corporations will set up Web Services with their suppliers and dealers. Finally, after experience has been gained in controlled situations, corporations will begin to deal with enterprise-to-enterprise Web Services discovery and business-to-business secure interoperability.

These steps roughly correspond to secure interoperability between tiers, then between technologies, and finally between companies. We will discuss each of these in turn.

Between Security Tiers

Just how important are the security tiers in the Web Services paradigm? To answer this question, we need to determine whether Web Services security is enforced across the security tiers, or whether security tier interoperability is supported by the underlying message transport after a Web Services connection has been made. A distributed Web Services scenario that depicts the three security tiers is shown in Figure 10.1.

The scenario in Figure 10.1 is as follows. A Web Services client calls a Web server in the "demilitarized zone" (DMZ) between two firewalls. That client has to be authenticated, so we definitely have a perimeter tier boundary that the Web Services message will cross. The next hop moves the message from the perimeter to, say, an application server in the mid-tier. This call could be over a traditional HTTP transport from the Web server to an application server, or the Web server could access the application server in the mid-tier using SOAP. The former case relies on HTTP transport for secure interoperability, while the latter, SOAP-based, case puts the secure interoperability problem into the sphere of Web Services.

Why would you use Web Services within the mid-tier, as in the examples in the previous paragraph? There are more performance-efficient ways to build calls between applications. However, performance is not the sole, or even prime, driving force in all situations. In many cases, speed of implementation is more important. The choice between getting an application up and running in days and doing so in weeks or months is a no-brainer—management will opt for the shorter time to implement.

When a message is received at the target site, the request could have been made by means of the Web Services protocol or by the more traditional transport protocols: TCP/IP, RMI, or DCOM. The former method presents a Web Services security interoperability problem, while the latter is a traditional security interoperability problem between tiers. The same choices are present when the message moves from the mid-tier to the back-office tier. Let's take a deeper look at the anatomy of these requests in each of the tiers. Before we examine each tier boundary, let's look briefly at the reason why you would want to combine different technologies in the first place.

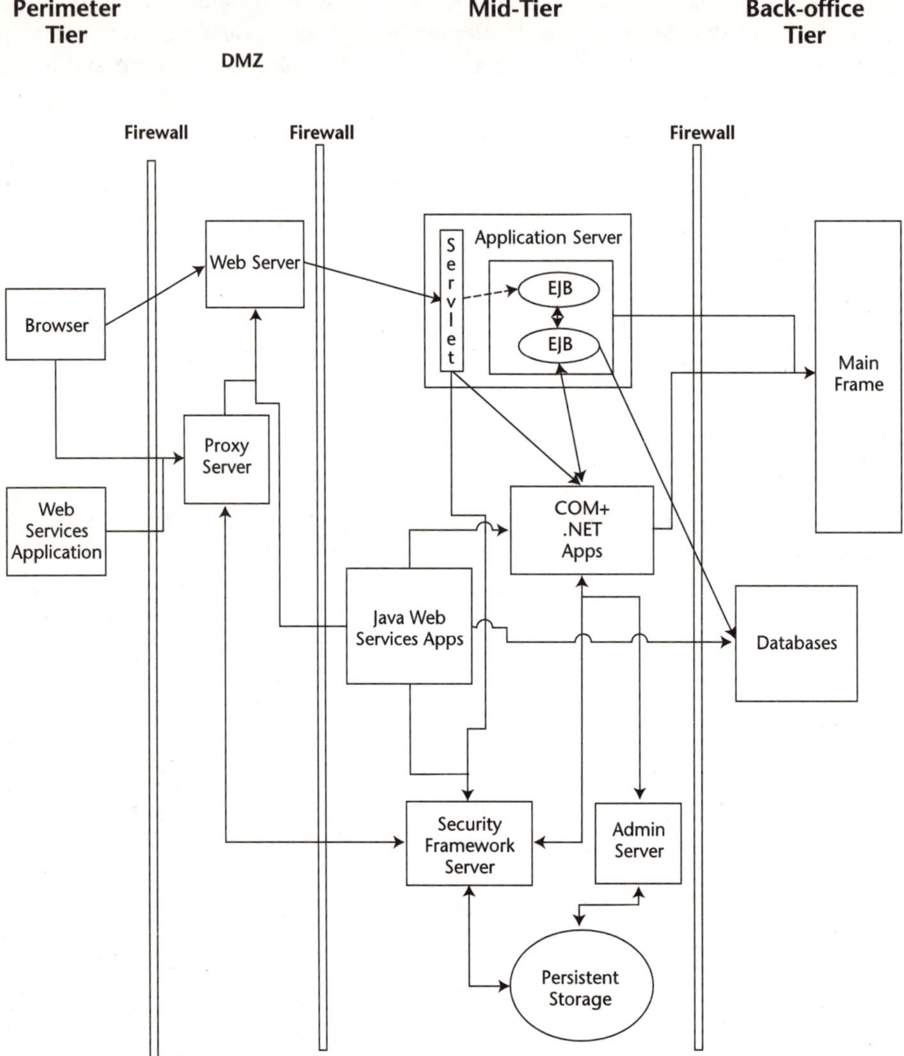

Figure 10.1 Multitier Web Services scenario.

Layered Security

As Web Services become more extensive, many architectures will allow external clients to access their enterprise using an external browser or an application using SOAP over HTTP. The initial question is which application should receive the incoming call? The first thing that comes to mind is the Web server. But is this the correct entry point into your system?

For example, EJB application servers are also prepared to receive requests from external HTTP clients. Servlets in a typical application server can be derived from an HTTP servlet base class supplied by the container, which has methods for extracting usernames and cookies from the incoming HTTP header. This information can then be used to authenticate the user who is attempting to access the system. Once an EJB servlet has processed the HTTP request and made subsequent calls to the enterprise beans, the beans can provide fine-grained authorization of the request and can direct a request to layers deeper in your enterprise. So you might be tempted to expose your application server as a Web Service.

But do you want to permit direct access from external clients to an application server in the DMZ or in the mid-tier? The answer should be no, based on the principle that we have been expounding; you should have multiple layers of defense (also known as *security in depth*). An outer layer of defense should protect the application server from external requests. You want to prevent an attacker from breaking into your application server, which provides sensitive services. Thus, we strongly recommend perimeter security as an important first layer, but it should not be the only layer in your overall defense.

It is better to use Web server technology in the DMZ, which then accesses other tiers, for example, an EJB application server, COM+ server, or CORBA server in your mid-tier. In all probability, you will have a mixture of two or three of these systems in your mid-tier. Finally, these mid-tier technologies will most probably use traditional databases and/or a mainframe in your back-office tiers.

If an attacker breaks your security in the perimeter, he or she should be stopped in the secondary layers. We repeat our mantra about having multiple layers of defense: The first layer of perimeter defense is in the DMZ, which will receive your Web Services calls and make primary authentication and authorization decisions. The second layer of defense is authentication verification and authorization in your mid-tier applications. The third layer of defense occurs at your back-office applications.

Since the DMZ is your first line of defense, it is necessary to keep the security functionality straightforward and relatively easy to analyze from a security point of view. This does not mean the security mechanisms should be weak. In fact, making security easy to analyze allows security experts to uncover potential security problems and thus results in stronger security.

Perimeter Security

The perimeter is defined by your outer firewall. By necessity, Web Services requests that enter into your enterprise cross the perimeter boundary. Previously, most of these requests were from a browser. In the Web Services paradigm, we find that the pendulum has swung back to a preponderance of applications making these requests, since the Web Services paradigm is directed more toward application-to-application interaction, moving the human being out of the loop.

This move to applications has some implications when we look at the problem of single sign-on (SSO), that is, the ability to log on once and access multiple applications, multiple times, without having to log on for each access. Attempting to do authentication in combination with SSO from a browser is quite difficult to accomplish, as we discussed in Chapters 5, "Security Assertion Markup Language," and 6, "Principles of

Securing Web Services." The reason is that browsers are limited in their capabilities. A quick summary of the problem follows. Since the HTTP protocol is stateless, the target uses cookies to keep the state and puts some information in the cookie that references the fact that the client has been authenticated. Once we have done that, we have moved our problem from being that of a secure channel (that is, SSL) to being that of protecting the cookie, which browsers are not very good at.

The change from browsers to applications makes SSO more challenging because of the difficulty of getting an application to log on without involving a human being. On the other hand, it permits a more robust SSO authentication paradigm. Applications can keep state, that is, the authentication evidence, and thus a client application can supply the authentication proof transparently for each access. Alternately, the client and target can set up a security session where both sides establish a mutual security context, exchanging a secret or a session id with each message. As we described in Chapter 6, with Web Services you can use confidentiality and/or digital signatures for portions of the message to provide end-to-end security rather than point-to-point security such as SSL. However, you have to employ mechanisms in the perimeter layers to operate on the security context provided by the Web Services client application.

Present-day perimeter applications, such as Web servers, do not supply the necessary security mechanisms for Web Services out of the box. A basic Web server is only capable of handling the security of simple HTTP requests for Web pages. You can go further and add a perimeter SSO product, such as Netegrity's SiteMinder or RSA's ClearTrust. However, many of today's perimeter products use proprietary credentials that lock you into their product. Proprietary credentials make it difficult, if not impossible, to mix and match products to find the best of the breed for a given use, and do not encourage the changing of security products as new threats and solutions come on to the scene.

When a proprietary security credential is passed to another vendor's product, that vendor cannot use the credential without creating some handcrafted code to interpret the proprietary format. Additionally, in some cases, such as when the proprietary information is encrypted with the first vendor's proprietary encryption key, you cannot even construct a handcrafted solution to use the first vendor's security credentials. Thus, you don't have interoperability. SAML, which we discussed in Chapter 5, is intended to provide an interoperable solution by defining a standardized security context, that is, a SAML assertion. However, the vendors would have to incorporate SAML assertions into their products. This requirement exposes a conflict between a vendor's desire to lock their customers into their product and the requirements of their customers, who want interoperability so that they can use the best security product for the particular problem at hand.

The minimum functionality that is needed to get basic security interoperability is to have a security context that has the following characteristics:

- It is independent of any one computing platform and programming language.
- It is based on a generally accepted standard.
- It is broadly defined so that it can hold all the security information that needs to be transferred between disparate endpoint applications.

SAML has very good potential to address these requirements and enable secure interoperability between applications and tiers. Note that SAML is not the only solution to the security interoperability problem or even the complete solution in the Web Services world. However, SAML does meet the basic minimum described by these three criteria and is well matched with Web Services.

Let's say that a Web Services client sends a request to your Web Services-enabled system, and the message contains a SAML authentication assertion signed by a trusted third party. Is a SAML assertion by itself sufficient for you to trust the authentication of the request from that client? The answer is probably no. How do you know that the assertion has not been stolen and sent by an impostor? You don't, unless some other means has been used to establish trust. One or more of the end-to-end security principals that we put forth in Chapter 6 can be used to establish trust in the client. For example, the client could sign the Web Services message with its private key, thus giving the target the capability of verifying the signature. Verifying the message signature will ensure that the client created the message that included the SAML assertion. The target also needs to ensure that data in any reply is only accessible to the real client, and not an impostor. The most secure way to ensure that data is only readable by the original client is to encrypt the critical parts of the reply message using the public key of the client, based on the XML Encryption and WS-Security specifications.

While the steps that we have outlined to secure a request from a security-enabled Web Services client can deliver a secure message to our service, this approach may not be feasible, depending on your application platform. For example, you might be using a third-party security product that does not support SAML, WS-Security, or even SOAP. In that case, you would need to use an approach similar to that described in Chapters 8, "Securing .NET Web Services," and 9, "Securing Java Web Services," where we described using the capabilities of existing Microsoft and Java security mechanisms to support Web Services security.

Another approach in the perimeter tier is to use a software Web Services firewall as a front end (proxy) to protect your Web server. A Web Services firewall proxy can receive a SOAP request and perform initial checks, including parsing the SOAP message, examining the message for correct form, determining whether it uses security algorithms of sufficient strength, and recognizing that an RPC or XML document is contained in the SOAP message. The proxy can then extract the relevant security information and use the retrieved authentication evidence to carry out authentication of the principal and potentially perform coarse-grained authorization of the principal's requested action on a resource.

The proxy may call a security server to perform the detailed security checks. One of the reasons that we recommend separating the functionality into scanning work by the proxy and security policy checks by the security server is that this provides a high-performance proxy. This is accomplished by permitting the proxy to quickly reject badly formed messages and direct low-security requests, such as those for read-only pages, directly to the Web server. A second reason for the split is that we want to remove the security policy functionality from the DMZ and place it behind a second firewall. Figure 10.2 shows the perimeter proxy model.

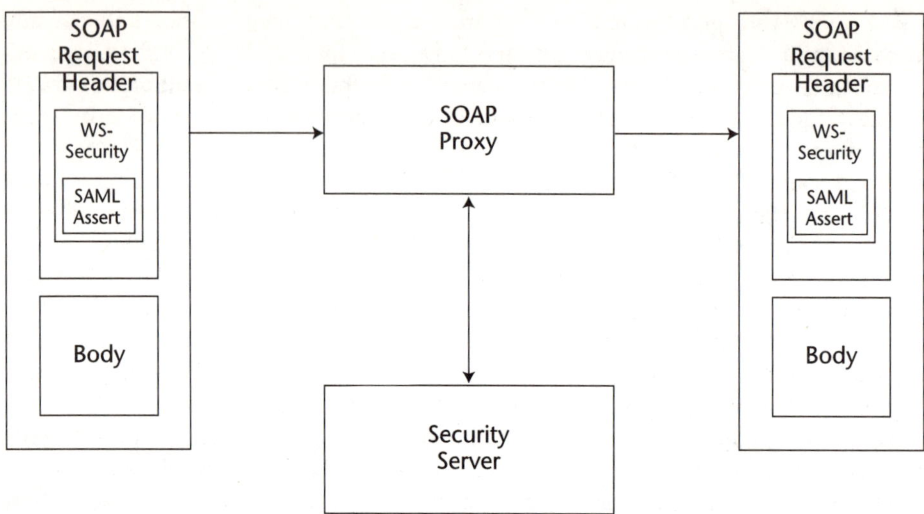

Figure 10.2 Perimeter proxy for Web Services.

The scenario in Figure 10.2 is as follows: A SOAP request containing a SAML assertion as a token in a WS-Security element, with both contained in the SOAP security header, arrives at the proxy. The proxy calls into the security server, which validates all the security aspects of the SOAP message, performs authentication and course-grained authorization, and potentially adds a second header to the WS-Security for consumption by a mid-tier application, and redirects the message to the appropriate application in the mid-tier.

The Web Services firewall proxy itself can be a software component and, as such, it could be located separately from your Web server, or be integrated into it. There are new products on the market from several vendors that provide this type of security, including offerings from Quadrasis/Xtradyne, Vordel, and Westbridge Technologies.

Mid-Tier

While the perimeter is your first line of defense, it should not be your only one. Once a Web Service request passes the perimeter, it goes to the sweet spot of your system, the mid-tier. This is where your business logic and much of your decision logic lie. When the SOAP message reaches this tier, an RPC call embedded in the SOAP message could be instantiated, and the risk of compromising your business data increases. Each application must have the ability to defend itself.

A second reason for protection in the mid-tier is that this area is the most complex of all your computational areas. Mid-tiers contain a mixture of computing models, EJB, COM+, .NET, and individual applications of all kinds. A single message may traverse many paths through the mid-tier, depending on the particular workflow that is to be accomplished. You should have different levels of authorization, depending on what the risk exposure could be for a given operation.

As one example, let's take a look at an EJB application server in your mid-tier. Your application container has the capability of giving you finer-grained control over who can access what by means of its attributes and security policies. At the same time, the application server gives you the ability to handle large numbers of users as well as the ability to assign policies to objects at run time. While all this is happening at the application server inside the mid-tier boundary, there are also a number of traditional applications that may act as helper functions in both the mid-tier and back-office tier.

The most straightforward way for an EJB container to implement its access control is to use the information from the method permissions in its deployment descriptor; that is, ascertain what role can access what method. However, method permissions are issued on a per EJB basis, which can cause administrative problems when the enterprise has thousands of beans and the organization has to add another role or change an access rule. This static approach is not optimal for the dynamic nature of Web Services.

A large amount of security data might need to be administered if fine-grained control is required by your policy. To make administration feasible, you may need a more scalable security policy than the one typically provided by EJB security. For example, traditional Java Application Server access control, that is, method permissions in EJB, requires that each bean have its own method-permission list in the deployment descriptor, whereas we would prefer that attributes be managed independently of an individual EJB. More sophisticated security policies permit hierarchical collections of EJBs so that it is easier to administer very large numbers of beans or other resources. Another type of scaling challenge arises because application servers need to map large numbers of users to roles. Authentication and attribute services, as defined in the SAML model, are a solution to this scaling problem. We'll investigate this solution a little later in the chapter.

Security between Distributed Models

Today, the bulk of the protection is found in the perimeter and not at the boundary between the perimeter and the mid-tier. It should be noted that this boundary transition to mid-tier applications such as EJB or COM+ is not standardized, although the building blocks are there (that is, WS-Security and SAML). Enforcing all security at the perimeter with coarse-grained authorization reduces the scaling problem that we brought up in the previous section. However, as we've pointed out in previous chapters, insiders acting in the mid-tier corporate network commit many of the reported security violations. With the advent of Web Services in e-commerce, you will be permitting customers or other businesses inside your mid-tier, which vastly increases the number of de facto insiders. Given these facts, it becomes clear that the likelihood that a Web Services client will break your security and thus gain access to your internal network is dramatically increased. Also, don't neglect the possibility that a disgruntled employee could substitute a malicious or badly written component in a container or a COM+ application that would let a Web Service client do harm in your mid-tier.

The choice between when Web Service calls are made and when one of the more traditional interchanges between applications is made becomes less obvious in the mid-tier. A certain message might come into the mid-tier as a SOAP Web Service call to an application server, then one of the beans may make a .NET call to a COM+ application, which may make a call to a C or COBOL application wrapped by CORBA that then retrieves the data from a database. This brings up the question, "Should you use different security technologies as your message moves through this complex path?" Generally the answer is no—you should avoid different security technologies whenever possible. Security is complex enough without trying to manage a security technology for every type of application in your organization. (We'll give you an approach to handle multiple security models later in this chapter when we introduce the concept of a security middleware framework.)

We have seen organizations where security is handled by requiring each programmer to roll his or her own security into the application. Again, this is a very bad idea for two reasons:

1. Business programmers are not security experts and should not be depended upon to produce foolproof security.
2. Many times, in a complex message flow, the security of an individual application depends on the security in the applications preceding it and following it in the message flow.

When you are making calls between different types of applications, especially if the call is to an application in another company or to an application supplied by a provider that you have not dealt with before, the risk level increases. The success of the security, in either case, depends on the security model being understood by the disparate applications.

Interoperability between Java and .NET Platforms

A common request for secure interoperability is, "Can you provide the ability for Web Services in Java, such as Sun JWSDP and IBM Web Sphere, to interoperate with .NET-based services?" The quick answer is that when all of the security models support common models like WS-Security and SAML, the interoperability problem will be almost, but not quite, solved.

These new security specifications, which are still evolving, will allow applications to send and receive a security context that both the sender and receiver can understand and act upon. Since the Web Services message, including the security data, is in XML, the message is platform- and language-independent. However, even when these specifications are widely deployed there will be a few problem areas to be addressed.

The interoperability problem areas that remain are relevant for any middle tier application platform, whether it is based on Java or .NET. The first problem is the potential inability of a target to understand the attributes that are sent from the client. The second problem is related to federation. The federation problem has to do with the separation of the authentication and authorization domains between the two companies. The last problem is the fact that products are just beginning to implement the WS-Security specification. It's this last problem that is the stickiest in the near term. Note that even in the long term not all applications will support Web Services security. We will discuss solutions to each of these problems later in this chapter.

On the positive side, a recent demonstration of secure interoperability between IBM and Microsoft products at the XML Web Services One conference shows the momentum and direction of Web Services. If two major competing vendors can reach this goal, we have good potential to achieve general Web Services secure interoperability. The Web Services Interoperability (WS-I) consortium, to which these and many other companies belong, is dedicated to Web Services interoperability, giving further promise for interoperability solutions.

Back-Office Tier

The last security tier to be addressed is the tier where legacy applications, such as mainframes, databases, and nondistributed applications, reside. The mid-tier applications will probably have a need for additional data at some point in the workflow. Normally, this data is held in back-end relational databases. In many cases, this corporate data, such as accounting data, customer information, or employee information, has existed in the system long before any of the new technologies, such as Web Services, came on the scene. The protection scheme for such data will, in all probability, have a different format from the protection scheme used in the newer Web Services applications and may require authentication data that is disjoint from that used in the perimeter and the mid-tier.

A well-known approach for bringing legacy applications into the distributed, object world is to wrap the legacy applications with CORBA. In addition, Java 2 Enterprise Edition (J2EE) defines the Java Connector Architecture for connecting to existing enterprise systems. One could use these technologies to form a bridge between the Web Services and legacy applications. In addition, you will need to map to the specific security data needed by any legacy security that exists. Another approach is to wrap these applications with Web Services interfaces and have the implementation of the Web Services make direct calls to legacy applications.

In the future, many of these legacy applications will be upgraded to support Web Services. For example, Oracle and IBM are actively implementing Web Services environments, which we would expect would also include Web Services security mechanisms.

Interoperable Security Technologies

Now that you have been introduced to some of the security problems underlying interoperability between the security tiers, we will look at the interoperability issues for the security services: authentication, security attributes, authorization, security context, and delegation.

Authentication

When your perimeter applications implement authentication, the Web server process needs to pass a compatible security token that your interior object model can interpret and use. Authentication would no longer be a problem if all of the technologies used a compatible authentication context.

If your containers or applications do not support the chosen authentication token format, then you will have to build a bridge between the two security systems. However, there is one token format, namely SAML assertions, that is gaining interest in part because it can solve this interoperability problem.

To think about how authentication may be extended to support Web Services, we consider the following Java-based scenario: You have a container that receives a SOAP message at its built-in HTTP servlet. The Web Services message contains a SAML token in a WS-Security element. You want to make a call from that application to another application, and the target application does not support WS-Security or SAML. The solution entails using an authenticator that knows how to verify a SAML assertion and accept that assertion as proof of authentication, as we describe later in this chapter. You might have to build the authenticator yourself, or you might use a third-party authentication service, as described in the SAML specification. Note that standard definitions for these services are still in progress.

A servlet in your Web server receives a SOAP message containing a WS-Security element from the perimeter tier. The servlet could validate the message itself, but to do this the servlet would need all of the technology to support the token formats defined in WS-Security, which would make the servlet's implementation too complex. Therefore, the servlet should pass the SOAP message to a *security authority*. We'll describe one form of a security authority later in the chapter, namely an EASI framework, which we introduced in Chapter 1. The security framework should have the full range of WS-Security technologies and should be able to authenticate messages, validate SAML credentials if present, and validate any signatures intended for the servlet. The framework should also have the ability to construct, insert, remove, and validate SOAP headers, and support XML digital signatures and encryption. The Web server could then pass the SOAP message to the mid-tier where the target application server could also use an EASI framework to validate the message and decrypt relevant portions of the message.

Before we look further at the EASI framework solutions, we will delve into other security technologies, including security privilege attributes, authorization, and delegation.

Security Attributes

Security attributes are intimately tied to authorization because most authorization decisions are based on the attributes of the principal making a request to perform some action on a resource. You could use the name, that is, identity, of the principal to make an authorization decision. However, this approach does not scale well when you have thousands or millions of principals. In this case, attributes such as groups or roles are necessary. Security attributes can also be looked upon as the security policy connection between the initiating client and the target, since attributes are used by the target to make its decision about what access permissions should be granted to the client. As long as the target and the client agree on the syntax and semantics of the attributes, the relationship holds.

Authorization models differ in the privilege attributes they support. For example, EJB and COM+ only support a username and roles, whereas other authorization security models support usernames and roles as well as a number of additional attribute types such as groups, security clearance, and many others.

In Web Service applications, which potentially can support more complex attribute models, attributes may be assigned to a client principal by an external attribute authority (AA) and transmitted to the target in an attribute token, for example, a WS-Security element containing a SAML attribute assertion.

When making a call from a client application that supports one set of attributes to a target application that supports a different set of attributes, the target could potentially ignore or misinterpret attribute types. For example, the role attributes defined for a hospital application (say, doctor, nurse, administrator) have different meanings from those defined for an insurance company (say, agent, doctor, manager, administrator). Note that even though both organizations have doctor and administrator roles, the privileges associated with the identical role names may be quite different. To avoid the mismatch of attributes, the target application can use the client's identity to look up a set of locally defined attributes. For example, the insurance company could maintain insurance-related attributes for all hospital employees who need to access insurance information. A huge administrative headache can result when the target must store and maintain all the attributes of all the foreign identities that might want to access it.

The target application could use the authenticated identity of the client to go to an AA that it trusts, and request the attributes of the named client in the format and with the semantics that the target application understands. The target application must establish mutual authentication with the AA and/or have a trust relationship with the AA. If these conditions are met, the AA can return the proper mapped attributes to the server. But this has pushed the scaling problem over to the AA, which eventually ends up being quite complex. Commercial third-party AAs should become available in the future to handle large-scale deployments. However, no one expects that there will be a single AA that will handle the world's attributes. This potentially leads to a hierarchy of AAs for different organization types and cross-certification of AAs for the different organizations.

Using AAs to store attributes for different organizations still does not address interoperability of attributes. We believe that *attribute mapping* will also be required for Web Services that span many organizations. In this approach, the client maps attributes in its domain to a set of generic attributes defined by an AA that both client and target subscribe to. Then, the target maps the generic attributes to specific attributes in the target's domain. Using our e-business example, a client may be ordering a product from a storefront. The client would map its attributes to the generic attributes defined by the retail domain. The storefront could then map to its specific attributes from the generic retail attributes. Later in the transaction flow, if the storefront wanted to send data to an outside accounting service, the storefront would then map to the generic attributes in the accounting domain, and the accounting service would map the received generic attributes of the accounting domain to its specific attribute set.

At this time, widespread generic attribute domains do not exist, so local groupings of these different attribute domains would need to be set up between cooperating parties—for example, a consortium of companies. It is hoped that, over time, these local sets in vertical markets will coalesce and develop into true generic domains, for example, representing the financial services industry or healthcare practices. Since we believe that most implementations of Web Services in the near term will be within a single company or between partners, local generic domains are quite feasible. As federated Web Services begin to be used between companies, we believe that attribute mapping will drive the need for generic attribute domains. We are already seeing this trend, in a limited sense, in the Liberty Alliance, which we introduced in Chapter 6. The Liberty Alliance maps users to an opaque handle, a type of generic attribute for the identity, and transmits the handle between partners. We'll look at the Liberty solution later in this chapter.

In a few cases, it's possible to avoid the difficulties of mapping attributes across domains. In the case where there is a dominant company that can dictate the behavior of its partners (for example, a large automobile manufacturer and its many suppliers), the dominant company can simply define a uniform set of attributes for all of its partners to use. There is also the remote possibility that all organizations will agree to one single worldwide set of attribute definitions, but we don't believe that such a definition would ever be achievable. Our assessment is that the best hope for a general solution to attribute interoperability is that attribute domains for specific areas of common interest are established, for example, the medical domain, the accounting domain, the retail domain, and so on.

Authorization

Authorization is an aspect of security where there is a great deal of Web Services standardization work in process using XML-based systems. In the traditional access control models, some authorization systems use a simple model. For example, J2EE uses method permissions (which are just a list of what roles can access what methods), whereas more complex systems use a combination of rights and domains. The details of role-based access control are given in Chapter 11, "Administrative Considerations for Web Services Security." In this chapter, we touch on the aspects of the interoperability problems related to access control. Since authorization takes place at the target, which has the responsibility to protect its resources, authorization itself is not an interoperability problem. However, the principal for whom the authorization is requested is defined and usually authenticated in the client. The information related to the principal must be passed to the target to be used in the authorization process. In the previous section, we discussed the problems associated with unambiguously transmitting the principal's attributes, which is the most common method of transmitting the information about the principal. But are there other methods.

The one feature that various security models have in common is the use of a user identity that can be used for authorization. Even with a user identity, there may still be a need to generate a mapping between two forms of a username. However, because the underlying principal is the same, this is just a matter of clarifying the form it takes, although it might mean an explicit listing of each form of the username. For example, an implementation that stores the user's login name in an LDAP tree uses an X.500 format. The login name in this case is the same name used in the implementation retrieval process, so the mapping can be done by an LDAP lookup. A more difficult name mapping exists when the principal name is in, say, a Kerberos format and the target stores the name in an X.500 format, which requires mapping tables between these different representations. Another problem with authorization using only the username is the administrative burden of managing a large number of users at the target.

There are some situations in which the target wishes to control and manage the users' identities, for example, when a large corporation has a number of suppliers or where an online store has its customers self-register. In such cases, the clients send their authentication evidence, and the services side handles every aspect of authentication and authorization. This simple central server model has few interoperability problems, since the entire burden of defining and managing all security policies rests with the target server.

Maintaining the Security Context

HTTP is the most common transport used for Web Services. HTTP defines a simple request/response model, which means that a request is sent from the client to the target, and then a response is sent back. The HTTP context is then closed, and a new context is opened for the next message. The difficulty of achieving security with this model is the problem of preserving the security context and the security session between the client and the service providers over multiple request/reply interactions. What makes preserving the security context and session important is the users' desire to login once and be able to access all their applications, that is, SSO. To give a user SSO, the system has to keep track of the user, that is, the user's context, over many different sessions, or else the user will need to login again to prove his or her identity, since that proof has been lost.

Implementations have gone to some length to preserve a security session and context. One of the more familiar means, when the client is a browser, is to use cookies. We discussed the security problems with using cookies in Chapter 6. Another approach is to use session identifiers saved in a cookie or preserved by the application. Some of the popular perimeter security products use proprietary formats and proprietary encryption for the cookie contents to preserve and protect the session identifiers. Needless to say, this last approach is not interoperable.

The positive aspect of Web Services with respect to interoperability at the transport layer is that they use commonly accepted transport mechanisms that are understood by most of the modern middleware technologies. The downside for Web Services security is that HTTP is stateless and there are no standard session models for Web Services.

WS-Security can be used to establish a security context across heterogeneous systems in a Web Services environment. WS-Security defines an element where security information, called a token, can be inserted. The specification also supports the signing and encrypting of portions of the enclosing SOAP message. Both of these capabilities can be used to support a distributed security context as it moves across heterogeneous applications.

To understand how WS-Security supports transporting the security context, we will discuss the security header block in WS-Security. There can be more than one security header block, one for different actors or, as the SOAP 1.2 specification calls them, roles, that are the targets for the message. Consequently, we can support different security for each of the different, heterogeneous targets that our message will access. WS-Security has defined some types of security information that can be contained within tokens in the security header, for example, username/password, Kerberos tickets, X.509 certificates, and SAML. A client application first determines what targets it wants to send a Web Services message to. The client can then decide and enforce what targets should be able to view what information, by encrypting certain parts of the message. If the client application deems that certain targets should only see parts of the message, it can then encrypt those parts of the message with the public key of that particular target for that part of the message. The net result is that only the specified services can see what the client wanted that service to see. In this way, the message can move through multiple hops, accessing different heterogeneous applications, while only revealing to each service what it wants that service to see.

As long as the applications along the path support the complex set of specifications, and the client knows what it wants to reveal to each service and what security requirements the service demands, WS-Security can be an effective way to establish a security context between applications. But until products mature, getting everything to work in all but the simplest cases will be a challenge. We believe that what is needed is middleware to handle the difficult security problems that we have described. We will discuss one such solution—a distributed security framework—in a later section. But first lets look at a common but difficult security problem for interoperability, namely, delegation.

Handling Delegation in Web Services

We originally explained delegation, its complexity, and its importance in securing multi-tier architectures in Chapter 7, "Security of Infrastructures for Web Services." At this stage of evolution, delegation is not supported by any of the leading Web Services security models. This does not mean that there is less of a need for delegation in Web Services, only that the problem has not yet been formally addressed by any of the Web Services standards bodies. In this section, we will point out some potential near-term approaches for delegation within Web Services using custom implementations, as well as the possible future directions for standard solutions. Chapter 11, "Administrative Considerations for Web Services Security," provides further guidance on when and how to use delegation.

An example of a delegation scenario is a Web Services client calling on an intermediate service such as a purchasing system, which calls on the accounting system to release the initiating client's financial data, again using Web Services. The client must be authorized by the purchasing system to buy the product, and the purchasing system acts as an intermediate for the initiating client so that the accounting system will release the client's financial data.

In constrained (or restricted) delegation, the client restricts which intermediates may use the client's credentials. In our example above, the client would only permit the purchasing system to act on its behalf; other applications would not be able to use the client's credentials. The intermediate's target, namely the accounting system, checks the validity of any calling intermediate and rejects a delegated call if it cannot validate that the call is from the purchasing system.

To give you an idea of how constrained delegation might be implemented in Web Services, we'll walk through an example delegation scenario. Figure 10.3 shows the general scenario of an initiating client object named P1 invoking on an intermediate object named P2 (the purchasing system). The intermediate P2 then invokes on a target object (the accounting system).

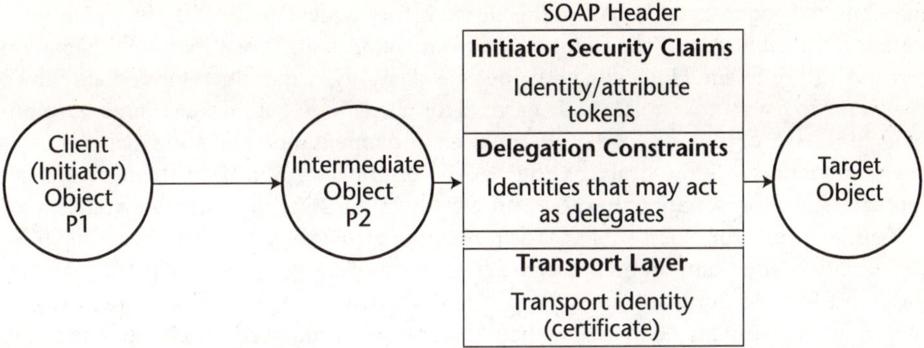

Figure 10.3 Delegation scenario.

Figure 10.3 also shows the credential tokens that may be passed from intermediate P2 to the target object as part of the SOAP header. In this example, the SOAP header transmits the *delegation constraints*, which identify the intermediates that are permitted to act as delegates, and the *initiator security claims*, which contain the identity and other attributes of the initiating client.

Although the standard WS-Security elements do not yet address constrained delegation, we can use a separate non-standard (but legal) WS-Security element that contains the identities of delegates. These identities define the intermediates that the client trusts to act as delegates on the client's behalf. Initiator security claims may be transmitted as usual in a standard WS-Security element (containing SAML or other tokens) as described in Chapter 4.

To ensure that the delegation constraints and initiator claims are bound to the SOAP message body, the initiating client should provide a digital signature based on both WS-Security elements as well as the SOAP message body.

The intermediate transmits its identity to the target object by the underlying secure transport layer, using, for example, an X.509 certificate via SSL.

The described implementation would work as follows for our delegation scenario: When the accounting system (target object) receives the SOAP message, it (1) verifies the identity of the purchasing system (intermediate P2) by SSL mutual authentication, (2) checks whether the purchasing system identity is in the delegation constraints list, and (3) verifies the digital signature on the WS-Security elements and message body. If these checks succeed, then the accounting system retrieves the initiating client from the initiator security claims and uses the initiating client's attributes to authorize the client's request.

It is also straightforward for this same approach to support the simplest type of delegation, namely impersonation. In this case, the initiating client makes the same request on the intermediate, but this time allows any target to impersonate the client by passing a wild card value for the delegation constraints. Without any constraints, there is nothing that prevents the intermediate from abusing the client credentials by making unauthorized requests on behalf of the client. If the request is low risk, for example, a request for a catalog, and the client doesn't care about its privacy, then impersonation may not be a problem. However, how does the client know that the intermediate can be trusted not to use its credentials to do harm to the client? Delegation constraints can eliminate this threat, at the price of a more complex implementation and security policy.

The current working draft of the SAML binding of WS-Security also has an approach for impersonation. In this approach, the requesting intermediate vouches for the verification of the client subject. The target must trust the intermediate to vouch for the identity of the client. In this case, the client has not delegated rights to the intermediate and has no control over who are trustworthy delegates. Consequently, this method will be applicable in cases where the only trust required is between the target receiver and the intermediate. Note that this working draft is ongoing, and the support for delegation may change before the standard is completed.

The SAML specification describes authentication, attribute, and authorization authorities, which could be designed to handle the requisite delegation functionality. However, these authorities are outside the scope of the present SAML specification and no details have been worked out, especially for the type of Web Services delegation problem that we have described in this section.

A possible alternative to delegation is for the client to send a signed SOAP request that contains portions encrypted with the public key of the target. By encrypting the data, the "tunneled" request will not be readable by any intermediates. This approach can be an effective way for a client to transmit requests through potentially untrustworthy intermediates. However, the approach will only work if there is no requirement for intermediates to access the encrypted data in the request. Additional countermeasures may need to be in place to prevent untrustworthy intermediates from launching replay attacks by resending the client request, further complicating the approach.

Transmitting encrypted data between a client and the ultimate recipient also requires that the client obtain the public keys of the recipients, and vice versa. This brings up the complexities of PKI. Although PKI technology has been around for some time, it is not trivial to implement, so it is usually used in situations where extensive security is required.

The client could get the public key of the targets by first retrieving the service name from the UUDI and then, using PKI, retrieving the public key from a certificate authority, using the service name. This is a somewhat ad hoc solution in that the service name must match the one the CA uses for that service, and the client also has to know the correct CA to ask for the key and trust that CA.

Delegation in Web Services is another of the reasons for our contention that Web Services will first be used and perfected within a single enterprise, on an intranet, and then used between a small number of partner companies, on an extranet. In these cases, there is a controlled environment, and issues relating to key management and trust can be worked out. Once people have experience with intranet and extranet Web Services security, we can move to Internet Web Services security. This does not mean that we cannot use Web Services security in the Internet today in constrained cases, but you should be aware that delegation across the Internet will be a risky proposition for some time to come.

We will now move on to describing how you would use an EASI framework as the security authority in your Web Services solution.

Using a Security Framework

We introduced the concept of an Enterprise Application Security Integration (EASI) security framework in the first chapter. We will look at a security framework as a means of solving the range of security interoperability problems associated with Web Services described in this chapter and as an early model of a SAML authority. So what, exactly, is an EASI framework? It's a flexible framework that integrates security technologies and products from multiple vendors across the perimeter, middle, and back-office tiers—both within a single enterprise and across multiple enterprise domains.

In our definition, a *security framework* is a middleware system that intercepts incoming messages before they reach the application and performs one or more security functions. As a result of these activities, the incoming request is either allowed to continue or it is denied. The activities that a security framework performs are those of authentication, attribute retrieval and mapping, authorization, and auditing. A framework should be able to carry out these activities between heterogeneous applications and security technologies, and it should know how to use the Web Services protocols that we have been discussing, that is, XML, SAML, WS-Security, digital signatures, XML Encryption, and PKI. Our overview in Chapter 1 portrayed an end-to-end solution for securing a message traversing a complete Web Services process from the client through the perimeter, through the mid-tier, and finally to the back-office tier. In this section, we will show how the framework uses the Web Services technologies that we have described in the earlier chapters.

Figure 10.4 will help you visualize the client and target security interactions that we describe. In this example, we assume a separate EASI framework for the client and the target and a variety of specialized security services that the framework uses. There are different variations of the EASI framework architecture, for example, both the client and the target could use the same framework if they were part of the same enterprise. However, the basic concepts of an EASI Framework remain the same regardless of its variation. That is, it reduces the need for custom-coded security, it offers a consistent security interface among disparate security products, and it facilitates the nondisruptive evolution of security services.

Client Use of EASI

A typical scenario for a Web Services activity using an EASI framework starts with the client authenticating itself with the EASI system, as shown in Figure 10.4. An EASI system is the complete implementation of an EASI framework that includes the administration and internal security between the different parts of the framework system. The EASI system may be controlled or run by a trusted third party. Alternately, the client could control the EASI system if the target Web Service trusts the client's EASI system to generate authentication assertions for users. In either case, the client would make a SOAP call, passing the authentication evidence to the EASI system, either as encrypted data in the WS-Security header or using point-to-point protection and mutual authentication, for example, SSL.

Since a minimum amount of security functionality is usually required to be in the client application, we recommend that the EASI client-side framework carry out all the client security work. Thus, the client would pass the SOAP message to the framework, where the signing, encryption, and authentication would be carried out. Note that this does not mean that the message has to be sent to remote parts of the framework. Efficient implementations of the framework permit processing of the message to be collocated with the client's host. Although you could do the security in the application, we strongly advise against putting the security at the application level, as we have stated repeatedly throughout this book. In addition, client-side applications are usually required to be simple to implement. Therefore, the more security that you want on the client side given this restriction, the more necessary a security framework becomes.

In this example, the SOAP message that is passed to the EASI framework is the message that will eventually be sent to the target. The EASI framework will use the authentication evidence to authenticate the user. The framework takes the incoming SOAP message and extracts the authentication data, then, using policy information set by the administrator, the framework chooses an authentication service to perform the actual authentication. By using an EAI approach for the framework, the authentication service could be switched to a different authentication service without perturbing the system.

The framework then creates a standard credential, for example, a SAML authentication assertion, and inserts the assertion into the proper WS-Security header. The framework signs and encrypts the parts of the message as dictated by the security policy or by the instructions received from the client. It then returns the secured SOAP message to the client for transport to the service.

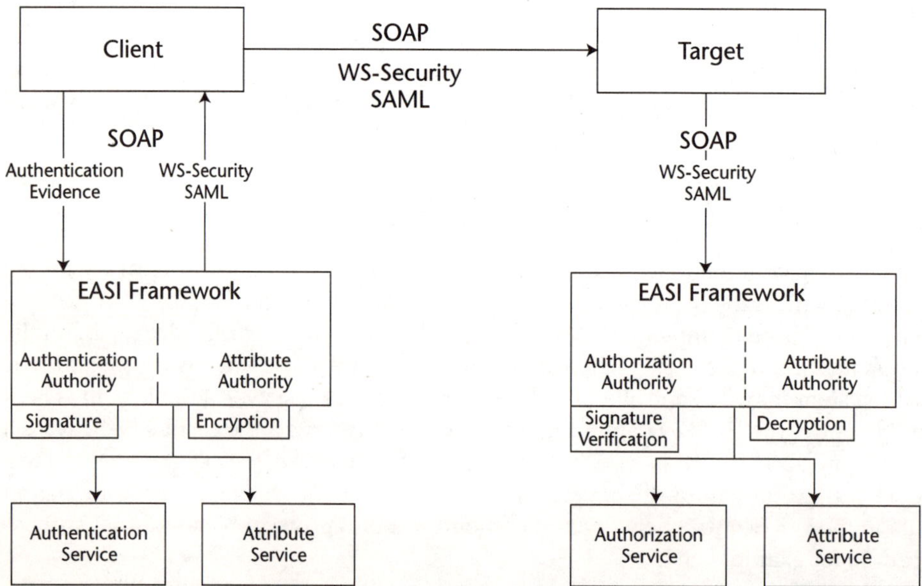

Figure 10.4 Security architectures using EASI frameworks.

There are a number of steps in the previous scenario for which standards have not been developed. For example, there are no standards for a request to a third-party authority that it sign or encrypt certain parts of a SOAP message as SAML has done for its assertions. Similarly, there are no standards to request that a third-party service authenticate itself using the evidence in the SOAP security header and insert proof of the authentication in the header. There is also the problem of attribute mapping, which we discussed earlier.

Although there are emerging approaches to providing general authentication services, such as Microsoft Passport and Liberty Alliance, the technology in this area is very immature. The lack of mature standards or products for the distributed authentication authorities point to the use of a framework that is local to the client. As some of the specification work is completed and third-party services become available, the framework can offload some of the tasks to a third party. However, the local client security service will still be needed to do some of the initial security work, such as protecting the message, vectoring the request to the appropriate third parties, coordinating the security data from the third parties, and auditing the activities.

Target Use of EASI

As shown in Figure 10.4, once the target has verified the message and mapped the appropriate attributes, the target calls on the framework to authorize the action that the client requests to perform on the resource.

The targets or providers of Web Services have security interoperability problems similar to those described for the client side. There is the request/response problem when using third-party authorities and establishing trust. The provider side of a Web Services system may also require specialized security services. Its security requirements are usually stricter and more complex than the client's, since it has the requirement to protect its resources, and its implementation is more complex, whereas the usual desire is to make the client lightweight.

The target-side interoperability problems lie with verifying the incoming message. To verify the message, the target must be able to interpret any authentication data that it receives from the client. (Recall our discussion of this problem in the Shibboleth context in Chapter 5.) Next there is the problem of attributes. Has the client done the correct mapping, and does the target trust the attributes sent from the client or does it want to pull the attributes from some repository? If the target wants to pull the attributes, from where does it get the attributes? The interoperable attribute problem has a lot of the same characteristics as the authentication problem. However, it is more complex because of the semantics associated with an attribute. A password is either correct or incorrect, but the same attribute does not necessarily imply the same privileges to the client and the target.

Securing the Example

We will use an EASI framework to extend our Web Services examples that we introduced in Chapters 8, "Securing .NET Web Services," and 9, "Securing Java Web Services." Figure 10.5 depicts the architecture of a solution based on an EASI framework.

The framework connects applications, presentation components, business components, and/or legacy components to third-party security services, which supply authentication, authorization, and other security services. Going back to our examples in Chapters 8 and 9, the framework could connect .NET or Java applications with each other or with various security services. There could be a variety of security services in the implementation: an authentication service from Microsoft, an authorization service from RSA, an attribute service from Verisign, or many others. In the EASI paradigm, this mix and match lets you choose the best security product for the service required, so any mixture of security services may be used. The framework, in addition to connecting the security products to the applications, maps Web Services security mechanisms to the traditional security solutions.

The application connects with the EASI framework by means of an adapter that calls the framework APIs. In our sample implementation of an EASI framework, we have supplied simple APIs (the Security API layer in Figure 10.5) for authentication, attribute retrieval, and authorization. These APIs hide the particular mechanism for transmitting the security information, for example, SAML assertions, from the developer. As a result, the developer does not have to know the intricacies of SAML.

Framework Authentication

The examples that we discussed in previous chapters assumed that client authentication was handled by existing browser to Web server security mechanisms. Alternatively, there are many situations where the EASI framework could be used for Web Services authentication. For example, a Web Services client may call into your Web Services system, passing the security evidence for authentication in a WS-Security token.

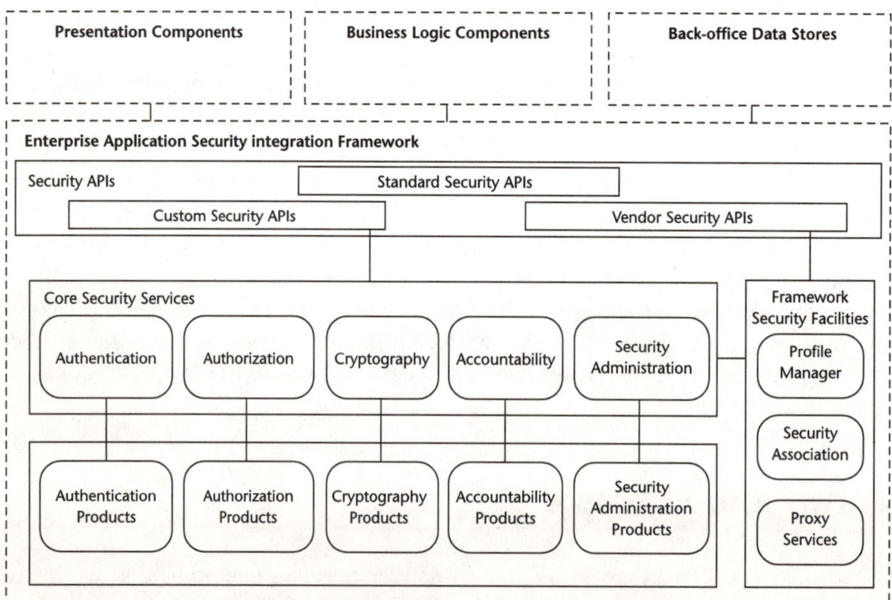

Figure 10.5 The EASI framework architecture.

We extend our examples from the previous chapters, assuming that the initiating client will authenticate at ePortal by passing a SAML authentication assertion via WS-Security to the EASI adapter for the Web Service. In this case, the adapter calls the verify API on the framework, passing it the SAML assertion in the form of an abstract token.

There are two ways to handle authentication in the Web Services example when the client sends a security-enabled SOAP message. The first is to have the application layer parse out the relevant security information and pass just the security evidence to the framework. There is some merit to this approach, because the application layer has to parse the SOAP message to determine what information the body contains. For example, the SOAP body may contain the methods that should be called on the Web Service.

However, in many cases it is not that straightforward. One complicating factor is that portions of the body may be encrypted. In this case, the application layer would have to understand how to handle XML encryption, which is no easy task. Some of the data may be integrity checked, that is, signed. In this case, the application will need to handle PKI and digital signatures. In addition, the authentication evidence may be in one of a number of different forms, for example, Kerberos or X.509 certificates. This approach forces the application to implement security logic, which is the very thing we want to avoid.

Since one of the basic concepts of an EASI framework is to relieve the application of becoming aware of the complexities of security, it would be better to pass the SOAP message to the framework and have the framework handle all the aspects of security. The framework could then extract the relevant security evidence, verify any signatures, verify the validity of the issuer of any assertions, and perform the authentication. However, passing the whole SOAP message to the framework could be prohibitively expensive. You will need to determine the right trade-off between efficiency and complexity of your Web Service applications.

Decryption and verification of the body of the SOAP message would normally be handled during an authorization call to the framework, since that is when you will need to use the information in the body. We'll cover this in the framework authorization section later in this chapter.

Note that the examples in the following subsections use sample APIs from a hypothetical framework implementation. Specific vendor implementations of an EASI framework will have different APIs for accessing the framework's functionality. However, the functionality required of an EASI framework is similar regardless of the syntax that it may use.

The authentication API of the EASI framework could look something like the following:

```
AuthenticationResponse
authenticate(
        String mechanism,
        String security_name,
        String authentication_data )
        throws AdapterException;
```

If authentication is based on the data in a SOAP message, the Web Services application would send the SOAP message in the *authentication_data* parameter, and the authentication *mechanism* would be SOAP. A SAML authentication assertion is returned in *AuthenticationResponse*. The documentation of the particular framework will describe the APIs that are supplied for passing the security data. Using this general API permits the EASI system to handle more than just SOAP, so that other authentication mechanisms may be accommodated.

Framework Attribute Handling

Going back to our example, if the user has been authenticated and the SAML assertion has passed verification, we next want to get the attributes for the user. The Web Services application will then call the get_attributes API on the EASI framework:

```
AttributeResponse
get_attributes( Token token )
        throws AdapterException;
```

where the token that is passed to the framework is the SAML authentication assertion and the *AttributeResponse* is a SAML attribute assertion. The framework parses the SAML authentication assertion, and using the information in the assertion, such as the subject name, calls the appropriate attribute service, which retrieves the attributes for subject. Alternately, when the framework receives the *get_attributes* call, it may map the SAML attribute request into a call to the persistent store that contains the user attributes.

The authentication assertion would be supplied to the target application either as a result of the authentication call or as part of the SOAP message. When the framework receives the attributes by either method just described, it constructs a SAML attribute assertion and passes this back to the Web Services application. The application then uses the attribute assertion to make an authorization call on the framework.

Framework Authorization

The Web Services application could use the attributes, passed to it by the framework, to enforce the authorization function defined on the .NET or Java platform, which is supplied by the application server. Alternately, the Web Services application could call the authorization API on the EASI framework, as follows:

```
AuthorizationResponse
get_authorization(
        Token         token,
        ScopedName    resource,
        ScopedName    action,
        NameValueMap instance_attributes )
        throws AdapterException;
```

The token parameter is the SAML attribute assertion. *ScopedName* is a structure containing the domain and the name itself. The resource identifies the data for which access is requested. The action is to access a specific method on the resource. This could be the *GetProductPrice* or *SetProductPrice* in our example. The framework will route the authorization call to the security service that has been set by policy and return the status of the authorization call in the *AuthorizationResponse*.

In this example, the *AuthorizationResponse* is a reference to an object that implements the following interface:

```
interface AuthorizationResponse
{
        public static final int ALLOWED;
        public static final int DENIED;
        public boolean access_allowed();
        public int get_reason();
}
```

Using the status of the authorization call, the Web Services application can then permit or deny access.

We mentioned earlier that, in the situation where the SOAP message contained encrypted portions of the body, it would be preferable for the framework to handle the decryption. This would be accomplished by passing the SOAP XML document to the framework in a helper function. There must be a trust relationship between the calling application and the framework, since we are decrypting potentially sensitive data.

The decryption could be accomplished by an API as simple as:

```
Token
decrypt(
        Token  token)
        throws AdapterException;
```

The *Token* would be the SOAP message and the return *Token* would be the decrypted SOAP message.

The XML Encryption specification from the W3C details how to encrypt and decrypt XML messages. This specification is referenced in WS-Security as the way to encrypt and decrypt SOAP messages. Consequently, when the SOAP document is sent to the framework, the framework will decrypt the portions of the body and replace the encrypted data with the decrypted XML text, following the XML Encryption specification.

Example Using JWSDP

Now that we have explained our example using an EASI framework, we will show you how you would use the framework with an extended version of our JWSDP example introduced in Chapter 9. Figure 10.6 depicts the architecture of this example. Here we see a JWSDP client at ePortal.com calling on a JWSDP servlet in eBusiness.com.

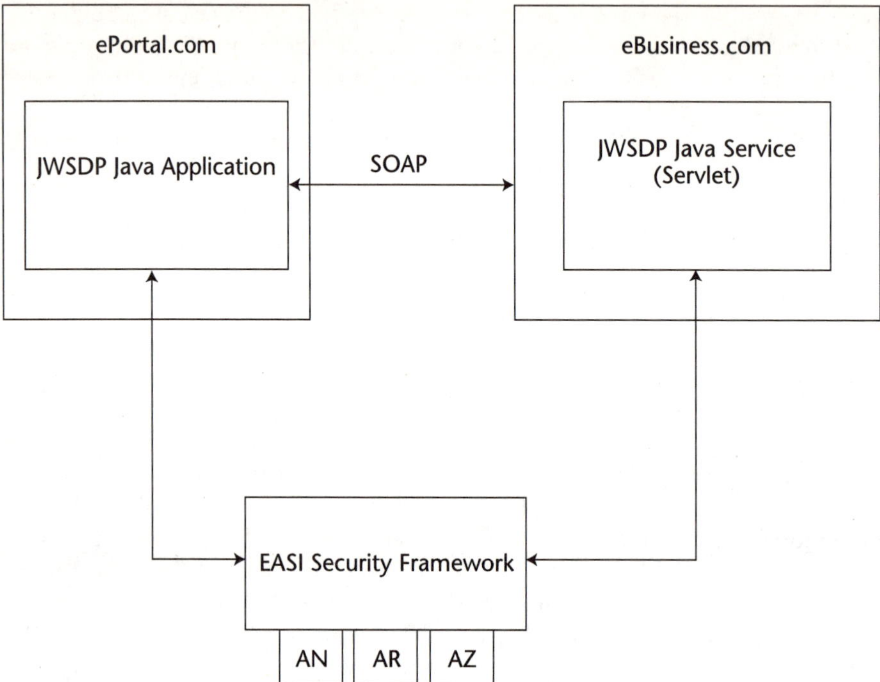

Figure 10.6 The EASI framework architecture using JWSDP.

StoreFront Client

We present the code from the previous chapter where our StoreFrontClient calls from ePortal using JAXM, now extended to use an EASI framework.

```
package com.StoreFront;
import javax.xml.soap.*;
import java.util.*;
import java.net.*;

public class StoreFrontClient {
public static void main(String [] args) {
try {
SOAPConnectionFactory scf =
    SOAPConnectionFactory.newInstance();
SOAPConnection con = scf.createConnection();

          // Call the security framework.
          // Get a reference to the framework using the approach
          // described by the framework. Then call the authenticate
          // method.
```

```
Token t = framework.authenticate("password", "joep",
 "apassword");

MessageFactory mf = MessageFactory.newInstance();
SOAPMessage msg = mf.createMessage();

        // Access the SOAP body object.
SOAPPart part = msg.getSOAPPart();
SOAPEnvelope envelope = part.getEnvelope();
SOAPHeader header = envelope.getHeader();

        // Create the header element request.
        // create a javax.xml.soap.Name "n" for the
        // security header
SOAPHeaderElement h = header.addHeaderElement(n);
       // Next add the Token element to the header
       // create a javax.xml.soap.Name "security element"
       // for the Header Child Element
SOAPElement sec_element = h.addChildElement(
                                    security_element );
       // There is no JWSDP API to attach an XML document
       // fragment to a SOAPElement. You will have to
       // traverse the Token t (WS-Security element) and add
       // each element to the header. It is best that
       // the framework you choose handle all this.
SOAPBody body = envelope.getBody();
Name bodyName = envelope.createName("request-prices",
          "RequestPrices", "http://ebusiness.com");
SOAPBodyElement requestPrices =
         body.addBodyElement(bodyName);

Name requestName = envelope.createName("getPrice");
SOAPElement request =
         requestPrices.addChildElement(requestName);
request.addTextNode("Send updated price list.");

msg.saveChanges();

         //Create the endpoint and send the message.
URL endpoint = new URL(
         "http://localhost:8080/grocery supplier/
                getProductPriceList");
SOAPMessage response = con.call(msg, endpoint);
con.close();

         //get contents of response
Vector list = new Vector();
SOAPBody responseBody = response.getSOAPPart().
getEnvelope().getBody();
Iterator it1 = responseBody.getChildElements();
         // get price-list element
```

```
38. while (it1.hasNext()) {
39.   SOAPBodyElement bodyEl = (SOAPBodyElement)it1.next();
40.   Iterator it2 = bodyEl.getChildElements();
              // get coffee elements
41. while (it2.hasNext()) {
42.   SOAPElement child2 = (SOAPElement)it2.next();
43.   Iterator it3 = child2.getChildElements();
              // get the price list
44. while (it3.hasNext()) {
45.   SOAPElement child3 = (SOAPElement)it3.next();
46.   String value = child3.getValue();
47.   list.addElement(value);
48. }
49. }
50. }
              //  Now that we have the contents of the response, we can
              //  do something with price list we received.
51. }
52. catch (Exception ex) {
53.   ex.printStackTrace();
54. }
55. }
56. }
```

Since we have described most of the program in the previous chapter, we will concentrate on the additions to use the EASI framework. The framework in this example constructs a header element corresponding to a user who is authenticated by the framework. In this example, on line 11 we call into the security framework to authenticate the user *joep*. (For simplicity, the example uses a hard-coded password, but note that this approach is a very poor security practice and is never recommended for deployment. A realistic implementation would obtain the password dynamically, as we discuss later.) The framework returns a header element containing a WS-Security/SAML element. The API for the call to the security framework is the authentication API that we presented in the previous section.

The actual order of the authentication call is not that important as long as it occurs before you return anything to the caller. A performance consideration when calling into the security framework for authentication is to make the call before you do any substantial work because the user may fail authentication. In this example, we retrieved the SOAP header in line 16 after calling the EASI framework for authentication on line 11. We're assuming in this example that the returned token is a WS-Security XML document that contains a SAML authentication and/or attribute assertion. The choice of assertion is determined by policy. The application programmer generally does not have to be concerned with this level of security detail. The returned string, the security SOAP header element, would be inserted into the header after line 18.

Note that this example only supplies the authentication proof, the SAML assertion, in the header element. A more extensive framework would also handle signing the header, cryptographically tying the header to the body, and encrypting portions of the SOAP message. In that case the API would look something like the following:

```
String authenticate (String mechanism, String security_name,
                     String authentication_data, String SOAP_message);
```

In this example API, the authentication *mechanism*, the *security_name*, and the *authentication_data* are the same as in the previous API. However, the complete SOAP message to be secured is passed to the security framework as the last parameter. The framework, using policy data set by the administrator, would authenticate the subject, create the correct SAML assertions, and put them into the WS-Security element. The framework would then not only digitally sign the SAML assertions, as before, but construct a digital signature over the header and body as instructed by the corporate security policy set in the framework's security policy database. Furthermore, if the policy so dictates, the framework would encrypt parts of the message before signing the header and body.

This more extensive framework API would be called after line 27 rather than after line 18, as before. The framework would return the SOAP message fully secured according to your corporate policy. The remaining client code constructs the SOAP body (lines 19-27), creates the URL to the service (lines 29-31), and sends the SOAP message, containing security tokens and potentially cryptographic data (line 32). We then retrieve the response from the service (lines 35-47) and use the results.

The extent to which the EASI framework supports a security policy is a very important criterion in your choice of framework vendor, if you go that route. The policy supported must give you the granularity and flexibility for signing and encryption that you require, and it should also be easy to administer.

In this example, we used password authentication, which means that you would need some code to get the user's password, probably by popping up a login prompt window. If the framework returned an exception, you would handle the exception in your catch clause. Whatever way you are informed of a failed authentication, you would stop processing and return an error. In the successful case, the framework should return a token, say a SAML assertion in a WS-Security XML document or a full SOAP message in the case of the more full-featured framework. There may be some additional information that you want to put in the header, but if you have purchased a good security framework, the few lines shown should be all that you need for security. With this knowledge of what a framework can and should do, you can examine the prospective security products you intend to employ. A good, well-thought-out security framework will make your Web Services secure with a minimum amount of effort by your company's programming team.

All of our discussion comes down to a few lines of code. But that's how frameworks should work. Since you are putting your security in the hands of the framework provider it is important that you question the prospective providers about the capabilities of their product and the way that it performs all the security functionality. We hope that the lessons of Web Services security that you learn throughout this book will prepare you to carry out this task. Remember that the ultimate responsibility for the security of your company and its data rests with you. You also need to know what is going on beneath the covers to judge how you can use the security middleware in an optimum manner.

StoreFront Service

We will use the same server code example as in the previous chapter, again extended by using an EASI framework.

```
1. public SOAPMessage onMessage(SOAPMessage message) {
2.   try {
3.      System.out.println("Here's the message: ");
                // Get the security framework using the means provided
                // by your framework provider and then call its
                // authorize method, passing the SOAP message.
4.      if (framework.authorize (message) {
                // Carry out the normal processing of the SOAP
                // message.

5.         message.writeTo(System.out);
              //Retrieve the SOAP envelope.
6.         SOAPEnvelope env = message.getSOAPPart().getEnvelope();
7.             SOAPHeader header = env.getHeader ();
8.             SOAPBody body = env.getBody ();
              // Do your normal processing of the SOAP message.
9.      } else {
              // Construct a SOAP fault.
10.      }
11.      return msg;
          } catch(Exception e) {
              logger.error(
                  "Error in processing or replying to a message", e);
              return null;
          }
      }
```

The SOAP message is passed to the onMessage JWSDP callback defined by the JAXM specification. If you have an EASI framework that handles all the security for Web Services, as we discussed in the client example, then the server simply calls the EASI framework's authorization method. The server passes the SOAP message to the framework using the authorization API. This is shown in line 4 of our example. Note that this API is simpler than that used in the previous example, because the full-featured framework should be able to discern the other parameters from the SOAP message. Using the WS-Security document extracted from the header, the framework will be able to verify the SAML assertion and make an access decision on whether the subject can perform the requested action on the resource. A less complete security framework may require that the server verify any signatures and/or decrypt portions of the document itself.

If the server gets a failure status from the security framework, the server denies access to the resource that the caller is requesting. If the requester is allowed to perform the action on the resource, the server creates the response and returns the response to the caller. Once again, if you have a complete EASI framework, you will save your programming team a lot of work for which they are not especially well equipped. In line with our security advice that security should be performed below the application layer in the middleware, we recommend the framework approach.

What Problems Should an EASI Framework Solve?

We've put forth the concept of an EASI framework as a potential solution to a number of the interoperability problems. This section will reiterate the discussion on EASI from Chapter 1 to pull together the basic types of problems that an EASI framework is intended to solve in light of our discussion of interoperability. The first part of the definition of an EASI framework involves the concept of EAI, Enterprise Application Integration. As we have said, EAI is a business level technology aimed at solving the problem of getting many different applications to work together smoothly, for example, enabling the output from an application to be used as the input to other applications. Basically, EAI solves the problem of reducing the many-to-many connectivity problem and the problem of semantic mismatches.

Distributed security has the same many-to-many connectivity and semantic mismatch problem as EAI. There are many third-party security products, each of which solves different parts of the security problem better than the others. As new solutions to particular security problems become available, you might want to switch products without perturbing your system. An EASI framework should support this flexibility. We discussed the problem of attribute mapping earlier in this chapter. An EASI framework should support this mapping either directly or by transparently calling an attribute mapping service. We talked about the problems associated with the security of SOAP messages: signing, encrypting, and creating the security elements, as well as the other side of these problems, verifying and decrypting elements. Once again, an EASI framework should either directly supply these functions or transparently call third-party products to solve these problems.

The bottom line is that a good EASI framework should:

- Substantially reduce the number of integrated connections between applications and security services (compared to custom point-to-point connections between applications and security services)
- Supply solutions for the set of problems that we discussed by having a means to transparently use third-party products
- Permit easy substitution of security services without perturbing your running system
- Supply internal solutions where third-party solutions are not readily available

Web Services Support for EASI

So far we have discussed how EASI can support Web Services security. However, we should also examine the reverse relationship: Can Web Services support EASI? That is, how could Web Services be used to connect an application securely to the EASI framework?

If we wished to use the full Web Services paradigm to connect with the EASI framework, we would have to discover the EASI service, determine what security methods to call, and ensure that the call to EASI was secure. The first two problems can be solved using UDDI and WSDL. The last problem could be solved by the EASI service requiring an SSL connection with mutual authentication. Since the EASI framework has to be a trusted entity and we want to minimize the security operations in the application, a point-to-point security connection is the best choice.

Why would you want to use Web Services for your connection to the EASI framework? Web Services use loose coupling via XML, whereas the EASI APIs we have described use tighter coupling. Loose coupling translates into faster development time for Web Services as opposed to better performance for the API approach. Both approaches have their advantages, so we believe that it is sensible to consider an EASI framework that uses *and* secures by means of both Web Services and by EAI techniques.

Making Third-Party Security Products Work Together

There are two problems that you will encounter when you are using many different security products and are trying to get them to work together:

1. Proprietary product credentials
2. Overlapping product functionality

With respect to the first problem, some third-party security products use proprietary techniques to create the evidence that is transferred from one application to another. For example, they may use a proprietary credential format, and some even encrypt the credential using a proprietary key format. This means that the credential from such a product cannot be used with another product. One way around this problem is to use the proprietary security to carry out the required functionality, for example, authentication, and then create a standardized credential based on, say, WS-Security and/or SAML, and use that structure to access another security product to do, for example, authorization. In some cases, you may need to carry both the standard credential and the proprietary credential, since the latter might be needed to access the initial proprietary security product at another application. For example, if you use one of the more popular security products for authentication, you will need certain proprietary data to use the same product for authorization. Further, unless you use that product for authentication, you cannot use it for authorization. Hopefully, as the open Web Services specifications gains traction, we will see these proprietary products switch to using the standardized credential before long.

Concerning the second problem, many of the security products try to address all aspects of security and do one function well while doing other security functions either poorly or not as well as other products. The solution to this problem is to use an EASI framework in conjunction with standardized credentials as we have discussed. This permits you to pick the best product for the particular security functionality that you need at the time.

Federation

Federation as applied to security is the ability of organizations (companies, divisions, or business units) to securely communicate while maintaining independent security policy repositories. For example, company A performs authentication using a trusted third party, which sends proof of the authentication to company B. Company B verifies the authentication proof and uses the privilege attributes in the proof to authorize the action of the principal whom the attributes represent. Federation primarily relates to coordination between authentication and authorization in two separate entities, with identities or privilege attributes as the coordinating pieces of evidence. Authorization by itself is usually not a federation problem, since only the target is involved in deciding whether a principal may perform some action on a resource once the target has the proper attributes for the requesting entity. There are additional security considerations when a third-party authority is used for authorization, but these do not introduce any new federation problems.

Digital signatures and encryption, which are part of the WS-Security specification, make solving the federation problem possible. In message-based security, the proof of who carried out the security actions is contained in the message itself. The target can unequivocally verify who constructed the security data, and if they trust the party who created that security data, use it confidently.

Distributed authentication is being addressed by a number of specification committees, such as the Liberty Alliance and Passport, but the distributed attribute problem is receiving considerably less attention. We believe that proper handling of distributed attributes is the key to solving the basic federation problem. Distributed delegation over multiple hops, as we explained earlier, is one of the problem areas that does not yet have a standardized solution. In many cases, the system design can avoid the use of delegation. Where this is not possible, you can use the approach we described earlier in this chapter.

In any large enterprise that expects to do business with a large number of customers, suppliers, or dealers, role-based access control (RBAC) is an important, time-tested solution to avoid the administrative problem of handling the profile data of each potential entity that will access its site. RBAC, as we will discuss in Chapter 11, uses security attributes. As we pointed out earlier, the attributes should come from either the client or a trusted third party; otherwise, the target system must administer all of the principals and their attributes, thus creating a significant scaling problem for the target. In addition, whether the attributes come from the client or from a third-party service, the problem of syntactic and semantic mismatch exists. An attribute mapping, as we described earlier, addresses the problem of mismatches between client and target attributes.

There is another solution to define how the target gets the client attributes. A CORBA specification, ATLAS, defines a protocol whereby the target directs the client to a third-party attribute service to translate the client attributes to ones that the target understands. ATLAS, however, still does not completely solve the federation problem. The attributes that the third party uses generally need to be semantically and syntactically understood by both the client and the target, and, as a result, there is still a need for attribute mapping.

Liberty Alliance, which we introduced in Chapter 6, is on its way to solving the authentication problem in constrained domains. In the next section, we will tie the explanation of the Liberty Alliance work more closely to the problems identified in this chapter.

Liberty Alliance

In this section, we give more details of the Liberty Alliance and compare Liberty Alliance support of federation to the requirements for federation that we described in the preceding section.

The basic architecture of a Liberty Alliance is what it calls a "circle of trust." In the circle of trust, there are three entity types defined: users, identity providers, and service providers. The user wants to obtain services from a set of service providers using SSO in a particular domain, that is, in a particular circle of trust. The identity provider is responsible for authenticating the user and, by using federation, supplying the service providers with proof of the authentication of the user. Figure 10.7 shows this relationship. When a user attempts to access a Liberty provider, that provider gets authentication proof from the identity provider, if the user has previously approved federation with that provider. The user will either have previously been authenticated to the identity provider or will be asked to log in. Once users have been authenticated, they can access any of the providers without further login.

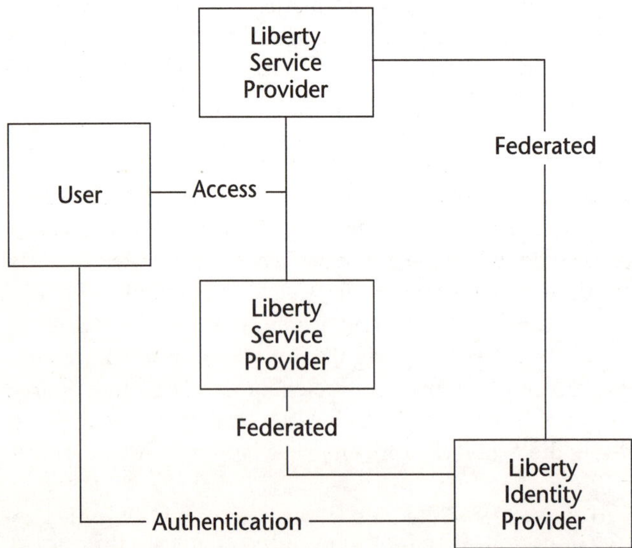

Figure 10.7 Liberty Alliance.

As in SAML, the actual authentication of the user by the identity provider is outside the scope of the Liberty specification. When a service provider accesses the identity provider for proof of authentication, the identity provider will return the proof of authentication in a SAML authentication assertion. In order to satisfy this set of requests, the Liberty Alliance uses the SAML artifact or HTTP POST protocol, giving the Liberty Alliance the same emphasis on Web SSO as SAML. Liberty also uses the SOAP binding. (It should be noted that the Liberty Alliance architecture does not make the same distinction between bindings and protocols that SAML does.) On the other hand, the specification does define a new protocol, the Liberty-enabled Client and Proxy Profile (LECP) that defines how Liberty-enabled clients may access identity and service providers. The proxy defined is the HTTP Wireless Application Protocol (WAP) gateway. The LECP profile moves the Liberty Alliance away from being strictly a perimeter profile.

While SAML may be thought of as a low-level definition of the security credential, the Liberty Alliance is a higher-level specification that uses SAML to implement many of its tasks. Taking this broader perspective, the Liberty Alliance defines a number of higher-level schemas that use SAML, as well as defining how the service and identity providers federate and use the circle of trust.

Two constructs that the Liberty Alliance elaborate on are SSO and the use of federation to implement SSO. To use SSO in all but the most trivial of cases the various services must be federated, that is, an authentication by one must be recognized by the other members of the federated group. The Liberty Alliance uses a master/slave relationship with respect to authentication, where the identity provider authenticates the user and supplies the authentication proof, the SAML authentication assertion, to the service providers upon request. Another important concept is that the Liberty Alliance protects the privacy of the user information between members of the circle of trust. The user is known to a service provider only by the user's local name, and the user's identity is exchanged by means of an opaque handle. In addition, the user has to explicitly permit federation between any of the services in a circle of trust before the user's information may be shared.

A useful adjunct that the Liberty Alliance defines is the concept of a global or single logout. Using this capability, one can log out at a single provider and that logout can be propagated to all the members of the circle of trust.

In addition to the basic transfer protocols, the Liberty Alliance defines schemas for establishing the relationships between the identity provider and the service providers, which the specification calls *metadata*. Metadata includes information such as the format of the user identity, the authentication method that can be used between the entities, name registration by which a provider can register a local username, and the protocols that can be used to authenticate the user.

One difference between Liberty and the federation requirements in this chapter is Liberty's use of individual identities rather than privilege attributes, which could lead to scaling problems for large user populations. Liberty Alliance does say that future releases will support attributes, although they do not discuss whether they will address attribute mapping. It should be noted that Liberty already has a simple form of mapping with respect to identities. The use of an opaque handle rather than the actual name is a type of generic attribute, although this is used primarily for privacy purposes.

Liberty has limitations that make it difficult to use for machine-to-machine federation that will become popular in the Web Services paradigm. For example, Liberty's reliance on the SAML browser profiles is not suitable for machine-to-machine interaction. We believe that they will need a more flexible security token container such as WS-Security with its extended capabilities. The use of WS-Security would permit more varied messaging-based exchanges beyond the browser-based profiles.

Liberty Alliance is a good first step in solving some of the federation problems, although its policies currently are constrained due to the lack of attribute support and the requirement of pair-wise agreements between the identity provider and each of the service providers. To Liberty's credit, it addresses additional problems such as privacy and consumer approval, which controls the unrestricted use of federated identities.

The Internet versus Intranets and Extranets

We have discussed the problems of Web Services security using the Internet and have stated our preference for using Web Services at this stage of their maturity in intranets and, in controlled cases, in extranets. The Internet is an uncontrolled environment, that is, anyone can potentially interact with anyone else over the Internet, which has its pluses and minuses. The pluses are well known: the Internet allows instant connectivity, cheaper cost of sales, easier interaction with customers, and many other advantages. The minuses have to do with securing the interaction with all these potential connections. While the Internet makes it easy for customers, suppliers, and business partners to connect and to do business, it also allows the bad guys to interact with your system. Thus you have to trade off the ease of use for your friends against the necessity of making it very hard for the bad guys to cause you harm by entering your system through the Internet. The goal of Web Services is to allow anyone to discover your services through UDDI and connect to you based on the information in the downloaded WSDL file that is supplied through the UDDI. On the other hand, the goal of Web Services security is to control who may access resources at a site.

Before Web Services are ready to be used ubiquitously on the Internet, we have to solve the interoperability problems. There are some solutions in place, but there still must be coordination between the requester and receiver until we get the full range of solutions standardized, used by the Web Services vendors, and working smoothly in the more controlled case. This coordination, for example, using attribute mapping, is easier to do on an intranet or extranet because you are not dealing with potentially unknown requestors. Our purpose in this chapter is to make you aware of these problems so that you can set up your system to handle them using the various techniques that we have described.

Summary

This chapter covered the subject of secure interoperability when using Web Services. We looked at where you might need to address interoperability both from the viewpoint of crossing the boundaries between security tiers and from the viewpoint of the standard security technologies of authentication, privilege attributes, and authorization.

We identified the need for a universally accepted security context as a major item required to make Web Services interoperability possible. Two other concepts are also necessary to enable interoperability: end-to-end security rather than point-to-point security and the use of standardization in solving the interoperability problem. The two most useful standards that we discussed are WS-Security, which supports end-to-end security, and SAML, which standardizes a credential format.

We also identified security attribute mapping as a technology necessary to enable security federation, that is, secure interaction between disparate organizations that have autonomous policies. We discussed the Liberty Alliance in relation to the requirements that we see for federation.

We discussed the use of an EASI framework as an important technology to enable solutions to the interoperability problem. We described how you would use such a framework and where it would fit into your architecture.

Finally, we suggested that Web Services would first be used in intranets and extranets rather than on the Internet because the solutions to the secure interoperability problems are more manageable when it's possible to coordinate between the various users of Web Services. We pointed out that the solutions to securely using Web Services over the Internet have not yet been fully standardized, and some are still under development.

The next chapter will look at how you would administer security in a Web Services environment and make your administration efficient and scalable.

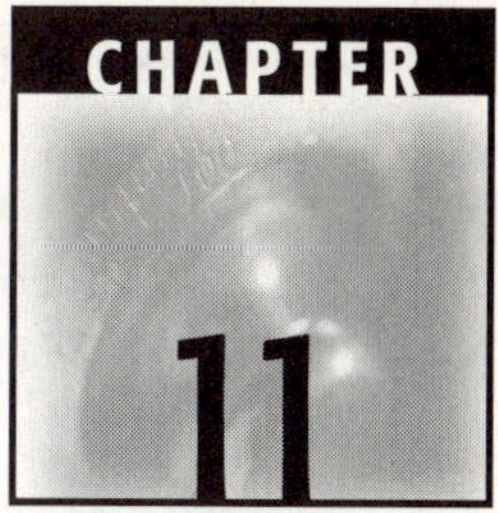

Administrative Considerations for Web Services Security

Up to this point, you've learned all about developing secure Web Services: from SOAP security, to security of the implementation platforms, to specific mechanisms for creating secure applications that utilize Web Services. The vital area left untouched is security administration. In this chapter, you will learn how to make security administration of Web Services efficient and scalable while supporting the security policies of your organization.

Introducing Security Administration

Once a system has been developed, deployed, integrated, and configured, the rest of your effort will be spent on operating (backing up, upgrading, patching, and so on) and administering it. Depending on the application domain and security requirements of your organization in general and the system in particular, as well as the administrative capabilities of the underlying middleware technology used for building the system, the cost of security administration could be anywhere from very high to extremely low. It's not a surprise that the typical case is closer to the higher end, but why is this so? Isn't it just a matter of specifying which users should have access to which resources in a system? What could be simpler than that?

The Security Administration Problem

In any interesting and useful system, there are too many objects to protect, too many users (also called subjects) using the system, and too many different ways in which they're using it. Moreover, objects tend to be created and deleted too frequently, users tend to come and go, and the only constant characteristic of business processes is their continuous change. Therefore it becomes very hard to keep the rules that control access up to date. Another thorny problem with any known simplistic approach is that administrators of large systems are not involved in system development and don't know each and every user. This makes it difficult for them to make correct decisions when writing security rules. How could an administrator know, for example, if user *abc* should have access to object *xyz* if they have never met? This is why researchers and practitioners have been investigating more scalable and human-friendly ways to administer protected systems, since the first multiuser systems came about. In the last 40 years, research has produced a plethora of approaches. Almost all of them, however, are based on two fundamental notions—grouping of objects and grouping of subjects. Administration starts to scale and make more sense when groups of subjects are granted access to groups of objects.

Subjects are grouped using subject attributes assigned according to specific criteria. Since these attributes are so critical—their possession could entitle somebody to access very valuable resources—they are assigned according to *user attribute assignment policies*, which have to be administered. Complex enterprise solutions frequently require the cooperation of several systems, resulting in the propagation of application requests from the client to the target through several intermediaries. Web Services are specifically designed to enable the processing of requests by multiple entities, or actors. Invocation chains introduce the need for policies governing the delegation of subject attributes (collectively referred to as credentials), namely *credential delegation policies*. Because security policies are never perfect, and in some application domains (e.g., healthcare) it is better to have too loose than too tight access control policies, a security audit is used to hold users accountable for their actions, even when they do have authority to access resources. *Security audit policies* specify what events should be recorded in security audit logs. Security audit, credentials delegation, user attribute assignment, and access control mechanisms depend on proper authentication of users. What authentication is proper and what isn't? This can vary from case to case (for instance, access from an emergency room versus access over the Internet), and it is the subject of yet another security policy, namely *authentication policy*.

Depending on the underlying technology, objects could be grouped in a number of ways. The example most familiar to everyone is grouping of files in a hierarchical directory structure, where access to any file in a directory requires access to the directory itself. However, this is not the only way to group objects. As we already discussed in Chapter 7, "Security of Infrastructures for Web Services," COM+ and EJB group objects by application. Both technologies support finer groupings of methods on objects, using permission groupings referred to as *roles*. CORBA pushes the envelope even further, abstracting object groups into policy domains, which can be as fine as one object and as coarse as several systems, and defining *required rights* that group methods on objects.

Besides administering access control, security administration also has to deal with other aspects of protecting system resources. For instance, when data is in transit between distributed parts of a system or between separate systems, access control mechanisms cannot help protect it—hence the need for cryptographic protection, which is subject to *data protection policies*.

What about Web Services?

There are two parts to security administration of Web Services: (1) administering the policies that govern protection mechanisms of enterprise Web Services, and (2) administering the advanced data protection features of the SOAP architecture. Depending on what capabilities of SOAP you use, one or both of these areas may be important to you. You might end up using Web Services as yet another middleware "glue" to integrate heterogeneous systems, either confined in one enterprise or department or interacting across organizational boundaries. In this case, you should only be concerned with the part of security administration that is common to any middleware technology and deals with administering all of the policies related to controlling access to enterprise Web Services. We will discuss this portion first.

The second part of security administration for Web Services deals with the advanced data protection features of SOAP—fine-grained cryptographic protection of data traveling in SOAP requests and responses—which distinguishes Web Services from other middleware technologies. Unlike point-to-point protection of all the data in the channels used for shipping requests and responses to and from distributed applications, selective encryption and signing of SOAP message elements enables end-to-end fine-grained protection in the face of multiple intermediary Web Services processing portions of a request or response. The data protection features of the SOAP architecture do not come for free. Not only is runtime support for it complex but also its administration could easily get out of hand. We leave discussion about administering data protection until the end of the chapter.

Administering Access Control and Related Policies

If you use Web Services as just another technology for integrating heterogeneous systems, you will discover that all of the concerns common to the security administration of most middleware are true in this case as well. The main objective boils down to finding a balance between scalability and expressiveness of access control and other security policies. Since access control usually becomes the most complex policy, we will devote nearly all of our attention to it. Other policies (auditing, credentials delegation, authentication) are frequently limited by the implementation mechanisms and have less demanding organizational requirements.

Your implementation platform for Web Services can take advantage of user attributes to make administration more efficient. No matter what access control model you employ, shrewd use of the attributes will make successful security administration possible.

Using Attributes Wisely

Security attributes allow you to group principals and apply the same security policies to such groups. You need to consider a number of points in order to use privilege attributes to your advantage. One is that care and thought must be put into deciding which attributes are assigned and allowed to which individuals, because this determines how these individuals, acting through applications, will be controlled by the security services. This further emphasizes the need for your organization to explicitly define the semantics assigned to a particular attribute. For example, what does the term *supervisor* mean in your organization? Is it any supervisor, or are there meaningful gradations of "supervisor" as that attribute applies to the security of the system? Furthermore, what are the semantics of a combination of attributes? Also, is a "clerk" in the Insurance Division semantically equivalent to a "clerk" in the Complaints Department, and so on?

In addition to assigning attributes to individuals, it may also be important to assign attributes to application entities that can control server applications. For example, you might have a Web Service that automatically forwards certain forms. In that case, this forwarding application might need certain attributes to access another Web Service to which the forms are forwarded. One approach might be to create an entity for that purpose, give it specific attributes, and use these attributes to determine access to that Web Service.

If you asked us to choose between using only few attributes or using many, we would recommend a point somewhere in the middle. Having too few groups, roles, and other attributes will not provide enough granularity in access control policies. On the other hand, with too many attributes, each attribute would be easy to understand, but the overall access control policy would be very complex. You will need to find your own happy medium in your particular environment. The number of attributes used for modeling security policies will also depend on the administration tools you are using and the training of your security administrators.

We recommend that you follow this list of rules for managing user security attributes:

- Because enterprises are dynamic, the security constraints represented in attributes and policy domains have to be continually modified and updated.
- The semantics of each attribute value must be clearly defined between any two disparate entities using it, so that both of them agree on the meaning of the attribute's value.
- Your organization needs to explicitly define the semantics assigned to a particular attribute (for example, "administrator") and to the mapping of attributes (for example, a "clerk" in the Insurance Division and a "clerk" in the Complaints Department).
- It may be important to assign attributes to entities that can control server applications (for example, applications that automatically forward certain forms).

Strive to find an optimum balance for your company between using too many attributes and too few, so as to be able to manage the complexity without losing the required level of granularity. "But," you might be asking, "how will I know how to tie together user attributes and security policies?" It is true that attributes alone don't buy you much. At the end of the day, they are used in access control and related policies. Currently, there is one technique that is believed to be quite successful in employing attributes for security administration of commercial enterprise systems that include Web Services: role-based access control (RBAC). This technique quite elegantly places one attribute type—role—into access control policies. Let us look at RBAC in more detail.

Taking Advantage of Role-Based Access Control

Access control based on roles has become so popular in the industry that today almost all security products claim to support the role paradigm. If you look at COM+, .NET, or EJB, for example, you will find the use of the term "role" all over the description of security APIs and the administration sections. All three technologies define APIs that allow an application to query the caller attributes using method *IsCallerInRole* or its equivalents. All three provide mechanisms for restricting access to objects and their methods only to principals with specified roles. No matter what your implementation platform is, there is a good chance that its security architecture uses the term "role." Unfortunately, depending on the technology, "role" could refer to very different concepts. Some technologies, such as EJB, define the meaning of this term. Some don't. You will see that not everyone can explain what RBAC means. To straighten things out and make sure there is no confusion about what we mean by roles and RBAC, the next section explains each of the RBAC models.

Overview of RBAC

RBAC (Sandhu et al. 1996) is a family of reference models in which permissions are associated with roles, and users are assigned to appropriate roles. Although groups and roles are closely related, and RBAC may be implemented in group-only systems such as Unix and MS Windows, the concepts of roles and groups are different. If used properly, a group usually represents organizational affiliation (for example, department, laboratory, division, or group of workers) or geographical location (company branch, building, floor, and even room). Examples of groups are Marketing Department, nuclear physics laboratory, computer support group, Dallas office, east building, and intensive care floor. A role can represent competency, authority, responsibility, or specific duty assignments. Role examples are clerk, VP, financial officer, and shift manager.

Some variations of RBAC include the capability to establish relations between roles, between permissions and roles, and between users and roles. There are four established RBAC reference models: unrelated roles ($RBAC_0$), role-hierarchies ($RBAC_1$), user and role assignment constraints ($RBAC_2$), and both hierarchies and constraints ($RBAC_3$). The RBAC models support three security principles in varying degrees:

Least privilege. Requires users to operate with the minimum set of privileges necessary to do their jobs.

Separation of duties. Requires that for particular sets of transactions, no single individual be allowed to execute all transactions within the set. A commonly used example is the separation of a transaction needed to initiate a payment from a transaction needed to authorize a payment.

Data abstraction. Requires security policies to be independent of the concrete representation and form of data and other valuable resources. In other words, RBAC models abstract the access to system-specific resources into system-independent access permissions. The permissions can represent anything you want. For example, they could mean the use of CPU time, modification of patient records, and even eating candies.

RBAC is an important concept for handling large-scale authorization policies. Most of the security community believes that eventually RBAC will prove to be more effective in security administration than other mainstream models, such as lattice-based *mandatory access control* (MAC) and owner-based *discretionary access control* (DAC), which are explained in the following sidebar.

Among the four RBAC reference models known in the security community, $RBAC_0$ is the base model. It only requires that a system supports the notions of users, roles, permissions, and sessions. There are no constraints on the assignment of permissions to roles and users to roles or on any relations among roles in $RBAC_0$. $RBAC_1$ has hierarchies of roles in addition to all the features of $RBAC_0$. $RBAC_2$ has constraints on the assignment of users to roles and permissions to roles, in addition to all the features of $RBAC_0$. $RBAC_3$ combines $RBAC_1$ and $RBAC_2$ and has both role hierarchies and constraints. See Figure 11.1 for an illustration of the relationships among RBAC models.

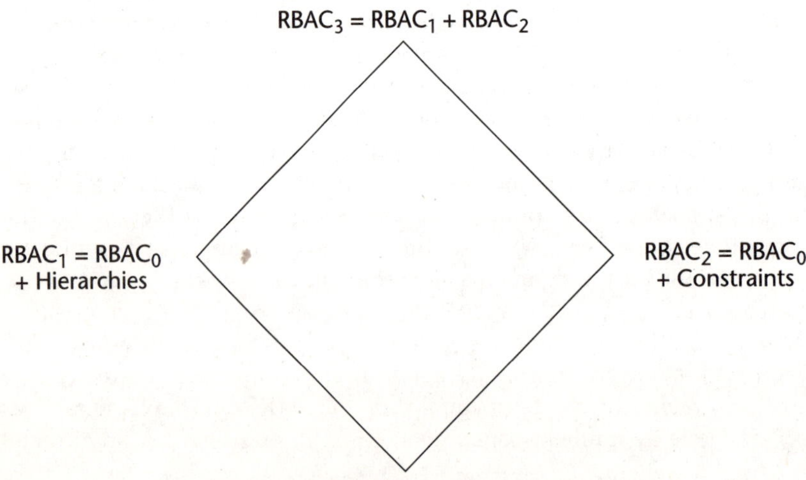

Figure 11.1 Relationships among RBAC models.

DAC AND MAC IN A NUTSHELL

There are several widely accepted access control models. Besides RBAC, two others are owner-based discretionary access control (DAC) (NCSC 1987) and lattice-based mandatory access control (MAC) (Bell and LaPadula 1975). Brief explanations of each are as follows.

The main premise of DAC is that individual users are owners of resources, and because of this they have complete discretion over who should be granted what access permissions for their resources. This is why DAC is often referred to as owner-based. In order for a user to access a resource, its owner should explicitly permit access to the resource by that user. Usually, DAC policies are implemented in the form of access control lists (ACLs), whereby each resource has an ACL administered by its owner. Because discretionary models are so generic and flexible, they easily suit access control requirements for any system. However, if the number of resources is large, then DAC administration becomes too expensive and burdensome for the resource owners. Another problem with the DAC model is that it's almost impossible to enforce consistent policies and determine what access is granted to a user. To do either of these tasks, you have to go through all the resources and analyze their ACLs.

In MAC, each user and resource is assigned a security level (for example, "confidential," "secret," or "top secret"). Security levels are usually partially ordered, thereby creating a "lattice." For instance, "secret" is higher than "confidential" and lower than "top secret." The sensitivity of the resource is reflected in its security level. The security level of a user, sometimes called "clearance," reflects the user's trustworthiness not to disclose sensitive information to users not cleared to have it. In MAC-based systems, a user is usually allowed to read only those resources that have the same security level as the user, or lower. For example, a "secret" cleared user can read "confidential" and "secret" information, but not "top secret" information. In addition, a user may write into a resource if the resource's security level is the same or higher than the security level of the user. Thus, the information can only "flow up" from lower levels to higher levels. This model is better at ensuring the consistency of organizational policies than owner-based DAC, as long as the security levels are assigned properly to the resources and users. However, it is not flexible and thus not very supportive of dynamic business workflow. Also, it's only concerned with information flow, which does not make it very suitable for service-based systems, such as today's businesses, in which services as well as information have to be protected.

According to the RBAC family of models, each login session is a mapping of one user to possibly many roles. When a user establishes a session by logging into the system and authenticating, the user selects what subset of roles assigned to the user by the user's administrator(s) should be activated for the duration of the session. The ability of a user in an ideal RBAC system to activate a subset of assigned roles is another feature that differentiates the concepts of roles and groups. The permissions available to the user are the union of permissions from all roles activated in that session. To enable data abstraction, RBAC treats permissions as uninterpreted symbols because their semantics are dependent on the implementation and system.

In the following subsections, we walk you through all four RBAC models and describe them.

$RBAC_0$: Just Roles

A system implementing the $RBAC_0$ model can be described using the following simple and ordinary elements (illustrated in Figure 11.2):

- Sets of users, roles, permissions, and sessions as described in the previous section
- Assignment of permissions to roles, a process that you can picture as a table with rows representing roles, columns representing permissions, and cells marked if the corresponding permission is assigned to the corresponding role, and unmarked otherwise
- Assignment of users to roles, which you can picture as a table with rows representing roles, columns representing users, and cells marked if the corresponding user is assigned to the corresponding role, and unmarked otherwise
- A way of determining which user runs a given session (this is abstracted in RBAC using the hypothetical function *user*(*s*), which receives the session ID as an argument and returns the user ID)
- A way of mapping a given session into a set of roles (this is abstracted in RBAC using the hypothetical function *roles*(*s*), which receives the session ID as an argument and returns a set of roles activated for that session)

That's it. The basic model is rather straightforward and is based on simple and natural concepts that we use in security every day: users, roles, sessions, and permissions.

When security professionals talk about roles, they often mention role hierarchies, which is exactly what $RBAC_1$ defines. Let's look at $RBAC_1$.

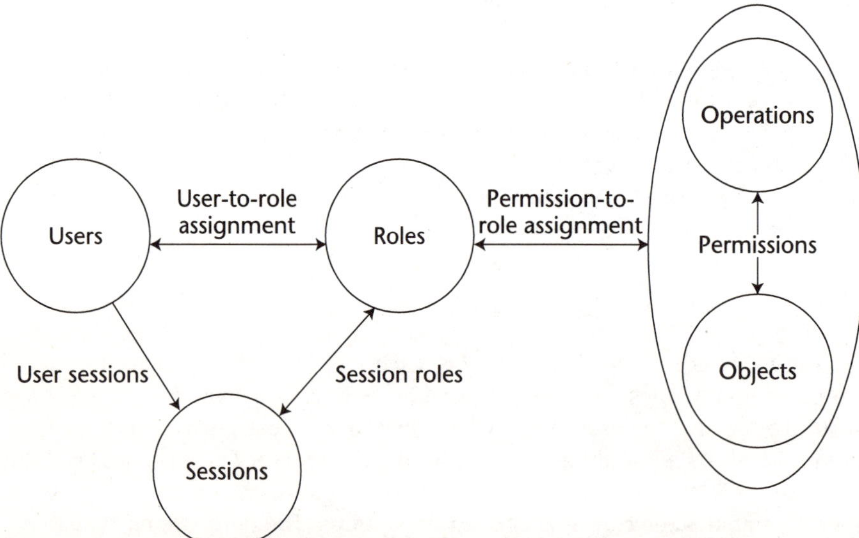

Figure 11.2 $RBAC_0$ model.

$RBAC_1$: Role Hierarchies

$RBAC_1$ is actually $RBAC_0$ with role hierarchies, shown in Figure 11.3, which is as powerful a concept as inheritance in object-oriented (OO) systems. We will explain why.

After working with roles for a while, you will find, if you haven't already, that some roles share responsibilities and privileges. By this, we mean that users assigned to different roles often need to perform the same operations. Moreover, a number of general operations within your company are usually performed by all employees. For example, in the case of eBusiness, everybody can look up all products and create a customer object, and staff members can do everything customers and members can, except settle orders and accounts. Consequently, you can improve the efficiency and provide for the natural structure of the company by utilizing the concept of role hierarchies defined in $RBAC_1$. A role hierarchy defines roles that have unique attributes and may be senior to other roles—that is, one role may be implicitly associated with the permissions that are associated with another "junior" role. If used appropriately, role hierarchies are a natural way of organizing roles to reflect authority, responsibility, and competency.

An example of a role hierarchy is shown in Figure 11.4. As you can see, the role "customer" is senior to the role "visitor." This means that members of the role "customer" are implicitly granted the permissions of the role "visitor" without the administrator having to explicitly assign all the permissions of visitors to customers. The more powerful roles are at the top of the diagram, and the less powerful roles are at the bottom. The roles at the top of the diagram are associated with the greatest number of permissions.

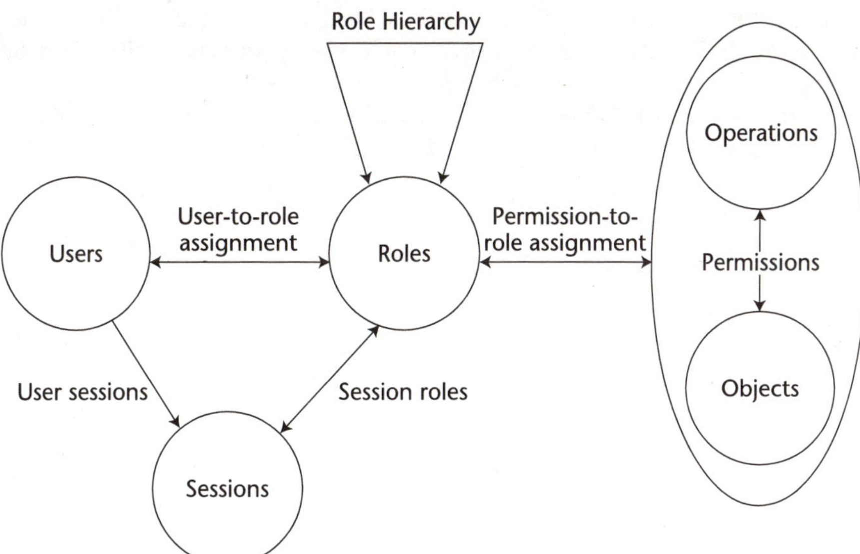

Figure 11.3 $RBAC_1$ model.

(Ferraiolo et al. 2001) © 2001 ACM, Inc. Reprinted by permission.

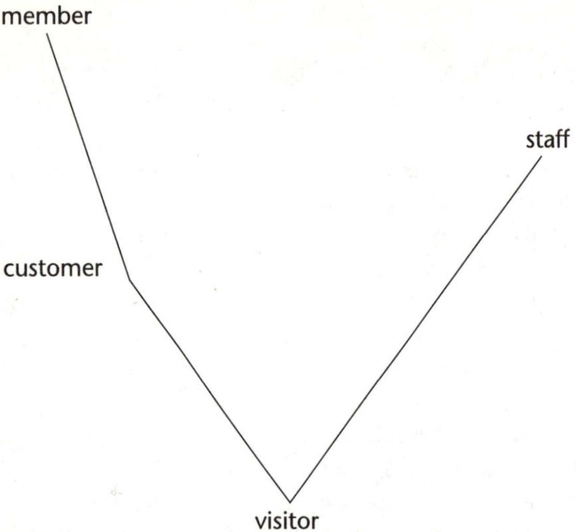

Figure 11.4 Role hierarchy for the eBusiness example.

If your security environment supports $RBAC_1$, you can reuse assignment of permissions to roles so that senior roles inherit permissions assigned to junior roles. Keep in mind that assignment of a user to a role allows the user to activate the role and all the roles junior to that role. For example, because we made the "member" role senior to "customer," a member can choose (if the technology is capable of supporting this feature) to have a "customer session." This is how RBAC supports the *principle of least privilege*. A better illustration of the principle would be a system administrator who activates the administrative role only when performing tasks that require administrative privileges, and performs other tasks as a regular user. The requirement to support the principle of least privilege is not always obvious, and you will run into situations where products do not implement such a feature. However, for some Web Service systems it could be a necessity.

$RBAC_2$: Constraints

Constraints in RBAC are predicates that apply to user-to-role and permission-to-role relations as well as to the hypothetical functions *user()* and *roles()*. They enable an implementation of the *separation of duties* principle, which requires that for particular sets of transactions, no single individual be allowed to execute all transactions within the set. A good example of separation of duties in the case of eBusiness is prohibiting staff members from settling orders (performing checkout, which pays for an order) for customers and members. Because staff can add products to orders for customers and members, they could potentially abuse their rights by shipping unwanted products to customers and members, and then charging their credit cards. To protect customers from such situations, eBusiness's security system enforces a constraint on the user-to-role relation that prohibits the assignment of staff members to the role "customer" or "member."

There are two types of separation of duties: static separation of duties (SSD) and dynamic separation of duties (DSD). An example of a SSD constraint was provided in the preceding paragraph. DSD relaxes some of the limitations of SSD. For example, with DSD, a user can be assigned to both "administrator" and "auditor" roles. These are, by nature, conflicting roles, because auditors inspect the work of administrators; however, only one role can be activated in each session. Thus, the user can act either as an administrator or an auditor, but not as both. RBAC2 enables SSD and DSD via constraints on various relations and functions.

Constraints on user-to-role relations are enforced by an implementation of user administration tools. Constraints on the functions *user()* and *roles()* are the responsibility of authentication environments. This is done when you want to make sure that your user attribute assignment policies help to enforce constraints that control which roles can be activated concurrently or how many users can activate a particular role at the same time (that is, role activation cardinality). Constraints on privilege-to-role relations are enforced by an implementation of security administration tools.

Before configuring your Web Service security to support $RBAC_2$, you'll need to make sure that the underlying platform:

- Implements $RBAC_0$
- Supports the enforcement of constraints on user-to-role relations by user administration tools
- Enforces user attribute assignment policies with the support of constraints on the functions *user()* and *roles()*
- Enables the enforcement of constraints on privilege-to-role relations by security administration tools

$RBAC_3$: $RBAC_1$ + $RBAC_2$

Illustrated in Figure 11.5, $RBAC_3$ is a combination of $RBAC_1$ and $RBAC_2$ as well as any additional constraints on the role hierarchy. For an implementation of a Web Service security technology to support $RBAC_3$, it should:

- Implement $RBAC_1$
- Implement $RBAC_2$
- Implement possible additional constraints on the role hierarchy

We've already discussed the requirements for the support of $RBAC_1$ and $RBAC_2$ by a Web Service security implementation. The implementation of additional static constraints on the role hierarchy is done by user administration tools. For dynamic constraints, in addition to the administration tools, supporting functionality is required in the authentication mechanisms.

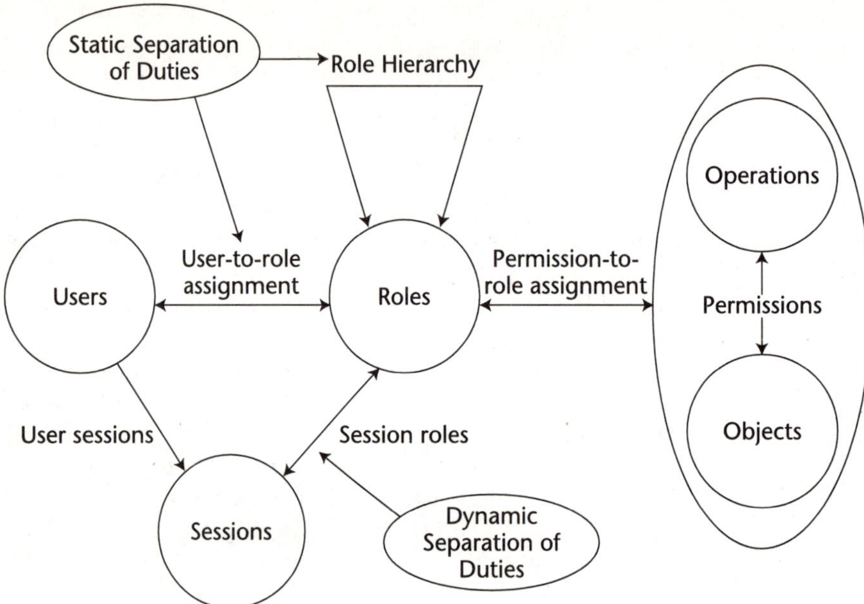

Figure 11.5 RBAC$_3$ model.
(Ferraiolo 2001) © 2001 ACM, Inc. Reprinted by permission.

Engineering Roles

If you decide to use RBAC, one of the major challenges related to security administration will be determining what roles to create, and which permissions and users to assign to which roles. The problem's intricacy is twofold. First, there are many choices for defining roles, and it may not be clear which will be the best for you. The obvious choice is to follow organizational structure. However, one could also base roles on responsibilities, competency, or workflow functions. Second, there is a risk of omitting some permissions so that no role will have them, or misassigning permissions so that the wrong roles will have them. How do you make sure that your roles are complete and that the right permissions are assigned? How do you avoid unnecessary proliferation of roles?

The problem is not yet well understood, and there is no solution that would let you engineer roles and permissions in a provably complete and optimal way. However, there are some suggested methods, and we will describe one recently developed by Epstein and Sandhu (Epstein 2001).

The cornerstone of their method is the introduction of three more abstraction layers between roles and permissions, to help identify which permissions should be assigned to which roles.

- *Job* is a type of work that a single role can perform. A role can perform more than one job. An example could be the role of a procurement clerk who performs jobs of ordering items and reporting purchasing statistics to management.
- All activities necessary to perform a job are grouped into a *workpattern*. Many jobs can map to the same workpattern, but we can only have one workpattern mapped to a job. Each workpattern is composed of a set of steps required by a single role to complete the work of the job. Let's go back to our example of a procurement clerk role. For the sake of simplicity, the ordering job has a workpattern that requires the steps of collecting orders from different departments over email, ordering items, notifying requestors over email of the received items, and distributing items to the corresponding departments. The reporting job has a workpattern that requires the steps of compiling statistics about requested, ordered, and received items and sending them to the manager via email.
- Each step of the workpattern is assigned to a *task*. In our example, the workpattern associated with the ordering job has the following tasks: collecting, ordering, emailing, and distributing. The reporting job workpattern consists of compiling and emailing. Notice that both workpatterns have the task of emailing, which can be consolidated into one task, provided that the permissions needed for emailing notifications and statistics are the same.

Once tasks are mapped to permissions, the whole picture for our example would look like the one in Figure 11.6. The important question that we did not answer so far is how to apply this method with three additional layers to engineer role-permission relationships. In other words, how do we come up with such a picture? There is no definitive answer yet, although Epstein and Sandhu acknowledge that whatever approach is taken, it falls into one of two categories: top-down (decomposition) or bottom-up (aggregation). For decomposition approaches, roles are defined first, and then the jobs with the corresponding workpatterns are identified by analyzing attributes, properties, and other characteristics of the roles. Then, each workpattern is analyzed to identify necessary tasks, and finally each task is decomposed into permissions. The aggregation approach requires the grouping of permissions, according to some type of organization, into larger sets that will be assigned to tasks, workpatterns, jobs, and eventually roles.

No matter which approach is employed, defining the specific criteria applied to the analysis will increase your productivity in the engineering of the layers. For example, you can use the following criteria:

- *Role Attributes* based on skill sets, business position description, branch location, and experience
- *Application Attributes* based on functionality, manageability, business domain, and interoperability
- *Permission Attributes* based on platform, technology, access type, application type, and capabilities

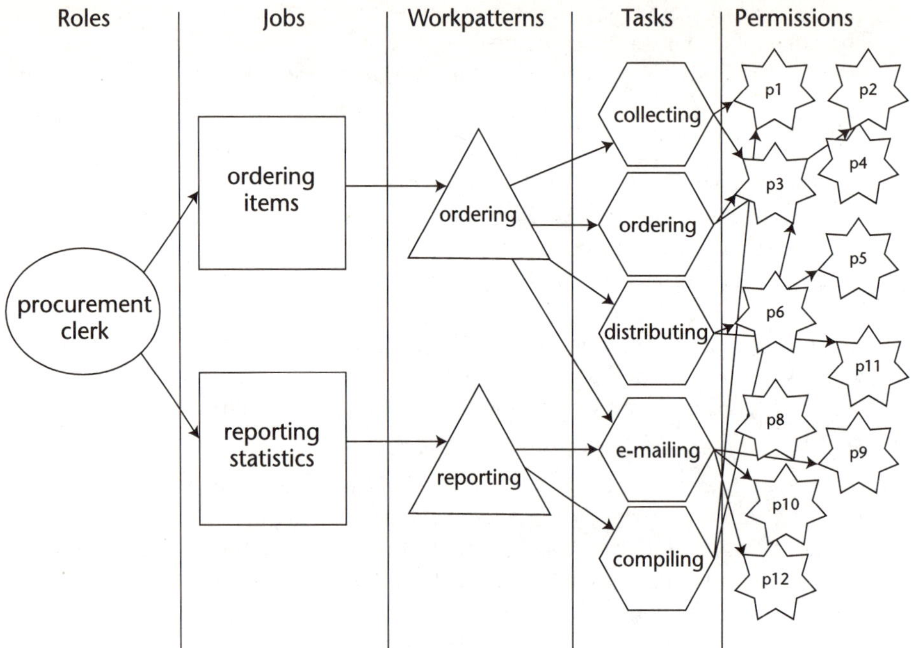

Figure 11.6 Role-permission mapping via jobs, workpatterns, and tasks.

While determining role responsibilities, you will eventually find that some roles are well defined and their responsibilities are documented, other roles are defined but documented poorly or not at all, and yet other roles and their responsibilities are neither defined nor documented. You will need to fill the gaps as part of the role-permission engineering process. While doing the analysis of the role responsibilities, you will identify related responsibilities and group them into jobs. Similar engineering at the layer of workpatterns and tasks should be done.

It is important to achieve a number of objectives in the engineering of role-permission relationships. First, try to minimize the number of elements used in role-permission assignments. Ideally, each element should be unique and, therefore, no set should contain duplicate entries. When you finish mapping the layers to permissions, you want to check if the layered elements map to the same set of permissions. If two elements are equivalent, then they will grant the same accesses to the functions of the application, and there may be no benefit to having both these elements that map to the same set of permissions. As a result, you might want to delete one element if you can reuse the other. For example, tasks *compiling* and *collecting* in Figure 11.6 map to the same permissions, *p1* and *p3*. For the sake of minimizing the number of elements in the mapping, these two tasks can be collapsed into one.

Once you complete the mapping, check also for its completeness by making sure that each role maps to at least one permission, and vice versa. The example in Figure 11.6 is incomplete because permission p8 is not mapped to any role, which means that under no circumstances will any role ever be granted this permission.

To summarize the objectives of engineering elements for each layer, you want to:

- *Reuse* elements previously defined at the same layer
- *Minimize* the number of elements by determining equivalent elements and striving to eliminate them
- Perform all the necessary work to ensure that there is a *complete* mapping of elements between layers

Engineering roles and role-permission assignments can be a daunting task, and security officers of large organizations spend months doing it. This section gave you a quick introduction and described one of the known approaches to start with. Once you take the first steps, you will discover your own techniques, which will fit the needs and peculiarities of your organization and the application domain of Web Services for which you need to administer.

RBAC Gotchas

Although we highly recommend using RBAC models in the security administration of your enterprise Web Services, we want you to recognize the limitations of RBAC (the model and its current implementations) and the difficulties accompanying it. RBAC is not a panacea. It won't solve all your security administration problems, and in some cases it could simply be the wrong approach. Just because the security mechanisms of the middleware platform underlying a Web Service support role-based security, it doesn't follow that it will necessarily fulfill your policy and management requirements.

As you can see from the previous section, engineering roles and identifying role-permission relationships is not a simple task. There is no definitive and comprehensive algorithmic approach for accomplishing it. This is why the Giga Group reports, in Penn (2002), that "many organizations struggle with the role definition process." It is also very easy to get on a slippery slope that will lead to role proliferation. Users have multiple roles to begin with, so you may end up with too many roles significantly increasing the administration overhead because each role's membership and permissions have to be managed. The more roles you have, the less effective your security administration is. On the other hand, having too few roles leads to granting unnecessary permissions to users and, as a result, violating the principle of least privilege. You will need to find your own middle ground, which will depend on the results of risk analysis for your particular system.

Also, administrators tend to define many roles solely to deal with exceptions to general policies, for which a rules-based approach would be more appropriate. RBAC has a tendency to be abused by many who attempt to express all the policies using roles, even when other attributes (group, certification, age, and so on) in combination with rules-based authorization could be more effective and more intuitive. A popular example is the role "18-years-or-older" in a public library that has to keep sexually explicit content from minors. With such a role, the library administrator has to assign it daily, to every registered patron who has just turned 18. Unless dynamic assignment to roles is implemented, a better way of granting authorizations would be via a rule that compares the user's date of birth with the current date.

Another problem with RBAC is due to its implementations in today's systems. Many role-based systems require the creation of static and manually maintained role attributes. As a person's responsibilities change and become reflected in other attributes, the role should change as well and retain consistency with the policy. As a consequence, each role becomes yet another item requiring administrative maintenance. A better way to go would be insertion of another indirection layer that would dynamically derive user roles from other attributes maintained by human resources or existing workflow systems. A quintessential example of such an approach is the architecture for the Resource Access Decision (RAD) authorization service (OMG 2001, Beznosov 1999), which allows some attributes of the requestor to be computed dynamically, depending on which resource is to be accessed. It has been shown (Barkley 1999) that RAD enables dynamic generation of resource-centric roles (for example, attending physician) in the context of a request regarding a particular resource (for example, the medical record of a specific patient).

Concluding Remarks on RBAC

Understanding available access control mechanisms is critical for protecting your Web Services applications. In the previous sections, we explained RBAC models and showed what functionality needs to be implemented in order to support RBAC. We also illustrated the discussion with examples for eBusiness.

As we've explained, for Web Services security mechanisms to support all four RBAC models, the authentication services need to support (and authentication policies have to express) roles and their hierarchies ($RBAC_1$). To support constraints ($RBAC_2$), the authentication infrastructure, backed by user attribute assignment policies, has to enforce them. You also need tools to administer user-to-role and role-to-permissions assignments with the necessary constraints imposed.

This section provided you with a framework for assessing implementations of RBAC models by Web Services security products. The framework described provides directions for Web Services security developers to realize RBAC in their systems, and also provides criteria for selecting implementations that support models from the RBAC families.

In the section on RBAC gotchas, we explained the limitations of the model and its popular implementations. In conclusion, we support the Giga Group's recommendations (Penn 2002) in regards to selecting a role-based security mechanism or system:

- It must at least support role hierarchies ($RBAC_1$).
- It must allow for a role to be dynamically determined according to other attributes associated with an identity rather than relying solely on a static user-to-role assignment.
- It must go beyond simple permission-to-role assignment and support rules for expressing access control policies that use other attributes of users, and, more importantly, to handle the exceptions to broad policies more efficiently.
- It must be integrated with the organizational workflow process for managing change as users move from role to role: determining deltas between two states and reconciling differences without having to hard-code the logic for each possible combination of changes.

To learn more about RBAC, go to:

- The RBAC Web site at the National Institute of Standards and Technology (NIST) at http://csrc.nist.gov/rbac/, where the concept originated. The site contains many very useful links on models, design, and implementations.
- The Laboratory for Information Security Technology Web site at http://www.list.gmu.edu, which is actively improving the model.
- The Association for Computing Machinery (ACM) Web site at http://www.acm.org/pubs/contents/proceedings/series/rbac, which contains the proceedings on the RBAC workshop, which is now renamed to Symposium on Access Control Models and Technologies (SACMAT).

Delegation

Described in detail in Chapter 7, delegation is a difficult and capricious beast to handle, not only in terms of its implementation, but also in its administration. Your policies on credentials delegation, which determine when and what delegation to use, should play in concert with other policies that support the task of access control. As a case in point, we use delegation in the example described in Chapter 8, "Securing .NET Web Services," where the ASP.NET Web Service offloads the tasks of access control and auditing to the more capable COM+-based middle tier, by means of simple unconstrained delegation (a.k.a. impersonation).

When and How to Use Delegation

On one hand, delegation can be harmful to your system's security. On the other hand, in almost all complex systems, delegation is either needed or very difficult to replace with an alternate solution. In the rest of this section, we give you our recommendations in regard to using delegation in your Web Services applications, so that you will know what should be taken into consideration when you deploy and configure your Web Services security solution.

Delegation is an important issue to consider when building distributed applications. Although using delegation is tempting to many developers, we recommend avoiding the use of delegation except for auditing or for simple proxy cases, such as the one in the Chapter 8 example.

General Recommendations

As a general rule, delegation is dangerous because it may cause a single point of security failure. If an intermediate Web Service that is permitted to use delegated credentials has been compromised, an attacker can abuse that trust and potentially cause serious system damage. Impersonation is the most dangerous form of delegation, and we recommend avoiding it whenever possible. Constrained delegation is much safer because the number of trusted intermediates is limited. However, even that form of delegation can be abused and should be avoided whenever possible.

For the best security, we recommend that each intermediate Web Service should perform authentication and have its own credentials statically assigned, rather than using delegated credentials. An intermediate should be set up with sufficient privileges to access resources on behalf of any of its potential clients. For example, if the intermediate is accessing a database, the intermediate's credentials must be sufficient to access any client's database entry.

As a result of this approach, the first intermediate component, which is the only one that will have the original client's credentials, will need to enforce the required authorization and audit policies for that client. Without delegation, later Web Services in the call chain will not have access to the client's credentials and so will not be able to make security decisions based on the client's attributes. All components in the call chain should be properly authenticated in a pair-wise fashion to preserve end-to-end security along the entire invocation chain.

Avoiding delegation minimizes the number of required back-end user accounts, because each intermediate Web Service only uses a single identity for authorization to required resources. Thus, a significant additional benefit of avoiding delegation is the reduction of the duplicate back-end user accounts that mirror the perimeter-tier user identities.

Delegation can be used with acceptable risk for intermediates that are simple proxies, such as load balancers. In these limited cases, the proxy usually needs to be a small and highly efficient intermediary that does not contain the logic needed to enforce access control and audit policies. The proxy should pass along the unaltered client credentials to a subsequent intermediate for authorization checks.

Risks of Delegation

To enable delegation within Web Services without compromising the security integrity of the system, the intermediary receiving delegated credentials must be able to trust that the received credentials are authentic—otherwise an attacker could impersonate a trusted principal. Be sure to check whether your security underlying the Web Service not only supports delegation but also provides constraints on transmission of credential tokens, to prevent impersonation abuse. If delegation constraints are not in place, all application components must implicitly trust each other to use delegated credentials safely. For small collections of components within corporate network boundaries, this assumption may be reasonable. However, as the number of components grows, particularly as you start deploying Web Services for inter-enterprise applications, trusting all applications, including those of other organizations, becomes too risky.

If your company adopts Web Service security technologies that support constrained delegation, delegation can be used safely. Without this support, we recommend that you avoid using delegation. Furthermore, delegation of security credentials to systems outside of your enterprise is particularly dangerous and is never advisable, even if delegation constraints exist.

So far we have discussed how access control, user attribute assignment, and delegation policies should be administered in concert for your Web Services. As we explained at the beginning of this chapter, access control by itself is insufficient for protecting a system. No matter which access control model you choose, how granular you make the permissions, how diligent the army of the security administrators, it's not possible to make the access policy 100 percent correct. It appears feasible in theory or with small systems, but it is just impossible in real life. You need to use several security mechanisms to avoid being vulnerable to potential policy errors. Following access control, security audit is the next important aid.

Audit Administration

Security audit is generally considered a supplement to access control mechanisms, for those cases when access policies (or their enforcement) are not strict enough to make users accountable, thus allowing unauthorized access. With Web Services, you will often find it necessary to balance between (1) making your Web Service implementations security-aware and processing an overwhelming amount of audit data, and (2) resorting to other potentially unsafe techniques, such as delegation. This necessity is due to the coarse granularity of the service-oriented interfaces provided by Web Services. Unlike most middleware technologies, which enable fine-grained object-oriented computing, Web Services tend to have the same entry point for accessing resources with different access requirements. For instance, the Web Service of the eBusiness system has a *ShoppingCartService*, which supports methods for manipulating all shopping carts. Among the three ways to provide adequate security for shopping carts, thorough security auditing of accesses to shopping carts is one.[1]

Because of the supplementary nature of security audit and the risk of generating too much data, audit policies should be carefully tuned to strike the right balance. For example, since *ShoppingCartService* in eBusiness is vulnerable to attacks when customers read or modify the content of shopping carts owned by others, security audit of invocations on behalf of the *ShoppingCartService's* methods is necessary. It's often a challenging task, due to the limited capabilities of the audit mechanisms. In the ASP.NET implementation of eBusiness, file and URL are the only levels of audit granularity provided out of the box, which gives the security administrators two choices—to audit all of the requests on the eBusiness Web Service, or none of them. The other options are to program explicit audit in those methods, which is prone to all the problems of security-aware business logic, or to implement a special-purpose HTTP module to intercept requests and perform fine-grained security audit.

Audit decision mechanisms and security audit policies are similar to their access control counterparts. They face the same scalability, granularity, and expressiveness goals and can reuse solutions from the domain of access control, including the concept of roles and their hierarchies.

Authentication Administration

Authentication policies determine which authentication protocols should be used for what cases. For example, internal clients of a Web Service might be required to authenticate with Kerberos, and external users might have to utilize Microsoft Passport. Depending on the security requirements, factors other than client location might have

[1] The other two are making the Web Service security-aware and programming it to enforce fine-grained access control policies, or employing delegation so that the more capable middle tier could translate requests to separate protected objects, each representing a shopping cart.

to be taken into account. Such factors could be time of access (stronger authentication between 5:00 P.M. and 8:00 A.M.) or the sensitivity of the information accessed via a Web Service (patient's HIV data versus name). Again, the role the user wants to activate (regular "user" or "system administrator") is another example of a factor that could influence a decision on what authentication is required.

Depending on the security risks that your company faces, requirements for authentication policy granularity, scalability, and expressiveness will be different. Start with very basic policies and mechanisms (maybe just username and password), but make sure that your Web Services security is extensible to support advanced authentication policies.

How Rich Does Security Policy Need to Be?

Do you really need all the flexibility that the various security technologies permit? That depends on where you are in modeling your security. When you are first designing the security for your organization, we strongly urge you to keep it simple. Don't use all the power that the security mechanisms offer you. There is also a good chance that you will be using a number of different distributed technologies. The architecture can very quickly become so complicated that you will have a very difficult time assessing the security effects as a transaction ripples through your system.

In your first pass at your security architecture, determine whether a simple authorization model is sufficient for your needs. If you determine that some areas need more granularity, then plan to bridge into one of the more complex authorization languages.

When there is an existing distributed system, study the architecture to define areas where security administration is giving you trouble, and determine if you need more or less granularity or scale. Where you determine that the granularity is insufficient, redo parts of the system to use a more powerful (albeit more complex) security mechanism for the job. If there is a part of the system that uses simple access control policy and has become a security administration bottleneck, think about substituting it with a RBAC model. For example, you might have started out with all of your policies in one domain and now want to model your organizational structure with a hierarchy of domains, to better enforce your corporate security policy.

Conversely, if there is a part of the system in which the business logic is changed frequently, think about substituting a simpler model—for example, an ACL model designed to explicitly use authorization based on identity name, groups, and resources.

When examining your architecture, determine which resources you are trying to protect and who needs access. This means that you will need to have a thorough knowledge of your system and of what the various applications are designed to accomplish. Only when you have this complete understanding can you make judgments about the balance between simple and complex access control models. Obviously, security is not the only criterion, but it is an important part of the picture. Too little security, and you put your resources at risk; too much security, and you can create unnecessary performance penalties as well as make the system high-maintenance. Another of our mantras bears repeating: security is risk management.

Administering Data Protection

Data protection can be implemented in the simple point-to-point (also referred to as connection-oriented) way or in the more powerful (but at the same time a great deal more complex) end-to-end message-oriented fashion. If you find point-to-point protection of the data traveling between your Web Services sufficient, then you are in the safe zone. Most distributed computing technologies implement point-to-point protection of communication channels. For example, a secure channel protocol such as SSL is a commodity nowadays. IPSEC is gaining more acceptance in the world of VPNs and is moving to network endpoints. To administer some products for the protection of communication channels, it is only necessary to select acceptable, preferred, and default cryptographic mechanisms and their parameters. In COM+ and CORBA, even those choices are hidden from the security administrators, who can select only whether data integrity and/or confidentiality are subject to protection.[2] It's not that simple with end-to-end data protection.

If the flow of your Web Service transactions is such that (1) a protected message may be passed to several parties, and each may affect the message content, and/or (2) portions of the message are meant for one recipient but not for another, then you are stepping into the treacherous zone of end-to-end data protection. As we described in Chapter 6, "Principles of Securing Web Services," XML Encryption and XML Signature—whose use for SOAP is specified by the WS-Security language (Atkinson 2002)—work together to provide end-to-end data protection.

The advantages of XML Encryption and Signature are that portions of a SOAP message can be encrypted and signed. The encrypted portions of the message may or may not overlap with those signed. This means, for example, that a message containing an offer to sell some product can include encrypted payment instructions that should be hidden from the potential buyer. At the same time, the entire message can be signed so that the buyer can verify the seller's signature on the offer. Although WS-Security specifies some rules to lower the risks of different intermediaries "stepping" on each other, there does not seem to be a well-defined algorithmic process of selectively encrypting and signing some parts of a message while passing it from one Web Service to another. Because products that implement WS-Security are very new, the industry has little experience in implementing Web Services based on this standard, and their administration is not yet well understood. Data protection solutions based on WS-Security should be treated with caution, and we advise restricting their deployment until production quality implementations are available.

The other accepted methods for end-to-end data protection are CMS or S/MIME. Although not designed for XML, they protect text-based information on the entire message. This might be adequate for protecting data authenticity and integrity by signing messages, but not for confidentiality protection, because each intermediary would have to decrypt the whole message before it could do any processing—a technique no better than readily available point-to-point protection. Administration of CMS and S/MIME is generally reduced to the administration of the infrastructure needed for retrieval and management of the keys for signing/verifying and encrypting/decrypting SOAP messages.

[2] CORBA, as was explained in Chapter 7, allows the specification of some other protection capabilities, such as authenticity and replay detection.

Overall, the techniques for data protection in Web Services fall either in the group of easy to administer (all point-to-point solutions as well as CMS and S/MIME) or complex to administer (XML-aware protections such as WS-Security profile of XML Encryption and Signature for SOAP). At the same time, there are no generally accepted models of administration for both groups, unlike access control administration, and you will find different paradigms in different products.

Making Web Services Development and Security Administration Play Well Together

All the actors in the big picture have to play well together—the security policies to be enforced, the security decision and enforcement mechanisms to be used, and the Web Services interfaces, as well as the mid-tier systems to which Web Services provide access. To create a secure, usable, and efficient system, you need to get rid of the illusion that you can develop Web Services, mid-tier systems, security mechanisms, and the policies without keeping in mind each component's capabilities. With today's state of the technologies, you will need to strike a compromise for any distributed system, and particularly for a secure Web Service.

Let's take access control as an illustration. Fine-grained policies require either low-level interfaces, a security-aware application, or a mid-tier implementation of fine-grained access control. Each of the options has drawbacks that might outweigh the benefits. In our example with the eBusiness *ShoppingCartService* that provides access to shopping carts, if the access policy requires that only the user who created a shopping cart can view and change it, and only staff can view it, there are the following options for implementation:

- Design the Web Service so that each instance of a shopping cart is handled by a separate instance of *ShoppingCartService*. This is possible theoretically by creating on the fly a separate endpoint for each shopping cart, but it is usually impractical with the current state of Web Services technologies.
- Implement an access control interceptor (in the form of an HTTP module in ASP.NET, for example) that would inspect the cart identification key parameter, look up the owner of the cart by the key, and compare it with the identity of the requestor. This is more realistic than the previous method. However, since shopping carts live short periods and can be created/deleted often, such access control logic could become very difficult to implement efficiently.
- Make the implementation of *ShoppingCartService* security-aware and let it enforce the decisions (preferably made by an authorization server). Somewhat less complex than the previous option, because it avoids parsing SOAP requests, this approach necessitates programming of the enforcement logic in all the methods that deal with shopping carts, which dramatically increases the system maintenance cost in the long run. This choice is also prone to obvious errors (such as forgetting to code the enforcement logic) by business programmers, leading to security holes.

- Since the mid-tier system, which implements most of the business logic accessed via a Web Service, could support (as in the case of the COM+-based example described in Chapter 7) each shopping cart represented by a separate object, it is possible to avoid most drawbacks of the previous options by enforcing fine-grained access control in the mid-tier. The solution would require adjustment of the access control settings on each shopping cart object, and delegation of the requestor's credentials from Web Service to the mid-tier.

As can be seen from the example, you need to align the security policies to be administered, the system design, and the security mechanisms, depending on what compromise is acceptable for the business requirements and security risks of your system. To this end, we recommend engineering business and security requirements for your Web Service system at the same time. If you also evaluate the capabilities in terms of performance, performance scalability, security, and other "ilities" up front, your project will have an even better chance for success.

Why are general system requirements and design being discussed in a chapter on security administration? Administration, particularly for security, eventually becomes the major factor in the system's maintenance costs. The ease and effectiveness of the system security administration is determined by the risks analysis and the design decisions made during the course of the system specification and development. To make your system's security administration a success, architects need to think early in the development cycle about how security policies are going to be enforced and administered.

Summary

Although Web Services are new, the administration of Web Services security can profit from the security knowledge that has been accumulating for years. You can categorize the way Web Services are used as similar to the way you use any other middleware with RPC and document-oriented processing. When multiple (possibly mutually suspicious) middleware intermediaries cooperate in business processing of documents, then the security administration of middleware and Web Services will be very similar.

Security administration of Web Services functioning as middleware leverages the relatively rich experience, as well as the knowledge body, of engineering and administering middleware security. The main task, namely controlling access to the protected resources, is accomplished by access control and supporting mechanisms: authentication, credentials delegation, and user security attribute assignment. To engineer a system useful for real-life tasks, you also need to combine access control with security audit. The administration effectiveness of all of these mechanisms is determined by how well you are able to group protected resources, such as the Web Services and their data, to group the users and programs acting on behalf of the users, and to balance between the expressiveness of the security rules and the complexity of the resulting policies.

This chapter discussed one popular model successfully used for achieving scalability without significantly compromising granularity and expressiveness: role-based access control (RBAC). You've learned the four RBAC variations and the approach for engineering role-to-permission assignment for large organizations. Like any other technique, RBAC is not without limitations and drawbacks. While designing RBAC for your Web Services security mechanisms and their administration, you should be aware of problems your security administrators will face.

A very powerful, and at the same time complex, mechanism for composing secure solutions from multiple systems is credentials delegation. As a general rule, delegation is dangerous because it may cause a single point of security failure. Impersonation is the most dangerous form of delegation, and we recommend avoiding it whenever possible. Constrained delegation is much safer because the number of trusted intermediates is limited. However, even that form of delegation can be abused and should be used only when absolutely necessary. Furthermore, delegation of security credentials to systems that are outside of your enterprise is particularly dangerous and is never advisable, even if delegation constraints exist.

Administration of point-to-point connection-oriented data protection is relatively simple, since key management and cryptographic mechanism selections are the bulk of its complexity. Administering end-to-end message-oriented data protection and access control of SOAP messages is much more challenging. These challenges are due to (1) the multitude of possible choices, (2) the lack of mature products implementing the new WS-Security and SAML specifications, and (3) insufficient experience in the technology among vendors and end users. Therefore, we recommend caution when using WS-Security and SAML implementations, until the industry in general and your organization in particular develop enough knowledge to tackle administration of security in SOAP messages.

To make Web Service development and security administration play well together, you need to align the security policies to be administered, the system design, and the security mechanisms. The alignment depends on what risk is acceptable, as driven by the business requirements for your system. To this end, we recommend engineering business and security requirements for your Web Service system in parallel. If you also evaluate the capabilities in terms of performance, performance scalability, security, and other "ilities" up front, your project will have even better chances for success. In our final chapter, we will bring these system issues together with security and discuss how to plan and build a secure Web Services architecture.

CHAPTER

12

Planning and Building a Secure Web Services Architecture

This book has taken you through many aspects of building secure Web Services applications. In Chapter 1, "Overview of Web Services Security," we first gave you an introduction to Web Services security issues and explained the need to unify Web Services security technologies. Chapter 2, "Web Services," provided an overview of Web Services, and Chapter 3, "Getting Started with Web Services Security," got you started with the fundamentals of security as they apply to Web Services. We then moved into the details of the technology, describing XML security in Chapter 4, "XML Security and WS-Security," the Security Assertion Markup Language (SAML) in Chapter 5, "Security Assertion Markup Language," the principles of Web Services security in Chapter 6, "Principles of Securing Web Services," and the security of middleware infrastructures that support Web Services in Chapter 7, "Security of Infrastructures for Web Services." Based on this background, we went through examples describing how you can create secure Web Services, both for .NET and Java environments in Chapters 8, "Securing .NET Web Services," and 9, "Securing Java Web Services." We covered more advanced topics on interoperability of Web Services security in Chapter 10, "Interoperability of Web Services Security Technologies," and administration of Web Services security in Chapter 11, "Administrative Considerations for Web Services Security."

We've given you a lot of information about many different technologies, and we know that with so many pieces for you to put together, it's not easy to know where to start. Our final chapter will hopefully make your job easier by looking at the big picture of defining an integrated Web Services security architecture. First, we summarize the challenges of Web Services security that we've examined in this book. We take a step back from the detailed analysis of technologies needed to create secure Web Service applications and look at the general principles for integrating security applications. Based on these principles, we then discuss how to deploy Web Services applications in the context of planning a security architecture. We describe how Web Services security relates to other security technologies used in the perimeter, middle, and back-office tiers of the enterprise. In this context we go through each of the steps that are needed to achieve end-to-end Enterprise Application Security Integration (EASI) for Web Services. We use ePortal and eBusiness as our case study for applying EASI.

Web Services Security: The Challenges

We saw in Chapters 1 and 2 that Web Services have the potential to finally attain the elusive goal of e-business: application interoperability across lines of business and enterprises, regardless of the platform, application programming language, or operating system (OS). Cross-platform communication among businesses takes the original vision of electronic data interchange (EDI) to the next level. Web Services provide access to valuable business service opportunities that never existed before because the data was trapped in networks behind firewalls.

Web Services may have great potential, but they also have a huge problem: they are too open. Companies need to limit access to their valuable resources, whether they are patient records, credit card numbers, or manufacturing designs. Enterprises want to collaborate and share information, but not at the expense of giving away all of their assets. Companies need to keep their guard up and stay suspicious of whom they communicate with. They want to share just enough information, but not too much.

Security Must Be In Place

Before Web Services will be successful, security must be in place. Companies will never be willing to open up their internal corporate networks without the proper countermeasures. If companies don't take this approach, there are several "bad things" that can happen:

External Attacks. E-business applications exchange information that is highly valuable—this isn't about ordering a book from your browser at home. E-business is about companies exchanging thousands of patient records or trading stocks worth millions. For Internet-based Web Services, attacks on these systems can be mounted from any desktop machine in the world using very simple software tools.

Internal Attacks. We've known for years that presumed trustworthy insider employees perform most security violations. They might be setting a trap door so they can access corporate data after they leave the company. They might be committing fraud by creating fictitious customers to trade stocks or order manufactured goods.

What's So Tough About Security for Web Services?

Security architects have known about the vulnerabilities we've described for a long time. What makes Web Services different? Plenty:

- Web Services are designed to be open and interoperable. Since firewalls are set up to let HTTP traffic through, Web Service requests via HTTP pass through firewalls with ease, leaving the internal network exposed.
- Web Services are all about connecting chains of applications together. A Web Service client communicates to one application, which proxies (delegates) the request to others downstream. Security technologies based on PKI are point-to-point, which work great for client/server communication but are completely inadequate for securing chains of applications. Web Services require security technology that establishes trustworthy security associations in multitier environments.
- The different companies participating in Web Service transactions all use different security products and technologies that don't interoperate. This situation leaves companies with three options: turn off security (too risky), agree on a single security technology (too expensive), or translate and use a bridge between technologies (not always easy, but the best choice—more on this later).

What Is Security?

When moving from an application view to an architecture view, you first need to determine what security problem you are trying to solve. New system-level security requirements may surface that are not apparent when looking only at your Web Services application. Different systems vary their emphasis on security; some service providers believe that availability is most important for their systems, even if it's at the expense of data confidentiality. Others make data integrity the most critical requirement.

Your first course of action in planning an integrated security solution is to decide exactly what security means to you. Examining business-level drivers for security is the first step of this process. Once you know what your business needs are, you can then identify the security technologies that best meet your company's needs. We'll talk further about security requirements for ePortal and eBusiness in the *Determining Requirements* section of this chapter.

When developing a Web Services security architecture, you need to take more into account than just your own business needs. E-business applications commonly cut across many different companies or lines of business, forming security policy federations. E-commerce sites depend on outside services to check the validity of credit card purchases. Supply chain management requires sensitive manufacturing data to be shared among many participants. If you are developing Web Service applications that are deployed across many different companies, be prepared to work with each of the companies to define cross-company security agreements. Each company will need to maintain its own autonomy to manage and administer its own security. At the same time, they must also work under some constraints to share security data, such as SAML assertions and public key certificates. You should also be prepared for lawyers to be involved because serious liabilities accompany federated security agreements across companies.

In addition to identifying your security requirements, you also need to determine the level of *trustworthiness* needed in your system. That is, you need a sufficient level of confidence that your architecture is as secure as you want it to be. Checking that the applications in your system function as required is well understood—you perform component and integration testing until you are confident that the system behaves correctly. Security testing, however, is much more subtle.

Security is a negative property—when we say that a system is secure, we mean that the chance of something bad happening (that is, a security compromise) is very small. It is very difficult to show that nothing bad can happen in a system without performing exhaustive testing, which is impractical for all but the simplest systems. The difficulty of security testing has been demonstrated many times over the years. Programs such as Web browsers and operating systems may be widely used by millions of people without incident. Then one day, someone discovers a security flaw that was in the program all along. That program, which functioned normally and was previously perfectly acceptable, is now fatally flawed. In this case, functional testing may have been adequate although the program is clearly not trustworthy.

Building Trustworthy Systems

Traditionally, computer security has worked effectively in systems in which sensitive data could be isolated and protected in a central repository. Web Services promote the opposite philosophy by making distributed data widely accessible across large networks. Simply put, the more accessible data is, the harder it is to protect. Ordinarily, it's a good idea to keep your crown jewels locked up in a vault. Web Services encourage you to pass them around to all your friends for safekeeping.

The traditional notion of computer security is embodied in the concept of a trusted computing base (TCB). The TCB consists of the hardware and software mechanisms that are responsible for enforcing the security policy, which defines when a user may access a resource. The TCB must be:

- Tamper proof
- Always invoked (nonbypassable)
- Small enough to be thoroughly analyzed

The TCB is usually implemented within an OS or client/server environment that is under strict configuration control. This architecture permits very tight security because the TCB is the mediator through which all user accesses to resources must pass. Everything within the TCB is trusted to enforce the security policy; everything outside of the TCB is untrusted. Figure 12.1 illustrates a traditional TCB.

Web Services applications are built on distributed component middleware, such as COM+, EJB, and CORBA, which we described in Chapter 7. Distributed component systems have a more complex security architecture than the traditional TCB, as shown in Figure 12.2. Security functionality (the shaded areas of the diagram) in component systems is distributed throughout the architecture rather than residing in a central TCB. Because Web Services applications are heterogeneous, security may be implemented differently on different platforms. Security might be enforced by the application components, middleware, OS, hardware, or any combination thereof. Some platforms may contain a great deal of code that is trusted to enforce the security policy, whereas other platforms may have very little.

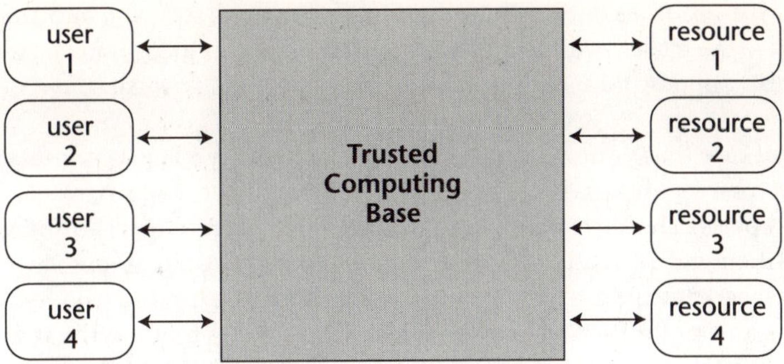

Figure 12.1 Traditional TCB.

Distributing security in this manner means that a particular distributed application may be secure, but that fact is hard to confirm. In a distributed Web Services architecture, the combining of all of this trusted code together theoretically embodies a *distributed TCB*. But is this really a distributed TCB? Probably not. It may be tamper proof and always invoked, but it may not be small enough to be analyzed easily. That's a concern because if we can't analyze the system, we can't be certain that the valuable data is being protected.

Some security traditionalists believe that it is not possible to build highly secure distributed component systems. We disagree and question whether a TCB model is even appropriate for distributed component environments. Although we agree with the philosophy of TCBs, which is that TCBs are great for enforcing security, they aren't sufficiently flexible to support Web Services architectures. This book presents a number of techniques that integrate security into a distributed Web Services environment. Although the end result of our approach does not resemble a traditional TCB model, we do recommend an integrated approach that is consistent with TCB principles and simplifies the analysis of distributed system security.

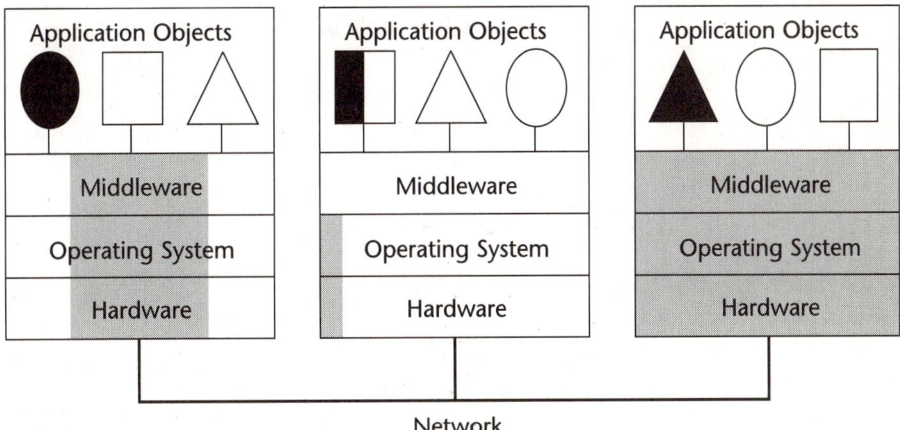

Figure 12.2 Distributed component security architecture.

By relying on security products rather than building your own security into the application, you increase the trustworthiness of your system. You can focus your security efforts on configuring and administering those security products instead of writing security code.

So how do you make sure that your system security is trustworthy? This is not easy to achieve, and perfect trustworthiness is generally impossible. The best approach is to leave security to the experts. Their systems won't be perfectly secure either, but they have one advantage—their code is likely to be exercised by lots of people, so the flaws are more likely to have been detected. Security experts should also be more sensitive to common programming errors (buffer overflow is a classic example) that are the root cause of many flaws, so their systems should be better tested and more robust.

If you can't find a commercial solution to your security needs and you have to roll your own, be prepared to spend a lot of effort to establish the trustworthiness of your code. Define a specialized security test plan and a security specification that is separate from functional testing. Remember that you'll probably never know if an attacker exploits a security vulnerability in your system, so get the most assurance you can. For the best confidence in your security solution, hire an outside group that specializes in security assessments and penetration testing, and let them thoroughly examine what you have built.

Security Evolution—Losing Control

Defining the security technologies needed for a single application can be straightforward because most things are under your control. When moving to a Web Services architecture view, however, you most likely will *not* have complete control over the selection of security technology.

Enterprises have to deal with multiple security products and technologies for several reasons. First, most large companies today have decentralized control over information technology (IT) in general and over security technology specifically. Although there may be a central IT group, it usually does not mandate what security must be used across the enterprise. Each business application group goes out in search of the best security technologies and deploys them independently to meet their own business needs. Second, companies want to use Web Services to interoperate with their suppliers, customers, and partners through business-to-business (B2B) marketplaces that have their own security requirements. Third, companies must cope with changing technology. Over time, all companies need to migrate to new security technologies to protect themselves against new threats and to maintain their competitive advantage.

The multitude of security technologies won't cause a problem until the various groups want to hook their applications together using Web Services, which they eventually will want to do to solve an e-business need. When interoperability is attempted, security is invariably one of the major obstacles because of incompatible technologies. The basic solution seems simple enough: some of the applications could change security technologies to match up with the others. The cost of this evolution can be expensive and time-consuming and can require major changes to the applications. When working across different enterprises, it's unlikely that one company will be willing to bear the cost of changing their security to match a partner's approach.

Public Key Infrastructure (PKI) authentication is an example of an evolving security technology. Although PKI is not widely used for authenticating clients today, it is just a matter of time before we see its widespread use as the cost of smart cards continues to drop. Can your Web Services applications migrate to PKI authentication without major modifications? If they can't, they have not been designed to handle security evolution.

The best way to deal with evolving security technologies is through a security framework. We presented the concept of an EASI framework in Chapter 1, and we'll describe how the framework applies to ePortal and eBusiness later in this chapter.

Dealing with the "ilities"

Getting a single isolated application to function properly is not a big challenge. Getting it to work in the context of a Web Services architecture that needs to behave predictably day in and day out is a major undertaking. It's the nonfunctional system requirements, the "ilities," that make system building so tough. We're talking about issues like manageability, extensibility, reliability, availability, scalability, and, of course, security. (We know security doesn't end with "ility," but who's perfect?)

Security has a major impact on the other "ilities." Security is a challenge for manageability because security adds complexity to a system. Security policy, in fact, is one of the most difficult aspects of system management. Security affects system extensibility, as we just explained in the previous section on security evolution. Security also affects system reliability; in particular, a security service can be a single point of failure if it is not properly designed. Security and availability go hand in hand because availability is itself an aspect of security in many systems. Denial-of-service attacks that consume system resources are common, and security mechanisms need to be in place to protect against these kinds of attacks. In addition, the proper configuration of a security policy is critical to ensure availability; if the security service denies access when it shouldn't, the entire system will be unavailable. Scalability, like reliability, is also greatly affected by the security solution. All sensitive application data must pass through security enforcement code; if the security architecture is not designed to scale, a bottleneck will result. We'll explore the relationship of security and the other "ilities" later in this chapter.

EASI Principles for Web Services

Security could easily be the downfall of Web Services. No company will be willing to deploy unsecured Web Services, but an approach based on a single security product is inadequate. Where do you go from here?

To solve the problem of Web Services security, enterprises need a solid application security architecture in place based on the principles of Enterprise Application Security Integration (EASI). We introduced EASI in Chapter 1; we now expand on the concept to guide us in our integration of Web Services security applications. We recommend that you follow basic principles of EASI when you define your own Web Services security architecture.

We've learned these rules over the years as we applied EASI techniques to many large customers' problems in banking, telecommunications, and manufacturing. We described a set of principles in our first book (Hartman, Flinn, and Beznosov 2001). In this book, we have extended our original enterprise security integration principles so they align well with Web Services requirements. We use these principles later in this chapter to guide our definition of the example Web Services security architecture.

Security Architecture Principles

We begin our list of EASI principles for Web Services with some general guidelines for defining Web Services security architectures.

Trust No One

Web Services applications are implemented by multitier chains of requests, and consequently are much more complex than the client-server model. A client request bounces through many applications, so there are many points of vulnerability. As a result, corporate auditors have difficulty establishing end-to-end system trustworthiness because the systems don't match the centralized TCB paradigm we described earlier.

A common simplistic model of trust is to have a security enforcement point at the perimeter firewall, and then assume that all Web Services applications are equally trustworthy to protect all data. This approach relies on a dangerous assumption, since firewalls usually permit Web Services HTTP traffic to pass through. If one component is compromised in this scenario, then the entire set of distributed components is vulnerable.

Transport security mechanisms, such as SSL or Internet Protocol Security (IPSEC), and message-oriented mechanisms such as XML Signature are inadequate by themselves in multitier environments because they cannot secure a chain of requests—they only secure two endpoints.

A better approach is to view collections of Web Services components as mutually suspicious islands—if one collection of components is compromised, then others will still be safe. In a mutually suspicious architecture, authentication isn't only for people. Each component that is a part of a request chain should be authenticated on its own.

To secure a multitier architecture, you need end-to-end security that supports passing security credentials across many different applications, and products that securely link users' credentials among systems to establish mutual trust. Defining a security architecture for distributed trust and controlled delegation is an advanced topic, and products that support these abilities are just beginning to enter the market. The best solution we've seen so far is to build Web Services security on the combination of WS-Security and SAML, which allows security credentials to be passed and validated at each component in the multitier architecture.

Enable Interoperability

You can't pick a single vendor product to solve Web Service security problems because your corporate customers and partners will pick different ones. Your Web Services architecture needs to have the ability to interoperate with other Web Services even when they use incompatible security technologies.

We've seen that there are many excellent point security solutions, but we're quite confident that no single vendor product will ever satisfy all security requirements and dominate the marketplace. Because there are so many possible vendor security solutions out there, proprietary technologies can make interoperability extremely difficult.

The best way to enable interoperability is to use vendor-neutral standards. Although security standards for Web Services are still in progress, they are well on their way. WS-Security and SAML are the key standards in this area. WS-Security provides a standard way to protect Web Services message traffic, while SAML standardizes how credentials may be passed across multiple applications. These two complementary standards when used together go a long way toward supporting Web Services secure interoperability in a vendor-neutral way.

Modularize Security

Web Service security technology will continue to evolve, so it's important that you don't get roped into one vendor's product. All companies need to have the flexibility to mix and match security technologies without recoding their Web Service applications.

As we discussed in Chapter 1, developers have the tendency to write their own security implementations within their application. We think this is a practice that should be avoided whenever possible. Developers cannot easily maintain the fragmented security embedded in each application, and their security tends to be fragile, requiring major rewrites when the security needs change. Look to enforce authentication, authorization, and cryptography at the lowest practical level in the architecture. The least desirable location is within the application, although some policies cannot be enforced anywhere else. By pushing security down to the lower layers of the architecture, you're more likely to produce robust common security mechanisms that can be shared across many applications.

The best approach is for applications to use standard APIs, such as those described in Chapter 7, to support the modular "plug and play" of security components from different vendors. A standard security API defines a virtual security service that insulates applications from dependencies on any specific vendor product.

Security Policy Principles

We continue our list of EASI principles for Web Services with some security policy guidelines for Web Services security architectures:

Authentication: balance cost against threat. The best authentication isn't for everyone. The most secure authentication, such as public key certificates on smartcards, is probably too expensive to deploy and manage for many applications. If authentication techniques are *too* strong, people may just give up and not use the system. It's better to have authentication that people will use rather than building a secure boat anchor. Single sign-on (SSO) is an example of this principle; no one likes to log in more than once.

Authorization: application driven. Authorization policies aren't really implemented to protect URLs or files: they protect business data that resides in those files. A lot of time and money is wasted on blindly setting up security products that do little to protect important application data. When you secure a system, don't lose sight of the fact that the most important thing to understand is the purpose of the business application. Once you understand what the business application is for and what security failures you are worried about, you can then figure out the best way to protect the data. (Application-driven authorization does *not* mean that the authorization policy should be implemented within the application. See the preceding *modularize security* principle.)

Accountability: audit early, not often. Auditing is expensive in distributed systems, so for performance reasons, it's better to do it as little as possible. Unlike authorization, it's preferable to push the source of an audit event to the *upper* layers of the architecture near the application. Low-level auditing (for example, at the OS level) is extremely difficult to analyze because it takes a combination of several low-level events to create a single business transaction. Low-level auditing is fine for discovering an attack on your OS, but correlating low-level audit data across multiple audit logs to detect an application attack can be close to impossible. As a result, the most effective auditing is done as soon as an application recognizes that a potentially dangerous event has occurred.

Security administration: design collections and hierarchies for scale. Web Services applications are all about managing huge numbers: millions of users and resources, thousands of servers. The best way to deal with large numbers is to collect users and resources into groups and make those groups hierarchical. (We discuss this topic in Chapter 11.) By defining collections, administrators can set policies on lots of users and resources at the same time and delegate security responsibilities across many administrators. Note that collections do not just contain people—services and data also should be grouped to handle scale.

Determining Requirements

For the rest of this chapter, we will consider the following scenario: ePortal and eBusiness wish to collaborate to offer an online storefront provided by ePortal, and supported by eBusiness for product and pricing information as well as order processing. ePortal is a Microsoft development shop and relies on Windows and ASP.NET technology (as described in Chapter 8) to secure its Web Services application. eBusiness does most of its development on Unix and uses the BEA WebLogic J2EE environment (as described in Chapter 9) to secure its Web Services application. eBusiness uses Oracle 9i database servers to store product and customer data.

ePortal and eBusiness realize that a security strategy needs to be in place as part of their joint Web Services offering. They recognize that their individual approaches to security have not considered how they might interoperate with other companies, and they realize they each need a more structured approach to ensure that their joint Web Services offering is secure.

The companies have experienced security IT groups that understand perimeter security, such as firewalls, network security, intrusion detection, and OS hardening. However, these groups are not accustomed to application-level security issues, and they do not understand middleware, such as Web Services, .NET, or J2EE. ePortal and eBusiness have good business application development groups that are experienced in building distributed component systems. As these groups build more sophisticated applications such as this joint e-commerce application, the development groups know that security is a critical issue. The development groups have looked to their security IT departments to supply the infrastructure for securing Web Services applications, but security IT doesn't know how to help.

Meanwhile, management in both companies is worried about the business risk of the initiative. Management will only approve the new joint business offering if adequate security is in place. ePortal wants to pass the online orders to eBusiness without jeopardizing the security of the customers' transactions. eBusiness wants to be sure that the customer orders coming from ePortal are trustworthy. Both companies are looking for reassurance that they have the best security practices in place to protect them against fraud, lawsuits, and other business risks. Both companies also want to maintain their business autonomy and are not interested in making major investments to change or align their security technologies.

Fortunately, ePortal and eBusiness management realizes that the way out of its predicament is to encourage each company's security IT and business application development groups to work together and create an interdisciplinary approach based on EASI. Each company creates an EASI task force that has members from their security IT and application groups; the task forces create corporate security frameworks that are the basis of their enterprise security strategies.

Each company's EASI task force works independently from the other company's—ePortal and eBusiness each define their own Web Services security architectures. They want to ensure that their architectures will be able to interoperate with a minimum of collaboration between the two companies. Their separate frameworks support the current deployment of the joint application and ensure that the companies' Web Services applications can interoperate securely. The frameworks will also evolve over time to encompass new security technologies as the companies build new applications and integrate with new business partners.

For ePortal and eBusiness, creating the application code that implements the functions described in Chapter 1 is the easy part. The companies then need to address many of the issues we discussed earlier as they plan the e-commerce application integration and deployment. We'll first address the system-level requirements, both security and nonfunctional, that must be considered when integrating the ePortal and eBusiness applications. Based on these requirements, the technical teams define the security architecture in terms of security APIs, protocols, and security policies.

Let's first look at the overall requirements for ePortal and eBusiness in terms of functional, security, and nonfunctional requirements. Functional requirements define how the applications should behave in terms of their basic functionality; that is, implementing a system that allows various customers to select and order goods over the Internet. Security requirements define the ePortal and eBusiness system security properties, which by now should be familiar to you. Our example has several different business-level security requirements that need to be enforced by the systems. We admittedly contrived our example to combine many security concerns into one simple example, but these security requirements are illustrative of common security issues that we have encountered in real-life businesses. Nonfunctional requirements define the other required system behaviors, the "ilities," beyond functional and security requirements.

Functional Requirements

Because this is a security book, we're going to assume that the ePortal and eBusiness developers know how to build a correctly functioning application. The basic description of the online storefront example's functionality was provided in the *Example of a Secure Web Services Architecture* section in Chapter 1. This should be all you need to know about what the example does. As a quick recap, a customer first authenticates to the ePortal storefront, and then gets a list of products and prices. The customer then places orders for products into his or her account and sometime later settles the order with a credit card number. In addition to the basic ordering interactions, the application interfaces also support administering customer and member accounts, and setting product prices. The e-commerce services provided by ePortal are primarily implemented by eBusiness. ePortal accesses the eBusiness services over the Internet via SOAP over HTTP (or HTTPS). eBusiness stores information about products and prices, and also performs the processing of the orders received by ePortal.

ePortal Security Requirements

Let's take a look at the security requirements from the perspective of ePortal. As a starting point, we should point out that it's frequently very difficult to tell exactly where functional requirements stop and security requirements begin. In many e-business applications, the primary purpose of the application is a financial transaction, which is fundamentally about security. Even so, it's important to try to make the distinction between security and functionality whenever possible. Why bother? As discussed previously in this chapter, one of our basic principles of EASI is to modularize security in the architecture. We separate security from application functionality so we can allow the security infrastructure to work for us. It's far better to let a robust security product enforce security for your application than to reinvent the wheel.

Limit Visitor Access

First, ePortal would like to permit access for unauthenticated visitors, as long as that access is strictly limited. If casual Web surfers happen to stumble across ePortal, they should be welcomed and should not immediately encounter the "Enter User ID and Password" warning that might scare them off. Of course, if the casual visitor is welcomed, so is the hostile attacker because it will be very difficult to distinguish between someone who is "just browsing" and a hacker looking for a security hole.

To address this issue, ePortal permits unauthenticated visitors to view an unrestricted part of the ePortal Web site. On this portion of the site, visitors may see a list of products but they may not see prices. ePortal does not pass any requests from visitors to eBusiness.

This rather open philosophy could leave ePortal open to problems, such as denial-of-service attacks, where a coordinated attack might flood the site with so many requests for product information that it would slow down or stop service to legitimate users. Firewalls and proactive intrusion detection products at ePortal may be used to detect, filter, and minimize the damage caused by these kinds of attacks. Fortunately for eBusiness, ePortal takes the brunt of these attacks.

Eliminate Administration of New Customers

A second business-driven security requirement is to minimize the burden on ePortal's security administrators wherever possible. One of the drivers of e-business is the desire to reduce the number of staff required to support customer interactions. This goal would be defeated if companies had to add administrative security staff to just deal with customers. As a result, a common model used is *self-registration,* in which the user adds himself or herself as a new customer. For the ePortal application, unauthenticated users are allowed to create themselves as new customers, so administrator intervention is not required.

Again, this open approach may be good for business, but it does open up ePortal to possible attacks. The self-registration program must be carefully written to check the credentials of new users before admitting them as customers. For example, ePortal requires a credit card to be supplied, and the ePortal application sends a request to eBusiness for some basic credit checks on the card to reduce the chance that the card has been lost or stolen. The self-registration program must be a highly trusted security-aware application because it will be interacting with the underlying security service to create new authenticated principals. Consequently, the self-registration program must be well tested to ensure that it is trustworthy; if a hacker could exploit an error in this code, he or she could create new users at will, which would not make ePortal or eBusiness very happy.

If eBusiness could prove that ePortal built an insecure self-registration program, there would probably be grounds for a lawsuit. eBusiness has a great deal to lose if ePortal fails to authenticate its users properly.

Grant Members More Access

The next business requirement for ePortal is to give its members access to special product deals that are not available to ordinary customers. The distinction between customers and members could have been made within the eBusiness application, but ePortal needs to maintain all information about its own users.

To address this requirement, we set up a simple role-based access control (RBAC) policy, as we discussed extensively in Chapter 11. ePortal defines a role hierarchy for visitors, customers, members, and staff. The role hierarchy simplifies administration for customers and members because it allows ePortal staff to grant additional privileges to a user simply by switching the user's role. ePortal does not actually enforce the RBAC access rights; that is eBusiness's job, as we will see in the next section.

Secure Exchange with eBusiness

The final business requirement, and the most important from a Web Services point of view, is for ePortal to pass Web Services requests securely from authenticated users to eBusiness. This exchange is the basis of the business relationship between ePortal and eBusiness, so both companies will pay close attention to ensure that the exchange provides an adequate basis for mutual trust.

The companies decided that the proper division of security responsibility in this case means that ePortal is responsible for authenticating users and eBusiness is responsible for protecting information about products, prices, and orders. This division makes business sense, since ePortal is customer facing, and eBusiness maintains the back-office business services.

ePortal must have a highly secure way to pass user security context information, including the authenticated user identity and role, along with each Web Service request to eBusiness. Since ePortal and eBusiness exchange this information over the Internet, the Web Services request must be passed in a trustworthy fashion so that ePortal can be sure that the request is only accessible to eBusiness, and eBusiness can be sure that the request came from ePortal and that no attacker tampered with the request while it was in transit. Since we already know that ePortal and eBusiness are using different Web Services and incompatible security technologies, it's also important that the exchange of the security context be based on a common standard.

eBusiness Security Requirements

Now that we've seen security from ePortal's point of view, we turn our attention to the security requirements for eBusiness. You will notice that several are naturally complementary with ePortal's requirements.

Secure Exchange with ePortal

As we just discussed, ePortal will pass Web Services requests securely to eBusiness. eBusiness requires the security context information in the received Web Service requests to enforce access control on valuable resources, so it's crucial that eBusiness be able to trust the security information in each request.

eBusiness also needs to be able to interpret the security context information that it receives from ePortal. Interpreting the security data may seem like an obvious issue, but it can be surprisingly difficult in business-to business (B2B) scenarios like this one. ePortal will pass user identity and role information in the security context of the request, but eBusiness may need to be able to translate the context before it can use it to enforce security.

For example, eBusiness may be supporting hundreds of other portal Web sites in addition to ePortal. Although ePortal defines the roles of visitor, customer, member, and staff, the other portals may use other definitions to distinguish customers, for example, bronze, silver, gold, and platinum. In this case, eBusiness must map the incoming attributes from each portal site into a set of local attributes that eBusiness uses to enforce policy. (See Chapter 10 for additional discussion on interoperability and attribute mapping.)

Limit Visitor Access

A second business requirement for eBusiness is to require all requests to its site to be from authenticated users. eBusiness needs to protect its sensitive business data about products, prices, and orders residing on the eBusiness site, and unauthenticated users have no legitimate reason to access this information. Visitors from ePortal are unauthenticated, so if eBusiness receives a request from ePortal from a user with a visitor role, eBusiness will reject the request.

Grant Members More Access

The next business requirement for eBusiness is to give ePortal members access to special product deals that are not available to ordinary customers. To address this requirement, eBusiness uses the mapped roles supplied by ePortal to enforce access to resources. eBusiness uses an RBAC policy that grants a basic set of access rights to all users who are customers. We then set up a role hierarchy that grants additional rights to users who are members; they are allowed to see prices for special products.

Protect the Accounts of Each Individual

eBusiness wants to ensure that the data in every customer and member account is protected so that one individual cannot access another individual's account. However, strictly speaking, this business requirement is not needed to protect eBusiness because if a customer accidentally pays for the wrong account, eBusiness still gets paid. The requirement is mainly to ensure the privacy of everyone's account information.

Privacy is a particular kind of security policy that protects user data. Unlike an enterprise security policy, which is controlled by a company to protect its own corporate data, a privacy policy is controlled by an individual to protect his or her own personal data. The view that privacy data should be controlled by an individual might surprise you because today there are few constraints placed on U.S. companies to regulate the sharing of their huge stores of consumer data. In most cases, these companies do not have genuine privacy policies in place. The trend we see, as driven by emerging government regulations all over the world, is to give back to consumers the control of their own data. Companies hold data on behalf of individuals, and those individuals will eventually dictate who is allowed to see their data and for what purpose.

Privacy is a rapidly growing topic in its own right and is too big and complex to address in this book. We will summarize by pointing out that the security mechanisms that have been explained in this book are also used to protect the privacy of an individual's data. Cryptography, such as the use of Secure Sockets Layer (SSL), protects the data privacy as it travels over the Internet. Access policies control who in a corporation is permitted to have access to an individual's private data.

To ensure privacy, eBusiness wants to enforce fine-grained access control to customer and member accounts. After looking at a variety of products, we have decided that access control at the level of individual accounts will be enforced by the back-office database server. The security policy in the database server ensures that individuals can only get access to their own accounts stored as database records.

Administrator Control of Critical Functions

eBusiness also wants to ensure that certain critical application functions are only controlled by its administrative staff. Only eBusiness is allowed to set prices and to administer customer and member accounts. (As we will see in a moment, however, even staff members have limits on what they can do.) Product pricing is central to this application and must be highly controlled; if a hacker could break in and set product prices, it would be a disaster.

We enforce this policy by only allowing staff members to access the set price operation on products.

Restrict Administrators' Abilities

Finally, eBusiness wants to limit the ability of its own administrative staff to commit fraud. In particular, eBusiness does not want to allow its staff to settle an order (for example, pay for an order using a credit card). If a staff member could settle orders, he or she would be able to manipulate a customer account in any fashion. The staff member might be tempted to create a fictitious customer account, and then use a stolen credit card number from another account to order merchandise. The goods could be shipped to a location of the staff member's choice and then be resold, making the fraudulent purchases very difficult to trace.

Preventing eBusiness's staff from settling orders is an example of a *separation of duties* policy. Separation of duties policies, as we described in Chapter 11, distribute trust among several people, making it less likely that a compromise will occur. In this case, for example, the staff member could still commit fraud by colluding with a person outside of the company who would pose as the fictitious customer. Although this approach might be possible for one or two people, the number of people required for a large-scale operation makes it likely that the staff member would get caught. We enforce this policy by only allowing customers and members to access the settle order operation on customer shopping carts.

Nonfunctional Requirements

The nonfunctional requirements that ePortal and eBusiness want to address are manageability, extensibility, reliability, availability, and scalability. All of these topics have many complex aspects, and because this book is not a complete guide to system architecture, we will not attempt to cover them in depth. However, we will address the relationship between each of these topics and security. In particular, we will discuss the nonfunctional requirements that ePortal and eBusiness impose on their security services.

Manageability

ePortal and eBusiness want to ensure that security is easy to manage in operational use. The enterprise security architecture should support a management framework for its components, users, resources, and enabling technology. The enterprise security architecture should also support centralized and delegated administration of security components. The framework standardizes the management approach for many security components, including:

- Monitoring
- Failure restart
- Installation of software upgrades
- Administration
- Auditing for accountability

Extensibility

ePortal and eBusiness have a variety of requirements for the extensibility of the security architectures and the applications. The security architectures should have the ability to support different security policies and extend those policies over time. The systems should have the flexibility to adjust to changed circumstances (such as new business policies and procedures) without requiring changes to the ePortal or eBusiness application code. If an application does need to change, the security architecture should be able to accommodate application changes without making major changes to the security infrastructure.

In addition, ePortal and eBusiness need to be able to respond quickly to a rapidly changing business environment. As a result, the security architectures should be able to evolve over time because of:

- Changes in demand for the ePortal and eBusiness application services
- Corporate reorganizations, acquisitions, mergers, or partnerships
- Introduction of new security technologies

Reliability

The ePortal and eBusiness enterprise security architectures must be highly reliable systems because of their critical role in ensuring the security of the e-commerce application. ePortal and eBusiness want to ensure that the security services are at least as reliable as the application. In this context, reliability means the ability of the system to continue operations without failure. Typically, the reliability of a system is measured in terms of mean time to failure (MTTF) and mean time to repair (MTTR).

In practice, security service reliability is dependent on the reliability of the underlying software and hardware. ePortal and eBusiness ensure security software reliability by purchasing products from reliable security vendors that have good quality control procedures in place and well-demonstrated track records of success. ePortal and eBusiness ensure hardware reliability by using redundant architectures that avoid a single point of failure. Software and hardware redundancy also supports availability and scalability, so we explore the topic further in the next two sections.

Availability

ePortal and eBusiness want to ensure that their systems are always available. The e-commerce site must be accessible 24 hours per day, 7 days per week. The site must continuously support large numbers of transactions per second and, typically, subsecond response times.

The high-availability plan considers the entire security architecture to identify and reduce any single points of failure. Included in the availability plan are network components, firewalls, Web servers, security policy servers, and the application server components. The availability considerations apply to both software and hardware components in the architecture. To ensure high availability, the enterprise security architectures incorporate the following capabilities:

- Redundancy of software and hardware
- Failover (automated, hot standby, cold standby)
- Disaster recovery
- Replication
- Backups
- Load balancing

Scalability

Scalability requirements for ePortal and eBusiness's enterprise security architectures are driven by their business application requirements. Because eBusiness expects to continue to grow, the companies want to be sure that all applications will be able to expand to handle larger volumes of customer orders. Scalability describes the ability of a system to support variations in the size of its workload without design changes.

The multitiered Web Services architectures that are the basis of ePortal and eBusiness applications include two features that directly improve performance and scalability:

Load balancing. Application server middleware hides the server's actual location, facilitating the allocation of processing loads across multiple mid-tier servers. The mid-tier servers can act as concentrators for client connections and thus manage growth in the number of concurrent client data requests.

Hardware and software architecture flexibility. Decoupling the business logic from the presentation, data access, and security logic permits flexibility in allocating the software components to physical computing resources. The components can reside on the same platform or be distributed across several platforms.

Overview of ePortal and eBusiness Security Architectures

We now move to our example and talk about using what you have learned to see what is necessary to implement ePortal and eBusiness's Web Services security infrastructure. Of course, implementing and deploying a large enterprise's e-commerce security is a major effort with many details to be decided. We will not go into the detailed design decisions for a full deployment; instead, we will focus on helping you understand the requirements of an end-to-end secure deployment. Although the focus of this book is Web Services, there are other security mechanisms that are necessary to enforce end-to-end security. Therefore, in this final chapter, we present a high-level view touching briefly on a number of different security subjects.

To provide end-to-end security and meet ePortal and eBusiness's requirements, their security architectures must encompass perimeter, mid-tier, and back-office security. Perimeter security provides the first level of defense against external attacks, and makes sure that only authenticated and authorized users may access the corporate network. Security within the enterprise, that is, mid-tier security, addresses security in applications and their underlying infrastructure. Without mid-tier security measures, there is no protection against insider attacks. Insiders include anyone who has access to internal network resources, including Web Services customers and partners. Back-office security protects the large stores of valuable corporate resources that reside on legacy systems and databases.

The security architectures of ePortal and eBusiness implement most of the principles espoused in this book, albeit in a somewhat simple example to enhance clarity. ePortal's application security architecture relies on a commercial Web SSO security product to authenticate Web users and control access to HTML pages, and Microsoft security mechanisms in ASP.NET, COM+, and Windows 2000 to secure the middle tier. eBusiness's application security architecture uses security built into the iPlanet Web server and WebLogic J2EE application server, and secures the back office using the security enforcement mechanisms of Oracle 9i.

Both ePortal and eBusiness use SAML and WS-Security to provide a trustworthy Web Services connection between the companies and to pass the user's security context. Products (including one from our company, Quadrasis) that can provide this support in a standard, vendor-neutral way are now reaching the market.

We derived the security architectures for ePortal and eBusiness described here from the case studies on .NET in Chapter 8 and J2EE in Chapter 9. Note, however, that we have changed the previously described architectures to allow them to interoperate in this chapter. In particular, the case studies assumed for simplicity that both ePortal and eBusiness were using a uniform underlying technology (either .NET or J2EE). In this chapter, we remove this constraint so that we can explore the more complex issues involved with implementing security interoperability across different Web Services and security technologies.

Figure 12.3 shows the ePortal and eBusiness security architectures, and how they work together to provide the online storefront service.

Next, we give you an overview of how the ePortal and eBusiness services work together to provide security for their online storefront offering. We'll walk you through the steps of a typical interaction, starting with a customer request:

1. The customer running a browser client, a desktop machine, selects a URL on the ePortal.com Web server to request a service, such as getting a product price.
2. The ePortal.com Web server checks to see if the requested URL requires an authenticated client. If it does, the Web server requires an SSL-protected connection with the browser (HTTPS) and requests the authentication credentials, such as a username and password.
3. The customer provides the username/password over HTTPS. (Alternately, if the request comes from a Web Service client application on eBuyer.com, the client application provides the username/password over HTTPS.)

4. The ePortal.com Web server passes the authentication credentials to the Web SSO product. If the authentication is successful, the Web SSO product returns a security token that may be returned to the client in a cookie later. The ePortal.com Web server may optionally enforce a coarse-grained authorization check on the URL in the request.
5. If the user request can be serviced locally on ePortal.com, the ePortal.com Web server passes the request to the StoreFront middle tier server running on COM+. The Web server uses impersonation supported by ASP.NET and IIS to make the request on behalf of the user. The StoreFront middle tier uses COM+ security (as described in Chapter 7), which in turn relies on Windows OS security, to enforce access control on the user request to the StoreFront middle tier. The result is returned to the user, as described in Step 13.
6. If the user request cannot be serviced locally on ePortal.com, the ePortal.com Web server creates a SAML assertion as a token contained in a WS-Security document (as explained in Chapter 10) that represents the customer and role.
7. The ePortal.com Web server constructs a SOAP request containing the WS-Security/SAML document and sends the request via HTTPS over the Internet to eBusiness.com.
8. The eBusiness.com Web server receives the SOAP request from ePortal.com and validates the WS-Security/SAML document in the SOAP header to ensure that it has not been tampered with, has not expired, and comes from a trustworthy source (that is, from ePortal.com).
9. The eBusiness.com attribute mapping service maps the incoming attribute (that is, the role) to a role to be used within eBusiness.com. The eBusiness.com Web server may also optionally enforce a coarse-grained authorization check on the SOAP request.
10. The eBusiness.com Web server then forwards the SOAP request containing the WS-Security/SAML document to the StoreFrontService on the J2EE application server. (The eBusiness.com Web server does not need to use impersonation because the identity and role of the user are contained in the SAML assertion.) The application server container extracts the username and role from the SAML assertion and sets up the JAAS context (as described in Chapter 7).
11. The J2EE application server enforces method-level authorization on the Enterprise Java Bean, based on the role in the request and the method permissions defined for the bean (as described in Chapter 7).
12. The bean calls the database to look up the pricing information. The bean uses delegation to make the database request on behalf of the customer. The database server enforces role-based access control for the requested database record, using the customer's identity and role.
13. The information is returned through the same path to ePortal.com and to the customer. The ePortal.com browser returns the response, which may contain a cookie, with the SAML assertion for subsequent single sign-on use across multiple SSL sessions.

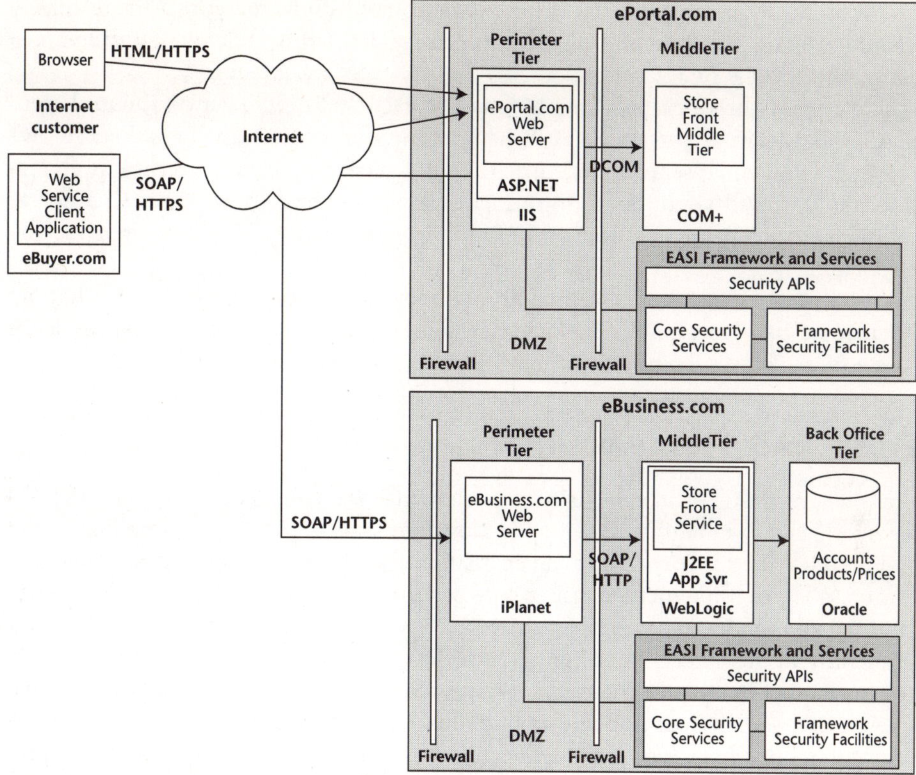

Figure 12.3 ePortal and eBusiness security architectures.

Applying EASI

Once ePortal and eBusiness have defined the functional, security, and nonfunctional requirements for the Web Services application, it's time to determine how to apply the EASI framework. We apply the concepts of EASI to define the security architectures for ePortal and eBusiness. The framework helps us structure our strategy for enforcing security and will guide us in choosing the kinds of products that we will need. These products will be used to implement the steps that we described above for ePortal and eBusiness to support secure interactions with customers.

As discussed in Chapter 1, the EASI framework specifies the interactions among the security services and the application components that use those security services. The framework security APIs define common, vendor-neutral APIs that encapsulate product-specific interfaces and permit the mixing and matching of a variety of different vendors' security products. The EASI APIs are called explicitly by some security-aware ePortal and eBusiness components, such as the ePortal Web Server code, and implicitly by most of the other components. We implement the EASI framework APIs primarily based on existing standard and de facto interfaces defined by Microsoft and the Java Community Process (JCP), among others.

There are new products reaching the marketplace that define vendor-neutral security APIs that align well with EASI. When defining your own EASI architecture, we recommend that you research new entries into the market, since this is a rapidly changing technology, and vendors are introducing new products all the time. Chapter 10 provides additional information on defining generic EASI APIs to support secure interoperability.

In the following sections, we give an overview of the EASI frameworks that are implemented by ePortal and eBusiness. We then describe how each company's EASI framework addresses their security requirements as defined previously.

ePortal EASI Framework

To implement the ePortal's security requirements, we will define the ePortal EASI framework shown in Figure 12.4. Application components that implement the tiers of the ePortal use the security APIs that encapsulate the underlying security services. The security APIs are implemented using core security services and framework security facilities that support these services.

Normally, at this stage, ePortal would select a specific set of commercial products to implement all of the required services. Because there is a broad choice of products that implement these services and we intend this book to be relevant for a variety of deployed architectures, we don't always name specific security products. We do provide some examples of alternate security products later in this chapter.

Application Components

ePortal contains the customer-facing components of the online storefront. ePortal uses Microsoft application products, including ASP.NET, IIS, and COM+ to build its Web server and associated services. These applications access the security services via the APIs listed next. Because most of ePortal's environment is built on Microsoft technology, the applications typically need not access the security functions explicitly. Microsoft generally tightly couples security enforcement with its applications, which means that security is enforced with little or no developer effort. (This approach, however, makes it more difficult to replace the security mechanisms in many Microsoft products.)

The ePortal Web server services requests from customers, and if a request can be serviced locally on ePortal, the Web server passes the request to the StoreFront middle tier server running on COM+. If the user request cannot be serviced locally on ePortal, the ePortal forwards to eBusiness the request containing the WS-Security/SAML token created by calling the SAML service API.

Security APIs

The security APIs are the interfaces that all ePortal applications use for security support. The APIs selected by ePortal are primarily based on Microsoft products since they are designed to work well with the ASP.NET, IIS, and COM+ application platforms.

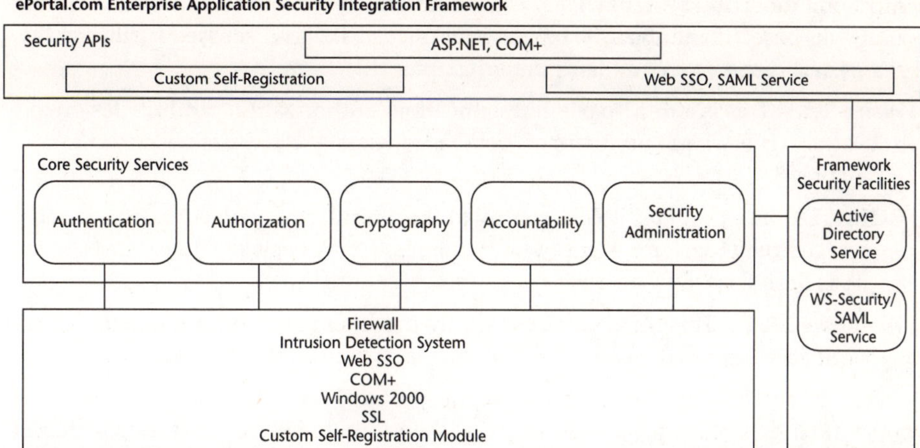

Figure 12.4 EASI framework for ePortal.

The ePortal EASI security APIs are implemented using the following standard, vendor, and custom interfaces:

ASP.NET, COM+. These are authentication, authorization, and cryptography APIs that are built on Microsoft products and generally need not be called explicitly by applications.

Custom self-registration. This is a custom-designed security administration API that the Web server calls to create a new customer.

Web SSO. This consists of authentication and authorization APIs that are called by the Web server to authenticate and authorize HTTP requests from the customer to the Web server. EASI provides vendor-neutral APIs to the Web SSO interfaces, which are generally proprietary and product-specific. The EASI APIs are designed to integrate easily with Web servers using standard plug-ins.

SAML service. This is a framework facility API that is called by the Web server to create a new WS-Security/SAML token that is passed to eBusiness.

Core Security Services

The core security services support the implementation of the framework security APIs based on specific security products. ePortal has selected the products in the following list to implement its system:

Firewall. This provides coarse-grained protection from external hostile attackers, ensuring that only HTTP traffic gets through to ePortal. In conjunction with IDS, which follows, firewalls can provide protection against hostile denial-of-service attacks. Firewalls are discussed further in the *Perimeter Security* section later in this chapter.

Intrusion detection system (IDS). IDS monitors and potentially prevents hostile attacks based on anomalous behavior or misuse. IDS is discussed further in the *Perimeter Security* section later in this chapter.

Web SSO. This is a third-party authentication/authorization product designed to scale to very large numbers of Web-based users. Web SSO is described in Chapter 3.

COM+. Com+ provides access control at the granularity of object methods and enforced by underlying Windows 2000 access control lists (ACLs). COM+ security is described in Chapter 7.

Windows 2000. This Microsoft OS security provides support for file- and device-based access control.

SSL. This public key-based cryptographic protocol provides transport-level data confidentiality, integrity, and mutual authentication. SSL support is provided by the Microsoft IIS environment. SSL is described in Chapter 3.

Custom self-registration module. An ePortal-developed module creates new customers. To successfully permit the creation of a new customer, the module requires that the user provide a credit card number, which the module passes to eBusiness for a credit check.

Framework Security Facilities

The framework security facilities provide support for the core security services. ePortal has selected the products in the following list to implement its system:

Active Directory service. This Microsoft LDAP-based directory service supports user and application security profile storage and retrieval. LDAP directories are described further in the *LDAP Directory Service* section of this chapter.

WS-Security/SAML service. This service provides support for generating and verifying standard interoperable security tokens based on SAML assertions embedded in WS-Security documents.

Addressing ePortal Requirements

We previously described ePortal's security requirements in terms of its responsibilities for providing the customer-facing portion of the online storefront. ePortal has the responsibility for maintaining information about its customers in terms of who they are, how they will be authenticated, and what roles they have. ePortal also needs to pass this authentication information to eBusiness in a trustworthy fashion so that eBusiness can enforce access control on the back-office resources supporting the storefront. We next describe how the ePortal EASI framework supports each of ePortal's security requirements.

Limit Visitor Access

When it permits unauthenticated user access to its Web site, ePortal needs to protect against denial-of-service attacks by hackers who might flood the Web site with spurious (but legitimate) HTTP requests. If the ePortal Web server is spending all of its time handling spurious requests, it will respond very slowly (if at all) to legitimate requests.

ePortal uses the framework security services to protect against external attacks such as denial-of-service attacks. ePortal installs its Web server in a "demilitarized zone" (DMZ) between two firewalls. The DMZ provides some isolation of the Web server from both the external Internet and the internal ePortal corporate network. The firewalls prevent whole classes of attacks made by using ports and services that are not relevant to this Web server (Simple Mail Transfer Protocol [SMTP], for example). The firewall can also filter traffic from IP addresses that are known to be hostile. ePortal installs an IDS in conjunction with the firewall to take a more proactive stance against external attacks. The IDS can detect patterns of attack, for example bursts of requests from a particular IP address at rates that are much higher than what would be expected from a person using a browser. The IDS can detect and alert the ePortal administrator to a potential attack, and can help the company take preemptive action by instructing the firewall to filter requests that appear to be hostile. We discuss firewalls and IDS further in the *Perimeter Security* section later in this chapter.

ePortal allows unauthenticated visitors to view an unrestricted portion of the ePortal Web site. ePortal does not allow visitors to view information that is only intended for members, such as product prices.

ePortal uses the COM+ and Windows 2000 framework security services to enforce access control that prevents visitors from viewing member-related information. The Web server uses impersonation supported by ASP.NET and IIS to take on a prespecified unauthenticated Windows 2000 anonymous OS identity (Chapter 8 discusses this topic further). When the Web server passes the request to a COM+ component in StoreFront middle tier, COM+ security provides method-level access control. COM+ security relies on the Windows 2000 OS to enforce this authorization check. Specifically, Windows 2000 defines access control lists (ACLs) on COM+ components that define which components can be accessed by the anonymous users.

Eliminate Administration of New Customers

ePortal provides self-registration support to minimize the burden on ePortal's security administrators. A visitor may enroll as a member by selecting a URL offered by the ePortal Web server. The Web server gathers user information from the user (protected by SSL), including the user's credit card number and proposed username and password. The Web server sends this information to an ePortal custom self-registration module implemented in COM+. The COM+ component sends a special Web Service request to eBusiness via the ePortal Web server to request a credit check. The Web server secures this Web Service request like any other request to eBusiness, using a special distinguished identity to indicate that the request is the ePortal self-registration application. If the check passes and the requested username and password are acceptable, the self-registration module component calls the Web SSO administrative API to create a new authenticated customer, which creates a user profile and stores it in the Active Directory service for later authentication checks. (We further describe this general topic in the *Self-Administration* section later in this chapter.)

Grant Members More Access

ePortal provides access to additional services by authenticating users based on a simple RBAC policy, with a role hierarchy for visitors, customers, members, and staff. ePortal uses several framework services to support this security requirement.

SSL establishes a secure session that provides transport-level data confidentiality. SSL ensures that the username and password passed from a client to the ePortal Web server are protected from external eavesdroppers who might be on the Internet.

The ePortal Web server passes the username and password to the Web SSO product authentication API. If the authentication is successful, the Web SSO authentication API returns a security token representing the authenticated user. This token may be returned to the client in a cookie, or it may be held by the Web Server. If the cookie is returned to the client, the client may use the cookie across multiple SSL sessions without reauthentication, as long as the token has not expired. If the Web Server does not return the token to the client, the client will need to reauthenticate itself each time the SSL session is broken. The cookie-based approach is more convenient for the user, but it does leave the cookie exposed on the client's machine and could be used by someone else using the same machine. By avoiding the cookie, we have a more secure approach, but the reauthenticating may be inconvenient for the user if the SSL session gets broken very often during a long connection.

Once the user is authenticated, the ePortal Web server will accept requests from the user. The Web server could use the Web SSO authorization API to make authorization checks on each requested URL, but this might be overkill since we also enforce authorization on COM+ components as well as at eBusiness. The Web SSO authorization could enforce a coarse-grained authorization check on the URL if needed for static Web content information that is not implemented with COM+ components or via an eBusiness service.

For requests that can be serviced locally on ePortal by COM+ components, the Web server impersonates the user identity, as supported by ASP.NET and IIS, and sends the request to the COM+ server. The server enforces method-level security based on Windows OS ACLs, which requires that the identity of the user correspond to a Windows OS identity. This approach won't work very well for customer identities since our self-registration module only defines new Web SSO identities rather than Windows OS identities. We would rather not have to maintain Windows OS identities for customers, which might number in the millions. (The trade-offs of using various access control methods in .NET are discussed in Chapter 8.)

However, for operations on small numbers of users, such as our administrative staff, Windows OS identities rather than Web SSO identities will work fine. (Self-registration of administrators would be a bad idea!) As a result, COM+ security will restrict access to administrative operations to a few administrators. COM+ will also allow anonymous users to access generic product information (but not prices), as we previously described in the section on limited visitor access. All other operations, such as getting product prices or settling an order, are passed to eBusiness for access control.

Secure Exchange with eBusiness

ePortal sends sensitive product-ordering SOAP requests to eBusiness, so we must ensure that requests are passed securely from authenticated users through ePortal to eBusiness. ePortal also needs to send the user identity and role information to eBusiness in a standard way that allows eBusiness to interpret this information, even though eBusiness and ePortal use different Web Services and security products.

We again rely on SSL to establish a secure session, this time between ePortal and eBusiness. SSL provides data confidentiality and integrity to ensure that no attacker can eavesdrop or manipulate the sensitive information in the order. ePortal and eBusiness use mutual certificate-based SSL authentication to ensure that both parties know who is at the other end of the session.

To pass user security context information to eBusiness, ePortal uses a SAML assertion within a WS-Security document. The ePortal Web server calls the framework SAML service API, passing it the Web SSO security token that was previously created for the user. The WS-Security/SAML service uses the security token to look up the user's identity and role information in Active Directory. The WS-Security/SAML service then creates a SAML attribute assertion that contains the user's identity and role, and is signed using ePortal's public key as the issuer of the assertion. WS-Security is then used to embed the SAML attribute assertion in the SOAP header of the request. WS-Security may be used to encrypt and sign the contents of the SOAP request, but in this simple example, we rely on SSL to provide this level of protection. (The various options for using WS-Security and SAML are described in Chapters 4, 5, 6, and 10.)

eBusiness EASI Framework

Next, we turn our attention to how we implement the security requirements for eBusiness. We start by discussing the EASI framework for eBusiness, as shown in Figure 12.5. As in the case of ePortal, we refrain from naming specific security products so that this example can be illustrative of a number of deployed architectures.

Application Components

eBusiness contains the back-office business components of the online storefront. eBusiness provides support for product pricing and order processing, and is built on the iPlanet Web server, BEA WebLogic J2EE application server, and Oracle 9i database server. The applications access the security services via the security APIs described in the next section. Unlike the Microsoft-based ePortal environment that provides both the application platform and security enforcement, most of the eBusiness applications explicitly call the EASI security APIs. These APIs are called via security-aware code either in the applications or in interceptor code that is integrated with the application platforms.

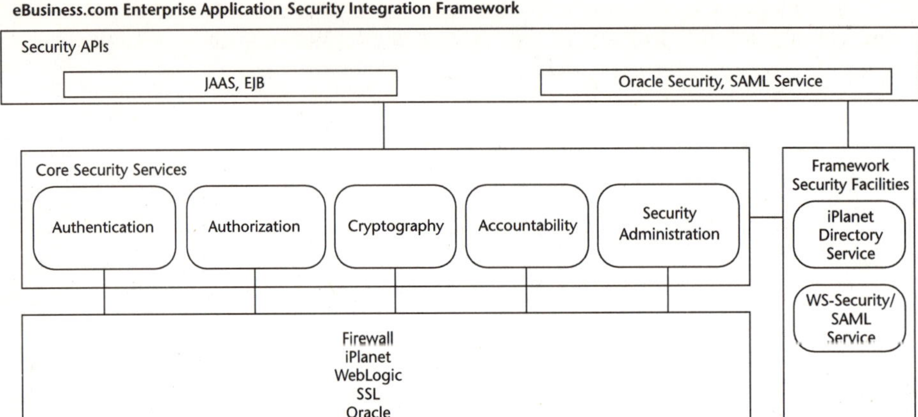

Figure 12.5 EASI framework for eBusiness.

The eBusiness receives a SOAP request from ePortal, and after validating the request, passes that request to the StoreFrontService on the J2EE application server. The J2EE application server components implement the eBusiness services. To access persistently stored information on product prices or orders, J2EE components access database records stored on the Oracle server.

In contrast to ePortal, eBusiness is not at all interested in providing these services directly to large numbers of users, such as consumers. The customers of eBusiness are companies like ePortal that handle the direct relationship to large numbers of individuals. This approach allows eBusiness to concentrate on what they do best, which is handling large volumes of business transactions from a relatively small number of customer corporations.

Security APIs

The eBusiness applications use the EASI security APIs to implement the required security services. eBusiness has implemented the EASI APIs to align with Java-related standards, namely the Java Authentication and Authorization Service (JAAS) and Enterprise Java Beans (EJB). In addition, eBusiness uses vendor-specific interfaces as supported by the Oracle database.

The eBusiness EASI security APIs are implemented using the following standard, vendor, and custom interfaces:

JAAS, EJB. These are authentication, authorization, and cryptography APIs that are built on Java 2 Enterprise Edition (J2EE) products. These APIs are designed to be extensible by developers so they can define new security functionality when needed. See Chapter 7 for more details on these interfaces.

Oracle Security. This is an authentication API to enforce security on the database records. This API allows the J2EE application server to act as a proxy for the user when sending a database query, as we describe in the *Protect the Accounts of Each Individual* section later in this chapter.

SAML service API. This is a framework facility API that is called by the Web server to validate a new WS-Security/SAML token that is received from eBusiness and extract attribute information from that token.

Core Security Services

The core security services support the implementation of the framework security APIs based on specific security products. eBusiness has selected the products in the following list to implement its system:

Firewall. This provides coarse-grained protection from external hostile attackers, ensuring that only HTTP traffic gets through to eBusiness. Since eBusiness communicates with a relatively small number of corporate customers, eBusiness sets up a conservative firewall policy that permits communication only with authenticated clients coming from the IP addresses of its customer sites. This approach significantly limits the exposure of eBusiness to hostile denial-of-service attacks.

iPlanet. This is a Web server that has built-in authentication/authorization enforcement. Although most Web server products have similar built-in security support, this level of security enforcement is generally not used for large deployments because of its scalability and administration limitations. However, since eBusiness is servicing a modest number of corporate clients rather than millions of consumers, the security features built into a Web server are more than adequate. Web server security is discussed in Chapter 3.

WebLogic. This provides access control at the granularity of object methods and enforced by the WebLogic J2EE application server, based on method permissions. J2EE security is described in Chapter 7.

SSL. This public key-based cryptographic protocol provides transport-level data confidentiality, integrity, and mutual authentication. SSL support is provided by the iPlanet Web server, WebLogic application server, and Oracle database server environments. SSL is described in Chapter 3.

Oracle. This is a database server that provides extensive support for authentication, authorization, and cryptography to protect database records.

Attribute mapping. This is a service that maps incoming attributes (such as roles) to a set of roles that can be used locally by eBusiness to enforce its role-based authorization policy. Attribute mapping is described further in Chapter 10.

Framework Security Facilities

The framework security facilities provide support for the core security services. eBusiness has selected the products in the following list to implement its system:

iPlanet directory service. The iPlanet LDAP-based directory service supports user and application security profile storage and retrieval. LDAP directories are described further in the *LDAP Directory Service* section of this chapter.

WS-Security/SAML service. This provides support for generating and verifying standard interoperable security tokens based on SAML assertions embedded in WS-Security documents.

Addressing eBusiness Requirements

As we discussed previously, since eBusiness provides the back-office services to support the storefront, the eBusiness's security requirements also focus on the back office. We next describe how the eBusiness EASI framework supports each of eBusiness's security requirements.

Secure Exchange with ePortal

When eBusiness receives a SOAP request from ePortal, eBusiness needs to know that the request is on behalf of a particular customer. In addition, eBusiness must ensure that the request came from ePortal. We rely on SSL to establish the secure session between ePortal and eBusiness and to provide mutual certificate-based authentication between the applications.

The eBusiness Web server relies on the WS-Security/SAML service to verify that the incoming request contains a valid token in the SOAP header. The WS-Security/SAML services verify the digital signature on the token to ensure that it has not been tampered with and that it has not expired. The services also verify that the token was signed and issued based on a certificate from a known, trustworthy source, namely ePortal. This check provides the basis for the federated security policy; eBusiness is willing to trust any customer identity and role that is asserted by ePortal. eBusiness does not need to reauthenticate ePortal's customers because eBusiness trusts that ePortal has previously performed acceptable authentication checks.

Because we use WS-Security/SAML to provide the security information in the SOAP request, we have eliminated security technology dependencies between ePortal and eBusiness. In particular, eBusiness does not need to know that ePortal uses .NET and a Web SSO product to authenticate customers. In fact, ePortal could change its implementation of security at any point without needing to inform eBusiness. The only common security technologies that are required of both ePortal and eBusiness are the ability to create and interpret standard WS-Security/SAML tokens, and the ability for eBusiness to verify the signature of the token based on ePortal's public certificate.

As part of the business agreement that ePortal and eBusiness set up in advance, ePortal explained how it maintains its categories of users, in particular, the roles of visitor, customer, and member. eBusiness maps the attributes internally because it needs to enforce distinct access control policies for its different corporate customers. For example, another portal customer, say eMarket, defines roles of bronze, silver, gold, and platinum for its users, which have no relationship to ePortal's roles.

eBusiness needs to be able to partition the policies for the different portals to make sure that one set of portal users cannot get improper access to another portal's resources. To implement the partitioning, eBusiness defines attribute-mapping rules to prepend a portal identifier onto each incoming role so that the roles associated with each portal will be in a separate namespace. These rules are stored in the iPlanet directory server for use by the attribute-mapping service. In our example, eBusiness defines roles from ePortal and eMarket such as eportal:member and emarket:gold. This allows eBusiness to set up separate access control policies for its corporate portal customers. Further, the approach allows eBusiness to disambiguate roles when two portals happen to pick the same names.

Limit Visitor Access

eBusiness needs to ensure that all requests to its site are from authenticated corporate customers. Because eBusiness contains valuable information about products, prices, and orders for many different corporations, unauthenticated users have no reason to need direct access to this site.

The eBusiness Web server enforces this requirement, as supported by the SSL and WS-Security/SAML services. If an incoming SSL session is not authenticated or a WS-Security/SAML token is not signed by a known, trusted corporation, eBusiness immediately rejects the request.

Grant Members More Access

eBusiness grants ePortal members access to special product details that are not available to customers. The eBusiness WebLogic J2EE application server enforces this RBAC policy based on the method permissions defined in the EJB deployment descriptor, as explained in Chapter 7. First, code in the application server container extracts the mapped role out of the WS-Security/SAML token that is part of the SOAP request. The code uses the extracted role to set up the JAAS context.

When subsequent calls on the methods in the EJB are made, the container enforces the access policy based on the role. Methods on beans that give access to special product details may be called only by members, not general customers.

Protect the Accounts of Each Individual

In addition to protecting corporate data, eBusiness has a legal responsibility to maintain the privacy of all individuals who are using the service. ePortal relies on eBusiness to protect personal customer data for ePortal; if eBusiness fails to do so, ePortal would probably sue eBusiness for negligence.

We start with SSL to establish the confidentiality between ePortal and eBusiness so that consumer data is kept private as it travels over the Internet. However, SSL by itself is inadequate to enforce the privacy requirement. We also need to protect the customer data that resides on the eBusiness servers.

As we discussed in Chapter 7, it's difficult to enforce fine-grained access policies that restrict users to their own data. eBusiness could build security-aware EJB applications to do this, but this would take a lot of effort and would result in a lot of trusted code in the applications.

As an alternate approach, we rely on the Oracle database to enforce the fine-grained access control needs for privacy. Databases such as Oracle 9i have many mechanisms for advanced access control (Oracle 2002) for ensuring that users can only see their own database records.

Historically, back-office databases have been able to enforce fine-grained access control, but they have not been able to connect seamlessly with middle tier products. In particular, enforcing fine-grained access control on a database generally required a separate database login for each individual user. However, having another login defeats the purpose of a multitier architecture, where authentication is performed on a separate system. Passing users' login information for database access is not an option in our example. ePortal enforces authentication on a separate system from eBusiness; eBusiness does not have access to any of the users' authentication information. It is not feasible in the eBusiness security architecture to require a user to directly authenticate to the database.

Fortunately, we can address this obstacle by using the eBusiness EASI framework and advanced database functionality. In the case of Oracle 9i, we use a feature known as *proxy authentication* (Oracle 2002). Proxy authentication allows the EJB application to be authenticated to the database server as an application and use delegation to speak on behalf of a user. First, the EJB authenticates itself to the database server (in this case using a public key certificate). Next, the EJB extracts the mapped user identity and attribute information from the WS-Security/SAML token that it received in the SOAP request. Then, the EJB establishes a lightweight session with the database server, passing the user's identity and role information as the requestor.

Using the proxy authentication feature, the database server trusts that the EJB has already performed an authentication check on the user making the request. The database server will then enforce an access control policy based on the individual user's identity and role information. In addition, the database policy can be set up to restrict the ability of an application to proxy users, so that the EJB is only permitted to request user information from selected users (say, only from ePortal users, but not from eMarket's).

We hide the details of the setup behind the eBusiness EASI framework APIs so that we do not have to embed special-purpose security code within the EJB application. As far as the J2EE application server is concerned, it is making a typical Java Database Connectivity (JDBC) call to the database server. Behind the scenes, the EASI framework has established the authentication between the EJB and the server and set up the user proxy information.

By using proxy authentication, we have completed the long chain of end-to-end trust. Back on ePortal, the Web server trusted the Web SSO product to perform the authentication check. That authentication check was the basis of trust for the creation of the SAML assertion within the WS-Security document. ePortal transmitted the WS-Security/SAML token within the SOAP request to the eBusiness Web server, which determined if it trusted the ePortal to speak on behalf of the user in the request. The eBusiness Web server then passed the mapped request on to the J2EE application server that had to trust the WS-Security/SAML token to set up the JAAS context. Finally, the application server used proxy authentication so that the database server would trust the application server to speak on behalf of the user. Hopefully, it is crystal clear by this time why multitier Web Services go well beyond the abilities of traditional client/server security!

Administrator Control of Critical Functions

eBusiness must ensure that application functions are controlled by its administrative staff. To enforce this requirement, we use the role-based policy defined for the J2EE application server. Local eBusiness staff are authenticated within the internal network directly to the application server, and are assigned the role of staff. We use method permissions on the product price and account interfaces to ensure that only users who are staff members are authorized to call methods on these interfaces.

Restrict Administrators' Abilities

Finally, eBusiness restricts the abilities of its own staff to commit fraud by prohibiting staff from settling (paying for) orders. This policy is very straightforward to enforce using the EJB application method permissions. We simply require that the callers accessing the settle order operation on shopping carts must be customers or members, and not staff.

Since eBusiness staff do not create customers and members (that activity takes place at ePortal), it would require the collusion of the staff from both companies to commit fraud. Although this type of attack is still possible, we have limited it to scenarios that are more difficult to set up and, hopefully, easier to detect.

Deploying Security

ePortal and eBusiness have put a lot of effort into planning and building their Web Services architectures. They have separately defined security requirements for each of their corporate application platforms, and jointly agreed on how they will collaborate to provide a secure online storefront. They have identified how their security architectures depend on each other and where the security of one company relies on the trustworthiness of the other. They have used EASI frameworks to define the security APIs and to implement the supporting security services from a variety of vendor products as well as custom-developed services.

The final step to ensure success is a well-thought-out deployment of the ePortal and eBusiness architectures. In this section, we provide some background on related security technologies that support the deployment of a secure Web Services architecture. We examine how the security technologies in the perimeter, middle, and back-office tiers contribute to the implementation of a fully operational system. We conclude with a discussion of the use of security policy servers and the increase in system architecture complexity caused by new security technologies.

Perimeter Security

Both ePortal and eBusiness rely on perimeter security mechanisms as a first line of defense before a request reaches the Web server. The two technologies in use are firewalls and intrusion detection systems. We will describe how these types of products may be deployed in support of perimeter security.

Firewalls/VPNs

A firewall protects one network from another. The benefits realized through the use of firewalls as the first line of defense include increased security assurance and intrusion alert capabilities. Examples of firewall products are Checkpoint Firewall-1, Cisco PIX, and Raptor Eagle. The placement of firewalls on a network is critical to its ability to provide security. All network traffic must pass through a firewall before being allowing onto a protected network. If network traffic is permitted to enter a protected network by any other means, the protection could be compromised.

With the advent of e-commerce and the greater use of Web Services and distributed computing, firewalls are not as effective as when systems in the perimeter were not permitted into a company's mid-tier or were only allowed to access a few computers that were not connected to the corporate network, such as an FTP server or an HTTP server that returned static Web pages. Traditional firewalls, for the most part, are designed to keep people out of your system. Web Services want to allow people into your system. That said, firewalls still play an important part in your system's defense.

The main job of perimeter firewalls is to direct traffic to a few systems, which in turn can examine requests and possibly do some authentication and authorization. This firewall may be a router, which directs traffic according to an IP address or a specific destination, such as an FTP server. The perimeter firewall may also be a little more complex and examine messages to determine if they are HTTP messages, and then direct those messages through its HTTP port to the HTTP server.

Typically, as in the case of both ePortal and eBusiness, a DMZ is created to facilitate access from public networks to publicly available services (that is, Web servers, public File Transfer Protocol (FTP) servers, and so on) without compromising the private internal corporate network. The basic configuration of the firewalls in a DMZ is a pair of firewalls with the publicly available services running on a subnetwork that is isolated between the firewalls. The pair of firewalls may be configured for redundancy so that a backup firewall can take over if a primary firewall fails. Firewalls may also be set up within an enterprise to separate groups of machines into *security enclaves*.

There is a new category of perimeter security product, called a software XML firewall, that is designed to work in conjunction with the packet-level firewall products discussed here. A software XML firewall is a proxy that typically sits in the DMZ behind the external firewall and in front of the Web or application server. XML firewall proxies can make up for the limitation of traditional packet-level firewalls that cannot prevent the tunneling of SOAP requests through HTTP. XML firewall proxies filter Web Services requests and enforce authentication and authorization on those requests. There are new products on the market from several vendors that provide this type of security, including offerings from Quadrasis/Xtradyne, Vordel, and Westbridge Technologies. We discuss this topic in more detail in Chapter 10.

Virtual private networks (VPNs) allow a trusted network to communicate with another trusted network over open networks such as the Internet. Although a VPN was not used in our example, we could have considered its use to improve security between ePortal and eBusiness. VPN technology provides seamless and transparent communication between systems on the Internet, while maintaining both the privacy and the integrity of the communicated data. A VPN does this by creating a secure point-to-point tunnel between two network entities, such as enterprise gateways, or from a client's desktop to a protected enterprise application. Data transmitted through this tunnel is both encrypted and authenticated. VPNs are useful for telecommuting employees and for communication with partners and business customers. Companies frequently implement VPNs to reduce network costs by allowing secure use of public networks.

Firewalls/VPNs provide the following security support:

Authentication. Firewalls provide coarse-grained authentication that is typically used to allow access to trusted networks based on IP or port addresses. Firewalls also support authentication mechanisms based on tokens (for example, RSA SecurID). VPN technology provides a means of protecting and securing authentication data (such as passwords) as the data traverses open networks.

Authorization. Firewalls/VPNs provide coarse-grained packet filtering based mainly on protocols and ports as well as other simple criteria, such as content-based filtering or protocol vectoring. The primary purpose of firewall authorization is to limit client access to specified servers and ports, for example, limiting a browser client to communicating only via HTTP to a Web server within the DMZ.

Firewalls typically use a set of security proxies to initiate a connection; each security proxy is designed to listen for specific types of connection attempts. In addition to built-in application proxy services, firewalls may also support implementation of custom proxy-based services.

Firewalls are also designed to protect against a broad range of external security and denial-of-service attacks, such as IP address spoofing, Transmission Control Protocol (TCP) SYN flooding, Simple Mail Transfer Protocol (SMTP) weaknesses, port scanning, and downloaded Java applets, among many others.

Accountability. Firewalls/VPNs generally provide extensive logging capabilities for attempted access. Firewall audits should, of course, be used to provide logging of attempted attacks.

Security administration. Firewalls/VPNs provide administrative tools to define firewall policies that are stored within an internal database.

Intrusion Detection

As you recall, ePortal decided to deploy an intrusion detection system (IDS) to protect against external attacks. An IDS monitors and potentially prevents attempts to break into or otherwise compromise a system component. Without an IDS in place, the likelihood of detecting an intrusion is greatly diminished. There are two basic models of intrusion detection: *anomaly detection* and *misuse detection*. Anomaly detection looks for activity that is different from a user or system's normal behavior. Misuse detection looks for activity that corresponds to known intrusion techniques (signatures) or system vulnerabilities.

Intrusion detection systems typically provide:

- Monitoring and analysis of user and system activity
- Auditing of system configurations and vulnerabilities
- Assessment of the integrity of critical system and data files
- Recognition of activity patterns reflecting known attacks
- Statistical analysis for abnormal activity patterns
- Operating system audit trail management with recognition of user activity reflecting policy violations

An IDS may be either network- or host-based. A network-based IDS typically monitors the network for attempts to exploit known network security threats, whereas a host-based IDS monitors servers and their critical applications and data for abuse and misuse. Although a host-based IDS is not as fast as its network counterpart, it does offer advantages that a network-based system cannot match. These strengths include stronger forensic analysis, a closer focus on host-specific event data, and lower entry-level costs.

There are two basic types of host-based monitoring:

A *network monitor* checks incoming network connections on a host by monitoring packets that attempt to access the host before the packets are passed to the networking layer of the host, which could represent a threat. (Note that a network monitor is different from network-based intrusion detection, because a network monitor only looks at network traffic coming to the host it is running on, and not all traffic passing through the network.) The IDS responds to network connections that represent some kind of intrusion attempt. An example of a product that performs this type of port monitoring is RealSecure Agent by ISS. The RealSecure engine runs on dedicated workstations to provide network intrusion detection and response.

A *host monitor* checks files, file systems, logs, or other parts of the host for suspicious activity that might represent an intrusion attempt (or a successful intrusion). Many host monitors come with the capability to alert systems administration staff regarding problems found. For Windows NT systems, the Event Log Monitor (ELM) displays a consolidated view of all the Windows NT event logs for the workstations and servers being monitored. It provides the capability to create custom views of grouped events, in which each view is dynamically updated as new events occur in the network. In addition to monitoring the Windows NT event logs, ELM monitors services, processes, and performance counters and generates alerts when things start to go wrong.

Mid-Tier Security

Web Services security depends primarily on the mid-tier security infrastructure. We described the security of the most common middleware technologies, namely CORBA, COM+, .NET, and J2EE, extensively in Chapter 7. We used several of these in our ePortal and eBusiness example, so we won't discuss them further here.

There are other specialized security products that we did not use in our example but that may be relevant to your Web Services application. One category of product to consider is *entitlement servers*, which can provide fine-grained access controls for the middle tier. CrossLogix3, which supports SAML, is an example of an entitlement server. These products are still new, so we recommend carefully evaluating this technology before performing any serious deployment.

An entitlement is a business access rule that describes the decision criteria applied when a user attempts to access an application resource. Entitlement management addresses administering and maintaining various permissions, roles, privileges, and login rights for an organization's information systems users, including suppliers, partners, customers, and employees. Resources include client/server applications, back-office legacy applications, and Web pages.

Entitlements originated in the financial services world, and they may be best suited for that class of business applications. However, the basic entitlements model appears to be very general, and vendors believe that their approach is applicable to most other environments.

Back-Office Security

Common back-office security technologies are database security and mainframe security. We gave some background on how eBusiness used database security in support of its Web Services security architecture. For simplicity, our examples did not use mainframe security, but it is common in many large enterprise deployments, so we touch briefly on this topic here.

Several products may be used to secure resources on a mainframe. As a representative sample, we discuss the basic capabilities of Computer Associates ACF2. ACF2 can protect and control all security aspects of the IBM mainframe environment. ACF2 provides security to the OS/390 business transaction environment including Unix system services and applications, as well as the IBM Websphere application server. ACF2 provides streamlined administration, single-point user sign-on, and platform/network level security and auditing.

Authentication. ACF2 supports the basic authentication mechanism of userID/password and can also be integrated with many other authentication mechanisms, including one-time password substitutes, smartcards, LDAP, and PKI certificates. ACF2 supports *user exits* that may be tailored to provide custom authentication checks. User exits are points within the ACF2 product that permit calls to an external program, giving the security administrator control over the authentication and authorization processes.

Authorization. ACF2 provides very extensive and customizable authorization policies that focus on the mainframe environment. For example, datasets, CICS transactions, and terminal resources can all be under the direct control of the ACF2 security product.

ACF2 provides a role-based approach to mainframe security; a user can be associated with one or more roles. Administrators can be granted authority to maintain a limited number of users and resources, and may be granted access to a limited set of administrative actions.

Cryptography. Using Kerberos and DCE, ACF2 provides the means to secure communications between OS/390 environments and open systems, including MQSeries messages and TCP/IP.

Accountability. ACF2 provides extensive platform- and network-level security auditing facilities as well as external audit reduction and reporting tools.

Security administration. ACF2 provides administrative tools to maintain security policies for the mainframe. The policies are stored within internal databases; user information can also be made accessible via LDAP.

Using a Security Policy Server

From an application developer's point of view, security is enabled by linking into a security library and having the middleware take care of it. However, in order for the security service to be able to enforce security, the security service needs to have access to policies and rules to know what actions to take for a client that wants to access a given resource. These policies and rules are typically defined for authentication, authorization, cryptography, and auditing. Any attack that compromises these policies could result in a breakdown of the security of the system, so you can see the necessity of protecting access to setting the policy data. A separate server, usually called a security policy server, is associated with some persistent store for the data, such as a database commonly accessed via LDAP.

Setting the security policy is a very sensitive process because it is the basis of your security. Having a separate server to handle security removes the procedure from the security run time and permits independent additions, updates, and modifications to the security data, making security administration a very secure procedure. The server can be physically protected and all remote access, such as Telnet, FTP, and rlogin can be disabled, allowing only secure interactions with the security policy server.

Self-Administration

One of the biggest challenges of security in an e-business environment is the ability to manage the security data for the business. ePortal could have thousands or millions of users. Human operators can maintain some of this security information, but ePortal needs to automate a vast majority of this data. Because the bulk of the data is related to the customer base, we will automate that data input by having a system that permits a user to register and change his or her personal data online.

The application that registers users must be heavily protected. We do not want one user to modify, or even view, another user's data. It's not only customers that we have to protect the system against. We also need to ensure that a random employee cannot access anyone's data. For example, a devious employee may register as a customer, buy a large amount of our products, and then change his access identity to that of a supervisor in accounting. With this bogus access identity, the employee could then change his charge to a credit. If he could break the administrative system, he could assume any identity and do anything he wanted with our system.

So how do we protect ourselves against this kind of an attack? There is a series of steps that you should take:

1. Use a security system that supports a protected administration subsystem.
2. Deploy this system on a separate machine.
3. Shut off remote access by unsecured or weakly secured means, such as Telnet, rlogin, and FTP. Also, do not install any remote access programs, such as pcAnywhere. You want to limit access to this machine.
4. Physically protect the machine and allow only cleared personnel, such as your security administrator, to log in to the machine.
5. Put very tight access controls on the administration programs.

We don't want to give the customer the rights to change his or her data directly on the security policy server because that would allow access to the administrative system itself. Although we could protect against inappropriate access at the administrative security policy server, a more secure way to prevent access is to only permit security administrators access to that server. Therefore, the application that we described in the previous paragraph will be "owned" by the security administrator. This is accomplished by the security administrator's logging into the system with authentication evidence known only to the security administrator, and then starting the application. In ePortal, we could require token-based authentication to log in to any application that has access to the administrative system. Consequently, not only does the security administrator have to supply a password to decrypt the data, but the authentication evidence is also physically separate from the computer; that is, it's a token.

Large-Scale Administration

There are several ways of performing administrative tasks on the security policy server. A common one is to use a GUI interface that supports graphical capabilities to aid the administrator in carrying out administrative tasks. Another method is to use secure batch tools, which can take information from another source, for example, a mainframe, and perform periodic updates. Finally, if the security product supports an administrative API, it's also possible to write a custom security-aware application that makes calls to the API. In all these cases, only the security administrator should be allowed access, using protections similar to those we described for ePortal.

For all but small companies, the amount of security data is usually very large, and maintenance is a major task. When ePortal reaches its million customer milestone, there will be a lot of customer security data. Security administrative tools are provided by your application platform supplier; so check the administrative capabilities that your vendor gives you to be sure that they will support maintenance of your security data as your business grows. As you well know, customers are always changing something, whether it is their credit cards, billing addresses, or even their names. So don't underestimate the work entailed in security data maintenance.

An important requirement of the security administrative service for a large installation is the ability to have multiple security policy servers. You don't want one point of failure in a critical task like security. This means that the application platform supplier should have solutions for supporting simultaneous changes by different administrators on these various security policy servers. Support for simultaneous updating includes solving all the problems of input timing conflicts, transaction rollback, failover, and replication.

One of the biggest problems that your security service must solve for you is synchronization between multiple security administrators. eBusiness expects to have a number of security policy servers located in different countries, and each of these different locales will have different security administrators. The problem to be solved is what happens when two or more of these administrators attempt to change the same set of security data. Does the system support atomic input of the data? Does it support notification between the administrators of an attempt at simultaneous input and a way for them to choose the correct input? This is a difficult problem, but there has been a lot of work on these types of problems in computer science. The bottom line is to determine what support your potential security provider has supplied, how well they have implemented the solution, and whether the solution meets your needs. Neglecting this area can lead to severe problems as your installation grows to enterprise scale.

Storing Security Policy Data

As you might imagine, ePortal and eBusiness will have quite a bit of security data if their plans work out to have millions of customers, thousands of products, and hundreds of suppliers, to say nothing of the number of ePortal and eBusiness employees. Security policy data has to be kept on all these entities. This naturally leads you to think of some sort of database and, of course, securing the persistent store. A popular form of data store that is used by a number of security providers is the LDAP directory service; other data stores for security policies include databases and file systems. We discuss each of these alternatives next.

LDAP Directory Service

More and more companies are releasing LDAP-based directories, for example, iPlanet, Oracle, Microsoft, IBM, and Novell. In addition, a number of the security systems support LDAP directories as a persistent store for security data. There are a couple of reasons for this. An LDAP directory presents a hierarchical data store, which matches the structure of the data from a security system, and LDAP supports SSL protection and both username and password and certificate authentication, again matching the protocols used in many security systems.

Let's first take a look at user data. In security systems, users are identified by X.500 names, which have a hierarchical data structure. For example, Mary Jones might have an X.500 name of CN=Mary Jones, CITY=Burlington, ST=MA, and C=US. Using this schema for the X.500 customer names allows us to break down our customers by country, state, city, and individual. Figure 12.6 shows the hierarchical nature of ePortal's customer persistent store.

This hierarchical schema for an LDAP directory tree is supported by the LDAP APIs and is used for more than security purposes. For example, it can be used for employees' telephone numbers, office numbers, and other business-related information. At ePortal, we break our customers down by each level in the hierarchy, for example, by country, state, and so on, so that we can use this breakdown to help ePortal in its marketing. Another use is to help us in delivery of customer purchases. As ePortal and eBusiness grow, we can automatically keep track of geographic growth and use this information to choose the location for distribution centers.

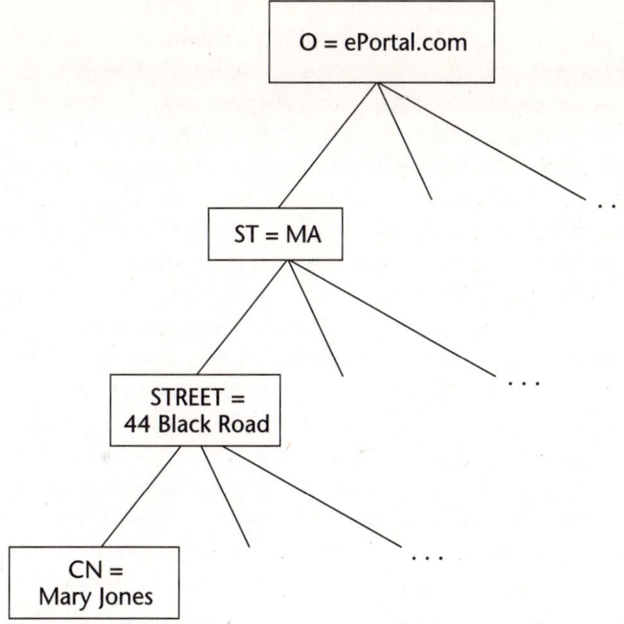

Figure 12.6 ePortal customer LDAP schema.

On the security side, the type of schema used for our customers matches the format of the customer names in their X.509 SSL certificates, making this a seamless match as we move toward client certificates. In addition to the node names in the LDAP structure, each node can hold a set of attributes, which are key/value pairs. (This is another example of an overloaded name. An LDAP attribute is not a security policy attribute, although a security policy attribute could be placed in an LDAP attribute value field.) LDAP attributes are where the telephone numbers and office numbers are stored.

Your security service could define a password attribute in the Common Name (CN) LDAP node and use that attribute to store the user's password, preferably in encrypted form. In order to store the password, the LDAP schema has to be expanded. The schema is controlled by an object class, which lists the required and allowed attributes; for example, the schema that we used for our customers is the Person Object Class. This object class requires the CN and the surname (SN). So, in addition to CN=Mary Smith, the security service has to have SN=Smith. But back to the password. The security provider could define a derived object class from the Person class and define an allowed attribute Password, or it could use a standard derived class that contains the password attribute. The reason that it may define its own object class is so it can define additional attributes, for example, a unique customer ID. In our case, we wanted our own schema in order to have the flexibility to add other marketing attributes.

If your security provider uses LDAP, there are a few things that you should look for in their LDAP implementation. We have seen some instances in which the provider uses one of the standard fields for its own use—for example, putting the password in an attribute field that it *guessed* its customers would not use. Because you will probably be using the LDAP store for uses other than security, such as the other uses in ePortal, be careful, because you might have a need for this same field either now or in the future.

A second thing to look out for is the type of connection between the security policy server and the LDAP server. LDAP supports SSL and simple password protection. If your security service does not use SSL and the LDAP server is distributed, that is, not on the same physical machine as the security service, then your security data is passed in the clear and is susceptible to snooping. The preferred security approach is to use a system that supports an SSL connection to the LDAP server. As usual, this should be looked at from a risk management point of view. What problems would you face if your security policy data was compromised? Be sure to check the type of connection from the service to the LDAP server that your security provider supports.

Not all your sensitive data will be handled by the LDAP server, even if that is your persistent store for your security policy data. In our analysis of our security system, we realize there is a distinction between policy data and functional data. Specifically, we transmit users' credit card numbers as functional data, whereas our policy data includes information such as user passwords. In the eBusiness design, the credit card numbers are stored in the back-office tier in a relational database, and the connection to that database uses security service protection, including SSL protection. User passwords are stored in encrypted form in the LDAP server and are passed as security policy data. At eBusiness, our risk assessment is such that we cannot afford to have our security policy data, for example, user passwords, compromised. Therefore, we demand a security service that supports an SSL connection when passing policy data. An alternate solution would be to have the LDAP server on the same physical machine as the security policy server and to isolate that machine. However, this limits the distributed capabilities of LDAP.

Relational or Object Databases

Most LDAP implementations use a database beneath the LDAP APIs to store security data. Therefore, there is not a big difference in the persistent store for your security data whether your security service provider uses a database directly or through LDAP. The provider's choice is reflected in the system-level effects, such as performance and fault tolerance. The provider's choice of persistent store could also show up in other ways, such as additional costs if you have to pay for a third-party persistent store or the replication, distribution, and failover capabilities of the security system as a whole.

There is one security aspect of the provider's choice of persistent store that we discussed in the previous section, which is how the transmission of the security policy data is protected. Just as with LDAP, the connection with the database chosen by your security provider must supply a secure channel to that database. This might be harder for the provider using an older database and thus might be skipped. However, it is critical that you find out what protection scheme the provider is using for this connection and make sure that it meets your security requirements.

The provider might be doing its own encryption of the data. If so, find out what encryption algorithms it is using and what type of key exchange it is using. The algorithms may be too weak and easy to break, or they may not be acceptable in the countries in which you are or may be doing business. Another question to ask is: Can you change the algorithms and substitute new ones? In general, it is better if the provider uses a standard security connection rather than rolls its own, but the provider may have a good reason to use its own system.

File Systems

Another way that the security service provider could store security policy data is by using the file system. This can be the least-secure method, depending on what additional protection schemes the system is using. In many cases, the provider's protection of the file system only relies on operating system protection—for example, setting the protection on a file to an operating system administrative owner.

There are two problems associated with a security service that relies on the security capabilities of the file system:

- Attackers have studied operating systems' security in depth and have discovered their weaknesses. Although these weaknesses are addressed as they become publicly known, operating systems are very complex beasts, and this complexity works against developing a secure operating system.
- The programs that write to the file system store must have the permissions to access that store and are thus susceptible to compromise themselves.

Our general advice is to shy away from a security service that relies solely on operating system protection for its persistent store, and look to solutions that combine operating system and cryptographic protection.

Securing UDDI and WSDL

Throughout this book, we have been concentrating on the security service itself with an implicit focus on securing the application. However, this is not the complete story. In any distributed system, including Web Services-based systems, there is an infrastructure of supporting services that are necessary to make the system work.

One of the most ubiquitous services is the directory used to find other services; in Web Services terminology, this is known as the Universal Description, Discovery and Integration (UDDI) registry. Your client application has to magically find a server that has implemented the service that you want to call. What if the UDDI returns to your client a WSDL file for a bogus service? How do you know whether you are really talking to a legitimate UDDI registry and not a fraudulent one?

We regrettably have to say that implementations do not always secure these services. This can leave a big security hole in your system, which could very well be exploited by malicious attackers. So once again, we advise you to use the information that we provide and find out what infrastructure services are supplied by your application platform vendor or vendors and also find out whether and how they have secured them.

Security Gotchas at the System Architecture Level

In addition to paying attention to the way your security service provider implements and secures the underlying services, you should pay attention to the overall operation of the security service as a whole. The two main system areas that can be severely affected by the addition of security are scaling and performance. We'll touch on each of these areas in the next two subsections.

Scaling

The security solutions for distributed systems usually employ a security policy server to handle requests for authentication, authorization, and audit policies. Let's take a look at what a security policy server is expected to do and why it can be a critical item in affecting the scaling capabilities of your system. There are two competing principles at work. On one hand, you want to be able to centrally administer your security data. On the other hand, funneling all the maintenance and requests through one server, especially for large, highly interactive companies like ePortal and eBusiness, can put an extreme load on that one server, to say nothing of the single point of failure that a lone security policy server would impose on the system. Another aspect is the geographic distribution of the system in which you would want security policy servers distributed. The latter two requirements point to multiple security policy servers, whereas the first is most easily satisfied by a single security policy server.

One way for multiple security policy servers to act as a central point of administration is for them to be stateless or to support very little state, which can be coordinated between the different security policy servers. A second requirement of multiple security policy servers is that maintenance be coordinated. For example, when our system administrator in London wants to update the same policy that our system administrator in New York wants to update, the security system should handle the multiple steps of a policy update from the two administrators as a separate, atomic update for each administrator. Because this could wind up in a last update wins situation, there needs to be notification of the updates between the distributed authorities.

The solutions to this class of problems are known, but they are not easy to implement. Therefore, this is another area that you should look at closely; that is, how your security provider has implemented solutions to this scaling problem.

Another potential scaling problem for a heavily distributed system is key management, which is how the system stores and retrieves the cryptographic keys needed for encryption and integrity. There are commercial systems that your security provider can use such as those from RSA, Entrust, Verisign, and Baltimore Technologies.

Performance

When discussing performance, the phrase that comes to mind is, "There's no free lunch." In order to have effective security in a distributed system, work has to be done by the system, which means computing time. Once again, risk management comes into the picture. The tighter and finer-grained you want the security to be, the bigger the performance hit.

For the same level of security, there are a number of factors that can affect the performance of the security system. Some of these include:

- Encryption algorithms
- Underlying transport
- Policy granularity
- Caching

As discussed in Chapter 3, there are two types of encryption: public key and secret key. Secret key encryption is much faster than public key encryption, but secret keys do not scale as well as public keys. In each of these encryption types, different algorithms have different performance characteristics. When encrypting large amounts of data, implementations usually exchange a secret key using a public key to protect the key exchange. The details of encryption are too arcane for most, so our suggestion is to look at the performance numbers for the systems under consideration and compare them with those of other systems.

The implementation of the underlying application platform transport is another mechanism that can seriously affect performance because the security system itself is distributed and uses the transport to do its work and get the data it needs.

The more finely grained the policy, the more work the security system must do and thus the slower the performance. This is a trade-off that you can use when designing your overall security system. For example, in some cases performing authorization at the application level is appropriate, whereas in other cases authorization at the interface or even method is required for adequate security.

Caching can boost performance by orders of magnitude if it is well integrated into a security service. For example, an access decision could entail multiple trips to the security policy server and from there to the persistent store for each piece of data. This offers multiple opportunities for caching the data to improve performance. However, caching can cause a security problem if not done properly. For example, if a break-in is discovered, you will want to flush the cache or that party or parties will continue to have access until the cache times out. If your provider has not implemented an emergency cache flush, you will have to bring your whole system down to remove the cached values. Another problem with a badly designed caching system is the lack of control over the timing of updates to the security data values. Has your provider given you the ability to control the updates to the cache?

In the end, what you, the user of a security service, are concerned with is the overall performance in your environment. It's the job of the security provider to balance the performance of the system against the functionality of the security. It's your job to assess the overall performance of the system. However, the security and system trade-offs in the various parts of the system make the subject of performance highly complex. Therefore, be sure that the performance characteristics that you examine match the type of work that your system will be asked to do. A performance number that measures the performance of calling the same method 100,000 times is not very useful if your system does separate method calls to a large number of methods with very little repetition.

Finally, it is best to get performance numbers from a third party. However, these are hard to get, so you will probably have to do your own comparative performance tests. There is a need for companies that perform independent security performance tests of distributed application server environments, and we expect to see them entering the industry market soon.

Summary

In this chapter, we first took a step back from our detailed analysis to look at how to define a Web Services security architecture. We began by discussing the challenges of Web Services security. We talked about issues such as interacting securely across system boundaries, trustworthiness, and security evolution. We then provided some EASI principles for Web Services, and defined the security requirements for ePortal and eBusiness based on those principles. We went through ePortal's and eBusiness's approaches to building their online storefront as a case study in deploying security. We discussed ePortal's and eBusiness's functional, security, and nonfunctional requirements. We finished by describing how we used EASI to define flexible security frameworks for the companies.

The EASI framework helped us structure our strategy for enforcing security and provided guidance for us on the kinds of products needed to satisfy Web Service security requirements. Based on the definition of the frameworks, we provided an overview of the ePortal and eBusiness security architectures, and described how they worked together to secure the online storefront. We then described security deployment issues related to supporting security technologies used in the perimeter, middle, and back-office tiers of the architecture.

Another component of an enterprise security system, the security policy data itself, is often neglected in the discussion of enterprise systems. We discussed this unglamorous part of security and pointed out the problems that can arise from the need to maintain large amounts of security policy data. We also discussed methods for isolating and maintaining this data. One component used by a number of security service providers is the security policy server. We looked at some of the problems and solutions associated with security policy servers.

We ended our discussion with two additional problems that are present in any large distributed system—scaling and performance—and how they are exacerbated by adding security to a system. We alerted you to be on the lookout for these problems and to ensure that the solutions your security system providers use to alleviate them meet your requirements.

Web Services security continues to move at "Internet speed," so the most valuable and lasting approach is to understand how security is established in a distributed system and to then use this knowledge to choose a current security technology that satisfies your needs. To that end, we concentrated on providing you with the practical theory and understanding of the underlying security functionality of Web Services. We placed this model in the bigger picture of end-to-end security. For updates on the latest developments in Web Services security technology, we encourage you to visit our Web site at www.wiley.com/compbooks/Hartman.

Web Services security is a very broad and complex topic. When you started reading this book, you may have thought that securing a Web Service required nothing more than using SSL to encrypt data sent between two applications. By now you realize that Web Services security covers a whole variety of technology and interoperability issues that span the entire system architecture. Now that you have a good grasp of Web Services security, we hope that you will use this knowledge when designing and building a robust, secure enterprise architecture. The principles that you have learned will also serve you well in choosing among security products that your company may contemplate purchasing and in making the numerous trade-offs that you will face when putting together your own enterprise security architecture. Distributed security is a rapidly changing field, but by learning the fundamental hows and whys of Web Services security, you will be able to understand and critically assess the applicability of new security specifications, ideas, and products.

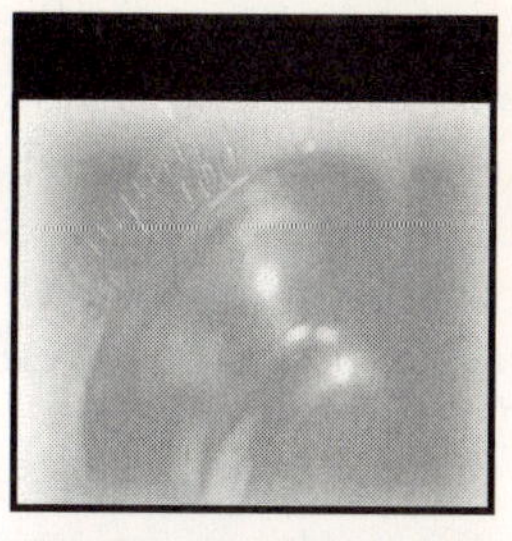

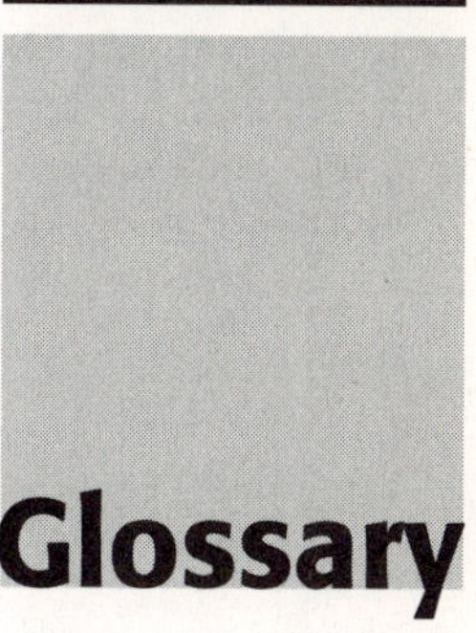

Glossary

access control Protection of resources against unauthorized access.

Access Control List (ACL) An association with each resource structure that lists subjects that have access rights for a particular resource.

Access matrix A conceptual model, first introduced by Butler Lampson in his milestone work "Protection" (Lampson 1971), which helps developers to describe access control policies and mechanisms. In the matrix, there is a row for each subject and a column for each object, and each cell specifies access rights granted to the subject for the corresponding object.

accountability mechanisms Security mechanisms that make sure that subjects are held accountable for their actions toward the system resources and services.

ACF2 Access Control Facility 2, an add-on security software package for mainframes from Computer Associates.

ACL *See* Access Control List.

active server pages (ASP) A scripting environment for Microsoft Internet Information Server in which you can combine HTML, scripts and reusable ActiveX server components to create dynamic web pages (FOLDOC 2002).

API *See* Application Programming Interface.

application assembler A role in an EJB lifecycle, which is responsible for combining enterprise beans into larger deployable application units by inserting the application assembly instructions into the deployment descriptors of one or more EJB JAR files provided by the bean provider(s).

Application Programming Interface (API) An interface or calling convention by which an application program accesses other programs.

application server A computing environment used for hosting component-based distributed business applications.

ASP *See* active server pages.

assurance A measure of confidence that the security features and architecture of an information system accurately mediate and enforce the security policy.

asymmetric cryptography A modern branch of cryptography (popularly known as public key cryptography) in which the algorithms employ a pair of keys (a public key and a private key) and use a different component of the pair for different steps of the algorithm (FOLDOC 2002).

audit *See* Security audit.

authentication The process of establishing the authenticity of the claimed subject identity.

authorization The process of making access control decisions.

availability A property of an information system consisting of the ability to deliver services and data when they are needed.

B2B Business-to-business.

backward trust evaluation A CSIv2 term that refers to the evaluation of delegation trust based on the rules of the target.

bean An abbreviated name for an Enterprise Java Bean.

bean deployer A role in an EJB life cycle that is responsible for taking one or more EJB JAR files produced by a bean provider or application assembler and deploying the enterprise beans contained in these files in a specific enterprise environment.

bean provider A role in an EJB lifecycle that is responsible for producing enterprise beans in the form of EJB JAR files containing one or more enterprise beans. The JAR files include Java classes that implement the enterprise bean's business methods, definitions of the bean's remote and home interfaces, and the deployment descriptor.

class A named description of a set of objects that share the same attributes, operations, relationships, and semantics.

client stub An element generated by the IDL compiler as part of the client code that acts as a proxy of the object for the client. The client code calls a locally residing stub, which makes calls on the rest of the ORB, using interfaces that are private to, and presumably optimized for, the particular ORB core.

COM+ The next generation (after COM) in the evolution of Microsoft distributed computing architecture. It integrates Microsoft Transaction Server into COM and provides a messaging alternative, based on Microsoft Message Queue technology, for COM calls.

component The fundamental building block of distributed software applications. Each component has one or more interfaces that provide the points of entry for calling programs. An interface, which is defined in terms of operations (also called methods), encapsulates a component and ensures that a component is modular.

composite delegation A form of delegation in which both the client privileges and the immediate invoker's privileges are passed to the target, so that both the client privileges and the privileges from the immediate source of the invocation can be individually checked.

confidentiality A security property ensuring that information is disclosed only to the authorized subjects.

constrained delegation Synonymous with controlled delegation.

container A rich runtime environment that provides an array of application services, allowing the application developer to concentrate on building the application rather than the supporting infrastructure.

controlled delegation A form of delegation in which a client can impose constraints on what privileges can be delegated to what intermediates. Also known as constrained delegation or restricted delegation.

cookie A small piece of information sent by a Web server to be stored on a Web browser so it can later be read back from that browser.

CORBA Common Object Request Broker Architecture. CORBA is an open, vendor-independent specification for an architecture and infrastructure that computer applications use to work together over networks.

CORBA Security (CORBASec) The CORBA Security service as defined in OMG 2000a.

credentials A container for a subject's security attributes.

CSIv2 Common Secure Interoperability version 2 (CSI, 2000). A recent addition to the CORBA security specification that defines a protocol for transmitting authentication and authorization data over IIOP.

DAC *See* Discretionary Access Control.

Data Encryption Standard (DES) A popular encryption algorithm standardized by the U.S. National Bureau of Standards. It is a product cipher that operates on 64-bit blocks of data, using a 56-bit key. It is defined in the Federal Information Processing Standards (FIPS) 46-1 (1988), which supersedes FIPS 46 (1977). DES is identical to the ANSI standard Data Encryption Algorithm (DEA) defined in ANSI X3.92-1981 (FOLDOC 2002).

data tier A tier in the enterprise computing architecture that usually consists of database servers and mainframe-based repositories providing access to data.

DCE *See* Distributed Computing Environment.

DCOM *See* Distributed Component Object Model.

delegation A feature of distributed systems that allows intermediate servers to act on behalf of the originating subject.

demilitarized zone (DMZ) A part of the network that is neither part of the internal network nor directly part of the private network. Typically, this is the area between the public network (such as the Internet) access router and the enterprise bastion host, although it can be located between any two policy-enforcing areas.

denial of service Prevention of authorized access to a system resource or the delaying of system operations and functions (TIS 2000).

deployer *See* bean deployer.

deployment descriptor A file that provides both the structural and application assembly information about the enterprise beans in the EJB JAR file.

DES *see* Data Encryption Standard.

digital certificate A certificate document in the form of a digital data object (a data object used by a computer) to which is appended a computed digital signature value that depends on the data object (TIS 2000).

digital signature A value computed with a cryptographic algorithm and appended to a data object in such a way that any recipient of the data can use the signature to verify the data's origin and integrity (TIS 2000).

directory service A distributed service that provides the ability to look up objects by their keys or attributes.

Discretionary Access Control (DAC) An access control model based on "restricting access to objects based on the identity of subjects or the groups to which they belong. The controls are discretionary in the sense that a subject with a certain access permission is capable of passing that permission (perhaps indirectly) on to any other subject" (DoD 1985).

Distributed Component Object Model (DCOM) Microsoft's extension of their Component Object Model (COM) to support objects distributed across a network. DCOM has been submitted to the IETF as a draft standard (FOLDOC 2002).

Distributed Computing Environment (DCE) A computing environment standardized by the Open Group that provides the following integrated facilities: Remote Procedure Call, Directory Services, Security Service, Threads, Distributed Time Service, and Distributed File Service.

DMZ *See* demilitarized zone.

document type definition (DTD) A description of the markup elements available in any specific type of XML or SGML document.

DTD *See* document type definition.

EAI *See* Enterprise Application Integration

EASI *See* Enterprise Application Security Integration

e-business The use of the Internet technology to help businesses streamline processes, improve productivity, and increase efficiency. E-business enables companies to easily communicate with partners, vendors, and customers, connect back-end systems, and conduct commerce in a secure manner.

ebXML A joint activity by *OASIS* and the United Nations Center For Trade Facilitation and Electronic Business (UN/CEFACT), whose goal is to define standards for the formatting and transmission of electronic commerce data, describe business processes, and negotiate business terms and responsibilities. It is hoped that by assuming Internet standard protocols and using *XML* that the cost of implement ebXML will be less than the cost of *EDI*.

e-commerce Commerce conducted electronically with the use of the Internet technology. It includes an online display of goods and services, ordering, billing, customer service, and the handling of payments and transactions.

EDI *See* Electronic Data Interchange.

EDIFACT *See* Electronic Data Interchange for Administration, Commerce and Transport.

EJB *See* Enterprise JavaBeans.

electronic data interchange (EDI) The exchange of standardized document forms between computer systems for business use (FOLDOC 2002).

Electronic Data Interchange for Administration, Commerce and Transport (EDIFACT) ISO's 1988 standard (ISO 9735) for electronic data interchange for administration, commerce and transport. It defines application-layer syntax. It was amended and reprinted in 1990. The document is available from ISO's Web site (FOLDOC 2002).

encryption The cryptographic transformation of data (called "plaintext") into a form (called "ciphertext") that conceals the data's original meaning to prevent it from being known or used. If the transformation is reversible, the corresponding reversal process is called "decryption," which is a transformation that restores encrypted data to its original state (TIS 2000).

Enterprise Application Integration (EAI) A methodological approach supported by a set of technologies that allows flexible integration of applications in order to support enterprise business processes.

Enterprise Application Security Integration (EASI) A special case of Enterprise Application Integration that enables the use of many different security technologies, and, as a result, provides the framework for secure EAI.

Enterprise JavaBeans (EJB) Architecture for component-based distributed computing from Sun. Enterprise beans are components of distributed transaction-oriented enterprise applications.

entitlement A business access rule that describes the decision criteria applied when a user attempts to access an application resource.

entitlement management Administration and maintenance of the various permissions, roles, privileges, and login rights for an organization's information systems users, including suppliers, partners, customers, and employees. Resources include client/server applications, legacy applications, and Web pages.

entitlement server A particular type of authorization server that can provide entitlement-based fine-grained access control for the mid-tier.

eXtensible Access Control Markup Language (XACML) A specification for expressing access control policies over the Internet.

Extensible Markup Language (XML) A markup language standardized by the W3C that defines a simple dialect of SGML suitable for use on the Web.

extranet the extension of a company's intranet out onto the Internet, for example, to allow selected customers, suppliers and mobile workers to access the company's private data and applications via the World Wide Web. This is in contrast to, and usually in addition to, the company's public Web site, which is accessible to everyone (FOLDOC 2002).

federation A system in which each party retains most of its authority and agrees to afford the other limited rights.

firewall A hardware device or a software program running on a secure host computer that protects networked computers from intentional hostile intrusion, which could result in a security breach.

forward trust evaluation A CSIv2 term that refers to the evaluation of trust based on rules provided by the caller.

framework A set of services, designs, architectures, or systems that embodies an abstract solution to a number of related, concrete problems.

hacker A person who enjoys the intellectual challenge of creatively overcoming or circumventing limitations (FOLDOC 2002). Frequently, malicious intruders are also called hackers.

HTML *See* Hypertext Markup Language.

HTTP *See* Hypertext Transfer Protocol.

HTTPS *See* Hypertext Transfer Protocol, Secure.

Hypertext Markup Language (HTML) Built on top of SGML, a hypertext document format used on the WWW.

Hypertext Transfer Protocol (HTTP) A client/server TCP/IP protocol used on the WWW for the exchange of HTML documents.

Hypertext Transfer Protocol, Secure (HTTPS) A variant of HTTP used for connecting to HTTP servers using SSL.

IDL *See* Interface Definition Language.

IETF *See* Internet Engineering Task Force.

IIOP *See* Internet Inter-ORB Protocol.

IIS *See* Internet Information Server.

impersonation The act whereby one principal assumes the identity and privileges of another principal without restrictions and without any indication visible to recipients of the impersonator's calls that delegation has taken place (OMG 2000a). There is still debate over this definition. For consistency, we use the CORBASec definition.

initiator A client who originated a chain of client/server calls.

integrity A security property ensuring that information is modified only by the authorized subjects.

interceptor An object that provides one or more specialized services at the ORB invocation boundary based upon the context of the object request (OMG 2000a).

interface A boundary across which two systems communicate. In software systems, an interface is an agreed upon convention used for interprogram communications, including function calls.

Interface Definition Language (IDL) A language used for defining interfaces to distributed objects accessible via middleware. It's often used to refer specifically to the IDL defined by the OMG as part of CORBA.

intermediate An object in a call chain that is neither the initiator nor the final target.

Internet Engineering Task Force (IETF) A large, open international community of network designers, operators, vendors, and researchers whose purpose is to coordinate the operation, management, and evolution of the Internet and to resolve short- and mid-range protocol and architectural issues (FOLDOC 2002).

Internet Information Server (IIS) Microsoft's Web server and FTP server for Windows platforms.

Internet Inter-ORB Protocol (IIOP) A standard protocol used for communications between CORBA-compliant ORBs over TCP/IP networks. IIOP is defined as part of CORBA.

Internet Protocol (IP) A connectionless, best-effort packet switching protocol used at the network layer for the TCP/IP protocol suite. IP provides packet routing, fragmentation, and reassembly.

Internet Protocol Security (IPSEC) A protocol that provides security for the transmission of sensitive information over unprotected networks such as the Internet. IPsec acts at the network layer, protecting and authenticating IP packets sent between participating devices (FOLDOC 2002). IETF documents related to the IPsec can be found at http://www.ietf.org/ids.by.wg/ipsec.html.

Internet Server Application Programming Interface (ISAPI) Microsoft's programming interface between applications and their Internet Server. Active Servers created with ISAPI extensions can be complete in-process applications themselves, or can "connect" to other services. ISAPI is used for the same sort of functions as Common Gateway Interface (CGI) but uses Microsoft Windows dynamic link libraries (DLL) for greater efficiency. The server loads the DLL the first time a request is received and the DLL then stays in memory, ready to service other requests until the server decides it is no longer needed. This minimizes the overhead associated with executing such applications many times (FOLDOC, 2002).

Internet service provider (ISP) A company that provides other companies or individuals with access to, or presence on, the Internet (FOLDOC 2002).

Interoperable Object Reference (IOR) A CORBA object reference in a format specified by CORBA that enables interoperability of object references.

intrusion detection A process of monitoring and analyzing system events for the purpose of finding and providing real-time or near real-time warning of attempts to access system resources in an unauthorized manner.

IOR *See* Interoperable Object Reference.

IP *See* Internet Protocol.

IPSEC *See* Internet Protocol Security.

ISAPI *See* Internet Server Application Programming Interface.

ISP *See* Internet service provider.

J2EE *See* Java 2 Platform, Enterprise Edition.

J2SE *See* Java 2 Platform, Standard Edition.

Java 2 Platform, Enterprise Edition (J2EE) Sun's Java platform for multitier server-oriented enterprise applications. The basis of J2EE is EJB (FOLDOC 2002).

Java 2 Platform, Standard Edition (J2SE) Sun's core Java platform for clients and servers.

Java Web Services Developer Pack (JWSDP) An integrated toolset that, in conjunction with the Java platform, allows Java developers to build, test, and deploy XML applications, Web services, and Web applications. The Java WSDP provides Java standard implementations of existing key Web services standards, including WSDL, SOAP, ebXML, and UDDI, as well as important Java standard implementations for Web application development such as JavaServer PagesTM (JSPTM pages) and the JSP Standard Tag Library (Sun 2002a).

JWSDP *See* Java Web Services Developer Pack.

Kerberos A system developed by project Athena at the Massachusetts Institute of Technology and named for the three-headed dog guarding Hades. It implements a ticket-based, peer entity authentication service and an access control service distributed in a client/server network environment, using passwords and symmetric cryptography.

lattice A partially ordered set in which all finite subsets have a least upper bound and greatest lower bound.

lattice-based MAC An access control model based on comparing security classifications (which indicate how sensitive or critical system resources are) with security clearances (which indicate subjects that are eligible to access certain resources). It's called "mandatory" because a subject that has clearance to access a resource may not, just by its own volition (that is, at its discretion), enable another subject to access that resource. Because a system of security labels (a general name for classifications and clearances) constitutes a lattice, the model is called lattice-based.

LDAP *See* Lightweight Directory Access Protocol.

least privilege principle A security principle that requires users to operate with the minimum set of privileges necessary to do their jobs.

legacy security Security infrastructure and technologies that are developed and deployed by the enterprise to support an old enterprise architecture and that do not satisfy the requirements of the current enterprise architecture.

Lightweight Directory Access Protocol (LDAP) A protocol for accessing online directory services, which defines a relatively simple protocol for updating and searching directories running over TCP/IP.

Mandatory Access Control (MAC) *See* lattice-based MAC.

method An association between a name and a procedure, routine, or some other action execution, which is encapsulated in an object in an object-oriented programming language (for example, Java) or other computing environment (for example, EJB).

method permission A permission to invoke a specified group of methods of the enterprise beans' home and remote interfaces. Method permissions are defined in the corresponding sections of an EJB deployment descriptor.

middle tier A tier in the enterprise computing architecture between the perimeter and data tiers. The middle tier consists of business applications that implement business logic.

middle tier (mid-tier) security A security infrastructure that protects mid-tier systems.

middleware Software that mediates between an application program and a network by managing the interactions between disparate applications across the heterogeneous computing platforms.

mid-tier *See* middle tier.

MIME See Multipurpose Internet Mail Extensions.

Multipurpose Internet Mail Extensions (MIME) A standard for multipart, multimedia electronic mail messages and World Wide Web hypertext documents on the Internet. MIME provides the ability to transfer nontextual data, such as graphics, audio, and faxes. It is defined in the following IETF RFCs: 2045, 2046, 2047, 2048, and 2049 (FOLDOC 2002).

.NET Framework Microsoft's environment for building, deploying, and running applications.

nonrepudiation The provision of evidence that prevents a participant in an action from convincingly denying his responsibility for the action (OMG 2000a).

OASIS *See* Organization for the Advancement of Structured Information Standards.

object "A unique instance of a data structure defined according to the template provided by its class. Each object has its own values for the variables belonging to its class and can respond to the messages (methods) defined by its class" (FOLDOC 2002). In the context of security, object is a synonym for resource.

Object Management Group (OMG) A consortium founded in 1989 by 11 companies to create a component-based software marketplace by hastening the introduction of standardized object software. In 2000, it had about 800 members. The organization's charter includes the establishment of industry guidelines and detailed object management specifications to provide a common framework for application development. The major technologies developed by the OMG members are CORBA and UML.

object reference A data structure used as a handle through which a client requests operations on the corresponding object.

Object Request Broker (ORB) The core part of CORBA middleware that facilitates communications among distributed objects. An ORB is responsible for finding remote objects, handling parameter passing, and returning results, among other things.

OMG *See* Object Management Group.

operation A CORBA equivalent to a method in object-oriented programming languages.

ORB *See* Object Request Broker.

Organization for the Advancement of Structured Information Standards (OASIS) A not-for-profit, global consortium that drives the development, convergence, and adoption of e-business standards. Members themselves set the OASIS technical agenda, using a lightweight, open process expressly designed to promote industry consensus and unite disparate efforts. OASIS produces worldwide standards for security, Web services, XML conformance, business transactions, electronic publishing, topic maps, and interoperability within and between marketplaces. Its Web page is www.oasis-open.org.

owner-based DAC A Discretionary Access Control model in which for each resource there is a subject who is said to be the resource's owner and who manages the resource's access rights.

PAC *See* Privilege Attribute Certificate.

perimeter tier A tier in the enterprise computing architecture that usually consists of Web servers implementing presentation logic.

perimeter tier security A security infrastructure protecting enterprise resources at the perimeter tier.

policy domain *See* security policy domain.

presumed trust Trust based solely on the assumption that the environment and all its entities are trustworthy. In the context of CSIv2, presumed trust is the acceptance of the client identity based solely on the fact of its occurrence and without consideration of the intermediate's authentication identity. The presumption is that communications are constrained such that only trusted entities are capable of asserting an identity to the target security system.

principal A user or programmatic entity with the ability to use the resources of a system. Synonymous with subject.

privilege *See* privilege attribute.

privilege attribute A security attribute that need not have the property of uniqueness, and thus that may be shared by many users and other principals. Examples of privilege attributes include groups, roles, and clearances.

Privilege Attribute Certificate (PAC) A digital certificate that contains privilege attributes of a principal with any associated information needed for delegation and other controls.

profile A set of data describing security and other attributes of a user or application.

proxy A hardware device or software program acting on behalf of or representing other hardware devices or software programs in computing interactions.

proxy server A server acting as a *proxy*.

public key cryptography A popular synonym for asymmetric cryptography.

pull model A way of obtaining a subject's credentials by looking them up in the security environment using some unique information about the subject, such as its identity.

push model A way of providing a subject's credentials to a target by embedding them into the context of the client's request.

RACF *See* Resource Access Control Facility.

RAD *See* Resource Access Decision.

reference monitor An access control concept that refers to an abstract machine that mediates all access to objects by subjects (NCSC 1988).

Remote Method Invocation (RMI) Part of the Java programming language library, which enables a Java program running on one computer to access the objects and methods of another Java program running on a different computer (FOLDOC 2002).

repudiation Denial by one of the entities involved in an action of having participated in all or part of the action.

Resource Access Control Facility (RACF) IBM's large system security product available for multiple virtual storage (MVS) and virtual machine (VM) operating system environments.

Resource Access Decision (RAD) A specification of application-level authorization services from the OMG. The specification text is available from the OMG as document number dtc/00-06-07.

restricted delegation Synonymous with controlled delegation.

right A named value conferring the ability to perform actions in a system. Access control policies grant rights to principals (on the basis of their security attributes); in order to make an access control decision, access decision functions compare the rights granted to a principal against the rights required to perform an operation (OMG 2000a).

RMI *See* Remote Method Invocation.

RSA A public key cryptosystem for both encryption and authentication, invented in 1977 by Ron Rivest, Adi Shamir, and Leonard Adleman. Its name comes from their initials (FOLDOC 2002).

SAML *See* Security Assertion Markup Language.

SDMM *See* Security Domain Membership Management.

secret key cryptography Synonymous with symmetric cryptography.

Secure European System for Applications in a Multi-Vendor Environment (SESAME) A European research and development project that was started in the late 1980s. It is also the name of the technology that came out of that project. This technology defines components of a security architecture that provide the underlying bedrock upon which full managed security products can be built using the following services defined by the architecture: authentication, authorization, confidentiality, integrity, and auditing.

Secure Multipurpose Internet Mail Extensions (S-MIME) A specification for secure electronic mail. S-MIME was designed to add security to e-mail messages in MIME format. The security services offered are authentication (using digital signatures) and privacy (using encryption) (FOLDOC 2002).

Secure Sockets Layer (SSL) An Internet protocol (originally developed by Netscape Communications, Inc.) layered above TCP that uses connection-oriented end-to-end encryption to provide data confidentiality service and data integrity service for traffic between a client (often a Web browser) and a server. Optionally, it can provide peer entity authentication between the client and the server (TIS 2000).

Security Assertion Markup Language (SAML) XML-based format and protocol for exchanging authentication and authorization requests and responses.

security association The shared security state information that permits secure communication between two entities (OMG 2000a).

security attributes The characteristics of a subject (user or principal) that form the basis of the system's security policies governing that subject.

security audit The independent examination of records and activities to ensure compliance with established security policies.

security authority An entity that establishes security policies.

security-aware application An application that uses security APIs to access and validate the security policies that apply to it. Security-aware applications may directly access security functions that enable the applications to perform additional security checks and fully exploit the capabilities of the security infrastructure.

security context The security object that encapsulates the shared state information representing a security association (OMG 2000a).

security domain *See* security policy domain.

Security Domain Membership Management (SDMM) An upcoming specification (OMG 2001a) from the OMG that will define the interfaces necessary for run-time retrieval of object domain membership information, as well as object security attributes that can be used for various security policy decisions.

security enclave A group of machines within an enterprise that is separated from the rest of the enterprise by firewalls.

security policy A set of rules and practices that specify or regulate how a system or organization provides security services to protect sensitive and critical system resources (TIS 2000).

security policy domain A set of objects to which a security policy applies for a set of security-related activities and that is administered by a security authority. The objects are the domain members. The policy represents the rules and criteria that constrain activities of the objects to make the domain secure (OMG 2000a).

security self-reliant application An application that does not use any of the security services provided by a security framework. A security self-reliant application may not use the security services because it has no security relevant functionality and thus does not need to be secured or because it uses separate independent security functions that are not part of the defined ESI security framework.

security trustworthiness The ability of a system to protect resources from exposure to misuse through malicious or inadvertent means.

security-unaware application An application that does not explicitly call security services, but that is still secured by the supporting environment (for example, an EJB or CORBA Container).

self-administration An approach in user administration in which users handle many of their own administrative functions rather than relying on an administrator within the enterprise to do it for them. Self-administration provides better service for customers at a lower cost, but comes with significant security risks.

separation of duties principle A security principle requiring that for particular sets of transactions, no single individual be allowed to execute all transactions within the set.

server skeleton Code, usually automatically generated by IDL compilers, that handles parameters and returns results, passing to and from a middleware object.

SESAME *See* Secure European System for Applications in a Multi-Vendor Environment.

SGML *See* Standard Generalized Markup Language.

simple delegation A type of delegation in which the client permits the intermediate to assume its privileges, using them for access control decisions and delegating them to others. The target object receives only the client's privileges and does not know who the intermediate is (when used without target restrictions, it is known as impersonation).

Simple Mail Transfer Protocol (SMTP) A protocol defined in IETF RFC 821, used to transfer electronic mail between computers over *TCP*. It is a server-to-server protocol, so other protocols are used to access the messages (FOLDOC 2002).

Simple Object Access Protocol (SOAP) An XML-based format for exchanging data in a decentralized, distributed environment. It consists of three parts: an envelope that defines a framework for describing what is in a message and how to process it, a set of encoding rules for expressing instances of application-defined datatypes, and a convention for representing remote procedure calls and responses (W3C 2002d).

Simple Public-Key GSS-API Mechanism (SPKM) A GSS-API mechanism defined in IETF RFC 2025 (Adams 1996), which is based on a public key, rather than a symmetric key, infrastructure.

single sign-on (SSO) A technology, product, or solution that enables user-transparent authentication to different applications.

S-MIME *See* Secure Multipurpose Internet Mail Extensions.

SMTP *See* Simple Mail Transfer Protocol.

SOAP *See* Simple Object Access Protocol.

SPKM *See* Simple Public-Key GSS-API Mechanism.

SSL *See* Secure Sockets Layer.

SSO *See* single sign-on.

Standard Generalized Markup Language (SGML) An international standard that defines a generic markup language for representing documents.

subject An active entity in the system; either a human user principal or a programmatic principal.

symmetric cryptography A branch of cryptography involving algorithms that use the same key for two different steps of the algorithm (such as encryption and decryption or signature creation and signature verification) (TIS 2000).

target object (target) The recipient of a CORBA request message. Also, the final recipient in a delegation call chain. The only participant in such a call chain that is not the originator of a call (OMG 2000a).

TCB *See* trusted computing base.

TCP *See* Transmission Control Protocol.

TCP/IP A stack of Transmission Control Protocol over Internet Protocol. It's often used to refer to the entire suite of protocols (such as HTTP, SSL, IIOP) based on this stack.

technology domain A part of an enterprise security infrastructure in which common security mechanisms are used to enforce security policies.

TLS *See* Transport Layer Security.

TMEP *See* Transport Message Exchange Pattern.

token An abstract concept used for passing a property or its evidence between cooperating entities.

traced delegation A type of delegation in which the client permits the intermediate object to use its privileges and delegate them. However, at each intermediate object in the chain, the intermediate's privileges are added to privileges propagated to provide a trace of the delegates in the chain (OMG 2000a).

Transmission Control Protocol (TCP) A transport layer protocol built on top of Internet Protocol. It provides full-duplex, process-to-process connections with reliable communication, flow control, multiplexing, and connection-oriented communication.

Transport Layer Security (TLS) An Internet protocol that in version 1.0 is effectively SSL version 3.1. TLS, as opposed to SSL, which is an IETF standard.

Transport Message Exchange Pattern (TMEP) A template used to describe the exchange of messages between *SOAP* nodes.

trust The extent to which someone who relies on a system can have confidence that the system meets its specifications; that is, that the system does what it claims to do and does not perform unwanted functions (TIS 2000).

trusted computing base (TCB) The totality of the hardware and software mechanisms that are responsible for enforcing the security policy. The TCB must be tamperproof, always invoked (nonbypassable), and small enough to be thoroughly analyzed. The TCB is usually implemented within an operating system that is under strict configuration control. This architecture permits very tight security because the TCB is the mediator through which all user accesses to resources must pass. Everything within the TCB is trusted to enforce the security policy; everything outside of the TCB is untrusted.

trustworthiness *See* security trustworthiness.

UDDI *See* Universal Description, Discovery, and Integration.

UML *See* Unified Modeling Language.

unconstrained delegation Synonymous with impersonation.

Unified Modeling Language (UML) A third-generation modeling language standardized by the OMG and used to specify, visualize, construct, and document the artifacts of an object-oriented software-intensive system under development.

Uniform Resource Identifier (URI) The generic set of all names and addresses, which are short strings that refer to objects (typically on the Internet). The most common kinds of URI are URLs and relative URLs. URIs are defined in IETF RFC 1630.

Uniform Resource Locator (URL) A standard way of specifying the location of an entity, typically a Web page, on the Internet.

Uniform Resource Name (URN) A standard syntax for naming resources on the Internet. URNs are intended to serve as persistent, location-independent, resource identifiers and are designed to make it easy to map other namespaces (which share the properties of URNs) into URN-space. URN format is defined in IETF RFC 2141.

Unitary Login A security service that provides secure storage and retrieval of sensitive authentication data (for example, passwords); typically used to access back-end and database systems.

Universal Description, Discovery and Integration (UDDI) An architecture for Web services integration. It contains standards-based specifications for service description and discovery.

Universal Unique Identifier (UUID) A unique 128-bit number used to identify an object on a network.

unrestricted delegation Synonymous with impersonation.

URI *See* Uniform Resource Identifier.

URL *See* Uniform Resource Locator.

URN *See* Uniform Resource Name.

UUID See Universal Unique Identifier.

virtual private network (VPN) A restricted use, logical (that is, artificial or simulated) computer network that is constructed from the system resources of a relatively public, physical (that is, real) network (such as the Internet), often by using encryption (located at hosts or gateways) and often by tunneling links of the virtual network across the real network (TIS 2000).

VPN *See* virtual private network.

W3C *See* World Wide Web Consortium.

WASP *See* Web Application and Services Platform.

Web Application and Services Platform (WASP) A platform-independent, standards-compliant set of infrastructure products offered by Systinet (www.systinet.com) for building Web Services solutions.

Web Service An application that exposes a programmatic interface using standard Internet protocols. Web services are designed to be used by other programs or applications rather than by humans.

Web Services Description Language (WSDL) An XML format for describing Web services. WSDL specification defines a language for describing the abstract functionality of a service, as well as a framework for describing the concrete details of a service description.

Web Services Toolkit (WSTK) A software toolkit from IBM that supports the development of Web Services applications.

World Wide Web Consortium (W3C) The main standards body for the World Wide Web. W3C works with the global community to establish international standards for client and server protocols that enable online commerce and communications on the Internet. It also produces reference software. W3C was created by the Massachusetts Institute of Technology (MIT) on October 25, 1994. W3C is funded by industrial members, but its products are freely available to all (FOLDOC 2002).

WSDL *See* Web Services Description Language.

WS-Security A specification describing how to attach signature and encryption information, as well as security tokens, to SOAP messages.

WSTK *See* Web Services Toolkit.

X.500 An ITU-T recommendation that is one part of a joint ITU-T/ISO multipart standard (X.500-X.525) that defines the X.500 Directory, which is a conceptual collection of systems that provide distributed directory capabilities for OSI entities, processes, applications, and services. (The ISO equivalent is IS 9594-1 and related standards, IS 9594-x.)

XACML *See* eXtensible Access Control Markup Language.

XML *See* Extensible Markup Language.

XML Schema A language used with *XML* markup specifications to describe data structure, constraints on content, and data types. It was designed to provide more control over data than is provided by *DTDs*.

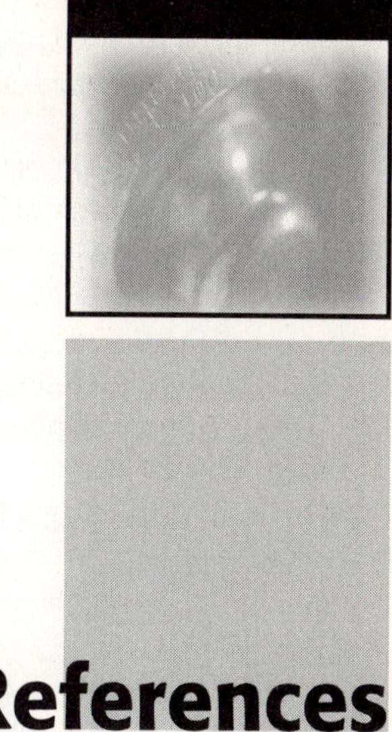

References

Abadi, M., et al. "A Calculus for Access Control in Distributed Systems." DEC, http://citeseer.nj.nec.com/64113.html, 1991.

Amoroso, Edward. Fundamentals of Computer Security Technology. Upper Saddle River, NJ: Prentice Hall, 1994.

Angeline, Dennis. "Architectural Overview of the Common Language Runtime." In *Microsoft Research - University Programs 2001*. Multi-University Research Laboratory, Redwood, WA, http://murl.microsoft.com/LectureDetails.asp?717, 2001.

ANSI. "X9.31-1998, Digital Signatures Using Reversible Public Key Cryptography for the Financial Services Industry (rDSA)." American National Standards Institute, 1998a.

ANSI. "X9.62-1998, Public Key Cryptography for the Financial Services Industry: The Elliptic Curve Digital Signature Algorithm (ECDSA)." American National Standards Institute, 1998b.

Atkinson, Bob, et al. "Web Services Security (WS-Security) v1.0." IBM, Microsoft, Verisign, http://msdn.microsoft.com/library/default.asp?url=/library/en-us/dnglobspec/html/ws-security.asp, 2002.

Barkley, John, Konstantin Beznosov and Jinny Uppal. "Supporting Relationships in Access Control Using Role Based Access Control." In *Proceedings of ACM Role-Based Access Control Workshop*, pp. 55-65, Fairfax, Virginia, October 1999.

Bell, D. E. and L. J. LaPadula. "Secure Computer Systems: Unified Exposition and Multics Interpretation." Bedford, MA: MITRE, 1975.

Berghel, Hal. "Digital Village: Caustic cookies." In *Communications of the ACM*, Vol. 44, pp. 19-22, http://doi.acm.org/10.1145/374308.374320, 2001.

Beznosov, Konstantin, et al. "A Resource Access Decision Service for CORBA-based Distributed Systems." In *Proceedings of Annual Computer Security Applications Conference*, pp. 310-319, Phoenix, Arizona, USA, http://www.acsac.org/1999/abstracts/fri-b-0830-beznosov.html, December 1999.

Blakley, Bob, *CORBA Security:An Introduction to Safe Computing with Objects*. Addison-Wesley, Reading, 1999.

Bos, B. "XML in 10 Points." W3C, http://www.w3c.org/XML/1999/XML-in-10-points, 2001.

Box, Don. "A Brief History of SOAP." XML.com, http://xml.com/lpt/a/2001/04/04/soap.html, 2002.

Brown, Keith. "Building a Lightweight COM Interception Framework Part 1: The Universal Delegator." *Microsoft Systems Journal*, January 1999.

Brown, Keith, *Programming Windows Security*. Upper Saddle River, NJ: Addison-Wesley, 2000.

Cover, R. "The XML Cover Pages - XML Overview." Coverpages, http://xml.coverpages.org/xml.html, 2002.

CSI. "Common Secure Interoperability, Version 2, Final Submission." Object Management Group. Document number orbos/00-08-04, www.omg.org, 2000.

Epstein, Pete and Ravi Sandhu. "Engineering of Role/Permission Assignments." In *Proceedings of 17th Annual Computer Security Applications Conference*, pp. 127-136, New Orleans, Louisiana December 10-14 2001.

Erdos, M. Cantor, S. "Shibboleth-Architecture DRAFT v04." http://middleware.internet2.edu/shibboleth/docs/draft-internet2-shibboleth-arch-v04.pdf, Internet2/MACE and IBM, November 2001.

Ferraiolo, David F., et al. "Proposed NIST Standard for Role-Based Access Control." *ACM Transactions on Information and System Security* 4(3): 224-274, http://ite.gmu.edu/list/journals/tissec/p224-ferraiolo.pdf, 2001.

Flynn, P. "The XML FAQ, v. 2.1 (2002-01-01)." (Ed. Flynn P), http://www.ucc.id/xml/, 2002.

FOLDOC. "Free Online Dictionary of Computing." www.foldoc.org, 2002.

Garguilo, J. J. and Paul Markovit. "NIST Special Publication 500-231, Guidelines for the Evaluation of Electronic Data Interchange Products." National Institute for Standards and Technology, 1996.

Gittler, Frederic and Anne C. Hopkins. "The DCE Security Service." *Hewlett-Packard Journal* 46(6): 41-48, http://www.hp.com/hpj/dec95_41.pdf, 1995.

Gollmann, Dieter, Computer Security. John Wiley & Sons, 1999.

Grimes, Richard, *Professional DCOM Programming*. Wrox Press Inc., Birmingham, UK, 1997.

Hartman, Bret, Donald J. Flinn, and Konstantin Beznosov, *Enterprise Security With EJB and CORBA*. New York: John Wiley & Sons, Inc., 2001.

Heffner, Randy. "Planning Assumption: Giga's Model for Enterprise Application Security Integration." Giga Information Group, June 22, 2001, http://www.gigaweb.com.

Howard, Michael, Marc Levy, and Richard Waymire, *Designing Secure Web-based Applications for Microsoft Windows 2000*. Redmond, WA: Microsoft Press, 2000.

IBM and Microsoft. "Security in a Web Services World: A Proposed Architecture and Roadmap", http://msdn.microsoft.com/library/default.asp?url=/library/en-us/dnwssecur/html/securitywhitepaper.asp, 2002.

IBM, Microsoft, and Verisign. "Web Services Security (WS-Security), Version 1.0, April 5, 2002." http://www-106.ibm.com/developerworks/webservices/library/ws-secure/, 2002b.

IETF. "RFC 1510, The Kerberos Network Authentication Service, V5." 1993.

IETF. "RFC 2195, IMAP/POP AUTHorize Extension for Simple Challenge/Response." Internet Engineering Task Force, ftp://ftp.isi.edu/in-notes/rfc2195.txt, 1997a.

IETF. "RFC 2222, Simple Authentication and Security Layer (SASL)." Internet Engineering Task Force, ftp://ftp.isi.edu/in-notes/rfc2222.txt, 1997b.

IETF. "RFC 2245, Anonymous SASL Mechanism." Internet Engineering Task Force, ftp://ftp.isi.edu/in-notes/rfc2245.txt, 1997c.

IETF. "RFC 2478, The Simple and Protected GSS-API Negotiation Mechanism." Internet Engineering Task Force, ftp://ftp.isi.edu/in-notes/rfc2478.txt, 1998.

IETF. "RFC 2246, The Transport Layer Security Protocol version 1.0." Internet Engineering Task Force, ftp://ftp.isi.edu/in-notes/rfc2246.txt, 1999.

IETF. "RFC 2616, Hypertext Transfer Protocol - HTTP 1.1." Internet Engineering Task Force, ftp://ftp.isi.edu/in-notes/rfc2616.txt, 1999a.

IETF. "RFC 2630, Cryptographic Message Syntax." Internet Engineering Task Force, ftp://ftp.isi.edu/in-notes/rfc2630.txt, 1999b.

IETF. "RFC 2633, S/MIME Version 3 Message Specification." Internet Engineering Task Force, ftp://ftp.isi.edu/in-notes/rfc2633.txt, 1999c.

IETF. "RFC 2808, The SecurID SASL Mechanism." Internet Engineering Task Force, ftp://ftp.isi.edu/in-notes/rfc2808.txt, 2000a.

IETF. "RFC 2831, Using Digest Authentication as a SASL Mechanism." Internet Engineering Task Force, ftp://ftp.isi.edu/in-notes/rfc2831.txt, 2000b.

IETF. "RFC 3156, MIME Security with OpenPGP." Internet Engineering Task Force, ftp://ftp.isi.edu/in-notes/rfc3156.txt, 2000c.

IETF. "X.509 Authentication SASL Mechanism." Internet Engineering Task Force, http://www.ietf.org/internet-drafts/draft-ietf-ldapext-x509-sasl-03.txt, 2000d.

IETF. "SASL GSSAPI mechanisms." Internet Engineering Task Force, http://www.ietf.org/internet-drafts/draft-ietf-cat-sasl-gssapi-05.txt, 2001.

IETF. "IP Security Protocol (ipsec) Charter." IETF, http://www.ietf.org/html.charters/ipsec-charter.html, 2002.

IETF. "Secure Remote Password SASL Mechanism." Internet Engineering Task Force, http://www.ietf.org/internet-drafts/draft-burdis-cat-srp-sasl-06.txt, 2002a.

IETF. "RFC 3281, An Internet Attribute Certificate Profile for Authorization." Internet Engineering Task Force, ftp://ftp.rfc-editor.org/in-notes/rfc3281.txt, 2002b.

ISO. "ISO 8879: 1986(E), Information processing - Text and Office Systems - Standard Generalized Markup Language (SGML)." International Organization for Standardization, 1986.

Kindel, Charlie and Brown. "Distributed Component Object Model Protocol (DCOM/1.0)." Redmond, WA, Microsoft Corporation, 1998.

Kreger, Heather. "Web Services Conceptual Architecture." p. 41. IBM Software Group, http://www.ibm.com/software/solutions/webservices/pdf/WSCA.pdf, 2001.

LaMacchia B. A., S. Lange, M. Lyons, R. Martin, and K. T. Price. *.NET Framework Security*, 1st ed, Reading, MA: Addison Wesley Professional, 2002.

Lampson, B. W. "Protection." In *Proceedings of 5th Princeton Conference on Information Sciences and Systems*, pp. 437, Princeton, 1971.

Lampson, Butler, et al. "Authentication in Distributed Systems: Theory and Practice." In *Proceedings of ACM Symposium on Operating Systems Principles*, pp. 165-182, Asilomar Conference Center, Pacific Grove, California, http://citeseer.nj.nec.com/lampson92authentication.html, October 13-16 1991.

Levitt, Jason. "From EDI To XML And UDDI: A Brief History Of Web Services." *Information Week*, http://www.informationweek.com/story/IWK20010928S0006, 2001.

Lowy, Juval. "Windows XP: Make Your Components More Robust with COM+ 1.5 Innovations." *MSDN Magazine*, http://msdn.microsoft.com/library/default.asp?url=/library/en-us/dnmag01/html/ComXP.asp, 2001.

Microsoft. "IP Security for Microsoft Windows 2000 Server." Microsoft Corporation, http://msdn.microsoft.com/library/default.asp?url=/library/en-us/dnw2k/html/msdn_ip_security.asp, 1999.

Microsoft. "Step-by-Step Guide to Mapping Certificates to User Accounts." Microsoft, http://www.microsoft.com/windows2000/techinfo/planning/security/mappingcerts.asp, 2000.

Microsoft. "Web Services Description Language (WSDL) Explained, July 2001." Microsoft Corporation, http://msdn.microsoft.com/library/default.asp?url=/library/en-us/dnw2k/html/msdn_ip_security.asp, 2001.

Microsoft. "IIS Authentication." Microsoft, http://msdn.microsoft.com/library/default.asp?url=/library/en-us/vsent7/html/vxconIISAuthentication.asp, 2001a.

Microsoft. "Microsoft .NET Passport." http://www.microsoft.com/myservices/passport, 2001b.

Microsoft. "SOAP Toolkit 2.0: Guidelines and Limitations." Microsoft Corporation, http://msdn.microsoft.com/library/default.asp?url=/library/en-us/soap/htm/soap_guidelines_9soj.asp, 2001c.

Microsoft. "Web Services Development Kit" Microsoft, http://msdn.microsoft.com/webservices/building/wsdk/default.asp, 2002.

Microsoft. "WSDL Specification Index Page." Microsoft, http://msdn.microsoft.com/library/default.asp?url=/library/en-us/dnwsdl/html/wsdlspecindex.asp, 2002a.

Microsoft. *Building Secure ASP.NET Applications.* http://msdn.microsoft.com/library/en-us/dnnetsec/html/secnetlpMSDN.asp, 2002b

Moats, R. "RFC 2141: URN Syntax." IETF, http://www.ietf.org/rfc/rfc2141.txt, 1997.

NCSC. "A Guide to Understanding Discretionary Access Control in Trusted Systems." National Computer Security Center, 1987.

Netscape, "Persistent Client State, HTTP Cookies." Netscape, http://wp.netscape.com/newsref/std/cookie_spec.html.

Neuman, B. Clifford and Theodore Y. Ts'o. "Kerberos: An Authentication Service for Computer Networks." p. 6. Marina del Ray, CA: University of Southern California, Information Sciences Institute, 1994.

NIST. Federal Information Processing Standards (FIPS) 46-1. 1988.

NIST. "FIPS Pub 186-2 Digital Signature Standard (DSS)." National Institute of Standards and Technology, http://csrc.nist.gov/publications/fips/fips186-2/fips186-2.pdf, 2000.

NIST. "FIPS Pub 198 HMAC - Keyed-Hash Message Authentication Code." National Institute of Standards and Technology, http://csrc.nist.gov/publications/fips/fips198/fips198a.pdf, 2000.

NIST. "Specification for the Advanced Encryption Standard (AES)." FIPS 197, http://csrc.nist.gov/publications/fips/fips197/fips-197.pdf, November 2001.

OASIS. "Assertions and Protocol for the OASIS Security Assertion Markup Language." http://www.oasis-open.org/committees/security/docs/cs-sstc-core-01.pdf, 31 May 2002.

Ogbuji, Uche. "Using WSDL in SOAP applications: An introduction to WSDL for SOAP programmers." Consultant, Fourthought, Inc., http://www-106.ibm.com/developerworks/library/ws-soap/index.html?loc=wstheme, November 2000.

OMG. "Resource Access Decision Facility." Object Management Group, http://www.omg.org/cgi-bin/doc?formal/2001-04-01, 2001.

OMG. "Security Domain Membership Management Service, Final Submission." Object Management Group, http://www.omg.org/cgi-bin/doc?ptc/02-03-03, 2001a.

Oppliger, Rolf, *Authentication Systems for Secure Networks*. Boston: Artech House, 1996.

Orfali, Robert, Dan Harkey and Jeri Edwards, *Instant CORBA*. New York: John Wiley & Sons, 1997.

Orfali, Robert, Dan Harkley and Jeri Edwards, *Client/Server Survival Guide*. New York: Wiley Computer Publishing, 1999.

OSF. "Authentication and Security Services." 1996.

Parker, Tom and Denis Pinkas. "SESAME V4 - Overview." p. 61. SESAME, http://www.esat.kuleuven.ac.be/cosic/sesame/doc-ps/overview.ps, 1995.

Penn, Jonathan. "Role-Based Access Control Implementations Require Advanced Capabilities." p. 2. Cambridge, MA: Giga Information Group, Inc., 2002.

Pope, Alan, *The CORBA Reference Guide: Understanding the Common Object Request Broker Architecture*. Reading, MA: Addison-Wesley, 1998.

Ray, E. T. *Learning XML*. Sebastopol, CA: O'Reilly & Associates, 2000.

Roman, Ed, Scott Ambler and Tyler Jewell, *Mastering Enterprise JavaBeans*. New York: Wiley Computer Publishing, 2002.

Rescorla, Eric. *SSL and TLS: Designing and Building Secure Systems*. Reading, MA: Addison Wesley, 2000.

Rubin, William and Marshall Brain, *Understanding DCOM*. P T R Prentice Hall, http://www.phptr.com/ptrbooks/ptr_0130959669.html, 1999.

Ruh, William A., Thomas Herron and Paul Klinker, *IIOP Complete: Understanding CORBA and Middleware Interoperability*. Reading, MA: Addison-Wesley, 1999.

Ruh, William A., Francis X. Maginnis, and William J. Brown. Enterprise Application Integration: A Wiley Tech Brief. New York: John Wiley & Sons, 2000.

Russel, Debby and G.T. Gangemi, *Computer Security Basics*. O'Reilly & Associates, http://www.oreilly.com/catalog/csb/, 1991.

Sandhu, R., E. Coyne, H. Feinstein, and C. Youman. "Role-Based Access Control Models." *IEEE Computer* 29(2): 38-47, 1996.

Seely, Scott. "Building Industry Standard WSDL." Microsoft, http://msdn.microsoft.com/library/default.asp?url=/library/en-us/dnservice/html/service02062002.asp, February 4, 2001a.

Seely, Scott. "An XML Overview Towards Understanding SOAP." Microsoft Developer Network, http://msdn.microsoft.com/library/default.asp?url=/library/en-us/dnwebsrv/html/Xmloverchap2.asp?frame=true, November, 2001b.

Seely, Scott, *SOAP: Cross Platform Web Service Development Using XML*. Prentice Hall, http://vig.pearsoned.com/store/product/0,,store-562_banner-0_isbn-0130907634,00.html, 2002.

Shohoud, Yasser, "Introduction to WSDL." Learnxmlws, http://www.learnxmlws.com/tutors/wsdl/wsdl.aspx.

Siegel, Jon, *CORBA 3 Fundamentals and Programming*. New York: John Wiley & Sons, 2000.

Sit, Emil and Kevin Fu. "Inside Risks: Web cookies: not just a privacy risk." In *Communications of the ACM*, Vol. 44, p. 120, http://doi.acm.org/10.1145/383694.383714, 2001.

Slemko, Marc. "Microsoft Passport to Trouble." http://alive.znep.com/~marcs/passport/, 2001.

Smith, Richard. *Internet Cryptography*. Reading, MA: Addison Wesley, 1997.

Snell, James. "Web services insider, Part 1: Reflections on SOAP." IBM, http://www.ibm.com/developerworks/library/ws-ref1.html, April, 2001.

Sun. "Java Authentication and Authorization Service (JAAS)." Sun Microsystems, http://java.sun.com/products/jaas/index-14.html, 2001.

Sun. "Java Technology & Web Services Frequently Asked Questions." Sun Microsystems, http://java.sun.com/webservices/faq.html, 2002.

Sun, *Java Web Services Developer Pack Home Page*, http://java.sun.com/webservices/webservicespack.html, 2002a.

Tapadyia, Pradeep, *COM+ Programming: A Practical Guide Using Visual C++ and ATL*. Upper Saddle River, NJ: Prentice Hall PTR, 2001.

Tapang, Carlos C. "Web Services Description Language (WSDL) Explained." p. 28.Infotects, http://msdn.microsoft.com/library/default.asp?url=/library/en-us/dnwebsrv/html/wsdlexplained.asp, 2001.

Taylor, David, *Object Technology: A Manager's Guide*. Reading, MA: Addison Wesley Longman, http://www.amazon.com/exec/obidos/ASIN/0201309947/qid=1012272472/sr=1-1/ref=sr_1_10_1/103-8613496-5987843, 1997.

Thai, Thuan L., *Learning DCOM*. Sebastopol, CA: O'Reilly & Associates, 1999.

Thai, Thuan and Hoang Q. Lam, *.NET Framework Essentials*. Sebastopol, CA: O'Reilly & Associates, 2001.

TIS 2000 "Internet Security Glossary" The Internet Society. Request for Comments 2828, 1995.

UDDI.org. "UDDI Executive White Paper." UDDI, http://www.uddi.org/pubs/UDDI_Executive_White_Paper.pdf, November 14, 2001a.

UDDI.org. "UDDI Frequently Asked Questions (FAQ)." UDDI, http://www.uddi.org/pubs/UDDI%20FAQ%20Nov%202001%20draft%20v4.pdf, November 14, 2001b.

UDDI.org. "UDDI Overview." UDDI, http://www.uddi.org/pubs/UDDI_Overview_Presentation.ppt, September 6, 2001c.

UDDI.org. "UDDI Technical White Paper." UDDI, http://www.uddi.org/pubs/Iru_UDDI_Technical_White_Paper.pdf, September 6, 2001d.

UDDI.org. "UDDI Version 2.0 Data Structure Reference UDDI Open Draft Specification." v. 2.0, http://www.uddi.org/pubs/DataStructure-V2.00-Open-20010608.pdf, June 8, 2001e.

Vlist, Eric van der. "Using W3C XML Schema." XML.com, http://www.xml.com/lpt/a/2000/11/29/schemas/part1.html, September, 2002.

Wagner, Allen. "Developing a Custom Authentication Scheme in .NET." Microsoft Developer Network, http://msdn.microsoft.com/library/default.asp?url=/library/en-us/dncold/html/storagecustauth.asp, 2002.

W3C. "XML Path Language (XPath)." v. 1.0 Recommendation, http://www.w3.org/TR/1999/REC-xpath-19991116, November 16, 1999.

W3C. "Extensible Markup Language." v. 1.0 (Second Edition), http://www.w3.org/TR/2000/REC-xml-20001006, October 6, 2000.

W3C. "Canonical XML." v. 1.0, http://www.w3.org/TR/2001/REC-xml-c14n-20010315, March 15, 2001.

W3C. "Web Services Description Language (WSDL)." v. 1.1, http://www.w3c.org/TR/2001/NOTE-wsdl-20010315, March 15, 2001a.

W3C. "XML Pointer Language (XPointer)." v 1.0 Candidate Recommendation, http://www.w3.org/TR/2001/CR-xptr-20010911/, September 11, 2001b.

W3C. "XML Schema Part 0: Primer."http://www.w3.org/TR/2001/REC-xmlschema-0-20010502, May 2, 2001c.

W3C. "XML Schema Part 1: Structures." http://www.w3.org/TR/2001/REC-xmlschema-1-20010502, May 2, 2001d.

W3C. "XML Schema Part 2: Datatypes." http://www.w3.org/TR/2001/REC-xmlsch-2-20010502, May 2, 2001e.

W3C. "Decryption Transform for XML Signature." Candidate Recommendation, http://www.w3.org/TR/xmlenc-decrypt, March 4, 2002a.

W3C. "Exclusive XML Canonicalization." v 1.0 Candidate Recommendation, http://www.w3.org/TR/xml-exc-c14n/, July 18, 2002b.

W3C. "Namespaces in XML." v. 1.1 (Working Draft 3), http://www.w3.org/TR/xml-names11/, April, 2002c.

W3C. "SOAP Version 1.2 Part 0: Primer." Working Draft, http://www.w3.org/TR/2002/WD-soap12-part0-20020626/, June 26, 2002d.

W3C. "SOAP Version 1.2 Part 1: Messaging Framework." Working Draft, http://www.w3.org/TR/2002/WD-soap12-part1-20020626/, June 26, 2002e.

W3C. "SOAP Version 1.2 Part 2: Adjuncts." Working Draft, http://www.w3.org/TR/2002/WD-soap12-part2-20020626, June 26, 2002f.

W3C. "SOAP Version 1.2 Usage Scenarios." Working Draft, http://www.w3.org/TR/2002/WD-xmlp-scenarios-20020626/, June 26, 2002g.

W3C. "XML Encryption Requirements." http://www.w3.org/TR/xml-encryption-req, March 4, 2002h.

W3C. "XML Encryption Syntax and Processing." Candidate Recommendation, http://www.w3.org/TR/xmlenc-core/, March, 2002i.

W3C. "XML-Signature Syntax and Processing." http://www.w3.org/TR/xmldsig-core/, February 12, 2002j.

W3C. "XML-Signature XPath Filter." v. 2.0, http://www.w3.org/TR/2002/WD-xmldsig-filter2-20020425/, April 25, 2002k.

W3C and Internet Society. "XML-Signature Requirements W3C." W3C, Working Draft, http://www.w3.org/TR/xmldsig-requirements, October 14, 1999.

Winer, Dave. "Dave's History of SOAP." XML-RPC.com, http://www.xmlrpc.com/stories/storyreader$555, September 25, 1999.

SYMBOLS AND NUMERICS

A

E

K

L

M

N

X